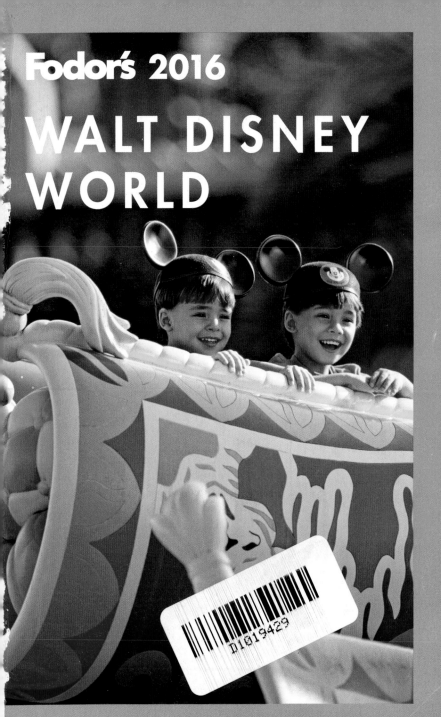

Fodor's 2016

WALT DISNEY WORLD

D1019429

WELCOME TO WALT DISNEY WORLD

Orlando vacations are events that often become part of family legend. Kids and parents swap Disney or Universal stories for years, fondly reliving favorite moments such as the first Butterbeer in Hogsmeade, the "Be Our Guest" dance with Belle, or the final battle between Buzz Lightyear and Zurg. Beyond the Wizarding Worlds and Fantasylands, there is a lot more to see in Orlando. Towns such as Mount Dora, Kissimmee, and Winter Park lure travelers away from the theme parks with fascinating museums, great shopping, and tempting freshwater lakes.

TOP REASONS TO GO

★ **Walt Disney World:** Quite simply, the magic of the Disney parks touches all who visit.

★ **Universal Orlando:** Islands of Adventure and Universal Studios are high-energy fun.

★ **Resorts:** Elaborately-themed resorts offer visitors fun and memorable experiences.

★ **International Drive:** Bustling strip with attractions like Fun Spot and Wet 'n Wild.

★ **Downtown Orlando:** Top restaurants, theater, and music create a thriving scene.

★ **LEGOLAND Florida:** A unique family-friendly theme park with fun rides, shows, and attractions.

Fodor's WALT DISNEY WORLD 2016

Publisher: Amanda D'Acierno, *Senior Vice President*

Editorial: Arabella Bowen, *Editor in Chief*; Linda Cabasin, *Editorial Director*

Design: Tina Malaney, *Associate Art Director*; Chie Ushio, *Senior Designer*

Photography: Jennifer Arnow, *Senior Photo Editor*; Mary Robnett, *Photo Researcher*

Production: Linda Schmidt, *Managing Editor*; Evangelos Vasilakis, *Associate Managing Editor*; Angela L. McLean, *Senior Production Manager*

Maps: Rebecca Baer, *Senior Map Editor*; Mark Stroud (Moon Street Cartography) and David Lindroth, *Cartographers*

Sales: Jacqueline Lebow, *Sales Director*

Marketing & Publicity: Heather Dalton, *Marketing Director*; Katherine Punia, *Publicity Director*

Business & Operations: Susan Livingston, *Vice President, Strategic Business Planning*; Sue Daulton, *Vice President, Operations*

Fodors.com: Megan Bell, *Executive Director, Revenue & Business Development*; Yasmin Marinaro, *Senior Director, Marketing & Partnerships*

Copyright © 2016 by Fodor's Travel, a division of Penguin Random House LLC

Writers: Rona Gindin, Jennifer Greenhill-Taylor, Jennie Hess, Joseph Hayes, Gary McKechnie

Editor: Perrie Hartz

Production Editor: Carrie Parker

ISBN 978-1-101-87838-5

ISSN 1531–443X

SPECIAL SALES

This book is available at special discounts for bulk purchases for sales promotions or premiums. For more information, e-mail specialmarkets@penguinrandomhouse.com.

PRINTED IN THE UNITED STATES OF AMERICA

10 9 8 7 6 5 4 3 2 1

CONTENTS

Fodor's Features

CONTENTS

MAPS

ABOUT
THIS GUIDE

Fodor's Recommendations

Everything in this guide is worth doing—we don't cover what isn't—but exceptional sights, hotels, and restaurants are recognized with additional accolades. **Fodor's**Choice★ indicates our top recommendations; and **Best Bets** call attention to notable hotels and restaurants in various categories. Care to nominate a new place? Visit Fodors.com/contact-us.

Trip Costs

We list prices wherever possible to help you budget well. Hotel and restaurant price categories from $ to $$$$ are noted alongside each recommendation. For hotels, we include the lowest cost of a standard double room in high season. For restaurants, we cite the average price of a main course at dinner or, if dinner isn't served, at lunch. For attractions, we always list adult admission fees; discounts are usually available for children, students, and senior citizens.

Hotels

Our local writers vet every hotel to recommend the best overnights in each price category, from budget to expensive. Unless otherwise specified, you can expect private bath, phone, and TV in your room. For expanded hotel reviews, facilities, and deals visit Fodors.com.

Top Picks	Hotels &
★ **Fodor's**Choice	**Restaurants**
	🏨 Hotel
Listings	⤵ Number of
✉ Address	rooms
✉ Branch address	¶⊙¶ Meal plans
☎ Telephone	✗ Restaurant
🖷 Fax	☙ Reservations
⊕ Website	🏛 Dress code
✎ E-mail	▭ No credit cards
🎟 Admission fee	⑤ Price
⊙ Open/closed	
times	**Other**
Ⓜ Subway	⇨ See also
⊹ Directions or	☞ Take note
Map coordinates	⚐ Golf facilities

Restaurants

Unless we state otherwise, restaurants are open for lunch and dinner daily. We mention dress code only when there's a specific requirement and reservations only when they're essential or not accepted. To make restaurant reservations, visit Fodors.com.

Credit Cards

The hotels and restaurants in this guide typically accept credit cards. If not, we'll say so.

EUGENE FODOR

Hungarian-born Eugene Fodor (1905–91) began his travel career as an interpreter on a French cruise ship. The experience inspired him to write *On the Continent* (1936), the first guidebook to receive annual updates and discuss a country's way of life as well as its sights. Fodor later joined the U.S. Army and worked for the OSS in World War II. After the war, he kept up his intelligence work while expanding his guidebook series. During the Cold War, many guides were written by fellow agents who understood the value of insider information. Today's guides continue Fodor's legacy by providing travelers with timely coverage, insider tips, and cultural context.

EXPERIENCE ORLANDO AND THE PARKS

1

WHAT'S NEW IN THE PARKS

Visitors see Orlando as a shiny vacation kingdom bolstered by cartoon characters. Residents see it as a city on the rise, with a stunning arts center in the heart of Downtown, an increasingly popular commuter rail line, a totally refurbished football stadium, a blossoming Downtown technology hub, and a brand new major league soccer stadium. Orlando is becoming an increasingly sophisticated destination.

Theme parks also are staying cutting-edge with interactive exhibits and high-tech attractions. Disney's new MyMagic+ Experience invites guests to manage their vacations by planning both online and with mobile tools; then they can use a special card or the MagicBand wrist band for everything from park admission and hotel entry to FastPass+ attraction appointments and food and merchandise purchases.

Walt Disney World

Adding a new look to the Magic Kingdom is the park's largest-ever expansion—to **Fantasyland,** with the opening of the Seven Dwarfs Mine Train family coaster. The redesign of this kid-friendly land allows guests to visit not one but three castles: the park's iconic and original Cinderella Castle, the new Beast's Castle that houses the lavish Be Our Guest Restaurant, and Prince Eric's castle where Under the Sea: Journey of the Little Mermaid features a voyage with Ariel. Fantasyland also boasts a double-the-fun Dumbo ride and a French cottage where Belle herself meets guests for a storybook "tale as old as time" in the Enchanted Tales with Belle attraction. The Princess Fairytale Hall, with its richly appointed greeting rooms in the Castle Courtyard, offers photo ops with Cinderella, Rapunzel, and visiting princesses like Snow White. In Adventureland, an interactive quest, A Pirates Adventure: Treasures of the Seven Seas, sends guests on a treasure hunt throughout Adventureland.

At **Downtown Disney,** the AMC Theater multiplex now offers six dine-in theaters with premium and casual dining experiences. Downtown Disney West Side turned the former Virgin Megastore building into Splitsville, a bowling mega-hangout across from House of Blues. Splitsville's menu, including beef-fillet sliders and sushi, adds to the entertainment center's upscale vibe. Meanwhile, Downtown Disney is in the midst of a multiyear transformation into Disney Springs. When it's completed, guests will find easier access with new parking garages; lots of new shopping, dining, and entertainment options; and open-air promenades along a waterfront. Epcot has its own thrill-a-minute custom-car adventure with the made-over, now-interactive Test Track by Chevrolet attraction.

Disney's luxury custom homes in the Golden Oaks community are built on ¼- to ¾-acre lots nestled beside the Magic Kingdom and Four Seasons.

Universal Orlando

Harry Potter became such a theme park star at Islands of Adventure that Universal Studios opened its own Potter playland: **The Wizarding World of Harry Potter—Diagon Alley,** in 2014. This entire new land is filled with eye candy and wonderful wizardry that can keep you entertained for hours, and its marquee attraction is based on a spinning and whirling ride through Gringotts Bank. Just across the lagoon, park guests can immerse themselves in Homer Simpson's hometown. As if the cartoon came to life, here you'll find the Lard Lad donut shop, Moe's Tavern, the famed

Come to Universal Studios to spend some quality time with your minions.

Kwik-E-Mart, and other iconic Springfield landmarks. **Transformers: The Ride 3-D** is an attraction packed with fast and furious explosions and attacks of an intergalactic battle between the Autobots and the Decepticons. Plus, Universal Studios introduced the daytime **Superstar Parade,** starring animated characters and street performers, and the evening film-and-firework extravaganza **Cinematic Spectacular: 100 Years of Movie Memories.**

SeaWorld, Discovery Cove, Aquatica
SeaWorld took a big PR hit with the release of the 2013 documentary *Blackfish,* and is looking at new ways to sustain their mission of celebrating marine life through the medium of a theme park. How it does this best is by presenting attractions like **Antarctica: Empire of the Penguin** and the park's **TurtleTrek,** which takes you on the underwater journey of a sea turtle via a 3-D film. But even before you get to the 360-degree domed theater, you walk past habitats filled with hundreds of freshwater and saltwater fish, gentle manatees, and more than a dozen sea turtles. At Discovery Cove, the main attraction isn't a show, but a calming and quiet natural vibe found in the tropical rain-forest environment that is **Freshwater Oasis,** which provides face-to-face encounters with playful otters and curious marmoset monkeys, and **SeaVenture** where you don a helmet equipped with a breathing apparatus so you can walk underwater through a reef filled with tropical fish and rays. In 2014, SeaWorld's third park, Aquatica, opened its new multislide thrill ride, **Ihu's Breakaway Falls,** named after a colorful gecko that serves as the water park's mascot.

WHAT'S WHERE

The following numbers refer to chapters.

2 Walt Disney World Resort. Disney invites you to four attraction-packed theme parks: Magic Kingdom, Animal Kingdom, Epcot, and Hollywood Studios, as well as two water parks, Blizzard Beach and Typhoon Lagoon. The lively Downtown Disney area is full of restaurants, shops, and diversions like the House of Blues and Cirque du Soleil. What else? Only a 220-acre sports complex, myriad hotels, full-service spas, golf courses, character meals, dinner shows, a wedding pavilion, and other experiences that are the stuff of dreams.

3 Universal Orlando. Universal Studios brings movies to life while Islands of Adventure delivers gravity-defying rides and special-effects surprises. Four on-site resorts offer themed accommodations, and CityWalk is the nightlife hub with restaurants, bars, movies, and clubs. For big-ticket concerts, stroll over to Hard Rock Live.

4 SeaWorld Orlando, Discovery Cove, and Aquatica. Marine life takes the stage at SeaWorld Orlando where killer whales and other marine mammals perform in meticulously choreographed shows and thrill seekers find their adrenaline rush on coaster and simulator attractions. Sister park Discovery Cove is a daylong, swim-with-the-dolphins beach escape. SeaWorld also invites you to a day of water play at Aquatica water park.

5 Wet 'n Wild. This long-popular water park in the heart of the International Drive corridor is more about big thrills than theming. With attraction names like Bomb Bay, Brain Wash, and The Storm, Wet 'n Wild promises a good time for adrenaline junkies of all ages.

6 Orlando and Environs. Those who venture beyond the parks to Downtown Orlando, International Drive, Kissimmee, and Winter Park discover new sights and experiences.

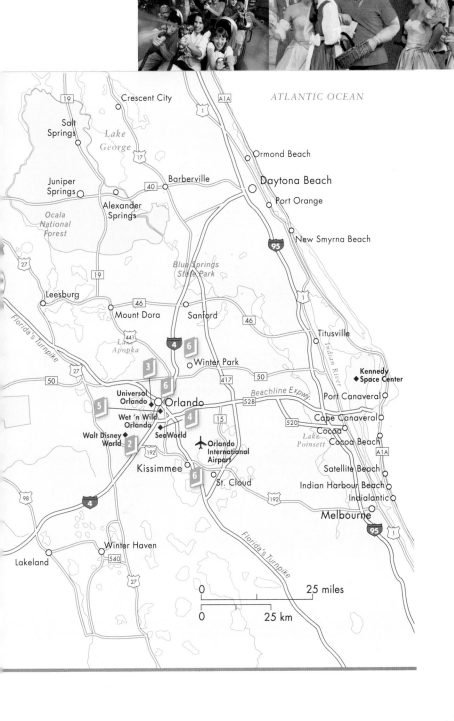

ATLANTIC OCEAN

Crescent City

Salt Springs

Lake George

Juniper Springs

Alexander Springs

Ocala National Forest

Barberville

Ormond Beach

Daytona Beach

Port Orange

New Smyrna Beach

Leesburg

Blue Springs State Park

Mount Dora

Sanford

Titusville

Lake Apopka

Winter Park

Kennedy Space Center

Universal Orlando

Orlando

Beachline Expwy.

Port Canaveral

Wet 'n Wild Orlando

Cape Canaveral

Walt Disney World

SeaWorld

Cocoa

Lake Poinsett

Cocoa Beach

Orlando International Airport

Satellite Beach

Kissimmee

Indian Harbour Beach

St. Cloud

Indialantic

Melbourne

Florida's Turnpike

Winter Haven

Lakeland

0 — 25 miles

0 — 25 km

ORLANDO TRANSPORTATION PLANNER

Getting Here

All the major and most discount airlines fly into **Orlando International Airport** (MCO ☎ 407/825–2001 ⊕ www.orlandoairports.net).

The **Beachline Expressway,** aka State Road 528, is a toll road that gets you from the airport to area attractions. Depending on the location of your hotel, follow it west, and either exit at SeaWorld for the International Drive (I-Drive) area or stay on it to Interstate 4, and head west for Disney and U.S. 192–Kissimmee or east for Universal and Downtown Orlando.

The **Central Florida Greenway** (☎ 407/690–5000 ⊕ www.oocea.com for toll info), **State Road 417,** also runs from the airport to Disney, but tolls are heftier.

Magical Express

If you're staying at a Disney hotel and flying on certain airlines, this free service will deliver your luggage from your home airport to your hotel (and back again) *and* shuttle you to and from your resort. You must book before departure (☎ 866/599–0951 ⊕ www.disneysmagicalexpress.com); have your flight information handy.

Getting Around

If you'll be on Disney property, you can use its buses, trams, boats, and monorails. If you're staying outside Disney—or want to visit a non-Disney attraction—options are cabs, shuttles (your hotel may have a free one), and rental cars. Some hotels have shuttles to and from Universal and SeaWorld, which don't have transit systems.

CABS, SHUTTLES, AND PUBLIC TRANSPORTATION

Many non-Disney hotels offer free airport shuttles. If yours doesn't, cabs from the airport to the Disney area run $55–$75. Try **Star Taxi** (☎ 407/857–9999) or **Yellow Cab Co.** (☎ 407/422–2222). **Town & Country Transportation** (☎ 407/828–3035) charges $75 one-way for a town car. The **Mears Transportation Group** (☎ 407/423–5566 ⊕ www.mearstransportation.com) offers shuttle and charter services throughout the Orlando area.The **I-Ride Trolley** (☎ 407/248–9590 ⊕ www.iridetrolley.com) serves most attractions in the I-Drive area (including SeaWorld). It won't get you to Disney, but it does have a stop about a half mile from Universal. The **LYNX** (☎ 407/841–5969 ⊕ www.golynx.com) bus system provides service in Orlando.

CAR RENTAL

Rates vary seasonally and can begin as low as $30 a day or $149 a week for an economy car (excluding 6.5% rental-car tax). If you're staying on Disney property but want to rent a car for a day, you might get a better daily rate if you reserve for two or more days and then return the car early. (Just be sure there aren't any penalties for this.)
■TIP→ Gas stations near the airport are pricey.

ROAD SERVICE

Dial *511 on your cell phone or 511 on a landline for traffic advisories (⊕ www.fl511.com). Dial *347 (*FHP) on your cell for the Florida Highway Patrol. Most Florida highways are also patrolled by Road Rangers, a free roadside service. The **AAA Car Care Center** (☎ 407/824–0976) near the Magic Kingdom provides emergency services, including free towing on Disney property, even for non-AAA members. Office hours are weekdays 7–7, Saturday 7–4, but trucks run whenever the parks are open.

Transit Times and Costs

AIRPORT TO:	BY SHUTTLE (PER PERSON)	BY TAXI/CAR
Magic Kingdom	30–45 mins; $36 round-trip (RT); $21 one way (OW)	35 mins; approx. $58 (taxi fare for up to 7 people)
Downtown Disney	30–45 mins; $36 RT; $21 OW	25–30 mins; approx. $51
Animal Kingdom/ Hollywood Studios	30–45 mins; $36 RT; $21 OW	35 mins; approx. $58
Universal	30–40 mins; $32 RT; $19 OW	20 mins; approx. $45
Kissimmee	30–45 mins; $48 RT; $27 OW	30 mins; approx. $56
I-Drive (midway)	30–40 mins; $32 RT; $19 OW	20 mins; approx. $35
Downtown Orlando	30 mins; $31 RT; $20 OW	20 mins; approx. $34
MAGIC KINGDOM TO:	BY SHUTTLE	BY TAXI/CAR
Downtown Disney	N/A (use Disney transportation)	10–15 mins; approx. $18
Animal Kingdom/ Hollywood Studios	N/A (use Disney transportation)	15 mins; approx. $17
Universal	25 mins; $20 RT	25 mins; approx. $43
Kissimmee	N/A	25–30 mins; approx. $28
I-Drive (midway)	N/A	30 mins; approx. $41
Downtown Orlando	N/A	40 mins; approx. $61
UNIVERSAL TO:	BY SHUTTLE	BY TAXI/CAR
Magic Kingdom	N/A	25 mins; approx. $43
Downtown Disney	N/A	20 mins; approx. $30
Animal Kingdom/ Hollywood Studios	N/A	30 mins; approx. $17
Kissimmee	30 mins; $19 RT	25 mins; approx. $45
I-Drive (midway)	25 mins; $16 RT	5–10 mins; approx. $10
Downtown Orlando	N/A	10 mins; approx. $25

Orlando Routes

Beachline Expressway: Toll road from the airport to I-Drive and Disney ($2.25). Also good for Universal, SeaWorld, and Space Coast.

Interstate 4: Main east–west highway between Tampa and Daytona; it follows a north–south track through Orlando, making for a little confusion. ■TIP➔ Think north when Interstate 4 signs say east (toward Daytona, say), and south when they say west (toward Tampa).

Key exits:

–Exit 64B: Magic Kingdom/U.S. 192; *heavy* peak-season traffic near this exit

–Exit 65: Animal Kingdom, ESPN Wide World of Sports

–Exit 67: Epcot/Downtown Disney, Typhoon Lagoon, Universal; less-congested exit

–Exit 68: Downtown Disney, Typhoon Lagoon

–Exits 71 and 72: SeaWorld

–Exits 72, 74A, and 75A: I-Drive

–Exits 74B and 75A: Universal Orlando Resort

Semoran Boulevard: One of the main roads to Orlando and Winter Park from the airport. Heavily traveled but moves well; plenty of amenities.

Spacecoast Parkway or Irlo Bronson Memorial Highway (U.S. 192): Runs east–west to Kissimmee. Continues east to the coast at Melbourne. Crosses Interstate 4 at Exits 64A and 64B.

WALT DISNEY WORLD AND ORLANDO TOP ATTRACTIONS

Magic Kingdom

(A) The magic of Disney begins on Main Street, U.S.A. where you are welcomed by a barbershop quartet serenade. Cinderella Castle beckons, and each magical land has classic attractions—from Adventureland's Pirates of the Caribbean to Tomorrowland's sleek Space Mountain. Children meet Mickey Mouse or their favorite princess, ride their first roller coaster, and fly high with Peter Pan and Dumbo.

Epcot

(B) Top reasons to visit begin with the hands-on Innoventions exhibits and end with the Soarin' "hang-gliding" adventure. History is entertaining at the American Adventure and Spaceship Earth. Count down to launch on Mission: SPACE. Dine at Via Napoli or other great restaurants at each international pavilion. End a day with fireworks at IllumiNations.

Disney's Hollywood Studios

(C) Film- and TV-inspired adventures lure audiences to the Indiana Jones Epic Stunt Spectacular!, Star Tours, and Toy Story Midway Mania! Thrill seekers get their kicks at Twilight Zone Tower of Terror and Rock 'n' Roller Coaster Starring Aerosmith. The Magic of Disney Animation highlights Walt and his cartoons.

Animal Kingdom

(D) Animals from several continents share the spotlight in habitats that mimic native environments. You'll see some critters from the open-air safari vehicles of Kilimanjaro Safaris; you'll spot others along landscaped trails. Shows like Festival of the Lion King draw crowds. Rides like DINOSAUR and Expedition Everest push the adrenaline envelope.

Universal Studios

(E) Universal is known for action, adventure, and now a touch of wizardry. Guests can wander through Diagon Alley, casting spells with pals from the Potter films, descend into the depths of Gringotts Bank, then hop on the train for Hogwarts. From Terminator 2: 3-D to Revenge of the Mummy and The Simpsons, attractions score points with fans of contemporary film and television.

Islands of Adventure

(F) The Wizarding World of Harry Potter allows fans of the book-and-film franchise to enter the hallowed halls of Hogwarts, wander through the village of Hogsmeade, buy Bertie Bott's Every-Flavour Beans™ at Honeydukes sweetshop, and then take the train to London and Diagon Alley. The other attractions in the park include the Amazing Adventures of Spider-Man and the Incredible Hulk Coaster. There's also whimsical Seuss Landing, perfect for fans of *The Cat in the Hat* and the *Star-Bellied Sneetches*.

SeaWorld and Discovery Cove

(G) Lagoons are populated by all manner of sea creatures, and shows are well done with a mixture of cute marine mammals, skilled trainers, and athletic divers. Kraken and Manta are first-rate coasters. The signature Discovery Cove experience is the chance to swim with dolphins.

I-Drive

7 miles northeast of Disney, this is a busy commercial strip with attractions such as the 400-foot-tall Orlando Eye, an observation wheel with 30 air-conditioned capsules from which guests can take in vast views of Central Florida. Other attractions include Madame Tussauds Orlando; SEA LIFE Aquarium with more than 5,000 sea creatures; Ripley's Believe It or Not! Odditorium; WonderWorks; Wet 'n Wild water park; and Fun Spot.

IF YOU LIKE

Thrill Rides

Many people love high-speed launches and stomach-churning multiple inversions. Simulator rides that produce similar results are just as popular. Strap on your seat belt and prepare for liftoff!

■ **Roller Coasters.** Coaster fans can't get enough of the Incredible Hulk at Islands of Adventure, Manta at SeaWorld, and Rock 'n' Roller Coaster at Disney's Hollywood Studios. There's also Expedition Everest at Animal Kingdom, Space Mountain at Magic Kingdom, Hollywood Rip Ride Rockit at Universal Studios, and SheiKra at Busch Gardens.

■ **Simulators.** Harry Potter and the Forbidden Journey at Islands of Adventure puts you on a virtual broomstick at Harry's right hand in a game of Quiddich. Universal Studios's Harry Potter and the Escape from Gringotts delves deep into the bank vaults and out over the rooftops with a fire-breathing dragon. Soarin' at Epcot gives you the sensation of hang gliding over California. Wild Arctic at SeaWorld takes you on a virtual helicopter ride above polar ice caps. The Simpsons Ride at Universal Studios is a cartoonish romp, and the Amazing Adventures of Spider-Man at Islands of Adventure uses 3-D technology to the max for high-voltage thrills. At DisneyQuest, Innovations at Epcot, and at WonderWorks you can "build" and ride your own simulated roller coaster.

■ **Wet Rides.** Hot Florida days and wet thrill rides go together like burgers and fries. Cool off at Journey to Atlantis at SeaWorld; Popeye & Bluto's Bilge-Rat Barges and Dudley Do-Right's Ripsaw Falls at Islands of Adventure; Splash Mountain at the Magic Kingdom; and Kali River Rapids at Animal Kingdom.

Special Effects and Interactive Fun

Bubbles burst on your nose. A 3-D Michael Jackson dances off the big screen. Cartoons come to life. Aliens attack. Anything's possible when theme-park attractions throw special effects, animation magic, and hands-on action into the mix.

■ **Theater Shows.** If you get a kick out of special-effects surprises in 3-D films, these top shows should be on your itinerary: Shrek 4-D at Universal Studios; It's Tough to be a Bug! at Animal Kingdom; Mickey's PhilharMagic at Magic Kingdom; Captain EO (with Michael Jackson) at Epcot; and Muppet*Vision 3-D at Hollywood Studios.

■ **Interactive Rides.** Competitive streak? These scored rides, complete with hands-on laser guns or spring-action shooters, are just the ticket: MEN IN BLACK: Alien Attack at Universal Studios; Toy Story Midway Mania! at Hollywood Studios; and Buzz Lightyear's Space Ranger Spin at Magic Kingdom.

■ **Audio-Animatronics.** Disney's Audio-Animatronics characters pop up in every park, and some of the figures can be quite convincing. Among the best: the wicked witch of the Great Movie Ride "Oz" sequence at Hollywood Studios; the President Obama figure at the Hall of Presidents and Captain Jack Sparrow of *Pirates of the Caribbean,* both at Magic Kingdom; and the monstrous yeti of Expedition Everest at Animal Kingdom.

■ **Cartoon Magic.** Animation brings characters to life on dozens of rides and attractions, from Homer and the aliens at Universal's The Simpsons Ride to Mushu of the Disney film *Mulan* at the Magic of Disney Animation in Hollywood Studios.

Animal Antics

Alligators don't just hang out in Orlando's many large lakes—they also headline gator-wrestling shows and whole-chicken feeding frenzies at Gatorland. If reptiles aren't your thing, consider the options.

■ **Natural Habitats.** Frolic with dolphins and snorkel amid stingrays at Discovery Cove's Dolphin Lagoon and the Grand Reef. SeaWorld's Wild Arctic and other attractions feature many animals and fish in re-created environments. At Animal Kingdom you'll see Bengal tigers along the Maharajah Jungle Trek, lowland gorillas at Pangani Forest Exploration Trail, and Galápagos tortoises at Discovery Island Trails. Myombe Reserve at Busch Gardens is a rain-forest environment with gorillas and chimps.

■ **Safaris.** Kilimanjaro Safaris at Animal Kingdom is a bumpy adventure in open-air vehicles through African habitats. No 20-minute safari is the same, as the elephants, hippos, lions, zebras, and other animals are constantly on the move. At Busch Gardens the off-road Rhino Rally safari passes crocs, rhinos, and hippos.

■ **Performances.** SeaWorld is the top park in which to see animals trained to entertain. Shamu makes a huge splash in the show One Ocean. Sea lions, otters, and walruses astound you at the Clyde and Seamore Take Pirate Island dramedy. At the Pets Ahoy show, dogs, cats, parrots, and even a pig play for laughs.

■ **Critter Connections.** At Rafiki's Planet Watch in Animal Kingdom are exotic-animal encounters and a petting yard with animals from around the world. At SeaWorld, you can feed and pet dolphins at Key West and stroke rays at Stingray Lagoon.

Parades, Fireworks, and Shows

Lights, fireworks, action! You'll get your fill at Orlando's theme parks.

■ **Daytime Pageants.** You can set your watch by the Magic Kingdom's daily 3 pm Disney Festival of Fantasy Parade. Mickey's Jammin' Jungle Parade is a safari of fun at Animal Kingdom. Universal's Superstar Parade boogies through the park with bubble machines, stunt performers, and popular characters like SpongeBob SquarePants.

■ **Nighttime Spectacles.** The Magic Kingdom's Wishes explodes nightly over Cinderella Castle, and the Main Street Electrical Parade with millions of twinkling lights charms crowds several times weekly along Main Street, U.S.A. Epcot's nightly IllumiNations combines music, flames, fireworks, and fountains in a 13-minute display of near-cosmic proportion. Get a seat early for Fantasmic! at Hollywood Studios, a 25-minute fireworks, laser, lights, and dancing-fountains show starring Sorcerer Mickey Mouse, which runs several times nightly during busy times and two or three times weekly in the off-season. Universal's Cinematic Spectacular—100 Years of Movie Memories gives a fireworks salute to a century of iconic films.

■ **Explosive Action.** The Eighth Voyage of Sindbad Stunt Show at Islands of Adventure juices up its story line with 25 minutes of physical stunt work, plus water explosions, flames, and fireworks. Indiana Jones Epic Stunt Spectacular! has dynamic action sequences straight from the film. Car, boat, and motorcycle stunts take the stage at the Lights, Motors, Action! Extreme Stunt Show (both at Hollywood Studios).

Luxury Resorts

Here are our favorite upscale lodging resorts that offer an array of amenities from first-rate service, fine food, and pampering spas to championship golf courses, attractive architecture, and a general ambience of luxury.

■ **Disney's Animal Kingdom Lodge.** One of the few places at Disney where the exotic animals strolling past your window are real. The soaring thatch-roofed lobby is breathtaking, and staff tell stories about their African homelands.

■ **Disney's Grand Floridian Resort & Spa.** A hotel in the Victorian style, complete with broad verandas, that allows guests to feel as though they've traveled back in time to an era when they were truly pampered.

■ **Four Seasons.** Inside Disney's gates, this award-winning resort comes with suites fit for royalty, accommodations for your nanny, views of all four Disney parks from the roof, a deluxe spa and golf course, and loads of special Disney bennies.

■ **Ritz-Carlton Orlando Grande Lakes.** A golf course, a spa, and chef Norman Van Aken's signature restaurant are just some of the jewels set in this luxury chain.

■ **Waldorf Astoria Orlando.** Although it's not an exact copy of the famed Manhattan original, it's a thoroughly updated ode to Waldorf luxury, with a deluxe spa, fine restaurants, and a championship golf course.

Family- and Budget-Friendly Stays

Families flock to this theme-park-oriented area, which means that there are endless budget options that can accommodate the entire clan.

■ **All-Star Sports, Music, and Movies Resorts.** Each section of these sprawling resorts is geared to a particular interest, providing fun for kids and a break for parents' wallets. The Music resort pays homage to genres from Broadway show tunes to country, jazz, and rock and roll; the pools are shaped like a guitar and a piano. In the Movies resort, huge characters from classic Disney films frame each building. The Sports resort celebrates baseball, football, basketball, and more, and has a pool shaped like a baseball diamond.

■ **Best Western Lake Buena Vista Resort.** Close enough to Disney to watch the fireworks from your balcony, this hotel has something for every member of the family: free Wi-Fi, free shuttles to Disney and outlet malls, and a fun pool. Best of all, it's within walking distance of Downtown Disney's entertainment complex.

■ **Fort Wilderness Resort Campground.** This relatively unknown and inexpensive part of Disney World offers a unique glimpse of Florida wilderness, along with entertainment, such as the ridiculously funny Hoop-Dee-Doo Musical Revue, which makes the kid in all of us erupt with laughter. If you don't have a tent, staff will provide one and put it up!

■ **Nickelodeon Suites Resort.** SpongeBob and Co. are as familiar to kids as Mickey and Minnie, and this reasonably priced hotel complex is near Disney but allows for an escape to something completely different.

Foodie Experiences

The Orlando dining scene does not consist only of hamburgers and hot dogs. You can also find five-star dining and creative cuisine mixed in among the sea of food courts and fast-food chains.

■ **Boma.** African-inspired dishes like spiced roasted chicken and curried-coconut seafood stew are a hit with parents and kids at this casual and excellent buffet in the Animal Kingdom Lodge.

■ **Luma on Park.** Under the deft guidance of chef Brandon McGlamery, over-the-top delicious takes on creative American fare are served in a stylish see-and-be-seen space right on Winter Park's tony Park Avenue.

■ **Primo.** Melissa Kelly's farm-to-table ethos is in full effect at the Orlando outpost of the chef's famed Italian-organic Maine restaurant. Here produce is grown in the hotel garden, so diners can expect all of the dishes to be prepared with the freshest ingredients.

■ **The Ravenous Pig.** From a charcuterie platter on which every salami is made entirely from scratch to a small inventive menu that changes every day based on what's fresh in the market (plus the best burger in town), this comfortable Winter Park gastropub is worth the drive.

■ **Victoria & Albert's.** One of the plushest dining experiences in Florida, this Disney resort restaurant serves up modern American cuisine with a seven-course prix-fixe menu that changes daily.

Theme Restaurants

Part of the fun of Orlando is the over-the-top theme parks, and the restaurants to match. Here are our favorite restaurants where ambience and decor are just as prized as what is on the plate.

■ **Cuba Libre.** This expansive eatery on International Drive replicates the streets of Cuba, and if you close your eyes, sip a mojito, and snack on some *papas rellenas,* you'll almost feel like you're in Havana.

■ **50's Prime Time Café.** Head back in time at this replica of a kitschy, classic American diner in Disney's Hollywood Studios. Clips of sitcoms like *I Love Lucy* and the *Donna Reed Show* play in the background as you chow down on comfort-food favorites like meat loaf and fried chicken.

■ **Sci-Fi Dine-In Theater Restaurant.** Dine in at this (fake) drive-in, also at the Studios, where standard American fare like salads, sandwiches, and burgers are served to you as you sit in a faux convertible and watch movie clips from classic sci-fi flicks from the '50s and '60s.

■ **Taverna Opa.** Taverna Opa on International Drive takes Greek dining to a whole new level. While sampling excellent Mediterranean fare, you are entertained by a fire-eating belly dancer. If the spirit moves you, dance around the dining room with a slew of fellow guests.

■ **Three Broomsticks.** Harry Potter fans should look no further than this fast-food restaurant designed to look like a tavern at the Wizarding World of Harry Potter attraction. Dining here feels like you're in the heart of Hogsmeade, rather than the heart of Islands of Adventure theme park.

SEASONAL AND HOLIDAY EVENTS

If you've been to Orlando and its parks and enjoyed the top attractions at least once, consider a special trip around one of the many festivals and events.

The year-end holiday season is particularly festive. Decorations go up and events begin around Thanksgiving and continue through early January. It pays to book a trip during the first few weeks of December, when there's a lull between Thanksgiving and Christmas crowds.

Winter

Candlelight Processional. Each holiday season between Thanksgiving and New Year's, a succession of celebrity narrators visit Disney to re-tell the story of Christmas before a full orchestra and large choir comprised of guest singers from local schools and churches. Presented at Epcot's American Gardens Theatre, the show is truly a spectacular with sing-along carols and a stirring performance of the Hallelujah Chorus from Handel's *Messiah*. The performance is free with admission (although you'll wait in a very, very long line)—or you can opt for the Candlelight lunch or dinner package, which includes a meal at one of Epcot's pavilions as well as VIP early-access seating. Prices change often; call in advance. ⊠ *World Showcase, America Gardens Theatre, Epcot.*

Grinchmas Wholiday Spectacular. The holiday season takes a curmudgeonly turn at Seuss Landing during Grinchmas, an Islands of Adventure stage show based on the Dr. Seuss classic *How the Grinch Stole Christmas*. An original Mannheim Steamroller musical score backs up a half dozen songs by an energetic and colorful cast including the Grinch and the Whos from Whoville. The stage show is only part of it. Stick around and this festive "Whobiliation" and the Grinch (as well as several

Whos) will be out on curving Seussian streets to say hello and pose for souvenir snapshots. ⊠ *Islands of Adventure.*

Mickey's Jingle Jungle Parade. During the year Disney's Animal Kingdom rocks with the Jammin' Jungle Parade, but during the holidays the parade is transformed into Mickey's Jingle Jungle Parade. While you can expect to see the "Fab Five" (Mickey, Minnie, Donald, Goofy, and Pluto) in their safari/holiday regalia, during the 15-minute rolling extravaganza, you'll also see Goofy in a Santa Claus outfit and floats featuring humongous presents and packages as well as many characters from *The Jungle Book*. Perhaps most impressive are the larger-than-life human-powered "animals" that first dazzled audiences on Broadway in *The Lion King*—animals that seem to have a mind of their own and often interact with park guests. ⊠ *Discovery Island, Animal Kingdom.*

Mickey's Very Merry Christmas Party. Disney's Magic Kingdom is just that: magic. Come here during scheduled evenings in November and December, and you'll discover Mickey's Very Merry Christmas Party spreads even more holiday cheer. On these evenings, add to the park's twinkling lights, fantasy architecture, and grandeur of Cinderella Castle a holiday parade, seasonal stage shows, fireworks, "snow" on Main Street, U.S.A., and platters of hot cocoa and cookies, and you've set the stage for some wonderful photographs as well as lifelong memories. And it's priced lower than a single day's park admission. ⊠ *Magic Kingdom.*

Osborne Family Spectacle of Dancing Lights. At Disney's Hollywood Studios, you can see the long-running holiday-time Osborne Family Spectacle of Dancing Lights from mid-November through early

January—although even when you see it you won't believe your eyes. As a sound track of holiday music plays, more than *5 million* colorful lights pulse in time, "snow" falls over the Streets of America, and Santa and his reindeer, angels, and toy soldiers add to the well-named spectacle. Now here's your Christmas present: the show is free with admission. ✉ *Streets of America, Disney's Hollywood Studios.*

The Polar Express Experience. Between mid-November and early January, SeaWorld's Wild Arctic attraction is transformed into The Polar Express Experience. Instead of a multisensory ride over the Arctic, you'll soar through and above classic scenes from the film based on the Caldecott-medal-winning book *The Polar Express.* SeaWorld's Christmas Celebration lineup also includes shows starring sea lions, otters, Shamu, and even the Sesame Street gang. ✉ *SeaWorld.*

Walt Disney World Marathon. Each January at least 40,000 athletes from around the globe lace up their running shoes during the Walt Disney World Marathon weekend. Donald, Mickey, and Goofy challenge racers to a half marathon, a full marathon, or both. Go the distance and you'll run through all four Walt Disney World theme parks, starting at Epcot, continuing on to the Magic Kingdom, Disney's Animal Kingdom, and then Disney's Hollywood Studios before heading back to the finish line at Epcot. There is also a 5K family fun run, a relay, kids' races, and a Health and Fitness Expo at ESPN Wide World of Sports Complex. In 2014, race officials added a 10K and the aptly named Dopey Challenge, in which participants run a 5K, 10K, half marathon, and marathon, totaling 48.6 miles. ✉ *Walt Disney World* ⊕ *www.rundisney. com.*

Spring

Mardi Gras at Universal Studios. During Mardi Gras at Universal Studios (select evenings between February and April), the spirit of New Orleans comes to Orlando. In addition to colorful floats, stilt walkers, New Orleans–style food and drinks, zydeco bands, and the distribution of nearly 2 million beads, there is a full calendar of concerts with headliners like Heart, Styx, the B52s, Kelly Clarkson, and Olivia Newton John. Best of all, all of it—the parades, shows, and performances—is free with park admission. ✉ *Universal Studios* ⊕ *https://www.universalorlando. com/Events/Mardi-Gras/.*

Winter Park Sidewalk Art Festival. One of Central Florida's most pleasant and anticipated events, since 1960 the juried Winter Park Sidewalk Art Festival has found posh Park Avenue and oak-shaded Central Park filled with paintings, sculptures, and myriad works of art displayed by more than 225 artists and exhibitors. In 2014, *Sunshine Artist* magazine ranked this number five in the nation in their list of Fine Art and Design Shows. Taking place during the third weekend of March, an estimated 350,000 visitors peruse this outdoor gallery, enhanced by food vendors, art workshops for children and adults, and the upscale shops of peaceful Park Avenue. If you're in the neighborhood, this art festival is a must. ✉ *Park Ave. and Central Park, Winter Park* ⊕ *www.wpsaf.org.*

Summer

City of Kissimmee July 4th Celebration. Starting at 5 pm on the shores of Kissimmee's Lake Tohopekaliga (aka Lake Toho), the city makes the most of the Fourth of July and its Lakefront Park with live music, entertainment, food, and children's events and activities. Just after 9 pm, the sky explodes with thunderous and colorful fireworks that rattle this still slow-paced cattle community on the doorstep of Disney. ✉ *Kissimmee.*

Fireworks at the Fountain. The focal point of Orlando isn't Cinderella Castle, it's the "Rainbow Fountain" at Downtown's Lake Eola, which was built in 1957 and refurbished in 2011. On all other nights of the year, the fountain is illuminated with a choreographed six-minute show set to music, with the colors and songs changing with the season. But on the 4th of July, the main event is a free celebration that begins in the afternoon with games, food, and live entertainment. Encircling the picturesque lake is a one-mile promenade that gives everyone a perfect vantage point to watch fireworks burst high above Lake Eola Park. ✉ *Lake Eola Park, Downtown Orlando.*

A Sci-Fi 4th of July. Launched in 2013, the Disney-planned community of Celebration teamed up with MegaCon (the renowned comic book, fantasy, gaming, and sci-fi convention) to create the Sci-Fi 4th of July; a festival-themed costume contest tied to a science fiction theme. The community celebration also features live music, games, and fireworks. ✉ *Celebration.*

Gay Days Orlando. In early June, Gay Days Orlando brings more than 150,000 members of the gay, lesbian, bisexual, and transgendered community to Orlando, primarily arriving to visit theme parks—although Disney makes a point to say they don't "officially sponsor or promote" the event. Gay Days also includes DJ parties, pool parties, music, and events throughout the metro area. ✉ *Orlando* ☎ *407/896–8431* ⊕ *www.gaydays.com.*

Fall

Epcot International Food & Wine Festival. For six weeks (late September through mid-November) the Epcot International Food & Wine Festival transforms the park into a food-and-wine wonderland with tasting seminars, culinary demonstrations, and a constant stream of celebrity chefs. Dine around the world at international marketplaces selling tasty bites, or splurge on wine schools and signature dinner events. Adding to the epicurean event is the Eat to the Beat concert series, featuring popular hit makers such as The Commodores, Pointer Sisters, Christopher Cross, and .38 Special. ✉ *World Showcase, Epcot* ⊕ *https://disneyworld.disney.go.com/ events-tours/epcot/epcot-international- food-and-wine-festival/.*

Halloween Horror Nights. Much more intense than your average haunted house, this extremely popular event incorporates all of the special effects and movie make-up skills you'd expect from one of the leaders in the horror genre. Each evening, the streets of Universal Studios are transformed into chill-inducing haunted houses and scare zones populated by characters from your worst nightmares. A new theme is introduced each year, but at heart this terror-rific event has a simple purpose: to attract teens and young adults who can't get enough of its heart-pounding horrors. Admission for this after-park-hours event is less than the price of regular park admission. ✉ *Universal Studios* ⊕ *www.*

halloweenhorrornights.com ⊙ *Select nights Sept. and Oct.*

Macy's Holiday Parade. If you're in New York, you can experience Macy's famous parade just once a year. Come to Universal Studios during the holidays and you can take in an abridged version of the parade every day of your visit. Featuring Macy's floats and balloons shipped to Orlando following the Big Apple event, the Universal Studios version features marching bands from across America, a Christmas tree lighting ceremony, and shines a spotlight on Barney, the Blues Brothers, and other Universal celebs. ⊠ *Universal Studios* ⊕ *www.universalorlando.com.*

Mickey's Not-So-Scary Halloween Party. As a marked contrast to the Universal's Halloween Horror Nights, at Disney's Magic Kingdom kids in costumes own the streets during their quest for treats (no tricks!) at Mickey's Not-So-Scary Halloween Party. The gently spooky celebration takes place on scheduled evenings throughout September and October. Party tickets are priced below regular park admission, and it's easier to meet the characters and avoid ride queues. ⊠ *Magic Kingdom.*

WALT DISNEY WORLD GREAT ITINERARIES

A trip to Walt Disney World can be . . . *interesting*. If you consider its size (more or less the size of San Francisco) as well as the variety of things to do (four theme parks, resort hotels and activities, recreation, attractions, restaurants, live shows, fireworks, golf, character breakfasts and greetings, parades, and a few hundred other choices for entertainment), it's easy to be overwhelmed. Take a breath, relax, and consider this approach.

If you have one day

If you have only one day to experience the essence of Disney, there's only one way to do it: visit The Magic Kingdom. Walt Disney's genius is on full display in this park adapted from his original at California's Disneyland, and you'll feel the pixie dust as soon as you step through the turnstiles.

Main Street, U.S.A. is a step into the past with horse-drawn streetcars rolling past, a barbershop quartet, and turn-of-the-20th-century buildings.

Ahead, the draw is Cinderella Castle, the focal point of the park. On your left, Adventureland features two must-sees: the Jungle Cruise and its wisecracking skippers and Pirates of the Caribbean, an entertaining boat ride that inspired the movie franchise.

Continue your clockwise walk and enter Frontierland where the standouts are the Big Thunder Mountain Railroad—a roller coaster mine train—and the Country Bear Jamboree. Liberty Square adjoins Frontierland with two more Disney classics: spooky Haunted Mansion and the inspiring Hall of Presidents.

A new and improved Fantasyland is next. A $400 million renovation completed in 2014 added new attractions including the Beast's Castle, Princess Fairytale Hall, and the Seven Dwarfs Mine Train to join it's

a small world and Dumbo the Flying Elephant, and the Carrousel.

Tomorrowland offers a retro-futuristic look in favorites like the Speedway and Space Mountain. Your round-trip complete, be sure to include time to watch a parade or circle the park via an authentic steam train.

If you have four days

If you have the good fortune to spend four days at Disney, you have to see each of its four theme parks. After visiting the Magic Kingdom on Day One, you can slow down the pace at Epcot—but be prepared for a lot of walking. The park is divided into two sections: Future World and the World Showcase, with the former—at the entrance to the park—opening an hour earlier than its neighbor. While it lacks the magic of the Magic Kingdom, Future World can be entertaining with high-tech demonstrations in the Innoventions areas, shows like Michael Jackson's Captain Eo, and the virtual hang-gliding adventure at Soarin'.

But what most Epcot visitors talk about is exploring the World Showcase. If travel abroad is out of your budget, you can test drive visits to exotic locations. At nearly every international pavilion—Canada, Great Britain, France, Morocco, Japan, United States, Italy, Germany, China, Norway, Mexico—there is usually entertainment (a movie, live show, street theater), a restaurant, art gallery, and a variety of gift shops. That evening, stick around for the grand finale. IllumiNations: Reflections of Earth is an over-the-top fireworks and laser show that wraps up the day with a dazzling finish.

On Day Three, plan a day at Disney's Hollywood Studios. Inspired by the Golden Age of the Silver Screen, the park ushers you in past classic Tinseltown landmarks. Must-sees here include the Muppet*Vision 3D, Star Tours: The Adventure Continues, Indiana Jones Epic Stunt Spectacular!, the mind-blowing Twilight Zone Tower of Terror, and the Lights, Motors, Action! Extreme Stunt Show. After dark, thousands of park guests flood into the Hollywood hills to watch the final show of the evening, Fantasmic!, a celebration of classic Disney films and characters accompanied by music, songs, water effects, and fireworks.

Day Four brings you to the Disney's Animal Kingdom, one of the most interesting parks you'll find. Two continents create the park. Africa is closest to the park entrance and includes several attractions. Festival of the Lion King is a wonderfully entertaining live show featuring classic moments from the iconic animated film as well as extremely talented gymnasts, fantastic floats, memorable songs, and cheering sections supporting the larger-than-life characters. And don't miss It's Tough to be a Bug! which you'll find in an underground theater below the Tree of Life, the park's focal point. The "4-D" film is a comedy that shows how insects affect our lives and includes sensations that'll make you shiver—and laugh.

Farther inside the park, the Kilimanjaro Safari is extremely popular since it offers a chance to see hippos, lions, giraffes, baboons, and more—but get there early since the wildlife is more active in the morning before the day gets too hot. Asia is filled with photo ops—and one incredible coaster. Expedition Everest takes you high into the Himalayas in search of the fabled yeti, and at the very peak of the mountain a surprise twist finds the entire coaster racing backwards through the

hills. Nearby, the Kali River Rapids offers similar thrills, but via a whitewater raft ride. Look for shows, animal encounters, street performers, and the retro amusement park thrills of DinoLand U.S.A. and you'll easily pack in a full day.

If you have seven days

If you can spend a full week at Walt Disney World, you'll enjoy a vacation that few have had the privilege to experience.

Follow the Day Four suggestions (above), then take the fifth to recharge and relax. That evening, head to Downtown Disney, take in a movie, go bowling at Splitsville, watch a live concert at the House of Blues, or the surreal show at Cirque du Soleil, La Nouba.

Wherever you place your "free day," you're now up to Day Six—and this is a good time to pay a return visit to your favorite theme park, especially if you purchased a multiple-day "all-parks" pass. Since you have a full day to explore, consider splitting up your time between two parks—perhaps Animal Kingdom for an early morning safari and Epcot or the Magic Kingdom to see that evening's fireworks display.

On Day Seven, start to wind things down. Theme parks are still an option, but it's also a good time to review the list of souvenirs you need to take home. That evening, make a reservation for dinner at the California Grill atop the Contemporary Resort (which is also a wonderful vantage point to watch fireworks over the Magic Kingdom), or go all out and dine at Victoria & Albert's at the Grand Floridian—one of the rare AAA Five Diamond restaurants in Florida.

What a week! Thanks, Walt!

ORLANDO GREAT ITINERARIES

AWAY FROM THE THEME PARKS

If you're like most visitors to Orlando, you've come for a theme park (or two or three). But if you need a break from them, have people in your group who aren't interested in them, or have an extra day or week, know that it's easy to get out and explore Central Florida, and that there are lots of things to do and see outside the parks. A stay in Orlando also puts you an hour from the eastern coast and 90 minutes from the Gulf of Mexico.

If you have one day

Head out mid-morning. If it's rainy or hot and humid, visit the Mennello Museum of Folk Art northeast of Downtown in Loch Haven Park. If you have kids, the Orlando Science Center, across the street, is a great alternative, and you can check to see what's playing at the adjoining Orlando Shakespeare Theater. If it's a nice day, explore the 50-acre Harry P. Leu Gardens, also northeast of Downtown Orlando, home to subtropical flora and a huge Floral Clock from Edinburgh, Scotland. Arrive for one of the day's first guided tours (they start at 10) of the Leu House Museum.

Head to Downtown's Lake Eola Park. A stroll around the lake brings views of the resident swans and waterbirds, along with the centerpiece fountain. Have a snack in the park's Relax Grill or at one of the many eateries nearby. After, go to happy hour at the bars or clubs of Orange Avenue At night, places like Venue 578, the Beacham, and the Social nightclubs are fun dance spots.

SHOPPING HIGHLIGHTS

If it's Saturday, head out early so you can start your spree at the Winter Park Farmers' Market, where there's free valet parking. Stalls sell locally sourced foods—including breakfast—and crafts. Regardless of the day, Park Avenue, a haven of shopping and dining, beckons. Boutiques and galleries—including Ten Thousand Villages and Timothy's—line the east side, opposite an oak-shaded park. An alfresco lunch will carry you through an afternoon of still more shopping. After spending the day shopping like a local, you should spend the evening dining like one. Head to Sand Lake Road for a plethora of multi-cultural cuisines—from Italian and Mediterranean to Thai, Mexican, Indian, and Hawaiian fusion.

If you have four days

You can continue your exploration of the museums at the Orlando Museum of Art in Loch Haven Park, with its stunning permanent collection of pre-Columbian artifacts from South and Central America. The Orange County Regional History Museum in Downtown offers several floors of family-friendly and gently educational local history. Winter Park's crowning jewel, the Charles Hosmer Morse Museum of American Art, houses the world's most complete collection of Tiffany windows, art glass, and ceramics. If you need some time outdoors, away from history-laden museum walls, take a picnic on Winter Park's scenic boat tour, which offers a pleasant two-hour voyage through lakes and canals, past luxurious homes and the campus of Rollins College, the Southsast's oldest halls of academe. Continuing the outdoor theme (of course, dependent on the weather), Central Florida's subtropical ecosystem contains lush natural greenery and wildlife that can be observed at several nearby state and local parks. The Audubon Center for Birds of Prey in Maitland houses injured eagles, hawks, owls, vultures, and more who cannot return safely to the wild. Just to the north is Wekiwa Springs State Park, where you can swim in crystal-clear waters that power up from the Florida Aquifer, or rent a canoe to slip silently along the river, to glimpse alligators, turtles, herons, eagles, cranes, deer, and even bears. Blue Spring State Park, a few miles farther north, is winter home to hundreds of manatees. A raised boardwalk meanders along the river to the springhead so you can observe the manatees and often their babies, without disturbing them.

Heading east from Orlando, you can be at the Kennedy Space Center in a little over an hour on SR528 (the Beachline Expressway, a toll road), which makes it a good day trip. Several Orlando tour companies have trips for about $100 per person, or if you have a car, it's an easy drive. The exhibitions on American space travel and the pioneer astronauts who were launched into space from "the Cape," as locals call it, have enthralled visitors since 1968. The IMAX 3-D films and Shuttle Launch Ride offer a fully immersive space experience. The right timing could have you viewing an actual SpaceX or Delta rocket rising from the nearby launch pads. With an overnight stay, you can lounge on the blissful beaches of Canaveral National Seashore, catch a wave like surfing legend (and local hero) Kelly Slater, or explore the adjacent 140,000-acre Merritt Island National Wildlife Refuge. There are also opportunities for horseback riding, hiking, bird-watching, and fishing. Cape Canaveral and Cocoa Beach make great bases, thanks to their coastal locations

and selection of hotels, restaurants, outfitters, and other amenities.

If you have seven days

After exploring the area's wildlife and space history, you could head southwest to the adjoining cities of Tampa and St. Petersburg, only about 90 minutes away on Interstate 4. They are perfectly reachable for a day trip, but the area's many attractions make Tampa, St. Petersburg, and other coastal towns worthy of an overnight stay or more. Big Cat Rescue center in North Tampa provides sanctuary for lions, tigers, and other large felines who have been abused, abandoned, or otherwise endangered. If you stay overnight, spend an evening in Ybor City, Tampa's Cuban enclave and a nightlife mecca, particularly along 7th Avenue, and enjoy dinner at the century-old Columbia restaurant. In the morning, head to a beach in St. Pete or Clearwater. Spend the day sunbathing or make an afternoon visit to St. Pete's Salvador Dalí Museum, where docents conduct free tours and can explain how works by the Spanish surrealist ended up in Florida.

Alternatively (or in addition), you can take a Segway tour of St. Pete, catch a spring training or Buccaneers game, bike along Tampa's Bayshore Boulevard Trail or Clearwater's Pinellas Trail, or hunt for shells at Caladesi Island State Park. A trip south to Sarasota lets you explore some fine art and circus lore at the John and Mable Ringling Museum of Art and the Ringling Circus Museum. Within the museum complex, be sure to visit the Ca' d'Zan, the Venetian-style mansion that was Ringling's home. The huge banyan tree in the expansive gardens is a spectacular photo spot.

ORLANDO WEDDINGS AND HONEYMOONS

Orlando and its theme parks have become increasingly popular shower, wedding, and honeymoon destinations. The area appeals to starry-eyed Gen Y couples and, more and more, older couples, some marrying for the second time and many bringing family and friends in for the wedding-vacation-reunion of a lifetime. They come from across the United States and throughout the world, and their ideas of the perfect wedding vary greatly.

One bride made an entrance in Cinderella's glass coach; her groom rode in on a white horse. A thrill-seeking couple took the free-fall plunge on the Tower of Terror at Disney's Hollywood Studios. Two couples, on separate occasions, tied the knot in the middle of their Walt Disney World Marathon run, exchanging vows in front of Cinderella Castle at the Magic Kingdom. Moonlight on the Ritz-Carlton lawn set the scene for another couple's romantic vow exchange, and a rooftop Orlando wedding wowed yet another couple's guests with a 360-degree view of the Downtown skyline and scenic Lake Eola Park.

Prewedding Events

Showers and bachelor and bachelorette parties are easy to arrange in a city where there's so much to do. At Disney, the Mad Hatter can show up for a bridesmaids' tea event at the Grand Floridian. Parties can begin with dinner and a wine tasting at Hannibal's wine cellar in Winter Park before moving on to a local nightclub. Grooms who stay at Portofino Bay like to party at Universal CityWalk because no driving is required—a ferry will shuttle them back to the hotel.

For rehearsal dinners (or wedding receptions), Disney pulls out the stops to stage events ranging from an after-hours

reception at the Lion King Theater in Animal Kingdom to an internationally themed event at one of the World Showcase countries in Epcot.

Weddings

You can opt for a traditional ceremony at Disney's Wedding Pavilion on the Seven Seas Lagoon by the Grand Floridian Resort & Spa. Designed with the charming features of a Victorian summerhouse, the pavilion is an airy room with a view of Cinderella Castle just across the lagoon. Alternatively, you can plan an informal beachside vow exchange at a lakeside Disney resort; a garden or gazebo ceremony; an over-the-top, Cinderella-style wedding; or a Broadway-themed blowout.

Downtown Orlando and historic Winter Park are popular wedding destinations as well, says Lora Ritzie Wardman, whose company (⊕ *www.loraritziewardman. com*) has planned weddings and events in Orlando for more than two decades. Elegant lakefront ceremonies are popular, Wardman said, and she coordinates many in a variety of waterfront pavilions and gardens, but she specializes in unique, vintage, and mod weddings in unique spots such as the rooftop of the Orlando Science Center. One of her weddings was even featured on MTV.

Other top wedding spots are Downtown's Orange County Regional History Center; the Mennello Museum of American Art in the city's Loch Haven area; and Casa Feliz, a historic Spanish home–museum in Winter Park.

According to Wardman, couples who hire her, whether for a traditional elegant ceremony, or one with an unusual theme, often like to hold the wedding ceremony and reception in one location, making Orlando the perfect choice. Theme-park

musicians and other performers often hire out for receptions at reasonable prices, and there's a lot of diversity, from zydeco and salsa bands to groups that specialize in swing music.

Heather Snively, owner of Weddings Unique (⊕ *www.weddingsunique.com*), says Orlando attracts a lot of couples planning second marriages, couples with children, and those seeking a wedding reunion–minivacation. Resort hotels like the Four Seasons, the Ritz, Waldorf Astoria, and Portofino Bay at Universal feature romantic backdrops for the ceremony, plus smaller ballrooms ideal for receptions.

The hotels can also support activities ranging from spa parties to golf outings for those in the wedding party. Snively and her team plan up to 40 weddings a year from soup to nuts, working closely with in-house resort coordinators to smooth out every detail and with travel agents to make arrangements for guest travel.

Honeymoons

Central Florida resorts cater to honeymooners with special packages. Honeymoon suites with whirlpools and other amenities create the backdrop for romance that's enhanced with extras like champagne and chocolate-covered strawberries. Resort pools with cabanas, beaches, waterfalls, swaying palms, and poolside margarita delivery make the subtropical setting seem as exotic as a tropical island.

Disney's Fairy Tale Honeymoons division helps you customize a vacation package and even offers a Honeymoon Registry if your guests wish to contribute to your postwedding getaway rather than give a traditional gift. There are package deals to be had at Walt Disney World resorts and at Disney's Vero Beach Resort. Some couples make their wedding dreams or vow renewals come true at sea, where the honeymoon follows immediately.

Planning Tips

If you're dreaming about a Central Florida wedding, keep these tips from the experts in mind:

■ If your budget can handle the expense, hire a reputable planner long before the big date. Though you'll pay a fee for your planner, he or she will be an advocate with barter power when dealing with vendors.

■ For a destination wedding, build in plenty of time to book travel arrangements and accommodations for all who plan to attend.

■ If your budget is tight, plan your Orlando wedding between Monday and Thursday during nonpeak season for the lowest hotel rates.

■ Split the wedding-planning tasks with your partner. If the groom is focused more on the reception's music, food, and beverages, the bride can focus on, say, wedding flowers and photography.

■ Let your wedding planner arrange romantic escapes from your guests, especially if you plan to wed *and* honeymoon in Orlando. If everyone's staying at the Gaylord Palms Resort or the Hard Rock Hotel, have your wedding planner book you a spa package at the Waldorf Astoria or Ritz-Carlton.

■ Start your research by visiting several Orlando-area wedding-planner websites; Visit Orlando at ⊕ *www.visitorlando. com/weddings*; and Disney's Fairy Tale Weddings & Honeymoons at ⊕ *www. disneyweddings.disney.go.com*.

DISNEY CRUISES

More than a dozen years after Disney Cruise Line (DCL) first set sail with the *Disney Magic* and the *Disney Wonder,* it launched its third ship, *Disney Dream,* in 2011. In 2012, the line's fourth ship, *Disney Fantasy,* debuted, expanding the line's cruise-ship guest capacity to more than 13,000. Disney made waves with innovations aboard the *Fantasy* and *Dream,* from its shipboard AquaDuck waterslide coasters, the first of their kind in the industry, to virtual portholes in inside staterooms that provide real-time views from outside the ship. In 2013, the Magic debuted a full renovation that included a new grand atrium lobby, the three-story AquaDunk thrill ride, and Marvel character experiences for the kids.

The cruise line continues to offer its popular excursions from Port Canaveral, Florida, to the Bahamas as well as to eastern and western Caribbean destinations with stops that include Grand Cayman, San Juan, Cozumel, St. Maarten, and St. Thomas. All Caribbean and Bahamian cruises include at least one stop at Disney's gem of a private island, Castaway Cay. DCL also offers a lineup of sailings to the Mediterranean and Alaska, and new itineraries include departures from Miami. A big Disney plus: you can combine an ocean getaway with a stay at Walt Disney World for a seamless land-and-sea vacation. You check in just once: your room key at your Disney resort hotel doubles as your boarding pass at Disney's terminal at Port Canaveral and the key to your stateroom. For reservations and information, call ☎ *800/951–3532* or visit ⊕ *www.disneycruise.disney.go.com.*

Cruise Packages

Packages include room, meals (there are extra charges at the exclusive restaurants though), and most shipboard activities, but not shore excursions or, generally, transportation to and from the ship. Prices vary greatly, depending on the package, the stateroom, the destination, the time of year, and which week you book. Perhaps due to the lack of income-generating casinos, or maybe due to the high quality of shows, service, and entertainment, a Disney Cruise Line voyage is more expensive than other lines, starting at about $450 per person for three nights, $460 for four nights, $575 for five nights, and $910 for seven nights based on double occupancy and not including taxes and fees.

Booking early may help you secure a better rate, but also a bargain may be obtained by booking at the last minute on a ship that hasn't filled. ■**TIP**➜ Dig **for a discount on your Disney cruise with a travel agent who specializes in cruises.** Find one at ⊕ *www.travelsense.org.*

Disney Cruise Line. To book any Disney cruise or to check into vessels, staterooms, shore excursions, and more, contact the Disney Cruise Line. ☎ *800/370–0097* ⊕ *www.disneycruise.com.*

Staterooms

Disney Magic and *Disney Wonder* each have 875 staterooms, 73% of which have ocean-view rooms and 44% of which have private verandas. *Disney Dream* and *Fantasy* are larger ships, with 1,250 staterooms each—88% are outside rooms, and 901 staterooms and suites offer private verandas.

Cabins are ranked by category and range from standard inside staterooms (category 11 on the *Fantasy* and *Dream*; categories 11 and 12 on the *Magic* or *Wonder*;

169–184 square feet, sleeps three to four) to deluxe family staterooms with verandas (category 4 on all ships, 256–304 square feet, sleeps five). Luxurious concierge suites are top of the line, with every amenity from whirlpool bathtubs to walk-in closets.

Budget-minded cruisers are often tempted to stick with the least expensive option, the inside stateroom, but this option lacks a valued amenity on Disney ships—the split bathroom. It features a vanity, sink, tub and shower in one area and a vanity, sink, and toilet in another—a real time-saver when it's time for you and your cabin mates to freshen up before excursions or evening dinners and shows.

Quite a few of the staterooms have a clever pull-down bunk-bed setup that saves space until bedtime and draws cheers from children. All rooms are elegantly appointed with natural wood furniture.

Disney does a commendable job of keeping rooms and much of the rest of the ship smoke-free while setting aside some deck, bar, and private veranda areas for smokers.

For Guests with Disabilities

Accessible staterooms for people with disabilities have ramps, handrails, fold-down shower seats, and handheld showerheads; special communications kits are available with phone alerts, amplifiers, and text typewriters. Assisted-listening systems are available in the ships' main theaters, and sign-language interpretation is offered for live performances on specified cruise dates.

Shore Excursions

At various ports of call, Disney offers between one and two dozen organized excursions, from snorkeling and diving to

THE PORT

In addition to the ships of DCL, Port Canaveral is also the home port for ships of Carnival Cruise Lines, Royal Caribbean, and Norwegian. To learn more about all cruises departing from Port Canaveral, visit ⊕ www.portcanaveral.com and click on links to each cruise line, or contact a travel agent or cruise discounter.

sightseeing and shopping. For example, at Grand Cayman you can visit a butterfly farm or sign up for a trip to Stingray City—not really a city, but a long sandbar where you can swim with hundreds of rays. During a stop at Cozumel you can explore the Mayan ruins of Tulum and strike a bargain for handcrafted Mexican hats, toys, and knickknacks. All activities are rated from "leisurely" to "strenuously active."

Adult Activities

Poolside games, wine tastings, and behind-the-scenes seminars are among the adults-only diversions. Each ship's spa is a don't-miss for those who need some pampering—book early!

For a romantic dinner, the intimate, adults-only **Palo** (*all ships*) offers sweeping ocean views. Expect a fantastic wine list and dishes such as grilled salmon with creamy risotto and grilled filet mignon with a port-wine reduction and Gorgonzola cheese sauce. Reserve early for this hot ticket. The champagne brunch is another great Palo dining event.

The decor in the *Dream*'s and *Fantasy*'s exclusive 80-seat restaurant, **Remy,** is a nod to the movie *Ratatouille,* and, of course, the cuisine is French inspired. The eight or nine tasting dishes served each night might include Kurobata pork

tenderloin and belly with corn ragout and wild turbot with lemon capers and spinach. Wine pairings are amazing; so are the pastries. Remy also has a champagne brunch. Book as far ahead of your trip as possible.

Children's Activities

On all four ships, there's nearly an entire deck reserved for kids. When you drop them off, use the onboard mobile phone service to stay in touch with the activities counselors. Babysitting is available on the *Wonder* for children ages 12 weeks to 3 years old at **Flounder's Reef Nursery** for $9 per hour (two-hour minimum) and $8 an hour for each additional sibling. Disney also offers a groundbreaking online service, Babies Travel Lite, which lets parents order all of their baby's travel products, including diapers and formula, and have them shipped to their stateroom before the cruise begins. Similar services are offered at the *Magic*'s, *Fantasy*'s, and *Dream*'s **It's a Small World Nursery.**

The well-run **Oceaneer Club** and **Oceaneer Lab** on each ship give parents a respite by providing nonstop activities for kids ages 3–12. Little ones have a ball in the **Club** playroom designed to look like Captain Hook's pirate ship. They can scramble around on a rope bridge, watch a Disney movie, and make crafts at the **Toy Story Boot Camp** (*Magic* and *Dream*) or **Pixie Hollow** (*Fantasy*). Counselors customize activities to kids within different age groups.

At the high-tech **Lab**, there are science experiments, sports challenges, and karaoke jams. Disney revamped its kids' program approach so that children have more options to tailor their experiences to their interests.

Tweens (ages 11–14) chill out at a getaway called **Edge** on each Disney ship; older teens (14–17) have their own hangout at **Vibe**. They can tune in to music, watch plasma-screen TVs, play board and video games, or just hang out and meet new friends. Organized activities for teens include trivia games and evening dance parties. Internet message, photo, and video posting also are available.

Restaurants

Coordinators arrange for you to alternate restaurants each night so you can sample a variety of offerings. Disney offers early and late dinner seatings, too. Early ones are best for families with small children. Also, look into the Dine and Play option, where servers speed up the kids' service, and then the ship's activity counselors whisk youngsters off so older family members can relax. If you miss your seating altogether, you can always find a casual dining option.

At **Animator's Palate,** scenes featuring Disney characters change from black-and-white to Technicolor as the meal progresses on the *Magic* and *Wonder*; on the *Dream* and *Fantasy,* diners are surrounded by an artist's studio where famous film scenes line the walls and fiber-optic "brush pillars" paint oversize ceiling "palettes" in vibrant colors. Dining is slightly more formal at **Lumiere's,** on the *Magic,* where beef tenderloin, lamb shank, and other entrées are served French style in a classic ocean-liner-style dining room.

At **Triton's,** on the *Wonder,* seafood, roast duck, pasta, and other selections are served in an elegant, art deco, under-the-sea-theme dining room. The *Dream*'s **Royal Palace** and the *Fantasy*'s **Royal Court** are inspired by Disney's princess films, with menus that may include crowned rack of lamb, beef Wellington, and other royal dishes. At the Caribbean-themed **Parrot Cay** restaurant (*Wonder*) and the new Rio de Janeiro–themed **Carioca's** *(Magic)*, the mood is casual and festive. On the *Fantasy* and *Dream*, **Enchanted Garden** is the whimsical, more informal rotation restaurant. Character breakfasts are offered one morning on most seven-nights-or-longer sailings.

After-Dark Entertainment

During a **Pirate Night event**, swashbuckling servers dish up Caribbean and Bahamian taste treats, a cup of grog, and (on seven-night cruises) a pirate bandana for every dinner guest. After dinner, you head off to a deck party where Captain Hook, Mr. Smee, and others appear for some high-spirited action, dancing, and fireworks.

Lavish shows and variety acts entertain families every night of every cruise. The big hit on *Disney Wonder* is *Toy Story: The Musical*, a larger-than-life stage version of the film classic. The Golden Mickeys on the *Wonder* is a high-tech salute to the animation of Walt Disney in the form of a Hollywood-style awards ceremony. *Twice Charmed: An Original Twist on the Cinderella Story* is a Broadway-style production on *Disney Magic* that begins where the original Cinderella story ended.

Disney Dreams: An Enchanted Classic, on the *Magic* and *Wonder,* is a sweet bedtime story starring Peter Pan, Aladdin, Ariel, and other Disney characters. It combines animation, pyrotechnic, and laser features, snow effects, and mechanisms that let characters "fly" more convincingly. The *Dream* produces the first full-scale musical revue dedicated to Disney's famous animated villains in *Villains Tonight!* Two new shows are popular on

the *Fantasy*: *Disney Wishes* and *Disney's Aladdin: A Musical Spectacle.* Each ship also has a **cinema** screening classic Disney films, and every guest has the opportunity to experience a show or film featuring digital 3-D enhancements.

There are also many things geared to adults. At the **Cove Café**, on all ships, you can enjoy gourmet coffee, watch TV, check email, and socialize. On the *Wonder,* the **Outlook Café** on Deck 10 has floor-to-ceiling windows with prime views. **After Hours,** the recently renovated nightlife district on the *Magic,* features **Fathoms** nightclub; O'Gill's Pub; and Keys, a piano bar. **Route 66,** the *Wonder*'s nightlife area, has the WaveBands dance club and the Cadillac Lounge piano bar. If you're looking for something more low-key, check out **Diversions,** a sports pub on both ships.

On the *Dream*, Disney expands its nightlife offerings at the **District**, with lounges, a pub, a sky bar, and a nightclub. *Fantasy* cruisers can visit the trendy clubs of **Europa**, influenced by European nightspots, including a rollicking Irish pub and a French champagne bar. Movie fans can see first-run films at the ships' plush Buena Vista Theatre, where full-length features really pop with digital 3-D technology.

Castaway Cay

Disney has its own private Bahamian island, Castaway Cay, with white-sand beaches, towering palms, and swaying hammocks—it's a key stop on many Disney cruises. You can relax on the beach or join a snorkeling or parasailing excursion.

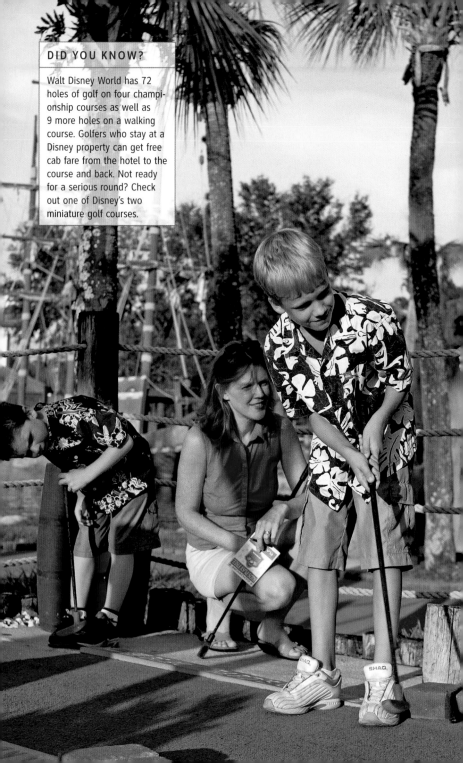

DOING ORLANDO AND THE PARKS RIGHT

by Jennie Hess

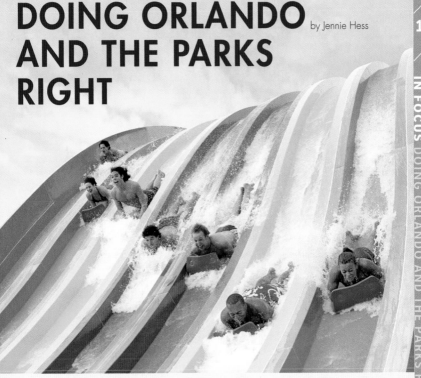

You don't have to wish upon a star to make all your Orlando vacation dreams come true. Your trip will be memorable, whether you're traveling with small children, tweens, teens, or the whole gang of friends or family; whether you're on your honeymoon or flying solo.

Gather (or cyber-gather) all your travel companions together to create a wish list. Then, as you create your itinerary, consider everyone's needs and plan accordingly.

Got small children? Know their theme-park limits to prevent meltdowns, and factor in time away from crowded parks for a laid-back visit to smaller attractions. And, to avoid disappointments, don't wait to get to the parks to determine ride height restrictions.

Teens and tweens may want to head for some rides on their own. Determine theme-park meeting locations, and be sure everyone carries a cell phone in case they encounter longer ride lines and delays.

If the guys are planning to hit the links and the gals want a spa day, don't wait until you're in town to reserve a tee time or a facial-mani-pedi package.

What follows are suggestions (and a few quick tips) on how you can do Orlando and the parks right—regardless of who's in your group. For more planning tips and insights, check out Chapter 1.

Taumata Racer, Aquatica

Shamu's Happy Harbor play area, SeaWorld

Pirates of the Caribbean, Magic Kingdom

FAMILIES WITH SMALL KIDS

Things will go more smoothly if you stick to routines. It's easier than you think. During naptime, for instance, you can relax on a bench while your toddler snoozes in her stroller and the rest of the family heads for a park attraction. Finding sights for wee ones is easy in the parks and outside.

Magic Kingdom. This is the top Disney destination for families with tots. Fantasyland has a treasure trove of age-appropriate attractions. Tom Sawyer Island lets squirmy kids burn up some energy.

SeaWorld. Dolphins, whales, and other marine mammals mesmerize young children. Most shows are captivating, and Shamu's Happy Harbor is a wet, wonderful play area.

Typhoon Lagoon. It sets an idyllic water-park scene for families with small children. Ketchakiddie Creek is a favorite splash zone.

Orlando Science Center. Exhibits—many of them interactive—at this center near downtown Orlando let kids experience science and the world around them.

Downtown Disney Marketplace. A kiddie carousel, splash fountains, a LEGO Imagination Center, Bibbidi Bobbidi Boutique (think princess makeovers) are among the attractions for kids.

FAMILIES WITH TWEENS

You and your tweens will have more fun together if you involve them in pre-trip planning. Let each child scope out best bets on Orlando- and theme-park Web sites, then gather to compare notes and create a rough itinerary. Here are a few suggestions to jumpstart the research.

Magic Kingdom. Who ever really outgrows this classic? Tweens love rides ending in "mountain"—Space, Splash, and Big Thunder. The Haunted Mansion and Pirates of the Caribbean are both cool.

Islands of Adventure. This theme-park will be a hit with tweens who love thrill rides and/or superheroes like Spider-Man. For muggle fans of J.K. Rowling's books, the Wizarding World of Harry Potter is a must-see.

Disney's Animal Kingdom. The exotic animals and safari are highlights, but so are scream-inducing Expedition Everest, DINO-SAUR, and Kali River Rapids.

Aquatica. This SeaWorld-affiliated water park has water-slide thrills and a tube slide through a Commerson's dolphin habitat.

Fun Spot. Tweens love the go-kart racetrack best, but the carnival-style rides and arcades are a big draw, too.

WonderWorks. Tweens can "build" their own coaster, and then ride it; lie on a bed of nails; and pilot a simulated fighter jet.

Incredible Hulk Coaster, Islands of Adventure

Sleuths Mystery Dinner Show, Orlando

FAMILIES WITH TEENS

Let teens make their own "gotta do" list and head out on their own. (Chances are at least some of the sights below will make it to every list.) Stay in touch by texting updates and meeting for meals.

Disney's Hollywood Studios. Teens rave about The Twilight Zone Tower of Terror and Rock 'n' Roller Coaster Starring Aerosmith. Competing in Toy Story Midway Mania! is another cool option.

Islands of Adventure. Older kids are drawn to the action here—from the Amazing Adventures of Spider-Man to the Incredible Hulk Coaster.

Universal Studios. Teens love Hollywood Rip Ride Rockit, Revenge of the Mummy, and The Wizarding World of Harry Potter.

Blizzard Beach and Wet 'n Wild. Blizzard stands out for its wintry theme, mix of thrills, and laid-back "beach" scene. Wet 'n Wild has loud music and big-thrill slides.

Universal CityWalk. It gets high marks for trendy shopping, movie theaters, and concerts. The theatrics of Blue Man Group is a big teen draw around the corner.

Spa with Mom. Mother-daughter facials and pedicures make for a fun morning or afternoon at Orlando spas like the Buena Vista Palace or Disney's Grand Floridian.

LARGE, MIXED GROUPS

Look into Disney's vacation-planning program, Grand Gatherings. Just remember that group members will be happier campers with some "me" time factored in. Here are some suggestions for shared and individual experiences.

Behind-the-Scenes Park Tours. Tours at SeaWorld, Magic Kingdom, Epcot, and Animal Kingdom are great shared experiences. Note that the more people you have on the expensive but oh-so-cool VIP tour at Universal, the better value it is.

Dinner shows. Some area favorites are Medieval Times in Kissimmee, Sleuths Mystery Dinner Show on I-Drive, and Disney's Hoop-Dee-Doo Revue.

Discovery Cove. Book a "beach" day here to share the experience of swimming with the dolphins. Meals and snacks are included.

Epcot. Everyone can fan out here to take in the attractions of Future World or World Showcase and then gather for dinner at a reserved table to share experiences.

Spa Visits and Golf Expeditions. These are perfect "breakaway" activities. And there are options for both at Disney and in the greater Orlando area.

Spring Training. In March, it's easy to arrange a group outing to a ballgame in one of several central Florida locations.

Cirque du Soleil – *La Nouba*

Disney's Animal Kingdom.

COUPLES

Let us count the ways to be romantic in Orlando . . . there are too many to list here. Even if the kids are along for the trip, you can carve out time together by using a hotel's sitter service or by packing the children off to a resort kids' club.

Victoria & Albert's. Splurge on a dinner fit for royalty at the Grand Floridian's elegant eatery, central Florida's only AAA Five-Diamond restaurant. Reserve months ahead.

Spa Treatments for Two. Top spas for couples pampering include those in the Ritz Carlton, Waldorf Astoria, Grand Floridian, Portofino Bay, Gaylord Palms, and Walt Disney World Dolphin, and the Four Seasons.

Cirque du Soleil. Hold hands and share the wonder of the surreal show, *La Nouba*, at Downtown Disney West Side

Wekiwa Springs State Park. Escape here for a picnic and/or to rent a canoe and share quiet time on the river.

Islands of Adventure and CityWalk. Plan a wild and crazy evening of roller-coaster thrills and then belly up to the bar for a cheeseburger in paradise at Jimmy Buffet's Margaritaville.

Lake Eola. Paddle a swan-shaped boat together at this lake in downtown Orlando. Then share flatbread and sip champagne at Eola Wine Company across the street.

SINGLES (OR GROUPS OF FRIENDS)

It's nice to have a traveling companion, but there's an advantage to visiting on your own—you can cover a lot more territory. Single but traveling with friends? You still may want to split up to sample from your own play list.

Animal Kingdom. Animal-loving singles can linger longer at this park to watch behaviors of many exotic creatures. Rough it on the excellent Wild Africa Trek for a fee.

Winter Park. On a day trip to this this town you can shop Park Avenue, take a scenic boat tour, and see the huge Tiffany collection at the Morse Museum of American Art.

Disney's Boardwalk. Let nostalgia take hold on a lakeside stroll. Or hop into a surrey or onto a bicycle built for two. Watch dueling pianos at Jellyrolls or a game at ESPN Club.

Run through the parks. Plan your visit in January and compete in the Walt Disney World Half- or Full Marathons—run both, and you'll go home with a Goofy medal as well as a Donald (half) and a Mickey (full)!

Tour new Worlds. Spend seven hours on Disney's Backstage Magic Tour of Magic Kingdom, Epcot, and Hollywood Studios. Or take one of SeaWorld's Spotlight tours into the penguin or dolphin backstage habitats.

WALT DISNEY WORLD

WELCOME TO WALT DISNEY WORLD

TOP REASONS TO GO

★ **Nostalgia:** Face it— Mickey and Company are old friends. And you probably have childhood pictures of yourself in front of Cinderella Castle. Even if you don't, nobody does yesteryear better: head to Main Street, U.S.A or Hollywood Boulevard and see.

★ **Memories in the Making:** Who doesn't want to snap selfies on the Dumbo ride or of Junior after his Splash Mountain experience? The urge to pass that Disney nostalgia on to the next generation is strong.

★ **The Thrills:** For some this means roller coasting to an Aerosmith sound track or simulating space flight; for others it's about cascading down a water-slide or going on safari.

★ **The Chills:** If the Pirates of the Caribbean cave doesn't give you goose bumps, try the Haunted Mansion or Twilight Zone Tower of Terror.

★ **The Spectacle:** The list is long—fireworks, laser-light displays, arcade games, parades . . .

1 Magic Kingdom. Disney's emblematic park is home to Space Mountain, Pirates of the Caribbean, and an expanded Fantasyl-and full of new experiences.

2 Epcot. Future World's focus is science, technology, and hands-on experiences. In the World Showcase, you can tour 11 countries without getting jet-lagged.

3 Disney's Hollywood Studios. Attractions at this re-creation of old-time Hollywood include Rock 'n' Roller Coaster Starring Aerosmith and Twilight Zone Tower of Terror.

4 Disney's Animal Kingdom. Amid a 403-acre wildlife preserve are an Asian-themed water ride, an African safari ride, a runaway-train coaster, and shows.

5 Blizzard Beach. Water thrills range from steep flume rides to tubing expedi-tions in the midst of a park that you'd swear is a slowly melting ski resort. There's plenty for little ones, too.

6 Typhoon Lagoon. Sandy beaches, oceanlike waves, and a themed water coaster invite castaways to enjoy a day of fun and relaxation. Take the kids on Bay Slides and don snorkels to explore Shark Reef.

CENTRAL FLORIDA

2

7 **Disney's Other Worlds.** Downtown Disney, the area soon to be known as Disney Springs, is the place to go for shopping, dining, and great entertainment from morning through late night. Disney's BoardWalk is a nostalgia trip, with bicycles built for two, surreys with fringe on top, pizza, bars, and a dance hall.

GETTING ORIENTED

Walt Disney World straddles Orange and Osceola counties to the west of Interstate 4. Four exits will get you to the parks and resort areas: 64B, 65, 67, and 68. To reach hotels along I-Drive, use Exit 72, 74A, or 75A.

Updated by
Jennie Hess

Mickey Mouse. Tinker Bell. Cinderella. What would childhood be like without the magic of Disney? When kids and adults want to go to *the* theme park, they're heading to Disney. Here you're walking amid people from around the world and meeting characters like Snow White and Donald Duck while rides whirl nonstop and the irrepressible "it's a small world" tune and lyrics run through your head. You can't help but believe dreams really do come true here.

The **Magic Kingdom** is the heart and soul of the Walt Disney World empire. It was the first Disney outpost in Florida when it opened in 1971, and it's the park that launched Disney's presence in France, Japan, Hong Kong, and Shanghai. For a landmark that wields such worldwide influence, the 142-acre Magic Kingdom may seem small—indeed, Epcot is more than double the size of the Magic Kingdom, and Animal Kingdom is almost triple the size when including the park's expansive animal habitats. But looks can be deceiving. Packed into six different "lands" are nearly 50 major crowd-pleasers, and that's not counting all the ancillary attractions: shops, eateries, live entertainment, character meet-and-greet spots, fireworks shows, and parades.

Nowhere but at **Epcot** can you explore and experience the native food, entertainment, culture, and arts and crafts of countries in Europe, Asia, North Africa, and the Americas. What's more, employees at the World Showcase pavilions actually hail from the countries the pavilions represent.

Epcot, or "Experimental Prototype Community of Tomorrow," was the original inspiration for Walt Disney World. Walt envisioned a future in which nations coexisted in peace and harmony, reaping the miraculous harvest of technological achievement. The Epcot of today is both more and less than his original dream. Less, because the World Showcase presents views of its countries that are, as an Epcot guide once put it, "as Americans perceive them"—highly idealized. But this is a minor quibble in the face of the major achievement: Epcot is that rare paradox—a successful educational theme park that excels at entertainment, too.

Disney's Hollywood Studios were designed to be a trip back to Tinseltown's golden age, when Hedda Hopper, not tabloids, spread celebrity gossip and when the girl off the bus from Ohio could be the next Judy Garland. The result is a theme park that blends movie-themed shows and attractions and high-tech wonders with breathtaking rides and Hollywood nostalgia. The park's old-time Hollywood atmosphere begins with a rosy-hued view of the moviemaking business presented in a dreamy stage set from the 1930s and '40s, amid sleek art-moderne buildings in pastel colors, funky diners, kitschy decorations, and sculptured gardens populated by roving actors playing, well, roving actors. There are also casting directors, gossip columnists, and other colorful characters.

Thanks to a rich library of film scores, the park is permeated with music, all familiar, all evoking the magic of the movies, and all constantly streaming from the camouflaged loudspeakers at a volume just right for humming along. The park icon for many years, a 122-foot-high Sorcerer Mickey Hat that served as a gift shop and Disney pin-trading station, towered over Hollywood Boulevard until it was removed in 2015.

Disney's Animal Kingdom explores the stories of all animals—real, imaginary, and extinct. Enter through the Oasis, where you hear exotic background music and find yourself surrounded by gentle waterfalls and gardens alive with exotic birds, reptiles, and mammals.

At 403 acres and several times the size of the Magic Kingdom, Animal Kingdom is the largest in area of all Disney theme parks. Animal habitats take up much of that acreage. Creatures here thrive in careful re-creations of landscapes from Asia and Africa. Throughout the park, you'll also learn about conservation in a low-key way.

Amid all the nature are thrill rides, a 3-D show (housed in the "root system" of the iconic Tree of Life), two first-rate musicals, and character meet and greets. Cast members are as likely to hail from Kenya or South Africa as they are from Kentucky or South Carolina. It's all part of the charm. New park areas based on the movie *Avatar* are expected to open in 2017, a fitting addition, since the film's theme of living in harmony with nature reflects the park's eco-philosophy.

Typhoon Lagoon and **Blizzard Beach** are two of the world's best water parks. What sets them apart? It's the same thing that differentiates all Disney parks—the detailed themes. Whether you're cast away on a balmy island at Typhoon Lagoon or washed up on a ski-resort-turned-seaside-playground at Blizzard Beach, the landscaping and clever architecture will add to the fun of flume and raft rides, wave pools, and splash areas. Another plus: the vegetation has matured enough to create shade. The Disney water parks give you that lost-in-paradise feeling on top of all those high-speed, wedgie-inducing waterslides. They're so popular that crowds often reach overflow capacity in summer. If you're going to Disney for four days or more between April and October, add the Water Park Fun & More option to your Magic Your Way ticket.

PLANNING

ADMISSION

At the gate, the per-person, per-day price for Magic Kingdom guests is $99 for adults (ages 10 and older) and $93 for children (ages 3–9). At Disney's other three parks, Epcot, Hollywood Studios, and Animal Kingdom, the per-person, per-day price is $94 for adults (ages 10 and older) and $88 for children (ages 3–9). You can buy tickets at the Ticket and Transportation Center (TTC) in the Magic Kingdom, from booths at other park entrances, in all on-site resorts if you're a guest, at the Disney store in the airport, and at various other sites around Orlando. You can also buy them in advance online—the best way to save time and money.

If you opt for a multiday ticket, you'll be issued a nontransferable pass that uses your fingerprint for ID. Hold your pass up to the reader, just like people with single-day tickets, and also slip your finger into the V-shaped reader. A new option, the MagicBand wristband, serves as park ticket, attraction FastPass+ ticket, and even hotel room key.

OPERATING HOURS

Walt Disney World operates 365 days a year. Opening and closing times vary by park and by season, with the longest hours during prime summer months and year-end holidays. The parking lots open at least an hour before the parks do.

In general, openings hover around 9 am, though certain attractions might not start up till 10 or 11. Closings range between 5 and 8 pm in the off-season and between 8 and 10, 11, or even midnight in high season. Downtown Disney and BoardWalk shops stay open as late as 11 pm.

EXTRA MAGIC HOURS

The Extra Magic Hours program gives Disney resort guests free early and late-night admission to certain parks on specified days—check ahead (⊕ *www.disneyworld.disney.go.com/calendars*) for information about each park's "magic hours" days to plan your early- and late-visit strategies.

PARKING AND IN-PARK TRANSPORT

Parking at Disney parks is free to resort guests; all others pay $17 for cars and $18 for RVs and campers. Parking is free for everyone at Typhoon Lagoon, Blizzard Beach, Downtown Disney, and the Board-Walk. Trams take you between the theme-park lots (*note your parking location!*) and turnstiles. Disney's buses, boats, and monorails whisk you from resort to park and park to park. If you're staying on Disney property, you can use this system exclusively. Either take a Disney bus or drive to Typhoon Lagoon and Blizzard Beach. Once inside the water parks, you can walk, swim, slide, or chill out. Allow up to an hour for travel between parks and hotels on Disney transportation.

Disney *Magic Your Way* Price Chart

TICKET OPTIONS								
TICKET	**1-DAY**	**2-DAY**	**3-DAY**	**4-DAY**	**5-DAY**	**6-DAY**	**7-DAY**	**10-DAY**
BASE TICKET								
Ages 10–up	$97–$105	$192	$275	$305	$315	$325	$335	$365
Ages 3–9	$91–$99	$179	$256	$285	$295	$305	$315	$345

Base Ticket admits guest to one of the four major theme parks per day's use.
Park choices are: Magic Kingdom, Epcot, Disney's Hollywood Studios, Disney's Animal Kingdom.
8- and 9-day tickets are also available.

ADD: Park Hopper	$50	$50	$50	$64	$64	$64	$64	$64

Park Hopper option entitles guest to visit more than one theme park per day's use. Park choices are any combination of Magic Kingdom, Epcot, Disney's Hollywood Studios, Disney's Animal Kingdom.

ADD: Water Parks Fun & More	$64 2 visits	$64 2 visits	$64 3 visits	$64 4 visits	$64 5 visits	$64 6 visits	$64 7 visits	$64 10 visits

Water Parks Fun & More option entitles guest to a specified number of visits to a choice of entertainment and recreation venues. Choices are Blizzard Beach, Typhoon Lagoon, DisneyQuest, Disney's Oak Trail golf course, and Wide World of Sports.

ADD: Both	$90	$90	$90	$90	$90	$90	$90	$90

Adding both the *Park Hopper* and *Water Park* option entitles guests to all the privileges under both sepcific options above.

MINOR PARKS AND ATTRACTIONS		
TICKET	**AGES 10–UP**	**AGES 3–9**
Typhoon Lagoon or Blizzard Beach 1-Day 1-Park	$58	$50
DisneyQuest 1-Day	$47	$40
Disney's ESPN Wide World of Sports	$16.50	$11.50
Cirque du Soleil's *La Nouba*	$63–$150	$52–$123

*All prices are subject to Florida sales tax

Get wet on the 12-story Summit Plummet at Disney's Blizzard Beach.

FASTPASS+

FastPass+ helps you avoid lines, and it's included in regular park admission. Using the new My Disney Experience app or FastPass+ kiosks in each park, you can select up to three attractions at one time; each appointment will give you a one-hour window within which you can experience each attraction. The FastPass+ appointments are loaded directly to your plastic theme-park ticket or your new MagicBand. It's best to make appointments only for the most popular attractions and to stick with the standby queue for attractions that aren't in such demand. Strategy is everything.

Guests can get FastPass+ reservations for some designated character greetings, parades, and shows. These "experience" FastPass+ reservations count just the same as those for the rides. You get three to start with (in a single park) and can add as many more as you have time for (and these can be in a different park if you have the Park Hopper option). Best FastPass+ practices are explained by the program. It will direct you to the attractions where FastPass+ is most helpful. If these attractions don't meet your family's specific needs—your kids are too young to ride coasters, for example—the program will also help you customize your FastPass+ selections.

DISNEY STRATEGIES

Keep in mind these essential strategies, tried and tested by generations of Disney fans.

■ **Buy tickets before leaving home.** It saves money and gives you time to look into all the ticket options. It also offers an opportunity for you to consider vacation packages and meal plans and to register with the My Disney Experience program and mobile app for vacation planning.

■ **Make dining reservations before leaving home.** If you don't, you might find yourself eating fast food (again) or leaving Disney for dinner. On-site restaurants, especially those featuring character appearances, book up months ahead, and you can reserve 180 days before you arrive.

■ **Arrive at least 30 minutes before the parks open.** We know, it's your vacation and you want to sleep in. But you probably want to make the most of your time and money, too. Plan to be up by 7:30 am each day to get the most out of your park visits. After transit time, it'll take you 15–20 minutes to park, get to the gates, and pick up your park guide maps and *Times Guide*.

■ **See top attractions in the morning.** And we mean *first thing*. Decide in advance on your can't-miss attractions, find their locations, and hotfoot it to them before 10 am.

■ **Use FastPass+.** The system is free, easy, more streamlined than ever with the new FastPass+ online prebooking system, and it's your ticket to the top attractions with little or no waiting in line. Even if you wait to book once you're in the park, you can now schedule up to three Fast-Pass+ events at one time; paper Fastpass tickets are obsolete. Instead, your attraction appointments are loaded onto your MagicBand or plastic ticket, whichever you choose to use.

■ **Use Baby Swap.** Disney has a theme-park "rider switch" policy that works like this: one parent waits with the baby or toddler while the other parent rides the attraction. When the ride ends, they switch places with minimal wait.

■ **Build in rest time.** Start early and then leave the parks around 3 or 4 pm, thus avoiding the hottest and often most crowded period. After a couple of hours' rest at your hotel, head back for a nighttime spectacle or to ride a big-ticket ride (lines often are shorter around closing time).

■ **Create an itinerary, but leave room for spontaneity.** Don't try to plot your trip hour by hour. If you're staying at a Disney resort, find out which parks have Extra Magic Hours on which days.

■ **Eat at off-hours.** To avoid the mealtime rush hours, have a quick, light breakfast at 7 or 8 am, lunch at 11, and dinner at 5 or 6.

OTHER DISNEY SERVICES

If you can shell out $360–$500 an hour (with a six-hour minimum), you can take a customized **VIP Tour** with guides who help you park hop and get good seats at parades and shows. These tours don't help you skip lines, but they make navigating easy. Groups can have up to 10 people; book up to three months ahead.

WDW Tours. Reserve with WDW Tours up to 180 days in advance for behind-the-scenes tours. Participant age requirements vary, so be sure to check before you book. ☎ *407/939–8687* ⊕ *www.disneyworld.com.*

Character meals. Mickey, Belle, and other characters sign autographs and pose for photos. Book through Disney's dining reservations line up to 180 days out; these hugging-and-feeding frenzies are wildly popular.

DISNEY CONTACTS

Cruise Line: ☎ *800/370–0097* ⊕ *www.disneycruise.com*

Dining Reservations: ☎ *407/939–3463*

Extra Magic Hours: ⊕ *www.disneyworld.disney.go.com/calendars*

Fairy-Tale Weddings: ☎ *321/939–4610* ⊕ *www.disneyweddings.disney. go.com*

Golf Reservations: ☎ *407/939–4653*

Guest Info: ☎ *407/824–4321*

VIP Tours: ☎ *407/560–4033*

WDW Travel Company: ☎ *407/828–8101*

Web: ⊕ *www.disneyworld.disney.go.com*

THE MAGIC KINGDOM

Whether you arrive at the Magic Kingdom via monorail, boat, or bus, it's hard to escape that surge of excitement or suppress that smile upon sighting the towers of Cinderella Castle or the spires of Space Mountain. So what if it's a cliché by now? There's magic beyond the turnstiles, and you aren't going to miss one memorable moment.

Most visitors have some idea of what they'd like to see and do during their day in the Magic Kingdom. Popular attractions like Space Mountain and Splash Mountain are on the lists of any thrill seeker, and the recently expanded Fantasyland is Destination One for parents of small children and seekers of moderate thrills like the new Seven Dwarfs Mine Train. Visitors who steer away from wilder rides are first in line at the Jungle Cruise or Pirates of the Caribbean in Adventureland.

It's great to have a strategy for seeing the park's attractions, grabbing a bite to eat, or scouring the shops for souvenir gold. But don't forget that Disney Imagineers—the creative pros behind every themed land and attraction—are famous for their attention to detail. Your experience will be richer if you take time to notice the extra touches—from the architecture to the music and the costumes. The same genius is evident even in the landscape, from the tropical setting of Adventureland to the red-stone slopes of Frontierland's Big Thunder Mountain Railroad.

Wherever you go, watch for hidden Mickeys—silhouettes and abstract images of Mickey Mouse—tucked by Imagineers into every corner of the Kingdom. For instance, at the Haunted Mansion, look for him in the place settings in the banquet scene.

Much of the Magic Kingdom's pixie dust is spread by the people who work here, the costumed cast members who do their part to create fond memories for each guest who crosses their path. Maybe the grim ghoul who greets you solemnly at the Haunted Mansion will cause you to break down and giggle. Or the sunny shop assistant will help your

TOP ATTRACTIONS

FOR AGES 7 AND UP

Big Thunder Mountain Railroad. An Old West–theme, classic coaster that's not too scary; it's just a really good, bumpy, swervy thrill.

Buzz Lightyear's Space Ranger Spin. A shoot-'em-up ride where space-ranger wannabes compete for the highest score.

Haunted Mansion. With its razzle-dazzle special effects, this classic is always a frightful hoot.

Pirates of the Caribbean. Don't miss this family cruise through pirate territory, especially if you're a fan of the movies.

Seven Dwarfs Mine Train. It's the newest coaster on the block, with train cars that swing to and fro during the rollicking, musical ride through a mine full of glittery gems.

Space Mountain. The Magic Kingdom's scariest ride zips you along the tracks in near-total darkness except for the stars.

FOR AGES 6 AND UNDER

Dumbo the Flying Elephant. The elephant ears get them every time, and the renovated ride offers double the number of pachyderm vehicles.

Enchanted Tales with Belle. Young girls and boys, and some parents, too, clamor to play characters from "Beauty and the Beast" in this well-done interactive story adventure.

The Magic Carpets of Aladdin. On this must-do for preschoolers, you can make your carpet go up and down to avoid occasional water spurts as mischievous camels spit at you.

The Many Adventures of Winnie the Pooh. Hang on to your honey pot as you get whisked along on a windy-day adventure with Pooh, Tigger, Eeyore, and friends.

Under the Sea: Journey of the Little Mermaid. Wander past waterfalls and tide pools into the cave beneath Prince Eric's Castle for some interactive fun and a clamshell ride through Ariel's story.

daughter find the perfect sparkly shoes to match her princess dress. You get the feeling that everyone's in on the fun; in fact, you wonder if they ever go home!

ORIENTATION AND PLANNING

GETTING ORIENTED

The park is laid out on a north–south axis, with Cinderella Castle at the center and the various lands surrounding it in a broad circle.

As you pass underneath the railroad tracks, symbolically leaving behind the world of reality and entering a world of fantasy, you'll immediately notice the charming buildings lining Town Square and Main Street, U.S.A, which runs due north and ends at the Hub (also called Central Plaza), in front of Cinderella Castle. If you're lost or have questions, cast members are available at almost every turn to help you.

MAGIC KINGDOM PLANNER
PARK AMENITIES

Baby Care: The quiet baby-care center is next to the Crystal Palace between Main Street and Adventureland. Rocking chairs and low lighting make nursing comfortable, though it can get crowded. Toddler-size toilets are a hit with tots. There are also changing tables, formula, baby food, pacifiers, diapers, and children's pain relievers. Most park restrooms also have changing tables.

Cameras: The camera center at Town Square Theater (formerly Exposition Hall), opposite City Hall, sells film, batteries, and digital memory cards. If a Disney photographer took your picture in the park, you can buy the photos here or pick up your PhotoPass to view and order them online. A 5-inch-by-7-inch photo costs $12.95 for the first print; the more prints you buy, the less each additional print costs. An 8-inch-by-10-inch costs $16.95 and less for each extra print. Or you can go completely digital with the $199 Memory Maker option to view and download all PhotoPass images. This area is a Mickey Mouse meet-and-greet spot and features the first-ever FastPass+ ticket to meet Mickey.

First Aid: The first-aid center, staffed by registered nurses, is beside the Crystal Palace. More than a dozen automated external defibrillators are across the park.

Guest Relations: To the left in Town Square as you face Main Street, **City Hall** houses Guest Relations (aka Guest Services), the Magic Kingdom's principal information center (☎ *407/824–4521*). Here you can search for misplaced belongings or companions, ask questions of staffers, and pick up a guide map and a *Times Guide* with schedules of events and character-greeting information. ■ TIP➔ **If you're trying for a last-minute lunch or dinner reservation, you may be able to book it at City Hall.**

Lockers: Lockers ($7 or $9 plus $5 deposit) are in an arcade under the Main Street railroad station. If you're park hopping, use your locker receipt to get a free locker at the next park.

Lost People and Things: Instruct your kids to talk to anyone with a Disney name tag if they lose you. **City Hall** also has a lost and found and a computerized message center, where you can leave notes for your companions in the Magic Kingdom and other parks.

Main Lost and Found: After a day, found items are taken to the Lost and Found office at the Ticket and Transportation Center. On Disney property, follow signs to Magic Kingdom and, at the toll plaza entrance, tell an attendant you are going to Lost and Found so you aren't charged for Magic Kingdom parking. The attendant will direct you to Lost and Found parking at the Transportation and Ticket Center location. There is no address that works with your GPS. ✉ *Ticket and Transportation Center [TTC]* ☎ *407/824–4245* ⊕ *www.disneyworld.com.*

Package Pick-Up: Have large purchases sent to Package Pick-Up at the Chamber of Commerce next to City Hall, so you won't have to carry them around. Allow three hours for the delivery. You also can have packages delivered to your Disney hotel.

Services for People with Disabilities: The Magic Kingdom gets decent marks from visitors with disabilities. Level entrances and ramps provide wheelchair access. Frontierland is the only area of the park, aside from Main Street, that has sidewalk curbs; there are ramps in several locations.

Pick up a *Guide for Guests with Disabilitie*s at Guest Relations. It gives mobility details and notes where you can use handheld-captioning, assisted-listening, video-captioning, and other devices (which are available for free but require a deposit). The guide also indicates which attractions have sign-language interpretation and when, which attractions don't permit service animals, and locations of designated "break" areas for animals.

At the hub by the Tip Board across from Casey's Corner, there's a large Braille map of the park. You can rent wheelchairs only at the park's entrance before passing under the train station for $12 daily, $10 a day for multiday rental. Electronic convenience vehicles (ECV) are $50 per day plus a refundable $20 security deposit. ■TIP➡ **Neither wheelchairs nor ECVs can be booked ahead, so arrive early to rent them—ECV availability is limited.**

Stroller Rentals: The Stroller Shop is near the entrance on the east side of Main Street. Single strollers are $15 daily, $13 for multiday rental; doubles are $31 daily, $27 for multiday rental.

Wait-time Updates: At the end of Main Street, on the left as you face Cinderella Castle, just before the Hub, is the **Tip Board**, a large board with constantly updated information about attractions' wait times.

PARK TOURS

Book any park tours ahead of your visit by calling ☎ *407/939–8687*.

Family Magic Tour. It's a two-hour "surprise" scavenger hunt in which your guide encourages you to find things that have disappeared. Disney officials don't want to reveal the tour's components—after all, it's the Family "Magic" Tour—but they will say that a special character-greeting session awaits you at the end of the adventure. Tours leave the Chamber of Commerce adjacent to City Hall in Town Square daily ($34 for adults and children 3 and up). ⊠ *Main Street, U.S.A.* ☎ *407/939–8687* 🖃 *$34* ☉ *Daily.*

Keys to the Kingdom Tour. The five-hour tour gives you a feel for the Magic Kingdom's layout and what goes on behind the scenes. The walking tour, which costs $79, includes lunch. Park admission must be purchased separately. No one younger than 16 is allowed. Tours leave from the Chamber of Commerce adjacent to City Hall in Town Square several times daily. Included are visits to "backstage" zones: the parade staging area, the wardrobe area, and other locations in the web of tunnels beneath the Magic Kingdom. ⊠ *Main Street, U.S.A.* ☎ *407/939–8687* 🖃 *$79* ☉ *Daily.*

Magic Behind Our Steam Trains. This tour, which gives you an inside look at the daily operation of the WDW railroad, became so popular that it was lengthened from two to three hours and is offered on six days. Tours begin at the front-entrance turnstile at 7:30 am Monday through

Saturday. Visitors 10 years old and up may participate. The cost is $54 per person, plus park admission. ☎ *407/939–8687* ➩ *$54* ⊘ *Mon.–Sat.*

Magic Kingdom guided tours. Several Disney-run Magic Kingdom guided tours are available. Ask about discounts when booking, and arrive 15 minutes ahead of time to check in. Park admission is required in addition to the tour fee unless otherwise noted. ☎ *407/939–8687.*

Walt Disney: Marceline to Magic Kingdom Tour. Walt Disney spent much of his early childhood in Marceline, Missouri, and this insider's walking tour offers insight into the boy who became the man behind the Disney kingdom. It also offers an insider's look at the design and operation of attractions. Open to ages 12 and up, tours ($30) leave from the Main Street Chamber of Commerce, next to City Hall, on Monday, Wednesday, Friday, and Saturday at 8 am. ⊠ *Main Street, U.S.A.* ☎ *407/939–8687* ➩ *$30* ⊘ *Mon., Wed., Fri., and Sat.*

VISITING TIPS

■ Try to come toward the end of the week, because most families hit the Magic Kingdom early in a visit.

■ Ride a star attraction during a parade; lines ease considerably. (But be careful not to get stuck on the wrong side of the parade route when it starts, or you may never get across.)

■ At City Hall, near the park's Town Square entrance, pick up a map and a *Times Guide,* which lists showtimes, character-greeting times, and hours for attractions and restaurants.

■ Book character meals early. Main Street, U.S.A's The Crystal Palace, A Buffet with Character has breakfast, lunch, and dinner with Winnie the Pooh, Tigger, and friends. All three meals at the Fairy Tale Dining experience in Cinderella Castle are extremely popular—so much so that you should reserve your spot six months out. The same advice goes for booking the full-service dinner at the new Be Our Guest Restaurant in the Beast's Castle in Fantasyland.

EXPLORING THE MAGIC KINGDOM

MAIN STREET, U.S.A

With its pastel Victorian-style buildings, antique automobiles ahoohga-oohga-ing, sparkling sidewalks, and an atmosphere of what one writer has called "almost hysterical joy," Main Street is more than a mere conduit to the other enchantments of the Magic Kingdom. It's where the spell is first cast.

You emerge from beneath the Walt Disney World Railroad Station into a realization of one of the most tenacious American dreams. The perfect street in the perfect small town in a perfect moment of time is burnished to jewel-like quality, thanks to a four-fifths-scale reduction, nightly cleanings with high-pressure hoses, and constant repainting. And it's a very sunny world, thanks to an outpouring of welcoming entertainment: live bands, barbershop quartets, and background music from Disney films and American musicals played over loudspeakers. Horse-drawn trolleys and omnibuses with their horns tooting chug along the street. Vendors in Victorian costumes sell balloons and popcorn. And

Cinderella's famous castle floats whimsically in the distance where Main Street disappears.

Although attractions with a capital A are minimal on Main Street, there are plenty of inducements—namely, shops and eateries—to while away your time and part you from your money. The largest of these, the Emporium, is often the last stop for souvenir hunters at day's end. At the Main Street Bakery, you can find your favorite Starbucks latte and a sandwich or baked treats like cupcakes and brownies. If you can't resist an interactive challenge while making your way through the park, head first to the Firehouse, next to City Hall, to join the legendary wizard Merlin in the Sorcerers of the Magic Kingdom role-playing game. For no extra charge, you can take ownership of special cards with "magic spells" that help you search for symbols and bring down Disney villains like Yzma and Kronk from the Disney film *The Emperor's New Groove*. Don't worry—you'll have time between fireball battles and cyclone spells to ride Space Mountain.

The Harmony Barber Shop lets you step back in time for a haircut ($15 for children 12 and under, $19 for anyone older). Babies or tots get free Mickey Ears, a souvenir lock of hair, and a certificate if it's their first haircut ever, but you pay $19 for the experience. At the Town Square Theater (formerly Exposition Hall), presented by Kodak, Mickey Mouse meets you for photos and autographs. And, for the first time in Disney history, you can pick up a FastPass+ appointment for such meet and greets. While you're here, stock up on batteries and memory cards or disposable cameras.

Walt Disney World Railroad. If you click through the turnstile just before 9 am with young children in tow, wait at the entrance before crossing beneath the station. In a few moments, you'll see the day's first steam-driven train arrive laden with the park's most popular residents: Mickey Mouse, Donald Duck, Goofy, Pluto, and characters from every corner of the World. Once they disembark and you've collected the stars' autographs and photos, step right up to the elevated platform above the Magic Kingdom's entrance for a ride into living history. All the locomotives date from 1928, the same year Mickey Mouse was created.

Disney scouts tracked down these vintage carriers in Mexico (where they transported sugarcane in the Yucatán), brought them back, and overhauled them. They're splendid, with striped awnings, brightly painted benches, authoritative "choo-choo" sounds, and hissing plumes of steam.

The 1½-mile track runs along the perimeter of the Magic Kingdom, with much of the trip through the woods and stops in Frontierland and Fantasyland. The four trains run at five-to-seven-minute intervals. **For people with disabilities:** You can remain in a standard wheelchair or transfer to one if you're in an ECV. Equipped for handheld-captioning. ■ TIP→ **The ride is a good introduction to the layout of the park; it's also great as relief for tired feet.** You can't load bulky strollers—like those Disney rents. Go mid-afternoon, when there's no line, or early, before 9 am, to greet Disney characters. ⊠ *Magic Kingdom* ☞ *Duration: 21* *mins or less depending where you disembark. Crowds: Moderate. Audience: All Ages.*

ADVENTURELAND

From the scrubbed brick, manicured lawns, and meticulously pruned trees of the Central Plaza, an artfully dilapidated wooden bridge leads to the jungles of Adventureland. Here, South African cape honeysuckle droops, Brazilian bougainvillea drapes, Mexican flame vines cling, spider plants clone, and three varieties of palm trees sway. The bright, all-American sing-along tunes that fill the air along Main Street and Central Plaza are replaced by the recorded repetitions of trumpeting elephants, pounding drums, and squawking parrots. The architecture is a mishmash of the best of Thailand, the Middle East, the Caribbean, Africa, and Polynesia, arranged in an inspired disorder that recalls comic-book fantasies of far-off places.

Once contained within the Pirates of the Caribbean attraction, Captain Jack Sparrow and the crew of the Black Pearl are brazenly recruiting new hearties at the Pirates League, adjacent to the ride entrance. You can get pirate and mermaid makeovers (for lots of doubloons) here. On a nearby stage furnished with pirate booty, the captain instructs scurvy dog recruits on brandishing a sword at Captain Jack Sparrow's Pirate Tutorial (several shows a day). And that's not all! At "A Pirate's Adventure: Treasures of the Seven Seas" park guests embark on an interactive quest with a pirate map and talisman to complete "raids" through Adventureland as they fight off pirate enemies along the way. Shiver me timbers—it's a pirate's life for ye!

Walt Disney's Enchanted Tiki Room. The latest version of Disney's first Audio-Animatronics attraction brings back the original show, Tropical Serenade. Winged hosts Jose, Fritz, Pierre, Michael, and the boys take you on a tour of the attraction while cracking lots of jokes. The original ditty "In the Tiki, Tiki, Tiki, Tiki, Tiki Room" is second only to "it's a small world" as the Disney song you most love to hate. Speaking of which, many people do hate this attraction, finding the talking birds obnoxious and the music too loud and peppy. But you can also hear old-timers singing along to "Let's All Sing Like the Birdies Sing," tweet, tweet tweet, tweet, tweet. **For people with disabilities:** Accessible for those in standard wheelchairs; equipped for handheld-captioning, audio description, and assisted-listening devices. ■ TIP→ **Go when you need to sit down with air-conditioning.** ✉ *Adventureland, Magic Kingdom* ☞ *Duration: 12 mins. Crowds: Moderate. Audience: All Ages.*

Jungle Cruise. Cruise through three continents and along four rivers: the Congo, the Nile, the Mekong, and the Amazon. The canopied launches are loaded, the safari-suited guides make a point of checking their pistols, and the *Irrawady Irma* or *Mongala Millie* is off for another "perilous" journey. The guide's shtick is surprisingly funny in a wry and cornball way, provided he or she has mastered the art of enunciation. Along the way, you'll encounter Disney's famed Audio-Animatronics creatures of the African veld: bathing elephants, slinky pythons, an irritated rhinoceros, a tribe of hungry headhunters, and a bunch of hyperactive hippos (good thing the guide's got a pop pistol). Then there's Old

Adventureland Adventure Number 1: Being shipwrecked with the Swiss Family Robinson and exploring their tree house.

Smiley, the crocodile, who's always waiting for a handout—or, as the guide quips, "a foot out."

The animals are early-generation and crude by Disney standards—anyone who's seen the real thing at the Animal Kingdom or even a good zoo won't be impressed. Unless you're an old-school Disney fan, the Jungle Cruise isn't really worth a FastPass+. **For people with disabilities:** Several boats have lifts that allow wheelchair access; equipped for assisted-listening. Sign language is provided some days. ■ TIP➔ **Go during the afternoon parade, but not after dark—you miss too much.** ⊠ *Adventureland* ☞ *Duration: 10 mins. Crowds: Heavy. Audience: All Ages.*

The Magic Carpets of Aladdin. Brightening the lush Adventureland landscape is this jewel-toned ride around a giant genie's bottle. You can control your own four-passenger, state-of-the-art carpet with a front-seat lever that moves it up and down and a rear-seat button that pitches it forward or backward. Part of the fun is dodging the right-on aim of a water-spewing "camel." The ride is short but a big hit with kids, who are also dazzled by the colorful gems implanted in the surrounding pavement. Parents must ride with toddlers. **For people with disabilities:** There's ramp access for guests in wheelchairs. If you're in an ECV, you must transfer to a standard wheelchair. ■ TIP➔ **FastPass+ is now available here but you may not need one, as lines move fairly quickly.** ⊠ *Adventureland* ☞ *Duration: 3 mins. Crowds: Heavy. Audience: All Ages.*

Pirates of the Caribbean. This is one of the few rides in the world that inspired a film (*Haunted Mansion* with Eddie Murphy was another) rather than the other way around.

Beast's Castle

Be Our Guest
Restaurant

Gaston's Tavern

Pete's Silly
Sideshow

Walt Disney World
Railroad Station

Under the Sea–
Journey of the
Little Mermaid

Ariel's
Grotto

Enchanted Tales
with Belle

Prince Eric's
Village Market

Casey Jr.
Splash 'N' Soak
Station

The
Barnstormer

FANTASYLAND

Big Top
Souvenirs

Dumbo the
Flying Elephant

Seven Dwarfs
Mine Train

Prince Charming
Regal Carrousel

Storybook
Treats

The Many Adventures
of Winnie the Pooh

The Friar's
Nook

Mad Tea
Party

Princess
Fairytale Hall

Cheshire
Cafe

Sir Mickey's

Fairytale
Garden

Cinderella's
Royal Table

Cosmic Ray's
Starlight Café

Tomorrowland
Speedway

Space
Mountain

Cinderella Castle

Bibbidi Bobbidi
Boutique

Dream Along
with Mickey

TOMORROWLAND

Central
Plaza

Auntie Gravity's
Galactic Goodies

ATM

Stitch's
Great Escape

Monsters, Inc.
Laugh Floor

The
Lunching
Pad

Astro Orbiter

Buzz Lightyear's
Space Ranger
Spin

Tomorrowland
Transit Authority
PeopleMover

Casey's Corner

Tomorrowland
Terrace

Walt Disney's
Carousel of
Progress

Plaza
Restaurant

Main Street
Bakery

MAIN
STREET
U.S.A.

Parade Route

Tony's
Town Square
Restaurant

Town
Square

Town Square Theater/
Camera Center

WDW Railroad Station

Lockers

Stroller &
Wheelchair
Rentals

Entrance
Turnstiles

ATM

Guest
Relations

Disney Resort
Bus Facility

Seven Seas
Lagoon

Ferry Landing

KEY	
✗	Restaurants
🚻	Restrooms
——	Rail Line
══	Monorail
••••	Parade Route

The gracious arched entrance soon gives way to a dusty dungeon, redolent of dampness and of a spooky, scary past. Lanterns flicker as your boat sails, and a ghostly voice intones, "Dead men tell no tales." Next, a deserted beach, strewn with shovels, a skeleton, and a disintegrating map indicating buried treasure prefaces this story of greed, lust, and destruction. You'll pass right through a water-mist screen featuring the maniacal mug of Davy Jones, complete with squirming tentacle beard and barnacle-encrusted hat. Emerging from a pitch-black tunnel after a mild, tummy-tickling drop, you're caught in the line of fire as a pirate ship cannon blasts away at a stone fortress. Look for Captain Barbossa, evil nemesis of Captain Jack Sparrow. Audio-2s pirates hoist the Jolly Roger while brave soldiers scurry to defend the fort—to no avail.

Politically correct nerves may twinge as the women of the town are rounded up and auctioned, but the wenches rule in another scene, where they chase roguish rapscallions with glee. The wild antics of the pirates—Captain Jack Sparrow pops up in several situations—result in a conflagration; the town goes up in flames, and all go to their just reward amid a catchy chorus of "A Pirate's Life for Me." **For people with disabilities:** Boarding requires transferring from a standard wheelchair to the ride vehicle; the very small flume drop may make the attraction inappropriate for those with limited upper-body strength or those wearing neck or back braces. Equipped for audio-description and handheld-captioning devices. ■ TIP➔ A FastPass+ is now available but not always necessary. It's best to ride in the heat of the afternoon, and lines move steadily. ⊠ *Adventureland* ☞ *Duration: 12 mins. Crowds: Moderate. Audience: All but Very Young Kids.* ✦

Swiss Family Treehouse. Inspired by the classic novel by Johann Wyss about the adventures of the Robinson family, who were shipwrecked en route to America, the tree house shows what you can do with a big faux tree and a lot of imagination. Disney detail abounds: the kitchen sink is a giant clamshell; the boys' room, strewn with clothing, has two hammocks instead of beds; and an ingenious system of rain barrels and bamboo pipes provides running water in every room.

As you clamber around the narrow wooden steps and rope bridges that connect the rooms in this split-level dwelling, take a look at the Spanish moss. It's real, but the tree itself—some 90 feet in diameter, with more than 1,000 branches—was constructed by the props department. The 300,000 leaves are vinyl. Toddlers unsteady on their feet may have trouble with the stairs. **For people with disabilities:** With its 100 steps and lack of narration, this attraction gets low ratings among those with mobility and visual impairments. ■ TIP➔ If you're with children 4 to 12 who like to explore, plan to climb while you're already in Adventureland. ⊠ *Adventureland* ☞ *Duration: Up to You. Crowds: Light to Moderate. Audience: All Ages.*

▌ NEED A BREAK? If you're looking for real refreshment and an energy boost, stop by **Aloha Isle**, where you'll find some of the tastiest and most healthful goodies. Try the fresh pineapple spears, or sip the popular Frozen Dole Whip or just

Adventureland Adventure Number 2: Gliding through the muggy, steamy Caribbean world of pirates. Yo ho ho!

some fruit juice, while you relax on one of the benches scattered around Adventureland.

FRONTIERLAND

Frontierland evokes the American frontier and is planted with mesquite, twisted Peruvian pepper trees, slash pines, and cacti. The period seems to be the latter half of the 19th century, and the West is being won by Disney cast members dressed in checked shirts, leather vests, cowboy hats, and brightly colored neckerchiefs. Banjo and fiddle music twangs from tree to tree, and snackers walk around munching turkey drumsticks so large that you could best an outlaw single-handedly with one. (Beware of hovering seagulls that migrate to the parks during cooler months—they've been known to snatch snacks.)

The screams that drown out the string music aren't the result of a cowboy surprising an Indian. They come from two of the Magic Kingdom's more thrilling rides: Splash Mountain, an elaborate flume ride, and Big Thunder Mountain Railroad, a roller coaster. The Walt Disney World Railroad tunnels past a colorful scene in Splash Mountain and drops you off between it and Thunder Mountain.

Fodor's Choice
★

Big Thunder Mountain Railroad. Set in gold-rush days, this thrilling roller coaster simulates a runaway train. It's a bumpy ride with several good drops (pregnant women and guests wearing back, neck, or leg braces should avoid this one). There are moments when you feel like you're going to fly right off the tracks. Overall it's more fun than scary, and you'll see kids as young as 7 lining up to ride. The train rushes and rattles past 20 Audio-Animatronics figures—mostly critters—as well as

$300,000 worth of genuine antique mining equipment, tumbleweeds, a derelict mining town, hot springs, and a flash flood.

The 197-foot mountain landscape is based on the windswept scenery of Arizona's Monument Valley, and thanks to 650 tons of steel, 4,675 tons of concrete, and 16,000 gallons of paint, it replicates the area's gorges, tunnels, caverns, and dry river beds. **For people with disabilities:** You must be able to step into the ride vehicle and walk short distances. Service animals aren't permitted. ■ TIP➔ **Use FastPass+ unless you go first thing in the morning or during a parade. The ride is most exciting at night, when you can't anticipate the curves and the track's rattling really sounds as if something's about to give.** ⊠ *Frontierland* ⌔ *Duration: 4 mins. Crowds: Absolutely. Audience: Not Small Kids.*

Country Bear Jamboree. Wisecracking, cornpone, lovelorn Audio-Animatronics bears joke, sing, and play country music and 1950s rock and roll in this stage show. Even timid youngsters love them. The emcee, the massive but debonair Henry, leads the stellar cast of Grizzly Hall, which includes the robust Trixie, who laments love lost while perching on a swing suspended from the ceiling; Bubbles, Bunny, and Beulah, harmonizing on "All the Guys That Turn Me on Turn Me Down"; and Big Al, the off-key cult figure who has inspired his own shopping kiosk. **For people with disabilities:** Wheelchair accessible; reflective captioning provided; equipped for assisted-listening devices. If you lip-read, ask to sit up front. ■ TIP➔ **Visit before 11 am, during the afternoon parade, or late in the day. Stand to the far left in the anteroom for the front rows and to the far right for the last row, where small kids can perch atop seats to see better.** ⊠ *Frontierland* ⌔ *Duration: 17 mins. Crowds: Moderate. Audience: All Ages.*

Fodor'sChoice
★
Splash Mountain. One of the most popular thrill rides after Space Mountain, this log-flume water ride was based on animated sequences in Disney's 1946 film *Song of the South*. Here the Audio-Animatronics creations of Brer Rabbit, Brer Bear, Brer Fox, and a menagerie of other Brer beasts frolic in bright, cartoonlike settings. Settle into the eight-person hollowed-out logs, and the fun begins.

As the boat carries you up the mountain, Brer Rabbit's silhouette hops merrily ahead to the tune of the ride's theme song, "Time to Be Moving Along." Every time some critter makes a grab for the bunny, your log boat drops out of reach. But Brer Fox has been studying his book *How to Catch a Rabbit,* and our lop-eared friend looks as if he's destined for the pot. Things don't look so good for the flumers, either. You get one heart-stopping pause at the top of the mountain—just long enough to grab the safety bar—and then the boat plummets about five stories at a 45-degree angle into a large, wet briar patch. It's enough to reach speeds of 40 mph—and makes you feel weightless. Clench your teeth and smile: as you begin to drop, a flashbulb pops. Another photographic memento for sale as you "Zip-a-Dee-Doo-Dah" your way to the next ride.

You may get wet, so plan accordingly. If you need to use Baby Swap you can take the young ones to a play area in a cave under the attraction; riders must be at least 40 inches tall. Do not ride if you're pregnant or have heart, back, or neck problems. **For people with disabilities:** You

Coasting down Splash Mountain in Frontierland will put some zip in your doo-dah and some water on your clothes.

must be able to step into the ride vehicle and walk short distances. Service animals aren't permitted. ■TIP➜ **Plan to use FastPass+ or ride when the park opens or during meal or parade times.** ⊠ *Frontierland* ☞ *Duration: 11 mins. Crowds: Yes! Audience: Not Small Kids.*

Tom Sawyer Island. Tom Sawyer Island is a playground of hills, trees, rocks, and shrubs. Most attractions are on the main island, where your raft docks. The Mystery Mine is like a secret passageway to exploration. Children love Injun Joe's Cave, where there are lots of columns and crevices from which to jump out and startle siblings. As you explore the shoreline on the dirt paths, watch out for the barrel bridge—the whole contraption bounces at every step.

On the other island is Fort Langhorn, a log fortress from which you can fire air guns with great booms and cracks at the passing *Liberty Belle* riverboat. **For people with disabilities:** With its stairs, bridges, inclines, and narrow caves, this attraction isn't negotiable by those using a wheelchair. ■TIP➜ **Get away from the crowds here. Watch toddlers closely, as it's easy to lose track of them.** ⊠ *Frontierland* ☞ *Duration: Up to You. Crowds: Light. Audience: Kids and Tweens.*

LIBERTY SQUARE

The rough-and-tumble Western frontier gently folds into Colonial America as Liberty Square picks up where Frontierland leaves off. The weathered siding gives way to solid brick and neat clapboard. The mesquite and cactus are replaced by stately oaks and masses of azaleas. The theme is Colonial history, which Northerners will be happy to learn is portrayed here as solid Yankee. The buildings, topped with weather vanes and exuding prosperity, are pure New England.

A replica of the Liberty Bell, crack and all, seems an appropriate prop to separate Liberty Square from Frontierland. There's even a Liberty Tree, a more than 150-year-old live oak, transported here from elsewhere on Disney property. Just as the Sons of Liberty hung lanterns on trees as a signal of solidarity after the Boston Tea Party, the Liberty Tree's branches are decorated with 13 lanterns representing the 13 original colonies. Around the square are tree-shaded tables for an alfresco lunch and plenty of carts and fast-food eateries to supply the goods.

NEED A BREAK?

Sleepy Hollow offers quick pick-me-ups in the form of funnel cakes, soft-serve ice cream, espresso drinks, and waffle sandwiches.

The Hall of Presidents. With the latest in Disney Audio-Animatronics (this attraction introduced the technology in 1971) this show tells a moving story of the bond between the presidents and "We, the People." Producers re-shot the accompanying film in high-definition video and added more than 130 images culled from the National Archives, Library of Congress, and other collections. A digital sound track, LED lighting, and narration by Morgan Freeman further enhance the experience. The film covers 220 years of U.S. history and emphasizes anecdotes about presidents who've reached out to people in times of strife. Both George Washington and Abraham Lincoln grab a bit of the spotlight, the latter by delivering his famous Gettysburg Address.

The best part of the show is a roll call of all 43 U.S. presidents. (Fun fact: Obama is officially the 44th president because Grover Cleveland is counted twice due to his having served nonconsecutive terms.) Each chief executive responds with a nod, and those who are seated rise (except for wheelchair-bound Franklin Delano Roosevelt, of course). The robots nod and whisper to each other as the roll call proceeds. During Obama's turn, he takes the presidential Oath of Office (recorded in the White House by Imagineers) and delivers a speech about the American Dream. Anyone interested in presidential artifacts will enjoy the wait in the lobby area, where First Ladies' dresses, presidential portraits, and even George Washington's dental instruments are on display. **For people with disabilities:** Wheelchair accessible; enter through a door on the right. Reflective captioning available; equipped for assisted-listening devices. ■ TIP→ **Visit anytime.** ⊠ *Liberty Sq.* ⌢ *Duration: 22 mins. Crowds: Moderate to Heavy. Audience: Not Small Kids.*

Fodor's Choice ★ **Haunted Mansion.** The special effects here are a howl. You're greeted at the creaking iron gates of this Gothic mansion by a lugubrious attendant, who has one of the few jobs at Disney for which smiling

Liberty Square's Haunted Mansion in lights—pretty scary or just pretty? You decide.

is frowned upon, and ushered into a spooky picture gallery. A disembodied voice echoes from the walls: "Welcome, foolish mortals, to the Haunted Mansion. I am your ghost host." An audio system with 30-plus surround-sound speakers ups the ghost-host fright factor. A scream shivers down, the room begins to "stretch," and you're off into one of Disney's classic attractions. ■TIP➔ Don't rush out of this room when other visitors depart; linger for some ghoulish bonus whispers.

Consisting mainly of a slow-moving ride in a cocoonlike "doom buggy," the Haunted Mansion is really scary only for younger children, and that's mostly because of the darkness. Everyone else will laugh while they gawk at the special effects. Watch the ghostly ballroom dancers, Madame Leota's talking head in the crystal ball, and ghostly footprints that move along a staircase. In the "bride in the attic" scene, keep an eye on the portraits. Just when you think the Imagineers have exhausted their bag of ectoplasmic tricks, you discover that your doom buggy has gained an extra passenger. This is a high-capacity, fast-loading ride, and lines usually move steadily. **For people with disabilities:** Those in wheelchairs must transfer to the "doom buggies" and take one or more steps; however, if you can walk up to 200 feet, you'll enjoy the preshow as well as the ride's sensations and eerie sounds. Equipped for handheld-captioning and audio-description devices. ■TIP➔ When you reach a fork in the queue before entering the mansion, go left through the cemetery for interactive graveyard fun. The Musical Crypt and Secret Library help you forget you're in line. Nighttime adds an extra fright factor. ⊠ *Liberty Sq.* ☞ *Duration: 8 mins. Crowds: Heavy. Audience: Not Small Kids.*

Continued on page 74

A MAN, A MOUSE, A LEGACY

By Jennie Hess

Walt Disney once said, "I only hope that we never lose sight of one thing—that it was all started by a mouse." His legendary mouse, Mickey, took the world by storm in 1928 in the theatrical debut of the animated short film *Steamboat Willie*. Today, Walt is Mickey, Mickey is Walt, and their legacy is legendary.

Above: Walt Disney; below: Mickey from *Fantasia*, 1940; right: *Pinocchio*, 1940

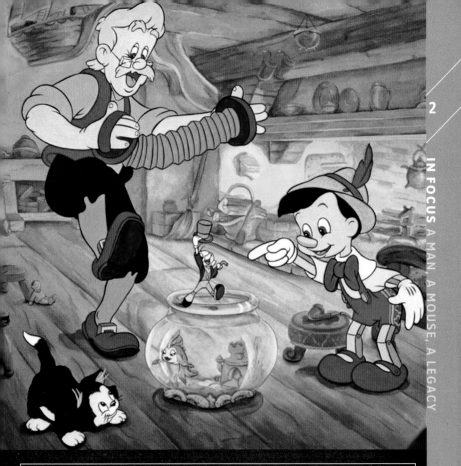

There's a tale still told (and disputed) that Walt imagined Mickey while on a train from New York to California, after a disastrous meeting where he lost the rights to a character called Oswald the Lucky Rabbit. Walt's friend and colleague, gifted Dutch cartoonist Ub Iwerks, first drew Mickey, but it was Walt who gave him a voice and personality.

He planned to name the mouse Mortimer, but his wife, Lilian, insisted the name didn't fit the cheerful little rodent.

The man behind the mouse, Walter Elias Disney, was born December 5, 1901, in Chicago. His early Midwestern years were spent nurturing his love of drawing. After driving an ambulance for the Red Cross in France during World War I, Walt returned to the States and worked for an ad company, where he met Ub.

Though Mickey appeared in the silent short *Plane Crazy* in May of 1928, the amiable mouse didn't really take a bow until the November debut of *Steamboat Willie*. Walt's use of synchronized sound made all the difference. By 1937, Walt and company had released their first animated feature-length film, *Snow White and the Seven Dwarfs*.

The many films that followed formed the creative and financial bedrock for a legacy of one theme park after another. But perhaps the greatest legacy of Walt and his mouse is that they both make memories for generation upon generation.

Shirley Temple presents Disney with one big and seven dwarf-size Oscars for *Snow White*, 1939; right: *Snow White*; *Steamboat Willie* poster, 1928

1920s–30s

A Mouse Is Born

Walt and his brother, Roy, establish a Hollywood studio in 1923. Animated shorts *Plane Crazy* and *Steamboat Willie*, starring both Mickey and Minnie, are released in 1928. Thereafter, Walt and his artists create dozens of Mickey shorts like 1930's *The Chain Gang*, when an orange pup named Pluto first appears.

Two years later, good-natured Goofy debuts as an audience extra in *Mickey's Revue*. His spasmodic laugh earns him a series of his own animated short films. Hot-tempered Donald Duck and his loyal girlfriend, Daisy, follow.

In 1937, America's first full-length animated feature,

Snow White and the Seven Dwarfs, becomes the highest-grossing feature of its time. *Gone with the Wind* doesn't blow by that record until 1939, the same year that Disney's groundbreaking feature earns a special Academy Award: one full-size Oscar and seven dwarf Oscars presented by Shirley Temple.

■ **Visit:** Walt Disney: One Man's Dream; The Magic of Disney Animation

Goofy

1940s–50s

Characters Come to Life

Fans of all ages flock to see successive hits, from *Pinocchio* and *Fantasia* (both 1940) to *Dumbo* (1941) and *Bambi* (1942). Though *Fantasia* is panned by some, it earns Academy Awards kudos for innovating in the area of visualized music—specifically, animation set to music by composers such as Bach, Tchaikovsky, and Beethoven and recorded under the direction of conductor Leopold Stokowski.

During World War II, the Disney studio springs to patriotic action with a series of military training and propaganda films. After the war, the animation wizards cast a spell over the

Left: *Dumbo* and *Lady and the Tramp;* right: entrance to Sleeping Beauty's Enchanted Castle, Disneyland, late 1960s

country with *Cinderella* (1950), *Alice in Wonderland* (1951), *Peter Pan* (1953), *Lady and the Tramp* (1955), *Sleeping Beauty* (1959), and others.

Walt's love for nature leads him to produce 13 True-Life Adventure films, eight of which win Oscars. Walt also brings his first live-action adventure film, *Treasure Island,* to the screen. He and his brother, Roy, begin dreaming up a new adventure altogether—Disneyland.

The first Disney theme park opens on July 17, 1955, in Anaheim, California. Many attractions and rides have Disney film themes. Drawing on his lifelong train infatuation, Walt encircles the park with the Disneyland Railroad.

■ **Visit:** Cinderella Castle

■ **Ride:** Prince Charming Regal Carrousel, Peter Pan's Flight, Dumbo the Flying Elephant, and Walt Disney World Railroad

■ **See:** Mickey's PhilharMagic

Cinderella Castle today

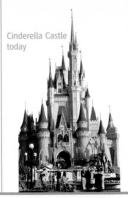

1960s–70s

A Magical New Frontier

In the early 1960s, Walt purchases 27,500 Orlando acres—an area twice the size of Manhattan. Sadly, he dies (December 1966) before Walt Disney World opens.

On October 1, 1971, the Magic Kingdom gates swing open, and a sleek monorail glides to the Contemporary and the Polynesian resort hotels. In November, a 640-acre western-style camping resort, Fort Wilderness, opens.

■ **Visit:** Magic Kingdom

■ **Ride:** The Monorail

Above: Disney Paris; Mickey hat; right: EPCOT's iconic Spaceship Earth

1980s–90s

A Worldlier Walt

Prior to his death, Walt begins work on what he hopes will be an ideal city. He names the project Experimental Prototype Community of Tomorrow. After the Magic Kingdom opens, Disney executives use some of Walt's ideas to create EPCOT Center. What opens in 1982 is the second Florida theme park—celebrating the world's cultures, the past, and the future—rather than an experimental community.

The 1980s are banner years for Disney Parks and Resorts. In 1983, the company's first international park—Tokyo Disneyland—opens. In 1989, Florida's third park, Disney-MGM Studios (later Disney's Hollywood Studios) premiers with celebrity fanfare. Not far from it, a new nightlife district, Pleasure Island, pumps up the volume, and Typhoon Lagoon crashes onto the scene with 6-foot waves and thrill-slide appeal.

The decade that follows is no less ambitious. In 1992 Euro Disney Resort (now Disneyland Paris) becomes the Mouse's second international destination; the first Disney cruise ships are launched from Port Canaveral, Florida; and the fourth Florida park, Disney's Animal Kingdom, earns raves for its authentic habitats. The icing on the Magic Kingdom's 20th anniversary cake? The animation studio is once again making big-screen hits with *Beauty and the Beast* (1991), *Aladdin* (1992), and *The Lion King* (1994)

■ **Visit:** Spaceship Earth at EPCOT; Beauty and the Beast—Live on Stage at the Studios; Kilimanjaro Safaris at Animal Kingdom; Typhoon Lagoon

Aladdin

FINDING MICKEY

A Hidden Mickey at Epcot

Hidden Mickeys began as an inside joke among Disney Imagineers, the creative folks behind the theme parks. When finishing an attraction, they'd slip a Mickey into the motif to see who might notice. You can get a list of Hidden Mickeys at any Guest Relations location, at ⊕www.allears.net, or at ⊕www.hiddenmickeys. org. Here are just a few to get you started, though:

Big Thunder Mountain Railroad (Magic Kingdom). As your train nears the station, look to your right for three rusty gears on the ground.

DINOSAUR (Animal Kingdom). Stare at the bark of the painted tree in the far left background of the wall mural at the entrance.

Haunted Mansion (Magic Kingdom). As you move through the ballroom, notice the Mouse-eared place setting on the table.

Spaceship Earth (Epcot). Mickey smiles down from a constellation behind the loading area.

Twilight Zone Tower of Terror (Hollywood Studios). In the boiler room, look for a water stain on the wall after the queue splits.

Finding Nemo's, Dory and Nemo

New Millennium

To Infinity and Beyond!

The new millennium sends the Mouse into overdrive. Hong Kong Disneyland opens (2005), as do several World attractions, among them one with a *Toy Story* theme, and two with a *Nemo* theme. Disney World also adds to its accommodations, bringing the total to 30,000 rooms, 3,200 Disney Vacation Club villas, and 800 campsites. New eateries like the Trattoria al Forno at Disney's Boardwalk open, as do luxurious on-Disney property resorts including Four Seasons Resort Orlando.

Looking ahead, it seems as if pixie dust will permeate the World for years to come. The Magic Kingdom's new Fantasyland is complete with everyone's newest favorite ride, the Seven Dwarfs Mine Train family coaster. Disney Cruise Line now sails with four ships including the newer *Disney Fantasy* and *Disney Dream*. The multimillion-dollar makeover of Downtown Disney to Disney Springs has brought new shops, restaurants, and entertainment, plus one much-needed parking garage and a second to open by 2016. By early 2017, Avatar Land is expected to open at Disney's Animal Kingdom.

Toy Story's Buzz Lightyear

Liberty Square Riverboat. An old-fashioned steamboat, the *Liberty Belle* is authentic, from its calliope whistle and the gingerbread trim on its three decks to the boilers that produce the steam that drives the big rear paddle wheel. In fact, the boat misses authenticity on only one count: there's no mustachioed captain to guide it during the ride around the Rivers of America. That task is performed by an underwater rail. The 1½-mile cruise is slow and not exactly thrilling, but there are lovely views of Tom Sawyer Island and surrounding attractions. Children like exploring the boat. Lines move quickly. **For people with disabilities:** Wheelchair accessible; enter through exit on right or left. ■ TIP➜ **Come when you need a break from the crowds. Check Times Guide—the riverboat is open seasonally.** ⊠ *Liberty Sq.* ☞ *Duration: 15 mins. Crowds: Light to Moderate. Audience: All Ages.*

FANTASYLAND

Walt Disney called this "a timeless land of enchantment," and Fantasyland does conjure pixie dust. Perhaps that's because the fanciful gingerbread houses, gleaming gold turrets, and, of course, the rides are based on Disney-animated movies.

Many of these rides, which could ostensibly be classified as rides for children, are packed with enough delightful detail to engage the adults who accompany them. Fantasyland has always been the most heavily trafficked area in the park, and its rides and shows are almost always crowded.

The good news is that Fantasyland has undergone the largest expansion in the park's history to offer several new attractions and experiences. Dumbo the Flying Elephant now is double the size, flying above circus-themed grounds that also include the Great Goofini coaster, starring Goofy as stuntman. There's also a Walt Disney World Railroad station in Fantasyland. And a circus-themed Casey Jr. Splash 'N' Soak Station provides water-play respite for kids. Ariel of *The Little Mermaid* invites you to her own state-of-the-art attraction, Under the Sea: Journey of the Little Mermaid. Disney princesses welcome you for a photo op in the glittering Princess Fairytale Hall. You can be part of the show when you join Belle, Lumiere, and Madame Wardrobe of *Beauty and the Beast* at the Enchanted Tales with Belle attraction for a story performance. Meanwhile, Beast may be brooding in his castle, where the Be Our Guest dining room beckons to lunch and dinner guests. And the musical Seven Dwarfs Mine Train family coaster opened in 2014 to complete the expansion.

You can enter Fantasyland on foot from Liberty Square, Tomorrowland, or via the Walt Disney World Railroad, but the classic introduction is through Cinderella Castle. As you exit the castle's archway, look left to discover a charming and often overlooked touch: Cinderella Fountain, a lovely brass casting of the castle's namesake, who's dressed in her peasant togs and surrounded by her beloved mice and bird friends.

From the southern end of Liberty Square, head toward the park hub and stop at the Disney PhotoPass picture spot for one of the park's best, unobstructed ground-level views of Cinderella Castle. It's a great spot for that family photo.

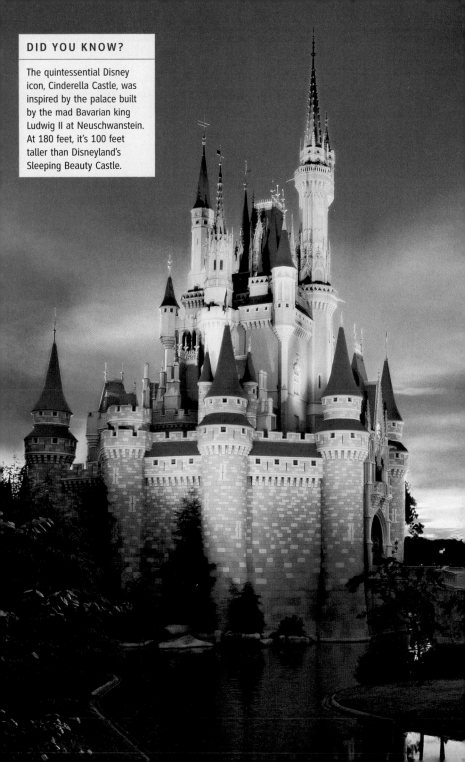

DID YOU KNOW?

The quintessential Disney icon, Cinderella Castle, was inspired by the palace built by the mad Bavarian king Ludwig II at Neuschwanstein. At 180 feet, it's 100 feet taller than Disneyland's Sleeping Beauty Castle.

Ariel's Grotto. Every mermaid princess should have a giant seashell throne, and that's where Ariel fans can meet the fashionably finned, red-headed beauty. Built into the rockwork of Prince Eric's castle, the grotto provides shade for those waiting in the queue and a more secluded experience for families who want to photograph or videotape the royal meet-up. ■TIP➔ Mermaid fans will be happy to know FastPass+ is now available. It's a natural to visit with young children before or after visiting Under the Sea: Journey of the Little Mermaid. ✉ *Fantasyland* ☞ *Duration: About 2 mins. Crowds: Yes. Audience: Young Kids.*

The Barnstormer. This coaster, which used to feature Goofy at his Wise-acre Farm, now stars the Great Goofini, stunt master—a perfect fit for Fantasyland's new Storybook Circus area. The twisting, turning roller coaster "flight" takes you high above the circus fun. It's perfect for young children's first thrill ride if they are 35 inches or taller. Circus props and themed posters tell Goofini's tale with references to some of the short films of Goofy's heyday. **For people with disabilities:** You must be able to walk a few steps from your wheelchair to board the ride. Service animals are not permitted. ■TIP➔ Book a FastPass+ or, first thing in the morning, take the Walt Disney World Railroad to Fantasyland and hop in line before the crowds arrive. ✉ *Fantasyland* ☞ *Duration: 1 min. Crowds: Heavy. Audience: All but Smallest Kids. Height minimum: 35 inches.*

Casey Jr. Splash 'N' Soak Station. The Casey Jr. circus train has just pulled into town, and train cars full of faux circus animals are taking a break in this circus-themed play area across from Dumbo the Flying Elephant. The critters may not be real, but they sure do put out a lot of water as children run hooting and squealing past spitting camels, spraying elephants, and other water hazards. **For people with disabilities:** Wheelchair accessible. ■TIP➔ While the kids cool off and burn energy, parents can take a break and grab a hot dog or soft pretzel from nearby carts. Pack towels and fresh clothing for cooler days. ✉ *Fantasyland* ☞ *Duration: As long as you like. Crowds: Moderate to Heavy. Audience: Young Kids.*

Cinderella Castle. Although often confused with Disneyland's Sleeping Beauty Castle, at 189 feet this iconic castle is more than 100 feet taller; and with its elongated towers and lacy fretwork, it's more graceful. Don't miss the elaborate mosaic murals on the walls of the archway as you rush toward Fantasyland from the Hub. The five panels, measuring some 15 feet high and 10 feet wide, were created from a million bits of multicolor Italian glass, silver, and 14-karat gold by mosaicist Hanns-Joachim Scharff. The mosaics tell the story of the little cinder girl as she goes from pumpkin to prince to happily ever after.

The fantasy castle has feet, if not of clay, then of solid steel beams, fiberglass, and 500 gallons of paint. Instead of dungeons, there are service tunnels for the Magic Kingdom's less-than-magical quotidian operations, such as Makeup and Costuming. These are the same tunnels that honeycomb the ground under much of the park.

Within the castle's archway is the **Bibbidi Bobbidi Boutique,** where the "royal treatment" transforms little girls age 3 and older into princesses

2

or divas. Hair and makeup are by a "Fairy Godmother-in-training." The valiant Knight Package offers a heroic alternative makeover that includes hairstyle, sword, and shield. If you have reservations to dine at **Cinderella's Royal Table,** you enter the castle by way of an ascending spiral staircase. You are attended by costumed waiters and joined by Cinderella and other princesses in one of Disney's most popular character-dining experiences. **For people with disabilities:** For those with limited mobility, elevator access to the dining experience is provided. ■TIP➔ Call or book online 180 days ahead, if possible, to reserve the character breakfast, lunch, or dinner known as Fairytale Dining. ✉ *Fantasyland.*

Dumbo the Flying Elephant. Based on the movie about the gigantic-eared baby elephant who learns he can fly, the ride consists of flying pachyderms, each packing a couple of kids and a parent. A joystick controls your Dumbo's up-and-down movement. A popular new feature for parents and children: the Big Top "play while you wait" indoor area chock full of climbing equipment for kids of most ages. As you enter the colorful circus tent, a Disney "ringmaster" hands you a pager that buzzes when it's your turn to join the ride queue. Parents can supervise tots in a small circus ring of play equipment while older kids burn up energy on multilevel climbers like the "Thrilling Tower of Flames." Adults enjoy the bench seating. **For people with disabilities:** If using a wheelchair, prepare to transfer to a ride vehicle. ■TIP➔ Get a FastPass+ if you're in a hurry; otherwise, let the kids enjoy the play area before riding. ✉ *Fantasyland* ⌚ *Duration: 2 mins. Crowds: Heavy. Audience: Young Kids.*

Fodor'sChoice
★
Enchanted Tales with Belle. Stroll the path through an artfully planted woodland and meadow to a rustic French cabin complete with waterwheel, where Belle's father, Maurice, tinkers with his inventions. The small homestead oozes Belle's provincial life, with a giant pot hanging in the fireplace and books stacked on a simple wooden chair. Inside her father's workshop, amid blueprints and tools, a giant gold-framed mirror hangs. A costumed cast member welcomes your group to the workshop (*Bonjour!*) and implores everyone to chant, "Take me back to the day Belle and Beast fell in love!" *Voilà!* The mirror becomes an animated screen straight from the Disney film *Beauty and the Beast* before transforming into a portal that leads to an elegant room of Beast's Castle. Inside, an Audio-Animatronic Madame Armoire encourages guests to grab props and play character roles from the "tale as old as time." Then, it's on to the library, where a spot-on Audio-Animatronic Lumiere holds court from the mantle. Families grab a cushy bench as a coiffed actress playing Belle joins guests to act out a scene from the enchanted tale. You'll dance around the room to "Be Our Guest," and you may shed a tear as the interactive story unfolds. This live performance gets to the heart of Disney storytelling, and every participant poses for photos with Belle before a very happy ending. **For people with disabilities:** Wheelchair accessible; equipped for handheld captioning and assisted listening. ■TIP➔ You can book a FastPass+ or visit while waiting for your Under the Sea: Journey of the Little Mermaid or other

See Lumiere chat with Belle at Enchanted Tales with Belle in Fantasyland.

nearby FastPass+ appointments. ⊠ *Fantasyland* ☞ *Duration: 15 mins. Crowds: Yes. Audience: All Ages; Perfect for Families.*

it's a small world. Visiting Walt Disney World and not stopping for this tribute to terminal cuteness—why, the idea is practically un-American. The attraction is essentially a boat ride through several candy-color lands, each representing a continent and each crammed with musical moppets, all madly singing. Disney raided the remains of the 1964–65 New York World's Fair for sets, and then appropriated the theme song of international brotherhood and friendship for its own. Some claim that it's the "revenge of the Audio-Animatrons," as 450 simplistic dolls differentiated mostly by their national dress—Dutch babies in clogs, Spanish flamenco dancers, sari-wrapped Indians waving temple bells, Swiss yodelers, Japanese kite fliers, Middle East snake charmers, and young French cancan dancers, to name just a few—parade past, smiling away and wagging their heads in time to the song. Now all together: "It's a world of laughter, a world of tears. It's a world of hope and a world of fears." Take enchanted tots through again if the line is short. **For people with disabilities:** You can board with your standard wheelchair through the designated entrance; if you use a scooter, transfer to one of the attraction's standard chairs available at the ride entrance. Equipped for handheld-captioning and audio-description devices. ▣ TIP➜ **FastPass+ is available but lines usually move quickly for those in the stand-by queue.** ⊠ *Fantasyland* ☞ *Duration: 11 mins. Crowds: Heavy. Audience: All Ages.*

Mad Tea Party. This carnival staple is for the vertigo addict looking for a fix. The Disney version is based on its own 1951 film *Alice in*

Wonderland, in which the Mad Hatter hosts a tea party for his un-birthday. You hop into oversize, pastel-color teacups and whirl around a giant platter. Add your own spin to the teacup's orbit with the help of the steering wheel in the center. Check out the soused mouse that pops out of the teapot centerpiece. **For people with disabilities:** If using a wheelchair, enter through the exit on right, then transfer to a ride vehicle. ■ TIP➜ FastPass+ is available but not recommended unless you can't resist a good fast spin. Lines move slowly. ⊠ *Fantasyland* ⌒ *Duration: 2 mins. Crowds: Moderate. Audience: Small Kids.*

Fodor'sChoice
★ **The Many Adventures of Winnie the Pooh.** The famous honey lover and his exploits in the Hundred Acre Wood are the theme for this ride. You can read posted passages from A.A. Milne's stories as you wait in line. Once you board your honey pot, Pooh and his friends wish you a "happy windsday." Pooh flies through the air, held aloft by his balloon, in his perennial search for "hunny," and you bounce along with Tigger, ride with the Heffalumps and Woozles, and experience a cloudburst. This ride replaced Mr. Toad's Wild Ride; look for the painting of Mr. Toad handing the deed to Owl. **For people with disabilities:** If using a scooter, see a cast member about transferring to a standard wheelchair for the ride. Equipped for handheld-captioning and audio-description devices. ■ TIP➜ Use a FastPass+ if crowds are heavy. ⊠ *Fantasyland* ⌒ *Duration: 3 mins. Crowds: Heavy. Audience: Small Kids.*

Mickey's PhilharMagic. Mickey Mouse may be the headliner here, but it's Donald Duck's misadventures—reminiscent of Mickey's as the sorcerer's apprentice in *Fantasia*—that set the comic pace in this 3-D animated film. As you settle into your seat, the on-screen action takes you behind the curtains at a grand concert hall where Donald and Mickey are preparing for a musical performance. But when Donald misuses Mickey's sorcerer's hat, he finds himself on a whirlwind journey that includes a magic carpet ride and an electrifying dip under the sea. And you go along for the ride. On the way you meet Ariel, Simba, Aladdin, Jasmine, Peter Pan, Tinker Bell, and others.

The film startles with its special-effects technology—you'll smell a fresh-baked apple pie, feel the rush of air as champagne corks pop, and get lost in the action on the 150-foot-wide screen. The 3-D film marks the first time that classic Disney characters appear in a computer-generated animation attraction. Some of the effects can startle small children, and some of the darker scenes are a bit muddy through the recycled 3-D glasses. **For people with disabilities:** There's a special viewing area for guests in wheelchairs. Reflective captioning is provided; equipped for assisted-listening and audio-description devices. ■ TIP➜ FastPass+ is offered, but it's a big theater, so waits aren't long. ⊠ *Fantasyland* ⌒ *Duration: 12 mins. Crowds: Heavy. Audience: All Ages.*

Peter Pan's Flight. This sweet indoor ride was inspired by Sir James M. Barrie's 1904 novel about the boy who wouldn't grow up, which Disney animated in 1953. Aboard two-person magic sailing ships with brightly striped sails, you soar into the skies above London en route to Neverland. Along the way you can see Wendy, Michael, and John get sprinkled with pixie dust while Nana barks below, wave to the Lost

MAGIC KINGDOM

NAME	Height req.	Type of Entertainment	Duration	Crowds	Audience	Tips
Adventureland						
Enchanted Tiki Room	n/a	Show	12 mins.	Light	All Ages	Visit when you need a refresher in a/c.
Jungle Cruise	n/a	Cruise	10 mins.	Heavy	All Ages	Use FastPass+ or come during the parade.
The Magic Carpets of Aladdin	n/a	Thrill Ride for Kids	3 mins.	Heavy	All Ages	Visit while waiting for a FastPass+ appointment.
Pirates of the Caribbean	n/a	Cruise	12 mins.	Moderate	All Ages	A good destination in the heat of the afternoon.
Swiss Family Treehouse	n/a	Walk-through	Up to you	Moderate	All Ages	Visit while waiting for a FastPass+.
Fantasyland						
★ The Barnstormer	35"	Thrill Ride for Kids	1 min.	Heavy	All but Young Kids	Ride early after hopping train to Fantasyland.
Dumbo the Flying Elephant	n/a	Thrill Ride for Kids	2 mins.	Heavy	Young Kids	New circus tent queue offers air-conditioned play area. FastPass+ available in a pinch.
★ Enchanted Tales with Belle	n/a	Show	15 mins.	Heavy	All Ages	Go while waiting for Mermaid FastPass+ appointment.
it's a small world	n/a	Cruise	11 mins.	Moderate to Heavy	All Ages	Tots may beg for a repeat ride; it's worth it.
Mad Tea Party	n/a	Thrill Ride for Kids	2 mins.	Moderate	Young Kids	Skip it if wait is 30 mins.
★ The Many Adventures of Winnie the Pooh	n/a	Thrill Ride for Kids	3½ mins.	Heavy	All Ages	Use FastPass+. Come anytime.
Mickey's PhilharMagic	n/a	3-D Film	12 mins.	Heavy	All but Young Kids	Use FastPass+ or arrive early or during a parade.
Peter Pan's Flight	n/a	Thrill Ride for Kids	2½ mins.	Heavy	All Ages	Try evening or early morning. Use FastPass+ first.
Prince Charming Regal Carrousel	n/a	Thrill Ride for Kids	2 mins.	Moderate to Heavy	Families	Come while waiting for Peter Pan's Flight FastPass+, during afternoon parade, or after dark.
★ Seven Dwarfs Mine Train	At least 38"	Thrill Ride	2½ mins.	Heavy	All but Young Kids	This ride recently opened use a FastPass+.
Under the Sea: Journey of the Little Mermaid	n/a	Ride-Through	7 mins.	Absolutely!	All Ages	You can get a FastPass+, but you'll miss the interactive queue.
Frontierland						
★ Big Thunder Mountain Railroad	At least 40"	Thrill Ride	4 mins.	Absolutely!	All but Young Kids	Use FastPass+. Most exciting at night when you can't anticipate the curves.

	Name	Height	Type	Duration	Crowds	Ages	Comments
	Country Bear Jamboree	n/a	Show	17 mins.	Moderate	All Ages	Visit before 11 am. Stand to the far left lining up for the front rows.
★	Splash Mountain	At least 40"	Thrill Ride with Water	11 mins.	Yes!	All but Young Kids	Use FastPass+. Get in line early, or ride during meal or parade time. You may get wet.

Liberty Square

	Name	Height	Type	Duration	Crowds	Ages	Comments
	Hall of Presidents	n/a	Show/Film	22mins.	Moderate	All but Young Kids	Visit anytime.
★	Haunted Mansion	n/a	Thrill Ride	8 mins.	Heavy	All Ages	Nighttime adds extra fear factor. FastPass+ now available.
	Liberty Square Riverboat	n/a	Cruise	15 mins.	Moderate	All Ages	Good for a break from the crowds.

Main Street U.S.A.

	Name	Height	Type	Duration	Crowds	Ages	Comments
	Walt Disney World Railroad	n/a	Railroad	21 mins.	Moderate to Heavy	All Ages	Board with young children for an early start in Frontierland or Fantasyland or hop on midafternoon.

Tomorrowland

	Name	Height	Type	Duration	Crowds	Ages	Comments
	Astro-Orbiter	n/a	Thrill Ride for Kids	2 mins.	Moderate to Heavy	All Ages	Skip unless there's a short line.
★	Buzz Lightyear's Space Ranger Spin	n/a	Interactive Ride	5 mins.	Heavy	All Ages	Come in the early morning and use FastPass+. Kids will want more than one ride.
	Monster's Inc. Laugh Floor	n/a	Film with special interactive effects	15 mins.	Heavy	All Ages	Come when you're waiting for your Buzz Lightyear or Space Mountain FastPass+.
★	Space Mountain	At least 44"	Thrill Ride	2½ mins.	You Bet!	All but Young Kids	Use FastPass+, or come at the beginning or the end of day or during a parade.
	Stitch's Great Escape	At least 40"	Simulator Exp.	15 mins.	Moderate to Heavy	All but Young Kids	Visit early after Space Mountain.
	Tomorrowland Speedway	32" to ride and 54" to drive	Thrill Ride for Kids	5 mins.	Moderate	Young Kids & Tweens	Come in the evening or during a parade; skip on a first-time visit; 32" height requirement to ride shotgun.
	Tomorrowland PeopleMover	n/a	Railroad	10 mins.	Light	All Ages	Come with young kids if you need a restful ride.
	Walt Disney's Carousel of Progress	n/a	Show	20 mins.	Light to Moderate	All Ages	Skip on a first-time visit unless you're heavily into nostalgia.

★ Fodor's Choice

Boys, spot the evil Captain Hook, and cheer for the ticktocking, clock-swallowing crocodile who breakfasted on Hook's hand.

Children—especially preschoolers—love this ride. Adults enjoy the dreamy views of London by moonlight. The downsides are the ride's brevity and its low-tech look. **For people with disabilities:** You must transfer from your wheelchair to the ride vehicle. Service animals aren't permitted. Equipped for handheld-captioning and audio-description devices. ■ TIP→ **Use FastPass+ here or ride early, late, or during the parade.** ☒ *Fantasyland* ☞ *Duration: 2½ mins. Crowds: Heavy. Audience: Small Kids.*

Pete's Silly Sideshow. No other Disney character meet-and-greet location is quite as much fun as Pete's Silly Sideshow, named after the Mickey Mouse archenemy created in 1925. But you won't meet Pete under this big top; instead, you'll grip and grin with Goofy, Minnie Mouse, Donald Duck, and his sweetheart, Daisy. Each character poses for photos and signs autographs against a sideshow backdrop: the Great Goofini, "Broken Bone Record Holder," in his stunt garb; the Astounding Donaldo dressed as a snake charmer; Minnie Magnifique, pretty in pink feathers, and her "pirouetting Parisian poodles," and Madame Daisy Fortuna with crystal ball as "seer of all fate and destinies." Two queues move guests along fairly quickly, and elaborate, themed backdrops offer extra fun photo ops. Strongman Pete does make a poster appearance. ■ TIP→ **Line up your FastPass+ for Enchanted Tales with Belle or Under the Sea: Journey of the Little Mermaid, then head back to the Storybook Circus area to meet these characters and ride Dumbo the Flying Elephant.** ☒ *Fantasyland* ☞ *Duration: About 1–2 mins per character meet and greet. Crowds: Yes, but double queue makes wait shorter. Audience: Young Kids.*

Prince Charming Regal Carrousel. This ride is great for families and for romantics, young and old. Seventy-two of the 90 dashing wooden steeds date from the original carousel built in 1917 by the Philadelphia Toboggan Company; additional mounts were made of fiberglass. All are meticulously painted, and each one is completely different. One wears a collar of bright yellow roses; another, a quiver of Native American arrows. Eighteen panels beneath the wooden canopy depict scenes from Disney's 1950 film *Cinderella*. As the ride spins, the mirrors sparkle, the fairy lights glitter, and the band organ plays favorite Disney movie tunes. **For people with disabilities:** If using a wheelchair, or if you have a service animal, check with a host for boarding information. ■ TIP→ **Lines move quickly. Come while waiting for your Peter Pan's Flight FastPass+ reservation.** ☒ *Fantasyland* ☞ *Duration: 2 mins. Crowds: Moderate to Heavy. Audience: Families.*

Fodor'sChoice ★ **Seven Dwarfs Mine Train.** Quick! Can you name all Seven Dwarfs in seven seconds? Sleepy, Doc, Grumpy, Bashful, Sneezy, Happy, and Dopey. Snow White's hard-working pals debut impressive Audio-Animatronics flair as they mine a steep mountain full of glittering gems and "Heigh-ho" their way into theme-park fans' hearts at the Seven Dwarfs Mine Train. Set amid a steep Enchanted Forest landscaped with red poppies, cedars, and birch trees, the long-awaited attraction is a visual feast of

LED-illuminated gems, playful woodland creatures, and beloved characters from Walt Disney's 1937 animated film classic, *Snow White and the Seven Dwarfs*. A rough-hewn entrance to the mine leads to a covered queue designed to keep riders occupied as they wend their way toward the train load area. Fun interactive diversions include animated "floating" gems that you can catch and match in a touch-screen jewel-washing trough. The musical family coaster serves up thrills, but no stomach-churning plunges, with cars that twist, climb, drop rapidly, and rock gently when slowing down for riders to enjoy the artfully crafted scene of the dwarfs at work in the mine. As the train rounds its final curve, you'll see Snow White dancing with her diminutive pals in the storybook cottage as the Wicked Queen, disguised as an old hag, lurks outside. The ride is not appropriate if you're pregnant or have heart, back, or neck problems. Expect this to be the highest-demand attraction in Disney World's four-park playbook for some time. **For people with disabilities:** You must transfer from wheelchair to ride vehicle. ■TIP➜ **Book your FastPass+ at the closest park kiosk if you didn't reserve it at the My Disney Experience website or mobile app. If circumstances deposit you in the stand-by queue, enjoy the clever hands-on activities along the way.** ✉ *Fantasyland* ☞ *Duration: 2½ mins. Crowds: Heavy. Audience: All but children under the 38-inch height minimum.*

Under the Sea: Journey of the Little Mermaid. The shipwreck theming, craggy grotto rockwork, waterfalls, lagoons, and magical landscape of this attraction draw you into Ariel's world long before you board a giant clamshell for a journey under the sea. As you wend your way through the long queue, you'll see starfish embedded in rocks, a sandy beach, palm trees, sea-grape plants, and other authentic seaside touches. Once inside the cavern beneath Prince Eric's Castle, you can join in an interactive game that plays out around every corner starring Scuttle the seagull and his animated crab pals. Through a cave portal, you'll enter the castle's stone hallways, where you hop aboard a clamshell ride vehicle and, thanks to cold air and light effects, feel the sensation of descending under the sea. You'll float past animated and Audio-Animatronic scenes from *The Little Mermaid* film, including a Broadway-style "Under the Sea" number with Sebastian conducting the undersea orchestra. There are fish conga lines and ominous scenes starring villainess Ursula but, of course, a fairy-tale ending is in store featuring Menken-Ashman show-stopper "Kiss the Girl." Most children love this ride, but some tots are afraid in the dark Ursula scene. **For people with disabilities:** Guests in scooters must transfer to a standard wheelchair to ride; equipped for handheld captioning and audio description. ■TIP➜ **You can get a Fast-Pass+, but you'll miss the fun of the interactive stand-by queue.** ✉ *Fantasyland* ☞ *Duration: 7 mins. Crowds: Absolutely! Audience: All Ages.*

TOMORROWLAND

The "future that never was" spins boldly into view as you enter Tomorrowland, where Disney Imagineers paint the landscape with whirling spaceships, flashy neon lights, and gleaming robots. This is the future as envisioned by sci-fi writers and moviemakers in the 1920s and '30s, when space flight, laser beams, and home computers were fiction, not fact. Retro Jetsonesque styling lends the area lasting chic.

Gamers who want a break from the crowds can find their favorite video challenges in the arcade attached to Space Mountain. SEGA race car, NASCAR, and Fast and Furious Super Bikes games draw tweens and teens; Lil' Hoops give young kids a manageable basketball challenge. Though Tomorrowland Transit Authority (TTA) PeopleMover isn't a big-ticket ride, it's a great way to check out the landscape from above as it zooms in and out of Space Mountain and curves around the entire land.

Astro Orbiter. This gleaming superstructure of revolving planets has come to symbolize Tomorrowland as much as Dumbo represents Fantasyland. Passenger vehicles, on arms projecting from a central column, sail past whirling planets; you control your car's altitude but not the velocity. The line is directly across from the entrance to the TTA PeopleMover. **For people with disabilities:** You must be able to walk several steps and transfer to the vehicle. ■ TIP→ **The line moves slowly; come while waiting for a Space Mountain FastPass+ appointment or if there's a short line. Skip on your first visit if time is limited.** ⊠ *Tomorrowland* ☞ *Duration: 2 mins. Crowds: Moderate to Heavy. Audience: All Ages.*

Fodor's Choice
★

Buzz Lightyear's Space Ranger Spin. Based on the wildly popular *Toy Story,* this ride gives you a toy's perspective as it pits you and Buzz Lightyear against the evil Emperor Zurg. You're seated in a fast-moving two-passenger Star Cruiser vehicle with an infrared laser gun and a centrally located lever for spinning your ship to get a good vantage point. Throughout the ride you shoot at targets to help Disney's macho space toy, Buzz, defeat the emperor and save the universe. You have to hit the targets marked with a "Z" to score, and the rider with the most points wins. To infinity and beyond! **For people with disabilities:** To board you must transfer to a standard wheelchair. Equipped for audio-description and handheld-captioning devices. ■ TIP→ **Use FastPass+ or go during a parade. If you're with kids, time the wait and—if it's only 15 or 20 minutes—ride twice so they can have a practice run.** ⊠ *Tomorrowland* ☞ *Duration: 5 mins. Crowds: Heavy. Audience: All Ages–Truly.*

Monsters, Inc. Laugh Floor. The joke's on everyone at this interactive attraction starring Mike Wazowski, the one-eyed hero from Disney-Pixar's hit film *Monsters, Inc.* In the 400-seat theater, you can interact with an animated Mike and his sidekicks in the real-time, unscripted way that the character Crush from *Finding Nemo* performs at Epcot in Turtle Talk with Crush at The Seas with Nemo & Friends. Here the premise is that Mike realizes laughter can be harnessed as a power source, and Mike's new comedy club is expected to generate power for the future. The more the audience yuks it up, the greater the power produced. You can text-message jokes from cell phones to the show's producer; they might even be used in the show. **For people with disabilities:** Wheelchair accessible. Sign language is available some days. Equipped for assisted-listening and video-captioning devices. ■ TIP→ **Skip the FastPass+ for this show; come when you're waiting for your Buzz Lightyear or Space**

In Tomorrowland, interplanetary travel is within your reach on the Astro Orbiter.

Mountain FastPass+ appointment. ⊠ *Tomorrowland* ⌛ *Duration: 15 mins. Crowds: Heavy. Audience: All Ages.*

Fodor's Choice ★ **Space Mountain.** The needlelike spires and gleaming, white, concrete cone of this 180-foot-high attraction are almost as much of a Magic Kingdom landmark as Cinderella Castle. Inside is what is arguably the world's most imaginative roller coaster. Although there are no loop-the-loops or high-speed curves, the thrills are many as you take a trip into the depths of outer space—in the dark.

You can pass the wait time playing big-screen interactive space games in the long, dark queue area. As you walk to the loading area, you'll pass whirling planets and hear the screams and shrieks of the riders, pumping you up for your own launch. Once you blast off, the ride lasts only two minutes and 38 seconds, with a top speed of 28 mph, but the devious twists and invisible drops in the dark make it seem twice as long. You can hear the screams from other cars, but you don't know where they are, adding an additional fright factor. Stow personal belongings securely. Not appropriate for pregnant women or guests wearing back, neck, or leg braces. **For people with disabilities:** You must be able to step into the ride vehicle and walk short distances. Guests in wheelchairs should see a cast member for boarding options. Service animals aren't permitted. ■TIP➜ **The wait can be long. Get a FastPass+, or come early, late, or during a parade.** ⊠ *Tomorrowland* ⌛ *Duration: 2½ mins. Crowds: You bet! Audience: Not Young Kids. Height minimum: 44 inches.*

Stitch's Great Escape. Once again, Disney seizes upon a hit film to create a crowd-pleasing attraction. The film is *Lilo & Stitch*, and the attraction

MAGIC KINGDOM KIDS TOUR

The Magic Kingdom is alive with thrilling distractions for young children, so let them take the lead now and then. Toddlers may want to jump from their strollers and dance along to the barbershop quartet on Main Street. Children who love to explore will have a ball scrambling around Frontierland and hopping a raft to Tom Sawyer's playground.

STOP AND SMELL THE ROSES
Head down Main Street, U.S.A, and, if you're lucky, the park's **Dapper Dan's barbershop quartet** will be harmonizing sweet tunes and tossing out one-liners from a small alcove along the street (check the park's *Times Guide* for performances). Young children are jazzed by the music and colorful costumes of these talented singers.

As you continue on, veer right toward the rose garden for a scenic picture spot where you can snap one of the prettiest shots in the park: the kids by the garden amid Mickey and Minnie topiaries, with Cinderella Castle in the background.

Fantasyland is dead ahead, and after you've soared on **Dumbo the Flying Elephant** and nabbed a FastPass+ for Under the Sea: Journey of the Little Mermaid or the new Seven Dwarfs Mine Train family coaster, head straight to Enchanted Tales with Belle where the kids get to participate. Then, try to catch a character performance in front of **Cinderella Castle** or during one of the daily parades or street parties.

PUT THE ZIP IN YOUR DOO-DAH
With little ones in tow, when it's time for food, fast is best. **Cosmic Ray's Starlight Café** is a high-energy quick stop with multiple choices for the entire family. Kids can head straight to the dance floor where Audio-Animatronics entertainer Sonny Eclipse keeps the tunes coming. After refueling, board the **Walt Disney World Railroad** at Main Street, U.S.A, Fantasyland, or Frontierland. While in Frontierland, too-short-to-ride kids can burn energy in the cavelike play area beneath **Splash Mountain** while parents take turns riding. And the short raft trip to **Tom Sawyer Island** is worth it for kids who like exploring. Not far from the Country Bear Jamboree, sure shots can take aim at Western-style targets in the often-missed **Frontierland Shootin' Arcade**—at about $1 per 35 shots, it's a blast for any aspiring sheriff.

BECOME THE CHARACTER
Get the makeover of a lifetime ($55–$195) at **Bibbidi Bobbidi Boutique,** in Cinderella Castle. Hair, nails, makeup—even a sprinkling of pixie dust—it's all here. At the **Pirates League,** in Adventureland by Pirates of the Caribbean, a scurvy sea-dog makeover ($29.95–$45) lets the inner buccaneer emerge. Don't want to be a pirate? Try the mermaid makeover ($35–$75).

After, be sure to catch a character meet and greet (see *Times Guide* for schedule) so the little rascals get all the hugs, autographs, photos, and magical memories they deserve.

If Pooh can, you can—enjoy a Main Street parade, that is.

is built around a backstory to the film about the mischievous alien, Stitch, before he meets Lilo in Hawaii. You're invited, as a new security recruit for the Galactic Federation, to enter the high-security teleportation chamber, where the ill-mannered Stitch is being processed for prison. In the form of a 3½-foot-tall Audio-Animatronics figure, Stitch escapes his captors and wreaks havoc on the room during close encounters with the audience in near-darkness. Sensory effects are part of the package. Beware the chili-dog "belch" odor and other tactile surprises.

Small children may be frightened by shoulder restraints, periods of darkness, and loud, startling noises. **For people with disabilities:** Guests in motorized scooters must transfer to an on-site standard wheelchair. Equipped for assisted-listening, handheld-captioning, and video-captioning devices. Guests with service animals should check with a host before entering. ■ TIP➡ **Come during a parade or whenever lines dwindle.** ✉ *Tomorrowland* ⏲ *Duration: 15 mins. Crowds: Moderate to Heavy. Audience: Not Young Kids. Height minimum: 40 inches.*

Tomorrowland Speedway. This is one of those rides that incite instant addiction in children and immediate regret in their parents. The reasons for the former are evident: the brightly colored Mark VII model cars that swerve around the four 2,260-foot tracks with much *vroom-vroom-vrooming*. Like real sports cars, the vehicles are equipped with rack-and-pinion steering and disc brakes; unlike the real thing, these run on a track. However, the track is so twisty that it's hard to keep the car on a straight course. Expect to spend a lot of time waiting your turn on the track and returning your vehicle after your lap. All this for a ride that achieves a top speed of 7 mph.

For people with disabilities: To drive the cars, you must be able to steer, press the gas pedal, and transfer into the low car seat. ■TIP➔ Don't waste a FastPass+ on this one; skip on a first-time visit unless you'll break your child's heart. ⊠ *Tomorrowland* ⌁ *Duration: 5 mins. Crowds: Moderate. Audience: Young Kids and Tweens. Height requirements: With an adult must be at least 32 inches; those who wish to drive must reach 54 inches.*

Tomorrowland Transit Authority PeopleMover. A reincarnation of what Disney old-timers may remember as the WEDway PeopleMover, the TTA PeopleMover gives you a nice, leisurely ride with great views of Tomorrowland, circling the Astro-Orbiter and gliding through the middle of Space Mountain. Disney's version of future mass transit is smooth and noiseless, thanks to an electromagnetic linear induction motor that has no moving parts, uses little power, and emits no pollutants. **For people with disabilities:** You must be able to walk several steps and step on and off of a moving ramp to transfer to a ride vehicle. Equipped for handheld-captioning and audio-description devices. ■TIP➔ Come to view Tomorrowland, to preview Space Mountain, if you have young children, or if you need a relaxing ride. ⊠ *Tomorrowland* ⌁ *Duration: 10 mins. Crowds: Light. Audience: All Ages.*

Walt Disney's Carousel of Progress. Originally seen at New York's 1964–65 World's Fair, this revolving theater traces the impact of technological progress on the daily lives of Americans from the turn of the 20th century into the near future. Representing each decade, an Audio-Animatronics family sings the praises of modern-day gadgets that technology has wrought. **For people with disabilities:** Wheelchair accessible; equipped for assisted-listening, handheld-captioning, audio-description, and video-captioning devices. ■TIP➔ Skip on a first-time visit unless you adore nostalgia. May close early or entirely in low season. ⊠ *Tomorrowland* ⌁ *Duration: 20 mins. Crowds: Moderate. Audience: All Ages.*

MAGIC KINGDOM SPECTACLES

Celebrate the Magic!. Before the popular Wishes fireworks show most evenings, and some nights twice, Cinderella Castle lights up to tell a story to park guests with the help of cutting-edge projector technology that wraps colorful images around the castle in sequences enhanced by music. For 10 minutes, the castle is a magical canvas that transforms into Alice's rabbit hole, Simba's savanna, and Dumbo's big top. Playful sequences feature popular Disney and Pixar characters, and even Walt Disney himself. Watch for seasonal updates like the villains' appearance around Halloween. **For people with disabilities:** Ask any cast member along Main Street for the best wheelchair viewing location; several areas are set aside. ■TIP➔ Try for a better view and some breathing room away from the crowds by migrating to one of the walkways that lead from the castle hub to Tomorrowland or Adventureland. ⊠ *Magic Kingdom* ⌁ *Duration: 10 mins. Crowds: Heavy. Audience: All Ages.*

Fodor'sChoice   **Disney Festival of Fantasy Parade.** Who'd want to miss a parade that deliv-
★   ers in 12 entertainment-packed minutes a lineup of Disney characters

and royalty, a Steampunk-inspired, fire-breathing dragon, elaborate towering floats, and handsome pairs of dancers twirling to some of Disney's best tunes? This newest daily 3 pm parade celebrates Walt's legacy with vignettes featuring the glamour, drama, and fun of classic films like *Sleeping Beauty* and *Peter Pan* while also catering to fans of contemporary box-office hits like *Brave* and *Frozen*. The colorful pageant of nine floats outperforms its predecessors with über-creative costuming, inventive float technology, a cast of nearly 100 gung-ho performers, and a musical score that invites singing along with familiar medleys. From the 50-foot-long topiary garden float of Disney royal couples led by dancers in swan-neck-collared ball gowns with iridescent feathers to the 32-foot-tall Airship float finale with Mickey and Minnie, the parade energizes spectators as it rolls past. A Lost Boy from *Peter Pan* may grab your hand and kiss it. A stilt-walker might lean into your camera for a snapshot. You'll hear viewers gasp or shout when the towering 53-foot-long, green-eyed Maleficent Dragon, created with help from Tony-award-winning designer Michael Curry, rears its head and spews flames. **For people with disabilities:** There are viewing areas for guests in wheelchairs along the route; ask any cast member for guidance. A sign-language schedule is available at Guest Relations. ■TIP→ **The parade runs from Frontierland to Town Square. Check your guide map for the complete route. Disney now distributes a limited number of Fast-Pass+ reservations, but book as far ahead as possible. Otherwise, find shade beneath a Frontierland porch at least an hour before showtime. If you've seen the parade, this is a good time to head for popular rides while crowds gather along the route.** ⊠ *Magic Kingdom* ☞ *Duration: 12 mins. Crowds: Heavy. Audience: All Ages.*

Dream Along with Mickey. The Cinderella Castle forecourt provides the perfect location for several daily performances of this Disney character spectacle starring Donald Duck, Mickey Mouse, Minnie Mouse, Goofy, and others. As the show begins, Donald is a "dreams-come-true" skeptic, but he has joined his optimistic pals anyway at a party where Disney princes and princesses dance in a romantic, dreamy number. There's adventure, too, when Peter Pan, pirates, and wenches take the stage. When pesky Disney villains crash the party, Donald decides to challenge evil and fight for the dreams of all his character friends and family. If you want to sit (and don't mind an obstructed view), arrive 30 to 40 minutes before showtime to get a seat on a bench. ■TIP→ **If you have children, plan to stand or sit on the pavement near the stage for an unobstructed view.** ⊠ *Magic Kingdom* ☞ *Duration: 20 mins. Crowds: Heavy. Audience: All Ages.*

Fodor'sChoice   **Main Street Electrical Parade.** The Main Street parade, with 23 illuminated
    ★   floats, 80 performers, and a half-million lights in all, first debuted at Disneyland in California in 1972. It lights up Magic Kingdom nights with plenty of power and its distinctive synthesizer-infused "Baroque Hoedown" musical theme. The lead float features Tinker Bell showering guests with 25,000 pixie-dusted points of light, and a finale float with a patriotic tribute that includes a majestic bald eagle shining with golden lights. Check *Times Guide;* the parade sometimes runs twice in one night and occasionally not at all. **For guests with disabilities:** Ask a cast

member for best wheelchair viewing. ■ TIP→ Use MyDisneyExperience. com to sign up before your visit for FastPass+ viewing, or take your place on the curb at least 40 minutes before the parade begins. ⊠ *Magic Kingdom* ⌒ *Duration: 20 mins. Crowds: Heavy. Audience: All Ages.*

FodorsChoice
★
Wishes. When the lights dim on Main Street and orchestral music fills the air, you know this fireworks extravaganza is about to begin. In Wishes, Jiminy Cricket's voice comes to life and tries to convince you that your wishes really can come true. He gets plenty of support from the Disney stars of classic films such as *Pinocchio, Fantasia, Cinderella,* and *The Little Mermaid.* Portions of famous film songs play over loudspeakers, and you hear the voices of film characters like Peter Pan and Aladdin as more than 680 individual fireworks paint the night sky. Oh, and don't worry that Tinker Bell may have been sealed in her jar for the night—she comes back to fly above the crowd in grand pixie-dust style. Check the *Times Guide* for performance time, which varies seasonally. ■ TIP→ You can book a FastPass+ ahead of your visit for best viewing. The Castle forecourt and surrounding bridges offer great views; or find a place near the front of the park for a quick postshow exit. ⊠ *Magic Kingdom* ⌒ *Duration: 12 mins. Crowds: Heavy. Audience: All Ages.*

2

EPCOT

Walt Disney said that Epcot would "take its cue from the new ideas and new technologies that are now emerging from the creative centers of American industry." He wrote that Epcot—never completed, always improving—"will never cease to be a living blueprint of the future, a showcase to the world for the ingenuity of American free enterprise."

But the permanent settlement that Disney envisioned wasn't to be. Epcot opened in 1982—16 years after his death—as a showcase, ostensibly, for the concepts that would be incorporated into the real-life Epcots of the future. (Disney's vision *has* taken an altered shape in the self-contained city of Celebration, an urban-planner's dream opened in 1996 on Disney property near Kissimmee.)

Epcot, the theme park, has two key areas: Future World, where most pavilions are collaborations between Walt Disney Imagineering and U.S. corporations and are designed to demonstrate technological advances through innovative shows and attractions; and the World Showcase, where shops, restaurants, attractions, and live entertainment create microcosms of 11 countries from four continents.

For years, Epcot was considered the more staid park, a place geared toward adults. But after its 10th anniversary, Epcot began to evolve into a livelier, more child-friendly park, with interactive fun at Innoventions and such "wow" attractions as Future World's Test Track, Mission: SPACE, and Soarin'.

There's something for everyone here. The World Showcase appeals to younger children with the Kidcot Fun Stop craft stations and the Norway pavilion's Princess Storybook Dining. Soarin', in the Land Pavilion, is a family favorite. And the Seas with Nemo & Friends—with one of the world's largest saltwater aquariums and a Nemo-themed ride—is a must-see for all. Adrenaline junkie? Don't miss Test Track presented

TOP ATTRACTIONS

The American Adventure. Many adults and older children love this patriotic look at American history; who can resist the Audio-Animatronics hosts, Ben Franklin and Mark Twain?

IllumiNations. This amazing musical laser-fountains-and-fireworks show is Disney nighttime entertainment at its best.

Mission: SPACE. Blast off on a simulated ride to Mars, if you can handle the turbulence.

Soarin'. Everyone's hands-down favorite: feel the sweet breeze as you "hang glide" over California landscapes.

Test Track. Design your concept car, then rev up to 60 mph on a hairpin turn in this wild ride on a Chevrolet proving ground.

MIND GAMES

Although several attractions provide high-octane kicks, Epcot's thrills are mostly for the mind. The park is best for school-age children and adults, but there's interactive entertainment for everyone at **Innoventions** and with the **Disney Phineas and Ferb: Agent P's World Showcase Adventure,** with starting points in several locations. Most attractions provide some diversions for preschool children. At the 11 **Kidcot Fun Stops,** younger children can try their hands at crafts projects—like designing a mask and adding special touches at each pavilion along the way.

by Chevrolet, where you can design your own custom concept car, then put it through its high-speed paces.

Wear comfortable shoes—there's *a lot* of territory to cover here. Arrive early, and try to stay all day, squeezing in extras like high-tech games at Innoventions and a relaxing meal. If you enter through International Gateway before 11 am, cast members will direct you to Future World, which usually opens two hours before World Showcase, or you can indulge in a latte and éclair at the France bakery, the sole quick-service eatery open early in World Showcase.

ORIENTATION AND PLANNING

GETTING ORIENTED

Epcot is composed of two areas: Future World and the World Showcase. The inner core of Future World's pavilions has the Spaceship Earth geosphere and a plaza anchored by the computer-animated Fountain of Nations. Also at the core is Innoventions, popular for its hands-on, high-tech exhibits, and immersion entertainment.

Six pavilions compose Future World's outer ring. Each of the three east pavilions has a ride and the occasional postride showcase; a visit rarely takes more than 30 minutes. The blockbuster exhibits on the west side contain rides and interactive displays; each exhibit can take up to 90 minutes for the complete experience.

World Showcase pavilions are on the promenade that circles the World Showcase Lagoon. Each houses shops, restaurants, and friendly international staffers; some have films or displays. Mexico offers a tame ride. Live entertainment is scheduled at every pavilion except Norway. Disney's monorail and buses drop you off at the main entrance in front of Future World. But if you're staying at one of the Epcot resorts (the BoardWalk, Yacht Club, Beach Club, Dolphin, or Swan), you can use the International Gateway entrance between World Showcase's France and U.K. pavilions.

EPCOT PLANNER

PARK AMENITIES

Baby Care: The baby-care center at Odyssey Center in Future World has rocking chairs and low lighting. The center sells formula, baby food, pacifiers, and disposable diapers. Changing tables are available here, as well as in all women's and some men's restrooms.

Cameras: Disposable cameras and memory cards are widely available, and you can use the Disney PhotoPass Service to gather memories throughout the park. Other photo services are available at the Imagination! pavilion.

First Aid: Staffed by registered nurses, first aid is in the Odyssey Center. More than a dozen automated external defibrillators are located across the park.

Guest Relations: To the right of the ticket windows at the park entrance and to the left of Spaceship Earth inside the park, these are the two locations where you can pick up schedules and maps. You also can get maps at the park's International Gateway entrance and most shops. Guest Relations will also assist with dining reservations, ticket upgrades, and services for guests with disabilities.

Lockers: Lockers ($7 and $9, with $5 refundable deposit) are at the International Gateway and to the west of Spaceship Earth. Coin-operated lockers also are at the bus information center by the bus parking lot.

Lost People and Things: Instruct children to speak to someone with a Disney name tag if you become separated. Guest Relations has a computerized message center for contacting companions in any of the parks.

Epcot Lost and Found: Located in the Guest Relations lobby east of Spaceship Earth. ✉ *Future World* ☎ *407/560–7500.*

Main Lost and Found Office: After one day, all articles are sent here and can be retrieved between 9 am and 7 pm daily. ✉ *Ticket and Transportation Center [TTC]* ☎ *407/824–4245.*

Package Pick-Up: Ask shop clerks to forward large purchases to Package Pick-Up at the Gift Stop in the Entrance Plaza and at the World Traveler at International Gateway. Allow three hours for delivery. You also can have packages sent to your Disney hotel.

Services for People with Disabilities: Accessibility standards are high. Many attractions and most restaurants and shops are fully wheelchair accessible. There are large Braille park maps at Guest Relations in Future World and International Gateway as well as to the left of the walkway from Future World to the World Showcase Plaza.

At Guest Relations there's a schedule for sign-language presentations at some of the park attractions; you also can pick up special devices for hearing- and sight-impaired visitors.

At World Showcase most people stroll around the promenade, but there are also Friendship boats, which require visitors using oversize wheelchairs or scooters to transfer to Disney chairs.

You can rent wheelchairs at the gift stop outside the main entrance, at the Stroller & Wheelchair Rental Shop to the left of Spaceship Earth, or at the International Gateway. A limited number of electronic convenience vehicles (ECV) are available only at the Stroller & Wheelchair Rental.

Wheelchairs are $12 daily, $10 for multiday rental. ECVs are $50 per day plus a refundable $20 security deposit. Arrive early, because neither conveyance can be reserved.

Stroller Rentals: You can rent strollers on the east side of the Entrance Plaza and at the International Gateway. Singles are $15 daily, $13 for multiday rental; doubles cost $31 daily, $27 for multiple days. Even preschoolers will be glad for a stroller in this large park.

PARK TOURS

Dolphins in Depth. At 9:45 am Dolphins in Depth ($199, neither park admission nor diving certification required) guides escort you from Epcot Guest Relations outside the main park entrance. Tours run Tuesday through Saturday and last about three hours. Participants must be 13 or older; a parent or legal guardian must accompany anyone under 18. ⊠ *Epcot* ☎ *407/939–8687* ✉ *$199* ⊘ *Tues.–Sat.*

Epcot Divequest. On the three-hour Epcot Divequest ($175, park admission not required or included) at the Seas with Nemo & Friends pavilion, you spend 40 minutes in the mammoth aquarium under the supervision of a master diver. The tour takes place Tuesday through Saturday in the afternoon. Guests 10 and up must have open-water adult scuba certification; children under 18 must dive with a parent or legal guardian. ⊠ *Epcot* ☎ *407/939–8687* ✉ *$175* ⊘ *Tues.–Sat.*

Epcot Seas Aqua Tour. For this tour ($140, no park admission required or included) you wear a flotation device and diving gear, but you remain on the water's surface. Anyone age 8 and older can join the tour (those ages 8–12 must be with a parent or legal guardian). Tours are limited to 12 guests, meet Tuesday through Saturday, and run about 2½ hours, with 30 minutes in the water. ⊠ *Epcot* ⊘ *Tues.–Sat.*

UnDISCOVERed Future World. This tour ($64, plus park admission) leaves at 9 am Monday through Friday from Guest Relations at the main entrance. The four-hour behind-the-scenes walk for guests 16 and older covers all Future World pavilions and some VIP lounges and backstage areas, including the Epcot marina where IllumiNations fireworks floats are docked. ⊠ *Epcot* ☎ *407/939–8687* ✉ *$64* ⊘ *Weekdays* .

VISITING TIPS

■ Epcot is so vast and varied that you really need two days to explore. With just one day, you'll have to be highly selective.

■ Go early in the week, when others are at Magic Kingdom.

EPCOT BY BOAT

Epcot is a big place at 305 acres; a local joke suggests that the acronym actually stands for "Every Person Comes Out Tired." But still, the most efficient way to get around is to walk.

To vary things, you can cruise across the lagoon in an air-conditioned, 65-foot water taxi. Also called

Friendship Boats, they depart every 12 minutes from two World Showcase Plaza docks at the border of Future World.

The boat closer to Mexico zips to a dock by the Germany pavilion; the one closer to Canada heads to Morocco. You may have to stand in line to board, however.

■ If you like a good festival, visit during the International Flower & Garden Festival (early March through mid-May) or the International Food & Wine Festival (late September through mid-November).

■ Once through the turnstiles at either the main Future World entrance or the back World Showcase entrance, make a beeline for the popular Mission: SPACE and Test Track (for fast-paced thrills) or the Seas with Nemo & Friends and Soarin' (for family fun). Or get a FastPass+ and return later.

EXPLORING EPCOT

FUTURE WORLD

Future World's inner core is composed of the iconic Spaceship Earth geosphere and, beyond it, a plaza anchored by the awe-inspiring computer-animated Fountain of Nations, which shoots water 150 feet skyward. Don't miss interactive fun at Innoventions.

Six pavilions compose Future World's outer ring. On the east side, they are the Ellen's Energy Adventure, Mission: SPACE, and Test Track. Each pavilion presents a single, self-contained ride and an occasional postride showcase; a visit rarely takes more than 30 minutes, but it depends on how long you spend in the postride area. On the west side are the Seas with Nemo & Friends, The Land, and Imagination! These blockbuster exhibits contain both rides and interactive displays; you could spend at least 1½ hours at each of these pavilions, but there aren't enough hours in the day, so prioritize.

■TIP→ Before setting out, look into the Disney PhotoPass at the Camera Center in the Entrance Plaza. It tracks photos of your group shot by Disney photographers, which you can view and purchase later at the center or online.

SPACESHIP EARTH

Balanced like a giant golf ball waiting for some celestial being to tee off, the multifaceted silver geosphere of Spaceship Earth is to Epcot what Cinderella Castle is to the Magic Kingdom. As much a landmark

Avenue of the Stars

MEXICO

[PROJECTED *FROZEN* ATTRACTION]

NORWAY

CHINA

Avenue of the Stars

Gran Fiesta Tour Starring The Three Caballeros

San Angel Inn
La Cava del Tequila

First Aid & Baby Care

Kringla Bakeri Og Kafe

Lotus Blossom Café

Reflections of China

Nine Dragons

Princess Storybook Dining at Royal Akershus Banquet Hall

Africa Coolpost

Saluting Africa Outpost

La Hacienda de San Angel and La Cantina Restaurant

GERMANY

Biergarten

Sommerfest

Boat Launch

Boat Launch

WORLD SHOWCASE PLAZA

World Showcase Lagoon

ITALY

Via Napoli Ristorante e Pizzeria

Tutto Italia

Tutto Gusto Wine Cellar

Boat Launch

WORLD SHOWCASE

Fife & Drum

ATM

America Gardens Theatre

Liberty Inn

AMERICAN ADVENTURE

Katsura Grill

Rose & Crown Pub & Dining Room

Yorkshire County Fish Shop

Teppan Edo & Tokyo Dining

Kabuki Cafe

JAPAN

UNITED KINGDOM

INTERNATIONAL GATEWAY

Boat Launch

Spice Road Table

Tangierine Cafe

Phineas & Ferb

Stroller & Wheelchair Rental

FRANCE

MOROCCO

Les Chefs de France

Restaurant Marrakesh

Monsieur Paul

L'Artisan des Glaces

Impressions de France

Les Halles Boulangerie & Pâtisserie

0   400 yards

0   400 m

as an icon, it can be seen on a clear day from an airplane flying down either coast of Florida.

Spaceship Earth ride. Inside the giant geosphere you are transported past a series of tableaux that explore human progress and the continuing search for better forms of communication. Oscar-winner Dame Judi Dench narrates the journey that begins in the darkest tunnels of time, proceeds through history, and ends poised on the edge of the future. Ten-time Emmy winner Bruce Broughton composed the musical score.

Audio-Animatronics figures present Cro-Magnon man daubing mystic paintings on cave walls, Egyptian scribes scratching hieroglyphics on papyrus, Roman centurions building roads, Islamic scholars mapping the heavens, and 11th- and 12th-century Benedictine monks hand-copying manuscripts. As you move into the Renaissance, there's Michelangelo and Gutenberg, and, in rapid succession, the telegraph, radio, television, and computer come into being. A family views the moon landing on TV, and soon the personal computer is born.

As your ride vehicle swings backward and descends slowly, touch screens ask how you envision your own future, then play back an animated, *Jetsons*-esque scenario based on the answers. Siemens, which presents the attraction, created a fun-packed postshow with high-demand interactive games. As you enter the postshow, watch the giant digital map screen to see your photo taken during the ride and posted in your hometown location.

For people with disabilities: You must be able to transfer to a standard wheelchair, then walk four steps to the ride vehicle. Guests with service animals should check with an attraction host for boarding information. The ride is equipped for handheld captioning and audio-description devices available at Guest Relations. ■TIP→ Ride while waiting for a Mission: SPACE or Soarin' FastPass+ appointment. Lines are longest in the morning and shortest just before closing. ⊠ *Future World, Spaceship Earth* ☞ *Duration: 15 mins. Crowds: Moderate to Heavy. Audience: All Ages.*

INNOVENTIONS

This walk-through attraction contains interactive exhibits that entertain kids (some are especially designed for preschoolers) and adults as they investigate the innovations now improving the world around us.

Innoventions. Innoventions is loaded with activities designed to entertain and inspire kids and adults, and it's a great place for families to play together. Take Sum of All Thrills, by technology company Raytheon, for instance. This is not your typical "design a coaster" ride. Here, you get your own multi-touch-screen table with math- and engineering-based tools (and simple instructions) to design and customize your bobsled, jet, or roller-coaster ride with corkscrews, inversions, and steep hills. Along the way, you'll apply math and engineering principles to measure the energy you need to make it over a hill. Then you and a partner get to climb aboard a robotic simulator for the high-def immersion ride that's as mild or as wild as you design it. At Habit Heroes presented by Florida Blue and Anthem Blue Cross and Blue Shield, you and your team tackle three interactive experiences designed to help you create a happier, healthier world through hydration, nutrition, and physical activity. In each scenario, you'll get to battle villainous hazards in your quest to save the world. StormStruck, presented by the Federal Alliance for Safe Homes, serves up severe weather that'll make you jump and duck in a 4-D theater. You have your own electronic buttons for voting on how you'd protect your property from future storms before the "big reveal" tells you whether you're right or wrong. Colortopia, presented by Glidden and new in 2015, offers color mixing-and-matching games and a creative experience where you can wield your own "magical paintbrush."

For people with disabilities: This attraction is completely wheelchair accessible—some exhibits inside this always-evolving attraction may require transferring from a wheelchair. Guests with service animals should check with an attractions host when entering. ■TIP➜ **Come before 11 am or after 2 pm. Sum of All Thrills and StormStruck draw crowds.** ⊠ *Future World, Innoventions* ⌁ *Duration: Up to You. Crowds: Moderate to Heavy. Audience: All Ages.*

NEED A BREAK?
Club Cool. With soft drinks going for more than $2 per cup at park concessions, Club Cool is the place to visit when you're thirsty and in the mood to be adventurous. Here Coca-Cola's bold red-and-white colors guide you to a room full of soda machines and logo merchandise. You can sample (for free) the cola king's products from around the world, including mainstays Vegitabeta from Japan and Beverly from Italy. Other refreshing sips are from Thailand, Africa, Brazil, and Peru. It's entertaining to watch kids' faces when their taste buds react to an unfamiliar flavor. ⊠ *Future World, Epcot.*

TEST TRACK

This pavilion is shaped like a giant disk. As you wait to enter the building for the high-speed ride, cars on the return track whiz past you. Outside, kids can get a soaking in the Cool Wash, an interactive water area that lets them pretend they're in a car wash.

Fodor's Choice ★
Test Track ride. The white-knuckle finale of this fan favorite is as thrilling as ever. Create a custom concept vehicle at an interactive design station, and then buckle up in a six-person SimCar to put the design through its paces in a neon-splashed, futuristic setting that surrounds the attraction's original hills and mountain switchbacks.

The High-Speed Test is last: your vehicle bursts through an opening in the Test Track building to negotiate a steeply banked loop at a speed of nearly 60 mph. At the special effects–laden postshow, you can check out how your custom car performed and create your own car commercial. The speeds and some jarring effects may prove unsettling. The ride isn't suitable for pregnant women or guests wearing back, neck, or leg braces.

For people with disabilities: Visitors in wheelchairs are provided a special area in which to practice transferring into the ride vehicle before actually boarding. One TV monitor in the preshow area is closed-captioned. Service animals aren't permitted on board. ■TIP➜ **If you use a FastPass+, you won't get to customize your vehicle—it will be a**

predesigned version. A Single Rider queue lets you skip a long wait. The ride won't function on wet tracks, so don't head here after a downpour. ⊠ *Future World, Test Track* ⏱ *Duration: 5 mins. Crowds: Heavy. Audience: Not Small Kids. Minimum height: 40 inches.*

MISSION: SPACE

The exterior of this pavilion has a sleek, futuristic look with a planetary theme. When the weather is warm enough, kids like to hop around in the fountain out front.

Fodor's Choice ★ **Mission: SPACE.** It took five years for Disney Imagineers, with the help of 25 experts from NASA, to design Mission: SPACE, the first ride ever to take people "straight up" in a simulated rocket launch. The story transports you and co-riders to the year 2036 and the International Space Training Center, where you are about to embark on your first launch. Before you board the four-person rocket capsule, you're assigned to a position: commander, navigator, pilot, or engineer. And at this point you're warned several times about the intensity of the ride and the risks for people with health concerns. Pregnant women and anyone with heart, back, neck, balance, blood-pressure, or motion-sickness problems shouldn't ride.

■TIP→ Many people exit this ride feeling nauseated and disoriented from the high-speed spinning, which is what makes you feel as if you're rocketing into space. These effects are often cumulative, so stick with one go-round.

For those who can handle the intense spinning, the sensation of liftoff is a turbulent, heart-pounding experience that flattens you against your seat. Once you break into outer space, you'll even feel weightless. After landing, you exit your capsule into the Advanced Training Lab, where you can play some very entertaining space-related games.

For people with disabilities: This ride requires a transfer from wheelchair to seat. Service animals aren't permitted to board. Video-captioning devices can be used on the ride; assisted-listening devices can be used in the postshow Training Lab. ■TIP→ Arrive before 10 am or use FastPass+ during peak season. Don't ride on a full stomach. ⊠ *Future World, Mission: SPACE* ⏱ *Duration: 4 mins. Crowds: You Bet! Audience: Not Small Kids. Minimum height: 44 inches.*

UNIVERSE OF ENERGY

The first of the pavilions on the left, or east, side of Future World, the Universe of Energy occupies a large, lopsided pyramid sheathed in thousands of mirrors—solar collectors that power the attraction inside.

Ellen's Energy Adventure. Comedian Ellen DeGeneres plays the lead role in this attraction that has fun with pop culture at the same time it gives a crash course in Energy 101. As Ellen naps and dreams, you'll meet Alex Trebek of *Jeopardy!* and Bill Nye, the Science Guy. Actress Jamie Lee Curtis, as Ellen's irritating former college roommate, and "Albert Einstein" himself play Ellen's game show challengers.

Your Energy 101 primer reveals the history of the universe—in one minute—on three 70-millimeter screens, 157 feet wide by 32 feet tall. Next the theater separates into six 96-passenger vehicles that lurch

2

into a primeval forest. Through this swampy, damp, (and chilly) landscape, apatosauruses wander, a tyrannosaurus fights it out with a triceratops, and pterodactyls swoop through the air. A terrified Ellen is even cornered by a menacing elasmosaurus.

The ride concludes with another film (sorely in need of an update) in which Ellen learns about the world's present-day energy needs, resources, and concerns. It's shown on three screens, each 30 feet tall, 74 feet wide, and curved to create a 200-degree range of vision. Does Ellen win in her *Jeopardy!* dream? You'll have to travel back in time for the answer.

For people with disabilities: This attraction is accessible to guests using standard wheelchairs and those who can transfer to them. Equipped for assisted-listening,

> **MISSION: SPACE CAUTION**
>
> Parents should exercise caution when deciding whether to let children ride Mission: SPACE. Even if your child meets the height requirement, she may not be old enough to enjoy the ride. In the capsule, you're instructed to keep your head back against the seat and to look straight ahead for the duration of the ride. (Closing your eyes or not looking straight ahead can bring on motion sickness.) Your role as a "crew member" also means you're supposed to hold on to a joystick and push buttons at certain times. All these instructions can confuse younger kids and get in the way of their enjoyment of the ride.

handheld-captioning, and audio-description devices. ■TIP➔ To experience the primeval landscape unspoiled by rows of modern heads, sit in the seats to the far left and front of the theater; to get these, position yourself similarly in the preshow area. ⊠ *Future World, Universe of Energy* ☞ *Duration: 45 mins. Crowds: Light to Moderate. Audience: All Ages, though a bit lengthy and possibly frightening for young children.*

THE SEAS WITH NEMO & FRIENDS

This pavilion has always been a draw with its 5.7-million-gallon aquarium filled with 65 species of sea life, including sharks, but it was reworked to capitalize on the popularity of the Disney-Pixar film *Finding Nemo.*

The Seas with Nemo & Friends. Hop into a "clamobile" and take a ride under the sea to look for Nemo, who has wandered off from Mr. Ray's class field trip. This ride adds clever fun to an aging, but relevant, attraction—an astonishing animation-projection effect makes it appear as if Nemo and his pals are swimming among the marine life of the actual Seas aquarium. As your ride progresses, Dory, Nemo's spacey sidekick, helps Bruce, Squirt, and other pals find him. After the ride, walk around the tank to Bruce's Shark World for some fun photo ops and shark facts, discover how dolphins communicate, and visit an endangered Florida manatee rehabilitation center.

For people with disabilities: Guests in standard wheelchairs can wheel onto an accessible "clamshell" vehicle; those in ECVs must transfer to a standard wheelchair or the ride vehicle. Equipped for audio-description

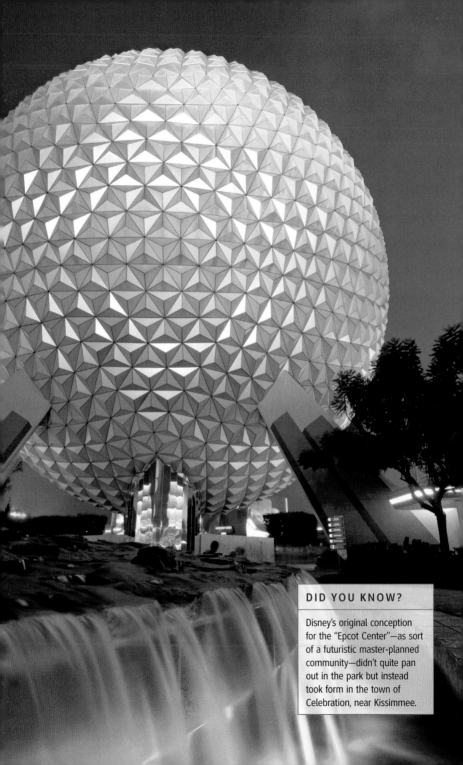

and handheld-captioning devices. ■TIP→ **Visit early or book a Fast-Pass+.** ✉ *Future World, The Seas with Nemo & Friends* ⏱ *Duration: Up to You. Crowds: Moderate to Heavy. Audience: All Ages.*

Turtle Talk with Crush. Head for the Sea Base area to line up for this real-time animated show starring Crush, the ancient sea turtle from *Finding Nemo*. Crush chats and jokes with kids so convincingly that young children, eyes wide as sand dollars, have walked up and touched the screen where Crush "swims." It's in a small theater and there's often a wait, but it's a hit with young children as well as their parents. **For people with disabilities:** The theater is wheelchair accessible, and assisted-listening devices can be used. ■TIP→ **Check the Times Guide for show schedule; use a FastPass+ or come early and prepare to be amazed.** ✉ *Future World, The Seas with Nemo & Friends* ⏱ *Duration: 15 mins. Crowds: Moderate to Heavy. Audience: Small Kids, but Great for All Ages.*

THE LAND
Shaped like an intergalactic greenhouse, the enormous, skylighted Land pavilion dedicates 6 acres and a host of attractions to everyone's favorite topic: food. You can easily spend two hours exploring here, more if you take one of the guided greenhouse tours available throughout the day.

NEED A BREAK? Talk about a self-contained ecosystem: The Land Pavilion grows its own produce, including tomatoes and cucumbers, some of which show up on the menu at the healthful **Sunshine Seasons** food court. Much of the fare is cooked on a 48-inch Mongolian grill. The eatery offers oak-grilled salmon, spicy stir-fries, and fish tacos. A sandwich shop delivers oak-grilled veggie sandwiches on fresh breads, and yummy turkey on ciabatta with chipotle mayonnaise. The salad shop wows with roasted beets and goat cheese over mixed greens, or a "power salad" of chicken, quinoa, and almonds—among other options. Wood-fired grills and rotisseries sizzle with chicken, pork, and salmon, and the bakery's pastries are sure bets. To avoid crowds, eat at nonpeak times—after 2 for lunch and before 5 or after 7 for dinner.

The Circle of Life. Featuring three stars of *The Lion King*—Simba the lion, Timon the meerkat, and Pumbaa the waddling warthog—this film delivers a powerful message about protecting the world's environment for all living things. Part animation, part *National Geographic*–like film using spectacular 70-millimeter live-action footage, Circle of Life tells a fable about a "Hakuna Matata Lakeside Village" that Timon and Pumbaa are developing by clearing the African savanna. Simba cautions about mistreating the land by telling a story of a creature who occasionally forgets that everything is connected in the great Circle of Life. "That creature," he says, "is man." The lilting accompaniment is Tim Rice's and Elton John's popular song, and James Earl Jones is the narrator.

For people with disabilities: Wheelchair accessible. Has reflective captioning and is equipped for assisted-listening and audio-description devices. ■TIP→ **It's enlightening for children and adults; a nap opportunity for toddlers. Squeeze in other attractions and see this before leaving.** ✉ *Future World, The Land* ⏱ *Duration: 20 mins. Crowds: Moderate. Audience: All Ages.*

EPCOT

NAME	Height Req.	Type of Entertainment	Duration	Crowds	Audience	Tips
Future World						
Captain EO (Imagination!)	n/a	3-D Film	18 mins.	Moderate to Heavy	All but Young Kids	Come in the early morning or just before closing. Take off the 3-D glasses if little kids get scared.
Journey into Imagination with Figment (Imagination!)	n/a	Ride-Through	8 mins.	Light	Young Kids	Ride after Captain EO. Warn toddlers about darkness at the end of the ride.
Ellen's Energy Adventure (Universe of Energy)	n/a	Ride-Through	45 mins.	Moderate	All but very Young Kids	Best seats are to the far left and front of the theater.
Innoventions	n/a	Walk-Through	Up to you	Moderate to Heavy	All Ages	Come anytime.
The Circle of Life (The Land)	n/a	Film	20 mins.	Moderate to Heavy	All Ages	Come early or for your toddler's afternoon nap.
Living with the Land (The Land)	n/a	Cruise	14 mins.	Moderate	All	The line moves quickly, so come anytime.
★ Soarin' (The Land)	At least 40"	Simulator Ride	5 mins.	Heavy	All but very Young Kids	Use FastPass+, or come early or just before closing.
The Seas with Nemo & Friends	n/a	Ride- and Walk-Through	Up to you	Moderate to Heavy	All Ages	Get Nemo fans here early in the morning.
Turtle Talk with Crush (The Seas with Nemo & Friends)	n/a	Animated Show	15 mins.	Moderate to Heavy	Young Kids and Families	Line up after "clamobile" ride.

Attraction	Height	Type	Duration	Crowds	Audience	Comments
★ Mission: SPACE	At least 44"	Thrill Ride	4 mins.	You Bet!	All but Young Kids	Come before 10 am or use FastPass+. Don't ride on a full stomach. A milder misson availabe for simulator-phobes.
Spaceship Earth	n/a	Ride-Through	15 mins.	Moderate to Heavy	All Ages	Ride while waiting for Mission: SPACE or Soarin' FastPass+ appointment or just before closing.
★ Test Track	At least 40"	Thrill Ride	5 mins.	Heavy	All but Young Kids	Come early or use FastPass+. The ride can't function on wet tracks, so don't come after a downpour.
World Showcase						
★ The American Adventure	n/a	Show/Film	30 mins.	Heavy	All Ages	Arrive 10 mins. before the Voices of Liberty are slated to perform.
America Gardens Theatre	n/a	Live Show	Varies	Varies	Varies	Arrive more than an hour or so ahead of time for holiday and celebrity performances.
Gran Fiesta Tour Starring the Three Caballeros	n/a	Cruise	9 mins.	Light to Moderate	All Ages	Especially good if you have young children.
Impressions de France	n/a	Film	20 mins.	Moderate	All Ages	Come anytime.
O Canada!	n/a	Film	14 mins.	Moderate to Heavy	All Ages	Stop in any time. Be prepared to stand for the film. No strollers permitted.
Reflections of China	n/a	Film	14 mins.	Moderate	All Ages	Come anytime. Be prepared to stand during the film. No strollers permitted.

★ **Fodor's**Choice

EPCOT FAMILY TOUR

A trip to Italy is on hold, but Mom knows she can find a taste of Venice in the World Showcase. Dad, the *Popular Mechanics* devotee, can't wait to check out Test Track and Innoventions. Each can have a great day—in his or her own way.

STRATEGIZE

Devise a plan before pushing through the Epcot turnstiles. Everyone will probably want to take off at Soarin' in The Land for the one-ride-fits-all thrill of simulated hang gliding (there are even special safety restraints for little ones). If your kids are too small for the height restrictions at Test Track, let Dad shift into overdrive while the rest of you play Innoventions games. Meet up with Dad at the Imagination! pavilion to see Michael Jackson circa 1980s dance his way through Captain EO, or head back to the Land for a Sunshine Seasons treat. Don't miss an under-the-sea ride at the Seas with Nemo & Friends before meeting the coolest dude of all at Turtle Talk with Crush.

GET YOUR WORLD SHOWCASE PASSPORTS

On the way into the World Showcase, let the kids get their own passports, complete with stickers, at any merchandise location. As you visit each country, they can get their passports stamped—not only fun, but a great keepsake. But before you cross the Future World border, stop and let young kids play in the dancing fountains if they're operating—it'll be one of their happiest memories. Bring a towel and a change of clothing, and you'll be happy, too.

FOR THE LITTLE ONES (AND MOM)

Younger children can be creative at Kidcot Fun Stops, where a Disney cast member gets them started on a craft activity, such as coloring a Carnivale-style mask on a stick. At each of 11 Fun Stops, the kids can add something to the mask, such as a Viking ship at Norway. Children love Mexico because they can ride the boats at Gran Fiesta Tour starring the Three Caballeros. Now it's your turn, Mom. Italy is right around the corner, and the kids can watch a juggler or comedy troupe in the courtyard while you taste some wine at Enoteca Castello or go shopping.

LIVE PERFORMANCES

The Beatles, the Rolling Stones, Elton John, and more: hear top hits by iconic British musicians when the tribute band British Revolution amps up the fun outside the United Kingdom showcase five days each week. Grab a bench or dance to favorite tunes. Young children are thrilled to explore hedge mazes that surround the gazebo stage.

Live entertainment is one of Epcot's strong suits—best shows for younger kids are the Jeweled Dragon Acrobats at China, Mariachi Cobre musicians at Mexico, Sergio the clown and juggler at Italy, and the JAMMitors percussion group at Future World East and West (check the daily *Times Guide*).

Living with the Land. A canopied boat cruises through three artificial biomes—rain forest, desert, and prairie ecological communities—and into an experimental live greenhouse that demonstrates how food sources may be grown in the future, not only on the planet but also in outer space. Shrimp, tilapia, eels, catfish, and alligators are raised in controlled aquacells, and tomatoes, peppers, squash, and other fruits and vegetables thrive in the Desert Farm area via drip irrigation that delivers just the right amount of water and nutrients to their roots. Gardeners are usually interested in the section on integrated pest management, which relies on "good" insects like ladybugs to control more harmful predators.

See Mickey Mouse–shaped fruits and vegetables (there may be pumpkins, cucumbers, or watermelons) nurtured with the help of molds created by the Land's science team; scientists also have grown a "tomato tree"—the first of its kind in the United States—that has yielded thousands of tomatoes from a single vine. Many of the growing areas are actual experiments-in-progress, in which Disney and the U.S. Department of Agriculture have joined forces to produce, say, a sweeter pineapple or a faster-growing pepper. The plants (including the tomato tree's golf-ball-size tomatoes) and fish that grow in the greenhouse are regularly harvested for use in The Land's restaurants. **For people with disabilities:** Those using an oversize wheelchair or ECV must transfer to a standard wheelchair. Equipped for handheld-captioning and audio-description devices. ■ TIP➜ The line moves fairly quickly, but you might want a FastPass+ appointment on a crowded park day. ⊠ *Future World, The Land ☞ Duration: 14 mins. Crowds: Moderate. Audience: All Ages.*

Fodor'sChoice **Soarin'.** If you've ever wondered what it's like to fly, or at least hang
★ glide, this attraction is your chance to enjoy the sensation without actually taking the plunge. It uses motion-based technology to literally lift you in your seat 40 feet into the air within a giant projection-screen dome.

As you soar above the Golden Gate Bridge, Napa Valley, Yosemite, and other California wonders, you feel the wind and smell pine forests and orange blossoms. Navy buffs get a kick out of swooping over a massive aircraft carrier. The accompanying score created by Jerry Goldsmith (*Mulan, Star Trek*) builds on the thrill, and the crispness and definition of the film, projected at twice the rate of a typical motion picture, adds realism.

The flight is so mild (and the view so thrilling) that even very timid children love it. **For people with disabilities:** Those with mobility impairments must transfer from their wheelchairs to the ride system. Equipped for video-captioning devices. Service animals aren't permitted on the ride. ■ TIP➜ Book your FastPass+ early or plan to wait an hour or longer in the standby queue. ⊠ *Future World, The Land ☞ Duration: 5 mins. Crowds: Heavy. Audience: All who meet the height requirement. Height minimum: 40 inches.*

IMAGINATION!

The focus is on the fun that can be had when you turn your imagination loose. The fanciful leaping fountains outside the pavilion make the point, as do the 3-D film Captain EO, the Journey into Imagination with Figment ride, and Image Works, a sort of interactive fun house devoted to music and art.

Captain EO. Directed by Francis Ford Coppola and produced by George Lucas, the 18-minute 3-D film stars pop legend Michael Jackson as Captain EO and Oscar-winner Anjelica Huston as the Supreme Leader of a colorless planet of droids from the dark side. After an opener that mimics space-fantasy action scenes from Lucas's epic *Star Wars* series, EO's motley crew of furry space creatures lands on the planet and magically transforms into an electronic band, prepared to shed light on the Supreme Leader and her robotic forces of darkness.

Music and light save the day as evil robot guards transform into dancers with hair and costumes straight from the '80s. Young children may be frightened by the dark nature of the film and its special effects.

For people with disabilities: The attraction is wheelchair accessible, although you must transfer to a theater seat to experience some special effects. Equipped with reflective captioning and for assisted-listening, video-captioning, or audio-description devices. The preshow area has closed-captioned TV monitors for the show intro featuring a behind-the-scenes look at how Lucas and Coppola made the film. Guests with service animals should check with a show host before entering. ■TIP➜ Come early or late, or get a FastPass+. ⊠ *Future World, Imagination!* ⏱ *Duration: 18 mins. Crowds: Moderate. Audience: Not Small Kids.*

Journey into Imagination with Figment. Figment, a fun-loving dragon, takes you on a sensory adventure designed to engage your imagination through sound, illusion, gravity, dimension, and color. After the ride—which could use some updating—you can check out Image Works, where several interactive displays allow you to further stretch your imagination. Although this ride is geared to smaller kids, be sure to prepare yours for a brief period of darkness.

For people with disabilities: Ride and Image Works are wheelchair accessible. Equipped for handheld-captioning and audio-description devices. ■TIP➜ Skip the FastPass+ and ride only if lines are short so you'll have plenty of time for preferred attractions on your list. ⊠ *Future World, Imagination!* ⏱ *Duration: 8 mins. Crowds: Light. Audience: Small Kids.*

WORLD SHOWCASE

Nowhere but at Epcot can you explore a little corner of nearly a dozen countries in one day. As you stroll the 1.3 miles around the 40-acre World Showcase Lagoon, you circumnavigate the globe-according-to-Disney by experiencing native food, entertainment, culture, and arts and crafts at pavilions representing countries in Europe, Asia, North Africa, and the Americas. Pavilion employees are from the countries they represent—Disney hires them as part of its international college program.

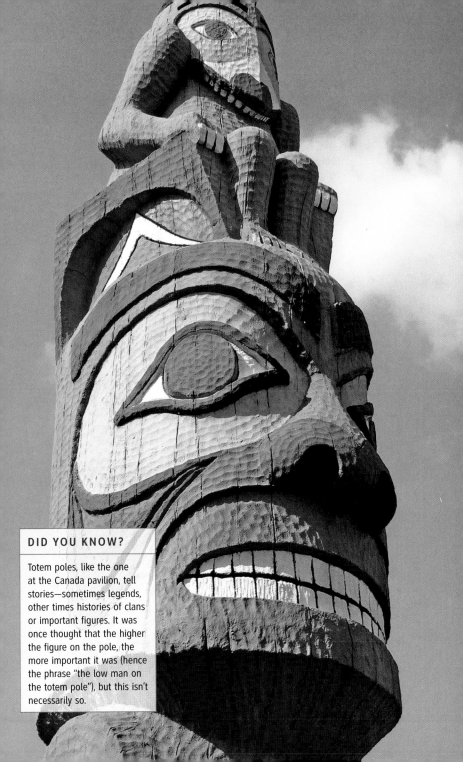

DID YOU KNOW?

Totem poles, like the one at the Canada pavilion, tell stories—sometimes legends, other times histories of clans or important figures. It was once thought that the higher the figure on the pole, the more important it was (hence the phrase "the low man on the totem pole"), but this isn't necessarily so.

Instead of rides, you have solid film attractions at the Canada, China, and France pavilions; several art exhibitions; and the chance to try your foreign language skills with the staff. Each pavilion also has a designated Kidcot Fun Stop, open daily from 11 or noon until about 8 or 9, where youngsters can try a cultural crafts project. Live enter-

WATER PLAY

Preschoolers love to play in the interactive fountains in front of Mission: SPACE and in the walkways between Future World and the World Showcase. Bring swimsuits and a towel!

tainment is an integral part of the experience, and you'll enjoy watching the incredibly talented Jeweled Dragon Acrobats in China and the Matsuriza Taiko drummers in Japan or laughing along with the mime and juggler in the Italy courtyard.

Dining is another favorite pastime at Epcot, and the World Showcase offers tempting tastes of the authentic cuisines of the countries here.

For People with Disabilities. Attractions at Mexico, American Adventure, France, China, and Canada are all wheelchair accessible, as are the plaza areas where shows are presented. Mexico's Gran Fiesta Tour boat ride also is wheelchair accessible; personal-translator units amplify sound tracks. Most of the live entertainment around the World Showcase features strong aural as well as visual elements.

EN ROUTE

A World Showcase Passport ($9.95) is a wonderful way to keep a kid interested in this more adult area of Epcot. The passports, available at vendor carts, come with stickers and a badge, and children can have them stamped at each pavilion. The World Showcase is also a great place to look for unusual gifts—you might pick up a Oaxacan wood carving in Mexico, a tea set in China, or a kimonoed doll in Japan.

CANADA

"Oh, it's just our Canadian outdoors," said a typically modest native guide upon being asked about the model for the striking rocky chasm and tumbling waterfall that represent just one of the pavilion's high points. The beautiful formal gardens do have an antecedent: Butchart Gardens, in Victoria, British Columbia. And so does the Hôtel du Canada, a French Gothic mansion with spires, turrets, and a mansard roof; anyone who's ever stayed at Québec's Château Frontenac or Ottawa's Château Laurier will recognize the imposing style favored by architects of Canadian railroad hotels.

Like the size of the Rocky Mountains, the scale of the structures seems immense; unlike the real thing, it's managed with a trick called forced perspective, which exaggerates the smallness of the distant parts to make the entire thing look gigantic.

You can browse shops that sell maple syrup; Canadian sports jerseys; and plush huggable bears, beavers, and huskies. Le Cellier Steakhouse is a great place for a relaxing lunch or dinner; due to its increasing popularity, book reservations far ahead.

O Canada! That's just what you'll say after seeing this CircleVision film's stunning opening shot—footage of the Royal Canadian Mounted Police surrounding you as they circle the screen. From there, you whoosh over

2

waterfalls, venture through Montréal and Toronto, sneak up on bears and bison, mush behind a husky-pulled dogsled, and land pluck in the middle of a hockey game. The only downsides: this is a standing-only theater, strollers aren't permitted, and toddlers and small children can't see unless they're held aloft. **For people with disabilities**: Wheelchair and ECV accessible; reflective captioning and equipped for assisted-listening and audio-description devices. ■ **TIP➔ Stop in on your stroll around World Showcase Promenade.** ✉ *World Showcase, Canada* ☞ *Duration: 14 mins. Crowds: Moderate to Heavy. Audience: All Ages.*

UNITED KINGDOM

The United Kingdom rambles between the elegant mansions lining a London square to the bustling, half-timber shops of a village High Street to thatch-roof cottages from the countryside. (The thatch is made of plastic broom bristles due to local fire regulations.) And, of course, there's a pair of iconic red phone booths.

The pavilion has no single major attraction. Instead, you wander through shops selling tea, Welsh handicrafts, and English lavender fragrance by Taylor of London. There's a store with Beatles T-shirts, CDs, and memorabilia. Next door is the Historic Research Center, where you can research your family name and purchase printed, hand-painted, or embroidered versions of your family coat of arms.

Outside, the strolling World Showcase Players coax audience members to participate in lowbrow versions of Shakespeare. There's also a lovely garden and park with benches in the back that's easy to miss—relax and kick back to the tunes of the British Revolution, a band known for its on-target Beatles and other Brit-band performances. Kids love to run through the hedge maze as their parents travel back in time to "Yesterday." Check the *Times Guide* and arrive 30 minutes early for a bench or 15 minutes early for a curb. Restrooms are near the red phone booths.

NEED A BREAK? Revive yourself with a pint of the best at the **Rose & Crown,** a pub where you'll jostle for space any evening the Hat Lady performs her piano magic. The dining room serves hearty fare for lunch and dinner (reservations often required). The outdoor terrace is one of the best spots for watching Illumi-Nations. Arrive at least an hour or so in advance for a seat. If you're in a hurry, grab fish-and-chips to go from Yorkshire County Fish Shop, then nab a lagoon-side table.

FRANCE

You don't need the scaled-down model of the Eiffel Tower to tell you that you've arrived in France, specifically Paris. There's the poignant accordion music wafting out of concealed speakers, the trim sycamores pruned in the French style to develop signature knots at the end of each branch, and the delicious aromas surrounding Les Halles Boulangerie & Pâtisserie bakeshop. This is the Paris of dreams, a Paris of the years just before World War I, when solid mansard-roof mansions were crowned with iron filigree, when the least brick was drenched in romanticism.

Here's a replica of the conservatory-like Les Halles—the iron-and-glass barrel-roof market that no longer exists in the City of Light; there's an arching footbridge; and all around, of course, there are shops. You can inspect Parisian impressionist artwork at Galerie des Halles; sample perfume at the Guerlain shop; and acquire a Julia Child cookbook or bottle of Pouilly-Fuisse at Les Vins de France. If you plan to dine at Les Chefs de France, make a reservation for a late lunch or dinner; the second-floor Monsieur Paul (dinner only) is a gourmet treat.

NEED A BREAK?

It's worth it to brave the lines at Les Halles Boulangerie & Pâtisserie, a large Parisian-style counter-service café. Have wine with a cheese plate, quiche, or sandwich on crusty French bread. Or go for a creamy café au lait and a napoleon. The new L'Artisan des Glaces ice cream–and-sorbet shop is praiseworthy for its ultracreamy treats that include an ice cream "martini" with Grand Marnier and flavor-customized ice-cream sandwiches made with brioche or French *macaron*.

Impressions de France. The intimate Palais du Cinema, inspired by the royal theater at Fontainebleau, screens this homage to the glories of the country. Shown on five screens spanning 200 degrees, in an air-conditioned, sit-down theater, the film takes you to vineyards at harvest time, Paris on Bastille Day, the Alps, Versailles, Normandy's Mont-St-Michel, and the stunning châteaux of the Loire Valley. The music sweeps you away with familiar segments from Offenbach, Debussy, and Saint-Saëns, all woven together by longtime Disney musician Buddy Baker. **For people with disabilities:** Wheelchair and ECV accessible; reflective captioning and equipped for assisted-listening and audio-description devices. ■TIP→ Visit anytime during your stroll around the World Showcase; theater seats are comfy and a great way to rest weary legs. ⊠ *World Showcase, France* ☞ *Duration: 20 mins. Crowds: Moderate. Audience: All Ages.*

MOROCCO

Walk through the pointed arches of the Bab Boujouloud gate and you're transported to this mysterious North African country. The arches are ornamented with wood carvings and encrusted with mosaics made of 9 tons of handmade, hand-cut tiles; 19 native artisans were sent to Epcot to install them and to create the dusty stucco walls that seem to have withstood centuries of sandstorms. Look closely and you'll see that every tile has a small crack or other imperfection, and no tile depicts a living creature—in deference to the Islamic belief that only Allah creates perfection and life.

Koutoubia Minaret, a replica of the prayer tower in Marrakesh, acts as Morocco's landmark. Winding alleyways—each corner bursting with carpets, brasses, leatherwork, and other wares—lead to a tiled fountain and lush gardens. A highlight is Restaurant Marrakesh. Enjoy couscous and roast lamb while a lithesome belly dancer makes for a pleasant diversion. One of the hottest fast-food spots in Epcot is Tangierine Café, with tasty Mediterranean specialties like pita-pocket lamb and chicken sliders, killer baklava, and share-worthy vegetable platters with hummus, tabbouleh, falafel, lentils, and couscous. Opened in 2014, Spice Road Table is the ideal lagoon-side spot for tapas and the best sangria in Orlando. All eateries are open for lunch and dinner. Restrooms on the France side of the pavilion offer quick access.

JAPAN

A brilliant vermilion torii gate, based on Hiroshima Bay's much-photographed Itsukushima Shrine, frames the World Showcase Lagoon and stands as an emblem of Disney's serene version of Japan.

Disney horticulturists deserve a hand for authenticity: 90% of the plants they used are native to Japan. Rocks, pebbled streams, pools, and pruned trees and shrubs complete the meticulous picture. At sunset, or during a rainy dusk, the twisted branches of the corkscrew willows frame a perfect Japanese view of the five-story winged pagoda that is the heart of the pavilion. Based on the 8th-century Horyuji Temple in Nara, the brilliant blue pagoda has five levels, symbolizing the five elements of Buddhist belief—earth, water, fire, wind, and sky.

The peace is occasionally interrupted by performances on drums and gongs. Mitsukoshi, an immense retail firm known as Japan's Sears Roebuck, carries everything from T-shirts to kimonos and rows of Japanese dolls. For lunch and dinner, you'll be entertained by the culinary feats of chefs at Teppan Edo (which carries on the chop-toss-applaud antics of the original Teppanyaki Dining Room). Tokyo Dining focuses on presentation of traditional ingredients and cuisine from Japan, including sushi. At the pavilion's rear is a sake tasting bar that you'll miss if you don't look for it.

AMERICAN ADVENTURE

In a Disney version of Philadelphia's Independence Hall, the Imagineers prove that their kind of fantasy can beat reality hands down. The 110,000 bricks, made by hand from soft, pink, Georgia clay, sheathe the familiar structure, which acts as a beacon for those across Epcot's lagoon. The pavilion includes an all-American fast-food restaurant, a shop, lovely rose gardens, and an outdoor theater. Restrooms are tucked away along the far left side of the restaurant, and a roomier, more modern restroom accommodation also is open by the gift shop.

NEED A BREAK? What else would you order at the counter-service **Liberty Inn** but burgers, apple pie, and other all-American fare? On a summer evening this is the place to get an ice-cream sundae before IllumiNations starts. On a chilly winter day, the hot cocoa is a hit. At the **Fife & Drum** along the promenade, you can pair a beer with a turkey leg for a satisfying snack.

Fodor'sChoice ★ **The American Adventure.** The pavilion's key attraction is this 100-yard dash through history, and you'll be primed for the lesson after reaching the main entry hall and hearing the stirring a cappella Voices of Liberty. Inside the theater, the main event begins to the accompaniment of "The Golden Dream," performed by the Philadelphia Orchestra. This show combines evocative sets, a rear-projection screen (72 feet wide), enormous movable stages, and 35 Audio-Animatronics players.

Morocco's open-air market is like something out of an Indiana Jones movie. It's a maze of shops selling straw bags, colorful carpets, leather goods, and, of course, ceramics.

Beginning with the arrival of the Pilgrims at Plymouth Rock and their grueling first winter, Benjamin Franklin and a wry, pipe-smoking Mark Twain narrate the episodes, both praiseworthy and shameful, that have shaped the American spirit. Each speech and scene seems polished like a little jewel. You feel the cold at Valley Forge. You're moved by Nez Percé Chief Joseph's forced abdication of Native American ancestral lands and by women's rights campaigner Susan B. Anthony's speech. You laugh with Will Rogers's aphorisms and learn about the pain of the Great Depression through an affecting radio broadcast by Franklin Delano Roosevelt. **For people with disabilities:** Wheelchair and ECV accessible; reflective captioning and equipped for assisted-listening and audio-description devices. ■ TIP→ Check your Times Guide and arrive 10 minutes before the Voices of Liberty are slated to perform, then head inside to enjoy the a cappella tunes. ⊠ *World Showcase, American Adventure* ☞ *Duration: 30 mins. Crowds: Heavy. Audience: All Ages.*

America Gardens Theatre. On the edge of the lagoon, directly opposite Disney's magnificent bit of colonial fakery, is this open-air, partially tree-shaded venue for concerts and shows. Most performances are hot tickets with themes tied to Epcot events, such as "Garden Rocks" concerts with pop legends during the March through May Epcot International Flower & Garden Festival and Eat to the Beat concerts during the late-September through mid-November Epcot International Food & Wine Festival. This is also the setting for the annual yuletide Candlelight Processional—a not-to-be-missed event if you're at WDW during the holidays. The Candlelight Dinner Package (available through Disney's dining reservations hotline) includes lunch or dinner in a select World

Showcase restaurant and preferred seating for the moving performance. Roomy new restrooms are now open behind the Kidcot Fun Stop. ■ TIP→ Arrive more than an hour ahead of time for holiday and celebrity performances. ⊠ *World Showcase, American Adventure* ⌕ *Duration: Performances vary. Crowds: Vary. Audience: Varies.*

ITALY

Architectural reproductions of Venice's Piazza San Marco and Doge's Palace are accurate right down to the gold leaf on the ringlets of the angel perched 100 feet atop the Campanile; the seawall stained with age, with barbershop-stripe poles to which two gondolas are tethered; and the Romanesque columns, Byzantine mosaics, Gothic arches, and stone walls that have all been carefully antiqued. Mediterranean plants such as grapevines, kumquat, and olive trees add verisimilitude. Shops sell Venetian beads and glasswork, leather purses, perfumes, olive oils, pastas, and Perugina cookies and chocolate kisses.

At Tutto Italia Ristorante, the cuisine—wines, handmade mozzarella, and fresh bread—is from several regions of Italy. Limited outdoor dining beneath umbrellas is lovely. The hot ticket is on the edge of the piazza: Via Napoli is a casual 300-seat pizzeria with wood-burning ovens and an airy, noisy dining room. Chefs use Caputo flour, San Marzano tomatoes, and fresh, handmade mozzarella to craft some of the best margherita pizza outside of Naples! The Tutto Gusto Wine Cellar is a cool escape for a glass of prosecco and a small plate.

Sergio, a clown–juggler, and the flag-throwing-to-live-music-group Sbandieratori Di Sansepolcro, bring crowds to the piazza several times each day. This is a great spot for viewing IllumiNations if you're in the vicinity.

GERMANY

Germany, a make-believe village that distills the best folk architecture from all over that country, is so jovial that you practically expect the Seven Dwarfs to come "heigh-ho"-ing out to meet you. If you time it right, you will spot Snow White as she poses for photos and signs autographs. The fairy tale continues as a specially designed glockenspiel on the clock tower chimes on the hour. You'll also hear musical toots and tweets from cuckoo clocks, folk tunes from the spinning dolls sold at Der Teddybär, and the satisfied grunts of hungry visitors chowing down on hearty German cooking.

The Biergarten's wonderful buffet serves several sausage varieties, as well as sauerkraut, spaetzle, and roasted potatoes, rotisserie chicken, and German breads, all accompanied by yodelers, dancers, and other lederhosen-clad musicians who perform a year-round Oktoberfest show. There are shops aplenty, including Die Weihnachts Ecke (the Christmas Corner), which sells nutcrackers and other Christmas ornaments. It's hard to resist watching the miniature trains that choo-choo along a garden track dotted with tiny villages. Restrooms are just steps away.

NEED A BREAK?

Sommerfest. Bratwurst and cold beer from the Sommerfest counter at the entrance of the Biergarten restaurant make a perfect quick and hearty lunch, while the apple strudel and Black Forest cake are ever-popular sweets. There's not much seating, so you may have to eat on the run. ✉ *World Showcase, Germany.*

Saluting Africa–Outpost. The Saluting Africa–Outpost, between Germany and China, isn't one of the 11 World Showcase pavilions, but kids love to test their drumming skills on bongos and other drums that invite players to improvise their own African folklore performances. Village Traders sells African handicrafts and—you guessed it—souvenirs relating to *The Lion King.* Buy an ice cream or frozen yogurt at the Africa Coolpost, and enjoy the break at a table by the lagoon. A cool mist is set up to offer respite on hot days. ✉ *World Showcase.*

CHINA

A shimmering red-and-gold, three-tier replica of Beijing's Temple of Heaven towers over a serene Chinese garden, an art gallery displaying treasures from the People's Republic, a spacious emporium devoted to Chinese goods, and two restaurants. The gardens—planted with a native Chinese tallow tree, water lilies, bamboo, and a 100-year-old weeping mulberry tree—are tranquil.

Piped-in traditional Chinese music flows gently over the peaceful hush of the gardens, which come alive with applause and cheers when the remarkable Jeweled Dragon Acrobats tumble into a roped-off area for their breathtaking act. At China's popular Nine Dragons Restaurant try the shrimp and chicken egg rolls or the peppery shrimp with spinach noodles; there are also several chicken and stir-fry favorites.

■ NEED A BREAK?

Lotus Blossom Café. The open-air Lotus Blossom Café offers some authentic Chinese fare: pot stickers, soups, and egg rolls. Entrées include orange chicken with steamed rice, vegetable curry, and a beef noodle soup bowl. The Joy of Tea cart along the promenade serves hot and cold tea, plus trendy green-tea frozen drinks, plum wine, beer, and cocktails. ✉ *World Showcase, China.*

Reflections of China. Think of the Temple of Heaven as an especially fitting theater for a movie in which sensational panoramas of the land and people are dramatically portrayed on a 360-degree CircleVision screen. Highlights include striking footage of Hong Kong, Shanghai, and Macao. This may be the best of the World Showcase films—the only drawbacks are that strollers aren't permitted and the theater has no chairs; lean rails are provided. ■TIP➜ Come anytime and, before the show, visit the Tomb Warriors gallery, where you can see replicas of the terra-cotta soldiers unearthed by farmers in Xi'an, China, in 1974. ✉ *World Showcase, China* ☞ *Duration: 14 mins. Crowds: Moderate. Audience: All Ages.*

NORWAY

Among the rough-hewn timbers and sharply pitched roofs here—softened and brightened by bloom-stuffed window boxes and figured shutters—are lots of smiling young Norwegians, all eager to speak English and show off their country. The pavilion complex contains a

The Temple of Quetzalcoatl (ket-zal-co-WAH-tal) at Teotihuacán (tay-o-tee-wah-CON), just outside Mexico City, is the model for the pyramid at the Mexico pavilion.

14th-century, fortresslike castle that mimics Oslo's Akershus, cobbled streets, rocky waterfalls, and a stave church modeled after one built in 1250, with wood dragons glaring from the eaves. The church houses an exhibit called "To the Ends of the Earth," which uses vintage artifacts to tell the story of two early-20th-century polar expeditions. It all puts you in the mood for the pavilion's shops, which sell spears, shields, and other Viking necessities perfect for next Halloween.

At Akershus Royal Banquet Hall, Princess Storybook Dining is a big deal. Visit the Norwegian *koldtbord* (buffet) for smoked salmon, fruit, and pastries, followed by a family-style hot breakfast of eggs, meats, and other treats served at the table. For lunch and dinner, you'll find traditional treats like chilled shrimp, salads, meats, and cheeses. Hot entrées served à la carte might include oven-roasted chicken breast, venison stew, or the traditional Scandinavian meatball dish called *kjottkaker*. Family-style dessert is a treat with three of the chef's sweet specialties.

■ TIP→ The restaurant is the only one in the park where you can dine with Disney princesses, who may include Aurora, Belle, or Snow White. You can reserve up to 180 days in advance, and we recommend booking as early as possible. However, you can always check at Guest Relations for seats left by cancellations.

NEED A BREAK?

Kringla Bakeri Og Kafe. You can order smoked salmon, sandwiches, and a vegetable torte, as well as wine, beer, and the potent Viking coffee at Kringla Bakeri Og Kafe. Sweet pretzels, pastries, and cookies satisfy sugar cravings. ⊠ *World Showcase, Norway.*

MEXICO

Housed in a spectacular Mayan pyramid surrounded by dense tropical plantings and brilliant blossoms, Mexico welcomes you onto a "moonlit" plaza that contains the Gran Fiesta Tour boat ride; an exhibit of pre-Columbian art; a very popular restaurant; and, of course, shopping kiosks where you can unload many, many pesos.

Modeled on the market in the town of Taxco, Plaza de los Amigos is well named: there are lots of friendly people—the women dressed in peasant blouses and bright skirts, the men in white shirts and dashing sashes—all eager to sell you trinkets from a cluster of canopied carts. The perimeter is rimmed with stores with tile roofs, wrought-iron balconies, and flower-filled window boxes. What to buy? Sombreros, baskets, pottery, jewelry, and maracas.

One of the pavilion's key attractions is the San Angel Inn, featuring traditional Mexican cuisine and wine and beer, and overlooking the faux-moonlit waterway traversed by Gran Fiesta Tour boats. The pavilion's La Cava del Tequila bar serves up tequila flights, exotic blended margaritas, and light snacks like guacamole with corn chips. The casual, outdoor La Cantina de San Angel is a 150-seat quick-service eatery adjacent to La Hacienda de San Angel, a 250-seat table-service restaurant with waterside view. You won't want to miss trying Mexican treats like the Queso Fundido, melted cheese with poblano peppers, chorizo, and tortillas, or La Hacienda mixed grill served with beans and fresh salsa.

FAMILY **Gran Fiesta Tour Starring the Three Caballeros.** In this attraction—which shines with the polish of enhanced facades, sound system, and boat-ride props—Donald teams with old pals José Carioca (the parrot) and Panchito (the Mexican charro rooster) from the 1944 Disney film *The Three Caballeros*. The Gran Fiesta Tour film sweeps you along for an animated jaunt as the caballeros are reunited for a grand performance in Mexico City. Donald manages to disappear for his own tour of the country, leaving José and Panchito to search for their missing comrade. **For people with disabilities:** The boat is accessible to guests using wheelchairs, but those using ECVs or oversize chairs must transfer to a Disney model. Equipped for handheld-captioning and audio-description devices. ■TIP➜ **It's worth a visit if lines aren't long, especially if you have small children, who usually enjoy the novelty of a boat ride.** ⊠ *World Showcase, Mexico* ☞ *Duration: 9 mins. Crowds: Moderate. Audience: All Ages.*

EPCOT SPECTACLE

Fodor'sChoice **IllumiNations: Reflections of Earth.** This marvelous nighttime spectacular
★ takes place over the World Showcase Lagoon every night before closing. Be sure to stick around for the lasers, lights, flames, fireworks, fountains, and music that fill the air over the water. The show's Earth Globe—a gigantic, spherical, video-display system rotating on a 350-ton floating island—is three stories tall with 180,000 light-emitting diodes. It houses six computer processors and 258 strobe lights and projects images celebrating the diversity and unified spirit of humankind. The

globe opens like a lotus flower in the grand finale, revealing a huge torch that rises 40 feet into the air as additional flames spread light across the lagoon. Nearly 2,800 fireworks shells paint colorful displays across the night sky.

Although there's generally good viewing from all around the lagoon, some of the best spots are in front of the Italy pavilion, on the bridge between France and the United Kingdom, on the promenade in front of Canada, at the World Showcase Plaza, and at La Hacienda de San Angel and La Cantina de San Angel in Mexico. **For people with disabilities:** During the show, certain areas along the lagoon's edge at Showcase Plaza, Canada, and Germany are reserved for guests using wheelchairs. ■ TIP→ Limited FastPass+ reservations are offered; otherwise, for best views, find your place 45 minutes in advance and send someone in your group for ice cream or other treats. ✉ *World Showcase* ☞ *Duration: 12 mins. Crowds: Heavy. Audience: All Ages.*

DISNEY'S HOLLYWOOD STUDIOS

The first thing you notice when you pass through the Hollywood Studios turnstiles is the laid-back California attitude. Palm-lined Hollywood Boulevard oozes glamour—but in a casual way that makes you feel as if you belong, even without your slinky Michael Kors jersey and Jimmy Choos.

When the park opened in May 1989 its name was Disney–MGM Studios. Disney changed the name in 2008 to broaden its appeal. Unlike the first movie theme park—Universal Studios in California—Hollywood Studios combined Disney detail with MGM's motion-picture legacy and Walt Disney's own animated classics. Imagineers built the park with real film and television production in mind, and during its first decade, the Studios welcomed films like *Ernest Saves Christmas* and TV shows like *Wheel of Fortune* to its soundstages.

The Animation Studios, too, were busy. Stories such as *Aladdin* and *Lilo & Stitch* came to life on the easels and computers of Disney's Florida animators. Though production has mostly halted at the park, you can enjoy plenty of attractions that showcase how filmmakers practice their craft. If you're wowed by action-film stunts, you can learn the tricks of the trade at the Indiana Jones Epic Stunt Spectacular! or the Lights, Motors, Action! Extreme Stunt Show. No trip to the Studios would be complete without a tour of the Magic of Disney Animation, where you can sit down and draw a character like Mickey or Donald.

In a savvy effort to grab a big piece of the pop-culture pie, in late 2008 Disney opened its own *American Idol* attraction, where performers earned audience votes to compete in a contest for a spot in the TV show's regional audition process. That show ran its course and closed in 2014. But big-hit attractions such as Toy Story Midway Mania! and new twists on old favorites like the 3-D Star Wars–themed simulator ride, Star Tours—The Adventures Continue keep the crowds happy.

2

TOP ATTRACTIONS

AGES 8 AND UP

Indiana Jones Epic Stunt Spectacular! The show's cast reenacts *Raiders of the Lost Ark* scenes with panache.

The Magic of Disney Animation. It's always fun to immerse yourself in Disney's world of animation.

Rock 'n' Roller Coaster Starring Aerosmith. Blast off to rockin' tunes on a high-speed, hard-core coaster.

Star Tours—The Adventures Continue. Prepare for a high-speed chase on this updated simulator thrill ride through multiple scenarios in the *Star Wars* galaxy.

Toy Story Midway Mania! 3-D glasses? Check. Spring-action shooter? Check. Ride and shoot your way through the midway with Buzz, Woody, and others.

Twilight Zone Tower of Terror. The TV classic theming of this free-fall "elevator" screamer is meticulous.

AGES 7 AND UNDER

For the First Time in Forever: A "Frozen" Sing-Along Celebration. Every audience member can "Let It Go" and sing along to the popular tunes from Disney's blockbuster film *Frozen.*

Beauty and the Beast—Live on Stage. Memorable music, talented performers, dancing kitchen objects, and a fairy-tale ending make this a must-see show.

Disney Junior—Live on Stage! The preschool crowd can't get enough of the characters here from Disney Channel shows like *Jake and the Never Land Pirates, Mickey Mouse Clubhouse,* Doc McStuffins, and Sofia the First.

Honey, I Shrunk the Kids Movie Set Adventure. Youngsters love to romp among the giant blades of grass and bugs.

Muppet*Vision 3-D. Children (and most adults) shriek with laughter during this 3-D movie.

ORIENTATION AND PLANNING

GETTING ORIENTED

The park is divided into sightseeing clusters. **Hollywood Boulevard** is the main artery to the heart of the park, and is where you find the glistening replica of Graumann's Chinese Theater.

Encircling it are **Sunset Boulevard,** the **Animation Courtyard, Mickey Avenue, Pixar Place, Commissary Lane, the Streets of America area,** and **Echo Lake**.

The entire park is 135 acres, and has fewer than 20 attractions (compared with Magic Kingdom's 40-plus). It's small enough to cover in a day and even repeat a favorite ride or two.

If you're staying at one of the Epcot resorts (BoardWalk, Yacht or Beach Club, Swan, or Dolphin), getting to the Entrance Plaza on a motor launch is part of the fun. Disney resort buses also drop you at the entrance.

If you're staying off-property and driving, your parking ticket will remain valid for parking at another Disney park later in the day—provided, of course, you have the stamina.

DISNEY'S HOLLYWOOD STUDIOS PLANNER

PARK AMENITIES

Baby Care: The small baby-care center next to Guest Relations has nursing and changing facilities. Formula, baby food, pacifiers, and disposable diapers are for sale next door at Movieland and at Oscar's Super Service. There are also diaper-changing areas in all women's rooms and some men's rooms.

Cameras: At the Darkroom (or next door at Cover Story) on Hollywood Boulevard, you can buy memory cards and disposable cameras. And if a Disney photographer takes your picture in the park, you can pick up a Disney PhotoPass from him or her that lets you see the pictures online. PhotoPass CD packages are $169.95 and $199.95, and you can purchase prints ($16.95 for an 8-inch-by-10-inch photo; other sizes available).

First Aid: The station is in the Entrance Plaza adjoining Guest Relations.

Guest Relations: You'll find it just inside the turnstiles on the left side of the Entrance Plaza. A FastPass+ kiosk is at the corner of Hollywood and Sunset boulevards.

Lockers: You can rent lockers at the Crossroads of the World kiosk in the center of the Entrance Plaza. The cost is $7 or $9 with a $5 refundable key deposit. The lockers themselves are at Oscar's Super Service.

Lost People and Things: Instruct your kids to go to a Disney staffer with a name tag if they can't find you. If you lose them, ask any cast member for assistance; logbooks of lost children's names are kept at Guest Relations, which also has a computerized message center where you can leave notes for companions.

Disney's Hollywood Studios Lost and Found: Report lost or found articles at Guest Relations. ⊠ *Hollywood Blvd.* ☏ *407/560–4666.*

Main Lost and Found: Seek out articles lost for more than one day here. ⊠ *Ticket and Transportation Center [TTC]* ☏ *407/824–4245.*

Package Pick-Up: You can ask shop clerks to forward purchases to your hotel if you're staying on Disney property or to Package Pick-Up next to Oscar's Super Service in the Entrance Plaza, so you won't have to carry them around. Allow three hours for delivery.

Services for People with Disabilities: The Studios' restaurants, shops, theaters, and attractions are wheelchair accessible, although there are boarding restrictions on some rides. Some theater-type attractions, including Muppet*Vision 3-D, have reflective captioning, and most other attractions are equipped for assisted-listening and video- or handheld-captioning devices. There are large Braille park maps near the Guest Relations lobby and near the Tip Board at Hollywood and Sunset. Note that restaurants don't have Braille menus.

You can pick up Braille guides ($25 same-day refundable deposit) and assisted-listening devices (also $25 deposit) and check on sign-language interpretation schedules at Guest Relations. Although interpreters appear only two days each week, you can request them (at least 14 days in advance) on other days by calling ☏ *407/824–4321* or TTY *407/827–5141.*

Oscar's Super Service, to the right in the Entrance Plaza, rents wheel-chairs ($12 daily, $10 multiday) and electronic convenience vehicles (ECVs; $50 per day plus a refundable $20 security deposit). Reservations aren't an option, so arrive early, especially to snag an ECV.

Stroller Rentals: Oscar's Super Service rents strollers. Single strollers are $15 daily, $13 for more than one day; doubles are $31 daily, $27 multiday.

DINNER AND A SHOW

Fantasmic! **Dinner Package.** Call or check ahead to visit on a day when you can see the after-dark *Fantasmic!* show, with its 30 powerful minutes of Disney characters, special effects, fireworks, flames, fountains, and even animation sequences projected onto water screens. If you're not crazy about the idea of arriving at the huge Hollywood Hills Amphitheater more than an hour ahead of showtime for a good seat, it's worth booking a *Fantasmic!* lunch or dinner package.

You get a prix-fixe meal at buffet-style Hollywood & Vine or a full table-service dinner at Hollywood Brown Derby or Mama Melrose's, along with a preferred-entry pass to the VIP seating area at the *Fantasmic!* show. Each dinner includes appetizer, entrée, dessert (the Brown Derby's grapefruit cake is a sweet-tart wonder), and a nonalcoholic beverage.

There's a small catch (well, actually, there are three):

If you choose to book dinner, allow plenty of time between your dining time and your arrival for showtime. (Disney recommends that you show up at the theater 30 or more minutes ahead of time to choose your seat).

The dinner package is offered only for the first show on peak nights when *Fantasmic!* is performed twice.

If it rains, *Fantasmic!* might be canceled. You still get dinner, but you lose out on seeing the show with preferred seating.

It's best to reserve the package 180 days or at least several months in advance. You'll have to provide a credit-card number and, if you cancel 48 hours or less before the show, your card will be charged $10 per person. ⊠ *Sunset Blvd.* ☎ *407/939–3463 reservations* ⌛ *$36–$57 adults, $13–$20 children 3–9 (prices vary by restaurant and exclude tax and gratuity).* ⊗ *Fantasmic! usually performed once nightly during off-peak seasons; twice nightly during holidays and other peak visiting times.*

VISITING TIPS

■ Visit early in the week, when most people are at Magic Kingdom and Animal Kingdom.

■ Check the Tip Board periodically for attractions with short wait times to visit between FastPass+ appointments.

■ Be at the Fantasmic! amphitheater at least an hour before showtime if you didn't book the lunch or dinner package.

■ Need a burst of energy? On-the-run hunger pangs? Grab a slice at **Pizza Planet** at Streets of America. Alternatively, **Hollywood Scoops ice cream** on Sunset is the place to be on a hot day.

EXPLORING DISNEY'S HOLLYWOOD STUDIOS

HOLLYWOOD BOULEVARD

With its palm trees, pastel buildings, and flashy neon, Hollywood Boulevard paints a rosy picture of 1930s Tinseltown. There's a sense of having walked right onto a movie set of old, with art-deco storefronts and roving starlets and nefarious agents—actually costumed actors known as the Citizens of Hollywood. Throughout the park, characters from Disney movies new and old—from *Mickey Mouse* to *Toy Story* friends—pose for photos and sign autographs.

Great Movie Ride. At the end of Hollywood Boulevard are the fire-engine-red pagodas of a replica of Graumann's Chinese Theater, where you enter this attraction. The preshow queue snakes through a screening room with continuously running clips from *Mary Poppins, Raiders of the Lost Ark, Singin' in the Rain, Fantasia,* and, of course, *Casablanca.* Turner Classic Movies recently collaborated with Disney to refresh the attraction's preshow; TCM host Robert Osborne offers insights into famous film moments of the silver screen in a preride video. Once you board the ride, Disney cast members dressed as 1920s newsboys (and girls) steer past a Hollywood Hills backdrop as you begin this tour of cinematic climaxes—with a little help from Audio-Animatronics, scrim, smoke, and Disney magic. Along the way you'll see Gene Kelly "Singin' in the Rain" as he clutches that immortal lamppost and Mary Poppins with her umbrella as her sooty admirers reprise "Chim-Chim-Cher-ee." A gangland shoot-out with James Cagney in *Public Enemy* is just around the corner. Gangsters or Western gunslingers (it depends on which tram you board) hijack your tram and whisk you off to a showdown. You'll meet some slimy characters from *Alien*—look up for truly scary stuff—before rolling onto the snake-ridden set of *Indiana Jones and the Temple of Doom,* where your hijacker attempts to steal an idol. We won't give away the scene stealer here.

Keep an eye out as Tarzan swings into action and Bogey bids Bergman goodbye with a "Here's looking at you, kid" by the plane to Lisbon. You'll know you're not in Kansas anymore with the Yellow Brick Road finale and the cackling imprecations by the Wicked Witch of the West. Remember to check out Dorothy's tornado-tossed house—you might spot the ruby slippers. The TCM-curated postshow video features an updated montage of famous film moments. **For people with disabilities:** You may remain in your wheelchair or ECV. Handheld captioning and audio description available. The sounds and effects on this ride might scare service animals, so check with a cast member before boarding. ■ TIP➔ FastPass+ is now offered, or you could stop here while waiting out another attraction appointment. ⊠ *Hollywood Blvd.* ☞ *Duration: 22 mins. Crowds: Moderate. Audience: All but Very Young Kids.*

SUNSET BOULEVARD

This avenue honors Hollywood with facades derived from the Carthay Circle, the Beverly Wilshire Theatre, and other City of Angels landmarks.

Beauty and the Beast—Live on Stage. This wildly popular stage show takes place at the Theater of the Stars, a re-creation of the famed Hollywood

Bowl. The actors playing a luminous Belle and delightfully vain Gaston sing with passion with a lively cast of characters and dancers. The enchanted prince (Beast) and household characters (Mrs. Potts, Chip, Lumiere, and Cogsworth) deftly navigate the stage despite their bulky costumes. Even some set pieces sway along during the charming "Be Our Guest" number. There's high drama during the mob scene and a sweet ending when ballroom dancers in frothy pink and purple waltz along with the fairy-tale couple.

As you arrive or depart, check out handprints and footprints set in concrete of the TV personalities who've visited Disney's Hollywood Studios. **For people with disabilities:** Wheelchair and ECV accessible and equipped for handheld captioning, audio description, and assisted listening. Sign language twice a week. ■ TIP➜ **Book a FastPass+ or line up at least 30 minutes prior to showtime. Performance times vary, so check the Times Guide.** ⊠ *Sunset Blvd.* ☞ *Duration: 30 mins. Crowds: Moderate to Heavy. Audience: All Ages.*

Fodor's Choice ★ **Rock 'n' Roller Coaster Starring Aerosmith.** Although this is an indoor roller coaster like Magic Kingdom's Space Mountain, the similarity ends there. With its high-speed launch (0 to 60 in 2.8 seconds), multiple inversions, and loud rock music, it generates delighted screams from coaster junkies, though it's smooth enough and short enough that even the coaster-phobic have been known to enjoy it. The vehicles look like limos, and the track resembles the neck of an electric guitar that's been twisted. Hard-driving rock tunes by Aerosmith blast from vehicle speakers to accentuate the flips and turns.

Pregnant women and guests with heart, back, or neck problems or motion sickness should skip this one. **For people with disabilities:** Guests using wheelchairs must transfer to a ride vehicle. Service animals aren't allowed. ■ TIP➜ **Ride when the park opens and try to book a FastPass+ to go again, especially if visiting with tweens or teens. Another way to avoid a wait—split up and try the Single Rider Queue.** ⊠ *Sunset Blvd.* ☞ *Duration: 1 min, 22 secs. Crowds: Huge. Audience: All but Young Kids. Height minimum: 48 inches.*

Fodor's Choice ★ **The Twilight Zone Tower of Terror.** After you enter the dimly lighted lobby of the deserted Hollywood Tower Hotel, then the dust-covered library, a lightning bolt zaps a TV to life. Rod Serling recounts the story of the hotel's demise and invites you to enter the Twilight Zone. On to the boiler room, where you board a giant elevator ride. The fifth dimension awaits, where you travel forward past scenes from the popular TV series. Suddenly, the creaking vehicle plunges into a terrifying, 130-foot free fall and then, before you can catch your breath, shoots quickly up, down, up, and down all over again. No use trying to guess how many stomach-churning ups and downs are in store—Disney's ride engineers have programmed random drop variations into the attraction for a different thrill every time.

Those who are pregnant or have heart, back, or neck problems shouldn't ride. **For people with disabilities:** You must have full upper-body strength and be able to transfer to a ride seat. Equipped for video captioning. Service animals can't ride. ■ TIP➜ **Get a FastPass+**

Earffel
Tower

Soundstages

Stage Lane

Lights, Motors, Action!
Extreme Stunt Show

Wandering Oaken's
Frozen Snowground

Toy Story
Midway Mania!

Walt Disney:
One Man's
Dream

Wandering Oaken's
Trading Post

PIXAR PLACE

MICKEY AVENUE

Studio
Catering Co.

Hey Howdy
Hey Take Away

Great Movie
Ride

STREETS OF
AMERICA

Honey, I Shrunk the Kids
Movie Set Adventure

ABC
Commissary

San Francisco Ave.

Sci-Fi Dine-In
Theater Restaurant

New York St.

S. Studio Dr.
(from World Dr.)

Premier Theater
"For the First Time
In Forever"

Muppet*Vision
3-D

The Writer's
Stop

COMMISSARY LANE

Min & Bill's
Dockside Diner

ATM

Echo Lake

ATM

Mama Melrose's
Ristorante
Italiano

Pizza Planet
Arcade

Tatooine
Traders

ECHO LAKE

Jedi Training
Academy

Star
Tours

50's Prime
Time Café

Tatooine Alley

Oasis
Canteen

Indiana Jones Epic
Stunt Spectacular!

Backlot
Express

Prospect Ave.

KEY

✗ Restaurants

🚻 Restrooms

•••• Parade Route

0   50 yards

0   50 m

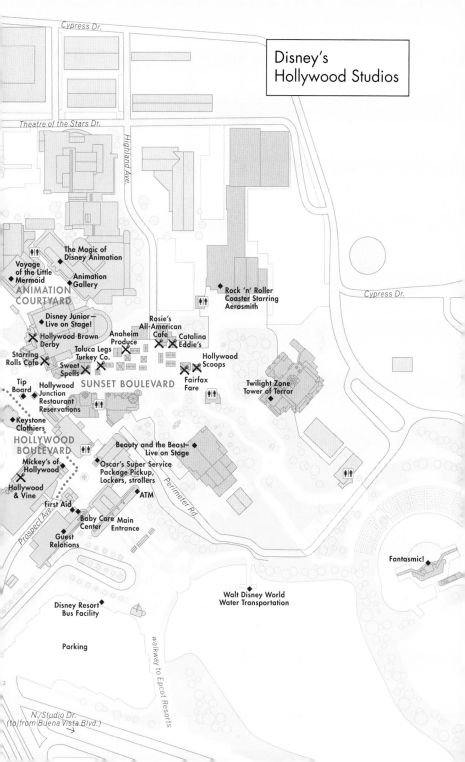

Disney's
Hollywood Studios

Cypress Dr.

Theatre of the Stars Dr.

Highland Ave.

Cypress Dr.

The Magic of
Disney Animation

Voyage
of the Little
Mermaid

Animation
Gallery

ANIMATION
COURTYARD

Rock 'n' Roller
Coaster Starring
Aerosmith

Disney Junior—
Live on Stage!

Rosie's
All-American
Cafe

Hollywood Brown
Derby

Anaheim
Produce

Catalina
Eddie's

Starring
Rolls Cafe

Toluca Legs
Turkey Co.

Hollywood
Scoops

Sweet
Spells

Tip
Board

Hollywood
Junction
Restaurant
Reservations

SUNSET BOULEVARD

Fairfax
Fare

Twilight Zone
Tower of Terror

Keystone
Clothiers

HOLLYWOOD
BOULEVARD

Mickey's of
Hollywood

Beauty and the Beast—
Live on Stage

Hollywood
& Vine

Oscar's Super Service
Package Pickup,
Lockers, strollers

Prospect Ave.

First Aid

ATM

Perimeter Rd.

Baby Care
Center

Main
Entrance

Guest
Relations

Fantasmic!

Disney Resort
Bus Facility

Walt Disney World
Water Transportation

Parking

walkway to Epcot Resorts

N. Studio Dr.
(to/from Buena Vista Blvd.)

reservation. Otherwise, come early or wait until evening, when crowds thin and it's spookier. ⊠ *Sunset Blvd.* ⏱ *Duration: 10 mins. Crowds: You Bet! Audience: All but Young Kids. Height minimum: 40 inches.*

ANIMATION COURTYARD

As you exit Sunset Boulevard, veer right through the high-arched gateway to the Animation Courtyard. Straight ahead are *Disney Junior—Live on Stage!*, the Magic of Disney Animation, and *Voyage of the Little Mermaid.*

Disney Junior—Live on Stage!. This is one of Walt Disney World's best shows for tots and preschoolers. A cast of Disney Channel characters joins the show's perky host, Casey, on a larger-than-life storybook stage. Puppets of Mickey Mouse, Goofy, and friends team up on the Mickey Mouse Clubhouse set to prep for Minnie's surprise birthday bash. In another skit, characters from Jake and the Never Land Pirates devise a clever way to thwart Captain Hook and defend their treasure chest. A third show segment features princess-in-training Sofia the First and Doc McStuffins. Sofia enlists sorcerer Mr. Cedric to cast a spell and make her father's royal ball a success. Meanwhile, Lambie's dance moves cause a bad case of "the rippies," cured only after Stuffy the Dragon and friends gather in Doc's office for some bubbly cheering-up fun.

Throughout the 24-minute show, preschoolers sing and dance along as the characters cha-cha-cha their way through the fun. Surprise special effects are icing on Minnie's birthday cake. **For people with disabilities:** Wheelchair and ECV accessible, equipped with preshow-area TV monitors with closed captioning, and equipped for assisted-listening, audio-description, and video- and handheld-captioning devices. ■TIP➜ FastPass+ is offered; or come early, when your child is most alert and lines are shorter. Be prepared to sit on the carpet. Don't miss character meet and greets before or after the show. ⊠ *Animation Courtyard* ⏱ *Duration: 24 mins. Crowds: Moderate to Heavy. Audience: Young Kids.*

The Magic of Disney Animation. More than any other backstage peek, this tour truly takes you inside the magic as you learn about the classical animation art behind Disney blockbuster hits like *Frozen.* You begin in a small theater with a performance of *Drawn to Animation,* in which an actor plays the role of an animator interacting with Mushu, the wisecracking character from *Mulan.* Depending on when you visit, new characters from upcoming Disney films may be introduced near the end of this show.

Then you enter a creative zone to play with computer touch screens. You can voice your favorite character and discover which one is most like you. Watch for popular costumed Disney toon stars to appear in this area for autographs and photos.

The final stop is the Animation Academy. Children and adults can participate as an artist explains how to draw the Disney character du jour—your sketch is your souvenir. As you exit, don't miss the collection of drawings and cels of characters from *Snow White, Fantasia,* and other classics. Here, too, are the actual Academy Awards that Disney has won for its animated films. The entire experience can take 15 to 30 minutes or more if you play at interactive exhibits or take part in the Animation Academy. **For people with disabilities:** Wheelchair and ECV accessible, has reflective captioning, and equipped for audio-description devices. ■TIP→ **Come early or late. To test your talents at Animation Academy, go there first or get in line quickly after the Drawn to Animation show. Toddlers may get bored.** ⊠ *Animation Courtyard* ⟳ *Duration: 15+ mins. Crowds: Moderate. Audience: All Ages.*

Voyage of the Little Mermaid. You join Ariel, Sebastian, and the underwater gang in this stage show, which condenses the movie into a marathon presentation of the greatest hits. In an admirable effort at verisimilitude, a fine mist sprays the stage; if you're sitting in the front rows, expect to get spritzed. Although this show is suitable for all ages, smaller children might be frightened by the dark theater and the evil, larger-than-life Ursula. **For people with disabilities:** Wheelchair accessible, has reflective captioning and preshow-area TVs with closed-captioning, and equipped for audio-description and assisted-listening devices. ■TIP→ **If you're not riding Rock 'n' Roller Coaster or Tower of Terror, come first thing and put FastPass+ to good use. Or wait until the stroller brigade's exodus later in the day.** ⊠ *Animation Courtyard* ⟳ *Duration: 15 mins. Crowds: Heavy. Audience: All Ages.*

MICKEY AVENUE

Walt Disney: One Man's Dream. One Man's Dream is a photo, film, and audio tour through Walt's life. For baby boomers, it's a real nostalgia trip to see Walt resurrected on film as his Wonderful World of Color intro splashes across the screen. There's also plenty of Walt memorabilia to view. One display showcases a towering Audio-Animatronics figure of Abraham Lincoln. Featured by Disney at the 1964–65 New York World's Fair in a "Great Moments with Mr. Lincoln" exhibit, the robotic president offers a transparent view of the mechanical innards that provide his movements. The film, hosted by Julie Andrews, at the end of your self-guided tour is 15 minutes long. **For people with disabilities:** Wheelchair and ECV accessible; has reflective captioning; and equipped for assisted-listening, handheld-captioning, and audio-description devices. ■TIP→ **Come while waiting for a Fast-Pass+ appointment at a high-demand ride like Rock 'n' Roller Coaster.** ⊠ *Mickey Ave.* ⟳ *Duration: 15+ mins. Crowds: Light to Moderate. Audience: Not Young Kids.*

PIXAR PLACE

Pixar Place is home to one of the park's biggest attractions, Toy Story Midway Mania! Where TV- and film-production soundstages once stood, warm brick facades welcome you to the land of Woody and Buzz. Open-air kiosks invite you to browse for themed toys and souvenirs. The brick building featuring Toy Story Friends is the place to mix and mingle with characters from the blockbuster movie *Toy Story.* Check schedules on your *Times Guide.*

Fodor's Choice
★

Toy Story Midway Mania!. Great toys like Mr. Potato Head, Woody, and Buzz Lightyear from Disney's hit film *Toy Story* never lose their relevance. The action here involves these beloved characters and takes place inside the toy box of Andy, the boy whose toys come to life when he's gone. Step right up and grab a pair of 3-D glasses before boarding your jazzed-up carnival tram. Soon, you're whirling onto the midway where you can use your spring-action shooter to launch darts at balloons, toss rings at aliens, and splatter eggs at barnyard targets.

You'll rack up points for targets hit and see your tally at ride's end. Try to hone a rat-a-tat shooting system to increase your score. Don't let Rex's fear of failure slow you down—shoot for the stars and you'll deserve a salute from the Green Army Men. **For people with disabilities:** Guests using ECVs must transfer to a standard wheelchair. Equipped for video-captioning and audio-description devices. Check with a host about boarding with a service animal. ■TIP➜ **It's so addictive, you might want to come first thing, ride, and get a FastPass+ for another go.** ⊠ *Pixar Pl.* ☞ *Duration: 7 mins. Crowds: Heavy. Audience: All Ages.*

STREETS OF AMERICA

It's fun to tour the New York and San Francisco sets here on foot so that you can check out the windows of shops and apartments, the taxicabs, and other details. If you're lucky (or smart enough to check the *Times Guide* show schedule), you'll join the street party for a performance by Mulch, Sweat & Shears—Live in Concert, as they play a 30-minute set of rock classics or rockin' seasonal tunes during holidays.

Honey, I Shrunk the Kids Movie Set Adventure. In this playground based on the movie, youngsters can slide down a gigantic blade of grass, crawl through caves, climb a mushroom mountain, and dodge sprinklers set in resilient flooring made of ground-up tires. All the requisite playground equipment is present: net climbs, ball crawls, caves, and slides. Because the area is enclosed, there's often a line to get in—but attraction hosts don't fudge on capacity limits, which maintains a comfort zone for those inside. **For people with disabilities:** Barrier-free, but uneven surfaces make maneuvering a wheelchair difficult. ■TIP➜ **Come when you've visited several attractions and your kids need to cut loose. Keep a close eye on toddlers—it's easy to lose track of them in the caves and on slides.** ⊠ *Streets of America* ☞ *Duration: Up to You. Crowds: Moderate. Audience: Young Kids.*

Lights, Motors, Action! Extreme Stunt Show. Here Disney show producers reveal the secrets behind Hollywood's greatest stunts, including heart-pounding car chases and explosions. The scene is a 177,000-square-foot Mediterranean village movie set inside a 5,000-seat, open-air theater. The premise? Filmmakers are producing a spy thriller, and the director is organizing out-of-sequence stunts. Heroes and villains perform high-speed spinouts, two-wheel driving, jumps, and high falls using various vehicles, including watercraft. Amid the action, you learn how filmmakers combine shots of various stunts to create a completed scene.

The show is pretty long, the benches are hard, some children become frightened by all the loud noises. Consider sitting toward the back in case you or your kids want to leave early. **For people with disabilities:** Wheelchair accessible and equipped for assisted-listening devices. ■TIP➜ **FastPass+ is offered but not recommended unless you're a huge stunt-action fan. For the best seats, check the Times Guide schedule** and line up 20 minutes before showtime. ⊠ *Streets of America* ☞ *Duration: 38 mins. Crowds: Moderate to Heavy. Audience: Not Young Kids.*

Muppet*Vision 3-D. You don't have to be a Miss Piggyphile to get a kick out of this combination 3-D movie and musical revue. All the Muppet characters make appearances, including Miss Piggy in roles that include the Statue of Liberty. In the waiting area, movie posters advertise the world's most glamorous porker in *Star Chores* and *To Have and Have More,* and Kermit the Frog in an Arnold Schwarzenegger parody, *Kürmit the Amphibian,* who's "so mean, he's green." Special effects are built into the walls and ceilings of the theater; the 3-D effects are coordinated with other sensory stimulation. **For people with disabilities:** Wheelchair accessible; has reflective captioning and preshow-area TVs with closed-captioning; and equipped for assisted-listening, video-captioning, and audio-description devices. ■ TIP→ Get your FastPass+ or arrive 10 minutes early. And don't worry—there are no bad seats. ⊠ *Streets of America* ☞ *Duration: 25 mins. Crowds: Moderate to Heavy. Audience: All Ages.*

ECHO LAKE

In the center of an idealized slice of Southern California is a cool, blue lake—an oasis fringed with trees, benches, and things like pink-and-aqua, chrome-trimmed restaurants with sassy waitresses and black-and-white TVs at the tables; the shipshape Min & Bill's Dockside Diner; and Tatooine Traders, where kids can build their own Lightsabers and browse a trove of Star Wars–inspired goods. You'll also find two of the park's longest-running attractions, the Indiana Jones Epic Stunt Spectacular! and Star Tours—The Adventures Continue, where a 3-D attraction transformation jazzes up the galaxy.

Fodor'sChoice **Indiana Jones Epic Stunt Spectacular!.** The rousing theme music from the
★ Indiana Jones movies heralds action delivered by veteran stunt coordinator Glenn Randall, whose credits include *Raiders of the Lost Ark, E.T.,* and *Jewel of the Nile.* Presented in a 2,200-seat amphitheater, the show starts with a series of near-death encounters in an ancient Mayan temple. Indy slides down a rope from the ceiling, dodges spears, avoids getting chopped by booby-trapped idols, and snags a forbidden gemstone, setting off a gigantic boulder that threatens to flatten him.

Next comes the Cairo street scene, circa 1940, where lucky audience members are chosen to perform as extras. When the nasty Ninja-Nazi stuntmen come out, you start to think that it's probably better to be in the audience.

Eventually Indy returns with his redoubtable girlfriend, Marian Ravenwood, portrayed by a Karen Allen look-alike. She's kidnapped and tossed into a truck while Indy fights his way free with bullwhip and gun, and bad guys tumble from every corner and cornice.

The actors do a commendable job of explaining their stunts, and you'll learn how cameras are camouflaged for trick shots. Only one stunt remains a secret: how do Indy and Marian escape the grand finale explosion? That's what keeps 'em coming back. **For people with disabilities:** Wheelchair accessible. Equipped for assisted-listening, audio-description, and handheld-captioning devices. There's sign language

DID YOU KNOW?

Pixar Place's Toy Story Midway Mania! combines the fun of a video game with 3-D technology *and* interaction with favorite *Toy Story* characters, like Mr. Potato Head. Man your spring-action shooter and take aim at playful targets along the colorful ride route. Scores are tallied at the end—will yours make you master of the midway?

interpretation twice weekly. ■TIP➜ Don't waste your FastPass+ here; there's plenty of room. Come at night to see the idols' eyes glow. ⊠ *Echo Lake* ☞ *Duration: 30 mins. Crowds: Moderate to Heavy. Audience: All but Very Young Kids.*

Fodor'sChoice **Star Tours: The Adventures Continue.** *Star Wars* fans, wield those light
★ sabers! This fan favorite multiplies the thrills with more than 50 ride scenarios powered up by Dolby 3-D video combined with motion-simulator technology. Here's the basic storyline: C-3PO and R2-D2, at the helm of a misappropriated spaceship, must navigate the galaxy with a rebel spy on board (it could be you!) while Imperial forces try to thwart the journey.

Each ride is different: you'll encounter multiple thrills from the *Star Wars* universe including the lush Wookiee planet Kashyyyk and the underwater world of Naboo. One flight propels you through a dangerous asteroid field before skimming the second Death Star construction zone. You may come face-to-menacing-mask with Darth Vader, or meet favorite sage Yoda. Other characters sprinkled throughout the different films include Admiral Ackbar, Chewbacca, and Boba Fett. Your 40-passenger Starspeeder 1000 rockets through space with enough high-speed twists, turns, and nosedives to guarantee that the Force is, indeed, with you.

Those who are pregnant or have heart, back, neck, or motion-sickness issues shouldn't ride. Children less than 40 inches tall may not ride. **For people with disabilities:** Guests using wheelchairs must transfer to a ride seat. Equipped for handheld-captioning and video-captioning devices. Service animals aren't allowed. ■TIP➜ Lines swell when the Indiana Jones show lets out. Use a FastPass+ or visit early or late. For the wildest ride, sit in the back. ⊠ *Echo Lake* ☞ *Duration: 6 mins. Crowds: Heavy. Audience: All but Young Kids.*

■ NEED A BREAK? Sweet tooth acting up? Funnel cakes and soft-serve ice cream are the ticket at the Oasis Canteen. If you're ready for a heartier bite, **Min & Bill's Dockside Diner** is the spot for a jumbo turkey leg or Italian sausage and a shake. You can even buy a beer here. Step right up to the counter.

HOLLYWOOD STUDIOS SPECTACLES

Fantasmic!. The Studios' after-dark show wows huge audiences with its special effects and Disney characters. The omnipresent Mickey, in his Sorcerer's Apprentice costume, plays the embodiment of Good in the struggle against forces of Evil, personified by Disney villains such as Cruella DeVil, Scar, and Maleficent. Animated clips of these famous bad guys (and gals), alternating with clips of Disney nice guys (and dolls), are projected onto screens made of water—high-tech fountains surging high in the air. The epic battle plays out amid water effects and flames, explosions, and fireworks worthy of a Hollywood shoot-'em-up. All this, plus the villainous action, is why small kids may find this show frightening.

DISNEY'S HOLLYWOOD STUDIOS

NAME	Height Req.	Type of Entertainment	Duration	Crowds	Audience	Tips
Animation Courtyard						
Disney Junior—Live on Stage!	n/a	Show	24 mins.	Moderate to Heavy	Young Kids	Come first thing in the morning, when your child is most alert and lines are shorter.
The Magic of Disney Animation	n/a	Tour	15+ mins.	Moderate	All Ages	Come in the morning or late afternoon. Toddlers may get bored.
Voyage of the Little Mermaid	n/a	Show	15 mins.	Heavy	All Ages	Come first thing in the morning. Otherwise, wait until after 5.
Echo Lake						
Indiana Jones Epic Stunt Spectacular!	n/a	Show	30 mins.	Moderate to Heavy	All but Young Kids	Come at night, when the idol's eyes glow. Sit up front to feel the heat of a truck on fire.
★ Star Tours 3-D—The Adventure Continues	At least 40"	Simulator Exp.	6 mins.	Heavy	All but Young Kids	Get a FastPass+. Sit in rear for wildest ride.
Hollywood Boulevard						
Great Movie Ride	n/a	Ride/Tour	22 mins.	Moderate	All but Young Kids	Come while waiting for FastPass+ appointment. Lines out the door mean 25-min. wait—or longer.
Mickey Avenue						
Walt Disney: One Man's Dream	n/a	Walk-Through/ Film	15+ mins.	Light to Moderate	All but Young Kids	See this attraction while waiting for a FastPass+ appointment.

Pixar Place

Toy Story Midway Mania!	n/a	Interactive Ride	7 mins.	Heavy	All Ages	Come early; use FastPass+.

Streets of America

Honey, I Shrunk the Kids Movie Set Adventure	n/a	Playground	Up to you	Moderate	Young Kids	Come after you've done several shows and your kids need to cut loose. Keep an eye on toddlers who can quickly get lost in the caves and slides.
Lights, Motors, Action! Extreme Stunt Show	n/a	Show	38 mins.	Heavy	All but Young Kids	For the best seats, line up for the show while others are lining up for the parade.
Muppet*Vision 3-D	n/a	3-D Film	25 mins.	Moderate	All Ages	Arrive 10 mins. early. And don't worry—there are no bad seats.
For the First Time in Forever A "Frozen" Singalong Celebration*	n/a	Actors, film, music	30 mins.	Heavy	All Ages	Check showtimes in Studio Times Guide.

Sunset Boulevard

Beauty and the Beast—Live on Stage!	n/a	Show	30 mins.	Moderate to Heavy	All Ages	Come 30 mins. before showtime for good seats. Performance times vary, so check ahead. FastPass+ available for show fans.
★ Rock 'n' Roller Coaster Starring Aerosmith	At least 48"	Thrill Ride	1 min., 22 secs.	Huge	All but Young Kids	Ride early, then use FastPass+ for another go later.
★ Twilight Zone Tower of Terror	At least 40"	Thrill Ride	10 mins.	You Bet!	All but Young Kids	Use FastPass+. Come early or late evening.

*This new show is expected eventually to move to Echo Lake area in old American Idol Theater. But no word on when.

★ **Fodor's**Choice

HOLLYWOOD STUDIOS KIDS TOUR

Young children always get a kick out of Hollywood Boulevard's wacky street performers and the park's energetic stage shows.

The minute you enter, head straight to Toy Story Midway Mania! and get in line (unless you made a FastPass+ reservation). Everyone loves this busy ride—even young children who have to learn how to operate their spring-action shooters to rack up midway points. If you can ride *and* come back for your FastPass+ reservation, you'll be your kids' hero.

Now take a deep breath and lead the little ones to hands-on activities inside the Magic of Disney Animation (where they'll first enjoy a short film) and Honey, I Shrunk the Kids Movie Set Adventure, where they can whoop their way through a larger-than-life playground.

Combine lunch with more playtime at the Disney Junior Play 'n Dine at Hollywood & Vine family buffet, where characters from Disney Junior: Live on Stage! mix and mingle with the children. Don't forget your camera and the kids' autograph books!

SEE THE CHARACTERS COME TO LIFE

Shows and attractions based on Disney films and TV series really grab young children. Check your *Times Guide* for performances of Beauty and the Beast: Live on Stage and

Disney Junior: Live on Stage! After tots and preschoolers have danced along at the Disney Junior show, they can meet the characters in the Animation Courtyard, then catch a Beauty and the Beast performance or watch Ariel "under the sea" in *Voyage of the Little Mermaid.*

Check other character greeting locations and times—the Green Army Men from *Toy Story* put the kids through their marching paces on Pixar Place; Mickey Mouse or *The Incredibles* stars might turn up at the Magic of Disney Animation. Make time to meet Phineas and Ferb near Mama Melrose's Ristorante Italiano. Then watch Kermit display his wry wit and Miss Piggy steal the show at Muppet*Vision 3-D. It's not easy being green. . . .

GRAB THE SPOTLIGHT

Jedi wannabes can suit up to clash with the Dark Force at Jedi Training Academy, which is scheduled throughout the day. At the ABC Sound Studio near Star Tours, children ages 4–12 should sign up early in the day for a chance to grab a light saber and let the Force be with them. During each 20-minute show, crowds gather and cheer the kids as they learn to "cut to the left shoulder, step back, and duck!" when clashing with a costumed Darth Vader. Needless to say, the Dark Force can't compete.

Arrive early at the Hollywood Hills Amphitheater opposite the Twilight Zone Tower of Terror. Check ahead for information on show days and times. This show often runs twice nightly during peak season; fewer times during nonpeak periods. **For people with disabilities:** Wheelchair and ECV accessible. Equipped with reflective captioning and for assisted-listening, hand-held captioning, and audio-description devices.
■ TIP➡ FastPass+ seating is now offered. If you didn't book it, arrive at least an hour early and sit toward the rear, near the entrance/exit. Or

HOLLYWOOD STUDIOS GROWN-UP TOUR

At the Studios, movie classics like *The Wizard of Oz* and *Casablanca* come to life on the Great Movie Ride, and the best of Disney animation—from *Toy Story* to *Beauty and the Beast*—is reborn as park attractions. The old small-screen favorite *The Twilight Zone* is taken to new heights, and Indiana Jones performs action-packed stunts to bring famous film moments to life.

FIND YOUR ADRENALINE RUSH
Two words—thrills and chills—define the top two attractions for older kids and adults. Head straight to Sunset Boulevard and grab the thrills at Rock 'n' Roller Coaster Starring Aerosmith, where multiple inversions, twists, and turns rock to the tune of "Dude (Looks Like a Lady)." Feel the chills at the Twilight Zone Tower of Terror, when something goes terribly wrong with your elevator car, and it veers off its ghostly course.

A quick walk to Echo Lake lands you in Wookiee territory, where you can climb aboard the Star Tours flight simulator for a wild flight to the Moon of Endor; 3-D upgrades and more than 50 different ride scenarios increase the thrill factor.

DISCOVER YOUR TALENT
Are you an actor, an artist, a singer, or a midway-game fanatic? If the Citizens of Hollywood Talent Agent doesn't get your number, you can try out your act at one of several park attractions.

At the Indiana Jones Epic Stunt Spectacular! 10 guests are chosen to perform as show extras (arrive early and get noticed). All those years filling notebooks with doodles might just have been training for the Magic of Disney Animation Academy experience. At Toy Story Midway Mania! join Woody and Buzz for a manic midway ride past moving targets that test your spring-action-shooter mettle.

LEARN TRICKS OF THE TRADE
Refuel at one of the park's many quick-service stands, let "Mom" serve you meat loaf and a peanut butter–and-jelly shake at the '50s Prime Time Café, or boost your image with a plush booth and a Cobb salad at the Hollywood Brown Derby.

Then stroll the Streets of America before queuing up for a seat at the Lights, Motors, Action! Extreme Stunt Show and a peek at how high-speed vehicle action is shot.

Back at Echo Lake, the Tune-In Lounge is a great place to grab a mojito or margarita before heading to the nighttime extravaganza Fantasmic! That's a wrap.

consider the lunch or dinner package, which includes a special block of seating for the show. If you sit in front rows you will get wet. ✉ *Sunset Blvd.* ☞ *Duration: 30 mins. Crowds: Heavy. Audience: Not Small Kids.*

For the First Time in Forever: A "Frozen" Sing-Along Celebration. Ever since the Disney film *Frozen* hit the jackpot, Disney's theme parks have been mining the blockbuster with character meet and greets, entertainment vignettes, and, now, a half-hour show that's packing the house up to 10 times a day. The show launched in the park's outdoor Premiere Theater along Streets of America and is expected to move into the cushier former American Idol theater. The show's comical emcees are two costumed

"Royal Historians" of Arendelle, who pepper the 30-minute show with witticisms as they narrate the *Frozen* story. Animated segments of the film accompany the narration on a giant screen as the story unfolds and the audience sings along to the film's playlist. Live actors portray Anna, Elsa, and Kristoff convincingly as they interact with the "historians" and audience. Kids in the audience rock the Academy Award–winning "Let It Go" most enthusiastically and can't resist the sweetly melodic "Do You Want to Build a Snowman?" Song lyrics, including those for Olaf's whimsical anthem, "In Summer," as well as "For the First Time in Forever," and "Love Is an Open Door," are displayed for the audience on two additional video screens. **For people with disabilities:** Wheelchair accessible. ■TIP→ **FastPass+ is available and recommended.** ⊠ *Echo Lake* ☞ *Duration: 30 mins. Crowds: Heavy. Audience: All Ages.*

2

ANIMAL KINGDOM

If you're thinking, "Oh, it's just another zoo, let's skip it," think again. Walt Disney World's fourth theme park, opened in 1998, takes its inspiration from humankind's enduring love for animals and pulls out all the stops. Your day will be packed with unusual animal encounters, enchanting entertainment, and themed rides that'll leave you breathless.

A large chunk of the park is devoted to animal habitats, especially the forest and savanna of Africa's Kilimanjaro Safaris. Towering acacia trees and tall grasses sweep across the land where antelopes, giraffes, and wildebeests roam. A lion kopje, warthog burrows, a zebra habitat, and an elephant watering hole provide ample space for inhabitants.

About 94 acres contain foliage like hibiscus and mulberry, perfect for antelope and many other species. The largest groups of Nile hippos and African elephants in North America live along the winding waterway that leads to the savanna. The generously landscaped Pangani Forest Exploration Trail provides roaming grounds for troops of gorillas and authentic habitats for meerkats, birds, fish, and other creatures.

Beyond the park's Africa territory, similar large spaces are set aside for the homes of Asian animals like tigers and giant fruit bats, as well as for creatures such as Galápagos tortoises and a giant anteater.

Disney Imagineers didn't forget to include their trademark thrills, from the Kali River Rapids ride in Asia to the fast-paced DINOSAUR journey in DinoLand U.S.A. Expedition Everest, the park's biggest thrill attraction, is a "runaway" train ride on a faux rugged mountain complete with icy ledges, dark caves, and a yeti legend. Next up: Imagineers are building a new land in the former Camp Minnie-Mickey location based on the blockbuster film *Avatar* and expected sequels.

Although you won't find a parade or a fireworks show, several live entertainment ensembles perform, including the popular Tam Tam Drummers of Harambe.

TOP ATTRACTIONS

AFRICA

Festival of the Lion King. Singers and dancers dressed in fantastic costumes representing many wild animals perform uplifting dance and acrobatics numbers and interact with children in the audience.

Kilimanjaro Safaris. You're guaranteed to see dozens of wild animals, including giraffes, gazelles, hippos, rhinos, zebras, and elephants, living in authentic, re-created African habitats. If you're lucky, the lions and cheetahs will be stirring, too.

ASIA

Expedition Everest. This roller coaster is a spine-tingling trip into the snowy Himalayas to find the abominable snowman. It's best reserved for brave riders 7 and up.

DINOLAND U.S.A

DINOSAUR. Extremely lifelike giant dinosaurs jump out as your vehicle swoops and dips. We recommend it for fearless kids 8 and up.

Finding Nemo: The Musical. Don't miss a performance of this outstanding musical starring the most charming, colorful characters ever to swim their way into your heart.

DISCOVERY ISLAND

Tree of Life: It's Tough to be a Bug! This clever and very funny 3-D movie starring Flik from the Disney film *A Bug's Life* is full of surprises, including "shocking" special effects. Some young children are scared of the loud noises.

TOUR

Wild Africa Trek. The price tag is hefty, but this behind-the-scenes wild-animal adventure is a memory maker.

The only downside to the Animal Kingdom layout is that walking paths and spaces can get very crowded and hot in the warmest months. Your best bet is to arrive very early and see the animals first before the heat makes them (and you) woozy.

Just before the park opens, Minnie Mouse, Pluto, and Goofy arrive at the iconic Tree of Life in a safari vehicle to welcome the first guests into the heart of the park. Let the adventure begin!

ORIENTATION AND PLANNING

GETTING ORIENTED

Animal Kingdom's hub is the Tree of Life, in the middle of Discovery Island. The park's lands, each with a distinct personality, radiate from Discovery Island. To the southwest, home of the former Camp Minnie-Mickey, Disney Imagineers are creating the new land of Pandora based on the *Avatar* film and upcoming sequels. The new area is expected to open in 2017. North of the hub is Africa, where Kilimanjaro Safaris travel across extensive savanna. In the northeast corner is Rafiki's Planet Watch with conservation activities.

Asia, with thrills like Expedition Everest and Kali River Rapids, is east of the hub, and DinoLand U.S.A brings *T. rex* and other prehistoric creatures to life in the park's southeast corner.

If you're staying on-site, you can take a Disney bus to the Entrance Plaza. If you drive, the $17 parking fee allows you to park at other Disney lots throughout the day.

Although this is technically Disney's largest theme park, most of the land is reserved for the animals. Pedestrian areas are actually quite compact, with relatively narrow passageways. The only way to get around is on foot or in a wheelchair or electronic convenience vehicle (ECV).

ANIMAL KINGDOM PLANNER

PARK AMENITIES

Baby Care: At Discovery Island you can stop in to nurse babies in the quiet baby-care center, which is equipped with rocking chairs and low lighting. There are changing tables, which are also available in restrooms (including some men's restrooms), and you can buy disposable diapers, formula, baby food, and pacifiers.

Cameras: You can buy film and digital memory cards at several shops throughout the park. If a Disney photographer takes your picture, sign up for a Disney PhotoPass—later, you can view and purchase the pictures online ($199 for full digital Memory Maker access) or at the park's photo center in the Oasis.

First Aid: The first-aid center, staffed by registered nurses, is in Discovery Island, and at least a dozen automated external defibrillators are in key park areas.

Guest Relations: This office will help with tickets at a window to the left just before you pass through the turnstile. Once you've entered, Guest Relations staffers in the Oasis can provide park maps, schedules, and answers to questions. They can also assist with dining reservations, ticket upgrades, and services for guests with disabilities.

Lockers: Lockers are in Guest Relations in the Oasis. Rental fees are $7 to $9 (depending on size) for a day plus a $5 key deposit.

Lost People and Things: Instruct your kids to speak to someone with a Disney name tag if you become separated. Lost children are taken to the baby-care center, where they can watch Disney movies, or to Guest Relations, whichever is closer. If you do lose your child, contact any cast member immediately and Disney security personnel will be notified.

Animal Kingdom Lost and Found: To retrieve lost articles on the same day, visit or call Lost and Found, which is at Guest Relations. ✉ *Oasis* ☎ *407/938–2785*.

Main Lost and Found: If more than a day has passed since you've lost something, contact the Main Lost and Found office at the Magic Kingdom Ticket and Transportation Center. ☎ *407/824–4245*.

Package Pick-Up: You can have shop clerks forward purchases to Package Pick-Up near the Main Entrance in the Oasis, so that you won't have to carry them around all day. Allow three hours for the journey. If you're staying at a Disney hotel, you also can have packages delivered there.

Services for People with Disabilities: Guests using wheelchairs will have ready access to restaurants, shops, and most attractions—including the Finding Nemo: The Musical theater in DinoLand U.S.A, and the Tree of Life theater showing *It's Tough to be a Bug!* (Theaters also are accessible to ECVs.) Some monitor-equipped attractions have reflective-captioning boxes.

Scripts and story lines for all attractions are available, and you can book sign-language interpreters with notice of two or more weeks. Large Braille park maps are by Guest Relations and near the Tip Board at the entrance to Discovery Island. Guest Relations is also where you can borrow assisted-listening, handheld-captioning, and video-captioning devices with a refundable deposit. Service animals are allowed in most, but not all, areas of the park.

You can rent wheelchairs ($12 daily, $10 for multiple days) and ECVs ($50 per day plus a refundable $20 security deposit) at Garden Gate Gifts in the Oasis. You can't, however, reserve these items, so arrive early to get one—particularly if you want an ECV.

Stroller Rentals: Garden Gate Gifts in the Oasis rents strollers. Singles are $15 daily, $13 multiday; doubles run $31 daily, $27 multiday.

TOURS

Animal Kingdom Guided Tours. For a closer look at the park's animals and habitats, call WDW Tours to reserve a behind-the-scenes tour. ☏ *407/939–8687.*

Backstage Safari. This tour ($72) takes an in-depth look at animal conservation, stopping at the state-of-the-art veterinary hospital and other behind-the-scenes areas. It's a great way to learn about animal behaviors and how handlers manage a diverse population of critters in captivity. The tour includes the park's Kilimanjaro Safaris ride, so you will see plenty of exotic creatures in their habitats. Participants must be at least 16 years old. ☏ *407/939–8687 ✉ $72 plus park admission ☼ Daily.*

Fodor'sChoice
★   **Wild Africa Trek.** You and 11 other guests will cover exciting new ground on this three-hour, walking-riding adventure into unexplored areas of the park. For a close-up view of the hippos, you'll wear a special vest with a harness that's tethered to a rail at the edge of a bluff. You'll cross a rope bridge above a pool of Nile crocodiles. Your exclusive open-air safari vehicle makes multiple stops for leisurely viewing of giraffes, wildebeests, cheetahs, and other creatures of the savanna. Burning all those calories pays off when breakfast or lunch treats are served (think prosciutto, Brie, fresh fruit) at the open-air Boma Landing on the edge of the savanna. The tour is good for anyone age 8 and older who's fit. Included in the admission price is a CD-photo souvenir of your trek. A portion of the tour price is donated to the Disney Worldwide Conservation Fund. ☏ *407/939–8687 ✉ $189–$249 depending on season; park admission also required ☼ Up to 8 times daily, beginning at 8 am.*

VISITING TIPS

■ Try to visit during the week. Pedestrian areas are compact, and the park can feel uncomfortably packed on weekends.

- Plan on a full day here. That way, while exploring Africa's Pangani Forest Exploration Trail, say, you can spend 10 minutes (rather than just two) watching vigilant meerkats stand sentry or tracking a mama gorilla as she cares for her youngster.

- Arrive a half hour before the park opens as much to see the wild animals at their friskiest (morning is a good time to do the safari ride) as to get a jump on the crowds.

- For updates on line lengths, check the Tip Board, just after crossing the bridge into Discovery Island.

- Good places to rendezvous include the outdoor Dawa Bar or Tamu Tamu Refreshments areas in Africa, in front of DinoLand U.S.A's Boneyard, or on one of the benches outside Expedition Everest in Asia.

EXPLORING ANIMAL KINGDOM

THE OASIS

This entrance makes you feel as if you've been plunked down in the middle of a rain forest. Cool mist, the aroma of flowers, playful animals, and colorful birds enliven a miniature landscape of streams and grottoes, waterfalls, and glades fringed with banana leaves and jacaranda. It's also where you can take care of essentials before entering. Here you'll find guide maps, stroller and wheelchair rentals, Guest Relations, and an ATM.

DISCOVERY ISLAND

The park hub and site of the Tree of Life, this island is encircled by Discovery River, which isn't an actual attraction but makes for attractive views from the bridge to Harambe and another between Asia and DinoLand U.S.A. The island's whimsical architecture, with wood carvings from Bali, lends charm and a touch of fantasy. The Discovery Island Trails that lead to the Tree of Life provide habitats for African crested porcupines, lemurs, Galápagos tortoises, and other creatures you won't want to miss.

You'll discover some great shops and good counter-service eateries here. Visitor services that aren't in the Oasis are here, on the border with Harambe, including the baby-care center and the first-aid center.

Fodor's Choice ★ **Tree of Life—*It's Tough to be a Bug!*.** A monument to all Earth's creatures, the park's centerpiece is an imposing 14 stories high and 50 feet wide at its base. Its 100,000-plus leaves are several shades of green fabric, each carefully placed for a realistic effect. Carved into its thick trunk, gnarled roots, and soaring branches—some of which are supported by joints that allow them to sway in a strong wind—are nearly 350 intricate animal forms that include a baboon, a whale, a horse, the mighty lion, and even an ankylosaurus. Outside, paths tunnel underneath the roots as the fauna-encrusted trunk towers overhead.

The path leads you inside the tree trunk, where you get a bug's-eye view of life. The witty 3-D film adventure *It's Tough to be a Bug!* is modeled on the animated film *A Bug's Life* from Disney-Pixar. Special effects spray you with "poison," zap you with a swatter, and even poke you with a stinger—all in good fun.

RAFIKI'S PLANET WATCH

Affection Section

Conservation Station

Habitat Habit!

Wildlife Express Train

SAFARI AREA

Wildlife Express Train

Pangani Forest Exploration Trail

AFRICA

Mombasa Marketplace

Kilimanjaro Safaris

Harambe Fruit Market

Kusafiri Coffee Shop & Bakery

Tusker House Restaurant

Festival of the Lion King

KEY

✕   *Restaurants*

🚻   *Restrooms*

••••   *Parade Route*

0   200 yards

0   200 m

Disney's Animal Kingdom

ASIA

Expedition Everest

Serka Zong Bazaar

Kali River Rapids

Anandapur Ice Cream Truck

Maharajah Jungle Trek

Finding Nemo— The Musical

Discovery River

Dino Diner

Primeval Whirl

Fossil Fun Games

Yak & Yeti Restaurant

Flights of Wonder

Boneyard

TriceraTop Spin

ATM

Chester Hester's Dinosaur Treasures

Upcountry

Beastly Kiosk

Bradley Falls

Mr Kamal's

Gardens Kiosk

Flame Tree Barbecue

Trilo-Bites

DINOLAND U.S.A.

The Dino Institute Shop

Dino-Bite Snacks

DinoSue

Tree of Life, It's Tough to Be a Bug!

DISCOVERY ISLAND

Disney Outfitters

Restaurantosaurus

DINOSAUR

Tamu Tamu Refreshments

Discovery Island Ice Cream

Discovery Island Trails

Tips and Showtimes

Isle of Java

Dawa Bar

Island Mercantile

Garden Gate Gifts

First Aid/ Baby Care Center

Pizzafari

Strollers & Wheelchairs

ATM

OASIS

Entrance

Lockers

Guest Relations

COMING SOON: AVATAR

Guest Relations

Rainforest Café

Although the show has something for all ages, it's very loud. Some effects frighten young children. **For people with disabilities:** Wheelchair accessible, but, to fully experience all the special effects, guests using wheelchairs should transfer to a seat. Equipped with reflective captioning and for audio-description and assisted-listening devices. If you have a service animal, check with a host before entering the theater. ■ TIP➜ **FastPass+ is offered; enter across from the Disney Outfitters store via the Discovery Island Trails.** ⊠ *Discovery Island* ☞ *Duration: 20 mins. Crowds: Moderate to Heavy. Audience: All but Young Kids.*

DINOLAND U.S.A

Just as it sounds, this is the place to come in contact with re-created prehistoric creatures, including the fear-inspiring carnotaurus and the gentle iguanodon. The landscaping includes live plants that have evolved over the last 65 million years. In collaboration with Chicago's Field Museum, Disney displays a complete, full-scale skeleton cast of Dino-Sue—also known as "Sue"—the 65-million-year-old *Tyrannosaurus rex* discovered near the Black Hills of South Dakota.

After admiring Sue, you can go on the thrilling DINOSAUR ride, play in the Boneyard, or take in the Finding Nemo: The Musical show at the Theater in the Wild. Kids will want to try the TriceraTop Spin and the Primeval Whirl family coaster, which has spinning "time machines." There's no need to dig for souvenirs at Chester and Hester's Dinosaur Treasures gift shop—all you need is your wallet.

NEED A BREAK?

Famished, but not much time for lunch? Make tracks for a counter-service burger and fries or a hearty salad at Restaurantosaurus and you'll be ready to take on *T. rex*.

The Boneyard. Youngsters can slide, dig, bounce, slither, and stomp around this archaeological dig site–cum–playground, the finest play area in any of the four Disney parks. In addition to a huge sand pit where children can dig for mammoth bones, there are twisting short and long slides, climbing nets, caves, and a jeep to climb on. Stomp on the dino footprints to make 'em roar. **For people with disabilities:** This fossil play maze is wheelchair accessible. ■ TIP➜ **Let the kids burn off energy here while waiting for a FastPass+ appointment. Or head over late in the day when kids need to run free.** ⊠ *DinoLand U.S.A.* ☞ *Duration: Up to You. Crowds: Moderate to Heavy. Audience: Young Kids.*

DINOSAUR. This wild adventure through time puts you face-to-face with huge dinosaurs that move and breathe with uncanny realism. When a carload of guests rouses a cantankerous carnotaurus from his Cretaceous slumber, it's showtime. You travel back 65 million years on a fast-paced, twisting adventure and try to save the last living iguanodon as a massive asteroid hurtles toward Earth. Exciting Audio-Animatronics and special effects bring to life dinosaurs like the raptor, pterodactyl, styracosaurus, alioramus, and compsognathus. Be prepared for a short but jolting drop toward the end of the ride.

Guests who are pregnant or have back, neck, or heart problems should avoid this very bumpy ride. The jostling and realistic carnivores may frighten young children. **For people with disabilities:** You must transfer from your wheelchair to board this ride. Equipped for video-captioning and assisted-listening devices. No service animals. ■TIP➜ **Come first thing in the morning or at the end of the day, or use FastPass+.** ✉ *Di-noLand U.S.A. ⌖ Duration: Under 4 mins. Crowds: Heavy. Audience: All but Young Kids. Height minimum: 40 inches.*

Timing Tip: Because of the proximity of the two attractions, Finding Nemo: The Musical is a good place to take younger kids while older siblings do Expedition Everest.

Fodor's Choice
★

Finding Nemo–The Musical. The performance of this fish tale is so cre-ative and fun that many have likened it to a first-rate Broadway show. Indeed, Disney Imagineers collaborated with several Broadway tal-ents to produce it. Original songs by Tony Award–winning *Avenue Q* co-composer-creator Robert Lopez and a-cappella musical *Along the Way* co-creator Kristen Anderson-Lopez add depth and energy. Michael Curry, who co-designed the character puppets of Broadway's *The Lion King*, also created this show's eye-popping puppetry.

Multigenerational humor, special effects, and larger-than-life puppets acted by gifted performers, dancers, and acrobats all bring you into Nemo's world. The sweet story remains the same as in the movie—Nemo and his father, Marlin, go on separate journeys that teach them how to understand each other. Zany Dory, with her memory lapses, Crush the sea turtle dude, tap-dancing sharks, and others give memo-rable supporting-role turns. **For people with disabilities:** Wheelchair accessible. Equipped with reflective captioning and for audio descrip-tion and assisted-listening devices. Check with Guest Relations for sign-language schedule. ■TIP➜ **Arrange a FastPass+ or arrive 30 to 40 minutes before showtime. Bring little kids here while older tweens and teens ride Expedition Everest.** ✉ *DinoLand U.S.A. ⌖ Duration: 40 mins. Crowds: Heavy. Audience: All Ages.*

Fossil Fun Games. A carnival-style midway in the middle of DinoLand U.S.A., this fun fair draws crowds with games like Whack a Packy-cephalosaur and the mallet-strength challenge, Dino-Whamma. The prehistoric fun comes at a price, however, and stone currency is not accepted. Prizes are mostly of the plush-character variety—you might win your sweetheart a stuffed Nala. **For people with disabilities:** Wheel-chair accessible. ■TIP➜ **It costs $4 a game, or $10 for 3 games. Bring a pocketful of change and a stash of ones.** ✉ *DinoLand U.S.A. ⌖ Dura-tion: Up to You. Crowds: Light. Audience: All Ages.*

Primeval Whirl. In a free-spinning, four-passenger vehicle, you head on a brief journey back in time on this outdoor open-air coaster, twisting, turning, and even venturing into the jaws of a dinosaur "skeleton." Crazy cartoon dinosaurs in shades of turquoise, orange, yellow, and purple pop up along the track bearing signs that warn "The End Is Near." More signs alert you to incoming "Meteors!" and suggest that you "Head for the Hills!"—coaster hills, that is. Halfway through the ride, your car seems to spin out of control and you take the next drop backward. The more weight in the vehicle, the more you spin.

Pregnant women or guests with back, neck, or heart problems should skip this one. **For people with disabilities:** Guests using wheelchairs

ANIMAL KINGDOM

NAME	Height Req.	Type of Entertainment	Duration	Crowds	Audience	Tips
Africa						
★ Festival of the Lion King	n/a	Show	30 mins.	Moderate	All Ages	Book a FastPass+ or arrive 30–40 mins. before showtime. Sit in one of the front rows to increase your kid's chance of being chosen to participate in a show number.
★ Kilimanjaro Safaris	n/a	Riding Tour	22 mins.	Moderate to Heavy	All Ages	Do this first thing in the morning or use FastPass+. If you arrive at the park late morning, save it for day's end, when animals may be more active.
Pangani Forest Exploration Trail	n/a	Zoo/Aviary	Up to you	Light to Moderate	All Ages	Come while waiting for your safari FastPass+; try to avoid coming at the hottest time of day, when the gorillas like to nap.
Asia						
★ Expedition Everest	At least 44"	Thrill Ride	2½ mins.	Huge	All but Young Kids	Arrive early or use FastPass+. This is the park's biggest thrill ride.
Flights of Wonder	n/a	Show	25 mins.	Light	All Ages	Arrive 15 mins. before showtime, and find a shaded seat beneath one of the awnings—the sun can be brutal.
Kali River Rapids	At least 38"	Thrill Ride	7 mins.	Heavy	All but Young Kids	Use your FastPass+ or come during the parade. You'll get wet.
Maharajah Jungle Trek	n/a	Zoo/Aviary	Up to you	Light to Moderate	All Ages	Come anytime.
DinoLand U.S.A.						
Boneyard	n/a	Playground	Up to you	Moderate to Heavy	Young Kids	Play here while waiting for DINOSAUR FastPass+, or come late in the day.

Attraction	Height	Type	Duration	Crowds	Audience	Notes
★ DINOSAUR	At least 40"	Thrill Ride	4 mins.	Heavy	All but Young Kids	Come first thing in the morning or at the end of the day, or use FastPass+.
Finding Nemo–The Musical	n/a	Show	40 mins.	Heavy	All Ages	Arrive 40 mins. before showtime or book a FastPass+. Take young kids here while older kids wait for Expedition Everest.
Fossil Fun Games	n/a	Arcade/Fair	Up to you	Light	All Ages	Bring a stash of ones to buy play tickets.
Primeval Whirl	At least 48"	Thrill Ride	2½ mins.	Heavy	All but Young Kids	Kids may want to ride twice. Take your first spin early, then use FastPass+ if the wait is more than 20 mins.
TriceraTop Spin	n/a	Thrill Ride for Young Kids	2 mins.	Heavy	Young Kids	Ride early while everyone else heads for the safari or while waiting for your FastPass+ appointment for DINOSAUR.
Discovery Island						
★ Tree of Life—It's Tough to Be a Bug!	n/a	3-D film	20 mins.	Moderate to Heavy	All but Young Kids	Do this after Kilimanjaro Safaris or Expedition Everest. Small children may be frightened at creepy crawly moments in the dark.
Rafiki's Planet Watch						
Affection Section	n/a	Petting Yard	Up to you	Light	All Ages	Pet exotic goats and other rare domesticated animals.
Conservation Station	n/a	Walk-Through	Up to you	Light to Moderate	All Ages	Wait for the critter encounter and learn how to protect endangered species.
Habitat Habit!	n/a	Trail Walk	Up to you	Light	All Ages	Watch cotton-top tamarins along this discovery trail.
Wildlife Express Train	n/a	Train Ride	5 mins.	Moderate	All Ages	Head straight to Affection Section with little kids to come face-to-face with domesticated critters.

must transfer to the ride vehicle. No service animals. ■TIP→ FastPass+ is recommended. **Kids might want to ride twice if the wait isn't long.** ⊠ *DinoLand U.S.A.* ☞ *Duration: 2½ mins. Crowds: Heavy. Audience: All but Young Kids. Height minimum: 48 inches.*

TriceraTop Spin. TriceraTop Spin is designed for playful little dinophiles who ought to get a kick out of whirling around this ride's giant spinning toy top and dodging incoming comets in their dino mobiles. "Pop!" goes the top and out comes a grinning dinosaur as four passengers in each vehicle fly in a circle and maneuver up and down. **For people with disabilities:** Wheelchair accessible, but guests using ECVs must transfer to standard wheelchairs. ■TIP→ **Ride early or take little ones while older kids are riding DINOSAUR or Primeval Whirl.** ⊠ *DinoLand U.S.A.* ☞ *Duration: 2 mins. Crowds: Heavy. Audience: Young Kids.*

ASIA

Meant to resemble an Asian village, this land is full of remarkable rainforest scenery and ruins. Groupings of trees grow from a crumbling tiger shrine, and massive towers—representing Thailand and Nepal—are the habitat for gibbons, whose hooting fills the air.

Fodor'sChoice
★

Expedition Everest—Legend of the Forbidden Mountain. A fierce yeti guards the route to Mt. Everest. Of course, you're willing to risk running across the big guy in your roller-coaster quest to reach the summit. So, you board an "aging," seemingly innocuous, 34-passenger, steam-engine train into the mountains. You roll past bamboo forests, waterfalls, and glacier fields as you climb higher through snowcapped peaks. Suddenly the train becomes a runaway, barreling forward then backward around icy ledges and through dark snowy caverns.

Nearly a mile of twists and turns cut through the dark mountain, and at one point your train plunges a harrowing 80 feet. Will you find the yeti? Buildings along the queue look like Himalayan mountain dwellings and teem with things like prayer flags, totems, and other artifacts from Tibet, Nepal, and the entire region.

Since the coaster is supposed to be less intense than, say, Space Mountain, brave children who meet the 44-inch minimum-height requirement can ride. Pregnant women or guests with back, neck, or heart problems shouldn't ride. **For people with disabilities:** You must transfer from your wheelchair to a ride vehicle; ask a cast member about the Transfer Practice Vehicle. No service animals. ■TIP→ **Unless you prefer to see the animals first, rush here as soon as the park opens and the wait isn't too long. Otherwise, grab a FastPast+ or choose the Single Rider Queue.** ⊠ *Asia* ☞ *Duration: 2½ mins. Crowds: Huge. Audience: Anyone 44 inches or taller.*

Flights of Wonder. This outdoor show area near the border with Africa has spectacular demonstrations of skill by falcons, hawks, owls, cranes, and other rare birds, which swoop down over the audience. Twenty species of birds are part of the show, including the bald eagle. **For people with disabilities:** Wheelchair accessible. Sign-language interpretation sometimes offered. Equipped for assisted-listening devices. ■TIP→ **Check the Times Guide for showtimes and arrive 15 minutes**

On Asia's Expedition Everest, you'll chug, twist, turn, and plunge up, through, and down Mt. Everest on nearly a mile of track. Oh, yeah, and beware of the yeti!

ahead to find a shaded seat beneath one of the awnings. ⊠ *Asia* ☞ *Duration: 25 mins. Crowds: Light. Audience: All Ages.*

Kali River Rapids. Asia's thrilling water adventure ride mixes the fun of a rafting experience with a solemn message to save pristine lands and animal habitats that are threatened by development. Aboard a round raft that seats 12, you run the Chakranadi River. After passing through a huge bamboo tunnel filled with jasmine-scented mist, your raft climbs 40 feet upriver, lurches and spins through sharp twists and turns, and then approaches an immense waterfall, which curtains a giant carved tiger face. Past rain forests and temple ruins, you find yourself face-to-face with the denuded slope of a logged-out woodland burning out of control. There are many more thrills, but why spill the beans?

You will get wet and you may get soaked. Unless you want to wring out your clothing in the nearest restroom afterward, bring a poncho. Better yet, bring a change of clothing in a plastic bag. The ride-height minimum is 38 inches. If you are pregnant or have heart, back, neck, or motion-sickness problems, sit this one out. **For people with disabilities:** Guests using wheelchairs must transfer to a ride raft. No service animals. ■ TIP→ **Use FastPass+ to avoid a long wait.** ⊠ *Asia* ☞ *Duration: 7 mins. Crowds: Heavy. Audience: All but Young Kids.*

Maharajah Jungle Trek. Get an up-close view of some unusual animals along this trail, including giant fruit bats that hang to munch fruit from wires and fly very close to the open and glass-protected viewing areas and Bengal tigers in front of a maharajah's palace ruins. The tigers have their own view (with no accessibility, of course) of Asian deer and black buck, an antelope species. At the end of the trek, you walk through an aviary with a lotus pool. Disney interpreters, many from Asian countries, are on hand to answer questions. **For people with disabilities:** Wheelchair accessible; equipped for audio-description devices. Guests with service animals should check with a host before entering the aviary. ■TIP→ **Come anytime. Crowds stay fairly light, as people are constantly on the move.** ⊠ *Asia* ☞ *Duration: Up to You. Crowds: Light. Audience: All Ages.*

AFRICA

The largest of the lands is an area of forests and grasslands, predominantly an enclave for wildlife from the continent. Harambe, on the northern bank of Discovery River, is Africa's starting point. Inspired by several East African villages, this Disney town has so much detail that it's mind-boggling to try to soak it all up. Signs on the apparently peeling stucco walls are faded, as if bleached by the sun, and everything has a hot, dusty look. For souvenirs with Disney and African themes, browse through the Mombasa Marketplace and Ziwani Traders.

NEED A BREAK?
The tantalizing aroma of fresh-baked cinnamon buns leads to the **Kusafiri Coffee Shop & Bakery**, where, after just one look, you may give in to the urge. These buns are worth the banknotes, and they pair well with a cappuccino or espresso. Kids may opt for a giant cookie and milk.

Fodor's Choice ★
Festival of the Lion King. If you think you've seen enough *Lion King* to last a lifetime, you're wrong, unless you've seen this show. Disney presents a delightful tribal celebration of song, dance, and acrobatics that uses huge moving stages and floats. The show's singers are first-rate; lithe dancers wearing exotic animal-theme costumes portray creatures in the wild. Timon, Pumba, and other *Lion King* stars have key roles. Once located in the park's former Camp Minnie-Mickey land (which now is part of the under-construction Avatar land), the show has moved to the new Harambe Theater in the park's Africa area. **For people with disabilities:** Wheelchair and ECV accessible; equipped for assisted-listening and handheld-captioning devices; sign-language interpretation is sometimes offered. ■TIP→ **FastPass+ is now offered. Without one, arrive 30–40 minutes before showtime. If you have a child who might want to go on stage, try to sit up front to increase his or her chance of getting chosen.** ⊠ *Africa* ☞ *Duration: 30 mins. Crowds: Moderate to Heavy. Audience: All Ages.*

Fodor's Choice ★
Kilimanjaro Safaris. A giant Imagineered baobab tree is the starting point for this adventure into the upcountry. Although re-creating an African safari in the United States isn't a new idea, this safari takes great pains to create an authentic environment, allowing you to observe rhinos, hippos, antelopes, wildebeests, giraffes, zebras, cheetahs, elephants, lions, and the like. There are illustrated game-spotting guides above the seats in the open-air safari vehicles, and as you lurch and bump over some 110 acres of savanna, forest, rivers, and rocky hills, you'll see most of the Harambe Reserve's 34 species of animals—sometimes so close you feel that you could reach out and touch them. It's easy to suspend disbelief here because the landscape and habitats are so effectively modeled and replenished by Disney horticulturists. Keep an eye out for

A silverback gorilla from Kilimanjaro Safaris

animal babies here and on the post-safari Pangani Forest Exploration Trail; the park's breeding programs have been extremely successful, with new additions including elephants, rhinos, okapi, giraffes, and several gorillas.

Parents should hang on tightly to their small tykes. The ride is very bumpy and should be avoided by expectant guests or those with heart, back, or neck problems. **For people with disabilities:** Wheelchair accessible, but ECV users must transfer to standard wheelchairs. Equipped for assisted-listening and video-captioning devices. Guests with service animals should check with a host for boarding information. ■ TIP→ **During the hottest months, come first thing in the morning when animals are most active, using FastPass+ if necessary. Otherwise come at day's end when it cools down a bit. For best photo ops, ask to be seated in the very last row of seats (you may have to wait for the next vehicle) where you can pivot for an unobstructed view of the animals you just passed.** ⊠ *Africa* ☞ *Duration: 18 mins. Crowds: Moderate to Heavy. Audience: All Ages.*

Pangani Forest Exploration Trail. Calling this a nature walk doesn't really do it justice. A path winds through dense foliage, alongside streams, and past waterfalls. En route there are viewing points where you can watch a beautiful rare okapi (a member of the giraffe family) munching the vegetation, a family and a separate bachelor group of lowland gorillas, hippos (which you usually can see underwater), comical meerkats (a kind of mongoose), exotic birds, and a bizarre colony of hairless mole rats. Native African interpreters are at many viewing points to answer questions. **For people with disabilities:** Wheelchair accessible

The Tree of Life is the iconic centerpiece of Disney's Animal Kingdom.

and equipped for audio-description devices. Guests with service animals should check with a host before entering. ■TIP➜ **Come while awaiting a Kilimanjaro Safaris FastPass+ appointment or just after you exit your safari vehicle; avoid coming at the hottest time of day, when the gorillas like to nap.** ⊠ *Africa* ☞ *Duration: Up to You. Crowds: Moderate to Heavy. Audience: All Ages.*

RAFIKI'S PLANET WATCH

While in the Harambe, Africa, section, board the 250-passenger rustic Wildlife Express steam train for a ride to a unique center of eco-awareness named for the wise baboon from *The Lion King*. Young children especially enjoy the chance to explore these three animal-friendly areas.

Affection Section. In this petting zoo, children and adults can pet and even borrow brushes to groom goats, sheep, donkeys, and other domesticated creatures. **For people with disabilities:** Guests must transfer from ECVs to standard wheelchairs. No service animals are allowed in this area. ■TIP➜ **If you visit at the right time, you might see pigs demonstrate how they've learned to paint with their snouts.** ⊠ *Rafiki's Planet Watch* ☞ *Duration: Up to You. Crowds: Light to Moderate. Audience: All Ages; Mostly Children.*

Conservation Station. This is a great place to meet some of the park's animal handlers and to gather round for a critter encounter. You'll learn about the park's veterinary care, ongoing research, and food preparation for hundreds of animal inhabitants. Interactive exhibits are simple fun for younger children and have messages about worldwide efforts to protect endangered species and their habitats. Here, you also can find out how to connect with conservation efforts in your own community.

ANIMAL KINGDOM GROWN-UP TOUR

When the park first opened, Disney went to great marketing lengths to be sure visitors would know that this is "Nahtazu" (as in "not-a-zoo"). Adults and older children needed assurance that there was plenty to do besides see animals. And there is. Several thrill rides, a hilarious 3-D-and-special-effects-laden film, and two Broadway-style shows with animal and conservation themes can fill a memorable day.

ADVENTURE SEEKERS WANTED

If a trip to the Himalayas is on your wish list, but your budget says dream on, make a beeline for Asia and **Expedition Everest.** If there's a wait for the attraction's high-speed train ride, the queue snakes through authentic rammed-earth and stacked-stone buildings of a Himalayan village, where museum-quality artifacts from Nepal and Tibet are worth browsing. While in Asia, pile into a **Kali River Rapids** raft for a white-water ride on the park's Chakranadi River.

Time-travel back to **DinoLand U.S.A** for a DINOSAUR journey through a primeval forest and white-knuckle encounters with carnivorous creatures like the razor-toothed carnotaurus, a swooping pterodactyl, and other menacing creatures of prehistoric doom.

If it's a cool day, the park's animals should be active, so head to Africa. Your **Kilimanjaro Safaris** open-air journey is a bumpy 20-minute quest for exotic-animal sightings, and you won't be disappointed. Adventurous guests with dollars to spare should sign up for the park's Wild Africa Trek. It's one of Disney's most thrilling guided tours.

EAT, SHOP, LAUGH

Dining can be an adventure, too, at **Tusker House Restaurant** in Africa, where a colorful buffet of vegetables and carved meats is enhanced with African-inspired chutneys, hummus, spiced tandoori tofu, and couscous salad. You can even sip on an African margarita or a sugar-cane mojito as you savor the exotic flavors.

Burn the calories during a shopping excursion to **Mombasa Market-place,** where you can buy a bottle of South African wine or pick up hand-painted dishes from Zimbabwe. Onward to Discovery Island for a stroll along Discovery Island Trails into the Tree of Life show It's Tough to be a Bug! Expect to laugh a lot.

DISCOVER ANIMAL ATTRACTION

Along the **Pangani Forest Exploration Trail,** you can view gorillas both through a glassed-in area and from a bridge as these magnificent primates move among the rocks and lush greenery.

Even though you feel safe from Bengal tigers on the **Maharajah Jungle Trek,** several raised viewing spots offer clear views with no glass or fence to mar your photos. Habitat backdrops like the Maharajah palace ruins create scenic props.

Before your day comes to a close, catch a **Flights of Wonder** performance to see hawks, eagles, and other imposing birds. If you can squeeze in only one live show, choose to take in the beautiful dance moves of "animal" performers at **Festival of the Lion King.**

For people with disabilities: Guest may remain in wheelchairs or ECVs. ■TIP→ This is a great place to begin a family conservation project. ⊠ *Rafiki's Planet Watch* ⌕ *Duration: Up to You. Crowds: Light to Moderate. Audience: All Ages.*

Habitat Habit!. On this educational wildlife trail that focuses heavily on animal conservation efforts, you get a close-up look at cotton-top tamarins (small white-headed monkeys) and their entertaining antics while you learn how to live with all the Earth's animals. The South American primates are named for their flowing white mane of hair. **For people with disabilities:** Wheelchair accessible. ■TIP→ Ask questions; the animal-care cast members enjoy telling you about these cute critters. ⊠ *Rafiki's Planet Watch* ⌕ *Duration: Up to You. Crowds: Light to Moderate. Audience: All Ages.*

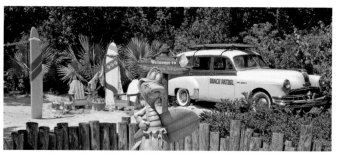

TYPHOON LAGOON

The beauty of Disney's water parks is that you can make either experience fit your mood. Like crowds? Head for the lounge chairs along the Surf Pool at Typhoon Lagoon or Melt-Away Bay at Blizzard Beach. Prefer peace? Walk past lush foliage along each park's circular path until you spot a secluded lean-to or tree-shaded patch of sand.

According to Disney legend, Typhoon Lagoon was created when the lush Placid Palms Resort was struck by a cataclysmic storm. It left a different world in its wake: surfboard-sundered trees, once-upright palms imitated the Leaning Tower of Pisa, and part of the original lagoon was cut off, trapping thousands of tropical fish—and a few sharks. Nothing, however, topped the fate of *Miss Tilly*, a shrimp boat from "Safen Sound, Florida," which was hurled high in the air and became impaled on Mt. Mayday, a magical volcano that periodically tries to dislodge *Miss Tilly* with huge geysers.

Ordinary folks, the legend continues, would have been crushed by such devastation. But the resourceful residents of Placid Palms were made of hardier stuff—and from the wreckage they created 56-acre Typhoon Lagoon, the self-proclaimed "world's ultimate water park."

ORIENTATION AND PLANNING

GETTING ORIENTED

The layout is so simple. The wave and swimming lagoon is at the park's center. Note that the waves are born in the Mt. Mayday side and break on the beaches closest to the entrance. Any attraction requiring a gravitational plunge starts around the summit of Mt. Mayday. Shark Reef and Ketchakiddee Creek flank the head of the lagoon, to Mt. Mayday's right and left, respectively, as you enter. The Crush 'n' Gusher water coaster is due right of Singapore Sal's.

You can take WDW bus transportation or drive to Typhoon Lagoon. There's no parking charge. Once inside, your options are to walk, swim, or slide.

WDW Information. Call WDW Information or check ⊕ *www.disney-world.com*'s park calendars for days of operation. ✉ *Blizzard Beach* ☎ *407/824–4321.*

TYPHOON LAGOON PLANNER

WHAT TO EXPECT

You can speed down waterslides with names like Crush 'n' Gusher and Humunga Kowabunga or bump through rapids and falls at Mt. Mayday. You can also bob along in 5-foot waves in a surf pool the size of two football fields or, for a mellow break, float in inner tubes along the 2,100-foot Castaway Creek. Go snorkeling in Shark Reef, rubberneck as fellow human cannonballs are ejected from the Storm Slides, or hunker down in a hammock or lounge chair and read a book. Ketchakiddee Creek, for young children, replicates adult rides on a smaller scale. It's Disney's version of a day at the beach—complete with friendly Disney lifeguards. Most people agree that kids under 7 and older adults prefer Typhoon Lagoon. Bigger kids and teens like Blizzard Beach.

During the off-season between October and April, Typhoon Lagoon closes for several weeks for routine maintenance and refurbishment.

PARKS AMENITIES

Dining: Picnicking is permitted, but coolers too large for one person to carry, glass containers, and alcoholic beverages not bought in the park are forbidden. There are tables at Getaway Glen, Typhoon Tilly's (near Shark Reef), and at pavilions across the park. You can always fork out $40–$60 a day, depending on the season, for a reserved spot at Getaway Glen, with chairs, an umbrella and small table, and four beach towels. Arrive early, though, and you can stake out a great spot for free. Park eateries and food stands have salads, burgers, pizza, and other treats, with a sweet emphasis on ice cream.

Dressing Rooms and Lockers: There are thatched-roof dressing rooms and lockers to the right on your way into the park. It costs $8 a day to rent a small locker and $10 for a large one; there's also a $5 deposit. There are restrooms in every nook and cranny. Most have showers and are much less crowded than the dressing rooms. If you forgot your towel, rent ($2) or buy one at Singapore Sal's.

First Aid: The small first-aid stand, run by a registered nurse, is on your left as you enter the park.

Guest Services: The staff at Typhoon Lagoon's Guest Services window outside the entrance turnstiles, to your left, can answer many questions. ■TIP→ **A chalkboard inside gives water temperature and surfing information.**

Lost People and Things: Ask about your misplaced people and things at the Guest Services window near the entrance turnstiles. Lost children are taken to an area by the Tip Board near the front of the park, where Disney cast members entertain them with games.

Private Patios: The park has a dozen premium, roped-off Beachcomber Shacks (patios, really) that groups of as many as six can rent. They generally offer shade and sun as well as plush loungers and other chairs, a table with an umbrella, and an ice chest with two bottles of water per guest (up to six). Each guest also gets two beach towels and a refillable soft-drink mug. The whole group gets a locker to share and an attendant to take and deliver food orders (cost of meals not included). The patios cost about $325 during peak season (usually March through late August), between $160 and $240 the rest of the year. Reserve (☏ 407/939–8687) well in advance or arrive very early to book one at High 'N Dry. In summer, any patio that isn't prebooked sells out within a half hour of the park opening.

Services for People with Disabilities: The paths connecting the different areas are wheelchair accessible, but most of the waterslides are not. There is, however, an elevator that takes you to the loading zone of the Crush 'n' Gusher water coaster. If you transfer from your chair to a raft or inner tube, you can float in Typhoon Lagoon Surf Pool or Castaway Creek.

Wheelchairs are available at the entrance turnstile area and are free with ID. You can trade a land-based wheelchair for chairs that go into the water by asking a lifeguard.

Supplies: You can get inner tubes at Castaway Creek and inner tubes, rafts, or slide mats at the rides. Borrow snorkel gear at **Shark Reef** (your own isn't allowed) and life vests at **High 'N Dry**. Near the main entrance is **Singapore Sal's,** where you can pick up free life jackets, buy sundries, and rent (or buy) towels and lockers.

VISITING TIPS

■ In summer, come first thing in the morning (early birds can ride several times before the lines get long), late in the afternoon when park hours run later, or when the weather clears after a thundershower (rainstorms drive away crowds). Afternoons are also good in cooler weather, as the water is a bit warmer. To make a whole day of it, avoid weekends, when locals and visitors pack in.

■ Women and girls should wear one-piece swimsuits unless they want to find their tops somewhere around their ears at the bottom of the waterslide.

■ Invest in sunscreen and water shoes. Plan to slather sunscreen on several times throughout the day. An inexpensive pair of water shoes will save tootsies from hot sand and walkways and from restroom floors.

■ Arrive 30 minutes before opening so you can park, buy tickets, rent towels, and snag inner tubes before the crowds descend, and, trust us, it gets very crowded.

EXPLORING TYPHOON LAGOON

Bay Slides. Kids scramble up several steps tucked between faux-rock formations, where a lifeguard sits to supervise their slide into Blustery Bay. The incline is small, but the thrill is great for young kids, who whoosh into the bay (sometimes into the arms of waiting parents). These two scaled-down versions of the Storm Slides are geared to kids shorter than 60 inches. ■TIP→ Kids really burn up energy going up the steps and down the slides repeatedly. Parents should be prepared for their wanting to ride over and over again. ⊠ *Typhoon Lagoon* ☞ *Duration: Up to You. Crowds: Light to Moderate. Audience: Small Kids.*

Castaway Creek. This circular, 15-foot-wide, 3-foot-deep, 2,000-foot-long waterway is chill. Snag an inner tube and float along a creek that winds through the park and around the Surf Pool and beaches. You pass through a rain forest that showers you with spray, you slide through caves and grottoes, you float by overhanging trees and flowering bushes, and you get dumped on at the Water Works with "broken" pipes. The current flows a gentle 2½ feet per second. Along the way there are five landing areas where you can hop in and out. **For people with disabilities:** Guests using wheelchairs must transfer to an inner tube. ■TIP→ A full circuit takes about 20 minutes, longer if you stop at one of the five lifeguard-manned launches. ⊠ *Typhoon Lagoon* ☞ *Duration: Up to 20 mins. Crowds: Vary by Season. Audience: All Ages.*

Fodor's Choice ★ **Crush 'n' Gusher.** If flume rides, storm slides, and tube races aren't wild enough for your inner thrill seeker, get ready to defy gravity on Disney's multipassenger water coaster. Designed to propel you uphill and down along a series of flumes, caverns, and spillways, this ride should satisfy the most enthusiastic daredevil. Keeping with park lore, Crush 'n' Gusher flows through what appears to be a rusted-out tropical fruit factory, weaving in and out of the wreckage and debris that once transported fruit through the plant's wash facilities. Three fruit spillways are aptly named Banana Blaster, Coconut Crusher, and Pineapple Plunger. Guests shouldn't ride if they are pregnant or have heart, back, or neck problems. **For people with disabilities:** An elevator takes guests using wheelchairs to the loading area; there's a short distance between this area and the ride. ■TIP→ Ride first thing in the morning before lines get too long. And don't forget to say cheese for the cameras! ⊠ *Typhoon Lagoon* ☞ *Duration: 1 min. Crowds: Moderate to Heavy. Audience: Anyone 48 inches or taller.*

Gangplank Falls. Families who climb Mt. Mayday for this ride are in for an adventure—more of an adventure than they might expect. Upon takeoff, a 6½-foot-long inflated raft plunges down the slide with impressive speed. It even gets bumpy at times along the 300-foot river. Not too scary for the tykes, and yet not a bore for parents, Gangplank Falls is great family fun! Those who are pregnant or have heart, back, or neck problems should sit this one out. ■TIP→ The inner tubes are heavy, so be sure to have at least two willing carriers. Also, be prepared to ride with two to four riders (five if some are smaller kids). ⊠ *Typhoon Lagoon* ☞ *Duration: 1 min. Crowds: Vary by Season. Audience: Not Small Kids.*

Humunga Kowabunga. There's little time to scream, but you'll hear just such vociferous reactions as the survivors emerge from the catch pool opposite Shark Reef. The basic questions are: want to get scared out of your wits in four seconds flat—and did you like it enough to go back for more? The three side-by-side Humunga Kowabunga speed

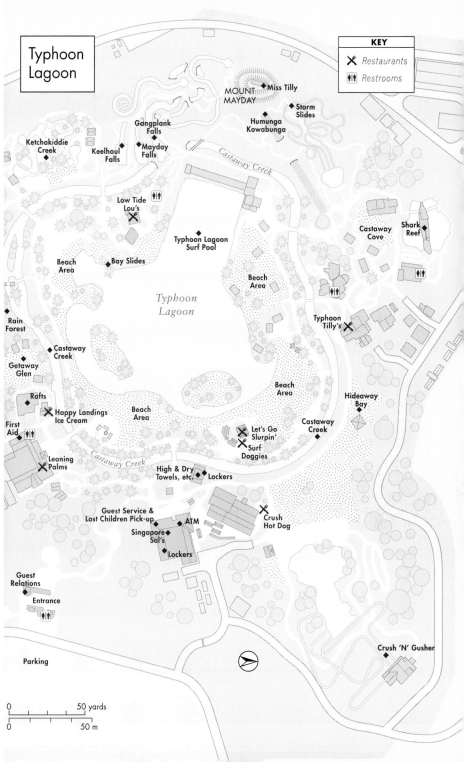

Typhoon Lagoon

KEY

✗ Restaurants
🚻 Restrooms

MOUNT MAYDAY

◆ Miss Tilly

◆ Storm Slides

◆ Humunga Kowabunga

◆ Gangplank Falls

◆ Mayday Falls

Ketchakiddie Creek

◆ Keelhaul Falls

Castaway Creek

🚻✗ Low Tide Lou's

◆ Typhoon Lagoon Surf Pool

Beach Area

◆ Bay Slides

Castaway Cove

◆ Shark Reef

🚻

Beach Area

🚻

Typhoon Lagoon

◆ Rain Forest

◆ Castaway Creek

Typhoon Tilly's ✗

Getaway Glen

Beach Area

◆ Rafts

Happy Landings Ice Cream ✗

First Aid 🚻

✗ Leaning Palms

Beach Area

Beach Area

◆ Castaway Creek

Hideaway Bay ◆

Castaway Creek

✗ Let's Go Slurpin'

✗ Surf Doggies

High & Dry Towels, etc. ◆ Lockers

Guest Service & Lost Children Pick-up

◆ ATM

✗ Crush Hot Dog

◆ Singapore Sal's

◆ Lockers

Guest Relations

Entrance 🚻

Parking

Crush 'N' Gusher

0 ——————— 50 yards

0 ——————— 50 m

slides deserve acclaim among thrill lovers, as they drop 214 feet downhill at a 60-degree angle in seconds. Oh yes, and then you go through a cave. In the dark. The average speed is 30 mph; however, you can really fly if you lie flat on your back, cross your ankles, wrap your arms around your chest, and arch your back. One caveat: the ride lasts only a few seconds—too short for us—and lines are often too long to requeue for another plunge. This ride isn't appropriate for guests who are pregnant or who have heart, back, or neck problems. ■TIP→ **Race against your friends or family; there are three slides at the top.** ✉ *Typhoon Lagoon* ☞ *Duration: 4 secs. Crowds: Heavy. Audience: Daring Souls 48 inches or taller.*

Keelhaul Falls. Do you need to chill out after the Mach 5 speeds of Humunga Cowabunga? Then venture up to Keelhaul Falls, a laid-back trip down the left side of Mt. Mayday. Just kick back and relax as your blue tube cruises down the 400-foot slide and splashes into the pool below. Keelhaul feels a little slow if you ride it right after Mayday Falls, so thrill seekers may be disappointed. Yet its winding path and scenic descent make for a satisfying ride. This ride isn't appropriate for guests who are pregnant or who have heart, back, or neck problems. ■TIP→ **Ride before or after Mayday Falls.** ✉ *Typhoon Lagoon* ☞ *Duration: 1 min. Crowds: Vary by Season. Audience: Not Young Kids.*

Ketchakiddee Creek. Typhoon Lagoon's play area for young children has slides, mini-rapids, faux sand castles, squirting whales and seals, bouncing barrels, waterfalls, sprinklers, and all the other ingredients of a splash fiesta. The bubbling sand ponds, where youngsters can sit in what seems like an enormous whirlpool bath, are special favorites. Little ones also love the tiny-scale tube ride. Small water cannons let kids engage in water-spray wars. Families can camp beneath lots of shady lean-tos when not in the water. **For people with disabilities:** Accessible for people using water-appropriate wheelchairs. ■TIP→ **Parents can take turns watching the kiddies here and riding the thrill slides.** ✉ *Typhoon Lagoon* ☞ *Duration: Up to You. Crowds: Light. Audience: Small Kids. Height requirements: Adults must be accompanied by a child under 48 inches and vice versa.*

Mayday Falls. This 460-foot slide in bright yellow inner tubes is the longest and bumpiest of the three falls. It's a long trek up to Mayday Falls—even higher than Keelhaul—but the increased speed and longer descent are well worth the climb. It's a relatively straight slide over the falls into a catchment, but it's not as thrilling as the up-and-down water

PARK VIEWS

Mt. Mayday. What goes down can also go up—and up and up. Climbing Mt. Mayday "[is] like climbing Mt. Everest," wailed one teenager about a climb that seems a lot steeper than an 85-foot peak should be. However, it's Mt. Everest with hibiscus flowers, a rope bridge, and stepping-stones set in plunging waters. The view encompasses the entire park. Lovers of white-water rafting should head to Mayday Falls, Keelhaul Falls, and Gangplank Falls at Mt. Mayday. These rides in oversize inner tubes plunge down the mountain's left side. They have caves, waterfalls, and intricate rockwork. ✉ *Typhoon Lagoon.*

From the wreckage—like that shown here—in the wake of a storm, Placid Palms Resort residents created 56-acre Typhoon Lagoon. Or so the story goes...

jets on the Crush 'n' Gusher. This ride isn't appropriate for guests who are pregnant or who have heart, back, or neck problems. ■TIP→ **While you're in the neighborhood, ride Keelhaul Falls, too.** ⊠ *Typhoon Lagoon* ↻ *Duration: 1 min. Crowds: Vary by Season. Audience: Not Young Kids.*

Shark Reef. If you felt like jumping into the tank at Epcot's The Seas with Nemo & Friends, make tracks for this 362,000-gallon snorkeling tank. The coral reef is artificial, but the 4,000 tropical fish—including rainbow parrot fish, sting rays, trigger fish, yellowtail damselfish, and amiable leopard and bonnet-head sharks (only 2 to 3 feet long)—are quite real. A sunken ship divides the reef; its portholes give landlubbers access to the underwater scene, though the windows are filmy and viewing is a bit blurry. During the warmest months (late March through September), adults and children (those under age 10 must be accompanied by an adult) can don personal supplied-air snorkeling equipment at no charge. Life vests are provided for weak swimmers. To prevent algae growth, Shark Reef is kept at a brisk 68°F, which is about 18° cooler than the rest of Typhoon Lagoon. For those who prefer a long, leisurely snorkel, this experience will be too brief. **For people with disabilities:** The sunken-ship viewing area is wheelchair accessible. ■TIP→ **This is popular, but even in the busy summer months the wait is often under 20 minutes.** ⊠ *Typhoon Lagoon* ↻ *Duration: Up to You. Crowds: Light to Heavy depending on season. Audience: Most Ages; children under 10 must be accompanied by an adult.*

Fodor's Choice ★ **Storm Slides.** Each of these three body slides is about 300 feet long and snakes in and out of rock formations, through caves and tunnels, and under waterfalls, but each has a slightly different view and offers a twist. The one in the middle has the longest tunnel; the others feature secrets you'll have to discover for yourself. Brace for splashdown on all three slides! Maximum speed is about 20 mph, and the trip takes about 30 seconds. These slides are not appropriate for guests who are pregnant or who have heart, back, or neck problems. ■TIP→ **Try each of the three slides for different twists.** ⊠ *Typhoon Lagoon* ⌒ *Duration: 15–20 secs. Crowds: Moderate to Heavy. Audience: Not Young Kids.*

Fodor's Choice
★

Typhoon Lagoon Surf Pool. This is the heart of the park, a swimming area that spreads out over 2½ acres and contains almost 3 million gallons of clear, chlorinated water. It's scalloped by coves, bays, and inlets, all edged with white-sand beaches—spread over a base of white concrete, as bodysurfers soon discover when they try to slide into shore. Ouch! The waves are the draw. Twelve huge water-collection chambers hidden in Mt. Mayday dump their load into trapdoors with a resounding whoosh to create waves large enough for Typhoon Lagoon to host amateur and professional surfing championships.

A piercing double hoot from *Miss Tilly* (the boat that purportedly landed at Mt. Mayday at the park's highest level) signals the start and finish of wave action: about every 2 hours, for 1½ hours, 5-to-6-foot waves issue forth every 90 seconds; the last half hour is devoted to moderate bobbing waves. Even during the big-wave periods, however, the waters in Blustery Bay and Whitecap Cove are protected. Surfers who don't want to risk a fickle ocean can surf here on certain days before the park opens. Instruction and a soft-sided surfboard are included in the $165 cost, and the surfing experience (ages 8 and older) lasts for 2½ hours. Reserve your waves by calling ☎ 407/939–7529. **For people with disabilities:** Accessible for people using water-appropriate wheelchairs. ■TIP→ **See the chalkboard at beach's edge for the day's wave schedule if you want to time your bodysurfing.** ⊠ *Typhoon Lagoon* ⌒ *Duration: Up to You. Crowds: Heavy. Audience: All Ages.*

NEED A BREAK?

Leaning Palms, to your left as you enter the park, has burgers, pizzas, turkey sandwiches, salads, beer, and, of course, ice cream and frozen yogurt. **Let's Go Slurpin'** is a beach shack on the edge of Typhoon Lagoon that dispenses frozen margaritas as well as wine and beer. **Typhoon Tilly's,** on the right just south of Shark Reef, serves sandwiches, salads, and snacks of all kinds and pours mostly sugary, nonalcoholic grog—though you can grab a Davy Jones "lager."

2

BLIZZARD BEACH

With its oxymoronic name, Blizzard Beach promises the seemingly impossible—a seaside playground with an alpine theme. As with its older cousin, Typhoon Lagoon, Disney Imagineers have created a legend to explain the park's origin.

The story goes that after a freak winter storm dropped snow over the western side of Walt Disney World, entrepreneurs created Florida's first downhill ski resort. Saunalike temperatures soon returned. But as the 66-acre resort's operators were ready to close up shop, they spotted a playful alligator sliding down the 120-foot-tall "liquid ice" slopes. The realization that the melting snow had created the world's tallest, fastest, and most exhilarating water-filled ski and toboggan runs gave birth to the ski resort–water park.

From its imposing ski-jump tower to its 1,200-foot series of rushing waterfalls, Blizzard Beach delivers cool fun even in the hot summertime. Where else can you wear your swimsuit on the slopes?

ORIENTATION AND PLANNING

GETTING ORIENTED

The park layout makes it fairly simple to navigate. Once you enter and rent a locker, you'll cross a small bridge over Cross Country Creek before choosing a spot to park your towels and cooler. To the left is the Melt-Away Bay wave pool. Dead ahead you can see Mt. Gushmore, a chairlift to the top, and the park's many slopes and slides.

If thrills are your game, come early and line up for Summit Plummet, Slush Gusher, and Downhill Double Dipper before wait times go from light to moderate (or heavy). Anytime is a good time for a dip in Melt-Away Bay or a tube trip around Cross Country Creek. Parents with young children should claim their spot early at Tike's Peak, to the park's right even before you cross the bridge.

Blizzard Beach

ATM
Park Entrance
Guest Services

Beach Haus

First Aid

Lockers

Guest Relations
Snowless Joe's
Frostbite Freddy's

Lost children at Guest Services

Lottawatta Lodge

Winter Summerland Mini Golf

Cooling Hut

Shade Shack

Tike's Peak

Cross Country Creek

Chairlift

Snow Balls

Cross Country Creek

Avalunch

Polar Pub

Lockers
I.C. Expeditions

Melt–Away Bay

Melt Away Bay

Cross Country Creek

Ski Patrol Training Camp

Warming Hut

Cave Entrance

Teamboat Springs

Chairlift
Toboggan Racers

Cave Entrance

Summit Plummet
Slush Gusher
Snow Stormers

MOUNT GUSHMORE

Downhill Double Dipper

Lockers

Runoff Rapids

Picnic Area

Cross Country Creek

0   50 yards
0   50 m

KEY	
✗	*Restaurants*
🚻	*Restrooms*

You can take WDW bus transportation or drive to Blizzard Beach. There's no charge for parking. Once inside, your options are to walk, swim, or slide.

BLIZZARD BEACH PLANNER

WHAT TO EXPECT

Disney Imagineers have gone all out here to create the paradox of a ski resort in the midst of a tropical lagoon. Lots of verbal puns and sight gags play with the snow-in-Florida motif. The centerpiece is Mt. Gushmore, with its 120-foot-high Summit Plummet. Attractions have names like Teamboat Springs, a white-water raft ride. Themed speed slides include Toboggan Racers, Slush Gusher, and Snow Stormers. Between Mt. Gushmore's base and its summit, swim-skiers can also ride a chairlift converted from ski-resort to beach-resort use—with multihued umbrellas and snow skis on their undersides. Older kids and devoted waterslide enthusiasts generally prefer Blizzard Beach to other water parks.

PARKS AMENITIES

Dining: You can't bring oversize coolers, glass containers, or your own alcoholic beverages into the park. Picnicking is welcome, however, and there are several pleasant pavilions and other spots, most notably the terrace outside Lottawatta Lodge. This is also where you can reserve your own picnic spot ($40–$60 for a day), which includes chairs (two of them loungers), an umbrella and small table, and four beach towels. Arrive early enough, and you'll snag your ideal spot in the park for free. You can get burgers, hot dogs, and salads at Lottawatta Lodge or other eateries and food stands. You could go for the usual snacks—snowballs or ice cream. But a truly sublime nibble is the melt-in-your-mouth mini-doughnut from the Mini Donuts stand across from Lottawatta Lodge.

Dressing Rooms and Lockers: Dressing rooms, showers, and restrooms are in the village area, just inside the main entrance. There are other restrooms in Lottawatta Lodge, at the Ski Patrol Training Camp, and just past the Melt-Away Bay beach area. Lockers are near the entrance, next to Snowless Joe's Rentals, and near Tike's Peak (the children's area and the most convenient if you have little swim-skiers in tow). It costs $8 to rent a small locker and $10 for a large one, and there's a $5 deposit. Note that there are only small lockers at Tike's Peak. The towels for rent ($2) at Snowless Joe's are tiny. If you forgot yours, you're better off buying a proper one at the Beach Haus.

First Aid: The first-aid stand, overseen by a registered nurse, is in the village, between Lottawatta Lodge and the Beach Haus.

Guest Services: Disney staffers at Blizzard Beach's Guest Services window, to the left of the ticket booth as you enter the park, can answer most of your questions. Get free life vests or rent towels and lockers at **Snowless Joe's**. Inner tubes, rafts, and slide mats are provided at the rides. Buy beach gear or rent towels or lockers at **Beach Haus. Shade Shack** is the place for a new pair of sunglasses.

Lost People and Things: Instruct youngsters to let a lifeguard know if they get lost. The lost-children station is beneath a large beach umbrella near the front of the park. And don't worry about the kids—a Disney cast member will keep them busy with activities.

Private Patios: The park has 14 Polar Patios to rent to groups of as many as six people. For $325 a day in peak season (usually March through late August) and between $160 and $240 other times of year, you get plush loungers, chairs, a table with umbrella, refillable beverage mugs, an ice chest with two water bottles per person, a group locker, and an attendant who will take your orders for and deliver lunch and snacks (food costs extra). It's best to book a patio far ahead of time (☎ 407/939–8687). If you arrive early enough, there might be an open patio; check at the Shade Shack.

SERVICES FOR PEOPLE WITH DISABILITIES

Most of Blizzard Beach's paths are flat and level. If you can transfer from your chair a short distance, you can also access all the waterslides except Summit Plummet. Or settle into a large inner tube and float in Cross Country Creek.

A limited number of wheelchairs—some suitable for the water—are available near the park entrance and are free if you leave an ID.

EXPLORING BLIZZARD BEACH

Chairlift. No subtropical skiing paradise would be complete without a chairlift, and this one is an attractive alternative to trekking to the top of Mt. Gushmore over and over again. The two-minute chairlift ascent is a great opportunity to scout out other slides and to enjoy the "ski beach" scenery. **For people with disabilities:** Guests using wheelchairs must transfer to a ride seat and subsequent attractions. A companion will have to meet you with the wheelchair at the base of Mt. Gushmore. ■ TIP→ If the wait is too long or you have children under 32 inches tall, hiking up is good exercise. ⊠ *Blizzard Beach* ⏱ *Duration: 2 mins. Crowds: Light to Moderate. Audience: Not Young Kids. Height requirement: At least 32 inches tall to ride.*

Cross Country Creek. Just grab an inner tube, hop on, and circle the entire park during a leisurely 25-minute float on this 3,000-foot-long creek. Along the way, you'll get doused with frigid water in an ice cave—wonderful on a steamy Florida day. Tubes are provided at seven launch sites, but they're not required. In fact, kids soon discover that the fastest and most enjoyable way to get around the park is to glide with the current and hop off at whichever landing they wish. **For people with disabilities:** Guests using wheelchairs must transfer to inner tubes. ■ TIP→ There are landings near most thrill rides, and moving through the park this way is oodles more fun than walking. ⊠ *Blizzard Beach* ⏱ *Duration: 25 mins. Crowds: Vary by Season. Audience: All Ages.*

Fodor's Choice **Downhill Double Dipper.** If you're on your way to Snow Stormers or Tobog-
★ gan Racers on the purple slopes, you may notice a cool-looking slide on the left. This is the Downhill Double Dipper, and it's well worth the stop. The best thing about this slide is that you are timed from blastoff to finish line! Competition may get heated as kids (48 inches or taller) vie for the glory of fastest speed slider, but even the least competitive

2

will enjoy tearing down Mt. Gushmore in their racing tubes. Expectant mothers shouldn't ride, nor should guests with heart conditions or neck or back problems. **For people with disabilities:** Guests using wheelchairs must transfer to the tube-launch site. ■ TIP→ Ride early; this popular purple-slope attraction gets crowded after lunch. (And, oh yeah—our fastest time was 5.89 seconds—can you beat that?) ⊠ *Blizzard Beach* ⌖ *Duration: Under 10 secs. Crowds: Heavy. Audience: Thrill Seekers 48 inches and taller.*

Melt-Away Bay. The park's main pool is a 1-acre oasis that's constantly fed by "melting snow" waterfalls. The man-made waves are positively oceanlike. If you're not a strong swimmer, stay away from the far end of the pool, where the waves originate. You can get temporarily stuck in a pocket even if your head is still above water. If you prefer to stay beached, there are plenty of recliner chairs spread out around the bay. This is where moms and dads often relax and watch their kids swim in the lifeguard-protected waters. **For people with disabilities:** Guests using water-appropriate wheelchairs can enjoy shallow waters here. ■ TIP→ Get an inner tube if you plan to venture to deeper waters, and arrive early if you want to find a shady spot (there are limited giant umbrellas). ⊠ *Blizzard Beach* ⌖ *Duration: Up to You. Crowds: Vary by Season. Audience: All Ages.*

Runoff Rapids. It's easy to overlook this three-track flume ride hidden on the far red slope of Mt. Gushmore. Yet if you have the courage to carry your tube all the way up to the top, you'll eventually come upon three twisting, turning 600-foot-long flumes—even one that's in the dark (keep in mind the tunnel slide is for single riders only, while the open slides are for one- or two-passenger tubes). Once you're in, it's way more fun than scary. Still, guests who are pregnant or who have heart, neck, or back problems should skip it. **For people with disabilities:** Guests using wheelchairs must transfer to inner tubes. ■ TIP→ It's worth riding both an open slide and the tunnel slide, but remember that the tunnel slide is only for single riders. ⊠ *Blizzard Beach* ⌖ *Duration: 35 secs. Crowds: Light to Moderate. Audience: Not Young Kids.*

Ski Patrol Training Camp. Preteens might want to spend most of their time on the T-bar drop, Cool Runners slides, and Snow Falls downhill body slide. In addition, there's a chance to take on the Thin Ice Training Course, a wide-open area where kids can jump from one slippery mogul to the next. The moguls really look more like bobbing baby icebergs, and kids don't mind when they miss a berg and plop into the pool. **For people with disabilities:** Guests using water-appropriate wheelchairs can enjoy wading areas here. ■ TIP→ The optimum time to come is early in the day or after a thunderstorm, when crowds thin out. That said, lines are often short at the zip-line drop and the iceberg obstacle course. ⊠ *Blizzard Beach* ⌖ *Duration: Up to You. Crowds: Light to Moderate. Audience: Tweens.*

Fodor's Choice ★ **Slush Gusher.** This speed slide, which drops through a snow-banked mountain gully next door to Summit Plummet on the green slopes, isn't quite as intimidating, but it's a real thriller nonetheless. Instead of one scream-inducing steep drop, the Slush Gusher features a fast, hilly descent to the base of Mt. Gushmore. While the Slush Gusher will not disappoint thrill seekers, it is perfect for those who want some adventure but tremble at the sight of Summit Plummet. For guests who are pregnant or who have heart, back, or neck problems, this ride is not recommended. **For people with disabilities:** Guests using wheelchairs must transfer to the slide. ■TIP→ **The earlier you ride, the better. On crowded days waits can last up to 90 minutes.** ⊠ *Blizzard Beach* ☞ *Duration: 15 secs. Crowds: You Bet! Audience: Not Young Kids; must be 48 inches or taller to ride.*

NEED A BREAK? Lottawatta Lodge—a North American ski lodge with a Caribbean accent— is the park's main emporium of fast food. Lines are long at peak feeding times. The Warming Hut, which is open seasonally, offers smoked turkey legs, salads, sandwiches, and ice cream. Specialty hot dogs, turkey legs, and salads are on the menu at Avalunch. Frostbite Freddy's and Polar Pub, on the main beach, both sell frozen drinks and spirits.

Snow Stormers. No water park would be complete without a meandering waterslide, and Blizzard Beach has one. Here three flumes, each 350 feet long, descend from the top of Mt. Gushmore along a switchback course of ski-type slalom gates on the purple slopes. Snow Stormers offers an exciting change of pace from the straight-down slides of the green slopes, and riders are in for a grand total of eight hairpin turns before finally splashing into the pool at the bottom. This ride isn't appropriate for guests who are pregnant or who have heart, neck, or back problems. **For people with disabilities:** Guests using wheelchairs must transfer to a toboggan-style slide mat with handles. ■TIP→ **This is a belly-down ride. Hold on tight!** ⊠ *Blizzard Beach* ☞ *Duration: 20 secs. Crowds: Moderate to Heavy. Audience: All Ages.*

Fodor'sChoice ★ **Summit Plummet.** This is Mt. Gushmore's big gun, which Disney bills as "the world's tallest, fastest free-fall speed slide." From Summit Plummet's "ski jump" tower at the very top of the green slopes, it's a wild 55-mph, 12-story plunge straight down, then into a tunnel before a whitewater splash landing at the end of the 360-foot-long run. It looks almost like a straight vertical drop, and you can't help but feel like a movie stunt double as you take the plunge. If you're watching from the beach below, you can't hear the yells of the participants, but you can bet many of them are screaming their heads off. The ride is not for guests who are pregnant or who have heart, back, or neck problems. ■TIP→ **Make this one of your first stops. The line will only get longer as the day goes on. (Summer-afternoon waits can be up to two hours.)** ⊠ *Blizzard Beach* ☞ *Duration: 10 crazy secs. Crowds: Absolutely. Audience: Not Young Kids; must be 48 inches or taller to ride.*

Teamboat Springs. Six-passenger rafts zip along green slopes in one of the world's longest family white-water raft rides. Since its original construction, it has doubled its speed of departure onto its twisting, 1,200-foot channel of rushing water, which ends with a refreshing waterfall dousing. This ride is a good place for kids too big for Tike's Peak to test more grown-up waters. Those who are pregnant or have heart, neck, or back problems should avoid this one. **For people with disabilities:** Guests using wheelchairs must transfer to the ride. ■ TIP→ This is an excel-lent ride for the whole family: there are no age or height requirements (other than "no infants"), tubes seat four to six people, and lines gener-ally move quickly. ⊠ *Blizzard Beach* ↺ *Duration: 1½ mins. Crowds: Moderate. Audience: Families.*

Fodor's Choice
★

Tike's Peak. Disney never leaves the little ones out of the fun, and this junior-size version of Blizzard Beach, set slightly apart from the rest of the park, has scaled-down elements of Mt. Gushmore, with sand, slides (including one with tubes), faux snow drifts, and igloolike tunnels. Par-ents can find sun or shade beneath lean-tos while watching over the little ones. Several lifeguards are on hand, but parents should still watch their youngsters at all times. **For people with disabilities:** Guests using water-appropriate wheelchairs can enjoy the wading areas. ■ TIP→ Stake out lounge chairs early, especially for a shady spot. If your tykes don't swim well, get them fitted with a free life vest, and pull your chair up to the water's edge. ⊠ *Blizzard Beach* ↺ *Duration: Up to You. Crowds: Vary by Season. Audience: Small Kids. Height requirement: Children shorter than 48 inches must be accompanied by adults.*

Toboggan Racers. Grab your mat, wait for the signal, and go. You and eight other racers whiz simultaneously down the watery trail on the purple slopes toward the finish line at the base of the mountain. The racing aspect and dips along the 250-foot-long slope make the ride fun, but it lacks the speed of single-rider green-slope rides like Slush Gusher. For a ride combining speed and friendly competition, check out the Downhill Double Dipper. Expectant mothers shouldn't ride, nor should guests with heart, neck, or back problems. **For people with disabilities:** Guests using wheelchairs must transfer to slide mats. ■ TIP→ It's more fun when you race family members or friends—up to eight people can ride at the same time. ⊠ *Blizzard Beach* ↺ *Duration: 10 secs. Crowds: Moderate to Heavy. Audience: Not Young Kids.*

DOWNTOWN DISNEY

East of Epcot and close to Interstate 4 along a large lake, this shopping, dining, and entertainment complex soon to be known as Disney Springs now has four areas: the Marketplace, West Side, The Landing, and Town Center. Major changes are under way for the build-out expected by early 2016 as new shops, restaurants, and promenades are completed. A much-needed, huge parking garage has opened, and another is under construction. You can rent lockers, strollers, or wheelchairs, and there are two Guest Relations centers.

EXPLORING

DisneyQuest. In a five-story virtual-reality mini-theme park at Downtown Disney West Side, DisneyQuest lets you pay a hefty cover to participate in high-tech virtual adventures and play video games. To be fair, you can play all day, and there are cutting-edge games and interactive adventures that make the admission worthwhile. It's also a great place for teens and older tweens (children under 14 must be accompanied by a guest age 14 or older).

In **Explore Zone,** fly through the streets of Agrabah with the help of a virtual-reality helmet on Aladdin's Magic Carpet Ride. Take a Virtual Jungle Cruise down the roiling rapids of a prehistoric world, and paddle (yes, *really* paddle) to adventure amid volcanoes, dinosaurs, and other Cretaceous threats. At Pirates of the Caribbean: Battle for Buccaneer Gold, you and the gang must brave the high seas and sink pirate ships to acquire treasure.

In the **Score Zone,** battle supervillains while flying, headset firmly intact, through a 3-D comic world in Ride the Comix. Escape evil aliens and rescue colonists during Invasion! An ExtraTERRORestrial Alien Encounter. Or hip-check your friends in a life-size Mighty Ducks Pinball Slam game.

In the **Create Zone** learn the secrets of Disney animation at the Animation Academy. Create your own twisted masterpiece at Sid's Create-A-Toy, based on the popular animated film *Toy Story.* Or, at Living Easels, make a *living* painting on a giant electronic screen. Thrills await at Cyberspace Mountain, where you can design your own roller coaster on a computer screen, then climb aboard a 360-degree pitch-and-roll simulator for the ride of your dreams. At Radio Disney SongMaker, produce your own hit.

Classic free-play machines like Pac Man reside in the **Replay Zone.** You can also sit with a partner in an asteroid cannon–equipped bumper car and blast others to make their cars do a 360-degree spin in Buzz Lightyear's AstroBlaster.

All attractions are wheelchair accessible, but most require transfer from wheelchair to the attraction itself. You can, however, wheel right onto Pirates of the Caribbean: Battle for Buccaneer Gold, Aladdin's Magic Carpet Ride, and Mighty Ducks Pinball Slam. Rent wheelchairs at the DisneyQuest Emporium or at Downtown Disney Marketplace Guest Relations ($12 per day for hand operated, plus $100 refundable credit-card deposit); electric chairs are $50 plus deposit at the Marketplace location only. Guide dogs are permitted in all areas but aren't allowed to ride several attractions. Strollers are *not* permitted.

Four attractions have height requirements: Cyberspace Mountain (51 inches), Buzz Lightyear's AstroBlaster (51 inches), Mighty Ducks Pinball Slam (48 inches), and Pirates of the Caribbean (35 inches). Little ones 2–7 can enjoy a Kids' Area on the fourth floor, where they can play smaller versions of video and other games like air hockey, basketball, and bowling.

Lost and Found is at the Guest Relations window and cash is available at ATMs inside the House of Blues merchandise shop not far from the DisneyQuest entrance. ⊠ *West Side* ☎ *407/828–4600* ⬛ *$45 adults, $39 children 3–9, excluding sales tax* ☉ *Sun.–Thurs. 11:30 am–10 pm, Fri. and Sat. 11:30 am–11 pm.*

Marketplace. In the Marketplace, the easternmost Downtown Disney area, you can meander along winding sidewalks and explore hidden alcoves. Children love to splash in fountains that spring from the pavement and ride the miniature train and old-time carousel ($2). Toy stores entice with creation-stations and too many treasures to comprehend. There are plenty of spots to grab a bite or sip a cappuccino along the lakefront. Most Marketplace shops, boutiques, and eateries begin opening at 9:30 am and stay open through 11 pm to midnight. ⊠ *Downtown Disney.*

The Landing. When it was a hopping nightlife destination called Pleasure Island, this area offered a mix of bars, comedy clubs, and dance spots. But the nightclubs are long closed, and the Island, renamed The

Downtown Disney

DISNEY'S
SARATOGA SPRINGS
RESORT & SPA

Village Lake

Parking

Paradiso 37

Water Taxi

Characters
in Flight

WEST SIDE

Parking

House
of Blues

Starbucks

Bongos
Cuban Café

Pin
trading

ATM

The
Smokehouse

House of Blues
Company Store

D Street

Orlando
Harley-Davidson

Cirque
de Soleil

ATM

Wolfgang
Puck Cafe

Sunglass
Icon

United World
Soccer

FoodQuest

Fit 2 Run

Hoypoloi

Candy
Cauldron

Lost & Found

Guest
Relations

Something
Silver

Stroller & Wheelchair
Rentals

Curl by
Sammy Duval

Sosa Family
Cigars

DisneyQuest

Haagen-Dazs

Splitsville
Luxury Lanes

AMC Downtown
Disney 24
(movie theaters)

Wetzel's Pretzels

DisneyQuest
Emporium

Pop
Gallery

Taxi Stand

Parking
Garage

Parking
Garage

Parking

Parking

- Bus Stop
- Disney Design-a-Tee
- Disney's Wonderful World of Memories
- The Art of Disney
- Wolfgang Puck Express
- The Spice & Tea Exchange
- Disney's Days of Christmas
- Mickey's Pantry
- Earl of Sandwich Restaurant
- Water Taxi
- Carousel
- Once Upon A Toy
- LittleMissMatched
- MarketPlace Fun Finds
- Disney's Pin Traders
- Rainforest Cafe
- Goofy's Candy Company
- Tren-D
- ATM
- Disney's PhotoPass Studio
- Stroller & Wheelchair Rentals
- Rainforest Cafe Retail Village
- Locker Rentals
- Lost & Found
- Marketplace Snacks
- MarketPlace Co-op
- ATM
- Guest Relations
- Ghirardelli Ice Cream & Chocolate Shop
- Arribas Brothers
- Waterside Stage
- Basin
- Fulton's Crab House
- MARKETPLACE
- World of Disney
- Taxi Stand
- The LEGO Store
- Portobello Country Italian Trattoria
- T-Rex Café
- Pollo Campero
- Bibbidi Bobbidi Boutique
- Cooke's of Dublin
- ATM
- THE LANDING
- Raglan Road Irish Pub & Restaurant
- Dino Store & Build-A-Dino by Build-A-Bear Workshop
- Apex by Sunglass Hut
- Shop for Ireland
- Sound Lion
- Taxi Stand
- Sanuk
- Art of Shaving
- Chapel Hats, Havaianas, Erin, McKenna's Bakery
- [Under Construction]
- Planet Hollywood
- Buena Vista Drive
- [Under Construction]

0   100 yards
0   100 m

KEY	
✕	Restaurants
👫	Rest rooms

Landing as part of the Downtown Disney redevelopment, is more of a family-oriented dining and entertainment district. Raglan Road Irish Pub & Restaurant celebrates more than a decade in this location offering great food by Raglan Road's Irish celebrity chef Kevin Dundon, indoor and patio dining, live Irish music, and traditional Irish step-dance performances every night and during weekend brunch. Paradiso 37 also welcomes diners indoors and alfresco. New to this area are Morimoto Asia, The BOATHOUSE, and other dining experiences. ⊠ *Downtown Disney.*

West Side. The main attractions in the hip West Side are the House of Blues music hall, Cirque du Soleil, Splitsville Luxury Lanes, Disney-Quest virtual indoor theme park and arcade, and a new Starbucks with covered patio overlooking the waterfront. You can also take a ride in the Characters in Flight helium balloon tethered here ($18 ages 10 and up, $12 ages 3–9), shop in boutiques, or dine in such restaurants as the Wolfgang Puck Café and Planet Hollywood. Shops open at 9:30 or 10:30 am, and closing time is between 11 pm and 2 am. The Splitsville entertainment center offers plenty of fresh fun with 30 bowling lanes on two floors, weekend DJs, and upscale eats like fillet sliders and sushi at indoor and outdoor tables. ⊠ *Downtown Disney.*

UNIVERSAL
ORLANDO

WELCOME TO UNIVERSAL ORLANDO

TOP REASONS TO GO

★ **The Variety:** Universal Orlando is much more than just a single Hollywood-themed amusement park. It's also the fantasy-driven Islands of Adventure (IOA) theme park; the clubs and restaurants of the CityWalk entertainment complex; and the upscale, on-site Hard Rock Hotel, Portofino Bay, and Royal Pacific resorts. Nearby Wet 'n Wild water park is also affiliated with Universal.

★ **Theme-Park Powerhouse:** Neither SeaWorld nor any of Disney's four theme parks can match the collective energy at Universal Studios and Islands of Adventure. Wild rides, clever shows, constantly updated attractions, and an edgy attitude all push the envelope here.

★ **Party Central:** Throughout the year, Universal hosts festive park-wide events such as Mardi Gras, Halloween Horror Nights, Grinchmas, the Summer Concert Series, and the Rock the Universe Christian-music celebration.

1 **Universal Studios Florida.** The centerpiece of Universal Orlando is a creative and quirky tribute to Hollywood past, present, and future. Overall, the collection of wild rides, quiet retreats, live shows, street characters, and clever movies (both 3-D and 4-D) are as entertaining as the motion pictures they celebrate. Another

plus, they're always adding something new—like the Wizarding World of Harry Potter: Diagon Alley.

2 **Islands of Adventure.** Certainly the most significant addition to any Orlando theme park came when IOA introduced an entire land dedicated to Harry Potter, which, in turn, sparked a substantial surge in attendance. Also at IOA

EXIT 77

Tropical Lake

Millenia Lake

Millenia Blvd.

Shingle Creek

Blvd.

W. Oak Ridge Rd.

Florida's Turnpike (Ronald Reagan Turnpike)

EXITS
75A (WESTBOUND)

Vanguard St.

Municipal Dr.

Carrier Dr.

Mandarin Dr.

Pomelo Dr.

Sand Lake Rd.

435

CENTRAL FLORIDA

Orlando

GETTING ORIENTED

3

Universal Orlando is tucked into a corner created by the intersection of Interstate 4 and Kirkman Road (Highway 435), midway between Downtown Orlando and the Walt Disney World Resort. Here you'll be about 15 minutes from each and just 10 minutes from SeaWorld.

are Spider-Man, the Hulk, velociraptors, the Cat in the Hat, and dozens of other characters that give guests every reason to head to the islands.

3 CityWalk. Even when the parks are closed (especially when the parks are closed), locals and visitors come to this sprawling entertainment and retail complex to watch movies; dine at

theme restaurants; shop for everything from cigars to surf wear; and stay up late at nightclubs celebrating the French Quarter, Jamaica, and the coolest clubs of NYC.

Updated
by Gary
McKechnie

Universal Orlando's personality is revealed the moment you arrive on property. Mood music, cartoonish architecture, abundant eye candy, subtle and overt sound effects, whirling and whizzing rides, plus a throng of fellow travelers will follow you to nearly every corner of the park. For peace and quiet, seek out a sanctuary at one of the resort hotels.

At a breathless pace, there's a chance you could visit both Universal parks in a single day, but to do that you'll have to invest in a UNIVERSAL EXPRESS PASS. Without it, you'll spend a good portion of that day waiting in line at the premium attractions. So allow two days, perhaps three; a day for each park and a "pick-up" day to return to your favorites at a leisurely pace. Which attractions are the main attractions? At both IOA and Universal Studios, it's definitely the Wizarding World of Harry Potter. That pairing along with The Mummy and The Simpsons attractions are always popular.

Universal Studios appeals primarily to those who like loud, fast, high-energy attractions—generally teens and adults. Covering 444 acres, it's a rambling montage of sets, shops, and soundstages housing themed attractions, reproductions of New York and San Francisco and London, and some genuine moviemaking paraphernalia.

When Islands of Adventure (IOA) first opened in 1999, it took attractions to a new level. Most—from Marvel Super Hero Island and Toon Lagoon to Seuss Landing and the Lost Continent—are impressive; some even out-Disney Disney. In 2010, IOA received well-deserved worldwide attention when it opened the 20-acre Wizarding World of Harry Potter. And in 2014 Universal Studios made another huge leap forward when it opened a full-scale version of Diagon Alley, complete with Gringotts Bank and a magical train that departs for IOA from Platform 9¾.

PLANNING

GETTING HERE AND AROUND

East on Interstate 4 (from WDW and Tampa), exit at Universal Boulevard (75A); take a left into Universal Orlando, and follow the signs. Heading west on Interstate 4 (from Downtown or Daytona), exit at Universal Boulevard (74B), turn right, and follow Hollywood Way.

Both Universal Studios and IOA require a lot of walking—a whole lot of walking. Start off by using the parking area's moving walkways as much as possible. Arrive early at either park, and you may be able to complete a single lap that will get you to the main attractions.

OPERATING HOURS

Universal Studios and IOA are open 365 days a year, from 9 am to 7 pm, with hours as late as 10 pm in summer and at holidays. Wet 'n Wild is also open 365 days a year, weather permitting, but with widely varying hours. Usually it's open from 9 to 6, with summer hours from 9:30 am until 9 pm. Call for exact hours.

PARKING

Universal's two garages total 3.4 million square feet, so *note your parking space.* The cost is $17 for cars and motorcycles ($5 after 6 pm and free after 10), $22 for RVs & buses, and $25 for preferred parking. Although moving walkways get you partway, you could walk up to a half mile to reach the gates. Valet parking ($15 for up to two hours, $35 for more than two hours) is much closer.

ADMISSION

The at-the-gate, per-person, per-day rate for either Universal Studios Florida or IOA is $96 (ages 10 and up) and $90 for children (ages 3–9). Far less expensive are multiday passes.

EXPRESS PASSES

The UNIVERSAL EXPRESS PASS ranges in price from about $35 off-season to around $80 in peak season. This pass gets you to the front of most lines and saves a lot of time. Keep in mind, the pass is for one use only at each attraction—a more expensive "unlimited" pass takes you to the head of the line again and again and again. If you're a guest at a Universal hotel, this perk is free; your room key serves as the pass.

UNIVERSAL DINING PLAN

If you prefer to pay in advance, Quick Service meals include one meal, two snacks, and a nonalcoholic beverage ($20). The kids' version covers a kids meal, one snack, and a beverage ($13). Universal Studios locations include Mel's Drive-In, Louie's Italian, Beverly Hills Boulangerie,

Universal Orlando Ticket Price Chart

TICKET OPTIONS				
TICKET	**1-DAY**	**2-DAY**	**3-DAY**	**4-DAY**
BASE TICKET				
Ages 10–up	$102	$149.99	$159.99	$169.99
Ages 3–9	$97	$139.99	$149.99	$159.99
Base Ticket admits guest to one park per day, either Universal Studios or Islands of Adventure.				
PARK-TO-PARK				
Ages 10–up	$147	$194.99	$204.99	$214.99
Ages 3–9	$142	$189.99	$194.99	$204.99
Park-to-Park Ticket allows guest to go back and forth between Universal Studios and Islands of Adventure; 7-day ticket available.				
ADD: CityWalk Party Pass	$12	Free	Free	Free
CityWalk Party Pass and Movie	$15	N/A	N/A	N/A
Meal and a Movie	$20.60	N/A	N/A	N/A
Meal and Mini-Golf	$22.48	N/A	N/A	N/A
CityWalk Party Pass gives guest one-night access to CityWalk clubs and venues (some of which require you to be at least 21). CityWalk Party Pass and Movie adds to that a free movie at the AMC Universal Cineplex 20.				
ADD: Wet 'n Wild to Universal Orlando Base Ticket (2-day)	$177.49 for adults, $167.49 for kids. (Plus $10 p/day for extra days)			
ADD: Wet 'n Wild to Part-to-Park ticket	$222.49 for adults, $212.49 for kids. (Plus $10 p/day for extra days)			
ADD: Universal Express Pass	Prices vary greatly by options and season; check website for details.			
Gives guest access to much shorter lines at Universal Studios and Islands of Adventure rides. (Note that this pass is included in the room rate at Universal Resort hotels.)				
All prices are subject to Florida sales tax				

Universal Orlando.

and the Classic Monsters Café. At Islands of Adventure, your choices are the Comic Strip Café, Croissant Moon, the Burger Digs, and Café 4.

UNIVERSAL TIPS AND ADVICE

Arrive early. Come as early as 8 am if the parks open at 9. Seriously. Better to share them with hundreds of people than with thousands.

Visit on a weekday. Crowds are lighter, especially fall through spring, when kids are in school.

Don't forget anything in your car. Universal's parking areas are at least a half mile from park entrances, and a round-trip hike will eat up valuable time. Consider valet parking. It costs $35 for longer than two hours before 6 pm (twice as much as regular parking), but it puts you much closer to Universal's park entrances and just steps from CityWalk.

Know the restrictions. A few things aren't allowed in the parks: alcohol and glass containers; hard-sided coolers; soft-sided coolers larger than 8½ inches wide by 6 inches high by 6 inches deep; and coolers, suitcases, and other bags with wheels. But if your flight's leaving later, you can check your luggage at the parks (unless you just leave them in your car).

Look into the Express Pass. Jumping to the front of the line with this pass really is worth the extra cost on busy days—unless you stay at a resort hotel, in which case front-of-line access is one of the perks.

Ride solo. At Universal some rides have a single-rider line that moves much faster than regular lines.

Get expert advice. The folks at Guest Services (aka Guest Relations) have great insight. The reps can even create a custom itinerary free of charge.

Check out Child Swap. At certain Universal attractions, one parent can enter the attraction, take a spin, and then return to take care of the baby while the other parent rides without having to wait in line again.

FOR PEOPLE WITH DISABILITIES

The *Studio Guide for Guests with Disabilities* (aka *Rider's Guide*) details attractions with special entrances and viewing areas, interpreters, Braille scripts, and assistance devices. In general, if you can transfer from your wheelchair unassisted or with the help of a friend, you can ride many attractions. Some rides have carts that accommodate manual wheelchairs, though not motorized wheelchairs or electronic convenience vehicles (ECVs).

CONTACTS

Universal ☎ *407/363–8000* ⊕ *www.universalorlando.com*

Universal Dining and Tickets ☎ *407/224–7840*

Universal (Loews Resorts) Room Reservations ☎ *877/819–7884*

Universal Vacation Packages ☎ *800/407–4275*

Wet 'n Wild ☎ *407/351–1800 or 800/992–9453* ⊕ *www.wetnwild.com*

UNIVERSAL STUDIOS

By Gary
McKechnie

Inspired by the California original and opened in Orlando in 1990 (when the city assumed it would become "Hollywood East"), Universal Studios celebrates the movies. The park is a jumble of areas and attractions. But the same is true of back-lot sets at a film studio. Suspend any disbelief you might have, and just enjoy the motion-picture magic.

At Production Central large soundstages house attractions based on TV programs and films like *Shrek, Despicable Me*, and *Twister*. Because it's right near the entrance it can be the park's most crowded area.

Here you see firsthand that not every film or program based in New York is actually shot in New York. Cleverly constructed sets mean that nearly every studio can own its own Big Apple. Universal is no exception. As you explore Production Central, a collection of sparkling public buildings, well-worn neighborhoods, and back alleys are the next-best thing to Manhattan itself.

As you enter the area known as San Francisco, you're roughly one-third of the way through the park. The crowds spread out, and the pace seems to slow. You can stop to see a show starring Beetlejuice or dine at the waterfront Lombard's Seafood Grille.

After passing scenes from San Francisco, you'll reach the land everyone is talking about: the Wizarding World of Harry Potter: Diagon Alley. What the books suggest and what filmmakers created, Universal has replicated right here—putting you in the middle of a fantastic fantasy-land. Just ahead, World Expo features two large attractions—MEN IN BLACK: Alien Attack and the Simpsons Ride. The scarcity of rides here is, however, offset by the colorful spectacle surrounding the Simpson's hometown of Springfield and the abundant attractions at Woody Woodpecker's KidZone. It matches the energy of toddlers and the under-10 crowd with diversions that include a junior-size roller coaster, a mini-water park, and a chance to meet E.T. and Barney the dinosaur. In

TOP ATTRACTIONS

AGES 7 AND UP

Harry Potter and the Escape from Gringotts. Getting into the vault at Gringotts Bank can be a challenge, but it's also a first-class adventure thanks to technology similar to that of The Transformers and IOA's Spider-Man and Harry Potter and the Forbidden Journey.

Hollywood Rip Ride Rockit. On this superwild coaster, you select the sound track.

MEN IN BLACK: Alien Attack. The "world's first ride-through video game" gives you a chance to compete for points by plugging away at an endless swarm of aliens.

Revenge of the Mummy. It's a jarring, rocketing indoor coaster that takes you past scary mummies and billowing balls of fire (really).

Shrek 4-D. The 3-D film with sensory effects picks up where the original film left off—and adds some creepy extras in the process.

The Simpsons Ride. It puts you in the heart of Springfield on a wild-and-crazy virtual-reality experience.

Transformers: The Ride 3-D. Universal Studios' version of IOA's fantastic Spider-Man experience, but this one features a rough-and-tumble encounter with the mechanical stars of the film franchise.

Universal Orlando's Horror Make-Up Show. This sometimes gross, often raunchy, but always entertaining demonstration merges the best of stand-up comedy with creepy effects.

AGES 6 AND UNDER

Animal Actors on Location! It's a perfect family show starring a menagerie of animals whose unusually high IQs are surpassed only by their cuteness and cuddle-ability.

Curious George Goes to Town. The celebrated simian visits the Man with the Yellow Hat in a small-scale water park.

A Day in the Park with Barney. Young children love the big purple dinosaur and the chance to sing along.

Hollywood, quiet parks and flashy Rodeo Drive really do make you think you've stepped into vintage Tinseltown.

All in all, Universal Studios fulfills its promise: to put you in the movies.

ORIENTATION AND PLANNING

GETTING ORIENTED

On a map, the park appears neatly divided into seven areas positioned around a huge lagoon. There's Production Central, which covers the entire left side of the Plaza of the Stars; New York, with street performances at 70 Delancey; San Francisco; the Wizarding World of Harry Potter: Diagon Alley; the futuristic World Expo; Woody Woodpecker's KidZone; and Hollywood.

What's tricky is that—because it's designed like a series of movie sets—there's no straightforward way to tackle the park. You'll probably make some detours and do some backtracking. To save time and shoe leather, ask theme park hosts for itinerary suggestions and time-saving tips. Here are a few of our own suggestions.

TOURING TIPS

We highly recommend you purchase your tickets online because it gives you plenty of time to consider your many options and includes a discount. Entering Universal Studios can be overwhelming as you and thousands of others flood through the turnstiles at once. Pick up a map in the entryway to CityWalk or by the park turnstiles and spend a few minutes reviewing it. Map out a route, find show schedules, and select restaurants. If a host is nearby, ask for insider advice on what to see first.

The "right" way. Upon entering, avoid the temptation to go left toward the towering soundstages, looping the park clockwise. Instead, head right—bypassing shops, restaurants, and some crowds to primary attractions like the Simpsons Ride and MEN IN BLACK: Alien Attack.

Photo ops. Universal Studios posts signs that indicate photo spots and show how best to frame your shot.

Rendezvous. Good meeting spots include Lucy: A Tribute, near the entrance; Mel's Drive-In, midway through the park on the right; and Beetlejuice's Graveyard Revue midway through the park on the left.

UNIVERSAL STUDIOS PLANNER

PARK AMENITIES

Baby Care: There are diaper-changing stations in many of the men's and women's restrooms, and a nursing station offers comfort and privacy at the park's first-aid station near the entrance. Baby supplies (diapers, food, wipes, and so on) are available at larger stores; ask for them at the counter, though, as they're not displayed on shelves.

Cameras: Just inside the main entrance, On Location is a shop with nearly everything you need for a picture-perfect vacation, including batteries, chargers, disposable cameras, and digital memory cards. This is also the pickup location for the souvenir photos taken in the park by Universal's squad of photographers.

First Aid: There are two first-aid centers: one just inside the turnstiles, to the right near the Studio Audience Center, and another directly across from the entrance to Beetlejuice's Graveyard Revue.

Guest Services: Get strategy advice *before* visiting by calling Guest Services at ☎ *407/224–4233.*

Lockers: Daily rates for lockers near the park entrance are $8 for a small unit and $10 for a larger one. There are free lockers near the entrances of some high-speed attractions (such as MEN IN BLACK: Alien Attack and Revenge of the Mummy), where you can stash your stuff before your ride; they're available to you for up to 90 minutes total.

Lost People and Things: If you plan to split up, be sure everyone knows where and when to reconnect. Staffers take lost children to Guest Services near the main entrance. This is also where you might find lost personal items.

Services for People with Disabilities: Universal has made it as easy as possible for guests with disabilities to enjoy the park. It starts when you arrive in the parking garage, where you can rent wheelchairs or ECVs before making the long trek to the park entrance (though there's also chair rental at the entrance), and extends to guidebooks with icons indicating which shows feature sign-language interpreters.

Guest Services (near the entrance just outside and inside the park) is the place to pick up assisted-listening and other devices, such as clickers that trigger closed-captioning. Other services include special viewing areas for people in wheelchairs, automatic doors, well-equipped restrooms, and walking areas for service animals. Be sure to pick up the *Studio Guide for Guests with Disabilities* (aka *Rider's Guide*), which is full of details on equipment and other services.

Accessibility information is posted at each attraction. Note that although ride lines can accommodate standard wheelchairs, often you'll be ushered into a waiting area while the rest of your party goes through the line. Many shows have seating to accommodate manual wheelchairs, but, in general, you'll have to transfer from your chair to ride vehicles.

Assisted-listening devices are available for Despicable Me, Shrek, Disaster!, Twister, MEN IN BLACK: Alien Attack, Transformers: The Ride 3-D, Terminator, Beetlejuice, Animal Actors, and A Day in the Park with Barney.

Stroller Rentals: Just inside the main entrance, there are strollers for $15 (single) and $25 (double) a day. You can also rent small kiddie cars ($18) or large ones ($28) by the day.

Wheelchair Rentals: You can rent manual wheelchairs ($12 per day) at the parking garages and inside the main entrance. Because there are limited quantities of electronic convenience vehicles (ECVs, available in the park for $50), reserve one in advance. A photo ID and a $50 deposit on a credit card are required for wheelchairs.

Where to Snack: The three restaurants on the Universal Dining Plan are **Mel's Drive-In,** a Happy Days–era soda shop–burger joint; **Louie's Italian Restaurant** (pizza, spaghetti, salads); and the **Classic Monsters Café** (pizzas, pasta, salads, rotisserie chicken). Also on the plan is **Beverly Hills Boulangerie** for breakfast croissants and pastries. Full-service restaurants include **Finnegan's Bar and Grill** (Irish pub) and **Lombard's Seafood Grille** (seafood).

Among the self-serve restaurants are **Richter's Burger Co.** (burgers, salads), **Schwab's Pharmacy** for ice cream, and the **Kid Zone Pizza Company** for pizza, chicken tenders, and other kid-geared dishes. At Diagon Alley, the Leaky Cauldron serves British pub fare, including cottage pie, bangers and mash, fish-and-chips, and cool, smooth mugs of Butterbeer. Near the Simpson's Ride, a strip called Fast Food Boulevard includes several Springfield-inspired eateries, including **Krusty Burger** (hamburgers, hot dogs), **Cletus' Chicken Shack** (chicken sandwiches, platters), the **Frying Dutchman** (fried seafood), **Luigi's Pizza, Lard Lad Donuts** (pastries, sweets), **Bumblebee Man's Taco Truck** (Mexican), and **Lisa's Teahouse of Terror** (salads, wraps, sandwiches). Want a cold one? Drop by **Moe's Tavern** for a Duff's beer or a Flaming Moe.

TOURS

VIP Tours. Universal has several VIP tours that are worthwhile if you're in a hurry, if crowds are heavy, if you're with a large group—and if you have the money to burn (prices leapt in 2014). The tours include extras like front-of-the-line access (that is, the right to jump to the head of the line). You can also arrange for extras like priority restaurant seating, bilingual guides, gift bags, refreshments at check-in, wheelchairs and strollers, and valet parking. Prices cited here do not include sales tax or park admission, and may edge up in peak seasons (or may not be available in peak season, so call ahead).

Here's what you'll pay in off-peak/peak seasons: Nonexclusive one-day tours (i.e., you'll tour with other park guests) cost $299/$369 per person for one park (five hours) and $329/$389 for two parks (seven hours). Then there are exclusive tours for your group only. If you're traveling with up to 10 people, consider splitting the cost of an eight-hour tour customized to your interests, which includes a sit-down lunch at the park of your choice. The eight-hour one-park exclusive price is $2,599/$2,899; two parks in eight hours will cost you $2,899/$3,199. What does $4,799/$4,999 get you? How about a two-day tour of both parks with backstage access and discussions on park history, decorating, and landscaping? And lunch. ☎ 407/363–8295 ⊕ *www.universalorlando.com.*

EXPLORING UNIVERSAL STUDIOS

PRODUCTION CENTRAL

Expect plenty of loud, flashy, rollicking rides that appeal to tweens, teens, and adults. Clear the turnstiles and go straight. You can use UNIVERSAL EXPRESS PASS at all attractions.

Despicable Me: Minion Mayhem. Even if you've never seen the hit animated film, it doesn't take long to fall for Gru, the Scourge of Humanity, in this wild virtual-reality chase through the movie. Two extremely funny (and cute) preshow rooms—Gru's living room and laboratory—set the stage for the 3-D ride. With help from his adopted daughters Margo, Edith, and Agnes (and ever-so-anxious minions), Gru reviews everyone to make sure they're ready to become minions. Sporting your "minion goggles" (aka 3-D glasses) you are transformed into minions for the ride itself, which is filled with close calls and colorful characters as you pursue the ever-elusive prize: the girls' gift for their dad on the one-year anniversary of their adoption. To celebrate, the ride exits into a minion disco. Of course. The 3-D experience, with preshows, lasts about 20 minutes (about five minutes on the ride itself). Not recommended for expectant mothers or anyone with motion sickness or back, neck, or heart problems. **For people with disabilities:** Closed-captioned devices are available; wheelchair guests may remain in their chairs; all guests must be more than 40 inches tall. ■TIP→ **Arrive early, late, or use a UNIVERSAL EXPRESS PASS. Go for the stationary seats if you think you'll suffer from motion sickness.** ⊠ *Production Central* ⟲ *Duration: 5 mins. Crowds: Heavy. Audience: All Ages. Height minimum: 40 inches.*

Fodor's Choice ★ **Hollywood Rip Ride Rockit.** Looking like an endless strand of spaghetti, this half-mile-plus coaster loops, twists, dives, and winds above and through Production Central. After you're locked into your seat, you'll select your personal sound track (choose from heavy metal, techno, country, rap, and pop) to accompany the video (starring you) that's shot as you scream your way along. And you will scream! It all starts as you're hauled nearly *17 stories straight up* before you drop nearly *17 stories straight down* before being lifted again into a towering loop and released into what seems like a never-ending series of twists, curves, sideways slings, and snap rolls at speeds up to 65 mph. By the time you return to the station, you might be woozy and a little spent—but you might spend a little more: the video with the sound track you selected is available for purchase. Off-season, the line never seems too bad. In season, consider using a Universal Express Pass. The ride isn't suitable for expectant mothers; anyone with neck, back, or heart problems; or people with a fear of heights. **For people with disabilities:** This does include closed-captioning, and guests using wheelchairs must transfer to a ride vehicle. ■TIP➔ **Come early or late or choose the single-rider line—and be sure to stow loose items in the available lockers.** ✉ *Production Central* ⏱ *Duration: 2 mins. Crowds: You Bet! Audience: Not Small Kids. Height minimum: 51 inches. Height maximum: 79 inches.*

Shrek 4-D. It's been years since the hit film premiered, but *Shrek* fans still line up at this animated 3-D saga. Mike Myers, Eddie Murphy, Cameron Diaz, and John Lithgow reprise their vocal roles as the swamp-dwelling ogre, Shrek; his faithful chatterbox companion, Donkey; Shrek's bride, Princess Fiona; and the vengeful Lord Farquaad (or rather his ghost). The preshow stars the Gingerbread Man, Magic Mirror, and the Three Little Pigs, and while this intro is slightly entertaining, at about 15 minutes long it's longer than the main attraction. Afterward, you're given OgreVision (aka 3-D) glasses through which to view Shrek as he attempts to rescue Fiona from Lord Farquaad. The adventure includes a battle between fire-breathing dragons and a pretty scary plunge down a virtual 1,000-foot waterfall—all made more intense by special theater seats and surprising sensory effects (mainly blasts of air and sprinkles of water) that create the "4-D" part. The ride can be unsettling for those with motion sickness—but fun as all get-out for everyone else. **For people with disabilities:** Equipped for assisted-listening devices. Those using wheelchairs don't need to transfer to a ride seat. There are, however, eight seats that allow guests with disabilities to fully experience the sensory effects. ■TIP➔ **Despite a capacity for 300, you may wait up to an hour to reach the preshow. Come early or late in the day. Accepts UNIVERSAL EXPRESS PASS.** ✉ *Production Central* ⏱ *Duration: 12 mins. Crowds: Heavy. Audience: All Ages.*

Transformers: The Ride 3-D. Based on the toy–turned–film franchise that's generated billions of dollars, Transformers: The Ride 3-D is now generating a lot of thrills and screams. Inside the stark industrial building that's the headquarters of NEST (Nonbiological Extraterrestrial Species Treaty), the attraction is the Universal Studios' equivalent of Islands of Adventure's ground-breaking Spider-Man (and that's a good thing.) After you board your transport, in a flash you're in an illusory

Universal Studios

Hogwarts Express to Hogsmead →

Beetlejuice's
Graveyard
Revue

First-Aid ✚
Canal St.
START

Revenge of
the Mummy

42nd St.
Louie's Italian
Restaurant

NEW YORK

Twister...
Ride It Out
STOP
5th Ave.
Parade Route

Finnegan's
Bar & Grill

57th St.
Park Ave.
Delancey St.
South St.

8th Ave.

The
Lagoon

Monster's
Cafe
Transformers:
The Ride 3D

South St.

**PRODUCTION
CENTRAL**

Amblin Ave.

Mel's
Drive-In

Sunset Blvd.

Blue Man
Group

Despicable
Me: Minion
Mayhem

Shrek 4-D

Parade Route

Vine St.

END

Hollywood
Rip Ride Rockit

Parade Route

Universal Orlando's
Horror
Make-Up Show

Nickelodeon Way

Lucy: A Tribute

Hollywood Blvd.

HOLLYWOOD

Beverly Hills
Boulangerie

Lockers

Strollers and
Wheelchairs

Plaza of the Stars

Terminator 2: 3-D

Lockers
Smart
Lockers

ATM
First-Aid

Guest
Services

Backlot Dr.

← TO ISLANDS OF
ADVENTURE (100 yards)

**Main
Entrance**

TO CITYWALK
(100 yards)

Knockturn
Alley

Harry Potter
and the Escape
from Gringrott's

Ollivanders

Leaky
Cauldron

THE WIZARDING
WORLD OF
HARRY POTTER—
DIAGON ALLEY

Fear Factor
Live

Disaster!

SAN FRANCISCO

Hogwarts
Express

The Knight Bus

The Embarcadero

San Francisco
Pastry Co.

Amity Ave.

Richter's
Burger Co.

Lombard's
Seafood Grille

The
Lagoon

MEN IN BLACK:
Alien Attack

Kang & Kodos'
Twirl 'n' Hurl

WORLD EXPO

Smart
Lockers

Exposition Blvd.

Fast Food
Boulevard

Moe's
Tavern

International
Food and Film
Festival

The Simpsons
Ride

Animal Planet Live!/
Animal Actors
on Location!

A Day in the
Park with Barney

WOODY
WOODPECKER'S
KIDZONE

0   50 yards

0   50 m

E.T. Adventure

Fievel's
Playland

Woody
Woodpecker's
Nuthouse Coaster

Curious George
Goes to Town

TO VINELAND RD. →

Celebrity Circle

Universal Blvd.

Hard Rock
Hotel

KEY	
• • • •	Parade route
✗	Restaurants
🚻	Restrooms

DID YOU KNOW?

On Production Central's Hollywood Rip Ride Rockit, you choose the sound track for your roller-coaster ride from songs within several genres of music. After the whole experience, you can buy a video of your ride with the music you selected.

world where 60-foot screens, fast-paced action, and plenty of 3-D effects ratchet up the excitement in a battle to save the planet as the heroic Autobots (including Optimus Prime and Bumblebee) try to keep the Allspark from falling into the hands of the evil Decepticons (ask your kids). Since you're wearing 3-D glasses, you ride through the attraction getting spun, twirled, splashed, spun, dropped, and faced with some tremendously realistic intergalactic encounters that rock and roll you through the Transformers' world. Very loud and very wild. The height minimum is 40 inches, and this ride isn't suitable for expectant mothers; anyone with neck, back, or heart problems; or people with a fear of heights. **For people with disabilities:** Guests using wheelchairs must transfer to a ride vehicle. ■**TIP**➔ **Come early or late, use UNIVERSAL EXPRESS PASS, or choose the single-rider line.** ✉ *Production Central* ⊕ *www.universalorlando.com* ☞ *Duration: 5 mins. Crowds: You Bet! Audience: Not Small Kids.*

WHAT'S NEW

Whether it's Despicable Me in 2012, or a real-life version of the Simpson's Springfield in 2013, Universal rarely takes a break from creating new lands and attractions. In 2013 the resort opened Transformers: The Ride 3-D, and in 2014 pleased muggles around the world with the premiere of Harry Potter's Diagon Alley as a bookend to the Island of Adventure's circa 2010 Hogsmeade village—with the two connected by a fantastic train journey that only adds to the magic. What's next? It's probably on the drawing board....

NEED A BREAK? In the heart of Production Central, the self-serve **Classic Monsters Cafe** resembles a mad scientist's lab. It offers wood-fired-oven pizzas, pastas, chef salads, four-cheese ravioli, and rotisserie chicken. Frankenstein's monster and other characters from vintage Universal horror films may make the rounds as you eat.

NEW YORK

Universal has gone all out to re-create New York's skyscrapers, commercial districts, ethnic neighborhoods, and back alleys—right down to the cracked concrete. Hidden within these structures are restaurants, arcades, gift shops, and key attractions. And, although they're from Chicago, the Blues Brothers drive from the Second City to New York City in their Bluesmobile for free performances at 70 Delancey. Here you can use UNIVERSAL EXPRESS PASS at Revenge of the Mummy and Twister.

Revenge of the Mummy. Action, adventure, and horror are in abundance in this $40 million spine-tingling thrill ride that combines roller-coaster technology, pyrotechnics, and some superscary skeletal warriors. The entrance is set up like the tomb of a pharaoh. You walk by Egyptian artifacts and through winding catacombs before boarding a multipassenger coaster car and zipping into the heart of a haunted labyrinth. "Dead" ahead, you're given the chance to sell your soul for safety and riches. Regardless of your decision, a guardian mummy sends you hurtling through underground passageways and Egyptian burial chambers where highlights include escaping a beetle-infested burial chamber, zipping backward through fog, and then racing full-tilt into the mummified mouth of Imhotep. Take note: you feel the 1.5 g-forces when flying uphill, and much of the ride takes place in the dark, which adds to its unforgettable intensity. Not good for expectant mothers or anyone with neck, back, or heart problems. **For people with disabilities:** Guests using wheelchairs must transfer to a ride vehicle. ■TIP➔ **Cut down on wait times: head for the single-rider line. Otherwise, use UNIVERSAL EXPRESS PASS or come early or late. Free lockers are available for loose items. Use them.** ⊠ *New York* ⌒ *Duration: 3 mins. Crowds: Heavy. Audience: Not Small Kids. Height minimum: 48 inches.*

Twister .. Ride It Out. After you proceed through a slow-moving line and hear a so-so discussion about the destructive force of tornadoes, you arrive in a standing-room theater—*and this is where the magic happens.* As you face a pastoral town setting, a make-believe windstorm builds in the distance and soon becomes an ominous five-story-high funnel cloud that weaves in from the background until it commands center stage. Amid the cacophony created by 110 decibels of wind noise, crackling electrical lines, and shattered windows, a truck, signs, car, and a cow earn frequent-flyer points by sailing across the stage. Then when the roof starts to blow off, your instinct is to head for the root cellar. Don't. Stay to marvel at the work of the special-effects masters who put this together, only to have it torn apart every few minutes. **For people with disabilities:** The theater is wheelchair accessible. Strong sound effects and assisted-listening devices make it possible for people with vision impairments to enjoy the show. ■TIP➔ **Use a UNIVERSAL EXPRESS PASS or come first thing in the morning or at closing.** ⊠ *New York* ⌒ *Duration: 3 mins. Crowds: Heavy. Audience: Not Small Kids.*

SAN FRANCISCO

This area celebrates the West Coast with the wharves and warehouses of San Francisco's Embarcadero and Fisherman's Wharf districts. *Use your UNIVERSAL EXPRESS PASS at both attractions.*

Beetlejuice's Graveyard Revue. Whew! This is *some* show. A Transylvanian castle is the backdrop for Beetlejuice, your ghost host who warms you up with snappy lines, rude remarks, and a heapin' helpin' of sarcasm—a theme that lasts throughout the performance. He then introduces the stars: Frankenstein's monster, his bride, the Wolfman, and Dracula. The creatures doff their traditional garb for glitzy, hip threads to sing hits by such diverse artists as Gloria Gaynor, AC/DC, Van Halen, and Springsteen, albeit with a few changes (e.g., "Jesse's Girl" would become "Frankie's Girl"). Ghoul Girl cheerleaders, Hip and Hop, up the weirdness factor and add sex appeal. This is the only place you'll see Frankenstein's monster pretending to play an electric guitar and shouting "Are you ready to rock, Orlando?" *We are not kidding.* Wayne Brady and Backstreet Boy Joey Fatone were once part of the cast. *We are still not kidding.* But despite (or because) of the far-fetched concept, it's a crowd favorite. **For people with disabilities:** The theater is wheelchair accessible and equipped for assisted-listening devices. Some shows feature a sign-language interpreter. ■TIP➔ **You can use UNIVERSAL EXPRESS PASS, but the amphitheater's high capacity means little chance of**

waiting. ✉ *San Francisco* ⊕ *www.universalorlando.com* ↻ *Duration: 25 mins. Crowds: Moderate to Heavy. Audience: Not Small Kids.*

NEED A BREAK? **Richter's Burger Co. (across from Beetlejuice) lets you drop in and dress up your own burger or grilled-chicken sandwich. It's pretty quick, pretty convenient, and there are seats inside and out.**

Disaster!. Packed with manic energy, tongue-in-cheek comedy, and some wild effects, here's how this two-part story unfolds: Since all of the movie's stars are in rehab, a harried production assistant must cast park guests for various roles in another blockbuster disaster film—*Mutha Earth.* After this guest star cast is selected, everyone moves to the special-effects set where disaster-movie producer Frank Kincaid (Christopher Walken) magically appears and interacts with the production assistant to explain his vision of a blockbuster film. From here, selected "guest stars" (park guests) are put through some stunt-filled paces before everyone boards San Francisco–style trams for a short ride through a tunnel. When the trams park at a subway station, a two-minute, 8.3-Richter-scale tremor begins; there are collapsing ceilings, blackouts, explosions, fire, and a massive flood that comes at you from every angle. The crazy thing about it is *you'd swear it was real!* At the end of the experience you get to see the hilarious "finished" film on the tram's monitors: the *Mutha Earth* trailer starring Dwayne "The Rock" Johnson as a heroic park ranger and your fellow guests as his costars. This ride isn't suitable for pregnant women or guests with heart, back, neck, or motion-sickness problems. **For people with disabilities:** If you use a standard-size wheelchair or can transfer to a ride vehicle, you can board this attraction. Service animals should not ride; sign-language interpreters are available at some shows. ■TIP→ Use UNIVERSAL EXPRESS PASS; otherwise, come early or late. ✉ *San Francisco* ⊕ *www.universalorlando.com* ↻ *Duration: 20 mins. Crowds: Often Heavy. Audience: Not Small Kids. Height minimum: 40 inches to ride without an adult.*

WORLD EXPO

At the far end of the park is a futuristic set of buildings containing a few of Universal Studios' most popular attractions, MEN IN BLACK: Alien Attack, the Simpsons Ride, and Kang & Kodos' Twirl 'n' Hurl, which offer fast admission with UNIVERSAL EXPRESS PASS.

Kang & Kodos' Twirl 'n' Hurl. Inspired by the intergalactic creatures that make an occasional appearance in Springfield, here's a new spin on an old favorite. About a dozen flying saucers encircle a towering statue of Kang (or Kodos), the one-eyed, fang-toothed, octopus-tentacled alien. Once you've climbed into your saucer the ride begins when, as at Seuss Landing's One Fish, Two Fish, Red Fish, Blue Fish, the spinning ride takes flight and whirls you and your co-pilot around Kang (or Kodos). Kids who love the opportunity to take the controls raise and lower the craft in hopes of avoiding the jets of water shot from surrounding poles. A pleasing, fun, low-thrill attraction that kids enjoy. ✉ *World Expo* ↻ *Duration: 3 mins. Crowds: Light to Medium. Audience: Small Kids and Up.*

MEN IN BLACK: Alien Attack. The preshow of "the world's first ride-through video game" provides the storyline: To earn membership in MIB you must round up aliens that escaped when their shuttle crashed on Earth. On board your vehicle with a few others, you enter the backstreets of a city where aliens pop out from windows, trash cans, and doorways. Fire at them with that laser gun mounted to your futuristic car, and since there's no limit to the number of shots you can take, blast away. Even though the gun's red laser dot is just a pinpoint, an onboard scoreboard helps you keep track of what you've hit. Aliens fire back at you, and if they score a hit it'll cause your car to spin out of control. Depending on the collective score, your ride will wrap up with one of 35 endings, ranging from a hero's welcome to a loser's farewell. All in all, it's pretty exciting. The spinning nature of the cars may cause dizziness, so use caution if you're prone to motion sickness. Don't ride if you have heart, back, or neck problems. **For people with disabilities:** Equipped for assisted-listening devices. Guests using wheelchairs must transfer to a ride vehicle. ■ TIP→ **In summer, waits may reach up to an hour. Come first thing or save time by splitting up and using the shorter single-riders line or by using UNIVERSAL EXPRESS PASS.** ⊠ *World Expo* ☞ *Duration: 4½ mins. Crowds: Heavy. Audience: Not Small Kids. Height minimum: 42 inches to ride without an adult.*

Fodor's Choice ★   **The Simpsons Ride.** As you enter this ride through Krusty the Clown's gaping mouth, and then receive a video greeting by citizens of Springfield, police chief Clancy Wiggum reminds you that if you must get sick, do it in your hat—and thus the tone is set for your arrival in one of television's most popular animated communities. The preshow explains that Krusty has expanded his empire to include a theme park, which his disgruntled former sidekick, Sideshow Bob, plans to sabotage. After a fairly tame start, your virtual train soars through virtual Springfield, plunging toward familiar businesses and buildings, and narrowly escaping disaster as Sideshow Bob tears up the tracks and sends you racing through wild scenes in a variety of locations such as Disney, SeaWorld—and hell. Several times you're saved by the split-second timing of an unexpected hero. If you have even a scintilla of motion sickness, this one will throw you for a colorful, cartoonish loop. Guests who are pregnant or who have heart, back, or neck problems shouldn't ride. **For people with disabilities:** Guests in wheelchairs must transfer to a ride vehicle. ■ TIP→ **Use UNIVERSAL EXPRESS PASS.** ⊠ *World Expo* ☞ *Duration: 6 mins. Crowds: Heavy. Audience: Not Small Kids. Height requirements: Must be at least 40 inches to ride; adults must accompany kids between 40 and 48 inches.*

WOODY WOODPECKER'S KIDZONE

With its colorful compilation of rides, shows, and play areas, this entire section caters to preschoolers. It's a pint-size Promised Land, where kids can try out a roller coaster and get sprayed, splashed, and soaked in a water-park area. It's also a great place for parents, since it gives them a needed break after nearly circling the park. All shows and attractions except Curious George and Fievel accept UNIVERSAL EXPRESS PASS.

Animal Actors on Location!. Animal shows are usually fun—and this one is better than most thanks to an arkful of animal stars. The tricks (or

Save the planet from interstellar invaders in World Expo's interactive MEN IN BLACK: Alien Attack. Zap aliens in city streets and compete with other guests to score points.

behaviors) they perform are mostly audience-participation segments, which makes it entertaining for young and old alike. You'll see birds, roosters, pigs, parrots, otters, ducks, dogs, and a skunk—and that's in just the first *two minutes*. Dogs demonstrate a range of thespian actions you've seen performed in movies and on television; a clever parrot has a knack for plucking cash from the outstretched hand of an audience member; and an orangutan seems the simian equivalent of Jerry Lewis as it plays opposite a straight-man trainer. The lineup of animals may vary, but the variety of scenes makes it like seeing several shows in one. Best of all, these are some of the cutest actors ever to hit the stage. **For people with disabilities:** The theater is equipped for assisted-listening devices and is wheelchair accessible. Some shows include a sign-language interpreter. ■ TIP→ **There's plenty of seating but come early for a good seat, or use UNIVERSAL EXPRESS PASS to get you in ahead of the crowd.** ⊠ *Woody Woodpecker's KidZone* ⌕ *Duration: 20 mins. Crowds: Moderate to Heavy. Audience: All Ages.*

Curious George Goes to Town. The celebrated simian visits the Man with the Yellow Hat in a no-line, no-waiting, small-scale water park. The main town square has brightly colored building facades, and the plaza is an interactive aqua playground that adults avoid but kids are drawn to like fish to water. Yes, there's water, water everywhere, especially atop the clock tower, which periodically dumps a mighty 500 gallons down a roof and straight onto a screaming herd of preschoolers. Kids love the levers, valves, pumps, and hoses that gush at the rate of 200 gallons per minute, letting them get sprayed, spritzed, splashed, and splattered. At the head of the square, footprints lead to a dry play area, with a rope climb and a ball cage where youngsters can frolic among thousands of foam balls. You can get into the act, sit it out on nearby benches, or take a few minutes to buy souvenir towels to dry off your waterlogged kids. **For people with disabilities:** Most of this attraction is barrier-free. ■TIP➔ Crowds are heavy mid-morning: come in late afternoon or early evening. Kids will get drenched; stash a bathing suit or change of clothing in a nearby locker. ⊠ *Woody Woodpecker's KidZone* ☞ *Duration: Up to You. Crowds: Moderate to Heavy. Audience: Small Kids.*

A Day in the Park with Barney. If your kids can't get enough of the big purple dinosaur, here he is again! A fairly long preshow features a goofy, kid-friendly emcee before you and your preschoolers enter a pleasant theater-in-the-round filled with brilliantly colored trees, clouds, and stars. Within minutes, the kids will cheer like baby boomers at a McCartney concert as their beloved TV playmate and Baby Bop dance and sing though clap-along, sing-along monster classics including "Mr. Knickerbocker," "If You're Happy and You Know It," and (of course) "I Love You." Following the very pleasing and thoughtful show and a chance to meet Barney up close, you exit to an elaborate play area with hands-on activities—a water harp, wood-pipe xylophone, and musical rocks—that propel the already excited kids to even greater heights. **For people with disabilities:** The theater is equipped for assisted-listening devices and is wheelchair accessible. ■TIP➔ Arrive 10–15 minutes early for a good seat—up close and in the center. UNIVERSAL EXPRESS PASS may be used here. ⊠ *Woody Woodpecker's KidZone* ☞ *Duration: 20 mins. Crowds: Light. Audience: Small Kids.*

E.T. Adventure. This well-meaning, circa 1990, ride is looking (and even smelling) a little tired, although you may still get a kick out of the take on Steven Spielberg's *E.T.* Once Spielberg himself advises you that it's your mission to help E.T. return to his planet, you board a bicycle mounted on a movable platform and fly 3 million light years from Earth, past a squadron of policemen and FBI agents to reach E.T.'s home. Here colorful characters climb on vines, play xylophones, and swing on branches in what looks like an alien Burning Man festival. Listen very closely for the payoff: having given your name to a host at the start of the ride, E.T. is supposed to bid you a personalized good-bye. This ride isn't suitable for guests with heart, back, neck, or motion-sickness problems. **For people with disabilities:** Guests with mobility issues must be in a standard-size wheelchair or transfer to a ride vehicle. Service animals aren't permitted. There's some sudden tilting and accelerating, but those for whom these movements are a concern can ride in E.T.'s orbs (spaceships) instead of the flying bicycles. ■TIP➔ Use UNIVERSAL EXPRESS PASS or come early. ⊠ *Woody Woodpecker's KidZone* ☞ *Duration: 5 mins. Crowds: Moderate to Heavy. Audience: All Ages. Minimum height: 34 inches.*

Fievel's Playland. Based on the Spielberg animated film *An American Tail,* this playground features larger-than-life props and sets designed to make everyone feel mouse size. An ingenious collection of massive boots, cans, and other ordinary objects disguise tunnel slides, water play areas, ball crawls, and a gigantic net-climb equipped with tubes, ladders, and rope bridges. A harmonica slide plays music when you

UNIVERSAL STUDIOS GROWN-UP TOUR

A stroll through Universal Studios will make you feel as if you've covered 3,000 miles in just a few hours. Hollywood is just a short walk from New York City; San Francisco is a stone's throw from the fictional Middle America of Springfield. The genius here is in the details, so take your time and notice the second-hand items in the windows of New York shops, for instance, or the cable-car tracks running through San Francisco.

SOUTH SIDE

Upon entering, don't head straight to Production Central; instead, turn right—onto Rodeo Drive. In a few steps you're in the heart of **Hollywood.** Although you'll probably drop into attractions such as Terminator 2: 3-D and Universal Orlando's Horror Make-Up Show, you can also have a soda at Schwab's or a hot dog at Mel's. Not even folks in the real Hollywood can do this. Notice the lovely Garden of Allah bungalows that look as if they were actually moved from Tinseltown.

Next stop: Springfield. Although **The Simpsons Ride** is a thrill, so is the amazing pop art that sets the stage for it. The facade is decorated like a carnival, with games of chance bordering the towering face of Krusty the Clown. Watch for the

kiosk that sells Squishees ("America's favorite icy goo") and take your time along Fast Food Boulevard where you'll have plenty of food ops—and photo ops—including Lard Lad (of donut fame), Moe's Tavern, and Bumblebee Man's taco truck. Really.

NORTH SIDE

Diagon Alley looks like a fashionable London district—but it's what's behind it that counts: a complete re-creation of Harry Potter's world.

San Francisco comes into view with cobblestone streets, redbrick buildings, and a waterfront inspired by Fisherman's Wharf.

New York captures nearly every borough. There are narrow alleys, fire escapes, a Chinese laundry, pawnshops, and secondhand stores. Round a corner and you'll see the Guggenheim Museum, newspaper offices, Italian restaurants, and Irish pubs. It's an amazing assemblage of styles, with clever signage, props, and effects.

Production Central takes you into the world of soundstages, movies, and TV shows. Look for the posters for the movies and albums being released by the stars of *Shrek* and other witty details.

At Universal Studios, the fun isn't just about the rides.

slide along the openings, and a 200-foot waterslide gives kids (and a parent if so desired) a chance to swoop down in Fievel's signature sardine can. It should keep the kids entertained for hours. The downside? You might have to build one of these for your backyard when you get home. **For people with disabilities:** Unfortunately, this ride isn't fully accessible to people using wheelchairs, although an elevator can transport wheelchairs to the top of the waterslide. ■ TIP→ **On hot days, come after supper to avoid waits for the waterslide. Kids will get drenched; stash a bathing suit or change of clothing in a nearby locker.**

UNIVERSAL STUDIOS

NAME	Height Req.	Type of Entertainment	Duration	Crowds	Audience	Tips
Hollywood						
Lucy: A Tribute	n/a	Walk-Through	15 mins.	Light	Adults	Save this for a hot afternoon or for on your way out.
Terminator 2 3-D	n/a	3-D Film/ Simulator Exp.	21 mins.	Heavy	All but Young Kids	Come first thing in the morning or use Express Pass.
★ Universal Orlando's Horror Make-Up Show	n/a	Show	25 mins.	Moderate	All but Young Kids	Come in the afternoon or evening. Young children may be frightened; older children eat up the blood-and-guts comedy.
Production Central						
★ Hollywood Rip Ride Rockit!	At least 51"	Thrill Ride	2 mins.	You Bet!	All but Young Kids	Come early, late, or use a Express Pass. Be patient.
Shrek 4-D	n/a	3-D Film	12 mins.	Heavy	All Ages	Come early or late, or use Express Pass.
New York						
Revenge of the Mummy	At least 48"	Thrill Ride	3 mins.	Heavy	All but Young Kids	Use Express Pass, or come first thing in the morning.
Twister...Ride It Out	n/a	Show/ Simulator Exp.	3 mins.	Heavy	All but Young Kids	Come first thing in morning or at closing. This "ride" involves standing and watching the action unfold.
San Francisco/Amity						
Beetlejuice's Graveyard Revue	n/a	Show	25 mins.	Light to Moderate	All but Young Kids	You can use Express Pass here, but there's really no need as there's little chance of a wait.
Disaster!	n/a	Thrill Ride	20 mins.	Heavy	All but Young Kids	Come early, before closing, or use Universal Express Pass. This is loud.
TRANSFORMERS	40"	3-D Thrill Ride	5 mins.	Heavy	All but Young Kids	No Express Pass. Come early.

Woody Woodpecker's KidZone

A Day in the Park with Barney	n/a	Show	20 mins.	Light	Young Kids	Arrive 10–15 mins. early on crowded days for a good seat—up close and in the center. Can use Express Pass.
Animal Actors on Location!	n/a	Show	20 mins.	Moderate to Heavy	All Ages	Stadium seating, but come early for a good seat. Express Pass accepted.
Curious George Goes to Town	n/a	Playground with Water	Up to you	Moderate	Young Kids	Come in late afternoon or early evening. Bring a towel.
E.T. Adventure	At least 34"	Thrill Ride for Kids	5 mins.	Moderate to Heavy	All Ages	Come early morning or use Express Pass.
Fievel's Playland	n/a	Playground with Water	Up to you	Light to Moderate	Young Kids	Generally light crowds, but there are waits for the waterslide. On hot days come late.
Woody Woodpecker's Nuthouse Coaster	At least 36"	Thrill Ride for Kids	1½ mins.	Moderate to Heavy	Young Kids	Come at park closing, when most little ones have gone home. Try Express Pass.

World Expo

★ MEN IN BLACK: Alien Attack	At least 42"	Thrill Ride	4½ mins.	Heavy	All but Young Kids	Solo riders can take a faster line, so split up. This ride spins. Use Express Pass.
The Simpsons Ride	40"	Thrill Ride/ Simulator Exp.	6 mins.	Heavy	All but Young Kids	Use Express Pass.

The Wizarding World of Harry Potter: Diagon Alley

Harry Potter and the Escape from Gringotts	42"	Simulator Exp.	5 mins.	Heavy	All but Young Kids	The single rider line moves fairly quickly.
Hogwarts Express–King's Cross Station	n/a	Railroad	10 mins.	Heavy	All Ages	You must have a Park-to-Park ticket

★ Fodor'sChoice

✉ *Woody Woodpecker's KidZone* ✆ *Duration: Up to You. Crowds: Light to Moderate. Audience: Small Kids.*

Woody Woodpecker's Nuthouse Coaster. Unlike the maniacal coasters that put you through zero-g rolls and inversions, this is a low-speed, mild-thrill version (top speed 22 mph) that makes it a safe bet for younger kids (who must be at least 36 inches tall) and action-phobic adults. It races (a relative term) through a structure that looks like a gadget-filled factory; the cars are shipping crates—some labeled "mixed nuts," others "salted nuts," and some tagged "certifiably nuts." Children generally love this low-level introduction to thrill rides (which is duplicated at Flight of the Hippogriff at the Wizarding World of Harry Potter). **For people with disabilities:** Guests using wheelchairs must transfer to a ride vehicle. ∎TIP➔ Use UNIVERSAL EXPRESS PASS and/or come at park closing, when most little ones have gone home. ✉ *Woody Woodpecker's KidZone* ✆ *Duration: 1½ mins. Crowds: Moderate to Heavy. Audience: Small Kids.*

HOLLYWOOD

The quintessential tribute to the golden age of the silver screen, this area to the right of the park entrance celebrates icons like the Brown Derby, Schwab's Pharmacy, and art deco Hollywood. There are only a few attractions here, and all except Lucy accept UNIVERSAL EXPRESS PASS.

Lucy: A Tribute. If you can't help smiling when you recall Lucy Ricardo stomping grapes, practicing ballet, gobbling chocolates, or wailing when Ricky won't let her be in the show, then a visit to this mini-museum and major gift shop will be a pleasant, nostalgic visit. The low-key attraction pays tribute to Lucille Ball through scripts, props, costumes, awards, and clips from the comedian's estate, and a challenging trivia quiz game on computer monitors has you trying to get Lucy, Ricky, Fred, and Ethel across the country to Hollywood. It's a fun place to take a break and spend time with one of the wackiest women of television, and the adjacent gift shop has Lucy souvenirs galore. **For people with disabilities:** This attraction is wheelchair accessible; the TV-show excerpts shown on overhead screens aren't closed captioned. ∎TIP➔ Save this for your way out or a hot afternoon. ✉ *Hollywood* ✆ *Duration: 15 mins. Crowds: Light. Audience: Adults.*

Terminator 2: 3-D. Entering the headquarters of the futuristic consortium Cyberdyne, a "community relations and media control" hostess greets your group and introduces the latest line of law-enforcing robots, but a slight snafu foreshadows what's ahead. After the preshow, you enter a theater to watch a James Cameron–directed 12-minute 3-D movie. The cyber-patrol goes haywire, and the excitement escalates courtesy of Schwarzenegger, icy fog, live actors, gunfights, and a chilling finale. Overall, it's a loud and fast-paced blend of nonstop action. Though some kids may be scared enough to require parental counseling, other visitors may feel that the franchise is a bit dated and the 3-D effects are few and far between. See for yourself and decide where you'd place it on the thrill-o-meter. **For people with disabilities:** The theater is wheelchair accessible and offers closed captioning as well as specialized sound through assisted-listening devices. ■TIP➡ If it's your first visit, skip this. UNIVERSAL EXPRESS PASS accepted. ⊠ *Hollywood* ⌇ *Duration: 21 mins. Crowds: Heavy. Audience: Not Small Kids.*

NEED A BREAK?

In the heart of Hollywood, **Schwab's Pharmacy** is a re-creation of the legendary drugstore where—studio publicists claim—Lana Turner was discovered. What you'll discover is a quick stop where you can order soda-fountain treats as well as hand-carved turkey and ham sandwiches.

Fodor's Choice
★

Universal Orlando's Horror Make-Up Show. This funny, highly entertaining show begins in an intriguingly creepy preshow area where masks, props, and rubber skeletons from classic and contemporary horror films and tributes to great makeup artists like Lon Chaney, Rick Baker, and Jack Pierce make a great backdrop for a horrifying family photo. Once inside the theater, your host brings out a special-effects expert who describes and shares some secrets about what goes into (and oozes out of) creepy movie effects (e.g., corn syrup and food coloring make for a dandy blood substitute). Despite the potentially frightening topic, most of the audience gets a kick out of the whole show, because the subject is handled with an extraordinary amount of dead-on humor. Older children, in particular, eat up the blood-and-guts stories. One-liners delivered with comedy-club timing, audience participation, knives, guns, loose limbs—all this goes into creating a flat-out fantastic show that entertains everyone. **For people with disabilities:** The theater is wheelchair accessible. Good scripts and good shtick mean that those with visual impairments can enjoy the show. ■TIP➡ If busy, use UNIVERSAL EXPRESS PASS or come in the afternoon or evening. Arrive about 15 minutes before showtime (doors close immediately after show starts). ⊠ *Hollywood* ⌇ *Duration: 25 mins. Crowds: Light. Audience: Not Small Kids.*

THE WIZARDING WORLD OF HARRY POTTER: DIAGON ALLEY

Hidden by a facade of London row homes, you may not think there's much to see. But when you spy an opening through a broken brick wall and step into Diagon Alley, you'll realize what an incredible blueprint J.K. Rowling created through her words. You can literally spend hours in this one district looking at the complete range of Potter-centric places: Universal Studios' version of Ollivanders wand shop; Weasleys' Wizard Wheezes (magical jokes and novelty items); the Magical Menagerie (all creatures furry, feathered, or scaly); Madam Malkin's Robes for All Occasions (wizard wear); Wiseacre's Wizarding Equipment; and Quality Quidditch Supplies. For practitioners of the Dark Arts, venture down Knockturn Alley and step inside Borgin and Burkes. For an appetizing break, stop at the Leaky Cauldron, the land's signature restaurant, or cool off at Florean Fortescue's Ice-Cream Parlour.

And when you're ready to head to Hogsmeade (conveniently located at the neighboring Islands of Adventure), make sure you have a park-to-park pass before stepping aboard the wonderful, magical Hogwarts Express—now departing to Islands of Adventure from Platform 9¾.

Harry Potter and the Escape from Gringotts. How do you know you've reached Gringotts Bank? Aside from a massive dragon perched on top of the building is the statue of a Gringotts goblin standing atop a towering stack of gold coins. Those two features alone will tell you that what lies ahead will be highly themed—and highly entertaining. The queue to the ride is an essential part of the attraction itself: you'll walk through the bank where a multitude of goblins are each working at their desks, diligently and wordlessly . . . eerie. Soon you're in a ride vehicle and after it departs the station it's only a matter of moments before Bellatrix Lestrange notices your presence and then does everything in her supernatural power to prevent you from traveling any farther. So from here on out, your vehicle will come face to 3-D face with a towering security detail that destroys the tracks and sends you deeper into the bank's recesses. Be warned that your first encounter with the one who shall not be named (aka Lord Voldemort) isn't your last. After he presents you with a fiery souvenir, he and Bellatrix return again—but they're no match for the scaly superhero who comes to your rescue. If you've ridden Universal's Spider-Man or The Transformers, you'll recognize the technology that blends virtual reality, 3-D effects, 4-D sensations, and gargantuan movie screens featuring scenes synchronized with the motion of your vehicle. Thankfully, this attraction tones down much of the volume and excess motion that pushes the envelope on the others, so it's enjoyable for everyone. **For people with disabilities:** Guests using wheelchairs must transfer to a ride vehicle. ■TIP➜ Be patient; UNIVERSAL EXPRESS PASS isn't accepted, but the single-rider line moves fairly briskly. ✉ *The Wizarding World of Harry Potter, Diagon Alley* ⊕ *www.universalorlando.com* ☞ *Duration: 5 mins (ride). Crowds: Yes! Audience: Everyone but Small Children. Height requirement: 42 inches minimum.*

Hogwart's Express–King's Cross Station. When Universal announced the Studios' Diagon Alley would connect to IOA's Hogsmeade via a train ride, many fans assumed an open-air train ride through the park's backstage area. But many people aren't nearly as creative as the geniuses at Universal. To reach Hogsmeade, you walk through an exact re-creation of a London rail station where a magical effect takes you to Platform 9¾. Even as the train pulls in, you're already being transported into another world. Settle into the compartment with other guests, and soon the ride is an attraction in itself. Chuffing out of the station, outside your window an owl follows you out of London, music plays, and you get the sense you're traveling hundreds of miles across the English countryside. Adding to the magic, silhouettes of Harry, Ron, and Hermione appear as the trio banishes dementors (and attempt to corral chocolate frogs). By the time Hagrid appears and you arrive in Hogsmeade, you really feel as if . . . *you've arrived in Hogsmeade.* ✉ *The Wizarding World of Harry Potter, Diagon Alley.*

3

ISLANDS OF ADVENTURE

More so than just about any other theme park, Islands of Adventure has gone all out to create settings and attractions that transport you from reality into the surreal. What's more, no one island here has much in common with any other, so in a way, a visit here is almost like a visit to half a dozen different parks.

IOA's unique nature is first revealed when you arrive at the Port of Entry and are greeted by a kaleidoscope of sights and a cacophony of sounds. It's all designed to put you in the frame of mind for adventure.

When you reach the central lagoon, your clockwise journey commences with Marvel Super Hero Island and its tightly packed concentration of roller coasters and thrill rides. Of special note is the amazingly high-tech and dazzling Amazing Adventures of Spider-Man. In just minutes you'll have experienced a day's worth of sensations—and you've only just begun.

Stepping into Toon Lagoon is like stepping into the pages of a comic book, just as entering the upcoming island, Jurassic Park, is like entering a research center where reconstituted dinosaur DNA is being used to create a new breed of *brontosaurus*.

You move from the world of science into the world of magic when you segue into the Wizarding World of Harry Potter. For the first time anywhere, you—and not just a few fortunate actors—can wander through the magnificently fictional, yet now very realistic, realm of the young wizard and his Hogwarts classmates and tutors. Beyond belief.

But that's not the end of it. In the Lost Continent the mood is that of a Renaissance fair, where crafters work inside colorful tents. It's as pronounced an atmosphere as that of the final island, Seuss Landing, which presents the incredible, topsy-turvy world of Dr. Seuss. It's a riot of colors and shapes and fantastic wildlife that pay tribute to the good doctor's vivid imagination.

TOP ATTRACTIONS

AGES 7 AND UP

Amazing Adventures of Spider-Man. Get ready to fight bad guys and marvel at the engineering and technological wizardry on this dazzling attraction.

Dudley Do-Right's Ripsaw Falls. Even if its namesake is a mystery to anyone born after the 1960s, everyone loves the super splashdown at the end of this log-flume ride dedicated to the exploits of the animated Canadian Mountie.

Harry Potter and the Forbidden Journey. This ride brings J.K. Rowling's books to life on a wild, virtual-reality adventure through Hogwarts and beyond with Harry, Hermione, and Ron.

Incredible Hulk Coaster. This superscary coaster blasts you skyward before sending you on seven inversions. It's hard to walk straight after this one.

AGES 6 AND UNDER

The Cat in the Hat. It's like entering a Dr. Seuss book: all you have to do is sit on a moving couch and see what it's like when the Cat in the Hat drops by to babysit.

Flight of the Hippogriff. Some of the younger Hogwarts "students" will enjoy this low-key coaster in Harry Potter's world.

Popeye & Bluto's Bilge-Rat Barges. This tumultuous (but safe) raft ride lets younger kids experience a big-deal ride that's not too scary—just wild and wet.

ORIENTATION AND PLANNING

GETTING ORIENTED

Getting your bearings at IOA is far easier than at its sister park, Universal Studios. Brochures in a multitude of languages are in a rack a few steps beyond the turnstiles. The brochures include a foldout map that will acquaint you with the park's simple layout (it's a circle). And, ahead by the lagoon, boards are posted with up-to-the-minute ride and show information—including the length of lines at the major attractions.

You pass through the turnstiles and into the Port of Entry plaza, a bazaar that brings together bits and pieces of architecture, landscaping, music, and wares from many lands—Dutch windmills, Indonesian pedicabs, African masks, restrooms marked "Loo's Landing," and Egyptian figurines that adorn a massive archway inscribed with the notice "The Adventure Begins." From here, themed islands—arranged around a large lagoon—are connected by walkways that make navigation easy. When you've done the full circuit, you'll recall the fantastic range of sights, sounds, and experiences and realize there can be truth in advertising. This park really *is* an adventure.

TOURING TIPS

Hosts. Just about any employee is a host, whether they're at a kiosk or attraction or turnstile. Ask them about their favorite experiences—and for suggestions for saving time.

Photo Ops. Islands of Adventure posts signs that indicate picture spots and show how best to frame your shot.

Retreat. Explore little-used sidewalks and quiet alcoves to counter IOA's manic energy.

Split the difference. If the park's open late, split the day in half. See part of it in the morning, head off-site to a restaurant for lunch (your parking ticket is good all day) then head to your hotel for a swim or a nap (or both). Return in the cooler, less crowded evening.

ISLANDS OF ADVENTURES PLANNER

PARK AMENITIES

Baby Care: There are diaper-changing stations in many of the men's and women's restrooms at IOA, as well as a nursing station for comfort and privacy at the first-aid station near the entrance. Baby supplies (diapers, food, wipes, and so on) are available at larger stores; ask for those items at the counter, though, as they aren't out on the shelves.

Cameras: Just inside the park, on your right after the turnstiles, is DeFoto's camera shop. It has nearly everything you need to make your vacation picture-perfect, including batteries, chargers, disposable cameras, cleverly themed photo frames, and digital memory cards. This is also IOA's pickup location for the souvenir photos taken by the active contingent of park photographers.

First Aid: There are two health-services/first-aid centers: one at the front entrance inside Guest Services, and another near Sindbad's Village in the Lost Continent. Just look for the Red Cross symbol on the building across from Oasis Coolers (or ask a park host).

Guest Services: Guest Services is right near the turnstiles, both before and after you enter Islands of Adventure (IOA). ☎ *407/224–6350* ⊕ *www. universalorlando.com.*

Lockers: There are $8-a-day lockers across from Guest Services at the entrance; for $10 a day you can rent a family-size model. You have unlimited access to both types throughout the day—although it's a hike back to retrieve things. Scattered strategically throughout the park—notably at the Incredible Hulk Coaster, Jurassic Park River Adventure, and Forbidden Journey—are so-called Smart Lockers. These are free for the first 45 to 75 minutes, $2 per hour afterward, and max out at $14 per day. Stash backpacks and cameras here while you're being drenched on a watery ride or going through the spin cycle on a twisty one.

Lost People and Things: If you've misplaced something, head to Guest Services in the Port of Entry. This is also where park staffers take lost children.

Services for People with Disabilities: Islands of Adventure has made an all-out effort to make the premises accessible for people with disabilities. Most attractions and all restaurants are wheelchair accessible, and all employees attend workshops on how to meet the needs of guests with disabilities. You may occasionally spot staffers using wheelchairs; many employees have had basic sign-language training. There's also a counter in Guest Services where you can pick up assisted-listening and other devices.

You can rent manual wheelchairs ($12 per day) and electronic convenience vehicles (ECVs; $50 per day) at the Port of Entry to the left after you enter the turnstiles. A photo ID and a $50 deposit on a credit card are required. Because it's a long way between the parking garages and the park entrance, you may want to rent a push wheelchair at the garages and then upgrade to an ECV when you reach the park entrance. Quantities of the latter are limited, so reserve in advance.

Even when the crowds are heavy, the park's avenues are wide enough to maneuver a wheelchair. Hosts and hostesses will direct you to a special attraction entrance or a special show seating area. Icons on the guide maps indicate which of the shows include an interpreter.

Assisted-listening devices are available for Cat in the Hat, Sindbad, Spider-Man, Incredible Hulk, Doctor Doom, Jurassic Park, and Poseidon's Fury.

Stroller Rentals: You can rent strollers ($15 per day for singles, $25 for doubles) at the Port of Entry to your left after the turnstiles. You can also rent kiddie cars—small ones for $18, and large ones for $28.

Where to Snack: If you prefer to pay in advance, Quick Service meals includes, for adults, one meal, two snacks, and a nonalcoholic beverage ($20). The kids' version ($13) includes one kids meal, one snack, and a nonalcoholic beverage. At Islands of Adventure, your choices are the Comic Strip Café (Asian, Italian, American, and fish), the Burger Digs (hamburgers, chicken sandwiches, chicken fingers, milk shakes), Café 4 (pizzas, subs, and salads), and Croissant Moon (deli sandwiches, panini, and pastries).

Other popular options include **Circus McGurkus Cafe Stoo-pendous** (chicken, pasta, pizza, burgers, salads) in Seuss Landing and, in Toon Lagoon, **Blondie's** (jumbo deli sandwiches). **Pizza Predattoria** and **Thunder Falls Terrace** (rotisserie chicken and ribs) are in Jurassic Park, and near the Port of Entry is the comparably more upscale **Confisco Grille,** with its steaks, salads, sandwiches, soups, pasta, and neat little pub. At IOA, the ultimate dining experience is the Lost Continent's **Mythos Restaurant.** Although its Continental dishes change seasonally, the warm, gooey, chocolate-banana cake is a constant.

EXPLORING ISLANDS OF ADVENTURE

MARVEL SUPER HERO ISLAND

The facades on Stanley Boulevard (named for Marvel's famed editor and co-creator Stan Lee) put you smack in the middle of an alternatively pleasant and apocalyptic comic-book world—complete with heroes, villains, and cartoony colors and flourishes. Although the spiky, horrific towers of Doctor Doom's Fearfall and the vivid green of the Hulk's coaster are focal points, the Amazing Adventures of Spider-Man is the must-see attraction. At various times Doctor Doom, Spider-Man, and the Incredible Hulk are available for photos, and sidewalk artists are on hand to paint your face like your favorite hero (or villain). All rides here accept UNIVERSAL EXPRESS PASS.

Amazing Adventures of Spider-Man. Already one of Universal's most popular attractions, when it was retooled with high-def animation it became even more of a must-see. The experience combines moving vehicles, 3-D film with the highest-definition resolution available, simulator technology, and special effects. After donning 3-D glasses, you board a special car that will pitch and roll as you get swept into weird all-encompassing cartoon battle. How weird? When Spider-Man lands on your car, you feel the bump; when Electro runs overhead, you hear his steps. You feel the sizzle of electricity, the frigid spray of water from Hydro Man, and the heat from a flaming pumpkin tossed by the Hobgoblin. No matter how many times you visit, you cringe when Doc Ock breaks through a brick wall, raises your car to the top of a skyscraper, and then releases it for a 400-foot free fall. The bizarre angles and perspectives really do make you feel as if you're swinging from a web. *Do not miss this one.* Youngsters accustomed to action TV shows should be fine, but timid kids won't. Not recommended if you're pregnant or have heart, back, or neck problems. **For people with disabilities:** Equipped for assisted-listening devices. Guests using wheelchairs must transfer to a ride vehicle. ■TIP➜ **Come early or at dusk—or most definitely head to the single-rider line. Be sure to check out the wanted posters of Spider-Man villains on the walls.** ⊠ *Marvel Super Hero Island* ⊕ *www.universalorlando.com* ☞ *Duration: 4½ mins. Crowds: Absolutely. Audience: All but Small Kids. Height requirements: 40 inches minimum; between 40 and 48 inches must be accompanied by an adult.*

Doctor Doom's Fearfall. Although the 200-foot-tall towers look really scary, the ride itself is just kind of scary (but still pretty cool). Several sets of four chairs wrap around the tower, and you and three fellow guests are seated and strapped in just out of the sight of other riders before the disembodied voice of Dr. Doom tells you the contraption is designed to extract fear he'll collect to use and rule the world. Without warning, all the chairs are rocketed to the peak, which jump-starts a surge of adrenaline as it rises, falls, rises and falls again in a very brief, but quite thrilling, experience. It's easy enough to have a second go as you can actually step off and get right back into line again. Guests who are pregnant or have heart, back, neck, or motion-sickness problems should sit this one out. **For people with disabilities:** Guests using wheelchairs must transfer to a ride vehicle. ■TIP➜ **Line moves fairly fast, though it's crowded early in the day; come late or use UNIVERSAL EXPRESS PASS.** ⊠ *Marvel Super Hero Island* ☞ *Duration: 1 min. Crowds: Light to Moderate. Audience: All but Small Kids. Minimum height: 52 inches.*

Incredible Hulk Coaster. Just seeing this attraction from the sidewalk is a thrill: its cars shoot out from a 150-foot catapult that propels them from 0 to 40 mph in less than *two seconds.* If this piques your interest, get in line where the wait for the prized front-row seats is the longest; however, every seat lets you experience flesh-pressing g-forces that match those of an F-16 fighter. You're whipped into an upside-down, zero-g position more than 10 stories up before being zipped into a dive at some 60 mph. You then race along the track before spinning through seven rollovers and making a plunge into two deep, foggy

Hogwarts Express
to Diagon Alley

Eighth Voyage
of Sindbad

Mystic
Fountain

Poseidon's
Fury

LOST
CONTINENT

Dragon
Challenge

Hogsmeade
Station

Triwizard
Spirit Rally

Fire Eater's
Grill

Hagrid's
Hut

Three
Broomsticks

Mythos

THE WIZARDING
WORLD OF
HARRY POTTER:
HOGSMEADE

Flight of the
Hippogriff

Harry Potter
and the
Forbidden Journey

Islands
of Adventure
Lagoon

Jurassic Park
Discovery Center

The Burger
Digs

Me Ship,
The Olive

TOON
LAGOON

Guest
Services

Jurassic Park
River Adventure

JURASSIC
PARK

Popeye & Bluto's
Bilge-Rat Barges

Pteranodon
Flyers

Blondie's

Camp
Jurassic

Comic
Strip
Cafe

Thunder Falls
Terrace

Dudley Do-Right's
Ripsaw Falls

Islands of Adventure

◆ First Aid

Circus McGurkus
Cafe Stoo-pendous ✕ 🚻

◆ One Fish, Two Fish,
Red Fish, Blue Fish

The High in the Sky Seuss
Trolley Train Ride!

Caro-
Seuss-el

◆ The Cat
in the Hat

TO
UNIVERSAL
STUDIOS →

🚻

If I Ran
the Zoo ◆

SEUSS
LANDING

🚻

🚻

Guest Services and
First Aid

PORT
OF ENTRY

TO
UNIVERSAL
CITY WALK →

✕ Confisco
Grill

◆ Lockers

🚻 ◆ Strollers and
Wheelchairs

◆ Smart
Lockers

◆ Incredible Hulk
Coaster

🚻

MARVEL
SUPER HERO
ISLAND

✕ Cafe 4

◆ Storm Force
Accelatron

✕ Captain
America
Diner

Doctor Doom's
Fearfall ◆

◆ Amazing
Adventures
of Spider-Man

🚻

0				50 yards
0				50 m

Hollywood Way

KEY	
✕	Restaurants
🚻	Restrooms

subterranean enclosures. Just when you think it's over—it's not. This coaster seems to keep rolling along well after you've exhausted your supply of screams and shrieks. Powerful. Pregnant women and people with neck, back, heart problems, or motion-sickness issues shouldn't ride. **For people with disabilities:** Guests using wheelchairs must transfer to a ride vehicle. ■ TIP➡ Come here first (effects are best in the morning and up front). Use UNIVERSAL EXPRESS PASS. Loose articles are not permitted, so stow things in a convenient locker. ⊠ *Marvel Super Hero Island* ↻ *Duration: 2¼ mins. Crowds: Yes! Audience: All but Small Kids. Minimum height: 54 inches.*

Storm Force Accelatron. On this whirling ride X-Men character Storm harnesses the weather to battle Magneto by having people like you board Power Orbs. Yes, the story line is that the containers convert human energy into electrical forces through the power of "cyclospin." Strip away the veneer, however, and what you've got seems like a faster version of Disney World's twirling teacups. Still, it's a high-adrenaline ride that's not for anyone who suffers from motion sickness. It's also not suitable for guests who are pregnant or who have heart, back, or neck problems. **For people with disabilities:** Guests using wheelchairs must transfer to a ride vehicle. ■ TIP➡ Ride whenever—except right after eating. Use UNIVERSAL EXPRESS PASS when needed. ⊠ *Marvel Super Hero Island* ↻ *Duration: 2 mins. Crowds: Light. Audience: All but Small Kids.*

TOON LAGOON

The main street, Comic Strip Lane, makes use of cartoon characters that are recognizable to anyone—anyone born before 1940, that is. Pert little Betty Boop, gangly Olive Oyl, muscle-bound Popeye, Krazy Kat, Mark Trail, Flash Gordon, Pogo, and Alley Oop are all here, as are the relatively more contemporary Dudley Do-Right, Rocky, Bullwinkle, Beetle Bailey, Cathy, and Hagar the Horrible. With its colorful backdrops, chirpy music, hidden alcoves, squirting fountains, and highly animated scenery, Toon Town is a natural for younger kids (even if they don't know who these characters are). All attractions here accept UNIVERSAL EXPRESS PASS except Me Ship, The Olive.

Dudley Do-Right's Ripsaw Falls. In the 1960s, Dudley Do-Right was recognized as the well-intentioned (but considerably dim) Canadian Mountie who somehow managed to always save the damsel and "get his man" (that is, foil the villain). But you don't need to be familiar with this character to enjoy this "waterlogged" attraction. The twisting, up-and-down flume ride through the Canadian Rockies begins with your mission to help Dudley rescue Nell, his belle, from the evil, conniving Snidely Whiplash. Tucked inside a hollow log, you'll drift gently down the stream before dropping through the rooftop of a ramshackle dynamite shack. After an explosive dive into a 400,000-gallon lagoon, you're not just damp—you're soaked. If the weather is cold or you absolutely must stay dry, pick up a poncho at Gasoline Alley, opposite the ride entrance, and store other items in a locker. This isn't suitable for guests who are pregnant, experience motion sickness, or have heart, back, or neck problems. **For people with disabilities:** Guests using wheelchairs must transfer to a ride vehicle. ■ TIP➡ Use UNIVERSAL EXPRESS PASS, and come in late afternoon, when you're hot as can be, or at day's end, when you're ready to head back to your car. Expect to get wet. ⊠ *Toon Lagoon* ☞ *Duration: 5½ mins. Crowds: Heavy in Summer. Audience: All but Small Kids. Height requirements: 44 inches minimum; under 48 inches must ride with an adult.*

NEED A BREAK?

Blondie's is home of the Dagwood—the jumbo club sandwich that's sold in sections (much too large for any one person to tackle). The eatery also sells cookies and Nathan's hot dogs (Chicago, chili, Reuben, slaw) as well as turkey, roast beef, and tuna sandwiches.

Me Ship, The Olive. Disguised as a teetering-tottering ship, this is actually a fantastic three-story playground. From bow to stern, there are dozens of participatory activities to keep kids busy as they climb around this jungle gym moored on the edge of Toon Lagoon. Toddlers enjoy crawling in Swee' Pea's Playpen, and with high-powered squirt guns, older children and their parents can take aim at unsuspecting riders twisting through the rapids over at Popeye & Bluto's Bilge-Rat Barges ride. The most excited participants are small kids who can't get enough of the whistles, bells, tunnels, and ladders. Check out the view of the park from the top of the ship. **For people with disabilities:** The playground area is wheelchair accessible. ■ TIP➔ Come in the morning or around dinnertime. ⊠ *Toon Lagoon* ☞ *Duration: Up to You. Crowds: Heavy. Audience: Small Kids.*

Popeye & Bluto's Bilge-Rat Barges. As with every ride at IOA, there's a story line here, but the real attraction is boarding the wide circular raft with 11 other passengers and then getting soaked, splashed, sprayed, or deluged as the watercraft bounces and bobs down and around the twisting stream. The degree of wetness varies, since the direction your raft spins may or may not place you beneath torrents of water flooding from a shoreline water tower or streaming from water guns fired with enthusiasm by guests at an adjacent play area. Pregnant women and guests with heart, back, neck, or motion-sickness problems should skip this one. **For people with disabilities:** Guests using wheelchairs must transfer to a ride vehicle. ■ TIP➔ Come first thing in the morning or an hour before closing. Use UNIVERSAL EXPRESS PASS, and stow your items in a locker if needed. ⊠ *Toon Lagoon* ☞ *Duration: 5 mins. Crowds: Heavy. Audience: All but Small Kids. Height requirements: 42 inches minimum; 42 to 48 inches must be accompanied by an adult.*

JURASSIC PARK

Pass through the towering gates of Jurassic Park and the music becomes slightly ominous, the vegetation tropical and junglelike. All of this, plus the high-tension wires and warning signs, does a great job of re-creating the Jurassic Park of Steven Spielberg's blockbuster movie (and its insipid sequels). The half-fun, half-frightening Jurassic Park River Adventure (the only attraction here that uses UNIVERSAL EXPRESS PASS) is the standout, bringing to life key segments of the movie's climax.

Camp Jurassic. Remember when you were content with just a swing set and monkey bars? Well, such toys have been replaced by themed play areas like this. Though the prehistoric camp is primarily for kids,

ISLANDS OF ADVENTURE

NAME	Height Req.	Type of Entertainment	Duration	Crowds	Audience	Tips
Jurassic Park						
Camp Jurassic	n/a	Playground	Up to you	Light to Moderate	All Ages	Come anytime.
Jurassic Park Discovery Center	n/a	Walk-Through	Up to you	Light	Young Kids to Teens	Come anytime.
Jurassic Park River Adventure	At least 42"	Thrill Ride with Water	6 mins.	Heavy	All but Young Kids	Use Express Pass. Come early or late.
Pteranodon Flyers	36" to 56"	Thrill Ride for Kids	2 mins.	Heavy	All Ages	Skip this on your first visit. 36" to 48" can ride but must do so with an adult.
Lost Continent						
Eighth Voyage of Sindbad	n/a	Show	25 mins.	Heavy	All but Young Kids	Stadium seating for everyone, but arrive at least 15 mins. early. Don't sit too far up front. Use Express Pass.
Poseidon's Fury	n/a	Walk-through Simulator Exp.	20 mins.	Heavy	All but Young Kids	Come at the end of the day. Stay to the left for best spot. Get in first row each time. Express Pass accepted.
Marvel Super Hero Island						
★ The Amazing Adventures of Spider-Man	At least 40"	Simulator Exp.	4½ mins.	Absolutely	All but Young Kids	Use Express Pass, or come early or late in day. Don't miss the bad guys in the wanted posters. Try it twice if you can.
Doctor Doom's Fearfall	At least 52"	Thrill Ride	1 min.	Light to Moderate	All but Young Kids	Use Express Pass, or come later in the day. Regardless, come with an empty stomach.
Incredible Hulk Coaster	At least 54"	Thrill Ride	2¼ mins.	Yes!	All but Young Kids	Come here first. Effects are best in the morning. The front row is best.
Storm Force Accelatron	n/a	Thrill Ride	2 mins.	Light	All but Young Kids	Come whenever—except right after eating.
Seuss Landing						

Attraction	Height	Type	Duration	Crowds	Audience	Strategy
Caro-Seuss-el	n/a	Thrill Ride for Kids	2 mins.	Moderate	All Ages	Use Express Pass, or end your day here.
The Cat in the Hat	n/a	Thrill Ride for Kids	4½ mins.	Heavy	All Ages	Use Express Pass here, or come early or at the end of the day.
High in the Sky Seuss Trolley Train Ride!	At least 34"	Railroad	3 mins.	Heavy	All Ages	Kids love trains, so plan to get in line! 34" to 48" can ride but must do so with an adult. Express Pass accepted.
If I Ran the Zoo	n/a	Playground with Water	Up to you	Heavy	Young Kids	Come toward the end of your visit.
One Fish, Two Fish, Red Fish, Blue Fish	n/a	Thrill Ride for Kids	2+ mins.	Heavy	Young Kids	Use Express Pass, or come early or late in day. Skip it on your first visit.
Toon Lagoon						
Dudley Do-Right's Ripsaw Falls	At least 44"	Thrill Ride with Water	5½ mins.	Heavy	All but Young Kids	Ride the flume in late afternoon to cool down, or at day's end. There's no seat where you can stay dry. Express Pass accepted.
Me Ship, The Olive	n/a	Playground	Up to you	Heavy	Young Kids	Come in the morning or at dinnertime.
Popeye and Bluto's Bilge-Rat Barges	At least 42"	Thrill Ride with Water	5 mins.	Heavy	All but Young Kids	Come early in the morning or before closing. You will get wet. Express Pass accepted.
The Wizarding World of Harry Potter						
Dragon Challenge	At least 54"	Thrill Ride	3 mins.	Heavy	All but Young Kids	Use Express Pass. Avoid if you're prone to motion sickness.
Flight of the Hippogriff	At least 36"	Thrill Ride for Kids	1 min.	Moderate	Young Kids	Keep an eye on the line, and come when there's an opening. Express Pass accepted.
★ Harry Potter and the Forbidden Journey	At least 48"	Walk-Through/Ride-Through/Thrill Ride	50 mins.	Yes!	All but Young Kids	Come early. Steer clear if you have a queasy stomach.
Hogwarts Express-Hogsmeade Station	n/a	Railroad	10 mins.	Heavy	All Ages	You must have a Park-to-Park ticket.

★ **Fodor'sChoice**

In the Jurassic Park Discovery Center, your kids might just learn something about dinosaurs that they didn't already know.

some adults join in, racing along footpaths through the forests, slithering down slides, clambering over swinging bridges and across streams, scrambling up net climbs and rock formations, and exploring mysterious caves full of faux lava. Watch for the dinosaur footprints; when you jump on them, a dinosaur roars somewhere (different footprints are associated with different roars). Also, look out for the watery crossfire nearby—or join in the shooting yourself. **For people with disabilities:** Much of this attraction is wheelchair accessible (its upper levels probably aren't). ■TIP➜ Great anytime. ⊠ *Jurassic Park* ☞ *Duration: Up to You. Crowds: Light to Moderate. Audience: All Ages.*

Jurassic Park Discovery Center. If there's a scintilla of information your kids don't know about dinosaurs, they can learn it here. There are demonstration areas where a realistic raptor is being hatched, and where you can see what you'd look like (or sound like) if you were a dino. In the Beasaur area ("Be-a-Saur"), you get a dinosaur's view of the world. There are numerous hands-on exhibits and a dinosaur trivia game, although the museumlike feel seems a little off-kilter at an amusement park. Burger Digs, the casual restaurant upstairs, is a nice place to take an air-conditioned break, and tables on the balcony overlook the lagoon. Step outside and a wide promenade affords a lovely perspective of the entire park. **For people with disabilities:** The attraction is fully wheelchair accessible. ⊠ *Jurassic Park* ☞ *Duration: Up to You. Crowds: Light. Audience: All but Small Kids.*

Jurassic Park River Adventure. Your excursion begins as a peaceful raft cruise on a mysterious river past friendly, vegetarian dinosaurs. Naturally, something has to go awry, and a wrong turn is all that it takes to float you into the Raptor Containment Area. Drifting into a research lab, you'll see that it's been overrun by spitting dinosaurs and razor-clawed raptors—and this is when things get plenty scary: straight ahead a towering, roaring T. rex with sharp claws and teeth the size of hams guards the getaway route. Just when you think you're about to become a Cretaceous period entrée, your raft slips down a tremendously steep 85-foot plunge that will start you screaming. Smile! This is when the souvenir photos are shot. Thanks to high-capacity rafts, the line moves fairly quickly. Not suitable for guests who are pregnant or who have heart, back, or neck problems. **For people with disabilities:** Guests using wheelchairs must transfer to a ride vehicle; assisted-listening devices are available. ■TIP➔ **Come early in the morning and/or use UNIVERSAL EXPRESS PASS.** ☒ *Jurassic Park* ☞ *Duration: 6 mins. Crowds: Heavy. Audience: All but Small Kids. Minimum height: 42 inches.*

NEED A BREAK? **Thunder Falls Terrace is open for lunch and dinner. Beneath towering ceilings in a spacious setting, one side is entirely glass, which makes it a great place to view the plunge at the adjacent Jurassic Park River Adventure. On a nice day, consider sitting outdoors next to the thundering waterfall and dine on barbecue ribs, wraps, chicken, turkey legs, soup, and salads. If Thunder Falls is too crowded, a short distance away are Burger Digs and Pizza Predattoria.**

Pteranodon Flyers. These prehistoric bird-style gondolas are eye-catching and may tempt you to stand in line for a lift. The catch is that this is a very slow, very low-capacity ride that can eat up a lot of your park time. Do it only if (1) your child asks, (2) you want a prehistoric-bird's-eye view of the Jurassic Park compound, or (3) you've been to the park a dozen times and this is the last ride to conquer. **For people with disabilities:** Guests using wheelchairs must transfer to a ride vehicle. ■TIP➔ **Crowds are usually perpetual, and since the ride loads slowly, waits can be quite a while. Skip this on your first visit.** ☒ *Jurassic Park* ☞ *Duration: 2 mins. Crowds: Heavy. Audience: All Ages. Height requirements: Between 36 and 56 inches tall; taller adults must be accompanied by a child who meets these height requirements.*

THE WIZARDING WORLD OF HARRY POTTER: HOGSMEADE

In mid-2010, Islands of Adventure fulfilled the fantasy of Harry Potter devotees when it unveiled the biggest theme-park addition since the arrival of Disney's Animal Kingdom in 1998. At the highly publicized premiere, even the actors from the Potter film franchise were amazed. Having performed their roles largely before a green screen, they had never seen anything like this. Neither have you. It's fantastic and unbelievable. The movie-magic-perfect re-creations of mythical locales such as Hogwarts and Hogsmeade Village are here, while playing supporting roles are a handful of candy shops, souvenir stores, and restaurants expertly and exquisitely themed to make you believe you've actually arrived in the incredible fantasy world of J.K. Rowling. Wands, candy, novelties, and more are unique to this magical land. Expect to be impressed—and to wait in line. Even if you owned a wand and were a

CLOSE UP

Hogsmeade Village

In Hogsmeade, the village that's the home of Hogwarts, you'll find the signature restaurant, Three Broomsticks, which serves traditional British fare (as well as an assortment of kids' meals), and the Hog's Head Pub, where you can down a pint of Butterbeer (tastes like cream soda, butterscotch, and shortbread cookies) or pumpkin juice (pumpkin, apple cider, and spices). The village is also a fantastic place to run errands and pick up sundries and pretend you're really in Harry Potter's world. Send a postcard or letter stamped with a novelty (and very real cancellation mark) at Owl Post before selecting (or being selected by) a magic wand at Ollivanders. If you can't get into Ollivanders due to the line, kiosks and small shops sell an impressive 25 different styles of wands at a profit-making price (about $30). Pick up some practical jokes (shrunken heads, extendable ears, screaming yo-yos) at Zonko's, and sample strange sweets at Honeydukes. But the best place to shop for Potterabilia is Dervish and Banges, where there are Hogwarts school uniforms, robes, scarves, T-shirts, and broomsticks—including the legendary Nimbus 2000. To explore even more of Harry's favorite haunts, board the train to Universal Studios' Diagon Alley. Much more than a train ride, it's an experience.

real wizard, the only attractions in this land that accept the UNIVERSAL EXPRESS PASS are Flight of the Hippogriff and Dragon Challenge. In fact, the land is so popular that in peak season it sometimes reaches capacity, and you have to wait for others to leave before you can enter. If you have a two-park pass, you can board the Hogwarts Express for a delightful train journey to Diagon Alley at Universal Studios.

Dragon Challenge. On this tandem roller coaster, the Chinese Fireball and Hungarian Horntail rocket you in a screaming, snap-crackle-pop half-mile ride along the rails. In the line watch for iconic elements from the Tri-Wizard Tournament, but when you get hung up in your seat (you're suspended beneath the track) get ready to be launched on one of the park's great rides. Each coaster is on a separate track, and when they rocket out of the station at the same time, it means they'll soon be rocketing *toward* each other at a combined speed of *120 mph*. Making it even more exciting, the coasters are programmed by computer to bring them just feet apart as they blaze through the track. This isn't appropriate for anyone with neck, back, or heart problems, or for anyone who is pregnant or suffers from motion sickness. **For people with disabilities:** Guests using wheelchairs must transfer to a ride vehicle. ■TIP➔ Make use of UNIVERSAL EXPRESS PASS. It's perfect for teens and adventurous tweens. ⊠ *The Wizarding World of Harry Potter ☞ Duration: 3 mins. Crowds: Heavy. Audience: All but Small Kids. Minimum height: 54 inches.*

Flight of the Hippogriff. This kid-friendly coaster is a simple way to introduce your children to the pleasures of g-force and vertigo. The queue takes you past Hagrid's hut and then onboard for a "training flight" above the grounds of Hogwarts Castle. On the brief journey, there

are some nice little twists and dips that'll give them a pint-size dose of adrenaline. This is an easy alternative to the Dragon Challenge, and one that should please parents and their kids. That said, this ride isn't appropriate for people with heart, back, or neck problems or who are prone to motion sickness. **For people with disabilities:** Guests using wheelchairs must transfer to a ride vehicle. ■**TIP**➔ **Bring smaller kids here while the older kids ride Dragon Challenge. Use UNIVERSAL EXPRESS PASS.** ⊠ *The Wizarding World of Harry Potter* ☞ *Duration: 1 min. Crowds: Moderate. Audience: Small Kids. Minimum height: 36 inches.*

WORD OF MOUTH

"The wait at Harry Potter's Forbidden Journey around 1 pm was just over an hour (can't use UNIVERSAL EXPRESS PASS for this one). Butterbeer is delicious, although pricey at $11 if you keep the plastic mug. It's available frozen or regular, and we decided the frozen was better. Harry Potter and Spider-Man were our favorite attractions except for our grandson who found some attractions including Harry Potter a bit too intense." –Jeff49

Fodor'sChoice ★ **Harry Potter and the Forbidden Journey.** Of all of Universal's rides, this is the one that really puts you in the movies. The queue leads you through the hallowed halls of Hogwarts to introduce you to the founders of the school and the story of the journey. Entering the academy, you'll see the sights you know from the books and films: Headmaster Dumbledore's office, Defence Against the Dark Arts classroom, Gryffindor common room, Room of Requirement, and the greenhouse. You'll also encounter the Sorting Hat, the One-Eyed Witch statue, and several talking portraits. Before you reach the actual ride, heroes Harry, Ron, and Hermione appear to persuade you to skip a lecture and follow them on a soaring journey. Thanks to a combination of live-action, robotic technology and innovative film making, your broomstick flight brings you face-to-face with a flying dragon and the Whomping Willow before being propelled into the heart of a Quidditch match. You also zip through a dozen scenes and encounter supporting characters Albus Dumbledore, Rubeus Hagrid, Draco Malfoy, and members of the Weasley family. All in all, a fantastic attraction—especially for fans of the series. Not suitable for those with neck, back, or heart problems. If you're pregnant or suffer from motion sickness, take a pass. **For people with disabilities:** Guests using wheelchairs must transfer to a ride vehicle. ■**TIP**➔ **Be patient; UNIVERSAL EXPRESS PASS isn't an option here, so relax and enjoy your tour of the school before boarding the ride.** ⊠ *The Wizarding World of Harry Potter* ☞ *Duration: 50–60 mins. Crowds: Yes! Audience: All but Small Kids. Height requirements: 48 inches minimum, 6 feet 3 inches maximum. Weight requirement: less than 250 pounds.*

Hogwart's Express–Hogsmeade Station. The trip to King's Cross Station at Universal Studios is distinctly different than the journey from Diagon Alley—but equally enjoyable. Inside the compartment, you can see the village and Hogwarts Castle from your window and when the train leaves the station the effect is amazing. Hagrid waves goodbye, centaurs gallop beside you, and Weasley brothers fly by on their broomsticks. As Hogwarts gradually disappears in the distance you can't help thinking you're really leaving a land known only to wizards. The journey lasts about four minutes, and when you see the streets of London you may think the fantasy is over–but it's not. You're only steps away from Diagon Alley where the magic is just getting started. ✉ *Wizarding World of Harry Potter, Islands of Adventure.*

LOST CONTINENT

Just beyond a wooden bridge, huge mythical birds guard the entrance to a land where trees are hung with weathered metal lanterns, and booming thunder mixes with chimes and vaguely Celtic melodies. Farther along the path, the scene looks similar to a Renaissance fair. Seers and fortune-tellers practice their trade in tents, and in a huge theater, Sindbad leaps and bounces all over Arabia. This stunt show and Poseidon let you bypass lines using UNIVERSAL EXPRESS PASS.

Eighth Voyage of Sindbad Stunt Show. The story line of this live stunt show is simple: Sindbad and his sidekick Kabob arrive in search of treasure, get distracted by the beautiful Princess Amoura, and are threatened by the evil sorceress Miseria. That's all you really need to know, and it's enough to get the good guy kicking off 25 nonstop minutes of punching, climbing, diving, leaping, and Douglas Fairbanks–ing his way through the performance. Kids are pleased with the action, and women are pleased with Sindbad. The downside is that it's sometimes hard to understand the stuntmen who (1) aren't exactly actors and (2) lip-sync to a script that's not always as funny as the writers intended. Still, you'll probably be satisfied by the water explosions, flames, and pyrotechnics that end with a daring, flaming high dive. Also, the 1,700-seat theater is a nice place to sit a spell and replenish your energy. **For people with disabilities:** The theater is wheelchair accessible and is equipped for assisted-listening devices. Some shows have sign-language interpreters. ■TIP➡ Find seats about 15 minutes before showtime. Don't sit too far up front—the experience is better a few rows back. ✉ *Lost Continent* ☞ *Duration: 25 mins. Crowds: Light. Audience: All but Small Kids.*

Poseidon's Fury. After a long walk through cool ruins guarded by the Colossus of Rhodes, a young archaeologist arrives to take you on a trek to find Poseidon's trident. Each chamber you enter looks interesting, and there's a story told in each one, but actually very little happens in most of them. Most of the time your group is simply walking through the ruins until the attraction attempts to bring the entertainment quotient up for the final scene. That comes after you've walked through a water vortex and enter the final hall where, on a 180-degree movie screen, actors playing Poseidon and his archenemy appear. As they shout at each other, a memorable fire- and waterworks extravaganza erupts all around you as massive waves crash and scorching fireballs fly. This finale is loud, powerful, and hyperactive. Is it worth the investment of time? Meh. Give it a whirl if you've done everything else. **For people with disabilities:** The theater is equipped for assisted-listening devices and is wheelchair accessible. ■TIP➡ Stay left against the wall as you enter, and position yourself opposite the central podium. In each succeeding section of the presentation, get into the very first

The Cat in the Hat, Circus McGurkus, and fish both red and blue are among the attractions geared to the under-7 set at Seuss Landing.

row, particularly if you aren't tall. ⊠ *Lost Continent* ☞ *Duration: 20 mins. Crowds: Heavy. Audience: All but Small Kids.*

SEUSS LANDING

This 10-acre tribute to Dr. Seuss puts you in the midst of his classic children's books. This means spending quality time with the Cat, Things 1 and 2, Horton, the Lorax, and the Grinch. From topiary sculptures to lurching lampposts to curvy fences (there was never a straight line in any of the books) to buildings that glow in lavenders, pinks, peaches, and oranges, everything seems surreal. It's a wonderful place to wrap up a day. Even the Cat would approve. All rides here except If I Ran the Zoo accept UNIVERSAL EXPRESS PASS.

Caro-Seuss-el. Ordinary horse-centric merry-go-rounds seem so passé compared with the menagerie on this one: the cowfish from *McElligot's Pool*, the elephant birds from *Horton Hatches the Egg*, and the Birthday Katroo from *Happy Birthday to You!* It's an entire ark of imaginary and interactive animals—indeed, the animals' eyes blink, and their tails wag. It may be a cliché, but there's a good chance you'll feel like a kid again when you hop aboard one of these fantastic creatures. You'll love it. **For people with disabilities:** Modified mounts let guests using wheelchairs ride without having to transfer to a ride vehicle. ■ TIP→ Use UNIVERSAL EXPRESS PASS, and/or make this a special end to your day. Lines move pretty well, so don't be intimidated. ⊠ *Seuss Landing* ☞ *Duration: 2 mins. Crowds: Moderate. Audience: All Ages. Height requirement: Children under 48 inches must be accompanied by an adult.*

The Cat in the Hat. Enter the pages of this classic book and you'll encounter a crazy cat ready to wreak havoc while your mom is out. As you

ISLANDS OF ADVENTURE FAMILY TOUR

As you go through IOA, try to pretend that you are not so much a park guest as you are a fledgling explorer and amateur sociologist (sometimes just watching people having fun *is* the fun). Imagine that you're taking in an entirely new world, rather than merely visiting a theme park.

In **Marvel Super Hero Island**, most guests race into the Hulk roller coaster and Spider-Man attractions. Instead, spend some time on the bridge or along the waterfront. Watch the frequent launching of the Hulk coaster, and perhaps study the visitors who've gathered for photos and autographs of Marvel superheroes.

In **Jurassic Park**'s Camp Jurassic, a series of paths loop through a prehistoric playground. Why not get lost for a while? Take time to explore the hallowed halls of Hogwarts and surrounding Hogsmeade village at the **Wizarding World of Harry Potter**. The **Lost Continent**, with its tents and crafters and colorful bangles, is yet another place to stop and take things in.

Toon Lagoon, the G-rated alternative to Super Hero Island, provides plenty of places to explore, including a marked path that lets you follow the trail of Billy (of *Family Circus* comic fame), who's wandered off on his own. At **Seuss Landing** find a quiet place to sit and spend some time just watching children (and adults). The closest thing here to a fountain of youth is spinning on a carousel, riding on a Seussian trolley, and meeting the fabled Cat in the Hat.

sit on a couch that spins, whirls, and rocks its way through the house, you'll roll past 18 scenes, 30 characters, and 130 effects. You're never alone. The mischievous cat appears balanced on a ball; hoists china on his umbrella; introduces Thing 1 and his wild sibling, Thing 2; and flies kites in the house while the voice of reason, the fish in the teapot, sounds the warning about the impending return of the family matriarch. As the tension builds, so does the fun—and kids love pointing out scenes from the book. This isn't the right ride for anyone who's pregnant; prone to motion sickness; or suffers from heart, neck, or back problems. **For people with disabilities:** The ride accommodates guests using wheelchairs and is equipped for assisted-listening devices. ■TIP→ Use UNIVERSAL EXPRESS PASS and/or come early or late. ⊠ *Seuss Landing* ⌁ *Duration: 4½ mins. Crowds: Heavy. Audience: All Ages. Height requirement: Under 48 inches must be accompanied by an adult.*

The High in the Sky Seuss Trolley Train Ride!. Colorful and quirky miniature Seussian trains on separate tracks embark on a slow and pleasing tour that provides an aerial view of the area, with Seuss-like narration along the way. You'll roll right through the Circus McGurkus Café Stoo-pendous and along the shores of the lagoon, where you can see the Sneetches as they enjoy the beaches. Fun for kids—and grown-ups, too. **For people with disabilities:** Guests using wheelchairs must transfer to a ride vehicle. ■TIP→ Kids love trains, so plan to get in line, especially if you have young ones. UNIVERSAL EXPRESS PASS is available here. ⊠ *Seuss Landing* ☞ *Duration: 3 mins. Crowds: Heavy. Audience: Small Kids. Height requirement: 34 to 48 inches must be accompanied by an adult.*

If I Ran the Zoo. In this interactive Seussian maze, kids can ditch the adults and have fun at their level. Here they encounter the trademarked fantasy creatures as they climb, jump, crawl, and push buttons to animate strange and wonderful animals. Park designers have learned that kids' basic needs include eating, sleeping, and getting splashed, so they've thoughtfully added some interactive fountains as well. **For people with disabilities:** The area is wheelchair accessible. ■TIP➜ If you can talk your kids into waiting, come at the end of your visit. ⊠ *Seuss Landing* ☞ *Duration: Up to You. Crowds: Heavy. Audience: Small Kids.*

One Fish, Two Fish, Red Fish, Blue Fish. Dr. Seuss put elephants in trees and green eggs and ham on trains, so it doesn't seem far-fetched that fish can circle "squirting posts" to a Jamaican beat. After a rather lengthy wait for what will seem like a very short experience, you climb into your fish and as it spins around a center pole, you (or your child) control its up-and-down motion. The key is to follow the lyrics of the special song—if you go down when the song tells you to go up, you may be drenched courtesy of the aforementioned squirting post. Then again, if the guests ahead of you miss their cue, the water's still spraying—and will likely splash you, too. Mighty silly, mighty fun. **For people with disabilities:** Modified mounts let guests using wheelchairs ride without having to transfer to a ride vehicle. ■TIP➜ Use UNIVERSAL EXPRESS PASS and/ or come early or late. Consider skipping it on your first visit. ⊠ *Seuss Landing* ☞ *Duration: 2+ mins. Crowds: Heavy. Audience: Small Kids. Height requirement: Under 48 inches must be accompanied by an adult.*

3

CITYWALK

With an attitude that's distinctly non-Disney, Universal has created nightlife for adults who want to party. The epicenter is CityWalk, a 30-acre entertainment-and-retail complex at the hub of promenades that lead to both Universal parks.

When it comes to retail, much of the merchandise includes things you can find elsewhere—and most likely for less. But when you're swept up in the energy of CityWalk and dazzled by the degree of window-shopping (not to mention the fact that you're on vacation and you're more inclined to spend), chances are you'll want to drop into stores selling everything from surf wear and cigars to tattoos and timepieces.

In addition to stores, the open and airy gathering place includes an over-the-top discotheque, a theater for the fabulous and extremely popular Blue Man Group, and a huge hall where karaoke's king. There's a New Orleans bar, a Jamaican reggae lounge, a casual Key West hangout, and, as of 2012, Hollywood Drive-In Golf, a pair of fun-filled 1950s sci-fi movie–themed miniature golf courses. On weeknights you find families and conventioneers; weekends a decidedly younger crowd parties until the wee hours.

Clubs have individual cover charges, but it's far more economical to pay for the whole kit and much of the caboodle. Choose a Party Pass (a one-price-all-clubs admission) for $11.99, or upgrade to a Party Pass-and-a-Movie for $15; a Party Pass-and-a-Meal for $21; a Movie-and-a-Meal for $21.95; or a Meal and a Mini-Golf Deal for $23.95.

At AMC Universal Cineplex, with its 20 screens (including IMAX), there's certain to be something you like—including nightly midnight movies. Meals (tax and gratuity included) are served at Jimmy Buffett's Margaritaville, the Hard Rock Cafe, and others. And as if these deals weren't sweet enough, after 6 the $15 parking fee drops to $5. Never-theless, it's a long haul from the garage to CityWalk—if you prefer, simply call a cab. They run at all hours. ☎ *407/354–3374, 407/363–8000 Universal main line* ⊕ *www.citywalkorlando.com.*

SEAWORLD, DISCOVERY COVE, AND AQUATICA

WELCOME TO SEAWORLD, DISCOVERY COVE, AND AQUATICA

TOP REASONS TO GO

★ **Animal Magnetism:** If you love animals—slick, shiny, feathery, or furry— SeaWorld, Discovery Cove, and Aquatica are where you want to be. No robotic wildlife here; just well-cared-for and talented dolphins, whales, seals, otters, penguins, cats, dogs. . . .

★ **A Slower Pace:** The shows and natural settings of SeaWorld and Discovery Cove let you enjoy a theme-park vacation without racing from one attraction to the next. Living in the moment is the lesson here.

★ **Getting Smarter:** No one leaves these parks without learning a little something about nature through shows, backstage tours, instructional signage, and well-versed educators and naturalists who are always ready to answer questions.

★ **Memories in the Making:** Chances are SeaWorld and Discovery Cove will afford you the chance to pet a penguin, feed a dolphin, or watch a 5-ton whale leap out of the water. You can't forget things like that.

1 SeaWorld. With the exception of a handful of thrill rides, the original park (which opened in 1973 to reroute visitors heading to the then recently opened Walt Disney World) maintains a slow and easy pace. Here it's all about clever shows, shaded sidewalks, and plenty of opportunities to enjoy the natural grace and intriguing personalities of marine life and other animals.

2 Discovery Cove. SeaWorld spun off this park to give you the chance to enjoy a lot more time (and to spend a little more cash) with the animals. A trip to this aquatic oasis feels like a trip to the islands; a daylong, all-inclusive experience that includes breakfast and lunch, drinks, a private beach, snorkeling equipment, and—for approximately an extra $100—the chance to swim with dolphins. Paradise.

TO WET 'N WILD &
UNIVERSAL STUDIOS

Universal Blvd.

EXIT 2

528

EXIT 1

EXIT 3A
AND
EXIT 3B

3 AQUATICA

Gateway Ave.

Orangewood Blvd.

International Dr.

1 SEAWORLD

423

0   1/4 mi

0   1/4 km

4

GETTING ORIENTED

SeaWorld is just off the intersection of Interstate 4 and the Beachline Expressway, equidistant from Universal Orlando and the Walt Disney World Resort, which are only about five minutes away. SeaWorld is also a mere 10 minutes from Downtown Orlando and 15 minutes from the airport. Discovery Cove is its own oasis across the street from SeaWorld. Aquatica, a little ways down the road from both, is the first of the three that you'll see after exiting the expressway.

3 Aquatica. SeaWorld's water park offers the chance to slip and slide at adrenaline-rush speeds, relax in the current of two wave pools, laze on a wide beach, and take the wee ones to pint-size play areas of their very own. All in all, there's something for everyone, showcased in a tropical, tiki-themed setting.

Updated
by Gary
McKechnie

Just as Walt Disney World and Universal Orlando are much more than just a single park, the same is true of SeaWorld. The original park—which includes the Shamu shows as well as presentations featuring dolphins and seals—has expanded to include Discovery Cove (an immersive tropical retreat), and Aquatica (a water park loaded with aquatic excitement). So, as you plan your vacation, consider that SeaWorld can easily fill a single day or, if you're really eager to take to the waters, perhaps a day or two more.

There's a whole lot more to SeaWorld and Discovery Cove than being splashed by Shamu. You can see manatees face-to-snout, learn to love a shark, swim with dolphins, and be spat at by a walrus. These two parks celebrate all the mammals, birds, fish, and reptiles that live in and near the ocean.

Then there's Aquatica, a wild water park that takes its cues from Sea-World and Discovery Cove in design and mood—marine-life motifs are everywhere. It also gives competitor water parks a run for their money with thrilling slides, broad beaches, calming rivers, and an area for small kids.

The park also takes some tips from the tropics. Right after you clear the parking lot, you see a tropical pastiche of buildings. Yup. That's definitely an island vibe you're detecting. Upon entering Aquatica, you feel as if you've left Central Florida for the Caribbean or Polynesia, even.

You might be drawn to the series of superfast waterslides (some of which conclude by sending you into serene streams), or you might feel the pull of the white-sand beaches beside the twin wave pools, where you can laze in the sun, venturing out every so often to try a ride or climb into an inner tube and float down a river. Whether you're spending the day at SeaWorld, Discovery Cove, or Aquatica, just go with it. Get into a groove, relax, and enjoy yourself at some of the most pleasant theme parks in Orlando.

PLANNING

GETTING HERE AND AROUND

Heading west on Interstate 4 (toward Disney) take Exit 72; heading east, take Exit 71. After that you'll be going east on the Beachline Expressway (aka Route 528), and the first right-hand exit leads you to International Drive. Turn left, and you'll soon see the entrance to Aquatica on your left. Sea Harbor Drive—leading to SeaWorld's entrance—will be on your right. To reach Discovery Cove, follow International Drive past Aquatica a half mile to the Central Florida Parkway and turn right. The park's entrance will be on your left.

OPERATING HOURS

SeaWorld opens daily at 9 am and usually closes at 7 pm, with extended hours during the summer and holidays. Hours at Discovery Cove also vary seasonally, although it's generally open daily from 8 to 5:30, with check-in beginning 30 minutes earlier—which is not a bad idea considering Discovery Cove serves a complimentary breakfast until 10 am. Aquatica is open at 9 am, with closing times varying between 5 and 9 pm, depending on the season. Allow a full day to see each attraction.

ADMISSION

SeaWorld, Discovery Cove, Aquatica, and Busch Gardens Tampa Bay fall under the SeaWorld Parks & Entertainment umbrella, and you can save by buying combo tickets. Regular one-day tickets to **SeaWorld** cost $95 (adults) and $90 (children ages 3–9), excluding tax, but if you order in advance over the phone or online, you'll save as much as $20 per ticket—which just may be the best money-saving option you'll find. Combo-park admission prices, which include 14 days at each park, are as follows:

SeaWorld/Aquatica Online *$89*

SeaWorld/Busch Gardens Tampa Online *$99*

SeaWorld/Aquatica/Busch Gardens Tampa Online *$109*

Flex Ticket (14 days at SeaWorld/Aquatica/Busch Gardens Tampa) *$345/$325*

Aquatica Online $37 (at the gate $56).

Reserve **Discovery Cove** visits well in advance—attendance is limited to about 1,000 a day. Tickets (with a dolphin swim) start at about $229 (off-season, in January and February) but are generally around $289. Forgo the dolphin swim and save approximately $80. This park has what's called dynamic pricing (meaning prices change by season, and also at other times without notice). Admission is less expensive the earlier you book (so call well in advance) and includes access to all beach and snorkeling areas and the free-flight aviary; meals and snacks; use of a mask, snorkel, swim vest, towel, locker, and sunscreen; parking; and a pass for 14 days of unlimited admission to SeaWorld Orlando and

Aquatica. Upgrade to an "ultimate" pass (about $20), which includes admission (and free transportation) to Busch Gardens Tampa.

Quick Queue Unlimited Passes. SeaWorld's Quick Queue passes (⌨ *$19–$35 per person, depending on season*) get you to the front of the line at major attractions and shows for one admission each. The higher-price unlimited pass is good for unlimited admissions. Neither Discovery Cove nor Aquatica has such a pass.

All-Day Dining Deal. Available at select SeaWorld restaurants (Voyager's Smokehouse, Seaport Pizza, Terrace Garden Buffet, The Spice Mill, Seafire Inn, and Mango Joe's), adults will pay about $30 and kids from $15 to chow down on an entrée, side dish, drink, and dessert for each meal. Skip it if you plan on having just one meal in the park.

PARKS TIPS

SMART SEAWORLD

Avoid weekend and school-holiday visits. These are the busiest times, so plan around them if you can.

Wear sneakers or water shoes—no heels or slip-on sandals. It may not seem like it, but there'll be a whole lot of walking as you roam from one end of the park to the other, stand in line, and walk through attractions.

Pack dry clothes. You can get wet just by being toward the front at the Shamu show or riding Journey to Atlantis. Alternatively, carry a rain poncho.

Budget for food for the animals. Participating in animal feedings is a major part of the SeaWorld experience, although it comes at a price: a small carton of fish costs $5.

Pick up a map-and-show schedule inside the entrance. SeaWorld has its show schedule down to a science. If you start by catching the show closest to the entrance, shortly after that one's over, guests are moving farther into the park to grab a seat at the next performance so you'll end up moving with the crowd. Instead, start off at a show farther inside the park so you are ahead of the crowds. Spend a few minutes planning so you can casually stroll from show to show and have time for learning, testing out thrill rides, *and* enjoying a leisurely meal.

Be open to learning. SeaWorld's trainers and educators are always at the ready to share information about the park's wildlife.

DISCOVERY DONE RIGHT

Make reservations well in advance. Prized June dates, for instance, can sell out in March. If there aren't openings when you call, though, don't despair. Call back often to inquire about cancellations.

Think about your eyewear. Park masks don't accommodate glasses, but there are a limited number of near- and far-sighted prescription masks (first-come, first-served) available. Just step into a booth and you'll be able to try on a few different pairs with different magnifications. If you don't mind risking lost contacts, just wear those beneath a non-prescription mask.

Don't bring your own wet suit or fins. Every guest must wear a Discovery Cove–issued wet suit or vest—not a bad idea, as the water can be cold.

Leave belongings in your locker. The plastic passes you're given are all you need to pick up your meals, soft drinks, and—if you're over 21—alcoholic drinks.

Be flexible when it comes to weather. If the weather on your reserved day looks like it'll be an all-day downpour, attempts will be made to reschedule your visit while you're in town. If that's not possible, you'll have to settle for a refund.

Have a dolphin relay a message. The Special Occasion Package enlists the help of a bottlenose dolphin to deliver love notes, wedding proposals, birthday or anniversary greetings, and the like.

AQUATICA ADVICE

■ **Buy tickets in advance.** Tickets bought ahead of time online or at another SeaWorld park allow early entry (and discounts) to Aquatica, which, in turn, increases your chances of hitting all the big-deal flume and tube rides—possibly more than once.

■ **Be open to animal encounters.** The Commerson's dolphins of Dolphin Plunge have scheduled feeding times, and you can see macaws perched on tree limbs and small mammals on display in Conservation Cabanas—usually attended to by knowledgeable educators.

■ **Pack beach supplies.** You'll save a few bucks by having your own towels, lotion, water shoes, and snacks.

■ **Take care of yourself.** Fight fatigue by eating a good breakfast, drinking plenty of water, and nibbling on high-energy snacks. Avoid sunburn by reapplying sunscreen often—even the waterproof stuff washes off.

■ **Save your soles.** Water shoes protect your feet from hot sand and sidewalks and the rough surfaces in some pools.

CONTACTS

Aquatica ☎ 888/800–5447 ⊕ *www.aquaticabyseaworld.com*

Busch Gardens Tampa ☎ 888/800–5447 ⊕ *www.buschgardens.com/bgt*

Discovery Cove ☎ 877/557–7404 ⊕ *www.discoverycove.com*

SeaWorld ☎ 888/800–5447 ⊕ *www.seaworld.com*

Parking. Parking is $17 for a car or motorcycle, $20 for an RV or camper. For $22 you can pull into one of the six Preferred Parking rows closest to the front gate. At Aquatica, cars and motorcycles are charged $12, RVs $16—although if you already have your parking slip from that day at SeaWorld, it's free. Parking is free at Discovery Cove.

SEAWORLD

Just as you wouldn't expect to arrive at Disney and see nothing but Mickey Mouse, don't expect to arrive at SeaWorld and see only Shamu. Only a few steps into the park you'll find baby dolphins and their mothers, a pool filled with stingrays, colorful flamingos, rescued sea turtles, rescued pelicans, and even rescued manatees. SeaWorld's objective is to educate as well as entertain.

You'll see how lumbering manatees live and what they look like up close; watch otters and seals perform slapstick routines based on their natural behaviors; learn about the lives of giant tortoises and sea turtles; and be absolutely amazed at the scope of marine life celebrated throughout the park.

Then there are the attractions, each and every one designed not only to showcase the marine world but also to demonstrate ways in which humans can protect the Earth's waters and wildlife. And, because there are more exhibits and shows than rides, the difference between SeaWorld and other theme parks is that you can go at your own pace, without that hurry-up-and-wait feeling. It's also worth noting that because shows, attractions, and exhibits are based primarily on nature and animals, designers have created a natural layout as well, with winding lanes and plenty of places to relax by the waterfront or beside bouquets of flowers. There's never a nagging urge to race through anything; indeed, the entire park encourages you to slow down and move at a casual pace. That said, theme parks like SeaWorld have been criticized by animal welfare groups. They argue that the conditions and treatment of marine life kept in captivity are harmful for the animals, and that human interaction further exacerbates this.

TOP SEAWORLD ATTRACTIONS

Antarctica: Empire of the Penguin. SeaWorld's latest attraction (and entire land, to boot), centers around a virtual-reality ride that follows a lone penguin through blizzards and past sea lions and into an ice cave where a colony of several hundred real-life penguins awaits your arrival.

Clyde and Seamore Take Pirate Island. Head for Sea Lion & Otter Stadium to watch this slapstick comedy routine starring an adorable team of water mammals and their trainers.

Kraken. Another fast and furious coaster takes you on a high-speed chase with a dragon. But the story-line doesn't matter as much as the fact that this one rockets you through some incredible loops.

Manta. SeaWorld likes to claim that this is two attractions in one: while waiting in line, you walk past 10 supercool aquariums filled with rays and fish. But the big thrill is the amazingly fast coaster you reach at the front of the line.

One Ocean. Although trainers no longer get into the water with the killer whales, SeaWorld's signature show can still impress and inspire the audience to care for the planet and its creatures.

Pets Ahoy. Anyone who has ever loved a pet (or just wanted one) simply has to see the talented cats, dogs, birds, and pig in this cute and clever show.

4

ORIENTATION AND PLANNING

GETTING ORIENTED

SeaWorld's performance venues, attractions, and activities surround a 17-acre lagoon, and the artful landscaping, curving paths, and concealing greenery sometimes lead to wrong turns. But armed with a map that lists showtimes, it's easy to plan an approach that lets you move fluidly from one show and attraction to the next and still have time for rest stops and meal breaks.

TOURING TIPS

Before investing in front-of-the-line Quick Queue passes (🎫 $19–$35), remember that there are only a handful of big-deal rides, and space is seldom a problem at shows.

If you bring your own food, remove all straws and lids before you arrive—they can harm fish and birds.

Arrive at least 30 minutes early for the Shamu show, which generally fills to capacity. Prepare to get wet in the "splash zone" down front.

In Discovery Cove make the aviary one of your first stops, since the 250-plus birds within will be more active in the morning. Check-in starts at around 7:30 am.

SEAWORLD PLANNER

PARKS AMENITIES

Baby Care: Diaper-changing tables are in or near most women's restrooms and in the men's restroom at the front entrance. Diaper-vending machines are in all changing areas and at Shamu's Emporium. Areas for nursing are alongside the women's restroom at Friends of the Wild gift shop and beside Shamu's Happy Harbor. Baby food is sold at most restaurants and at Sand Castle Toys and Treats. Rent strollers (*$15 for a single, $24 for a double per day*) at the information center.

First Aid: Staffed by registered nurses, first-aid centers are behind Stingray Lagoon and near Shamu's Happy Harbor. Discovery Cove's first-aid station is near the Photo Area entrance.

Guest Services: Ticket booths have become the new Guest Services (aka Guest Relations) center. If you ordered your tickets online, have questions about dining or attractions, or just need tickets to begin with, you can find it all here.

Information and Reservation Center: Right inside the entrance you can pick up the park map (which also has info on showtimes, services, and amenities); make dinner reservations; and buy tickets for Discovery Cove, Aquatica, and park tours.

Lockers: One-time-use, coin-op lockers ($1) are near flip-over coasters like Kraken and Manta, Journey to Atlantis, and Shamu's Happy Harbor as well as inside SeaWorld's main entrance. Also near the entrance, next to Shamu's Emporium, are day lockers ($8 small, $11 large per day). At Discovery Cove free lockers await you near the cabanas.

Lost People and Things: SeaWorld's Main Information Center operates as the park's Lost and Found. Lost children are brought here, and it's the place to report lost children. A park-wide paging system also helps reunite parents with kids. At Discovery Cove lost kids and items eventually find their way to the check-in lobby.

Package Pick-Up: If you buy something, you can have it sent to SeaWorld's Package Pick-Up, in Shamu's Emporium, or to the check-in lobby at Discovery Cove. Allow two hours for delivery.

Pet Care Center: SeaWorld's Pet Care Center, near the main entrance, accommodates dogs, cats, hamsters, and whatever other creatures guests are traveling with. Arrive with a copy of your pet's shot record, updated rabies tag, water bowl, food, and a toy or blanket to remind your pet of home. (Note that dogs must be walked at least once a day.) You can drop off your pet 30 minutes before the park opens and must pick it up 30 minutes before closing.

Services for People with Disabilities: Get info on services and rent standard wheelchairs ($12 daily) and electric wheelchairs ($50 daily) at SeaWorld's Main Information Center. Discovery Cove has some free wheelchairs equipped with huge balloonlike tires to cross the sand. Reserve one in advance. At both parks, aquariums, wading areas, theaters, and restaurants are wheelchair accessible. (Note that drinking straws aren't provided, out of concern for the safety of the animals.) Shops are level, but many are so packed with stuff that maneuvering in a wheelchair is a challenge.

EXPLORING SEAWORLD

A'Lure, the Call of the Ocean (Nautilus Theater). SeaWorld never holds back when it comes to stage shows, and this one, similar in style and feel to Cirque du Soleil, is no exception. It is framed by the story of a fisherman who falls overboard into a new world beneath the waves. The colorful, costumed inhabitants of this underwater kingdom astound the fisherman with their amazing talents on the trampoline, rocket themselves through hoops, and leap onto towering poles and stick to them like chameleons. Acrobats march into the audience with festive Chinese dragons, find wonderful new uses for hula hoops, and perform impressive feats with hanging strips of silk. You might want to see this show twice—there's so much taking place you're likely to miss some wonderful moments. **For people with disabilities:** Guests using wheelchairs have reserved seating at the rear of the theater. Assisted-listening devices are available. ■ TIP➡ **Although the auditorium seats more than 1,000 and you won't feel packed in, arrive at least 15 minutes early for a wider choice of seats. Reserved seats can be arranged through Signature Show Seating.** ⊠ *Nautilus Theater* ⊕ *www.seaworldparks.com* ☞ *Duration: 20 mins. Crowds: Heavy. Audience: All Ages.*

Blue Horizons (Dolphin Theater). The story is a fairy tale of sorts, starting with a young girl's fantasy of life in the sea, which is enough to lead off a high-energy, crowd-pleasing show that features high dives, dazzling dolphins, and astounding feats of "aquabatics." Dolphins execute perfectly coordinated leaps, arcs, and splashes. Performers ski atop the backs of two dolphins while another performer in a feathery bird costume performs an aerial ballet. Divers repeatedly leap from two high towers as two acrobats portraying the story's villains perform impressive and repeated synchronized jumps on bungee cords. It's active, it's exciting, it's beautiful, and it's a show that blends everything SeaWorld does best above and below the water. **For people with disabilities:** Ask an attendant about seating for wheelchair users toward the front. ■ TIP➡ **Arrive 20 minutes before showtime for the best seats, or invest in Signature Show Seating.** ⊠ *Dolphin Theater* ☞ *Duration: 20 mins. Crowds: Heavy. Audience: All Ages.*

Dolphin Cove. Dolphin Cove is a huge free-form pool where a few dozen Atlantic bottlenose dolphins skim around and nose up to the edge to be fed fish ($5 a tray) by generous guests. Once or twice a day, trainers will come out to host a scheduled feeding. Often a SeaWorld guide will offer a commentary about the dolphins' behaviors and remind everyone that the pool's residents enjoy having their sides rubbed and petted. Who doesn't? Be sure to walk to the far end of the lagoon where the walkway descends to a grotto to reveal an underwater view of the dolphins, providing an entirely new perspective that is both fascinating and entertaining—it's almost as if you're diving with the dolphins. **For people with disabilities:** This attraction is completely accessible to guests using wheelchairs. ■ TIP➡ **On your way to or from a show, come see the dolphins. If it's crowded, go shopping until the crowds disperse.** ⊠ *Key West at SeaWorld* ☞ *Duration: Up to You. Crowds: Light to Moderate. Audience: All Ages.*

Key West at SeaWorld. Dolphin Cove is within a laid-back area modeled after Key West, Florida's southernmost outpost (famous for spectacular sunsets and a festive mood). And although there are no distinct "lands" within SeaWorld, this Jimmy Buffett–style "island paradise" comes close. It contains individual tropical-style shows and attractions within its loosely defined borders. ⊠ *Key West at SeaWorld*

Dolphin Nursery. Although largely overshadowed by the more magnificent attractions, this large pool, which has been here since the park opened in 1973, continues to please guests by allowing them to watch dolphin moms and babies (with birth dates posted on signs) play and leap and splash. They say you can even observe the dolphin calves learning to communicate with their moms through clicks and vocalizations. Although you can't get close enough to pet or feed them, you can see them from just a few feet away. A host is usually on hand to answer questions. A popular answer? "No, you can't take one home." Hint: if you just *have* to touch a dolphin, head over to Dolphin Cove in the Key West section. **For people with disabilities:** Fully wheelchair accessible. ■TIP→ Get ready to lift up small kids so they can see into the pool. ⊠ *SeaWorld* ⌁ *Duration: Up to You. Crowds: Light. Audience: All Ages.*

Journey to Atlantis. SeaWorld's coaster offering is a hybrid, combining the elements of a high-speed water ride and a roller coaster with lavish special effects and a story line. The lost continent of Atlantis has risen in the harbor of a quaint Greek fishing village, and you board a Greek fishing boat to explore it. An ominous current tugs at your vessel, and an old fisherman (actually Hermes, the messenger of the gods, in disguise) offers a golden sea horse to protect you from the evil Sirens. The LCD technology, lasers, and holographic illusions are really cranked up during a watery battle between Hermes and Allura, queen of the Sirens. Amid this story, you experience frequent twists, turns, and short, shallow dives, as well as one hair-raising plunge that sends you nearly 60 feet into the main harbor (plan on getting soaked). This is followed by a final nosedive into S-shaped, bobsledlike curves. Although the ride is a little dated, it's still not for the faint of heart; anyone with back, neck, or heart problems; anyone who's pregnant; or anyone who dislikes the dark or enclosed spaces. **For people with disabilities:** You must transfer from your wheelchair to the ride vehicle. ■TIP→ Come first thing in the morning or about an hour before closing. Going at night is awesome, and if there's a wait at all, it will be short. Last resort: spring for a Quick Queue Pass. ⊠ *SeaWorld* ⌁ *Duration: 6 mins. Crowds: Heavy. Audience: Not Small Kids. Height minimum: 42 inches with an adult; 48 inches without.*

Fodor's Choice **Kraken.** As the park opens, many coaster lovers head straight for Kraken,
★ and when you see its loops and dips you'll know why. Named after an angry sea monster, this wickedly fast coaster takes you underground three times, lifts you higher (up to 149 feet), drops you longer, and spirals you faster than you'd expect. Kraken also packs a serious punch thanks to its floorless seats (your legs dangle loosely), seven inversions, and moments of weightlessness. The line for it moves pretty quickly because of a high seating capacity. Note that bags aren't allowed past

SeaWorld Orlando

← TO AQUATICA

Shark Encounter

Shark's Underwater Grill

Kraken

Pacific Point Preserve

Clyde and Seamore's Sea Lion High (Sea Lion & Otter Theater)

Spice Mill Café

Lockers

Antarctica: Empire of the Penguins

ATM

Pearl Dive

Lockers

Journey to Atlantis

Voyager Smokehouse

Antarctic Market

Seaport Pizza

Guest Services, Information Reservations and Show Schedules

Seaport Theater/ Pets Ahoy

THE WATERFRONT

Blue Horizons (Dolphin Theater)

Manta

Turtle Trek

Seafire Inn

Lockers

Dolphin Nursery

Pelican Preserve

Dolphin Cove

ATM

KEY WEST

ATM Lockers

Cypress Bakery

Stingray Lagoon

First Aid

Captain Pete's Island Eats

Key West at SeaWorld

Information and Reservations

SeaWorld Rescue

Parking

KEY

✘ Restaurants
🚻 Restrooms
ℹ️ Tourist information

The Terrace Garden Buffet

Nautilus Theater

Paddle boats

ATM

Games Area

Sea Carousel

First Aid

ATM

Arcade

Dine with Shamu

One Ocean (Shamu Stadium)

Baby Care Center

Shamu's Happy Harbor

Coconut Cove Snacks

Lockers

TO DISCOVERY COVE →

Sky Tower

Lagoon

Wild Arctic

Mango Joe's Café

ATM

Boardwalk

Atlantis Bayside Stadium

Sea Harbor Pavilions (Private Parties)

Education Program Entrance

Main Entrance/Exit

ATM

Ports of Call

Parking

0   100 yards

0   100 m

the turnstiles. It costs about 50¢ to leave them in a locker, but it's worth the investment. This is one cool coaster, though not for anyone with motion sickness or back, neck, or heart conditions. **For people with disabilities:** You must transfer from your wheelchair to the ride vehicle. ■ TIP➔ **Come as soon as the park opens—especially to snag front-row seats. Otherwise, use a Quick Queue pass (extra fee required) or come near closing or during a Blue Horizons show.** ⊠ *SeaWorld* ☞ *Duration: 6 mins. Crowds: Heavy. Audience: Not Small Kids. Height minimum: 54 inches.*

Fodor's Choice ★ **Manta.** While waiting in line for this incredible coaster, you're ushered past 10 aquariums containing more than 3,000 sea creatures, including 100 species of fish, graceful rays, sea dragons, and sea horses. This alone is fascinating, but this gentle encounter is followed by the sight of row after row of guests being locked down, strapped in, and firmly secured for what's about to happen. You'll be suspended horizontally (face down!) beneath a 12-foot, stingray-shaped, roller-coaster car, which leaps out of the station, attaining speeds of up to 56 mph on a ½-mile race of loops as it spins around and above the aquarium. At times you are so close to the water that the coaster's wings skim the surface. There are four inversions and a drop of more than 10 stories. Halfway through, the ride slows down a bit and you may think it's over—but it's not. There are even more twists and spins ahead. Kids will love the aquarium entrance; daring older children and adults will love the thrill of the ride. Avoid this ride if you're pregnant, suffer from motion sickness, or have back, neck, or heart problems. **For people with disabilities:** You must transfer to the ride seat, properly use the ride restraint, and be able to grip a harness with one hand. ■ TIP➔ **Come first thing or late in the day, or use a Quick Queue pass (extra fee required).** ⊠ *SeaWorld* ☞ *Duration: 6 mins. Crowds: You Bet! Audience: Not Small Kids. Height minimum: 54 inches.*

Fodor's Choice ★ **One Ocean (Shamu Stadium).** Within this stadium, SeaWorld's iconic mascot, Shamu, and other orcas star in a choreographed spectacle. For safety the trainers stay out of the water, which dilutes the thrills, but everything—not just the animals—still seems larger than life. A three-story whale-tail backdrop, enormous LED screens, a brilliant oceanic color palette, rhythmic music, and surround sound set the scene for the killer-whale performances. Celebrating how we and other creatures are all connected to the world we share, the show also incorporates fountains, an innovation inspired by regular interactions between whales and trainers, who have long used water hoses in play sessions. Perhaps you've heard tales of so-called soak zones? They exist. It takes only a wave of these creatures' massive flukes or a well-placed belly flop to throw gallons of water into the stands. Even in the upper reaches of the splash zones, you'll still get wet—fun at the time, but less so a few hours later if you didn't bring a change of clothes. If you've seen *Believe,* you may be disappointed; if not, this show may still be entertaining. **For people with disabilities:** If you're using a wheelchair, you and a companion can sit in a special area near the front-row soak zone, and others in your party can sit nearby. Assisted-listening devices are available. ■ TIP➔ **The show itself lasts about 25 minutes, but there's also** a 20-minute preshow, so plan accordingly. For an extra fee, reserve a seat through Signature Show Seating. ⊠ *Shamu Stadium* ☞ *Duration: 25 mins. Crowds: Moderate to Heavy. Audience: All Ages.*

Pacific Point Preserve. A nonstop chorus of "aarrrps" and "yawps" coming from behind Sea Lion & Otter Stadium leads you to the 2½-acre home of California sea lions and harbor and fur seals. This naturalistic expanse of beaches, waves, and huge outcroppings of upturned rock, designed to replicate the northern Pacific coast, has a calming effect. The area is roughly circular. Stroll around the edge of the surf zone, a favorite hangout for fun-loving pinnipeds, who swim up close for a share of the smelt you've just bought ($5) or flop over on their sides and laze in the Florida sun. On the far side of the complex you can walk down into a grotto where a large Plexiglas wall allows you to see them darting and diving and playing underwater. Priceless. **For people with disabilities:** This attraction is completely accessible to guests using wheelchairs. ■ TIP➜ **Come anytime. It shouldn't be too hard to find a place away from the crowds.** ⊠ *SeaWorld* ☞ *Duration: Up to You. Crowds: Light. Audience: All Ages.*

Pets Ahoy. About a dozen dogs, a dozen-plus cats, and an assortment of ducks, doves, parrots, and a pot-bellied pig (nearly all rescued from local animal shelters) are the stars of this lively, hilarious show. The animals perform complex stunts on a stage that looks like a seaside village. From stealing a string of sausages to driving their "girlfriends" on a date, these cute-as-a-button actors perform feats that are each more incredible than the last. Look around and you'll notice that the show is just as appealing to foreign guests; you don't have to speak English to enjoy what is essentially a live version of a silent movie. Stick around and you'll have a chance to shake paws with the stars. **For people with disabilities:** Special seating for guests using wheelchairs and assisted-listening devices are available. ■ TIP➜ **Gauge the crowds and arrive early if necessary.** ⊠ *SeaWorld* ☞ *Duration: 15–20 mins. Crowds: Moderate to Heavy. Audience: All Ages.*

Shamu's Happy Harbor. Sprawling, towering, and (for kids) beyond incredible, this 3-acre playground has places to crawl, climb, explore, bounce, and get wet. There's an adjacent arcade with midway games; there are pipes to crawl through; a tent with an air-mattress floor; and "ball rooms"—one for toddlers and one for grade-schoolers—with thousands of plastic balls to wade through. Keep on looking and you'll discover miniaturized thrill rides—roller coasters and spinning rides and an assortment of other rides that inject a pint-size dose of adrenaline. Then there are big sailing ships to explore and webbed ropes to climb and water to play in and around. For kids, this part of the park is worth the price of admission—they could be here for hours. **For people with disabilities:** Various areas offer different levels of clearance. Check with attendants about accessibility. ■ TIP➜ **Don't come first thing, or you'll never drag your child away; that said, it's busy here mid-afternoon or near dusk. Bring a towel to dry them off.** ⊠ *SeaWorld* ☞ *Duration: Up to You. Crowds: Heavy. Audience: Small Kids. Height minimum: 42 inches.*

SEAWORLD ORLANDO AND DISCOVERY COVE

NAME	Height Req.	Type of Entertainment	Duration	Crowds	Audience	Tips
SeaWorld						
Antarctica: Empire of the Penguins	48"	Tour/Thrill Ride	5 mins.	Heavy	All Ages	Come early.
A'Lure, the Call of the Ocean	n/a	Show	20 mins.	Heavy	All Ages	Plenty of seats, but arrive 15 mins. early for a wide selection.
Blue Horizons	n/a	Show	20 mins.	Heavy	All Ages	Arrive 20 mins. before showtime.
Dolphin Nursery	n/a	Aquarium	Up to you	Light	All Ages	Come during a Shamu show so the kids can be up front.
Journey to Atlantis	At least 42"	Thrill Ride with Water	6 mins.	Heavy	All but Young Kids	You can make a beeline here first thing or come about an hour before closing. But the best time for this is at night.
Key West at SeaWorld	n/a	Walk-Through/ Aquarium	Up to you	Light to Moderate	All Ages	If too crowded, wander until crowds disperse.
★ Kraken	At least 54"	Thrill Ride	6 mins.	Heavy	All but Young Kids	Get to the park when it opens and head straight to Kraken; otherwise, hit it near closing time or during a Blue Horizons show.
Manatees Rescue	n/a	Aquarium	Up to you	Light to Moderate	All Ages	Come during a Shamu show but *not* right after a dolphin show.
★ Manta	At least 54"	Thrill Ride with Water	6 mins.	You Bet!	All but Young Kids	Come first thing or late in the day, or purchase a Quick Queue pass for front-of-ride access.
Pacific Point Preserve	n/a	Aquarium	Up to you	Light	All Ages	Come anytime.
Pets Ahoy	n/a	Show	15–20 mins.	Moderate to Heavy	All Ages	Gauge the crowds, and come here early if necessary.
★ Sea Lion & Otter Stadium	n/a	Show	40 mins.	Heavy	All Ages	Sit toward the center for the best view, and don't miss the pre-show mime. Plenty of seats.

Attraction	Min. Height	Type	Duration	Crowds	Audience	Strategy
Shamu's Happy Harbor	n/a	Playground with Water	Up to you	Heavy	Young Kids	Don't come first thing in the morning, or you'll never drag your child away. Bring a towel to dry them off.
★ Shamu Stadium (One Ocean)	n/a	Show	25 mins.	Moderate to Heavy	All Ages	Show itself lasts 25 minutes, but there's a 30-minute pre-show; plan accordingly.
Shark Encounter	n/a	Aquarium	Up to you	Light to Moderate	All Ages	Come during the sea lion show.
Sky Tower	48"	Tour/Thrill Ride	6 mins.	Light	All Ages	Come whenever there's no line. Note the extra $4 charge, though.
Stingray Lagoon	n/a	Aquarium	Up to you	Moderate to Heavy	All Ages	Walk by if it's crowded, but return before dusk.
Turtle Point	n/a	Zoo	Up to you	Light	All Ages	Come anytime.
Wild Arctic	At least 42"	Simulator Exp./Aquarium	5+ mins.	Moderate to Heavy	All Ages	Come during a Shamu show. You can skip the ride if you just want to see the mammals.

Discovery Cove

Attraction	Min. Height	Type	Duration	Crowds	Audience	Strategy
Beaches	n/a	Beach Area	Up to you	Light	All Ages	Arrive early and head to the far side for a private spot.
★ Dolphin Lagoon	n/a	Pool	45–60 mins.	n/a	All but Young Kids	Be mindful of your appointment time.
Explorer's Aviary	n/a	Aviary	Up to you	Light to Moderate	All Ages	Come early, when the birds are most active.
Tropical Reef	n/a	Aquarium/Pool Area	Up to you	Light to Moderate	All Ages	Monitor crowds and come when they're lightest. Popular with teens.
Wind-Away River	n/a	Aquarium	Up to you	Light to Moderate	All Ages	When it gets hot, slip into the water. Popular with teens.

★ Fodor's Choice

SEAWORLD GROWN-UP TOURS

Strolling through SeaWorld is comforting. Quiet sidewalks and landscaped lanes abound. Indeed, a number of local senior citizens who were part of mall-walking clubs have learned that an annual pass gives them access to a very pleasant walk in the park—as well as a day filled with wonderful attractions. Follow in their footsteps on a walk of up to a mile, from west to east.

WEST SIDE STORY

The west side has most of the attractions—and the most paths. From the entrance, walk around the information center and to the left toward **Pelican Preserve**, where a flock of rescued pelicans are shuffling about.

Turn left into **Key West at SeaWorld**, where you can enjoy nature—first by feeding and petting the slippery skates at Stingray Lagoon and then by spending time with the residents of Dolphin Cove; be sure to head to the far end of the cove and drop down into the grotto, where a wide window reveals their underwater world. A little farther along, take your pick of **Turtle Trek** (home of turtles and manatees) and/or the **Blue Horizons** show at the Dolphin Theater. Afterward, loop back toward the entrance before peeling off to your left toward the **Waterfront** area. When you reach the shores of the lagoon, stroll past the **Sky Tower**—unless you'd like a bird's-eye view of the entire park. In that case, head on up and see the sights. You may also want to spend a few minutes watching the action at **Pearl Dive** before catching the show at the **Sea Lion and Otter Theater**. And be sure to explore **Antarctica: Empire of the Penguin** (both the land and the ride).

EAST SIDE STORY

Start at the **Seafire Inn**, a great place to grab a bite to eat and cool off. Head to the boardwalk and take it across the lagoon. This pleasing, uncongested walk brings you to the rear of **Shamu Stadium**, and although you can circle it in either direction, go right to avoid crowds of kids gathered at Shamu's Happy Harbor. If there's a show at the stadium, perfect. If not, not too far down the lane are the Nautilus Theater and the Cirque-style show, **A'Lure: The Call of the Ocean.** If your timing's off, after crossing the boardwalk just walk over to **Wild Arctic** where an observation area affords a glimpse of polar bears and walrus. Spend some time in the frozen North before returning to the sidewalk, which winds its way behind the Atlantis Bayside Stadium and back toward the park entrance and, all too soon, the real world.

Shark Encounter. Within a large, innocuous white structure are some thoroughly creepy critters: eels, barracuda, sharks, and poisonous fish. You may even spy a few creatures you've never seen (or even imagined) before, like the weedy sea dragon and his cousin, the leafy sea dragon, which look like branches of a tree. But the stars of the show are the sharks, and this attraction doesn't scrimp. The real fun comes when you enter large transparent corridors and see fish, eels, and a half dozen species of sharks slice gracefully through the water all around you—even overhead—which is a sensational new experience. Consider

There are bubbles but no toil and trouble with the Sea Witches of Sea World.

visiting the attraction in conjunction with a meal at the extraordinarily well-designed Sharks Underwater Grill, where you can order fresh fish and Floribbean cuisine while watching your entrée's cousins. **For people with disabilities:** Open spaces allow access to guests using wheelchairs. ■TIP→ **Spend at least 20 minutes here. Crowds are biggest when the adjacent sea lion and otter show gets out; time your visit accordingly.** ⊠ *SeaWorld* ☞ *Duration: Up to You. Crowds: Light to Moderate. Audience: All Ages.*

Sky Tower. The focal point of the park is this 400-foot-tall tower, the main mast for a revolving scenic double-decker observation platform. During the six-minute rotating up-and-down round-trip, you'll get the inside scoop on the park's history, its attractions, and surrounding sights. All in all, it's peaceful, relaxing, and gives you a new aerial perspective on SeaWorld and Orlando. Adjacent to it is Pearl Dive, a small area where you can sit and watch pearl divers snag oysters. **For people with disabilities:** The tower can accommodate two wheelchairs per cycle. ■TIP→ **Come whenever there's not a line, or use Quick Queue if necessary (extra fee required).** ⊠ *SeaWorld* ☞ *Duration: 6 mins. Crowds: Light. Audience: All Ages. Height minimum: 48 inches or accompanied by an adult for the tower trip.*

Stingray Lagoon. In this interactive hands-on exhibit (aka a shallow pool), dozens of circling stingrays are close enough to touch, as evidenced by the many outstretched hands surrounding the rim. Buy stingray delicacies (smelts, silversides, shrimp, and squid) available for $5 a tray, two for $9, three for $13 from the attendant. The best part is when the rays flap up for lunch, you can stroke their velvety skin.

Even though they have stingers, they won't hurt you—they just want food (and they're obligingly hungry all day). Check out the nursery pool with its baby rays. **For people with disabilities:** This attraction is easily accessible to guests using wheelchairs. ■TIP→ Walk by if it's crowded, but return before dusk before the smelt concession stand closes. ⊠ *SeaWorld* ☞ *Duration: Up to You. Crowds: Moderate to Heavy. Audience: All Ages.*

Turtle Trek. This walk-through attraction is a three-part experience that begins underground where wide windows reveal a pool inhabited by surprisingly graceful manatees. (SeaWorld, by the way, has rescued more manatees than anyone else in the world and has rescued an estimated 20,000 birds, fish, and animals since 1964.) Part two takes you to a room where rescued sea turtles can be seen swimming past as a host discusses the life cycle of these docile creatures. This bit of background leads to the final room, a domed 360-degree 3-D theater where you are introduced to Nyah, a sea turtle who defies the odds and scurries into the ocean after being hatched. From here, you follow Nyah through a series of near disasters until she returns to the beach to lay her own eggs. Note that the predators attempting to get at Nyah and her siblings may be too intense for kids, and the volume may be cranked up to rock-concert levels. If you have a tinge of motion sickness, hang on to the support rails, because the film makes it seem as if the world's gone topsy-turvy. ■TIP→ If you can't handle the virtual motion of the movie, skip the film and take a peek at the manatees and turtles from an outdoor observation area. If there's a long line, the fee-additional Quick Queue pass works here. ⊠ *SeaWorld* ☞ *Duration: 30 mins for entire experience; 7 mins for movie: Crowds: Moderate: Audience: All Ages.*

Wild Arctic. At this pseudo ice station, you embark on a soaring and swooping virtual helicopter ride that takes you over the Arctic and through some dangerously close calls (if you're sensitive to the very real rolls and pitches, you can opt out for a stationary virtual helicopter). Then you exit onto a long walk through interactive, educational displays which lead to above- and below-water stations where you can watch Beluga whales, polar bears, and groaning tusked walruses (some weighing as much as 3,000 pounds) hoisting themselves onto a thick shelf of ice. This is a diverse and cute collection of animals you certainly don't see every day, which makes this sneak peak at their lifestyle vastly entertaining. Those who are pregnant or who suffer from neck, back, or heart conditions or motion sickness should opt out of the virtual-helicopter part of the attraction. **For people with disabilities:** You must transfer from your wheelchair to the ride vehicle. ■TIP→ Come early, late, or during a Shamu show. You can skip the simulated helicopter ride if you just want to see the mammals. ⊠ *SeaWorld* ☞ *Duration: Up to You. Crowds: Moderate to Heavy. Audience: All Ages. Height minimum: 42 inches.*

The clear tunnel at Shark Encounter in Sea World takes you underwater and underneath the sharks.

ANIMAL ENCOUNTERS AND TOURS

SeaWorld has several programs that put you closer to the animals. Up-Close and Behind-the-Scenes tours last 60 to 90 minutes and cost about $10 to $50. The six-hour Expedition Tour starts at around $100 for adults and $80 for children (depending on the season) and includes reserved seating at shows; sea lion, dolphin, and ray feedings; Quick Queue Unlimited front of line access; and an All-Day Dining Deal. You'll join other park guests on this one. The seven-hour Private VIP Tour (limited to just your group) includes the same but adds preferred parking, and the meal is upgraded to the full-service Sharks Underwater Grill. Prices start at around $299 per person.

You can book tours up to three months in advance. For a list, check the SeaWorld website (⊕ *www.seaworld.com*) or call the park (☎ *407/ 351–3600*).

Behind the Scenes Tour. On this 90-minute program, you'll have a chance to see how SeaWorld's animal experts care for rescued manatees and sea turtles. Where else can you touch a shark, step inside a hidden polar bear den, and play with a penguin? From $29 adults, $9 children.

Beluga Interaction Program. For this program (starting from $119 and up, depending on season) you don a wet suit and assist a trainer in feeding Beluga whales, which average about 15 feet and 2,000 pounds. They're good-natured and well trained enough to respond to hand signals you learn from the trainer. FYI: The wet suits help protect guests from the frigid 55-degree water. Must be 10 or older; 14 and younger must be accompanied by an adult.

Dolphins Up Close. They're amazing animals, of course, and on this hour-long tour you'll be able to participate in a training session, touch a dolphin, and use hand gestures to prompt behaviors. From $59 adults, $39 children.

Marine Mammal Keeper Experience. The daylong keeper experience (from $399) is perhaps the ultimate SeaWorld offering. Your full day includes lunch, a T-shirt, seven consecutive days of park admission, and, perhaps, a lasting desire to become a SeaWorld trainer. After arriving at 6:30 am, you don a wet suit and then go to work with trainers to care for, feed, and train dolphins, manatees, sea lions, and Beluga whales. An unforgettable experience that includes plenty of photo ops and lasting memories.

Sea Lion & Otter Up Close Tour. If you'd like to spend some time with just about the cutest animals anywhere, this 60-minute tour focuses on the naturally funny sea lions and their svelte counterparts, otters. Snap a souvenir shot with a sea lion (and otter), and then make their day (and yours) by helping to feed buckets of fish to the sea lions and harbor seals at Pacific Point Preserve. From $39 adults, $19 children.

Sleepovers. These overnight events are arranged primarily for kids, with special programs designed specifically for Boy Scouts, Girl Scouts, and students from grades 2 to 12. During the summer, sleepovers are mainly geared to families with kids between kindergarten and fifth grade. Where will you bunk down for the night? The sleepovers are held at various locations, but always indoors beside a habitat for sharks, manatees, dolphins, Beluga whales, polar bears, penguins, or manta rays. The evening begins at 6 and includes a pizza dinner, a walk around the exhibit with a trainer, and ends with a continental breakfast. Expect to pay $95 for the experience, and park admission is included in the rate. Call ahead for reservations. ☎ *800/406–2244.*

VIP Tours. Two levels of special tours are offered with Expedition Sea-World (formerly the VIP Tour) ranging from $59 for children and $79 for adults. With that, you receive instant access to Manta, Kraken, Journey to Atlantis, Turtle Trek, Antarctica: Empire of the Penguin, and Wild Arctic plus reserved seating at the One Ocean, Blue Horizons, and Clyde and Seamore shows; a chance to feed sea lions, dolphins, and rays; and enjoy a meal at an All Day Dining Deal restaurant. Note that you'll be traveling with a group of up to 12. If you invest in the substantially more expensive Private VIP Tour (from $299 or, with park admission, from $349), it will be limited to you and your guests and included preferred parking, reserved seating at shows, and replace the buffet lunch with an upscale meal at Sharks Underwater Grill. Another plus is that the Private VIP Tour can be completely customized (i.e., if there are only adults, you can skip Happy Harbor and other kids' activities; if there *are* kids, then the tour will add stops just for them).

Wild Arctic Up Close Experience. On this hour-long program, you'll be able to interact with seals, walruses, and beluga whales. Trainers are there to take your questions—and you'll be delighted when you come face to snout with a whiskered walrus. Too cute! From $59 adults and children.

DISCOVERY COVE

4

If you were pleasantly surprised by the pace at SeaWorld, believe it or not, you'll find it's even slower at Discovery Cove. Here your mission is to spend an entire day doing nothing but savoring a 32-acre tropical oasis. It's a task made easier by an all-inclusive admission that covers all meals, towels, a wet suit, masks, sunscreen, and the option of springing for the highlight of the day: a unique swimming experience with a bottlenose dolphin.

Even without a dolphin encounter, you can have a great time splashing around coral reefs, swimming into a spacious aviary, floating down a quiet river, and lazing on a sandy beach beneath lovely palms. New in 2012, Freshwater Oasis is a tropical rain-forest environment of sparkling clear springs offering face-to-face encounters with playful otters and curious marmoset monkeys, while, thanks to a special diving helmet, SeaVenture lets you walk underwater through a reef filled with tropical fish and rays that you can literally reach out and touch.

ORIENTATION AND PLANNING

GETTING ORIENTED

Thanks to Discovery Cove's daily cap on crowds, it may seem as if you have the park to yourself. Navigating the grounds is simple; signs point to swimming areas, cabanas, or the free-flight aviary—aflutter with exotic birds and accessible via walkway or (even better) by swimming to it beneath a waterfall.

TOURING TIP

In Discovery Cove make the aviary one of your first stops, since the 250-plus birds within will be more active in the morning. Remember that check-in starts at 7:30 am, and the waterways open around 9.

TOP DISCOVERY COVE ATTRACTIONS

Dolphin Lagoon. You can swim at several areas, but this is the only place where you can get the signature swimming experience—with an Atlantic bottlenose dolphin.

Snorkeling Pools. There are three spots to snorkel—Serenity Bay, Freshwater Oasis, and the Grand Reef—and they may well be Discovery Cove's most underhyped attractions. It's a real thrill to float lazily and silently amid tropical fish, to swim beneath a waterfall into an elaborate aviary, and to dive down a few feet to peer at sharks and barracuda through the porthole of a wrecked ship. There's also on-site snorkeling instruction.

DISCOVERY COVE PLANNER

PARK AMENITIES

Baby Care: There's no primary baby care center, but there are nursing and changing facilities in locker and changing rooms.

Cancellations: If your plans change and you can't make it to Discovery Cove, cancel more than 30 days out and you'll receive a full refund; within 30 days of your reservation, you'll receive a one-time complimentary date change, which you can schedule for up to a year away.

First Aid: First-aid station is near the Photo Area entrance.

Guest Services: You can get information on meals, cabanas, lockers, dolphin swims, merchandise, souvenir photos, and other aspects of the park at the **Discovery Cove Check-In Lobby** when you arrive, or at Guest Services (**aka Guest Relations**) just after you enter.

Lockers: Free lockers await you near the cabanas.

Lost People and Things: Lost kids and items are usually turned over to Discovery Cove attendants, who bring them to the attendants at the Check-In Lobby.

Package Pick-Up: If you buy something, allow two hours for delivery.

Pet Care Center: If you arrive at Discovery Cove with a pet, plan on boarding it for a day ($15) at the Pet Care Center at SeaWorld.

Services for People with Disabilities: There are free wheelchairs equipped with huge balloonlike tires to cross the sand. Reserve one in advance over the phone or online and it'll be waiting for you when you arrive. At both parks, aquariums, wading areas, theaters, and restaurants are wheelchair accessible. (Note that drinking straws aren't provided, out of concern for the safety of the animals.) Shops are level, but many are so packed with stuff that maneuvering in a wheelchair is a challenge.

EXPLORING DISCOVERY COVE

Beaches. Lined with swaying palms, tropical foliage, quaint thatched huts, and speckled with shady umbrellas, hammocks, lounges, and beach chairs, this is where you claim your own private spot in the

Discovery Cove

WIND-AWAY RIVER

TO CENTRAL FLORIDA PKWY (500 feet); SEAWORLD (500 yards)

Check-in Lobby

Parking

EXPLORER'S AVIARY

FRESHWATER OASIS

WIND-AWAY RIVER

Guest Services

Photo Studio

BEACH AREA

WIND-AWAY RIVER

SERENITY BAY

Laguna Grill

BEACH AREA

Starfish Pool

Starfish Cabana

Sea Horse Pool

DOLPHIN LAGOON

Sea Horse Cabana

Sand Dollar Pool

Sand Dollar Cabana

West Beach

BEACH AREA

THE GRAND REEF

SeaVenture Underwater Walking Tour

KEY

Restaurants

✕

sand. Since the park's biggest selling point is its limited guest capacity, the most seductive aspect is lying in the sun and leaving the real world behind. For the most privacy, head to the far west end of Discovery Cove, where the beach chairs are more plentiful and private cabanas (from $60) are available. **For people with disabilities:** Modified beach wheelchairs are available. ■TIP➔ **With attendance limited to 1,000 guests, and plenty of sand to share, you should be fine. Just arrive early for the best spot.** ✉ *Discovery Cove* ☞ *Duration: Up to You. Crowds: Light. Audience: All Ages.*

Fodor's Choice
★

Dolphin Lagoon (Dolphin Swim). This is clearly the premier experience at Discovery Cove, but before you picture yourself frolicking alone with these playful creatures, remember that your "swim" is largely done alongside your fellow guests and is carefully supervised and restricted for the safety of both you and the dolphins. Despite the limitations, however, the attraction offers you the unique chance to touch, feed, play with, and even kiss a bottlenose dolphin, one of the most social and communicative marine animals. Before you can get into the lagoon, you'll attend a 15-minute orientation consisting of a film plus a few words from a dolphin trainer. Following the orientation, you and up to eight other guests will spend roughly 30 minutes interacting with one of a few dozen dolphins. Although you are only knee-deep in the water most of the time, it's surprisingly chilly, so you'll be grateful for the mandatory, Discovery Cove–provided wet suit.

When in the water, trainers teach you hand signals used to communicate with the dolphins and with them you can instruct your dolphin to roll over so you can touch its belly or signal it to leap into the air. Near the end of the session you have a chance to swim out to deeper water, catch hold of the dolphin's fin, and have it pull you back to shore—and you even get a moment to pose for a picture with your newfound friend. Be prepared for the photo finish: after you leave the water and return to the orientation cabana, the skilled trainers quickly transform into a determined souvenir-photo sales team. **For people with disabilities:** Alert staffers to your hearing, vision, or mobility issues when you're making reservations, and they'll have someone there to offer special assistance—signing or having a modified wheelchair at the ready. Note that the pool here is "zero entry," so there are no steps to contend with. ■TIP➔ **Be mindful of the appointment time on your badge. You don't want to miss the experience of a lifetime.** ✉ *Discovery Cove* ☞ *Duration: 45–60 mins. Crowds: N/A. Audience: Not Young Kids. Age requirement: 6 years and up; 6–12 must be accompanied by an adult.*

Explorer's Aviary. There are several entrances to this 12,000-square-foot birdhouse—three of which access the aviary from beneath waterfalls falling beside the Wind-Away River (otherwise, you can walk in from the beach). However you arrive, you will enter a sanctuary populated with more than 250 small exotic birds, including darting humming-birds, tiny finches, and honeycreepers. In the large-bird sanctuary, you get up close to perched toucans and wandering peacocks, red-legged seriema, and other colorful winged creatures that stand as tall as 4 feet. Look for attendants who have carts filled with complimentary fruit and feed that you can use to attract the birds. It's a beautiful experience—especially when a bird hops onto your shoulder to say hello. Get the camera ready. **For people with disabilities:** A pathway through the aviary accommodates wheelchairs. ■ TIP➜ **Come early in the morning when the birds are most active.** ⊠ *Discovery Cove* ☞ *Duration: Up to You. Crowds: Light to Moderate. Audience: All Ages.*

Freshwater Oasis. The oasis has a tropical theme and its lush landscaping is akin to a rain forest. Part of the experience is wading through a crystal-clear spring to reach an island populated by some outrageously cute marmosets (which are contained on the island thanks to a convenient moat). Swim a little farther and come nose-to-nose with otters, which frolic behind a nearly invisible wall of acrylic. Beyond the menagerie and beneath a canopy of cooling vegetation, there are watery trails to explore. It truly is a seductive setting and effortlessly evokes that soothing Discovery Cove experience. ⊠ *Discovery Cove* ☞ *Duration: Up to You. Crowds: Moderate. Audiences: All Ages.*

The Grand Reef. You can follow thousands of butterfly fish, angelfish, parrot fish, and a few dozen other species as you snorkel through this authentic-looking coral reef. Stingrays sail slowly and gracefully past and curious fish often come within touching distance—though when you reach out they scatter in nanoseconds. There's even an artificial shipwreck that, through a hole in its hull, reveals a separate pool filled with barracudas and sharks (they're out of reach, thanks to panels of Plexiglas). Even though you're hundreds of miles from the Caribbean, this is a wonderful, accessible substitute. If the sun is shining bright, good for you. The brighter the day, the more brilliant the underwater colors. **For people with disabilities:** Guests with mobility issues who can readily maneuver themselves with limited assistance can experience the reef. ■ TIP➜ **It's easy to monitor crowds; come when they're light. It's suitable for all ages, but teens and adults enjoy it most.** ⊠ *Discovery Cove* ☞ *Duration: Up to You. Crowds: Light to Moderate. Audience: All Ages.*

SeaVenture. If you've always wanted to experience the underwater world but don't have time for scuba lessons, SeaVenture is the solution. You don a dive helmet tethered to an air supply, which allows you to walk on the reef floor (about 15 feet deep), surrounded by schools of fish, sleek rays, and sharks. Even though the sharks are contained on the opposite side of lengthy panoramic panels of glass, you can't tell there's a partition, so the effect is chilling (so chilling, it makes a great souvenir photo). If you feel anxious, don't fret: guides float above you and beside you as you take your underwater stroll. The whole experience, including orientation, lasts about an hour, with about half the time spent on the underwater walk. At the end, you'll be handed a shaker filled with food. When you shake it and release its contents, you'll be instantly surrounded by a cluster of hungry fish. An unforgettable finish. The SeaVenture costs an extra $59. Some health restrictions apply. ⊠ *Discovery Cove* ☞ *Duration: 60 mins. Crowds: N/A. Audience: Not Young Kids. Age requirement: 10 years old; under 14 must be accompanied by a paying adult.*

Serenity Bay. A key to Discovery Cove's popularity is that it gives you time to do absolutely nothing. So if doing nothing means something to you, Serenity Bay is your place. This large pool of refreshingly clear, 80-degree water is ready when you are—or not—because maybe you'd prefer to just find a spot on the beach and soak up the sun. Take your pick. It's your vacation, and this is your bay. ⊠ *Discovery Cove* ⌁ *Duration: Up to You. Crowds: Light to Moderate. Audience: All Ages.*

Wind-Away River. As this river meanders through most of Discovery Cove, swimmers float lazily through different environments—a sunny beach; a dense, tropical rain forest; an Amazon-like river; a tropical fishing village; an underwater cave; and the aviary. The only drawbacks? The rough bottom of the river can annoy bare feet, and the too-often repeated scenery along the way can make it a little tedious. Still, this is a great option when you'd like a respite from the heat and a unique way to get around the park. **For people with disabilities:** Guests with mobility issues who can maneuver themselves with limited assistance can enjoy a tour of the river. ■ TIP→ **Slip in when it gets hot. All are welcome, but it appeals most to teens and adults.** ⊠ *Discovery Cove* ⌁ *Duration: Up to You. Crowds: Light to Moderate. Audience: All Ages.*

ANIMAL ENCOUNTERS

Trainer for a Day. This opportunity (from $428, but often $500-plus) rivals SeaWorld's Marine Mammal Keeper Experience. General admission includes meals, wet suit, and diving gear; this tour adds a gift bag, waterproof camera, trainer T-shirt, 30-minute dolphin swim, a private photo session with two dolphins, feeding fish in the Grand Reef, a meet and greet with tropical birds and small animals, and an almost exclusive (only eight guests in the entire lagoon) interaction that includes a "double-foot push" (two dolphins propel you across the lagoon by the soles of your feet). Ready for more? Shadow a trainer all day: head to the dolphin back area for a private tour and talk to trainers about how they teach and care for these amazing animals. Like other Discovery Cove admissions, this includes unlimited access to SeaWorld and Aquatica for 14 days. Call ahead to arrange a tour. ⊠ *Discovery Cove* ☎ *407/351–3600, 877/557–7404* ⊕ *www.discoverycove.com.*

AQUATICA

4

Just across International Drive from SeaWorld, Aquatica is the 60-acre water park that does a wonderful job angling water-park lovers away from Disney's Typhoon Lagoon and Blizzard Beach and Universal's Wet 'n Wild. And, sure, Aquatica has all the slides you'd expect, but it also has plenty of whimsical SeaWorld touches.

Aquatica takes cues from SeaWorld and Discovery Cove in design and mood. The park also takes its cues from the tropics. Right after you clear the parking lot, you see a tropical pastiche of buildings that may convince you your ship just sailed into the Caribbean. So go with it. Get into a groove, relax, and enjoy yourself. In addition to superslippery waterslides, there are quiet coves, phenomenally creative kids' play areas, lazy streams, and an atmosphere that is guaranteed to relieve your pre-vacation stress.

Ideally you'll have arrived with some snacks and drinks to combat the fatigue you'll feel after scaling to the tops of all those watery thrill rides. If not, fear not—there are plenty of places to find food and drink.

You should also be toting beach towels, sunscreen, and water shoes. Again, if not, fear not—there are a number of shops and kiosks where you can buy (or rent) all of this stuff and more.

Many of the rides have height restrictions, so if you're traveling with kids, have their heights checked at the Information Center, which you'll see right when you enter the park. Each child will be issued a colored wristband that alerts attendants to which rides are appropriate for him or her (or just look for the height requirement signposted at the entrance to each attraction—and check our reviews). If anyone in your group isn't comfortable in the water, this is also a good place to inquire about the swimming lessons that are offered.

After stashing excess supplies in a locker and generally settling in, it's time to explore. Unless it's peak season, several hours should be enough

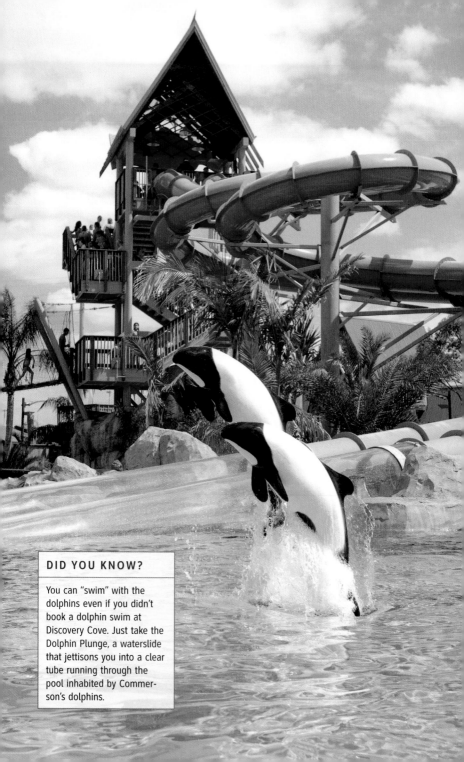

DID YOU KNOW?

You can "swim" with the dolphins even if you didn't book a dolphin swim at Discovery Cove. Just take the Dolphin Plunge, a waterslide that jettisons you into a clear tube running through the pool inhabited by Commerson's dolphins.

TOP AQUATICA ATTRACTIONS

Big Surf Shores and Cutback Cove. The lagoons here aren't too deep and are perfect for cooling off. About every 10 minutes, a series of small waves move across the lagoon, and while they're not large enough for surfing, they're big enough so you can bob around like a cork.

Dolphin Plunge. Aquatica's commercials showcase this attraction, where you slip through a winding string of pitch-black tubes and then a stretch of clear tubes through the Commerson's dolphins' habitat.

Tassie's Twisters. After hopping into an inner tube and sloshing at a high speed through an enclosed tube, you're flung into a huge circular basin and spiraled into a drain and down a slide.

Taumata Racer. Eight colorful tubes are lined up waiting for you. After a countdown, you launch yourself into your chute and, after a twisting-and-turning ride, end up on a long and slippery slide into the splashdown pool.

to visit each ride and attraction once or twice, and will also allow for some downtime, lazing on the beach, or enjoying a leisurely meal.

ORIENTATION AND PLANNING

GETTING ORIENTED

Initially, you might find it hard to get your bearings amid the towering slides, Caribbean palms, winding sidewalks, and the seemingly random layout of restaurants, rides, slides, and facilities. And there are no paper maps, only posted diagrams throughout the park. But in reality, the park is fairly easy to navigate—its layout forms a simple circle. The services (restaurants, changing rooms, shops) form a core around which the attractions are situated.

At the entrance, turn right and you'll be at the premier attraction, Dolphin Plunge; but after that you may want to do an about-face and head straight to the shores of the beach at Cutback Cove. This way, you can set up a base and then work your way to other attractions around the circle while remaining conveniently close to meals at Waterstone Grill and the Banana Beach Cookout.

TOURING TIPS

Be aware of the sun. Avoid sunburn by reapplying sunscreen (they suggest SPF 30) often—even waterproof sunblock washes off. For even more sun protection, rent a standard cabana (about $60) or go all out and splurge on the "ultimate cabana" for eight, which includes an all-day locker, bottled water, towels, and discount coupons for merchandise.

Be aware of your feet. Wear sandals or water shoes (or even socks) to protect your feet from hot sand, sidewalks, and rough pool surfaces. At the major thrill rides, a "sneaker keeper" offers a place to stash your footwear while you experience the ride.

Buy tickets in advance. Prepurchased tickets get you early entrance, and this head start will enable you to hit the major flume and tube rides more than once.

Commune with nature. You can catch Commerson's dolphins at feeding times; spot macaws on tree limbs; or see small mammals in the Conservation Cabanas, where docents answer questions. A variety of animals are on display around the park.

AQUATICA PLANNER

PARK AMENITIES

Baby Care: One nursing area is near the center of the park, by the towel- and locker-rental area and the changing rooms; another is at the far north end of the park, near Kata's Kookaburra Cove and Big Surf Shores. The nursing areas and several restrooms—for men and women—have fold-down changing tables. (Keep in mind that children still in diapers must also be wearing waterproof protectors.)

First Aid: A medical attendant is on duty during regular business hours at the first-aid station at the far end of the park between Kata's Kookaburra Cove and Big Surf Shores.

Information: The Main Information Center is at the park entrance, just past the ticket kiosks. Also at the entrance are an ATM, telephones, and restrooms. This is where you check out the posted park map and plan your approach. On the walkways outside the information center and leading into the park, attendants are stationed to help you get your bearings and point out where to find strollers and wheelchairs, help you with lost-and-found inquiries, and describe combination-ticket packages.

Lockers: There are three areas with unlimited-access lockers to rent for a day. One is near the splashdown area at Walhalla Wave and HooRoo Run; two others are at the center and far end of the park, where there are also nursing facilities. You pay $7 for a small locker (enough for one backpack) and $11 for a large one (for about two backpacks); there's also a $10 deposit, which is refunded when you leave. The central locker area also rents towels for $4 ($1 of which is refunded upon return).

Lost People and Things: Lost items and people are taken to a small tent called the Concierge Cabana, which is right by the entrance to the beach area.

Services for People with Disabilities: Aquatica was designed to accommodate people with mobility concerns. Paved pathways lead around the entire park; none of the river or family attractions has steps to contend with; and floats, life vests, and inner tubes make it easy for anyone to enjoy the park. This isn't to say there aren't challenges: regular wheelchairs can't handle the sandy beach areas, and several attractions involve climbing to the top of a high tower (although the stairs for each are accessible by ADA guidelines). Basic wheelchairs rent for around $12 a day; the motorized versions cost $50.

EXPLORING AQUATICA

Antarctica: Empire of the Penguins. SeaWorld's 4-acre "continent" centers around an attraction that's a fun-filled Arctic trek. After walking through a realistic ice floe, you leave the preshow and board a circular vehicle that glides, track-free, on a polar journey. Choose mild (no extra motion) or wild (a low-grade virtual-reality ride) as you follow the life of Puck the penguin as he travels through blizzards, past hungry sea lions, and through an ice cave. Eventually, you leave this virtual world and arrive in a massive real-life room where Puck's relations, a colony of approximately 250 always-entertaining Adélie, gentoo, king, and rock hopper penguins, are diving, waddling, and swimming like darts. Unlike the former attraction where the penguins lived behind Plexiglas, now you can step up to a low wall and watch them cavort in their private empire. All in all, this is a thoroughly entertaining educational experience. **For people with disabilities:** Guests using wheelchairs must transfer into the ride vehicle; a separate line is available if you'd prefer to bypass the ride and just visit the penguin exhibit. ⊠ *Aquatica* ↻ *Duration: 5 mins. Crowds: Moderate. Audience: All Ages. Height requirements: Riders must be at least 42 inches tall; between 42 and 48 inches accompanied by a supervising companion at least 14 years old. Guests under 42 inches may ride the less intense Mild Expedition.*

Big Surf Shores and Cutback Cove. These two side-by-side lagoons (aka wave pools) are perhaps the centerpiece of the park. Although the names suggest waves that surfers would fear, the large pool has only modest swells, and the small pool may even be closed if crowds are light. Still, both edge the park's popular white-sand beach and both are exceedingly pleasant locations where you can laze the day away. If you plan on spending a lot of time in the park and need to keep an eye on the kids, the wave pools make great bases of operation. ■ TIP→ **If you're establishing base camp here, arrive as early as possible and stake your claim on the beach.** ⊠ *Aquatica* ↻ *Duration: Up to You. Crowds: Vary by Season. Audience: Tweens and Up.*

Fodor's Choice
★
Dolphin Plunge. Thanks to the presence of Commerson's dolphins in the broad bay near the base of this attraction, this has become Aquatica's signature experience. The beginning of the ride is similar to that of other slides within the park. You whiz swiftly through an enclosed tube for about 250 feet, a long stretch that immerses you in darkness before the tube suddenly turns crystal clear. This clear shot affords a fleeting glimpse at the water that surrounds you, which happens to be the very same pool where the dolphins (which look like mini–killer whales) swim. You have to look fast to see them, though, because a split second later you're making your splashdown at the end of the line. In fact the best view of the dolphins may be from the walkway outside the ride or through an underwater pane of acrylic glass at the grotto. ■ TIP→ **Keep an eye on the line, and step up when it's light—likely very early or late.** ⊠ *Aquatica* ↻ *Duration: 1 min. Crowds: Absolutely. Audience: Tweens and Up. Height minimum: 48 inches. Loose articles must be removed prior to riding.*

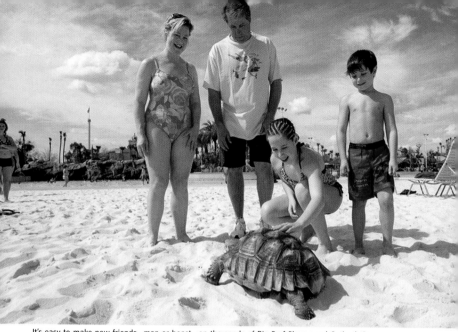

It's easy to make new friends—man or beast—on the sands of Big Surf Shores and Cutback Cove.

HooRoo Run/Walhalla Wave. One tower leads to these two attractions, each of which banks on the fact that, after climbing about 10 stories, you'd rather face your fears and *slide* back down than have to *climb* back down. At the top is a string of yellow rafts that can hold two adults and a child, though some passengers go solo. Walhalla is on your right, HooRoo on your left. After selecting a side, you and your fellow passengers slip into a raft and are pushed into the current by an attendant. Walhalla sends you circling around corners and banking to the edges of tight curves before sliding you into an enclosed tunnel. HooRoo keeps you out in the open, bouncing you down, down, down over a series of mogul-like slides. Either way you go, you'll want to go again and again and again. ■ TIP→ Come early or late—or be patient. ⊠ *Aquatica* ↻ *Duration: 30 secs. Crowds: Heavy. Audience: Tweens and Up. Height minimum: 42 inches; under 48 inches requires a life vest.*

Ihu's Breakaway Falls. New in 2014, this is billed as Orlando's "tallest, steepest, and only multi-drop tower." What's a multi-drop? Well, once you reach the top (80 feet up) there are four capsules to choose from, but no matter which one you select, you'll step inside and, as at Wet 'n Wild's Bomb Bay, you'll cross your arms and legs before a countdown of "3, 2, 1 . . ." signals it's time for the floor to "break away"—and for you to plunge straight down and into a nearly vertical 40-foot drop reaching speeds of 24 feet per second before you're pitched into a series of snaking, watery turns. Tips: At 420 feet, the orange tube is the longest. ⊠ *Aquatica* ↻ *Duration: Less than a min. Crowds: Vary by Season. Audience: Tweens and Up.*

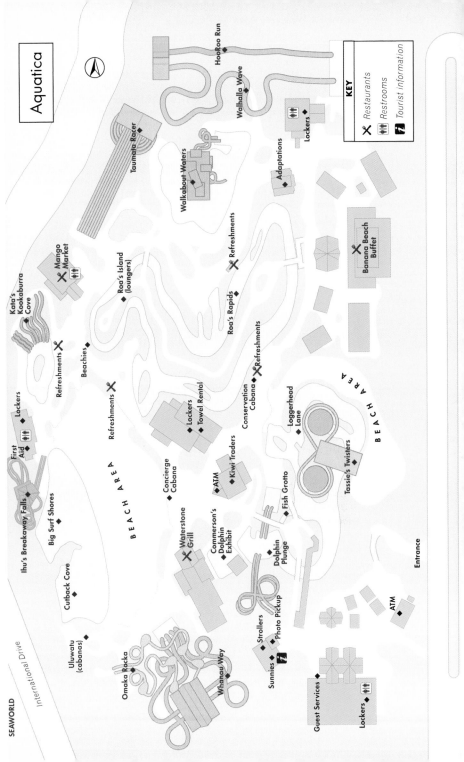

Aquatica

SEAWORLD

International Drive

KEY
✕ Restaurants
🚻 Restrooms
ℹ Tourist information

HooRoo Run
Walhalla Wave
Lockers 🚻
Adaptations
Taumata Racer
Walkabout Waters
Mango Market 🚻
Kato's Kookaburra Cove
✕ Refreshments
Roa's Island (loungers)
✕ Refreshments
Banana Beach Buffet ✕
Roa's Rapids
Beaches
✕ Refreshments
First Aid
Lockers 🚻
Ihu's Breakaway Falls
Big Surf Shores
Lockers
Towel Rental
Conservation Cabana ✕ Refreshments
Concierge Cabana
Cutback Cove
Kiwi Traders
ATM
Loggerhead Lane
BEACH AREA
Uluwatu (cabanas)
Waterstone Grill ✕
Commerson's Dolphin Exhibit
Fish Grotto
Tassie's Twisters
BEACH AREA
Omaka Rocka
Whanau Way
Dolphin Plunge
Strollers
Photo Pickup ℹ
Sunnies
Entrance
ATM
Guest Services
Lockers 🚻

Kata's Kookaburra Cove. If the sight of cool slides and water features finds you wondering who Kata's is meant for, look at the height restrictions. To visit this area, between the beach and Walkabout Waters, you must be under 4 feet tall (or accompanied by someone who is). Yes, the entire area of special pint-size slides, pools, and waterspouts is modified for the toddler set (the "deep end" is a modest 2 feet), but for them it's a big, fun world. Clear, inflatable floats give them a chance to drift about, looking cool. Plus it gives adults a chance to take a break. Be aware the smallest participants will need to wear swim diapers, available at the gift shop, and the Baby Care center is conveniently close. ✉ *Aquatica* ☞ *Duration: Up to You. Crowds: Moderate to Heavy. Audience: Small Kids. Height restrictions: Under 4 feet. Adults must be accompanied by a child no more than 48 inches.*

Loggerhead Lane. For a wonderful way to relax, you simply go with the current of this gently flowing stream, bobbing along on a double or single tube that drifts down and around the bend. Along the way, there's a spot where you can exit the river and enter the line for Tassie's Twisters. A little farther, the calm stream flows into a 10,000-gallon grotto filled with thousands of colorful fish and a view of the Commerson's dolphins. This is indeed a lazy river: there's next to no pull so you might have to paddle a bit, especially if you choose the turn that leads into the fish grotto. Guests under 48 inches must wear a life vest. ■ TIP➔ **Although there's plenty of river for everyone, try it when most people are at lunch.** ✉ *Aquatica* ☞ *Duration: Up to You. Crowds: Light. Audience: Tweens and Up.*

Omaka Rocka. Like the tentacles on a huge plastic octopus, a series of tunnels and tubes snake off the platform to provide multiple options for different starting points. Regardless of where you start, once you climb into an inner tube and slide into the slipstream you'll be riding and bouncing through some slick tubes, skimming past some half-pipe tunnels, and then sliding over some slippery moguls that splash you up on the side during some high-bank turns. Fast and furious. ■ TIP➔ **Keep an eye on the line, and hop in when it's short.** ✉ *Aquatica* ☞ *Duration: 1 min. Crowds: Heavy. Audience: Not Small Kids. Height minimum: 48 inches.*

Roa's Rapids. Even though it has "rapids" in its name, this attraction actually has a mild current that winds around numerous curves and "waterfalls" (really just sprays of water from the edge of the channel). Don a life vest and wade right in at either of two entrances (one red, the other blue, so you know where to exit). Then, whether you're traveling solo or hanging onto the kids, you simply go with the flow. Two advantages: there's no line, so you can always just drop right in, and you can go around and around for as long as you'd like. Guests under 51 inches tall are required to wear a life vest. ■ TIP➔ **Like Loggerhead Lane, there's plenty of river for everyone; still, come around lunchtime.** ✉ *Aquatica* ☞ *Duration: Up to You. Crowds: Light. Audience: All Ages.*

Tassie's Twisters. This is one of the weirdest attractions at Aquatica. Reaching it from Loggerhead Lane's lazy river, you go ashore, climb a tower, settle into an inner tube, and launch yourself into currents that carry you away at an impressive speed. But that's not the weird part. After that, the enclosed pipe you've been in delivers you to a massive basin, where you and your inner tube circle around and around and around and around like a soap bubble circling a bathtub drain. Eventually gravity takes over, and you slip through an opening in the side of the basin, straight into a short but thrilling slide into the splashdown pool. Strange and exciting. ■ TIP➡ Keep on eye on the line, and head upstairs when it's short. ⊠ *Aquatica* ☞ *Duration: 1 min. Crowds: Heavy. Audience: Tweens and Up. Height minimum: Under 48 inches requires a life vest, and you must be able to sit upright.*

Taumata Racer. In the aquatic equivalent of a bobsled run, you set yourself up on a blue mat at the opening of a large tube, and at the end of a countdown, you and the seven other racers beside you fling yourselves into the chutes. You then slide through 300 feet of enclosed twisting and turning tubes—but that's not the best part. Things really get going when you enter a stretch that's nearly pitch-black except for a small band of light beside you. After what seems like both an eternity and an instant, you reach the final drop and slide the last few yards into the splashdown pool. ■ TIP➡ If you can't see the end of the line, it's probably short—and it's time to head up. Eight lanes keep things moving along. ⊠ *Aquatica* ☞ *Duration: 30 secs. Crowds: Light to Moderate. Audience: Not Small Kids. Height minimum: 42 inches.*

Walkabout Waters. A colorful 60-foot "rain fortress" anchors 15,000 square feet of family slides, pools, climb- and crawl-through trails, and two humongous buckets that are filling up constantly and, just as constantly, dumping their contents on frolickers far below. This is a fantastically creative play space comparable to Shamu's Happy Harbor at SeaWorld. Kids that are too big for Kata's Kookaburra Cove are at home here—they treat it as the most amazing aquatic playground they've ever experienced. The slides attached to the play structure flow slowly enough for beginners (note that kids aren't permitted to ride on grown-ups' laps on this one), and supercharged water cannons add another level of fun. ■ TIP➡ Save this area for later, when you're worn out but the kids want to play. ⊠ *Aquatica* ☞ *Duration: Up to You. Crowds: Heavy. Audience: Young Kids. Height requirements: 36 to 42 inches for the main pool; over 42 inches for larger slides. Under 48 inches must wear a life vest on the larger slides.*

Whanau Way. Because water park guests can never get enough slipping and sliding, Aquatica offers this quadruple slide with an assortment of twists and turns. Depending on which tube you select, you'll enjoy a completely different experience. Like its partner slides, much of the attraction here is sliding straight into a darkened stretch; you know for sure that you're heading somewhere, but you're never exactly sure *where*. In the end, the answer reveals itself: you're heading down the final stretch on a long slide into the splashdown pool. Rinse and repeat. ■ TIP➡ Try it at lunchtime or near day's end. ⊠ *Aquatica* ☞ *Duration: 1 min. Crowds: Heavy. Audience: Not Small Kids. Height requirements: Riders must be at least 42 inches tall and able to retain an upright position unassisted; under 48 inches must wear a life vest.*

WET 'N WILD

5

WELCOME TO WET 'N WILD

TOP REASONS TO GO

★ **Year-round fun.** Pools are heated in cooler weather, so Wet 'n Wild is one of the few water parks in the country to stay open year-round.

★ **Dancing waters.** Where else can you spin through a watery 1970s disco but at Wet 'n Wild's Disco H2O?

★ **Sheer excitement.** Wet 'n Wild provides high-energy thrills with attractions that spin, drop, slosh, and twirl you through some amazingly creative splashy experiences.

★ **Sheer relaxation.** However, when you tire of climbing, walking, and swimming, Wet 'n Wild offers a sandy beach where you can laze the time away in a lounge chair and take a load off.

1 Surf Lagoon. The park's center area, Surf Lagoon and surrounding beach is the park's buffer zone and focal point.

2 West of Surf Lagoon. From the main entrance, the majority of high-speed slides and tube rides are on the left side of the park (along with the kid-friendly Blastaway Beach).

3 East of Surf Lagoon. On the right side of the park there are even more high-adrenaline rides, but they are offset by placid experiences such as the Lazy River and sanctuaries including the Riverside BBQ and tropical cabanas.

EXIT 75A

(northbound)

4

400

International Dr.

Gator Golf & ◆ Adventure Park

TO
ROUTE 435
(S. Kirkman Rd) →

International Dr.

WET 'N WILD

2

1

3

Universal Blvd.

Sandy Lake

0 ——————————— 1/8 mi

0 ——————————— 1/8 km

GETTING ORIENTED

If you arrive early, when crowds are light to moderate, you should have plenty of time to do each ride once, and possibly twice or more. From Surf Lagoon straight ahead, head counterclockwise to the most thrilling experiences (Bomb Bay, Der Stuka, The Storm) first. By the time you've circled the park, although you may be worn out your kids should still have plenty of energy to deplete at Blastaway Beach.

5

Updated
by Gary
McKechnie

When you were a kid, chances are all you needed for unlimited summer fun was a simple inflatable pool and a garden hose or sprinkler. Well, about the same time that you were growing up, so were water parks. They started with a few simple slides and are now the aquatic equivalents of megamalls.

It all began in 1977 with Wet 'n Wild, created by George Millay, who was also one of the founders of SeaWorld. Although it's now far from alone, Wet 'n Wild remains extremely popular thanks to its quality, service, and ability to create more heart-stopping waterslides, rides, and tubing adventures than its competitors. Indeed, new rides seem to be added like clockwork, old ones improved, and settings developed for the comfort of guests. There's a complete water playground for kids, numerous high-energy slides for adults, a lazy-river ride, and some quiet, sandy beaches on which you can stretch out and get a tan.

Speaking of high energy, this is a park that requires a lot of it. A day here is often a marathon of climbing steps, sliding, swimming, and splashing, though you may not notice just how much your stamina is being drained as you scamper from slide to slide. Plan to take breaks: laze in a beach chair and eat high-protein meals and snacks to maintain your strength. You can bring in a cooler for a picnic or eat at a restaurant in one of several food courts.

If you're not a strong swimmer, don't worry. There are plenty of low-key attractions, and all of the ride entrances are marked with warnings to let you know which ones are safe for you. Plus, during peak season, there are as many as 200 lifeguards on duty daily. Also note that all the pools (if not the rides) are ADA-compliant and are heated in cooler weather. This, combined with Orlando's temperate climate, means that Wet 'n Wild is one of the few water parks in the country to stay open year-round.

Surf's up!

TOP ATTRACTIONS

Bomb Bay: You drop through the floor of a cylinder and plummet down a nearly vertical slide—as they say, the first step is a doozy.

Brain Wash: Lighting effects and surreal sounds accompany your five-story drop and spin around a 65-foot domed funnel.

Disco H20: Why spin through a watery disco to a 1970s sound track? For the aquatic dance-hall

sensation that makes this ride so popular.

Lazy River: This calming stream is a good antidote to all the adrenaline.

The Storm: Nestled in an inner tube, you slip into a surreal spin around a massive basin that slowly but surely washes you—down the drain.

Surf Lagoon: If the beach is out of reach, take advantage of the sand and surf here.

PLANNING

PARK AMENITIES

Baby Care: There's no specific area for baby care at Wet 'n Wild, nor does the park rent strollers. There are changing stations in both men's and women's restrooms.

First Aid: The First-Aid Stand is between Surf Grill and Manny's Pizza.

Food: The **Wild Tiki Lounge,** a Polynesian restaurant-bar overlooking the lake, has a full menu, table service, and flat-screen TVs. If you're worn out from the attractions, chill out here. It's like being at a South Pacific resort. There's also **Manny's Pizza** (pizza, pasta, and subs), the **Surf Grill** (burgers, hot dogs, and more healthful choices like vegetarian burgers, baked potatoes, and salads), and the all-you-can-eat, seasonal **Riverside BBQ** ($19 adults, $11 children), where you can dine on chicken and pulled pork. Smaller kiosks sell cotton candy, ice cream, funnel cakes, and other carnival-style snacks.

Guest Services: Get maps and other information at Guest Services (aka Guest Relations), to the left as you enter.

Lockers: There are dressing rooms with lockers in three different sizes (personal $6/$3 deposit, standard $9/$3 deposit, family $11/$3 deposit) as well as showers and restrooms to the left of the entrance gates. Additional restrooms are on the island inside the lazy river and near the First-Aid Stand and the Surge.

Lost People and Things: The Lost and Found is at Guest Services, to the left just after you enter the park. This is also where lifeguards and other staffers take lost children.

Picnicking: You're welcome to bring coolers with food into the park, which has many picnic areas—both open and sheltered. Glass containers and alcoholic beverages are not permitted.

Wheelchair Rentals: Near the entrance, you can rent modified wheelchairs (they have large tires that can handle the sand) for $5 per day with a $25 refundable deposit. There are only a few of these, so arrive early if you

Brain Wash is one of Wet 'n Wild's most thrilling slides.

think you'll need one. Note that although many of the paths are flat and accessible, none of the rides accommodates people using wheelchairs.

ESSENTIALS

Admission: Basic admission is about $56 for adults (ages 10 and up) and $51 for children. Often you can find discounts in tourist magazines throughout the I-Drive area, but you may have better luck ordering your tickets online—and more time to consider the multiple ticket options. Different discounts apply to different ticket choices, i.e., 10% off, 14 consecutive days free, etc., but for Wet 'n Wild (as well as SeaWorld, Universal, and Disney) online purchases seem to be the best source for saving money and avoiding vacation time in line. Other money-saving options include military and college discounts and the FlexTicket, which bundles Wet 'n Wild with parks and attractions at Universal Orlando, SeaWorld, and Busch Gardens.

Parking: Costing $13 for cars, vans, and motorcycles and $17 for RVs and cars with trailers, parking is in a large lot along Universal Boulevard.

Wet 'n Wild: For general information, call Wet 'n Wild or visit online. ✉ *Wet 'n Wild* ☎ *407/351–3200 recorded information, 407/351–1800 park operations* ⊕ *www.wetnwildorlando.com.*

TOURING TIPS

■ Want to save a bundle? Admission drops to half price during the afternoon; exactly when depends on closing time, but can be as late as 5 pm in the summer. Call ahead for the magic hour. Even better, if you pay for a full-price ticket, you can return for free for 14 consecutive days. It's a great deal for families in town for an extended stay. You can see the big three (Disney, Universal, SeaWorld) during the day and return here in the evening.

■ When you arrive, it's a good idea to pick up a map, scan the park layout, and stake out a spot on the beach before heading on or in. To claim a prime beach spot, arrive at least 15 minutes before the park opens, or visit on a cloudy day. If it looks like rain all day, though, head elsewhere.

■ Men should wear a true bathing suit, and women should opt for a one-piece rather than a bikini. Cutoff shorts and garments with rivets, metal buttons, buckles, or zippers aren't allowed.

■ Wading slippers are a good idea—hot sidewalks and sandpaper-like pool bottoms can do a number on your feet—but put them in a locker or carry them when taking a plunge, since they can catch on slides.

■ Items too large to carry should be stashed in a locker. Some picnic tables have lockable containers (secured to the umbrella stand) that are just large enough to hold smaller items such as keys, glasses, and cell phones.

■ For extra privacy, a quiet oasis in the middle of the lazy river features cabanas with a fan, chaise longues, and a fridge stocked with a dozen bottles of water. It's a nice base for stowing your things, but the privilege costs some bucks. Depending on the time of the year, cabanas can go for a modest $60 to a high of $280 in the peak summer season. Don't want to get up? Servers will bring food to you.

■ Be patient with the lines here. Just when you think you've arrived, you discover there's another level or two to go.

■ To bypass lines at the popular rides, get an Express Pass (available seasonally), accepted at most rides. Prices change based on park attendance and time of day, so call Park Operations at ☎ *407/351–1800* for details. A limited number of passes are sold each day—all the more reason to get here early.

■ Okay. So you remembered your swimsuit and towel. But what about sunscreen? You can buy it and other necessities or souvenirs at the **Breakers Beach Shop**, near the park entrance. And if you did forget a towel, renting one here costs $4 with a $3 deposit. Rent a three-pack, though, and you save $2.

EXPLORING WET 'N WILD

Aqua Drag Racer. A pleasing but tranquil attraction called the Bubba Tub was given a warm send-off and replaced with this: A colorful line of four braided tubes. After climbing nearly 60 feet to reach the peak, you and your fellow racers lie flat on your own foam mats, line up, and with an "on your marks, get set, GO!" push off into your individual tube, flying six stories down in a twisting and turning sloshing path. As you near the finish line, there's daylight once again—just in time to see where you are in conjunction with your fellow racers. They say near the end you're traveling at 15 feet per second, but with all of the excitement, who's counting? ✉ *Wet 'n Wild* ⊕ *www.wetnwildorlando.com*

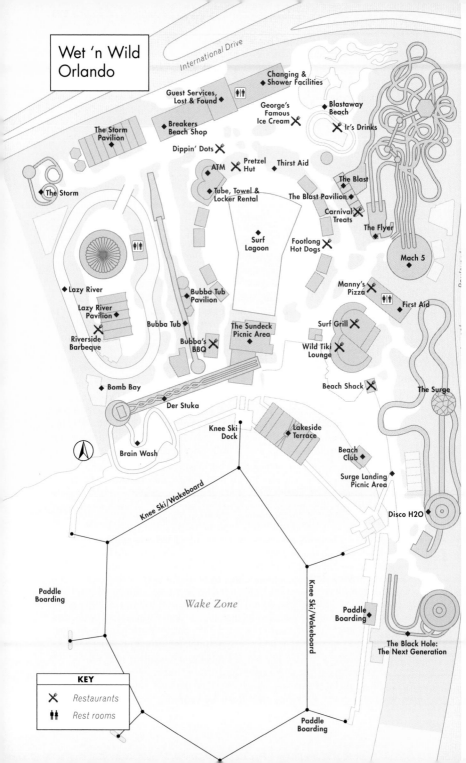

Duration: Less than 1 min. Audience: All but Small Kids. Height minimum: 42 inches.

The Black Hole: The Next Generation. Beneath a massive tower that looks like a UFO, you enter a darkened area that's sealed off from views of the outside world. From here, you're hurtled through the cosmos in a two-person "hydra-capsule" (aka an inner tube). All the while there's a dynamic display of lights flashing around you that ratchets up the drama. Chances are you'll scream your head off as you zip through space and experience the gravitational effects of wormholes and black holes before splashdown. ■TIP→ **Try it very early (or late), or invest in an Express Pass.** ⊠ *Wet 'n Wild* ⊕ *www.wetnwildorlando.com* *Duration: 1 min. Crowds: Heavy. Audience: Not Small Kids. Height minimum: 48 inches.*

The Blast. What's the story here? A pipe has ruptured, and the resulting deluge is enough to create this twisting and turning ride. Aboard a two-passenger inner tube, you and a friend will bump down a series of slides and drops and corners through explosive pipe bursts and drenching waterspouts that lead up to a final waterfall plunge. ■TIP→ **Keep an eye on the line, and hop on as soon as it gets short. Or you can use your Express Pass.** ⊠ *Wet 'n Wild* ⊕ *www.wetnwildorlando.com* *Duration: Under 1 min. Crowds: Heavy. Audience: Families. Height minimum: 48 inches; 36 inches with an adult.*

Blastaway Beach. If your kids get a thrill out of a simple waterslide, this may be the highlight of their vacation. It's an amazingly creative 15,000-square-foot section of the park dominated by a towering six-story sand castle that surpasses nearly everything a kid could expect. Adorned with flags and banners and surrounded by two pools that create an 85,000-gallon "moat," the castle is equipped with 15 slides and more than 160 soakers, water jets, waterfalls, water cannons, and huge buckets that fill and dump their contents on the guests below. All of this makes Blastaway Beach the best-equipped—not to mention largest—water playground in Florida. Even better, adults are welcome to join their kids in this splashtacular setting, but if you can't handle this much fun, rest easy: there's plenty of seating amidst lush, tropical landscaping. ■TIP→ **Come when you need a break but the kids still have energy.** ⊠ *Wet 'n Wild* ⊕ *www.wetnwildorlando.com* *Duration: Up to You. Crowds: Moderate to Heavy. Audience: Families.*

Fodor'sChoice
★ **Bomb Bay.** Lines move quickly here. Why? Because once excited guests reach the top, a lot of them chicken out and head back down the stairs. Here's why: You step inside a large enclosed capsule. The attendant looks through the glass door to make sure your arms and legs are crossed (thereby preventing wedgies) and punches a button to release the trapdoor. Then, like a bomb dropping out of a plane, you free-fall almost straight down for 76 feet before skimming down the long, steep slide. The force of the water on your feet, legs, and back rivals the emotional toll it took to take the plunge in the first place, but, oh, what a trip! ■TIP→ **Express Pass accepted here, but although the line might look long, it moves quickly so get on it anytime—if you dare to ride the ride, that is.** ⊠ *Wet 'n Wild* ⊕ *www.wetnwildorlando.com*

☞ *Duration: Under 1 min. Crowds: Heavy. Audience: Not Small Kids. Height minimum: 48 inches.*

Fodor's Choice
★
Brain Wash. At one of Wet 'n Wild's wildest thrill slides, you start by climbing into an inner tube designed for two or four passengers. With lights, video, and surreal sounds washing around you, you and your tube commit to a 53-foot vertical drop—but that's only half of it. Once you've survived the drop, you'll find yourself at the rim of a 65-foot domed funnel and swirl around its massive bowl before finally dropping through into water below. ■ TIP→ **Try it very early (or very late), or invest in an Express Pass.** ✉ *Wet 'n Wild* ⊕ *www.wetnwildorlando. com* ☞ *Duration: 1 min. Crowds: Heavy. Audience: Families. Height minimum: 48 inches; 36 inches if riding with an adult.*

Der Stuka. It's a steep slide with thrills similar to those of the adjacent Bomb Bay, but without the trapdoor drop. Despite that difference, *Der Stuka* ("Steep Hill" in German) is hard to beat for sheer exhilaration. After climbing the winding six-story platform, you sit down on a horizontal slide, nudge yourself forward a few inches, and then let gravity take over. Before you know it, you're hurtling down a 250-foot-long speed slide that will tax your back and test the security of your bathing suit. This one's a real scream. ■ TIP→ **Express Pass it, or try it very early (or very late).** ✉ *Wet 'n Wild* ⊕ *www.wetnwildorlando.com* ☞ *Duration: 1 min. Crowds: Moderate. Audience: Not Small Kids. Height minimum: 48 inches.*

Fodor's Choice
★
Disco H20. Here's something even the folks at Studio 54 never dreamed of: a four-person raft that floats into a swirling aquatic nightclub. Once you drift inside the 70-foot-tall building, your raft goes into a spin cycle as disco balls twirl, the lights flash, and the sounds of the '70s greatest hits reverberate. Incredibly, even with the numbing techno music, this is one of the park's most popular attractions. Weird, wet, and wild! ■ TIP→ **Try it very early (or very late), or invest in an Express Pass.** ✉ *Wet 'n Wild* ⊕ *www.wetnwildorlando.com* ☞ *Duration: 1 min. Crowds: Heavy. Audience: Families. Height minimum: 48 inches; 36 inches with an adult.*

The Flyer. If you've ever visited a ski resort during the summer, you've probably seen a toboggan run that you can take in a retrofitted sled. Well, that's kind of the same principle here, but with one difference: there's water, water everywhere. After getting onto your four-person toboggan, you'll slosh around and race into 450 feet of switchback curves and high-banked turns and down suddenly steep drops. The overall experience is similar to that of a real toboggan run—just much warmer and more refreshing. ■ TIP→ **Watch the line, and head over when the timing's right or invest in an Express Pass.** ✉ *Wet 'n Wild* ⊕ *www.wetnwildorlando. com* ☞ *Duration: 1 min. Crowds: Heavy. Audience: Families. Height minimum: 48 inches; 36 inches with an adult.*

Lazy River. Just settle into an inner tube for a peaceful trip down a gently moving stream, guided along by the slow current. As you bask in the sun, you drift past waterfalls, colorful flowers, and tropical greenery that grows so incredibly high. Along the way, you'll pass scenes of Old Florida (think rustic boat docks and retro billboards). This is a

AQUA

DRAG RACER

DID YOU KNOW?

Lane B of the Mach 5 water-slide is rumored to be the best. You decide by sliding down all three lanes—on your belly using a soft foam board.

great place to take a break when your body just can't handle any more climbing or free-falling. ■TIP→ **Come and go as you wish!** ⊠ *Wet 'n Wild* ⊕ *www.wetnwildorlando.com* ⟁ *Duration: Up to You. Crowds: Moderate. Audience: All Ages. Height minimum: Under 48 inches must wear a life vest (available for free).*

Mach 5. After grabbing a soft foam mat, you scale a few steps and arrive at one of three speedy waterslides. Conventional wisdom says that Lane B is the best, but it's possible all three are the same. Riding on your belly, you zip through some great twists, feel the sensation of hitting the high banks, and then splash down in a flood of water. ■TIP→ **Try it very early (or very late), or use an Express Pass.** ⊠ *Wet 'n Wild* ⊕ *www.wetnwildorlando.com* ⟁ *Duration: 1 min. Crowds: Moderate. Audience: Not Small Kids. Height minimum: Under 48 inches must wear a life vest.*

The Storm. From the top of the tower you'll see that two flumes are flowing with a torrent of water. No inner tubes or mats here! Just climb in, shove off, and, in the midst of a tidal wave, you start body surfing in a slow, curving arc. As your speed increases, you'll whirl around and around until you reach a 30-foot-diameter bowl and start spinning faster; like human-size soap suds whirling around a sink drain. After angular momentum has had its fun, you drop through a hole in the bottom of the bowl and into a small pool. Once you get your bearings, you may be tempted to climb up and do it again. ■TIP→ **Now's the time for Express Pass, or try this early in the day or later in the evening.** ⊠ *Wet 'n Wild* ⊕ *www.wetnwildorlando.com* ⟁ *Duration: 1 min. Crowds: Moderate. Audience: Not Small Kids. Height minimum: 48 inches.*

Surf Lagoon. Just past the turnstiles, this 17,000-square-foot lagoon is as close to a beach as you'll find in the park. With a zero-depth entry and a maximum depth of 6 feet, plus a wide beach, lounge chairs, and umbrellas surrounding it, it's generally packed. Every so often the lagoon is buffeted by 4-foot-high waves (which is why it's also known as the wave pool), eliciting screams of delight from kids. Adults are thrilled that the money they spent on floats, surfboards, and inner tubes was worth it. ■TIP→ **Anytime is fine.** ⊠ *Wet 'n Wild* ⊕ *www.wetnwildorlando.com* ⟁ *Duration: Up to You. Crowds: Moderate to Heavy. Audience: All Ages. Height minimum: Under 48 inches must wear an approved flotation device in the wave pool.*

The Surge. If you or your kids are too nervous for rides like Bomb Bay or The Black Hole, then this ride (which *borders* on exhilarating) may be a good alternative. You and up to three other passengers get into a giant raft and after going over the lip of the first drop, the raft zips down five stories while twisting and turning through steeply banked curves and zooming beneath waterfalls. It's a new definition of family fun. ■TIP→ **Try it very early (or very late), or invest in an Express Pass.** ⊠ *Wet 'n Wild* ⊕ *www.wetnwildorlando.com* ⟁ *Duration: Under 1 min. Crowds: Moderate. Audience: Families. Height minimum: 48 inches; 36 inches with an adult.*

Wake Zone. A molasses-slow line marks the entrance to this seasonal attraction (open May through September), which requires an extra $12 for an all-day pass. A moving cable with ski ropes attached encircles a large lake. After donning protective headgear and a life vest, you kneel on a knee skate or try to balance on a wakeboard, grab a ski rope, and are given the chance to circumnavigate the lake. The ½-mile ride includes five turns: roughly 75% of riders wipe out after the first one, and 90% are gone by the second. If you need help, ask the assistants for support; they want to see you go the distance and will suggest ways to help you make it around the lagoon (keep your arms in and lean forward). Riders who can stay afloat enjoy three laps per turn, but you can go back again and again. This is also where you can perfect your skills on a stand-up paddleboard (no height requirement). ■TIP➔ The extra fee means that the lines may be shorter (but not necessarily faster). The pass is good all day, so return when there's not a wait. ⊠ *Wet 'n Wild* ⊕ *www.wetnwildorlando.com* ☞ *Duration: 5 mins. Crowds: Moderate to Heavy in season. Audience: Teens and Adults. Height minimum: 56 inches.*

5

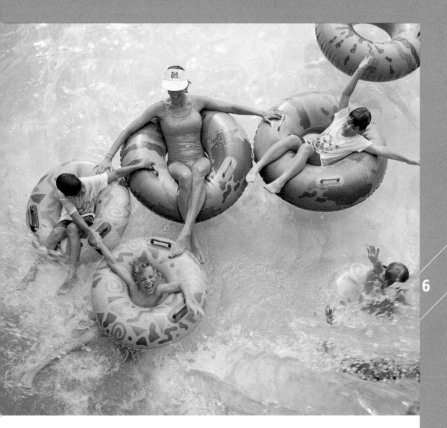

ORLANDO AND
ENVIRONS

WELCOME TO ORLANDO AND ENVIRONS

TOP REASONS TO GO

★ **Liberal Arts:** Orlando's theaters, including the new Dr. Phillips Center for the Performing Arts, host symphony orchestras, Broadway road shows, and local thespians of all types. Jazz, blues, world music, and rock are all part of the music scene. Area museums showcase folk art, Tiffany glass, and 14th- through 20th-century European and American paintings.

★ **The Sciences:** The Orlando Science Center has exhibits on human biology, technology, nature, and the stars. At WonderWorks, simulators let you survive an earthquake or pilot a jet.

★ **Cultivated Spaces:** Gardens devoted to historical blooms, camellias, azaleas, and roses are among the more refined outdoor offerings.

★ **Wild Places:** Experience Gatorland or see rescued winged creatures at the Audubon Center for Birds of Prey. Fish, boat, canoe, or swim in Wekiwa Springs State Park or Ocala National Forest.

1 Orlando. There's more to Orlando than theme parks: a thriving Downtown with ample opportunity to stay, eat, and play. Internationally recognized cultural events, theater, and the evolving music scene make Downtown more than just a stopping point.

2 Orlando Environs. Natural Florida beckons with some of the most unspoiled land and amazing sportfishing in the state. Several towns—Kissimmee, Mount Dora, and Winter Park among them—recall Old Florida *and* have great shopping, world-class museums, or both.

CENTRAL FLORIDA

GETTING ORIENTED

Central Florida runs from Tampa/St. Petersburg in the west through Orlando to the coastal attractions of Daytona Beach and Cape Canaveral on the east coast. Orlando is more or less equidistant, about 90 minutes by car to the Gulf of Mexico. Walt Disney World is not, contrary to advertising, in Orlando, but lies about 25 miles southwest of the city.

6

Updated by
Jennie Hess

Most Orlando locals look at the theme parks as they would an unruly neighbor: it's big and loud, but it keeps a nice lawn. Central Florida's many theme parks can become overpowering for even the most enthusiastic visitor, and that's when an excursion into the "other" Orlando—the one the locals know and love—is in order.

There are ample opportunities for day trips. If the outdoors is your thing, you can swim or canoe at Wekiwa Springs State Park or one of the area's many other sparkling springs, where the water remains a refreshing 72°F no matter how hot the day. Alternatively, you can hike, horseback ride, canoe, and camp in the Ocala National Forest.

If museums are your thing, charming Winter Park has the Charles Hosmer Morse Museum of American Art with its huge collection of Tiffany glass, and the Cornell Fine Arts Museum on the oak-tree-covered Rollins College campus. While in Winter Park, you can indulge in some high-end shopping and dining on Park Avenue or take a leisurely boat tour of the lakefront homes.

Got kids to educate and entertain? Check out WonderWorks or the Orlando Science Center, where you can view live gators and turtles. Even more live gators (some as long as 14 feet) can be viewed or fed (or even eaten) at Gatorland, just south of Orlando.

Do the kids prefer rockets and astronauts? Don't miss a day trip to Kennedy Space Center, where you can tour a rocket forest, sit in a space capsule, or see a space shuttle up close.

Kissimmee is a 19th-century cattle town south of Orlando that proudly hangs on to its roots with a twice-yearly rodeo where real cowboys ride bulls and rope cattle. The town sits on Lake Tohopekaliga, a favorite spot for airboat rides or fishing trips.

ORLANDO

Orlando is a diverse town. The Downtown area, though small, is dynamic, thanks to an ever-changing skyline of high-rises, sports venues, museums, restaurants, nightspots, a history museum, and several annual cultural events—including film festivals and a world-renowned theater fest. Downtown also has a central green, Lake Eola Park, which offers a respite from otherwise frantic touring.

Neighborhoods such as Thornton Park (great for dining) and College Park (an outpost of great dining) are fun to wander. Not too far to the north, you can come in contact with natural Florida—its manatees, gators, and crystal-clear waters in spring-fed lakes.

Closer to the theme-park action, International Drive, the hub of resort and conference hotels, offers big restaurants and even bigger outlet-mall bargains. Sand Lake Road, between the two, is Orlando's Restaurant Row, with plenty of exciting dining prospects.

GETTING HERE AND AROUND

Orlando is spread out. During rush hour, car traffic crawls along the often-crowded Interstate 4 (particularly now that the multibillion-dollar upgrade, expected to end in 2021, has begun), which runs to both coasts. If you're heading east, you can also take Route 528 (aka the Beachline), a toll road that heads directly for Cape Canaveral and points along the Space Coast; no such option leads west.

If you avoid rush-hour traffic, traveling to points of interest shouldn't take too much time out of your vacation. Winter Park is no more than 20 minutes from Downtown; International Drive and the theme parks are about 30 minutes away in heavier traffic. Orlando International Airport is only 9 miles south of Downtown, but it will take about 30 minutes via a circuitous network of highways (Interstate 4 west to Florida's Turnpike south to Route 528 east).

ESSENTIALS

Hospitals Florida Hospital ⊠ *601 E. Rollins St.* ☎ *407/303–5600* ⊕ *www. floridahospital.com.* **Orlando Regional Medical Center** ⊠ *1414 Kuhl Ave., Downtown Orlando* ☎ *321/841–5111* ⊕ *www.orlandohealth.com.*

Tourist Information Orlando Visitors Bureau ⊠ *8723 International Dr., Suite 101* ☎ *407/363–5872, 800/972–3304* ⊕ *www.visitorlando.com.*

EXPLORING

CENTRAL ORLANDO

Fodor's Choice
★

Harry P. Leu Gardens. A few miles outside of Downtown—on the former lakefront estate of a citrus entrepreneur—is this 50-acre garden. Among the highlights are a collection of historical blooms (many varieties of which were established before 1900), ancient oaks, a 50-foot floral clock, and one of the largest camellia collections in eastern North America (in bloom November–March). Mary Jane's Rose Garden, named after Leu's wife, is filled with more than 1,000 bushes; it's the largest formal rose garden south of Atlanta. The simple 19th-century Leu House Museum, once the Leu family home, preserves the

The 300-seat Dr. Phillips CineDome, a movie theater with an eight-story screen at the Orlando Science Center, offers large-format iWERKS films.

furnishings and appointments of a well-to-do, turn-of-the-20th-century Florida family. ⊠ *1920 N. Forest Ave., Audubon Park* ☎ *407/246–2620* ⊕ *www.leugardens.org* ⊠ *$10, free 1st Mon. of month* ☉ *Garden daily 9–5; guided house tours daily on hr and ½ hr 10–3:30; closed Dec. 25.*

FAMILY **Lake Eola Park.** This beautifully landscaped 43-acre park is the verdant heart of Downtown Orlando, its mile-long walking path a gathering place for families, health enthusiasts out for a run, and culture mavens exploring area offerings. The well-lighted playground is alive with children, and ducks, swans, and native Florida birds call the lake home. A popular and expanded farmers' market takes up residence on Sunday afternoon.

The lakeside Walt Disney Amphitheater is a dramatic site for concerts, ethnic festivals, and spectacular Fourth of July fireworks. Don't resist the park's biggest draw: a ride in a swan-shaped pedal boat. Up to five adults can fit comfortably into each. (Children under 16 must be accompanied by an adult.)

The Relax Grill, by the swan-boat launch, is a great place for a snack. There are also several good restaurants in the upscale Thornton Park neighborhood along the park's eastern border. The ever-expanding skyline rings the lake with modern high-rises, making the peace of the park even more welcome. The landmark fountain features an LED light-and-music show on summer evenings at 9:30. ⊠ *195 N. Rosalind Ave., Downtown Orlando* ☎ *407/246–4485 park, 407/246–4485 swan boats* ⊠ *Swan boat rental $15 per ½ hr* ☉ *Park daily 6 am–midnight; swan boats Sun.–Tues. 10–7, Wed.–Sat. 10–10.*

Central Orlando

0 1/2 mi
0 1/2 km

Lake Sylvan
Florida Mall ◆
Mall at Millenia ◆
Orlando Harley-Davidson ◆

Orlando Shakespeare Theater ◆
Rock & Roll Heaven ◆
Washburn Imports ◆
Wally's ◆
Bull and Bush Pub ◆
Bob Carr Performing Arts Centre ◆
Firestone Live ◆
The Social / Sky 60 ◆
Tanqueray's ◆
Chillers ◆
Monkey Bar ◆
Mad Cow Theatre ◆
Bösendorfer Lounge ◆
Dr. Phillips Performing Arts Center ◆
Amway Center
Parliament House Resort ◆

Orlando Executive Airport

TO ORLANDO INT'L AIRPORT via Route 436 (Semoran Blvd.)

TO WINTER PARK

CLOSE UP

Central Florida Art

There are a surprising number of world-class art museums in Central Florida—from Orlando and Winter Park to St. Petersburg and Sarasota; from sublime stained glass to surrealist paintings and folk art to circus folk.

Mennello Museum of American Folk Art, Orlando. The Mennello holds the nation's most extensive permanent collection of Earl Cunningham paintings, as well as pieces by many other "outsider" artists. Works by Wyeth, Cassatt, Eastman, and others have made their Central Florida debuts here.

Charles Hosmer Morse Museum of American Art, Winter Park. Known as the "Tiffany museum," the galleries contain the largest and most comprehensive collection of art by Louis Comfort Tiffany, including

stained-glass windows and lamps, blown-glass vases, and gem-studded jewelry.

Salvador Dalí Museum, St. Petersburg. Built upon the collection of an Ohio industrialist, this is the world's most comprehensive gathering of oils, watercolors, drawings, sculptures, photographs, and objets d'art by the Spanish surrealist. The museum moved into a new Dalí-inspired building in 2011, doubling its size.

FSU Ringling Center for the Cultural Arts, Sarasota. This artistic compound stars the John and Mable Ringling Museum of Art and the Ringling Circus Museum. Classical masters of art share space with sideshow memorabilia. Don't miss the enchanting scale model of a 1920s Ringling Bros. and Barnum & Bailey Circus.

Mennello Museum of American Folk Art. One of the few museums in the United States devoted to folk art has intimate galleries, some with lovely lakefront views. Look for the nation's most extensive permanent collection of Earl Cunningham paintings as well as works by many other self-taught artists. There's a wonderful video about Cunningham and his "curio shop" in St. Augustine, Florida. Temporary exhibitions have included the works of Wyeth, Cassatt, and Michael Eastman. At the museum shop you can purchase folk-art books, toys, and unusual gifts. The Mennello is the site of the annual Orlando Folk Festival, held the second weekend of February. ⊠ *900 E. Princeton St., Lake Ivanhoe* ☎ *407/246–4278* ⊕ *www.mennellomuseum.org* 🖀*$5* ☉ *Tues.–Sat. 10:30–4:30, Sun. noon–4:30.*

FAMILY **Orange County Regional History Center.** Exhibits here take you on a journey back in time to discover how Florida's Paleo-Indians hunted and fished the land, what the Sunshine State was like when the Spaniards first arrived, and how life in Florida was different when citrus was king. Visit a cabin from the late 1800s, complete with Spanish moss–stuffed mattresses and mosquito netting over the beds. Seminole Indian displays include interactive activities, and the Tourism Before Disney exhibit previews Florida's destiny as a future vacation mecca. Traveling exhibits bring modern technology and art to the museum. ⊠ *65 E. Central Blvd., Downtown Orlando* ☎ *407/836–8500, 800/965–2030* ⊕ *www.*

thehistorycenter.org 🖱 *$15; seniors, students $13; 5–12 $12; under 4 free* 🕐 *Mon.–Sat. 10–5, Sun. noon–5.*

FAMILY
Fodor's Choice
★

Orlando Science Center. With all the high-tech glitz and imagined worlds of the theme parks, is it worth visiting Orlando's reality-based science center? If you're a kid crazy about science, the answer is an overwhelming "yes." With exhibits about the human body, mechanics, computers, math, nature, the solar system, and optics, the science center has something for every child's inner geek.

The four-story internal atrium is home to live gators and turtles and is a great spot for simply gazing at what Old Florida once looked like. The 300-seat Dr. Phillips CineDome, a movie theater with a giant eight-story screen, offers large-format iWERKS films and planetarium programs. The Crosby Observatory and Florida's largest publicly accessible refractor telescope are here, as are several smaller telescopes; some weekends you can safely view spots and flares on the sun's surface.

Adults like the science center, too, thanks to events like the annual Science of Wine and Cosmic Golf Challenge; evenings of stargazing in the Crosby Observatory; live music, art, and film; and Otronicon, the annual interactive technology expo. ✉ *777 E. Princeton St., Lake Ivanhoe* ☎ *407/514–2000* ⊕ *www.osc.org* 🖱 *$19; senior, student $17; 3–11 $13; under 2 free; parking $5; tickets include all permanent and special exhibits, films, live science presentations, and planetarium shows* 🕐 *Daily 10–5; closed Wed, Easter Sun., Thanksgiving Day, Christmas Eve, and Christmas Day.*

INTERNATIONAL DRIVE AREA

FAMILY
Fun Spot America. Four go-kart tracks offer a variety of driving experiences. Though drivers must be at least 10 years old and meet height requirements, parents can drive younger children in two-seater cars on several of the tracks, including the Conquest Track. Nineteen rides range from the dizzying Paratrooper to an old-fashioned Revolver Ferris Wheel to the twirling toddler Teacups. Fun Spot recently expanded from 5 to 15 acres and now features Central Florida's only wooden roller coaster as well as the Freedom Flyer steel suspension family coaster, a kiddie coaster, and what's billed as the world's second-tallest (250 feet) SkyCoaster—part skydive, part hang-glide. The tallest, at 300 feet, is located at sister park Fun Spot USA, in Kissimmee. There's also an arcade. From Exit 75A, turn left onto International Drive, then left on Fun Spot Way. ✉ *5700 Fun Spot Way* ☎ *407/363–3867* ⊕ *www. funspotattractions.com* 🖱 *$39.95 for all rides (online discounts available) or pay per ride; admission for nonriders free; arcade extra; parking free* 🕐 *Apr.–Oct., daily 10 am–midnight; Nov.–Mar., weekdays noon–11, weekends 10 am–midnight.*

Ripley's Believe It or Not! Odditorium. A 10-foot-square section of the Berlin Wall. A pain and torture chamber. Two African fertility statues that women swear have helped them conceive. These and almost 200 other oddities (shrunken heads included) speak for themselves in this museum-cum-attraction in the heart of tourist territory on International Drive. The building itself is designed to appear as if it's sliding into one of Florida's notorious sinkholes. Give yourself an hour or two to

International Drive

EXIT 78

Conroy Rd.

Mall at Millenia

423

EXIT 77

Orlando Premium Outlets
International Drive

UNIVERSAL STUDIOS ORLANDO

Artegon Orlando

OAK RIDGE

EXIT 75

Outdoor World

Congo River

6

iFLY Orlando

EXIT 74B

Wet 'n Wild

TANGELO PARK

Lake Marsha

Dr. Phillips Blvd.

Lake Tibet

Apopka Vineland Rd.

Wallace Rd.

Spring Lake

EXIT 74A

Florida's Turnpike (Ronald Reagan Turnpike)

John Young Pkwy.

Sand Lake Rd.

482

435

Little Sand Lake

482

7

423

Lake Sheen

Big Sand Lake

◆ Pirate's Cove Adventure Golf

◆ Cafe Tu Tu Tango

4

ICEBAR ◆ Hawaiian Rumble
◆ Adventure Golf

8

B.B. King's Blues Club
Pointe Orlando

528

Turkey Lake Rd.

International Drive

EXIT 72

528

Beachline Expwy.

WILLIAMSBURG

Big Sand Lake

EXIT 71

SEAWORLD ORLANDO

Central Florida Pkwy.

WHISPER LAKES

VINELAND

Apopka Vineland Rd.

Palm Pkwy.

John Young Pkwy.

435

Orlando Premium Outlets
Vineland Avenue
◆

International Drive

Shingle Creek

423

535

Buena Vista Dr.

WALT DISNEY WORD

EXIT 68

417

535

Lake Bryan

4

EXIT 67

International Drive

536

417

Central Florida Greenway

0 ——————— 1 mi

0 ——————— 1 km

soak up the weirdness, but remember: this is a looking, not touching, experience; it might drive antsy youngsters—and their parents—crazy. ■TIP➜ Buy tickets online ahead of time, and you can get discounts. ⊠ *8201 International Dr.* ☎ *407/351–5803* ⊕ *www.ripleysorlando. com* 🖃 *$19.99; 4–12 $12.99; parking free* ☉ *Daily 9 am–midnight; last admission at 11 pm.*

NEED A BREAK? **Café Tu Tu Tango.** Here's something unusual: good tapas in a tourist area. With a light, breezy atmosphere (painters work in the Spanish Artist's loft as you eat) and small, shareable dishes (including Tango Alligator Bites), it's a great place for a quick snack while on I-Drive. ⊠ **8625 International Dr.** ☎ **407/248-2222** ⊕ **www.cafetutuftango.com.**

FAMILY **WonderWorks.** The building seems to be sinking into the ground .. at a precarious angle and upside down. Many people stop to take pictures in front of the topsy-turvy facade, complete with upended palm trees and broken skyward-facing sidewalks. Inside, the upside-down theme continues only as far as the lobby. After that, it's a playground of 100 interactive experiences—some incorporating virtual reality, others educational (similar to those at a science museum), and still others pure entertainment. You can experience an earthquake or a hurricane, land a space shuttle using simulator controls, make giant bubbles in the Bubble Lab, play laser tag in the enormous laser-tag arena and arcade, design and ride your own roller coaster, lie on a bed of real nails, and play baseball with a virtual Major League batter. ⊠ *9067 International Dr.* ☎ *407/351–8800* ⊕ *www.wonderworksonline.com/orlando* 🖃 *$26.99; seniors, 4–12 $20.99; laser tag and Outta Control Magic Comedy Dinner Show extra (online discounts available); parking $3–$9* ☉ *Daily 9 am–midnight.*

ORLANDO ENVIRONS

Although the small towns around Orlando aren't historic in a European sense, they reflect the early settlers' desire to capitalize on the subtropical climate—much as you and other visitors do today.

To the south lies Kissimmee, a former cattle town on Lake Tohopekaliga, one of Florida's largest, and a good place to go fishing or take an airboat ride. Kissimmee retains its ranching roots, with a twice-annual rodeo that's worth a visit.

Winter Park, to the northeast, offers a more intellectual look at Florida's past. The town exudes charm, with brick streets and Spanish moss–draped oaks. Park Avenue, the main drag, is lined with unique shops edged by a landscaped park. You can take a leisurely boat tour on waterways that snake through town or visit the large collection of Tiffany glass and other artworks in the Morse Museum of American Art.

To the northwest of Orlando is Mount Dora, built with citrus money in the 19th century. It's on Lake Dora, and the shops and restaurants lining its charming streets often have a water view.

Kissimmee's Lake Tohopekaliga (affectionately known as Lake Toho) is famous with fishers the world over. It's also great for wildlife spotting—an especially exhilarating experience when done from an airboat.

KISSIMMEE

18 miles south of Orlando, 10 miles southeast of Walt Disney World (WDW).

Although Kissimmee is primarily known as the gateway to Disney (technically, the vast Disney property of theme parks and resorts lies in both Osceola and Orange counties), its non-WDW attractions just might tickle your fancy. They range from throwbacks to old-time Florida to dinner shows for you and 2,000 of your closest friends. Orlando used to be prime cattle country, and the best sampling of what life was like is here during the Silver Springs Rodeo in February and June.

With at least 100,000 acres of freshwater lakes, the Kissimmee area brings anglers and boaters to national fishing tournaments and speedboat races. A 50-mile-long series of lakes, the Kissimmee Waterway, connects Lake Tohopekaliga—a Native American name that means "Sleeping Tiger"—with huge Lake Okeechobee in South Florida, and from there, to both the Atlantic Ocean and the Gulf of Mexico.

GETTING HERE AND AROUND

From Downtown Orlando it's easy to reach Kissimmee's main road, U.S. 192, from Interstate 4, Exit 64, just past the last Disney exit. Osceola Parkway (Toll Road 522) heads directly from Disney property, and Florida's Turnpike runs north–south through Kissimmee.

Kissimmee

DID YOU KNOW?

Old Town in Kissimmee—just one of many Orlando-area sights outside the theme parks—has several dozen shops, nine restaurants, 18 rides and attractions, and three or so antique-car shows a week.

ESSENTIALS

Visitor Information Experience Kissimmee. Get a travel guide and discount coupons here, in person or online. ✉ *215 Celebration Pl., Suite 200* ☎ *407/742–8200* ⊕ *www.experiencekissimmee.com/*. **Florida Fish and Wildlife.** To be able to catch those big Lake Toho bass, you need a license. ☎ *850/488–4676* ⊕ *www.myfwc.com/recreation* ✉ *Nonresident licenses: saltwater or freshwater $17 3-day, $30 7-day, $47 annual.*

⇨ *For information on Kissimmee hotels and restaurants, see "Where to Stay" and "Where to Eat."*

EXPLORING

FAMILY **Gatorland.** This campy attraction near the Orlando–Kissimmee border on U.S. 441 has endured since 1949 without much change, despite competition from the major parks. Over the years, the theme park and registered conservancy has gone through some changes while retaining its gator-rasslin' spirit. Kids get a kick out of this unmanufactured, old-timey thrill ride.

The Gator Gulley Splash Park is complete with giant "egrets" spilling water from their beaks, dueling water guns mounted atop giant gators, and other water-park splash areas. There's also a small petting zoo and an aviary. A free train ride is a high point, taking you through an alligator breeding marsh and a natural swamp setting where you can spot gators, birds, and turtles. A three-story observation tower overlooks the breeding marsh, swamped with gator grunts, especially come sundown during mating season.

For a glimpse of 37 giant, rare, and deadly crocodiles, check out the Jungle Crocs of the World exhibit. To see eager gators leaping out of the water to catch their food, come on cool days for the Gator Jumparoo Show (summer heat just puts them to sleep). The most thrilling is the first one in the morning, when the gators are hungriest. There's also a Gator Wrestlin' Show, and although there's no doubt who's going to win the match, it's still fun to see the handlers take on those tough guys with the beady eyes. In the educational Upclose Encounters show, the show's host handles a variety of snakes. Recent park additions include Panther Springs, featuring brother-and-sister endangered panthers, and the Screamin' Gator Zip Line (additional cost). This is a real Florida experience, and you leave knowing the difference between a gator and a croc. ✉ *14501 S. Orange Blossom Trail, between Orlando and Kissimmee* ☎ *407/855–5496, 800/393–5297* ⊕ *www.gatorland. com* ✉ *$26.99; 3–12 $18.99; discount coupons online* ☉ *Daily 10–5.*

FAMILY **Old Town USA.** A collection of shops and themed restaurants, Old Town was literally the heart of tourist Kissimmee before Disney moved in. With a new owner and the rickety-but-fun amusement park rides gone (Fun Spot next door takes up the slack), the 1950s theme is continued by magic shows in the Great Magic Hall; a haunted funeral parlor attraction; video game and shooting arcades; a laser-tag hall; go-karts and bumper cars; and weekly classic car shows. ✉ *5770 W. Irlo Bronson Memorial Hwy.* ☎ *407/396–4888* ⊕ *www.myoldtownusa.com/* ✉ *Free (admission and parking)* ☉ *Daily 10 am–11 pm (bars open until 2 am).*

Go gator! After a visit to authentic, rustic Kissimmee's Gatorland, you'll truly know the difference between a gator and a croc (and you'll see both).

LEGOLAND

50 miles southwest of Orlando.

LEGOLAND Florida. The quiet town of Winter Haven is home to numerous lakes and a waterskiing school. From 1936 to 2009, it was also home to the Sunshine State's first theme park, Cypress Gardens. Today the spot holds the world's largest LEGOLAND, set on 150 acres and built using nearly 56 million LEGOs. In addition to its 1:20-scale miniature reproductions of U.S. cities, the park features more than 50 rides, shows, and attractions throughout 10 different zones, as well as the marvelous botanical gardens from the original park. Opened mid-2013, the World of Chima presented by Cartoon Network invites guests into a fantastical world of animal tribal habitats anchored by an interactive water ride, the Quest for CHI. In Chima's new Speedorz Arena, participants compete to win a supply of the mystical CHI energy source. A 4-D movie and Chima-character meet and greets round out the experience.

The Danish toy company's philosophy is to help children "play well." And play they do, as LEGOLAND attractions are very hands-on. Kids can hoist themselves to the top of a tower, power a fire truck, or navigate a LEGO robot. Sights include huge LEGO dragons, wizards, knights, pirates, castles, roller coasters, racetracks, villages, and cities.

The cityscapes in Miniland USA fascinate children and adults, who delight in discovering what's possible when you have enough bricks. Miniland opens with Kennedy Space Center, where a 6-foot shuttle waits on the launch pad. Miami Beach features bikini-clad bathers and art deco hotels; St. Augustine and its ancient fort play into LEGO's

KISSIMMEE TOURS

Haunted Kissimmee. This 90-minute tour takes you through the shadowy streets and alleys of historic downtown. The community has amassed a huge store of paranormal activity over the years, and the docents who lead these outings know where the bodies are buried. ⊠ *804 Bryan St* 🕾 *321/251–5204* ⊕ *www.hauntedkissimmee.com* 🎫 *$19* ⊘ *Daily at 8:30 pm.*

Historic Downtown Kissimmee. Established well over a century ago, Kissimmee has a story rooted in the founding of the state. It was an important air base during World War II, and it was vital in the development of the Orlando cattle and orange industries. The visitors bureau sponsors chili cook-offs and a Tuesday evening farmers' market. You can learn more on the self-guided audio tour or map tour available at the Main Street Welcome Station or downloadable from the website. ⊠ *421 Broadway* 🕾 *407/846–4643* ⊕ *www.kissimmeemainstreet.com* ⊘ *Weekdays 9–5, Sat. 10–2.*

Kissimmee Swamp Tours. The 60- or 90-minute cruises in high-powered airboats take you through the marshes and swamps of Lake Kissimmee—home to hundreds of species of birds and other critters. ⊠ *4500 Joe Overstreet Rd., Lake Kissimmee, Kenansville* 🕾 *407/436–1059* ⊕ *www.kissimmeeswamptours.com* 🎫 *$49–$64.*

pirate theme; Key West's Mallory Square is accurate right down to the trained cats leaping through rings of fire. The rest of the United States is not ignored: New York City, Las Vegas, San Francisco, and Washington, D.C., appear in intricate detail. Visitors spend hours looking for amusing details hidden in each city, like New York's purse snatcher.

Among other highlights are LEGO Kingdoms, whose castle towers over a jousting area and a roller coaster where knights, damsels, dragons, and ogres are found; Land of Adventure, where you can explore hidden tombs and hunt for treasure; and the Imagination Zone, showcasing LEGO Mindstorms robots, where a giant head of Albert Einstein invites kids to explore and invent. Things get wild in LEGO Technic, the most active of the park's zones, where Test Track, Aquazone Wave Racers, and Technicycle let the family expend some energy. And Pirates' Cove provides a chance to sit in the shade and watch a full-size pirate battle, with actors wearing LEGO suits defending the huge ship from attacking pirates on water skis.

LEGOLAND Water Park features a wave pool; Build-a-Raft, where families construct a LEGO vessel and float down a lazy river; a 375-foot pair of intertwined waterslides that plunge riders into a pool; and a DUPLO toddler water play area. Not to be forgotten, Cypress Gardens, at the heart of the park, preserves one of Florida's treasures. Families can wander the lush, tropical foliage and gasp at one of the world's largest banyan trees.

The trip to Winter Haven is worth it. The rides, interactive games, gardens, water park, and other attractions will amuse and engage. Round-trip transportation from Orlando Premium Outlets, on Vineland

History You Can See

A long history, from early Native American occupants through Spanish, French, and British settlers, has left indelible marks on Central Florida. Add to that the influx of wealthy vacationers from the North and hopeful immigrants from Europe, and history comes alive in these repositories of knowledge.

DeSoto National Memorial, Bradenton. Hernando de Soto came ashore with his men and 200 horses near what is now Bradenton in 1539; this federal park commemorates that landing. From mid-December to late April, park workers dress in period costumes at Camp Uzita and demonstrate how European explorers lived.

Florida Holocaust Museum, St. Petersburg. A permanent History, Heritage, and Hope exhibit; an original boxcar; and an extensive collection of photographs, art, and artifacts give new perspective to one of the largest

collections of its kind. Conceived as a learning center for children, many of the exhibits avoid overly graphic content.

Tarpon Springs. Tarpon Springs has been the home of Greek sponge divers for more than 120 years, and the combination of sun, great food, and history can't be beat. Take time to visit St. Nicholas Greek Orthodox Cathedral, a replica of St. Sophia Cathedral in Constantinople.

Ybor City, Tampa. One of only four National Historic Landmark districts in Florida, Tampa's rollicking Cuban quarter has antique-brick streets and wrought-iron balconies, hand-rolled cigars, and fresh-roasted coffee. The neighborhood has become one of Tampa's hot spots, as empty cigar factories and social clubs have been transformed into boutiques, art galleries, restaurants, and nightclubs.

Avenue, leaves at 9 and costs $5. ✉ *One Legoland Way, Winter Haven* ☎ *877/350–5346* ⊕ *www.legoland.com* 🎫 *$84; seniors, 3–12 $77; parking $14* ⊙ *Hrs vary seasonally.*

BOK TOWER GARDENS

57 miles southwest of Orlando, 42 miles southwest of WDW.

Fodor'sChoice ★ **Bok Tower Gardens.** You'll see citrus groves as you ride south along U.S. 27 to the small town of Lake Wales and the Bok Tower Gardens. This appealing sanctuary of plants, flowers, trees, and wildlife has been something of a local secret for years. Shady paths meander through pine forests with silvery moats, mockingbirds and swans, blooming thickets, and hidden sundials. The majestic, 200-foot Bok Tower is constructed of coquina—from seashells—and pink, white, and gray marble. The tower houses a carillon with 60 bronze bells that ring out each day at 1 and 3 pm during 30-minute recitals that might include early-American folk songs, Appalachian tunes, Irish ballads, or Latin hymns. The bells are also featured in recordings every half hour after 10 am, and sometimes even moonlight recitals.

The landscape was designed in 1928 by Frederick Law Olmsted Jr., son of the planner of New York's Central Park. The grounds include the 20-room, Mediterranean-style Pinewood Estate, built in 1930 and open for self-guided touring. January through April, guides lead you on a 60-minute tour of the gardens (included in the admission price); tours of the inside of the tower are a benefit of membership ($100 and up). Take Interstate 4 to Exit 55 and head south on U.S. 27 for about 23 miles. Proceed past Eagle Ridge Mall, then turn left after two traffic lights onto Mountain Lake Cut Off Road, and follow the signs. ✉ *1151 Tower Blvd., Lake Wales* ☎ *863/676–1408* ⊕ *www.boktower. org* ☞ *$12–18; 5–12 $3–$8* ⊙ *Daily 8–6.*

WEKIWA SPRINGS STATE PARK

13 miles northwest of Orlando, 28 miles north of WDW.

FAMILY **Wekiwa Springs State Park.** *Wekiva* is a Creek Indian word meaning
Fodor's Choice "flowing water"; *wekiwa* means "spring of water." The river, springs,
★ and surrounding 6,400-acre Wekiwa Springs State Park are well suited to camping, hiking, picnicking, swimming, canoeing, and fishing. The area is also full of Florida wildlife: otters, raccoons, alligators, bobcats, deer, turtles, and birds.

Canoe trips can range from a simple hour-long paddle around the lagoon to observe a colony of water turtles to a full-day excursion through the less congested parts of the river, which haven't changed much since the area was inhabited by the Timacuan Indians. You can rent canoes ($16.98 for two hours and $3 per hour after that) in the town of Apopka, near the park's southern entrance.

The park has 60 campsites: some are "canoe sites" that you can reach only via the river, and others are "trail sites," meaning you must hike a good bit of the park's 13½-mile trail to reach them. Most, however, are for the less hardy—you can drive right up to them. Sites go for $60 a night with electric and water hookups.

To get here, take Interstate 4 Exit 94 (Longwood) and turn left on Route 434. Go 1¼ miles to Wekiwa Springs Road; turn right and go 4½ miles to the entrance, on the right. ✉ *1800 Wekiva Circle* ☎ *407/884–2008, 800/326–3521 campsites, 407/884–4311 canoe rentals* ⊕ *www. floridastateparks.org/wekiwasprings/default.cfm* ☞ *$2 per pedestrian or bicycle; $6 per vehicle* ⊙ *Daily 8–dusk.*

MOUNT DORA

35 miles northwest of Orlando, 50 miles north of WDW.

The unspoiled Lake Harris chain surrounds remote Mount Dora, an artsy valley community with a slow and easy pace, a rich history, New England–style charm, and excellent antiquing. Although the town's population is only about 12,000, there's plenty of excitement here, especially in fall and winter. The first weekend in February is the annual Mount Dora Art Festival, which opens Central Florida's spring art-fair

Wildlife-rich Wekiwa Springs State Park is a great place to camp, hike, picnic, canoe, fish, swim, or snorkel.

season. Attracting more than 250,000 people over a three-day period, it's one of the region's major outdoor events.

During the year there's also the annual Taste in Mount Dora event (April), a sailing regatta (April), a bicycle festival (October), a crafts fair (October), and many other happenings. Mount Dora draws large crowds during monthly antiques fairs (third weekend, except December) and thrice-yearly antiques "extravaganzas" (third weekends of January, February, and November) at popular Renninger's Twin Markets, an antiques center plus farmers' and flea markets.

GETTING HERE AND AROUND
Take U.S. 441 (Orange Blossom Trail in Orlando) north or take Interstate 4 to Exit 92, then Route 436 west to U.S. 441, and follow the signs.

ESSENTIALS
Tourist Information **Mount Dora Chamber of Commerce.** A historic train depot serves as the chamber's offices. Stop in and pick up a self-guided-tour map. Don't forget to ask about the trolley tour, during which a guide gives you the skinny on local historical spots and throws in a ghost story. ⊠ *341 Alexander St., at 3rd Ave.* ☎ *352/383–2165* ⊕ *www.mountdora.com* ⊙ *Weekdays 9–5, Sat. 10–4, Sun. 10–2; after hrs, maps on display at kiosk.*

EXPLORING
Lakeside Inn. Listed on the National Register of Historic Places, this country inn, built in 1883, overlooks 4,500-acre Lake Dora and is the oldest continuously operating hotel in the State of Florida. A stroll around the grounds, and the sight of seaplanes disembarking guests,

makes you feel as if you've stepped out of the pages of *The Great Gatsby*. You can book cruises and seaplane tours that leave from the inn's large dock. ⊠ *100 N. Alexander St.* ☎ *352/383–4101* ⊕ *www.lakeside-inn.com.*

FAMILY **Mount Dora Center for the Arts.** Local and national artists are highlighted in this lovely art center that grew out of the annual arts festival. The center is a focal point for the community, serving as headquarters of the arts festival, a gallery, a gift shop, and a place to take art lessons. ⊠ *138 E. 5th Ave.* ☎ *352/383–0880* ⊕ *www.mountdoracenterforthearts.org* ☉ *Gallery: weekdays 10–5.*

NEED A BREAK?

Pisces Rising. This upscale, New Orleans–themed seafood and steak house overlooks Lake Dora. It's open for lunch and dinner and offers a jazz brunch on Sunday, monthly wine dinners, and live entertainment Thursday through Sunday on its deck. ⊠ **239 W. 4th Ave.** ☎ **352/385–2669** ⊕ **www.piscesrisingdining.com** ☉ **Mon.–Thurs. 11:30–9, Fri. and Sat. 11:30–10, Sun. 11–9.**

6

WINTER PARK

6 miles northeast of Orlando, 20 miles northeast of WDW.

This peaceful, upscale community may be just outside the hustle and bustle of Orlando, but it feels like a different country. The town's name reflects its early role as a warm-weather haven for those escaping the frigid blasts of Northeast winters. From the late 1880s until the early 1930s, wealthy industrialists and their families would travel to Florida by rail on vacation, and many stayed, establishing grand homes and cultural institutions. The lovely, 8-square-mile village retains its charm with brick-paved streets, historic buildings, and well-maintained lakes and parkland. Even the town's bucolic 9-hole golf course is on the National Register of Historic Places.

On Park Avenue you can spend a few hours sightseeing, shopping, or both. The street is lined with small boutiques and fine restaurants and bookended by world-class museums: the Charles Hosmer Morse Museum of American Art, with the world's largest collection of artwork by Louis Comfort Tiffany, and the Cornell Fine Arts Museum, on the campus of Rollins College (the oldest college in Florida).

GETTING HERE AND AROUND

From Downtown Orlando, take Interstate 4 for 4 miles to Exit 87, and head east on Fairbanks Avenue for 3 miles to Park Avenue. LYNX Bus Nos. 102 and 443 run from the main depot to Winter Park.

ESSENTIALS

Bus Information LYNX Bus ✉ *455 N. Garland Ave., Downtown Orlando* ☎ *407/841–5969* ⊕ *www.golynx.com.*

Hospital Winter Park Memorial Hospital ✉ *200 N. Lakemont Ave.* ☎ *407/646–7000* ⊕ *www.floridahospital.com/winter-park-memorial.*

Visitor Information City of Winter Park ✉ *401 Park Ave. S* ☎ *407/599–3399* ⊕ *www.cityofwinterpark.org.*

TOUR

Scenic Boat Tour. Head east from Park Avenue and, at the end of Morse Boulevard, you'll find the launching point for this tour, a Winter Park tradition since 1938. The one-hour cruise takes in 12 miles of waterways, including three lakes and narrow, oak- and cypress-shaded canals built in the 1800s as a transportation system for the logging industry. A well-schooled skipper shares stories about the moguls who built their mansions along the shore and points out wildlife and remnants of natural Florida still surrounding the expensive houses. Cash or check only is accepted. ✉ *312 E. Morse Blvd.* ☎ *407/644–4056* ⊕ *www. scenicboattours.com* 🎟 *$12; 2–11 $6* ⊗ *Daily 10–4.*

⇨ *For information on Winter Park hotels and restaurants, see "Where to Stay" and "Where to Eat."*

EXPLORING

Albin Polasek Museum and Sculpture Gardens. Stroll along on a guided tour through gardens showcasing the graceful sculptures created by internationally known Czech sculptor Albin Polasek (1879–1965). The late artist's home, studio, galleries, and private chapel are centered on 3 acres of exquisitely tended lawns, colorful flower beds, and tropical foliage on the edge of Lake Osceola. Paths and walkways lead past classical life-size, figurative sculptures and whimsical mythological pieces. Inside the museum are works by Hawthorne, Chase, and Mucha. The Capen House, a historic 1885 building, has been moved to the grounds to be used for public events. ✉ *633 Osceola Ave.* ☎ *407/647–6294* ⊕ *www. polasek.org* 🎟 *$5* ⊗ *Tues.–Sat. 10–4, Sun. 1–4.*

Central Park. Given to the City of Winter Park by the Genius family (benefactors of the Morse Museum), this 11-acre green spot has manicured lawns, specimen plantings, a rose garden, a fountain, and a gazebo. If you take a seat and listen as the Amtrak passenger train rolls by the west end of the park, it's not hard to imagine how Winter Park looked and sounded in the late 19th century. The SunRail commuter train stops right amid the park, giving great car-free access to Downtown Orlando and during the packed art festivals. The Winter Park Farmers' Market draws people to the southwest corner on Saturday morning. If you don't want to browse in the shops across the street, a walk through the park beneath the moss-covered trees is a delightful alternative. ✉ *251 Park Ave. S.*

Fodor'sChoice
★
Charles Hosmer Morse Museum of American Art. The world's most comprehensive collection of work by Louis Comfort Tiffany—including immense stained-glass windows, lamps, watercolors, and desk sets—is in this museum, which also contains American decorative art and paintings from the mid-19th to the early 20th century.

Winter Park

Cady Way Park

Lake Berry

Lake Sylvan

Lake Mizell

Lake Osceola

Lake Maitland

Lake Virginia

Lake Killarney

Lake Bell

Little Lake Fairview

Lake Osceola

Winter Park Country Club

Kathmandu
Ten Thousand Villages
Shoooz on Park Avenue
Scenic Boat Tour
Timothy's Gallery

Central Park
Sassafras Sweet Shoppe
Farmers' Market
Park Plaza Gardens

Rollins College

Mead Botanical Gardens

426
426
426
423
423
527
17 92
17 92

Palmer Av.
Park Av.
Palmer Av.
Aloma Av.
Mizell Av.
Lakemont Av.
Osceola Av.
Park Av.
Pennsylvania Av.
Pennsylvania Av.
Webster Av.
Denning Dr.
Orlando Av.
Park Av.
Orlando Av.
Minnesota Av.
Fairbanks Av.
Fairbanks Av.
Clay St.
Formosa Av.
Orange Av.
Lee Rd.
Wymore Rd.
Adanson St.
Edgewater Dr.

EXIT 88
EXIT 87

0   1/2 mi
0   1/2 km

The Charles Hosmer Morse Museum of American Art is also known as the "Tiffany Museum" because of its extensive collection of art by Louis Comfort Tiffany.

Among the draws is the 1,082-square-foot Tiffany Chapel, originally built for the 1893 World's Fair in Chicago. It took craftsmen 2½ years to painstakingly reassemble the chapel here. Many of the works were rescued from Tiffany's Long Island estate, Laurelton Hall, after a 1957 fire destroyed much of the property. The 12,000-square-foot Laurelton Hall wing, opened in 2011, allows for much more of the estate's collection to be displayed at one time. Exhibits in the wing include architectural and decorative elements from Laurelton's dining room, living room, and Fountain Court reception hall. There's also a re-creation of the striking Daffodil Terrace, so named for the glass daffodils that serve as the capitals for the terrace's marble columns. ⊠ *445 N. Park Ave.* ☎ *407/645–5311* ⊕ *www.morsemuseum.org* ⊠ *$5; free Nov.–Apr., Fri. 4–8* ⊙ *Tues.–Sat. 9:30–4, Sun. 1–4; Nov.–Apr., Fri. until 8.*

Cornell Fine Arts Museum. On the Rollins College campus, this museum houses Florida's oldest art collection (its first paintings acquired in 1896)—one with more than 5,000 works, from Italian Renaissance to 19th- and 20th-century American and European paintings. Special exhibitions feature everything from Native American artifacts to Soviet propaganda posters. Outside the museum, a small but charming garden overlooks Lake Virginia. The museum is free to visit; free guided tours Saturday and Sunday at 1 pm. ⊠ *Rollins College, 1000 Holt Ave.* ☎ *407/646–2526* ⊕ *www.rollins.edu/cfam* ⊠ *Free* ⊙ *Tues.–Fri. 10–4, weekends noon–5.*

Hannibal Square Heritage Center. Almost crowded out by the glitz of new shops, restaurants, and art galleries is the original, once-thriving town of Hannibal Square, one of the oldest African-American communities in the country and home to Pullman porter families to this day. The Heritage Center hosts a permanent photographs and oral-history collection of the significant West Winter Park area. It's a touching and important memorial to a neighborhood that influenced American history. ⊠ *642 W. New England Ave.* ☎ *407/539–2680* ⊕ *www.hannibalsquareheritagecenter.org* ◻ *Free* ⊘ *Tues.–Thurs. noon–4, Fri. noon–5, Sat. 10–2.*

Kraft Azalea Garden. Enormous cypress trees shade this 5-acre public park on the shores of Lake Maitland, which is alive with heady color from January through March. The thousands of blooming azaleas (hence the name) make a perfect backdrop for romantic strolls, and sunset weddings are common at the park's exedra monument overlooking the lake. ⊠ *1365 Alabama Dr.* ☎ *407/599–3334* ⊕ *www.cityofwinterpark.org* ⊘ *Daily 8–dusk.*

NEED A BREAK?

Park Plaza Gardens. This elegant bistro at the Park Plaza Hotel has sidewalk tables and an atrium-style dining room. Though it specializes in seafood entrées, it also serves great sandwiches, beer on tap, an extensive wine selection, and offers great people-watching. ⊠ *319 Park Ave. S* ☎ *407/645–2475* ⊕ *www.parkplazagardens.com.*

6

MAITLAND

10 miles northeast of Orlando, 25 miles northeast of WDW.

An Orlando suburb with an interesting mix, Maitland is home to both the Florida Save the Manatee Society and one of Central Florida's larger office parks. A number of spectacular homes grace the shores of this town's various lakes, and there's a bird sanctuary and an art center.

GETTING HERE AND AROUND

Take Interstate 4 Exit 90A, then Maitland Boulevard east, and turn right (south) on Maitland Avenue.

EXPLORING

FAMILY **Audubon Center for Birds of Prey.** More than 20 bird species, including hawks, eagles, owls, falcons, and vultures, make their home at this wildlife rehabilitation center on Lake Sybelia. You can take a self-guided conservation tour with interactive exhibits and walkways through the wetlands, or you can call ahead for a private tour ($100), which includes up-close interaction with different birds in the center. There's an earnestness to this working facility, which takes in more than 800 injured wild birds of prey each year. Fewer than half of the birds can return to the wild; some permanently injured birds continue to live at the center and can be seen in the aviaries along the pathways and sitting on outdoor perches. From U.S. 17–92, turn west on Lake Avenue, then north on East Street. ⊠ *1101 Audubon Way* ☎ *407/644–0190* ⊕ *fl.audubon.org/audubon-center-birds-prey* ◻ *$5* ⊘ *Tues.–Sun. 10–4.*

Maitland Arts Center. Hidden down a tree-lined side street is this collection of 23 buildings in the Mayan Revival style—with Mesoamerican motifs—that contain an art gallery and artists' studios. Recognized by Florida as a historic site and on the National Register of Historic Places, the center was founded as an art colony in 1937 by American artist and architect André Smith (1880–1959), and it continues his tradition of art instruction and contains a major collection of his works. The center is part of the Art & History Museums Maitland, including the Maitland Historical Museum and the quirky telephone Museum. ⊠ *231 W. Packwood Ave.* ☎ *407/539–2181* ⊕ *www.artandhistory.org* ✏ *$3* ⊙ *Tues.–Sun. 11–4.*

Zora Neale Hurston National Museum of Fine Arts. This museum is in Eatonville, just a few minutes west of Maitland, the first African-American town to be incorporated after the Civil War. It showcases works by artists of African descent during five six-week-long exhibits each year, with one reserved for up-and-comers. The museum is named after former resident Zora Neale Hurston (1891–1960), a writer, folklorist, and anthropologist best known for her novel *Their Eyes Were Watching God*. This is the home of Zora Fest, a street festival and cultural arts and music event celebrating Hurston's life, which is held each year in late January. ⊠ *227 E. Kennedy Blvd., Eatonville* ☎ *407/647–3307* ⊕ *www.zoranealehurstonmuseum.com* ✏ *Donations accepted* ⊙ *Weekdays 9–4, Sat. 11–1.*

NEED A BREAK? **Jeremiah's Italian Ice.** There's always a long line in front of this little corner shop thanks to the fresh fruit ices and dozens of gelato flavors. It's also thanks to the pleasant staff, who give "pup cups" to well-behaved dogs. Bring your sweet tooth. ⊠ *111 S. Orlando Ave.* ☎ *407/599–9991* ⊕ *www.jeremiahsice.com.*

SANFORD

30 miles northeast of Orlando, 45 miles northeast of WDW.

At one time Sanford was the heart of Central Florida—a vital vacation spot and transportation hub on the St. Johns River. But that was before vacationers focused on Orlando and Walt Disney World. In an attempt to turn things around, Sanford has been slowly rebuilding its picturesque downtown overlooking Lake Monroe and increasing the size of its airport (Orlando–Sanford International), which is favored by flights from the United Kingdom.

EXPLORING

FAMILY **Central Florida Zoo and Botanical Gardens.** Sanford has had a zoo since 1923, and while there's nothing here to rival San Diego or New York, there's a certain charm about the place. In addition to 400-plus animals, including cheetahs, monkeys, and crocodiles, there's the ZOOm Air Adventure Park, with rope bridges and a zip line through the treetops, and the Wharton-Smith Tropical Splash Ground, a mini–water playground. The steam-powered 1/5-scale train that puffs around the zoo is as fun for adults as it is for kids. Take Interstate 4 to Exit 104 and turn left on U.S. 17–92; the zoo is on the right. ⊠ *3755 N.W. U.S. 17–92* ☎ *407/323–4450* ⊕ *www.centralfloridazoo.org* ✏ *$16.50; 3–12 $11.95; ZOOm Air and train extra; parking free* ⊙ *Daily 9–5.*

WHERE TO EAT

CHARACTER MEALS

Character meals are larger-than-life experiences that might be the high point of your child's visit to Walt Disney World or Universal. Mickey, Minnie, and more come alive and welcome your kids as if they were old friends.

These meals, ranging from Alice in Wonderland–themed tea parties to Mickey Mouse–hosted barbecues (and everything in between) are unique, one-on-one opportunities where characters pose for pictures and engage with the little ones. Kids adore hugging or getting an autograph from their favorites; even tots who may be shy at first will usually warm up to their most-loved character.

TOP PICKS FOR BREAKFAST

WALT DISNEY WORLD
Princess Storybook Dining at Akershus Royal Banquet Hall, Epcot. Belle, Jasmine, Snow White, the Little Mermaid's Ariel and many more princesses could appear at this medieval castle–styled Norwegian building.

Chef Mickey's Fun Time Buffet, Disney's Contemporary Resort. This breakfast combines space-age Disney styling with Mickey Mouse, Donald, and the gang, plus the ever-popular Mickey-shaped waffles.

'Ohana's Best Friends Breakfast with Lilo & Stitch, Disney's Polynesian Resort. The intergalactic Stitch and his human friend, Lilo, join your family in a tropical setting for this very popular breakfast. Every 30 minutes, Mickey and Pluto join in while kids parade around the restaurant with maracas and wide grins.

UNIVERSAL
Supterstar Character Breakfast, Universal Studios. SpongeBob SquarePants, Gru from Despicable Me, and E.B. from Hop are among the superstars who may stop by to say hi at Café La Bamba every morning.

TOP PICKS FOR LUNCH

WALT DISNEY WORLD
The Crystal Palace Character Meal, Magic Kingdom. A lovely Victorian setting is the perfect place for the old-fashioned and lovable Winnie the Pooh and friends to greet your kids. This is the only meal where you can find characters from the Hundred Acre Wood.

Disney Junior Play n' Dine, Disney's Hollywood Studios. The Hollywood & Vine Restaurant brings Disney Channel stars to life. Handy Manny and Agent Oso from Handy Manny, and June from Disney's Little Einsteins march around the room, singing and dancing to the delight of their energetic fans.

My Disney Girl's Perfectly Princess Tea Party, Disney's Grand Floridian Resort. Girls ages 3 to 11 enjoy the princess experience here. Dressing up is encouraged, and lunch, featuring tea and sandwiches, is served on china plates. Princess Aurora (Sleeping Beauty herself) will make an appearance. Little ones receive a special Disney Girl Princess doll, jewelry, a ribbon tiara, and a photo scrapbook page.

TOP PICKS FOR DINNER

WALT DISNEY WORLD
Mickey's Backyard BBQ, Fort Wilderness Resort. This dinner show has everything from dancing and foot-stomping country music with Cowboy Mickey Mouse, to finger-food goodies like hot dogs and smoked ribs.

Cinderella's Happily Ever After Dinner, Disney's Grand Floridian Resort. A dinner buffet of worldly cuisine is complete with Cinderella, Prince Charming, and their family (including the wicked steps) making the rounds.

UNIVERSAL
The Kitchen, Hard Rock Hotel at Universal Orlando. Scooby Doo and others appear on Saturday nights. The special Kids' Crib area supplies crayons and cartoon videos, allowing parents to have a break while everyone enjoys their meals.

Trattoria Del Porto, Loews Portofino Bay Hotel. Delectable Italian cuisine will please parents, while Bart Simpson and Scooby Doo may be on hand to distract the kids on Friday nights between 5:30 and 10 pm, which coincides with Pasta Cucina Kitchen, an all-you-can-eat experience where guests create their own pastas.

7

EPCOT INTERNATIONAL FOOD & WINE FESTIVAL

For seven autumn weeks, Epcot hosts the Epcot International Food & Wine Festival, attracting folks more interested in a fine phyllo than a photo op with Cinderella.

(Above) A wine and cheese tasting at the Epcot International Food & Wine Festival. (Bottom right) Diners at Epcot's Teppan Edo. (Top right) Marinated strawberries with basil served at the Argentina kiosk.

The festival is essentially a compendium of food- and beverage-related offerings, some free with the price of Epcot admission, others costing anywhere from $3.25 to a few hundred. You can attend mixology or cheese seminars, have cookbooks signed by authors, and sample tapas-size portions of foods from around the world. And that's just the basics. Throughout the event, Disney and guest chefs host brunches, lunches, and wine-pairing dinners at Epcot and in hotels, some posh, others festive, and yet more T-shirt-and-shorts-friendly. The headliners change annually but might include names like Jamie Deen, "Cake Boss" Buddy Valastro, or Andrew Zimmern. The festival's food and beverage lineup changes every year, too, so for more information and to make reservations (during festival season only, generally midsummer through early November), call ☎ 407/939–3378 or visit ⊕ *www.disneyworld.com/foodandwine*.

GARDEN OF EATING

So smitten are visitors with the Food & Wine Festival's food marketplaces that Epcot created similar "outdoor kitchens" for its annual Flower & Garden Festival. At the six-week springtime celebration of all things green and floral, snack-size foods inspired by the season and the garden are cooked "on stage" and served throughout the World Showcase—with paired beverages, of course.

SHOPPING FOR A SNACK

The heart of the Food & Wine Festival—and the most approachable event for hungry tourists on a budget—takes place around Epcot's World Showcase. Ordinarily a miniature world of 11 pavilions themed around one country apiece, the area takes on new life as 27 "international marketplaces" take up residence.

Most of the 27 marketplaces, from Brazil to South Korea, offer a taste of one country, selling approximately three appetizer-size food items and a few beverages that pair well—nearly all for $3.25 to $8 apiece. Indisputably popular creations like the cheddar soup ladled out endlessly at Canada are keepers; regulars might revolt if those were absent at any time. Still, a majority of the menu can change in a given year. Attendees who stop by every autumn might taste Belgian potato-leek waffles with braised beef (with a Stella Artois beer or Godiva-chocolate iced coffee) or Moroccan spicy shrimp roll with cilantro and mint sauce (with Guerrouane white wine) one time, an Irish fisherman's pie (with Bunratty mead honey wine) or a Korean lettuce wrap with roast pork and kimchi slaw (with a soju fruit slushy) another.

At a few marketplaces, a certain item is featured instead of a locale. The Desserts and Champagne booth, for instance, pours a bounty of bubbly and special sweets. A craft beer marketplace puts out several regional brews along with complementary snacks like spicy pimento cheese with crackers. And the all-American Hops & Barley Market often specializes in fare U.S. citizens can be proud of, such as baked lobster alfredo and carrot cake.

Lines tend to get very long, especially on weekends, when locals pour in for their regular fix of foreign fare, so consider timing your tour during the day or on a weekday evening, when most spots have shorter waits.

FESTIVAL OF THE SENSES

Several Saturday evenings throughout the festival, food and wine enthusiasts clad in cocktail attire saunter into the gala called Party for the Senses. Billed as a "grand tasting," the bash is a huge all-you-can-eat fancy-food fest. In a dramatically decorated, high-ceilinged room, 10 to 15 chefs from around the country host one food station apiece, serving a hearty appetizer-size portion of one passionately prepared dish. Some are Disney chefs eager to show their talents, and others are known nationally. Big names such as François Payard, Allen Susser, and Walter Staib have been known to participate. Live entertainment such as acrobats and vocalists—some years, from Cirque du Soleil's *La Nouba*—gives attendees something to watch while taking a break between bites. The price runs $149 to $299. Other Saturday nights, a similar gathering with food and entertainment will have a one-time theme, such as Dining through the Decades: A Tribute to Walt Disney.

Updated by
Rona Gindin

You'll find burger-and-fries combos everywhere in Orlando, yet the ambitious chefs behind Orlando's theme-park and independent restaurants provide loads of better options. Locally sourced foods, creative preparations, and clever international influences are all the rage here. Theme-park complexes have some of the best restaurants in town, or you may opt for a rental car to seek out the local treasures.

The signs of Orlando's dining progress is most evident in the last place one would look: Disney's fast-food outlets. Every eatery on Disney property offers a tempting vegetarian option, and kiddie meals come with healthful sides and drinks unless you specifically request otherwise. Chefs at Disney's table-service restaurants consult face-to-face with guests about food allergies.

Around town, locals flock to the Ravenous Pig, the Rusty Spoon, the Smiling Bison, and other gastropubs where the menu changes regularly; Luma on Park, a suave home of thoughtfully created cutting-edge meals; and any number of dining establishments competing to serve the very finest steak. Orlando's culinary blossoming began in 1995, when Disney's signature California Grill debuted, featuring farm-to-table cuisine and wonderful wines by the glass. Soon after, celebrity chefs started opening up shop. And in 2013, Disney completely revamped California Grill so it's a trendsetter once again.

Orlando's destination restaurants can be found in the theme parks, as well as in the outlying towns. Sand Lake Road is now known as Restaurant Row for its eclectic collection of worthwhile tables. Here you'll find fashionable outlets for sushi and seafood, Italian and chops, Hawaiian fusion and upscale Lebanese. Heading into the residential areas, the neighborhoods of Winter Park (actually its own city), Thornton Park, and College Park are prime locales for chow. Scattered throughout Central Florida, low-key ethnic restaurants specialize in the fare of Turkey, India, Peru, Thailand, Vietnam—you name it. Prices in these family-owned finds are usually delightfully low.

DINING PLANNER

WHERE SHOULD WE EAT?

With thousands of eateries competing for your attention, it may seem like a daunting question. But fret not—our expert writers and editors have done most of the legwork. The selections here represent the best this city has to offer—from hamburger joints to fine dining. Search "Best Bets" for top recommendations by price, cuisine, and experience. Or find a review quickly in the listings, organized alphabetically within theme park or neighborhood. Dive in and enjoy!

CONSIDERATIONS FOR DIFFERENT TYPES OF TRAVELERS

FAMILIES WITH YOUNG KIDS

If you're traveling with small children, you really should include a character meal. Walt Disney World offers breakfast, lunch, and dinner with characters at each of its four parks and some of its resorts. Some are buffets; others are family-style or à la carte. Regardless of the format, Mickey, Donald, Goofy, Chip 'n' Dale, Cinderella, and other favorites show up to sign autographs and pose for snapshots.

At Universal, character meals move around. Cafe La Bamba might feature characters from *Hop* and *Despicable Me*. Universal's hotels also have character dinners, including the Simpsons, on select nights.

When possible, reserve your spot far in advance.

■ TIP➜ If your young children are theme-park newbies, have your character meal near the end of a visit, so they'll be used to seeing the large and sometimes frightening figures.

Except for two, the ultraformal Victoria & Albert's and Christini's, all restaurants in and near the theme parks welcome children. Crayons, games, and kiddie menus are standard.

FAMILIES WITH TWEENS

Tweens are impressed by highly themed concepts. Consider the 50's Prime Time Café in Disney's Hollywood Studios, a kitschy 1950s-themed space where "Mom," the waitress, may make parents finish their vegetables. At the Sci-Fi Dine-In Theater nearby, guests eat in top-down convertible cars that face a big screen airing '50s and '60s sci-fi and monster trailers.

Universal's Islands of Adventure also has themed eateries based on superheroes or other classic characters. The Three Broomsticks replicates a Hogsmeade tavern, while Leaky Cauldron resembles a British pub. Both are boons for Harry Potter fans.

FAMILIES WITH TEENS

CityWalk is filled with high-energy themed eateries that teens love. In fact, local high schoolers tend to congregate in the CityWalk common areas on weekend evenings. The lively Hard Rock Cafe is a consistent favorite.

On the Disney boardwalk, the ESPN Club is a great choice for teen sports fans. Even its bathrooms are equipped with video monitors, so you don't have to miss a second of a great game.

COUPLES

Truly, you'd be hard-pressed to find more romantic restaurants than the ones on Disney property. Jiko, at the Animal Kingdom Lodge, pairs superb African-accented cuisine with an exceptional South African wine list and dramatic decor. If you really want to go all out, there's absolutely nothing like Victoria & Albert's, in the Grand Floridian. Treat yourself to a gourmet, seven-course prix-fixe meal to live harp music.

Outside the theme parks, Norman's, at the Ritz-Carlton, has a sophisticated dining room and impressive New World cuisine.

SINGLES OR GROUPS OF FRIENDS

Singles often dine at the bars of upscale-casual favorites, including Seasons 52, Prato, and Bonefish Grill. Groups enjoy the festive antics of International Drive's Taverna Opa, where visitors often find themselves dancing around the dining room.

LARGE GROUPS

Restaurants in theme-park hotels, in nearby convention hotels, on Sand Lake Road, and on International Drive have private party rooms for large groups more often than not. For an alternative, consider dinner shows. The food is plentiful and the entertainment keeps younger family members engaged. The luaus at Disney and Universal hotels are good for all ages, as is the wonderfully hokey Hoop-Dee-Doo Musical Revue at Disney's Fort Wilderness Resort.

Many off-park venues also offer themed dining with shows. The concepts range from medieval jousting on horseback to pirates to crime and comedy.

MEAL PLANS

Disney Magic Your Way Plus Dining Plan allows you one table-service meal, one counter-service meal, and one snack per day of your trip at more than 100 theme-park and resort restaurants, provided you stay in a Disney hotel. You'll also receive a refillable drink mug for use at your hotel's fast fooderies. For more money, you can upgrade the plan to include more; to save, you can downgrade to a counter-service-only plan. Used wisely, a Disney dining plan is a steal, but be careful to buy only the number of meals you'll want to eat. Moderate eaters can end up turning away appetizers and desserts to which they're entitled. Plan ahead, and use "extra" meals to your advantage by swapping two table-service meals for a Disney dinner show, say, or an evening at a high-end restaurant like California Grill.

Universal Meal Deal offers one sit-down and one quick-service meal at participating walk-up eateries inside Universal Studios and Islands of Adventure, plus a snack and soft drink. Daily prices are $52 and $18 (both parks) and must be purchased with a resort stay. A quick-service-only arrangement, with one meal a day, is $20 and $13. All-you-can-drink soft drinks are $12 daily for all.

WHAT IT COSTS				
	$	$$	$$$	$$$$
AT DINNER	under $15	$15–$21	$22–$30	over $30

Prices are per person for a median main course, at dinner, excluding tip and tax of 6.5%.

RESERVATIONS

Reservations are strongly recommended throughout the theme parks. Indeed, make reservations for Disney restaurants and character meals at both Universal and Disney at least 90 (and up to 180) days out. And be sure to ask about the cancellation policy—at a handful of Disney restaurants, for instance, you may be charged penalties if you don't give 24 to 48 hours' notice.

For restaurant reservations within Walt Disney World, call ☎ *407/939–3463 (WDW–DINE)* or book online at ⊕ *www.disneyworld.com/dining.* You can also get plenty of information on the website, including the meal periods served, price range, and specialties of all Disney eateries. Menus for all restaurants are posted online and tend to be up to date. For Universal Orlando reservations, call ☎ *407/224–9255* (theme parks and CityWalk) or ☎ *407/503–3463* (hotels). Learn about the complex's 50-plus restaurants at ⊕ *www.universalorlando.com/dining.*

In our reviews, reservations are mentioned only when they're essential or not accepted. Unless otherwise noted, the restaurants listed are open daily for lunch and dinner.

TIPPING AND TAXES

In most restaurants, tip the waiter 15%–20% of the food and beverage charges before tax. Tip at least $1 per drink at the bar, and $2 for valet parking.

WHAT TO WEAR

Because tourism is king around Orlando, casual dress is the rule. Flip-flops and cutoffs are acceptable in just about all fast-food and mid-price restaurants. Although it's best to dress up for the ritzier restaurants, don't be shocked to find diners beside you in Levi's and polo shirts. Men need jackets only in the most exclusive establishments; however, such establishments are strict about enforcing dress code. If you plan to eat at a nicer place, check on dress codes so you aren't caught unprepared and turned away at the door.

ABOUT OUR PRICE CATEGORIES AND MAPS

Prices in the restaurant reviews are the average cost of a main course at dinner or, if dinner is not served, at lunch; taxes and service charges are generally included.

Throughout the chapter, you'll see mapping symbols and coordinates (⊕ 3:F2) at the end of each review. Maps are within the chapter. The first number after the ⊕ symbol indicates the map number. After that is the property's coordinate on the map grid.

WALT DISNEY WORLD AREA

MAGIC KINGDOM

Dining options in the Magic Kingdom are mainly counter service, with a few delightful exceptions, and every land has its share of fast-food places selling burgers, hot dogs, grilled-chicken sandwiches, and salads. Each has a different regular and children's menu. The walkways are peppered with carts dispensing smoked turkey legs, popcorn, ice-cream bars, lemonade, bottled water, and soda. The Magic Kingdom's almost no-liquor policy (wine and beer is offered only during dinner at Be Our Guest) fits the theme park most suited for little kids. The spirits ban does not extend to the rest of Walt Disney World.

$$$
BRASSERIE
Fodor'sChoice
★

✕ **Be Our Guest.** Traverse a bridge flanked by gargoyles and gas lamps to reach the Beast's castle, home of this massive new restaurant with a *Beauty and the Beast* theme, French flair, and the Magic Kingdom's first and only wine and beer served at dinner. The 500-seat restaurant has three rooms: a gilded ballroom, whose ceiling sports cherubs with the faces of Imagineers' children; the tattered West Wing, with a slashed painting that changes from prince to beast during faux storms; and the Rose Gallery. Decor comprises French provincial furniture, suits of armor, and heavy drapes. Food, scratch-prepared on-site, includes pan-seared salmon, grilled steak, and maybe a pork rack with red wine au jus. The signature kids' soft drink comes in a light-up castle cup, and desserts, while sweet, are made without refined sugar. Be sure to accept a dollop of "the grey stuff"—it's delicious. Lunch is a no-reservations fast-casual affair with the likes of quinoa salad and a braised pork stew with mashed potatoes, ordered on a touch screen and delivered to the table. Ⓢ *Average main: $26* ✉ *Fantasyland* ☎ *407/939–3463* ⊕ *www. disneyworld.disney.go.com/dining* ⌕ *Reservations essential* ⊕ *1:B1.*

$$$$
AMERICAN

✕ **Cinderella's Royal Table.** Cinderella and other Disney princesses appear at this eatery in the castle's old mead hall; you should book reservations up to 180 days in advance to be sure to see them. The Fairytale Breakfast offers all-you-can-eat options such as lobster-crab crepes, and caramel apple–stuffed French toast. The Fairytale Lunch and Dinner, prix-fixe table-service meals, include entrées like gnocchi with roasted vegetables or roasted bone-in pork with sweet potato hash. When you arrive at the Cinderella Castle, a photographer snaps a shot of your group in the lobby. A package of photographs will be delivered to your table during your meal. Ⓢ *Average main: $59* ✉ *Cinderella Castle* ☎ *407/939–3463* ⊕ *www.disneyworld.disney.go.com/dining* ⌕ *Reservations essential* ⊕ *1:B1.*

$$$$
AMERICAN

✕ **The Crystal Palace.** A lovely Victorian setting is the perfect place for the old-fashioned and lovable Winnie the Pooh and friends to greet your kids via A Buffet with Character, offered here three meals a day. This is the only restaurant where you can find characters from the Hundred Acre Wood. Upscale goodies are served for adults while a separate children's spread features foods more appealing to them. At dinner, junior experiences cost from $20, adults $42. $ *Average main: $42* ✉ *Main Street, U.S.A.* ☎ *307/939–3463* ⊕ *www.disneyworld.com* ⚓ *Reservations essential* ✛ *1:B1.*

$$$$ ✕ **Liberty Tree Tavern.** This "tavern" is dry, but it's a prime spot on the
AMERICAN parade route, so you can catch a good meal while you wait. Order Colonial-period comfort food for lunch like hearty pot roast cooked with a Cabernet wine–and–mushroom sauce, or turkey and dressing with mashed potatoes. Dinner is the family-style Patriot's Platter, with turkey, carved beef, sliced pork, and sides. The restaurant is decorated in lovely Williamsburg colors with Early American–style antiques and lots of brightly polished brass. Each of the six dining rooms commemorates a historical U.S. figure, like Betsy Ross or Benjamin Franklin. $ *Average main: $32* ✉ *Liberty Sq.* ☎ *407/939–3463* ⊕ *www.disneyworld.disney. go.com/dining* ✛ *1:B1.*

$$$ ✕ **Tony's Town Square Restaurant.** Inspired by the animated classic *Lady*
ITALIAN *and the Tramp,* Tony's offers everything from spaghetti with meatballs to a New York strip steak with herb butter to garlicky shrimp scampi with sun-dried tomatoes. There's no wine list, but you can get the lemonade punch in a light-up collector's mug. The most tempting desserts are the chocolate cake with chocolate-hazelnut filling and the pistachio crème brûlée. If you can't get a table right away, you can watch *Lady and the Tramp* in the waiting area. $ *Average main: $25* ✉ *Main Street, U.S.A.* ☎ *407/939–3463* ⊕ *www.disneyworld.disney. go.com/dining* ✛ *1:B1.*

EPCOT

Epcot's World Showcase offers some of the finest dining in Orlando. Every pavilion has at least one and often two or even three eateries. Where there's a choice, it's between a relatively expensive full-service restaurant and a more affordable, ethnic fast-food spot, plus carts and shops selling snacks ranging from French pastries to Japanese ices—whatever's appropriate to the pavilion.

$$$$ ✕ **Akershus Royal Banquet Hall.** This restaurant has character buffets at all
SCANDINAVIAN three meals, with an array of Disney princesses, including Ariel, Belle, Jasmine, Snow White, Aurora, Mary Poppins, and even an occasional cameo appearance by Cinderella. The breakfast menu is American, but lunch and dinner find an ever-changing assortment of Norwegian specialties. Appetizers are offered buffet style, and usually include herring, goat-milk cheese, peppered mackerel, and gravlax (cured salmon served with mustard sauce) or *fiskepudding* (a seafood mousse with herb dressing). For your main course, chosen à la carte, you might try traditional ground pork and beef *kjottkake* (dumplings), venison stew, or a grilled pork chop with Jarlsberg mac and cheese. Aquavit, wine, and specialty drinks are offered. All meals are fixed price. $ *Average*

BEST BETS FOR ORLANDO AND THE PARKS DINING

If it can be fried and put under a heat lamp, you can probably find it in Orlando, but the dining scene both within the parks and the city itself has long transcended prototypical fast food. High-quality restaurants operate within the parks, Disney Springs, and several Orlando neighborhoods. Here are our top recommendations, organized by price, cuisine, and experience. The restaurants we consider the very best are indicated in the listings with the Fodor's Choice logo.

Fodor'sChoice★

4 Rivers Smokehouse, $

Be Our Guest, $$$

Boma—Flavors of Africa, $$$$

California Grill, $$$$

Christner's Prime Steak & Lobster, $$$$

Emeril's Orlando, $$$$

Flying Fish, $$$$

Hawkers, $$

Jiko, $$$$

K Restaurant & Wine Bar, $$$$

Luma on Park, $$$

Monsieur Paul, $$$$

Norman's, $$$$

Prato, $$$

Primo, $$$$

The Ravenous Pig, $$$$

The Rusty Spoon, $$$

The Smiling Bison, $$$

Todd English's bluezoo, $$$$

Victoria & Albert's, $$$$

By Price

$

4 Rivers Smokehouse

Anh Hong

Confisco Grille

Leaky Cauldron

$$

50's Prime Time Café

ESPN Club

Hawkers

Mythos

$$$

Be Our Guest

Bosphorous Turkish Cuisine

Cask & Larder

Emeril's Tchoup Chop

Les Chefs de France

Luma on Park

Prato

The Rusty Spoon

Sanaa

Seasons 52

The Smiling Bison

$$$$

Boma—Flavors of Africa

California Grill

Capa

Christner's Prime Steak & Lobster

Emeril's Orlando

Flying Fish

Jiko

K Restaurant & Wine Bar

Monsieur Paul

Norman's

Primo

The Ravenous Pig

Todd English's bluezoo

Victoria & Albert's

By Cuisine

AFRICAN

Boma—Flavors of Africa, $$$$

Jiko, $$$$

Sanaa, $$$

AMERICAN

50's Prime Time Café, $$

California Grill, $$$$

Cinderella's Royal Table, $$$$

Highball & Harvest, $$$

Luma on Park, $$$

The Ravenous Pig, $$$$

The Rusty Spoon, $$$

Seasons 52, $$

Victoria & Albert's, $$$$

Wolfgang Puck Grand Cafe, $$$$

ASIAN

Dragonfly, $$

Hawkers, $$

CONTINENTAL

The Venetian Room, $$$$

ECLECTIC

The Boheme Restaurant, $$$$

Café Tu Tu Tango, $$$

Citricos, $$$$

FRENCH

Be Our Guest, $$$

Les Chefs de France, $$$

Monsieur Paul, $$$$

IRISH

Finnegan's Bar & Grill, $$

Raglan Road Irish Pub, $$$

ITALIAN

Bice Ristorante, $$$$

Café d'Antonio, $$

Fiorella's Cucina Toscana, $$$

La Luce by Donna Scala, $$$

Mama Della's Ristorante, $$$

Peperoncino, $$$

Prato, $$$

Primo, $$$$

Tutto Italia Ristorante, $$$

JAPANESE

Kimonos, $$$

Shari Sushi Lounge, $$$

Tokyo Dining and Teppan Edo, $$$

LATIN

Columbia Restaurant, $$$

Cuba Libre, $$$

PIZZA

Via Napoli, $$$

SEAFOOD

Cityfish, $$

Flying Fish, $$$$

MoonFish, $$$$

Ocean Prime, $$$$

Oceanaire Seafood Room, $$$$

Todd English's bluezoo, $$$$

SOUTHERN

Cask & Larder, $$$

Highball & Harvest, $$$

Soco, $$$

STEAK HOUSE

Capa, $$$$

Christner's Prime Steak & Lobster, $$$$

Morton's The Steakhouse, $$$$

The Palm, $$$$

Shula's Steak House, $$$$

Yachtsman Steakhouse, $$$$

By Experience

BEST BUFFET

Biergarten, $$$$

Boma—Flavors of Africa, $$$$

Chef Mickey's, $$$$

Tusker House, $$$$

BEST VIEWS

California Grill, $$$$

Capa, $$$$

Sanaa, $$$

BEST DISNEY RESTAURANT

Be Our Guest, $$$

Boma—Flavors of Africa, $$$$

California Grill, $$$$

Flying Fish, $$$$

Jiko, $$$$

Monsieur Paul, $$$$

Victoria & Albert's, $$$$

BEST OFF-SITE RESTAURANT

K Restaurant & Wine Bar, $$$$

Luma on Park, $$$

Norman's, $$$$

Prato, $$$

Primo, $$$$

The Ravenous Pig, $$$$

SPECIAL OCCASION

Capa, $$$$

Norman's, $$$$

Ocean Prime, $$$$

Victoria & Albert's, $$$$

BEST SUNDAY BRUNCH

The Boheme Restaurant, $$$$

House of Blues, $$

K Restaurant & Wine Bar, $$$$

Soco, $$$

MOST ROMANTIC

Christini's Ristorante Italiano, $$$$

Norman's, $$$$

The Venetian Room, $$$$

Victoria & Albert's, $$$$

7

main: $48 ✉ *Norway Pavilion* ☎ *407/939–3463* ⊕ *www.disneyworld. disney.go.com/dining* ⌕ *Reservations essential* ✛ *1:D4.*

$$$$
GERMAN

✕ **Biergarten.** Oktoberfest runs 365 days a year here. The cheerful, sometimes raucous, crowds are what you would expect in a place with an oompah band. The menu and level of frivolity are the same at lunch and dinner. Mountains of sauerbraten, bratwurst, chicken or pork schnitzel, German sausage, spaetzle, apple strudel, Bavarian cheesecake, and Black Forest cake await you at the all-you-can-eat buffet. Patrons pound pitchers of all kinds of beer and wine on the long communal tables—even when the yodelers, singers, and dancers aren't egging them on. Prices change seasonally. ⑤ *Average main: $40* ✉ *Germany Pavilion* ☎ *407/939–3463* ⊕ *www.disneyworld.disney.go.com/dining* ⌕ *Reservations essential* ✛ *1:D4.*

$$$$
AMERICAN

✕ **Garden Grill.** Solid family-style dinner fare is served here as the restaurant revolves, giving you an ever-changing view of each biome on the Living with the Land boat ride. The restaurant offers all-you-can-eat family-style meals with visits from Chip 'n' Dale. Typical choices include beef, turkey, and a sustainable fish with trimmings, plus kiddie favorites like mac and cheese and oven-roasted chicken drumsticks. Except for the princess meals in Norway, this is the only Epcot restaurant that has Disney character meet and greets during meals. ⑤ *Average main: $42* ✉ *The Land Pavilion* ☎ *407/939–3463* ⊕ *www.disneyworld. disney.go.com/dining* ☾ *No lunch* ✛ *1:D4.*

$$$$
CANADIAN

✕ **Le Cellier Steakhouse.** This charming eatery with stone arches and dark woods has a good selection of Canadian wine and beer. Menu options are à la carte and include the signature cheddar cheese soup and filet mignon with wild-mushroom risotto and truffle–butter sauce. Of the many non-beef entrées, consider the seared lamb loin with mustard jus, and salmon with beluga lentils and bacon gastrique. As a side, add on any of three types of poutine. Desserts pay tribute to the land up north with crème brûlée made with maple sugar. ⑤ *Average main: $40* ✉ *Canada Pavilion* ☎ *407/939–3463* ⊕ *www.disneyworld.disney. go.com/dining* ✛ *1:D4.*

$$$
FRENCH

✕ **Les Chefs de France.** A busy, bustling brasserie with a plush look, this French café maintains its original spirit, which was created by three of France's most famous chefs at the time: Paul Bocuse, Gaston Lenôtre, and Roger Vergé. Classic escargots, a good starter, are prepared in a casserole with garlic butter; you might follow up with roasted breast and leg of duck confit with cherries, or grilled beef tenderloin with green peppercorn sauce. Make sure you finish with chocolate mousse. A three-course prix fixe option is often available. ⑤ *Average main: $27* ✉ *France Pavilion* ☎ *407/939–3463* ⊕ *www.disneyworld.disney. go.com/dining* ✛ *1:D4.*

$$$$
FRENCH
Fodor's Choice
★

✕ **Monsieur Paul.** A mere staircase away from Epcot's busy World Showcase, Monsieur Paul is a subdued and sophisticated fine dinery. It's owned by Chef Jerome Bocuse and named for his world-famous father, the Culinary Institute of America's Chef of the Century, Paul Bocuse. The restaurant is expensive and sophisticated—in odd juxtaposition to the rumpled clothing and sneakers of most diners—and a delightful diversion from the theme park's bustle. The menu is overtly French while incorporating the best of America. For example, the signature fish dish, which has "scales" of potato, braised fennel, and rosemary sauce, is made with Florida red snapper instead of the original's red mullet. Escargot is presented in large ravioli and a parsley cream. The seared scallops and roasted duck breast are especially interesting entrées. A three-course prix-fixe menu is often available. Although the service isn't as polished as the menu, it is heartening to hear the waitstaff converse in French. $ *Average main: $42* ⊠ *France Pavilion* ☎ *407/939–3463* ⊕ *www.disneyworld.disney.go.com/dining* ☽ *No lunch* ✛ *1:D4.*

$$$
BRITISH

╳ **Rose & Crown Pub & Dining Room.** If you're an Anglophile and you love a beer so thick you could stand a spoon up in your mug, this is the place to soak up both the suds and British street culture. "Wenches" serve up traditional English fare—fish-and-chips, cottage or shepherd's pie (ground lamb with onions, carrots, and peas, topped with mashed potatoes and cheddar cheese), and, at times, the ever-popular bangers and mash (sausage over mashed potatoes). Scotch egg makes a good appetizer. Vegetarians can always find one item adapted for them, such as vegetable cottage pie. For dessert, try the sticky toffee pudding. The terrace has a splendid view of IllumiNations. $ *Average main: $24* ⊠ *United Kingdom Pavilion* ☎ *407/939–3463* ⊕ *www.disneyworld. disney.go.com/dining* ✛ *1:D4.*

$$$
JAPANESE

╳ **Tokyo Dining and Teppan Edo.** Above the Mitsukoshi department store in Epcot's Japan pavilion are sister restaurants Teppan Edo, a teppan-yaki steak house where chefs do performance cooking at 20 grills, and Tokyo Dining, for sushi and pre-plated meals. Menu standouts at Teppan Edo include the filet mignon and the Tori chicken breast. It also has a small sushi selection and a kids' menu with Teppan-style chicken or shrimp with rice and veggies. The more stylish Tokyo Dining offers up tempura dishes, assorted sushi rolls, and grilled fish, chicken, or steak served with teriyaki or other sauces plus "sukiyaki beef rice." Both restaurants have something great to watch: Teppan Edo has the performing chefs; Tokyo Dining has a great view of the Japan pavilion. $ *Average main: $25* ⊠ *Japan Pavilion* ☎ *407/939–3463* ⊕ *www. disneyworld.disney.go.com/dining* ✛ *1:D4.*

$$$
ITALIAN

╳ **Tutto Italia Ristorante.** Tutto Italia may have an old-world look, but its menu is under the contemporary tutelage of Joachim Splichal, the prestigious Patina Restaurant Group's celebrity chef. Although freshened up significantly in recent years, the restaurant still has a certain formality, even though typical diners are wearing shorts, T-shirts, and flip-flops. Offerings include polenta with braised short ribs and meatballs, grilled salmon with shaved fennel salad, and rosemary chicken. Desserts include gelato and cannoli. Expect a wait at peak lunch and dinner times. Outdoor seating is available. An adjacent cavernous wine cellar, Tutto Gusto, has small bites and 200 wine options. $ *Average main: $27* ⊠ *Italy Pavilion* ☎ *407/939–3463* ⊕ *www.disneyworld. disney.go.com/dining* ⌕ *Reservations essential* ✛ *1:D4.*

$$$
PIZZA

╳ **Via Napoli Ristorante e Pizzeria.** When the Patina Restaurant Group decided to open a second Italian eatery in Epcot (the first was Tutto Italia Ristorante), they opted to specialize in authentic Neapolitan wood-fired pizza, importing the mozzarella from Italy and using only San

Marzano tomatoes. The result is crusty, thin pies topped with your choice of pepperoni; portobello and crimini mushrooms; or eggplant, artichokes, cotto ham, and mushrooms. The eggplant parmigiana is an outstanding alternative. ⑤ *Average main: $24* ⊠ *Italy Pavilion* ☎ *407/939–3463* ⊕ *www.disneyworld.disney.go.com/dining* ✛ *1:D4.*

DISNEY'S HOLLYWOOD STUDIOS

The Studios tends to have more highly themed restaurants than the other parks, and some serve good, imaginative food, too. Dinner packages that include the Fantasmic! after-dark show can be booked by phone or online, in person at a Disney hotel, or at the park's Guest Relations (aka Guest Services). With the package, you secure your reservation by credit card for dinner and then receive "designated seating" for the extravaganza. For a less expensive option, pick up a picnic dinner at Min & Bill's Dockside Diner as part of "A Taste of Hollywood to Go" It's available during the park's busiest seasons only.

$$ ╳ **50's Prime Time Café.** Who says you can't go home again? If you grew
AMERICAN up in middle America in the 1950s, just step inside. While *I Love Lucy*
FAMILY and *The Donna Reed Show* clips play on a television screen, you can feast on meat loaf, pot roast, or fried chicken, all served on a Formica tabletop. At $17, the meat loaf is one of the best inexpensive, filling dinners in any local theme park. Enjoy it with a malted-milk shake or root-beer float (or a bottle of wine). The place offers some fancier dishes, like grilled salmon with maple bourbon butter sauce, which is a good choice for lightish eaters. If you're not feeling totally wholesome, go for Dad's Electric Lemonade (rum, vodka, blue curaçao, sweet-and-sour mix, and Sprite), which is worth every bit of the $11.25 price tag. Just like Mother, the menu admonishes, "Keep your elbows off the table." ⑤ *Average main: $18* ⊠ *Echo Lake* ☎ *407/939–3463* ⊕ *www. disneyworld.disney.go.com/dining* ✛ *1:C5.*

$$$$ ╳ **Hollywood & Vine.** Disney Channel stars come to life at this restaurant
AMERICAN through its Disney Junior Play 'n Dine meals for breakfast and lunch. Handy Manny and Agent Oso from *Handy Manny*, along with friends of *Sofia the First* and *Doc McStuffins*, are among the cheerful characters marching around the room, singing and dancing to the delight of energetic fans. This is a great choice for toddlers. At night, the buffet format transforms into a more upscale all-you-can-eat affair with cooking stations. ⑤ *Average main: $35* ⊠ *Echo Lake* ☎ *407/939–3463* ⊕ *www.disneyworld.com* ✛ *1:C5.*

$$$$ ╳ **Hollywood Brown Derby.** At this reproduction of the famous 1940s
AMERICAN Hollywood restaurant, the walls are lined with movie-star caricatures, just as in Tinseltown. The specialty is the Cobb salad, which by legend was invented by Brown Derby founder Robert Cobb; the salad consists of finely chopped lettuce enlivened by loads of tomato, bacon, turkey, blue cheese, chopped egg, and avocado, all tossed table-side. Other menu choices include grilled salmon with golden lentils, applewood-smoked bacon, and green onions topped with fennel and citrus salad, and herb-crusted grilled loin of lamb. Dining with an Imagineer is a special option; you will have lunch or dinner with one of Disney's creative

engineers while enjoying a set-price four-course meal including soup, salad, entrée, and dessert. If you request the Fantasmic! dinner package, make a reservation for no later than two hours before the start of the show. $ *Average main: $31* ⊠ *Hollywood Blvd.* ☎ 407/939–3463 ⊕ *www.disneyworld.disney.go.com/dining* ✢ 1:C5.

$$$ ✕ **Sci-Fi Dine-In Theater Restaurant.** If you don't mind zombies leering at
AMERICAN   you while you eat, then head to this enclosed faux drive-in, where you can sit in a fake candy-color '50s convertible and watch trailers from classics like *Attack of the Fifty-Foot Woman* and *Teenagers from Outer Space*. The menu includes choices like steak and garlic-mashed potatoes, an Angus or veggie burger, shrimp with whole-grain pasta, and a huge Reuben sandwich with fries or cucumber salad. End with a hot-fudge sundae. $ *Average main: $23* ⊠ *Commissary La.* ☎ 407/939–3463 ⊕ *www.disneyworld.disney.go.com/dining* ✢ 1:C5.

DISNEY'S ANIMAL KINGDOM

Disney's Animal Kingdom is far from a foodie destination, but Disney's highly themed zoo does offer variety, including an African-theme buffet, a Chinese restaurant with table service, and surprises like a tea stand, a fruit market, and, at times, picnic lunches packaged to go.

$ ✕ **Flame Tree Barbecue.** This counter-service eatery is one of the rela-
FAST FOOD   tively undiscovered gems of Disney's culinary offerings. There's nothing fancy here, but you can dig into ribs and pulled-pork sandwiches. For something with a lower calorie count, try the smoked turkey sandwich served with cranberry mayo or a great barbecued chicken served with baked beans and coleslaw. The outdoor tables, set beneath intricately carved wood pavilions, make great spots for a picnic, and they're not usually crowded. $ *Average main: $12* ⊠ *Discovery Island* ⊕ *www. disneyworld.disney.go.com/dining* ⚹ *Reservations not accepted* ✢ 1:A4.

$$$$ ✕ **Tusker House.** This restaurant offers all-buffet dining three meals a day,
AFRICAN   and a Donald's safari-theme character crew complements the African-
FAMILY   esque decor and menu. Tusker House offers healthier fare like curry chicken, *peri-peri* (African hot pepper) marinated salmon, strip loin rubbed with *berbere* (an African spice mix), and saffron-infused root vegetables, along with the standard kids' fare. This restaurant has a large vegetarian selection. $ *Average main: $42* ⊠ *Africa* ☎ 407/939–3463 ⊕ *www.disneyworld.disney.go.com/dining* ⚹ *Reservations essential* ✢ 1:A4.

$$$ ✕ **Yak & Yeti.** The location of this pan-Asian cuisine, sit-down eatery—
ASIAN   the only full-service restaurant inside Disney's Animal Kingdom—certainly makes sense. It's just at the entrance to the Asia section, in a two-story, 250-seat building that is pleasantly faux-Asian, with cracked plaster walls, wood carvings, and tile mosaic tabletops. Standout entrées include seared miso salmon, roasted duck with orange-wasabi glaze, and tempura shrimp with jasmine rice and chili-plum sauce. Also tasty, if not authentically Asian, are the baby back ribs with a hoisin barbecue sauce and sweet chili slaw. $ *Average main: $22* ⊠ *Asia* ☎ 407/939– 3463 ⊕ *www.disneyworld.disney.go.com/dining* ✢ 1:A4.

7

DOWNTOWN DISNEY

Downtown Disney is a shopping and dining complex broken into three sections: Marketplace, which is known more for its shopping but boasts quite an array of restaurants; Pleasure Island, originally a nightlife center that, at this writing, has plenty of dining, shopping, and entertainment options; and West Side, with its enviable lineup of dining spots plus entertainment venues. By 2016, the area will be doubled in size and renamed Disney Springs. There is no cover charge to enter any part of the enterprise.

$$
AMERICAN

✕ **House of Blues.** You're unlikely to like this place unless you enjoy listening to high-decibel music during your meal. But if you do, this is a great spot to chow down from an eclectic menu that offers everything from ribs to shrimp and grits to a tasty chicken Caesar salad. The Juicy Lucy is a bacon cheeseburger with jalapeño and chipotle mayo. A worthy dessert is the bourbon-white-chocolate-banana-bread pudding. The Gospel Sunday Brunch offers a Southern cooking buffet and live gospel music. For a quicker meal, visit the quick-service barbecue counter The Smokehouse. $ *Average main: $21* ✉ *West Side, 1490 E. Buena Vista Dr.* ☎ *407/934–2583* ⊕ *www.houseofblues.com* ✛ *1:F4.*

$$$
IRISH

✕ **Raglan Road Irish Pub.** An authentic Irish pub in Downtown Disney seems oxymoronic, particularly when that pub seats 600 people. But if Irish grub's your thing, Raglan's is the place to go. The shepherd's pie served here is of higher quality than the usual version, prepared with beef and lamb and jazzed up with house spices. And you don't have to settle for plain fish-and-chips (though you can for $19); there's also baked salmon with smoked salmon and maple glaze; shiitake risotto; and lamb shanks braised with rosemary jus. Massive and ornate bars, imported from Ireland and more than a century old, help anchor the pub. The entertainment alone makes this place worth the visit. The house bands play nightly, and a troupe of Irish dancers performs every evening and during Rollicking Raglan Sunday Brunch. Another band plays outside for guests dining alfresco. A store called Shop for Ireland sells Irish merchandise. $ *Average main: $23* ✉ *Downtown Disney, 1640 E. Buena Vista Dr.* ☎ *407/938–0300* ⊕ *www.raglanroadirishpub.com* ✛ *1:F4.*

$$$$
AMERICAN

✕ **Wolfgang Puck Grand Cafe.** There are lots of choices here, from wood-oven pizza at the informal Puck Express to fine-dining meals in the upstairs formal dining room. There's also a sushi bar and an informal café; the café is quite literally a happy medium, and may be the best bet for families hoping for a bit of elegance without the pressure of a formal dinner. At Express try the butternut squash soup or the Margherita pizza. At the café, mid-price entrées like rosemary chicken and bacon-wrapped meat loaf are winners, and you can always have a personal pizza, such as barbecued chicken with smoked mozzarella. The dining room offers creative entrées like smoked pork chop with maple brown butter. $ *Average main: $32* ✉ *West Side, 1482 E. Buena Vista Dr.* ☎ *407/938–9653* ⊕ *www.wolfgangpuckcafeorlando.com* ✛ *1:F4.*

WALT DISNEY WORLD RESORTS

MAGIC KINGDOM RESORT AREA

$$$$
AMERICAN

✕ **1900 Park Fare.** Disney characters delight guests throughout the day at this sprawling, though dainty, lobby restaurant. Mary Poppins and friends join guests during the Supercalifragilistic Breakfast, posing for pics while cheerful tunes are played on an antique organ called Big Bertha. The buffet features omelets made to order. Midday, the Mad Hatter reigns at the Wonderland Tea Party, for kids only. "Tea" consists of apple juice and cupcakes served by Alice and a very silly Hatter. Dress-up is encouraged but not required. Games and stories fill the hour for the 25 attendees from 4 to 12, who leave with an autographed photo. Dinner is home to Cinderella's Happily Ever After Dinner, a buffet of worldly cuisine complete with Cinderella, Prince Charming, and their family (including wicked steps) making the rounds. $ *Average main: $42* ⊠ *Grand Floridian Resort & Spa, 4401 Floridian Way* ☎ *407/939–3463* ⊕ *www.disneyworld.com* ◷ *No lunch* ✛ *1:B1.*

$$$$
AMERICAN
Fodor'sChoice
★

✕ **California Grill.** The view from the surrounding Disney parks from this 15th-floor restaurant—the World's signature dining establishment since 1995—is as stunning as the food, especially after dark, when you can watch the nightly Magic Kingdom fireworks. The space has stylish mid-century modern furnishings and chandeliers, while the exhibition kitchen is so well equipped that it has a cast-iron flat grill designed specifically for cooking fish. Expect locally sourced foods where possible, made-from-scratch items such as the house-made charcuterie sampler appetizer, and many items cooked in the wood-fired oven. Sushi is a highlight, alongside creative, globally inspired entrées. Specialties include oak-fired fillet of beef with heirloom tomato risotto, and scallops with piquillo pepper rouille. $ *Average main: $42* ⊠ *Contemporary Resort, 4600 N. World Dr.* ☎ *407/939–3463* ⊕ *www.disneyworld. disney.go.com/dining* ⚞ *Reservations essential* ◷ *No lunch* ✛ *1:B1.*

$$$$
AMERICAN

✕ **Chef Mickey's.** This is the holy shrine for character meals, with Mickey, Minnie, or Goofy around for breakfast and dinner. Folks come here for entertainment and comfort food, not a quiet spot to read the *Orlando Sentinel.* The breakfast buffet includes "pixie-dusted" challah French toast, mountains of pancakes, and even a breakfast pizza. The dinner buffet doesn't disappoint with Thai-curry-chipotle barbecue chicken, roasted ham, and spice-rubbed beef sirloin. Finish off your meal at the all-you-can-eat dessert bar of sundaes. $ *Average main: $47* ⊠ *Contemporary Resort, 4600 N. World Dr.* ☎ *407/939–3463* ⊕ *www. disneyworld.disney.go.com/dining* ◷ *No lunch* ✛ *1:B1.*

$$$$
ECLECTIC

✕ **Citricos.** Although the name implies that you'll be eating lots of local citrus specialties, you won't necessarily find them here (unless you count the Solerno Prosecco Cocktail made with orange juice, or the veal chop's citrus butter). But you will find an ambitious menu that's fundamentally American with influences of southern Europe's low-fat, high-flavor cuisines, namely Tuscan, Provençal, and Spanish-Mediterranean. Standout entrées include the oak-grilled swordfish with citrus-marinated shellfish, and the red wine–braised beef short ribs with hand-harvested mushrooms.

The wine list, one of Disney's most extensive, includes vintages from around the world. $ *Average main: $42* ⊠ *Grand Floridian Resort & Spa, 4401 Floridian Way* ☎ *407/939–3463* ⊕ *www.disneyworld.disney. go.com/dining* ⌦ *Reservations essential* ⊗ *No lunch* ✢ *1:B1.*

$$ ✕ **Fort Wilderness Pavilion.** Mickey's Backyard BBQ is a dinner show in an
BARBECUE　open-air pavilion that has everything from dancing and foot-stomping country music to finger-food goodies like hot dogs and smoked ribs. Cowboy Mickey Mouse is the star of the show. $ *Average main: $55* ⊠ *Campsites at Disney's Fort Wilderness Resort, 4510 Fort Wilderness Trail* ☎ *407/939–3463* ⊕ *www.disneyworld.com* ⌦ *Reservations essential* ⊗ *No lunch* ✢ *1:C1.*

$$$$ ✕ **Garden View Tea Room.** Girls ages 3 to 11 enjoy the princess experience
BRITISH　with Mom (or Dad). Dressing up is encouraged, and an early lunch, featuring tea and sandwiches, is served on china plates (apple juice, peanut butter, and ham-and-cheese sandwiches for the little darlings; cheeses and finger sandwiches for adults). Princess Aurora (Sleeping Beauty herself) may make an appearance. Little ones receive a special Disney Girl Princess doll, jewelry, a ribbon tiara, and a photo scrapbook page, a nice parting gift considering the hefty cost. The price is for a child-adult duo. From 2 pm to 5 pm daily, the space serves a traditional afternoon tea. $ *Average main: $275* ⊠ *Grand Floridian Resort & Spa, 4401 Floridian Way* ☎ *407/939–3463* ⊕ *www.disneyworld.com* ⌦ *Reservations essential* ⊗ *Closed Tues. and Sat.* ✢ *1:B1*

$$$$ ✕ **Narcoossee's.** The dining room, with Victorian-style columns, high
SEAFOOD　ceilings, and hardwood floors, makes a great place not only to enjoy "coastal cuisine"—especially steaks and seafood—but to gaze out at the nightly fireworks over the Seven Seas Lagoon. The menu changes regularly. Typical choices are wild Alaskan halibut and the surf-and-turf centerpiece: a butter-poached lobster tail and a tender grilled filet mignon. The name of the place, incidentally, was not coined by Disney Imagineers; it's the name of a river and a small Central Florida town, both of which predate Disney. Diners should note that no tank tops or cut-offs are permitted. $ *Average main: $54* ⊠ *Grand Floridian Resort & Spa, 4401 Floridian Way* ☎ *407/939–3463* ⊕ *www.disneyworld. disney.go.com/dining* ⊗ *No lunch* ✢ *1:B1.*

$$$$ ✕ **'Ohana.** 'Ohana offers two thoroughly entertaining, though incred-
SOUTH PACIFIC　ibly different, experiences. Early in the day, the Best Friends Breakfast
FAMILY　with Lilo & Stitch is destination-worthy. The intergalactic Stitch and a human sidekick join families for the morning meal, and Mickey and Pluto join in periodically while kids parade around the restaurant with maracas and wide grins. At night, the Polynesian-themed restaurant serves family-style all-you-can-eat meatfests plus lo mein, dumplings, and stir-fries. The kids have coconut-rolling contests using brooms, and even dads are known to try out the hula hoops between courses. $ *Average main: $36* ⊠ *Polynesian Village Resort, 1600 Seven Seas Dr.* ☎ *407/939–3463* ⊕ *www.disneyworld.com/dining* ⊗ *No lunch* ✢ *1:B2.*

$$$$ ✕ **Victoria & Albert's.** At this ultraposh award-winning Disney restaurant,
MODERN　a well-polished service team will anticipate your every need during a
AMERICAN　gourmet extravaganza. This is one of the plushest fine-dining experi-
Fodor'sChoice　ences in Florida, with an ambience so sophisticated that children under
★　10 aren't on the guest list. The seven-course, prix-fixe menu changes

daily, and you'd do well to supplement the $150 tab with a $65 wine pairing. Appetizer choices may include wild turbot with toasted capers and preserved lemon, and masago-crusted scallop with coconut-curry broth. Entrées may feature veal with chanterelles or Australian Kobe-style beef with oxtail ravioli. For most of the year, there are two seatings, at 5:45 and 9 pm. In July and August, however, there's generally just one seating at 6:30 pm. For a more luxe experience, reserve a table in the intimate Queen Victoria Room or at the Chef's Table, which have more courses (10 to 12) and a bigger bill ($250, wine pairing $105). ⑤ *Average main: $200* ⊠ *Grand Floridian Resort & Spa, 4401 Floridian Way* ☎ *407/939–3862* ⊕ *www.victoria-alberts.com* ⚑ *Reservations essential* 🎩 *Jacket required* ⊗ *No lunch* ✛ *1:B1.*

EPCOT RESORT AREA

$$
AMERICAN
✕**Big River Grille & Brewing Works.** Strange but good brews, like Rocket Red Ale, Southern Flyer Light Lager, Steamboat Pale Ale, and Gadzooks Pilsner, abound here at Walt Disney World's only microbrewery. You can dine inside among the giant stainless-steel brewing tanks or sip your suds outside on the lake-view patio. The menu emphasizes meat and fish, with pork ribs dry-rubbed and topped with Rocket Red barbecue sauce, a flame-grilled meat loaf made with ground beef and Italian sausage, and grilled Atlantic salmon fillet with dill butter. The garlic mashed potatoes are a perfect accompaniment. ⑤ *Average main: $19* ⊠ *BoardWalk Inn, 2101 Epcot Resorts Blvd.* ☎ *407/560–0253* ⊕ *www.bigrivergrille.com* ✛ *1:C4.*

$$$$
SEAFOOD
FAMILY
✕**Cape May Cafe.** With the feel of a New England seafood house—the type your grandma might enjoy—this bustling spot features popular buffet meals. For breakfast, Goofy and other cast classics visit tables while families help themselves to American classics from waffles to sausage links from the buffet. In the evening, seafood is the star of the show. Instead of characters, diners dote over steamed mussels, fried clams, and seafood chowder. ⑤ *Average main: $38* ⊠ *Beach Club Resort, 1800 Epcot Resorts Blvd.* ☎ *407/939–3463* ⊕ *www.disneyworld.com/dining* ⊗ *No lunch* ✛ *1:C4.*

$$
AMERICAN
✕**ESPN Club.** Not only can you watch sports on a big-screen TV here (the restaurant has about 100 monitors), but you can also periodically see ESPN programs being taped in the club itself and be part of the audience of sports-radio talk shows. Food ranges from a variety of half-pound burgers, made with Angus chuck (and one topped with Cajun crawfish salad), to Philly cheesesteaks and *char siu* sliders. If you want an appetizer, try the Pub Nachos, crispy corn tortilla chips piled high with barbecued pulled pork, spicy chili, shredded cheddar cheese, cheddar cheese sauce, sour cream, pico de gallo, and sliced jalapeños. This place is open quite late by Disney standards—until 1 am daily. Beware, the place can be pretty loud during any broadcast sports event, especially football games. ⑤ *Average main: $17* ⊠ *BoardWalk Inn, 2101 Epcot Resorts Blvd.* ☎ *407/939–3463* ⊕ *www.disneyworld. disney.go.com/dining* ✛ *1:C4.*

7

$$$$
SEAFOOD
Fodor's Choice
★
✕ **Flying Fish.** One of Disney's best restaurants, Flying Fish is whimsically decorated with murals along the upper portion of the walls that pay tribute to Atlantic seaboard spots of the early 1900s. This is a place where you put on your "resort casual" duds to "dine," as opposed to putting on your flip-flops and shorts to "chow down." The chefs take the food so seriously that the entire culinary team takes day trips to local farms to learn their foodstuffs' origins. Flying Fish's best dishes include potato-wrapped red snapper, which is so popular it has been on the menu for several years, and oak-grilled salmon. Groups of up to six can sit at the counter that directly faces the exhibition kitchen for a five-course wine tasting menu. The restaurant serves breakfast during the busiest tourist seasons only. $ *Average main: $36* ⊠ *BoardWalk Inn, 2101 Epcot Resorts Blvd.* ☎ *407/939–2359* ⊕ *www.disneyworld. disney.go.com/dining* ☉ *No lunch* ✛ *1:C4.*

$$$$
AMERICAN
FAMILY
✕ **Garden Grove.** With twinkling lights hung amid the branches of its oversized 25-foot signature tree, this restaurant, designed to resemble New York's Central Park, specializes in character meals. At dinner nightly, guests dine on classic American fare like prime rib while Goofy and his buddies make their rounds. Seafood buffets are featured Friday and Saturday evenings. Weekend mornings, Pluto leads the fray as families fuel up on day starters from raisin bread French toast to lobster omelets. The restaurant is open for lunch but without characters. $ *Average main: $34* ⊠ *Walt Disney World Swan, 1200 Epcot Resorts Blvd.* ☎ *407/934–1618* ⊕ *www.swandolphinrestaurants.com* ✛ *1:C4.*

$$$
JAPANESE
✕ **Kimonos.** Knife-wielding sushi chefs prepare world-class sushi and sashimi but also other Japanese treats like soups and salads at this sleek hotel sushi bar, where bamboo-style floor tiles and dark teakwood furnishings create an inviting environment. Popular rolls include the Dragon Roll (giant shrimp and tuna), Dancing Eel Roll (faux crab, avocado, and eel), and the Bagel Roll (smoked salmon, cream cheese, and cucumber). Cocktails are a draw here, too, along with entertainment in the form of nightly karaoke. $ *Average main: $24* ⊠ *Walt Disney World Swan, 1200 Epcot Resorts Blvd.* ☎ *407/934–1609* ⊕ *www. swandolphinrestaurants.com/kimonos* ⌦ *Reservations not accepted* ☉ *No lunch* ✛ *1:C4.*

$$$$
STEAKHOUSE
✕ **Shula's Steak House.** The hardwood floors, dark-wood paneling, and pictures of former Miami Dolphins coach Don Shula make this restaurant resemble an annex of the NFL Hall of Fame. Among the best selections are the porterhouse and prime rib. Ambitious diners may be interested in the 48-ounce porterhouse challenge: finish the dish and you get a signed picture of coach Don Shula, plus your name will be displayed on a virtual plaque on the restaurant's website. If you're not a carnivore, go for the daily market fish or the huge (up to 4 pounds) Maine lobster. $ *Average main: $79* ⊠ *Walt Disney World Dolphin, 1500 Epcot Resorts Blvd.* ☎ *407/934–1362* ⊕ *www. swandolphinrestaurants.com/shulas* ☉ *No lunch* ✛ *1:C4.*

$$$$
SEAFOOD
Fodor's Choice
★
✕ **Todd English's bluezoo.** Celebrity chef Todd English oversees this cutting-edge seafood eatery, a sleek, modern restaurant that resembles an underwater dining hall, with blue walls and carpeting, aluminum fish along the wall behind the bar, and bubblelike lighting fixtures.

The menu is creative and pricey, with entrées like the 2-pound Maine "Cantonese lobster," fried and tossed in a sticky soy glaze, and the daily "dancing fish," cooked on an upright rotisserie with an apple-soy marinade. If you don't care for fish, you can opt for seasonal chicken or steak preparations. The children's menu is especially good. ⑤ *Average main: $44* ✉ *Walt Disney World Dolphin, 1500 Epcot Resorts Blvd.* ☎ *407/934–1111* ⊕ *www.thebluezoo.com* ◷ *No lunch* ✛ *1:C4.*

$$$ ✗ **Trattoria al Forno.** Themed as an old-time Italian home along a board-
ITALIAN walk, this Disney hotel restaurant melds new and old, from the homey yet plush decor with contemporary touches to the menu, where authentic dishes are refreshed for today's tastes. Share the sliced meat platter, served with olives and house-pickled vegetables, and split a pizza topped with fennel sausage, salame piccante, and more of those pickles. The campanelle pasta is a pesto dish with potatoes that even nonvegetarians will enjoy, and the shrimp with anchovy butter on polenta is indulgent. Entrées include braised beef Bolognese with homemade pasta, chicken parmigiana, and whole-roasted fish. All the wines are from Italy. End with a grappa, limoncello, or digestif. ⑤ *Average main: $27* ✉ *BoardWalk Inn, 2101 Epcot Resorts Blvd.* ☎ *407/939–3463* ⊕ *www. disneyworld.com* ◷ *No lunch* ✛ *1:C4.*

$$$$ ✗ **Yachtsman Steakhouse.** Aged beef, the attraction at this casual steak
STEAKHOUSE house in the upscale Yacht and Beach Club, can be seen mellowing in the glassed-in butcher shop near the entryway. The chefs are proud of their beef in this woodsy, family-friendly spot, and the quality seems to prove it. Meats are hand-cut on the premises. The 12-ounce New York strip with peppercorn-brandy sauce and white cheddar twice-baked potato is quite tasty, but at $49, it's not soft on the wallet. Other menu options include porterhouse, filet mignon, and a fish dish, such as ahi tuna with barley congee and Thai green curry. An artisanal cheese platter and nice selections of dessert wines and Scotches round out the menu. ⑤ *Average main: $45* ✉ *Yacht and Beach Club, 1700 Epcot Resorts Blvd.* ☎ *407/939–3463* ⊕ *www.disneyworld.disney.go.com/ dining* ◷ *No lunch* ✛ *1:C4.*

DOWNTOWN DISNEY RESORT AREA

$$$ ✗ **Olivia's Café.** This is like a meal at Grandma's—provided she lives in
AMERICAN Key West and likes to gussy up her grub with trendy twists. The menu ranges from a shrimp pasta with vegetables in a tomato broth to pork chops with smoked Gouda fondue and a side of multigrain rice and broccolini. Desserts are indulgent, such as the banana-bread-pudding sundae with bananas Foster topping and vanilla ice cream. The outdoor seating, which overlooks a waterway, is a nice place to dine anytime the midsummer heat is not bearing down. ⑤ *Average main: $25* ✉ *Old Key West Resort, 1510 N. Cove Rd.* ☎ *407/939–3463* ⊕ *www.disneyworld. disney.go.com/dining* ✛ *1:E3.*

ANIMAL KINGDOM RESORT AREA

$$$$
AFRICAN
Fodor's Choice
★

✕ **Boma—Flavors of Africa.** Boma takes Western-style ingredients and pre-pares them with an African twist—then invites guests to walk through an African marketplace–style dining room to help themselves at the extraordinary buffet. The dozen or so serving stations have entrées such as roasted pork, Durban-style chicken, spice-crusted beef, and fish served with tamarind and other robust sauces; intriguing salads; and some of the best hummus this side of the Atlantic. Don't pass up the soups, as the coconut-curry seafood stew is excellent. The zebra dome dessert is chocolate mousse covered with white chocolate and striped with dark chocolate. All meals are prix fixe, and prices change seasonally. The South African wine list is outstanding. $ *Average main: $40* ⊠ *Animal King-dom Lodge, 2901 Osceola Pkwy.* ☎ *407/939–3463* ⊕ *www.disneyworld. disney.go.com/dining* ♨ *Reservations essential* ☉ *No lunch* ✛ *1:A5.*

$$$$
AFRICAN
Fodor's Choice
★

✕ **Jiko.** The name of this restaurant means "the cooking place" in Swahili, and it is certainly that. The dining area surrounds two big, wood-burning ovens and a grill area where you can watch cooks in North African–style caps working on your meal. The menu here is more African-inspired than purely African, but it does include authentic flavors in appetizers like peri-peri chicken flatbread and wild boar tenderloin with mealie pap and chakalaka. Menu items often change, but entrées might include scallops with Senegal black-eyed pea salad, or spicy Botswana-style beef short ribs with cassava-potato puree. The restaurant offers dozens of wines by the glass, including a large selection of South African vintages. Ask about the Wednesday wine tastings. $ *Average main: $40* ⊠ *Animal Kingdom Lodge, 2901 Osceola Pkwy.* ☎ *407/939–3463* ⊕ *www.disneyworld. disney.go.com/dining* ♨ *Reservations essential* ☉ *No lunch* ✛ *1:A5.*

$$$
AFRICAN

✕ **Sanaa.** Most of the flavors are from India, yet Sanaa is really a cel-ebration of the Spice Islands—locales off the coast of Africa that for cen-turies hosted traders from the world's corners. Exotic yet approachable lunches and dinners make it a true find on the outer edges of the Disney empire; views of zebras and giraffes right out the picture windows are another draw. Potato-pea samosas as an appetizer sampler are good starters. For the main course, be sure to try the tandoori shrimp or the "Slow-cooked in gravy" sampler with two of five protein options. There is a reservations-only Dine with an Animal Specialist program consist-ing of a four-course meal and fascinating company. $ *Average main: $26* ⊠ *Animal Kingdom Villas—Kidani Village, 3701 W. Osceola Pkwy.* ☎ *407/989–3463* ⊕ *www.disneyworld.disney.go.com/dining* ✛ *1:A5.*

UNIVERSAL ORLANDO AREA

With dozens of restaurants, including the world's largest Hard Rock Cafe, Universal Orlando is a mecca for those seeking a meal, plain or fancy. Islands of Adventure has from one to six eateries—not all of them strictly burger-and-fries affairs—in each of its lands. Universal Studios Florida has yet more places for lunch and dinner. And at CityWalk, a dining, retail, and entertainment complex that you have to pass as you leave the two theme parks, you'll find even more tempting eateries. In fact, CityWalk recently added several new eateries, including the highly themed Mexican concept Antojitos, the sushi-burger duo Cowfish, and a so-called artisan pizza place.

UNIVERSAL STUDIOS

Behind-the-scenes movie action is the theme at Universal Studios Florida, and dining options are purposely cliché versions of restaurants you might see on the silver screen: an old-fashioned Italian joint, a '50s drive-in, an Irish pub, and a seafood house, for example. Be sure to snack on a sundae at a replica of Schwab's Pharmacy, where many starlets were "discovered." For Harry Potter fans, Leaky Cauldron is a must.

$$$ ✕ **Cafe La Bamba.** In the relaxed L.A. backdrop of the Hollywood Hotel, AMERICAN La Bamba is an unfussy sprawling spot that hosts Universal's Superstar Character Breakfast. The stars may vary, but *Hop* and *Despicable Me* faves tend to join Nickelodeon staples. Guests often follow the characters after the meal as they join the Superstar Parade. Expect pre-plated American breakfast staples for your meal. Park admission is required. ⑤ *Average main: $26 ⊠ Hollywood, 6000 Universal Blvd.* ☎ *407/224–9255 ⊕ www.universalorlando.com ⊗ No dinner ✛ 2:D1.*

$$ ✕ **Finnegan's Bar & Grill.** In an Irish pub that would look just right in IRISH downtown New York during the Ellis Island era, Finnegan's offers classic Irish comfort food like shepherd's pie, corned beef and cabbage, bangers and mash (sausage and mashed potatoes), and fish-and-chips, plus Guinness on tap and a five-beer sampler. If shepherd's pie isn't your thing, opt instead for a steak, burger, entrée salad, or sandwich. Irish folk music, sometimes live, completes the theme. ⑤ *Average main: $16* ⊠ *New York ☎ 407/363–8757 ⊕ www.universalorlando.com ✛ 2:D1.*

$ ✕ **Leaky Cauldron.** British pub staples are fitting fare for Diagon Alley's BRITISH restaurant, which complements those hearty meals with kooky-sounding beverages from the Harry Potter books like Tongue-Tying Lemon Squash, Otter's Fizzy Orange Juice, and Fishy Green Ale (it's minty, with blueberry-flavored filled boba). Order at the counter, then be seated; a microchip in your "candlestick" will tell servers where to bring the grub. The Ploughman's Platter, with its cheeses, Scotch eggs, and apple-beet salad is food enough for two average eaters. English sausages can be had in toad-in-the-hole, bangers and mash, or a sandwich with three-mustard mayo. The fish-and-chips has an excellent flaky crust; the cod is flown in daily. End with the indulgent sticky toffee pudding. ⑤ *Average main: $14 ⊠ Diagon Alley ☎ 407/224–9716 ⊕ https://www. universalorlando.com ⌂ Reservations not accepted ✛ 2:D1.*

$$ ✕ **Lombard's Seafood Grille.** Fresh fried fish, fried shrimp, and assorted other SEAFOOD takes on seafood are the specialty at this restaurant designed to resemble a Fisherman's Wharf warehouse from 19th-century San Francisco. You can also get a Boursin steak sandwich with fried onion strips, hamburgers, chicken sandwiches, and big salads. The New England clam chowder is a standout, especially for the price. ⑤ *Average main: $15 ⊠ San Francisco* ☎ *407/224–6400 ⊕ www.universalorlando.com ✛ 2:D1.*

$ ✕ **Mel's Drive-In.** At the corner of Hollywood and Vine is a flashy '50s AMERICAN eatery with a pink-and-white 1956 Ford Crown Victoria parked out in front. For burgers and fries, this is one of the best choices in the park,

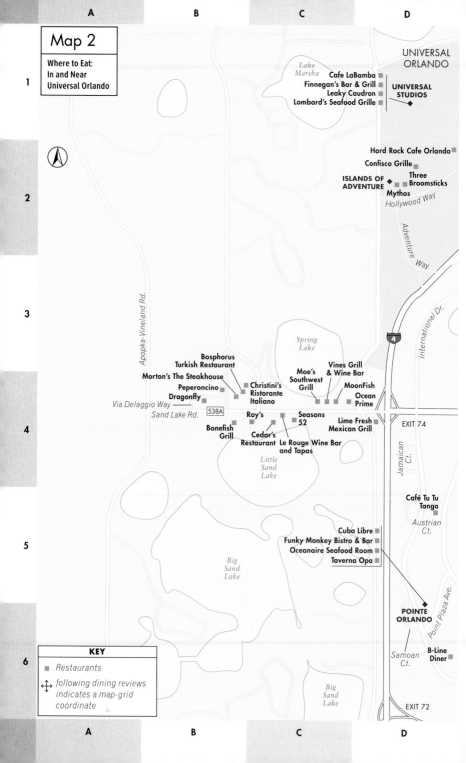

Map 2

Where to Eat: In and Near Universal Orlando

UNIVERSAL ORLANDO

Lake Marsha

Cafe LaBamba
Finnegan's Bar & Grill
Leaky Caudron
Lombard's Seafood Grille

UNIVERSAL STUDIOS

Hard Rock Cafe Orlando
Confisco Grille
ISLANDS OF ADVENTURE
Three Broomsticks
Mythos

Hollywood Way

Adventure Way

International Dr.

I-4

Spring Lake

Bosphorus Turkish Restaurant
Morton's The Steakhouse
Peperoncino
Dragonfly
Christini's Ristorante Italiano

Moe's Southwest Grill
Vines Grill & Wine Bar
MoonFish
Ocean Prime

Via Delaggio Way
Sand Lake Rd.
538A

Roy's
Bonefish Grill
Cedar's Restaurant
Le Rouge Wine Bar and Tapas
Seasons 52
Lime Fresh Mexican Grill

EXIT 74

Jamaican Ct.

Little Sand Lake

Café Tu Tu Tango

Austrian Ct.

Cuba Libre
Funky Monkey Bistro & Bar
Oceanaire Seafood Room
Taverna Opa

Big Sand Lake

POINTE ORLANDO

Point Plaza Ave.

Samoan Ct.

B-Line Diner

Big Sand Lake

EXIT 72

KEY

- Restaurants
- ⟷ following dining reviews indicates a map-grid coordinate

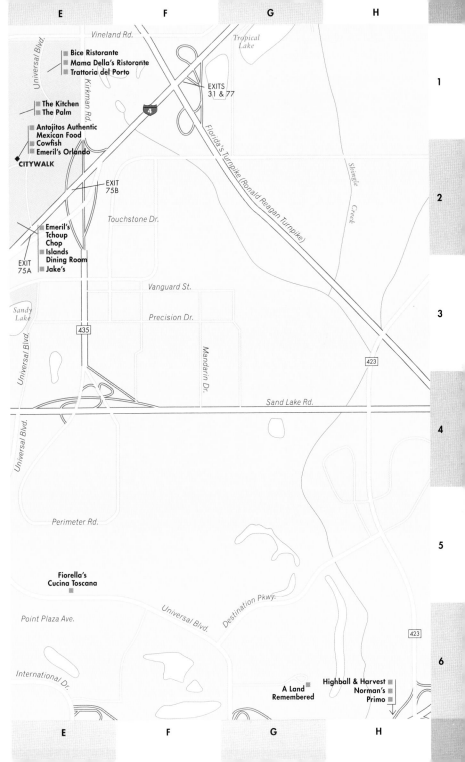

and it comes complete with a roving doo-wop group during peak seasons. You're on vacation, so go ahead and have that extra-thick shake or the decadent chili-cheese fries. Mel's is also a great place to meet up, in case you decide to go your separate ways in the park. ⑤ *Average main: $11* ✉ *Hollywood* ☎ *407/363–8766* ⊕ *www.universalorlando. com* ⚞ *Reservations not accepted* ✛ *2:D1.*

ISLANDS OF ADVENTURE

Here the food always fits the "island," from green eggs and ham at Seuss Landing (open seasonally) to an otherworldly grotto in the Lost Continent to the barbecue fare on tap in the Wizarding World of Harry Potter's Hogsmeade Village.

$ ✕**Confisco Grille.** You could walk right past this full-service restaurant
AMERICAN   without noticing it, but if you want a good meal and sit-down service, don't pass by too quickly. The menu is American with international influences. Entrées include pad Thai, grilled or blackened fresh fish of the day with mashed potatoes and sautéed spinach in a lemon-butter-cilantro sauce, and penne puttanesca—the vodka-cream tomato sauce is enhanced with sausage, Kalamata olives, fried pepperoncini, and roasted garlic. Wash it all down with refreshing sangria, available by glass, pitcher, and half pitcher. ⑤ *Average main: $13* ✉ *Port of Entry* ☎ *407/224–4404* ⊕ *www.universalorlando.com* ✛ *2:D2.*

$$ ✕**Mythos.** The name may be Greek, but the dishes are eclectic. The
ECLECTIC   menu includes such mainstays as pad Thai and pan-seared salmon with lemon-basil butter. The building itself—which looks like a giant rock formation from the outside and a huge cave (albeit one with plush upholstered seating) from the inside—is enough to grab your attention, but so do sandwiches like crab-cake sliders and roast beef panini with caramelized yellow onions, roasted red peppers, and pepperoncini. Mythos also has a waterfront view of the big lagoon in the center of the theme park. Except during the busiest weeks, the restaurant is open only for lunch. ⑤ *Average main: $15* ✉ *The Lost Continent* ☎ *407/224–4533* ⊕ *www.universalorlando.com* ⊗ *No dinner* ✛ *2:D2.*

$ ✕**Three Broomsticks.** Now Harry Potter fans can taste pumpkin juice
BRITISH   (with hints of honey and vanilla) and Butterbeer (sort of like bubbly butterscotch cream soda, or maybe shortbread cookies). They're on the menu along with barbecue and British foodstuffs at this Hogsmeade restaurant modeled after the fantasy books. Rickety staircases and gaslit chandeliers set the tone for the counter-service restaurant, where families gobble down ample portions of shepherd's pie, fish-and-chips, turkey legs, and Cornish pasty. In the adjacent Hog's Head pub, a faux hog's head sneers now and then. The breakfast menu has American and British staples. ⑤ *Average main: $12* ✉ *Wizarding World of Harry Potter* ☎ *407/224–4233* ⊕ *www.universalorlando.com* ⚞ *Reservations not accepted* ✛ *2:D2.*

CITYWALK

Restaurants, bars, clubs, shops, live entertainment, and movie theaters make Universal CityWalk an attraction on its own. The upbeat expanse serves as the entrance to both Universal Orlando theme parks—you can't reach the parks from the parking lot without walking through—and is an after-dark destination for tourists and locals alike.

$$
MEXICAN

✕ **Antojitos Authentic Mexican Food.** The massive Antojitos brings the specialties of Mexican cantinas and food carts to CityWalk. The outside looks like it's been spray-painted with shocking pastels. Inside, the grand two-story space is chic yet rustic, sparse but dotted with Mexican folk art. Neon sculptures on the ceiling depict hip versions of Day of the Dead figures. Start with guacamole, made table-side, and follow up with beer- and chili-braised pork tacos topped with pineapple and guajillo salsa. End with a coffee crème brûlée with churros or the molten dulce cake. The restaurant stocks 200 tequilas. $ *Average main: $17* ✉ *6000 Universal Blvd.* ☎ *407/224–2807* ⊕ *www.universalorlando.com* ☉ *No lunch* ✛ *2:E2.*

$$
BURGER

✕ **The Cowfish.** Burgers, sushi, and a combo the founders call "burgushi" bring Universal-goers to this contemporary second-story restaurant. The setting is flashy, with colorful booths and playful decor touches complementing an array of video screens showing schools of fish swimming by, aquarium-style. Unwind with a cocktail like Buffalos and Bacon, a bourbon-cherry liqueur combo garnished with candied bacon. The rolls and burgers defy traditional rules, mixing and matching so, for example, a sushi roll might be a sushi roll—or it might have filet mignon layered in. And a burger might be a hunk of ground beef, or it could have peanut butter, banana, and bacon. $ *Average main: $15* ✉ *6000 Universal Blvd.* ☎ *407/224–9255* ⊕ *www.thecowfish.com* ✍ *Reservations not accepted* ☉ *No lunch* ✛ *2:E2.*

$$$$
CAJUN
Fodor's Choice
★

✕ **Emeril's Orlando.** The popular eatery is a culinary shrine to Emeril Lagasse, the famous TV chef who occasionally makes an appearance. And although the modern interior of the restaurant with its 30-foot ceilings, blond woods, second-story wine loft, and lots of galvanized steel looks nothing like the French Quarter, the hardwood floors and linen tablecloths create an environment befitting the stellar nature of the cuisine. Entrées, which change frequently, may include andouille-crusted pan-roasted redfish with creole meunière sauce, apple cider–glazed pork "ham" chop with mascarpone grits, and mango barbecue swordfish with andouille-potato hash. Reservations are usually essential, but there's a chance of getting a walk-in seating if you show up for lunch (11:30 am) or early for dinner (5:30 pm). $ *Average main: $33* ✉ *6000 Universal Blvd.* ☎ *407/224–2424* ⊕ *www.emerils.com* ✍ *Reservations essential* ✛ *2:E2.*

$$$
AMERICAN

✕ **Hard Rock Cafe Orlando.** Built to resemble Rome's Colosseum yet surprisingly sophisticated inside, this 1,000-seat restaurant—the largest Hard Rock Cafe in the world—is huge, yet getting a seat at lunch or dinner can still require a long wait. The music is always loud and the walls are filled with rock memorabilia. Burgers are made from ground beef and brisket. Barbecued meats are smoked on-site. And entrées include

7

a cowboy rib eye and grilled Norwegian salmon. $\boxed{\$}$ *Average main: $23* ⊠ *6050 Universal Blvd.* ☎ *407/351–7625* ⊕ *www.hardrockcafe.com* ✛ *2:D2.*

UNIVERSAL HOTELS

$$$$
ITALIAN

✕ **Bice Ristorante.** Trendy, pricey Bice is the Orlando unit of an international upscale chain of Italian restaurants. Bice (pronounced "BEACH-ay") is an Italian nickname for Beatrice, as in Beatrice Ruggeri, who founded the original Milan location of this family restaurant in 1926. But the word "family" does not carry the connotation "mom and pop" here, where cream-colored starched linens set the stage for sophisticated cuisine. The restaurant retains its frescoed ceilings, marble floors, and picture windows overlooking great views of the artificial (but appealing) bay just outside. The food is expensive (a simple pasta with spicy tomato sauce is $19), but some of the entrées that seem worth it include the grilled swordfish with Sicilian caponata and the veal scallopine with lemon-caper sauce. Pastas and salads are available in half portions upon request. The amaretto cheesecake is a splendid dessert. $\boxed{\$}$ *Average main: $34* ⊠ *Loews Portofino Bay Hotel, 5601 Universal Blvd.* ☎ *407/503–1415* ⊕ *www.orlando.bicegroup.com* ☾ *No lunch* ✛ *2:E1.*

$$$
SOUTH PACIFIC

✕ **Emeril's Tchoup Chop.** The bold interior decor—with lots of bamboo, bright glazed tile, an exposition kitchen, and a long zero-edge pool with porcelain lily pads running the length of the dining room—is just as ambitious as the food at Emeril Lagasse's Pacific-influenced restaurant. Following the theme of the Royal Pacific Resort, Lagasse melds his signature bold flavors with Asian- and Polynesian-fusion tastes. A *robata* (charcoal) grill that heats to 1,000°F churns out appetizers and side dishes; try the pork belly. Entrées change regularly, but representative dishes include Hawaiian-style snapper with ginger, cilantro, and sesame soy sauce; and a grilled pork chop with apple cider ginger butter. Sushi varieties are offered. For dessert, get the Hawaiian-style *malasadas* doughnuts. They're served with three sauces in plastic bottles; you insert the tip into the donuts and squirt in the fillings yourself. $\boxed{\$}$ *Average main: $29* ⊠ *Loews Royal Pacific Resort, 6300 Hollywood Way* ☎ *407/503–2467* ⊕ *www.emerils.com* ⚲ *Reservations essential* ✛ *2:E2.*

$$$
ASIAN FUSION
FAMILY

✕ **Islands Dining Room.** An airy room with a tropical decor and menu items inspired by the Pacific Rim, Islands not only serves breakfast and dinner, it also has a play area that keeps tots entertained. On Monday, Wednesday, and Thursday nights, diners are treated to visits from assorted characters such as Scooby Doo and Shaggy—at no extra cost. On some evenings, the restaurant hosts the Wok Experience, where guests can create their own stir-fry combos. $\boxed{\$}$ *Average main: $22* ⊠ *Loews Royal Pacific Resort, 6300 Hollywood Way* ☎ *407/503–3463* ⊕ *www.loewshotels.com* ☾ *No lunch* ✛ *2:E2.*

$$$
AMERICAN
FAMILY

✕ **Jake's American Bar & Grill.** From noon through the evening, Jake's is more of a gastropub with an air-flight theme, but every morning the cozy space welcomes characters and the guests who adore them. Character breakfasts here are buffet-style, and the costumed entertainers might be from The Simpsons, Scooby-Doo, or Despicable Me. Menus later in the day range from burgers to kale salad and orange-braised duck legs.

Adults enjoy karaoke on Thursday nights and musicians on Friday and Saturday. $ *Average main: $27* ⊠ *Loews Royal Pacific Resort, 6300 Hollywood Way* ☎ *407/503–3463* ⊕ *www.universalorlando.com* ✥ *2:E2.*

$$$$
MODERN
AMERICAN
FAMILY

✕ **The Kitchen.** Contemporary yet comfy, this hotel restaurant tends to straddle various worlds. Its menu has comfort food with creative upscale twists. It's so family-friendly as to have a dedicated Kids' Crib area that supplies toys and cartoon videos, yet is sophisticated enough to please discerning parents. On Wednesdays and Saturdays from 6 to 9 pm, Shrek, Gru, the Minions from *Despicable Me,* or other quirky characters are apt to wander in and get the crowd going. Magic Men make appearances Fridays from 6 to 10 pm. Pricing is à la carte. $ *Average main: $31* ⊠ *Hard Rock Hotel, 5800 Universal Blvd.* ☎ *407/503–3463* ⊕ *www.hardrockhotelorlando.com* ✥ *2:E1.*

$$$
ITALIAN

✕ **Mama Della's Ristorante.** This playfully themed Italian restaurant happens to have excellent food. The premise is that you're eating at a home-turned-restaurant owned by an Italian woman. That woman, Mama Della, is played by an actress, whose warmth enhances the experience (as does the serenade by an accordionist, guitar player, and vocalist). The menu features Italian classics like chicken parmigiana and lasagna as well as more ambitious dishes like salmon with fennel sofrito and braised lamb with eggplant caponata. Outdoor seating on the patio provides a view of the hotel's nightly *Musica Della Notte* (Music of the Night) opera show. $ *Average main: $30* ⊠ *Loews Portofino Bay Hotel, 5601 Universal Blvd.* ☎ *407/503–3463* ⊕ *www.loewshotels.com* ⊗ *No lunch* ✥ *2:E1.*

$$$$
STEAKHOUSE

✕ **The Palm.** With its dark-wood interior and hundreds of framed celebrity caricatures, this restaurant resembles its famed New York City namesake. For most diners the steaks are the star of the show. Aged beef is the predominant house specialty, but the gargantuan lobsters are nearly as popular as the fine steaks. For fish lovers, salmon is a nice choice, as it is broiled and served with mango salsa. Crab cakes, another option, are made of jumbo-lump crabmeat and paired with chipotle tartar sauce. The Italian specialties are top-notch versions of favorites like veal parmigiana. $ *Average main: $42* ⊠ *Hard Rock Hotel, 5800 Universal Blvd.* ☎ *407/503–7256* ⊕ *www.thepalm.com* ⊗ *No lunch* ✥ *2:E1.*

$$$
ITALIAN
FAMILY

✕ **Trattoria del Porto.** Italian cuisine will please parents, while Bart Simpson or Scooby-Doo may be on hand to distract the kids, at this casual hotel restaurant with a dedicated children's play area. Characters appear on Friday nights between 6 and 10 pm, coinciding with "Pasta Cucina" ($26 adult, $12 child), an all-you-can-eat experience where guests create their own pasta dishes. À la carte or buffet breakfast is offered daily. $ *Average main: $26* ⊠ *Loews Portofino Bay Hotel, 5601 Universal Blvd.* ☎ *407/503–3463* ⊕ *www.loewshotels.com/portofino-bay-hotel* ⊗ *No lunch. No dinner Tues. and Wed.* ✥ *2:E1.*

7

ORLANDO METRO AREA

KISSIMMEE

Although Orlando is the focus of most theme-park visitors, Kissimmee is actually closer to Walt Disney World. It offers a huge number of dining choices, many of which are of the "burger barn" variety in accordance with the area's budget lodging options, but there are notable exceptions. While the restaurants featured here are minutes from Walt Disney World's southern tip, allow about 15 to 25 minutes to travel from WDW or about 35 minutes from International Drive.

$$$$
STEAKHOUSE

✕ **Old Hickory Steakhouse.** This upscale steak house is designed to look like rustic cabins in the Everglades. Beyond the playful facade is a polished restaurant with a classic steak-house menu—cowboy rib eye, porterhouse, and center-cut fillet, supplemented by rack of lamb, veal porterhouse, and wild salmon, all priced for the hotel's convention-goers. The chef gets creative with appetizers like braised pork belly with black-eyed pea succotash, but most are standards such as onion soup, shrimp cocktail, and wedge salad. Artisanal cheese plates are on the menu, and desserts are interesting, such as fudge-dipped derby pie. ⑤ *Average main: $47* ⊠ *Gaylord Palms Resort, 6000 W. Osceola Pkwy., I–4 Exit 65* ☎ *407/586–1600* ⊕ *www.gaylordpalms.com* ☾ *No lunch* ✛ *1:E6.*

CELEBRATION

If this not-so-small town with early-20th-century-style homes and perfectly manicured lawns reminds you a bit of Main Street, U.S.A, in the Magic Kingdom, it should. The utopian residential community was created by Disney, with all the Disney attention to detail. Every view of every street is warm and pleasant, though the best are out the windows of the town's Market Street–area restaurants, most of which face a pastoral (though man-made) lake. Homes here are on the expensive side, and restaurants reflect the upscale nature of the local customers. To get here, take Interstate 4 to Exit 64 and follow the "Celebration" signs.

$$
ITALIAN

✕ **Café d'Antonio.** The wood-burning oven and grill are worked pretty hard here, and the mountains of hardwood used in the open kitchen flavor the best of the menu—pizza, grilled fish and chicken, steaks and chops, and even the lasagna. A standout is the wood-fired veal chop stuffed with prosciutto, fontina, and spinach. For a less expensive meal, you can pick your own ingredients for a personal wood-oven pizza. The terrace overlooking the lake is enclosed and air-conditioned. ⑤ *Average main: $21* ⊠ *691 Front St.* ☎ *407/566–2233* ⊕ *www.antoniosonline.com* ✛ *1:E6.*

$$$
SEAFOOD

✕ **Celebration Town Tavern.** This New England–cuisine eatery, operated by a family with Boston roots, has a double personality. The interior is a brass, glass, and dark-wood-paneling kind of place, while the outside patio has table seating plus the Paddy O' Bar. The food ranges from landlubber treats like baby back ribs, prime rib, and half-pound burgers (from $8) to exquisite seafood including Ipswich clams, lobster rolls, Boston scrod, and 2-pound lobsters (all flown in from Boston), plus, on occasion, a salute to the Sunshine State with Florida stone crabs in season. While the place has a polished demeanor, there are plenty of menu choices right out of a working-class Boston bar—meatball hoagies, Philly cheesesteak sandwiches, and Buffalo-style chicken wings. For dessert there's great—what else?—Boston cream pie. $ *Average main: $27* ⊠ *721 Front St.* ☎ *407/566–2526* ⊕ *www.thecelebrationtowntavern.com* ✣ *1:E6.*

$$$
LATIN AMERICAN
✕ **Columbia Restaurant.** Celebration's branch of this family-owned high-end chain is generally as good as the original in Tampa, which has been operating for a century now. Start with the garlic shrimp or the empanadas stuffed with beef, raisins, and olives. For your main course, zero in on the paella—either *à la Valenciana,* with clams, shrimp, scallops, squid, chicken, and pork mixed into tasty yellow rice; or the *paella campesina,* a "farmer's" paella from Spain, with no seafood but with beef, pork, chorizo, and chicken. The best dessert, *brazo gitano cien anos* (sponge cake with strawberries that is soaked in syrup and Spanish sherry and flambéed table-side), was created for the restaurant chain's 100th anniversary in 2005, and is well worth its price just for the show. $ *Average main: $29* ⊠ *649 Front St.* ☎ *407/566–1505* ⊕ *www.columbiarestaurant.com* ✣ *1:E6.*

$
AMERICAN
✕ **Market Street Café.** The menu at this upscale diner ranges from breakfast classics served all day, like French toast and the house-special baked-potato omelet, to comfort classics like beef Stroganoff and homemade chicken potpie. In addition to a hearty version of the quintessential American hamburger (best enjoyed with a creamy milk shake), there are also salmon and portobello burgers for the cholesterol wary. An outdoor seating section in front of the restaurant makes for a pleasant dining destination. $ *Average main: $12* ⊠ *701 Front St.* ☎ *407/566–1144* ⊕ *www.market-street-cafe.com* ✣ *1:E6.*

INTERNATIONAL DRIVE

A number of restaurants are scattered among the hotels that line International Drive—the best along the manicured area near the Convention Center, at the very northern tip near the outlet stores, and in upscale convention hotels. Many are branches of chains, from fast-food spots to theme coffee shops and up, but the food here can be quite good. To get to the area, take Interstate 4 Exit 72 or 74A. Count on it taking up to half an hour from the Kissimmee area or from a WDW property.

$$
AMERICAN
✕ **B-Line Diner.** As you might expect from its location in the Hyatt Regency, this slick modern diner is not exactly cheap, but the salads, sandwiches, and griddle foods are tops. The classic combo—a thick, juicy burger with fries and a milk shake—is done beautifully. And there are lots of selections you'd never expect to find here, like an appetizer of potato chips with blue-cheese sauce and rosemary and an entrée of citrus-baked grouper with warm quinoa. It's open 24 hours, so if you crave a Reuben or Oreo chocolate mousse cake at 3 am, B-Line is the place to go. $ *Average main: $20* ⊠ *Hyatt Regency Orlando, 9801 International Dr.* ☎ *407/284–1234* ⊕ *orlando.regency.hyatt.com* ✣ *2:D6.*

$$$
ECLECTIC
✕ **Café Tu Tu Tango.** The food here is served tapas-style—everything is appetizer size but plentiful, and relatively inexpensive. If you want a

compendium of cuisines at one go, try the black-bean soup with cilantro sour cream, guava barbecue-glazed pork ribs, hazelnut-lemongrass fish, and spiced alligator bites. The wine list includes more than 35 wines from several countries, with all but a handful by the bottle and the glass, and 50-plus craft beers. The restaurant is designed to resemble an artist's loft; artists paint at easels while diners take a culinary trip around the world. Belly dancers, flamenco dancers, Bolivian dancers, and African drummers are among the entertainers who perform in the evening. Thanks to a patio, diners can also share their small plates alfresco. Ⓢ *Average main: $23* ✉ *8625 International Dr.* ☎ *407/248–2222* ⊕ *www.cafetututango.com* ✛ *2:D5.*

$$$ ✗ **Cuba Libre Restaurant & Rum Bar.** The dining rooms at this Cuban res-
CUBAN taurant feel as if they're movie sets of Old Havana, with dramatic touches upstairs and down. Carved second-level balconies, "weathered" facades, and stained glass replicate the Cuban city. Start your meal with a meat-filled arepa rellena corn cake or a platter of two to four empanadas filled with savory ground beef and olives, chicken, cheese, or pork. For the main course, consider the *churrasco a la Cubana* (grilled skirt steak) with a lemon-onion sauce plus a watercress-mushroom escabeche salad. Go traditional with a pressed Cuban sandwich, which is part of classic platter with black bean soup, salad, and chips, or a good version of the traditional Latin dish *ropa vieja*, shredded beef brisket with tomatoes, bell peppers, and onions in a red wine sauce. Ⓢ *Average main: $28* ✉ *Pointe Orlando, 9101 International Dr.* ☎ *407/226–1600* ⊕ *www.cubalibrerestaurant.com* ☽ *No lunch* ✛ *2:D6.*

$$$ ✗ **Fiorella's Cucina Toscana.** The Tuscan cooking at this quiet little eat-
ITALIAN ery—tucked behind the Orange County Convention Center in the Westin Imagine—is worth the short trip. The decor is vibrant, with dark woods accented by bright, custom-made glass flowers. Worthy dinner selections include lobster ravioli with crabmeat and brown butter, and chicken with prosciutto, sage, mushrooms, and a Marsala wine sauce. Finish your meal with the delectable tiramisu. Ⓢ *Average main: $26* ✉ *Westin Orlando Universal Boulevard, 9501 Universal Blvd.* ☎ *407/233–2950* ⊕ *www.fiorellasorlando.com* ✛ *2:D6.*

$$$ ✗ **Funky Monkey Bistro & Bar.** Funky Monkey brings to the Convention
ECLECTIC Center area an enticing mix of creative American cuisine, sushi, interesting wines, and occasional entertainment—including Friday- and Saturday-night drag shows. Fried goat cheese, soy-ginger glazed pork tenderloin, and salmon lo mein are typical choices. For a respite from touristy watering holes, grab a seat at the low-key bar and sip a glass of Chardonnay with a plate of seasoned-rice "monkey balls." There is a second Funky Monkey in Orlando's colorful Mills 50 neighborhood; it has a warmer, more romantic atmosphere. Ⓢ *Average main: $29* ✉ *Pointe Orlando, 9101 International Dr.* ☎ *407/418–9463* ⊕ *www.funkymonkeywine.com* ☽ *No lunch Sun.* ✛ *2:D6.*

$$$$ ✗ **Oceanaire Seafood Room.** Don't let the 1930s-era ocean-liner interior fool
SEAFOOD you: as theme restaurants go, this place is a good one, packing everything from—depending on the season—Canadian walleye, Costa Rican swordfish, or Ecuadorian mahimahi. The straightforward preparation here—grilled or broiled, brushed with lemon butter—is welcome. The

chefs change the menu every day based on what's fresh. Lobster bisque is a standout, as is the chilled shellfish platter and the day's fish specialties. Make sure to save room for the baked Alaska, which is flamed at the table. $ *Average main: $46* ✉ *Pointe Orlando, 9101 International Dr.* ☎ *407/363–4801* ⊕ *www.theoceanaire.com* ⊗ *No lunch* ✛ *2:D6.*

$$$ ✕ **Taverna Opa.** This high-energy Greek restaurant bills itself as offer-

GREEK ing "fun with a capital F—Not Just Dining, It's an Experience!" Here the ouzo flows like a mountain stream, the Greek (and global) music almost reaches the level of a rock concert, and the roaming belly dancers actively encourage diners to take part in the mass Zorba dancing, which often happens on the tops of dining tables. The only thing missing is the Greek restaurant tradition of throwing dinner plates, made up in part by the throwing of small paper napkins, which sometimes reaches near-blizzard level. The food, by the way, is also excellent. Standouts include traditional staples like spanakopita, *saganaki* (the traditional flaming cheese appetizer), *avgolemono* (lemony chicken-rice soup), and per-haps the most famous Greek entrée, moussaka. Family-style meals for groups of four and up are available at $33 and $44 per person. The best dessert is the baklava. $ *Average main: $27* ✉ *Pointe Orlando, 9101 International Dr.* ☎ *407/351–8660* ⊕ *www.opaorlando.com* ✛ *2:D6.*

SOUTH ORLANDO

$$$$ ✕ **A Land Remembered.** The name of this award-winning restaurant (from

STEAKHOUSE a novel about Florida by Patrick Smith) is somewhat enigmatic, but then so is the location (in the golf clubhouse of the Rosen Shingle Creek resort). But if you're a steak lover, you'll find this place worth seeking out. Notable choices include the 20-ounce chateaubriand for two carved table-side and the best seller, a 20-ounce Harris Ranch Prime bone-in rib eye, perhaps with a shared appetizer of collard greens braised in Gator Drool beer, or mac and cheese with big lobster chunks. If you don't like beef, you're still in a good place here, with choices that include cedar plank–broiled fish with onion-and-chive butter, and lamb Tequesta, rubbed with roasted garlic and dry mustard. Starters can be elegant, like steak tartare, or Floridian, like Cajun-spiced frog legs with mango-rum glaze. $ *Average main: $58* ✉ *Rosen Shingle Creek, 9939 Universal Blvd.* ☎ *407/996–9939* ⊕ *www.landrememberedrestaurant.com* ⊗ *No lunch* ✛ *2:G6.*

$$$ ✕ **Highball & Harvest.** Modern spins on Southern staples is the crux of

SOUTHERN this sprawling restaurant, where scratch cooking by Ritz chefs is the rule. Cocktails are handcrafted; even the ice is shaved from a block to order. The Southern Spread is a starter to share with pimento cheese, house-pickled veggies, and smoked fish dip. Dinner entrées change regu-larly and might include fig-glazed ribs, a skirt steak marinated in Book-er's bourbon, or the signature Pig-n-Potatoes, a hash of egg, potato, and pork cheek. Sticky toffee pudding and homemade donuts are choice sweets. In the lounge area, a specially designed eight-seat table hosts private cocktail tasting events. $ *Average main: $25* ✉ *Ritz-Carlton Orlando Grande Lakes, 4012 Central Florida Pkwy.* ☎ *407/393–4422* ⊕ *www.grandelakes.com* ✛ *2:H6.*

CLOSE UP

Popular Chain Restaurants

When all you want is a quick bite, consider these chain restaurants. They seem to crop up everywhere, and all have tables where you can sit for a few moments before heading back out to the shops and attractions.

Anthony's Coal-Fired Pizza: Thin-crust pizzas with generous toppings like arugula and pepperoni are baked—charred, really—in a coal-fired oven. The chicken wings are also popular in these bustling spaces near Restaurant Row and in Altamonte Springs. ⊕ www. anthonyscoalfiredpizza.com

Arepas El Cacao: What began as a food truck is now a mini-chain of four spiffy, colorful fast-fooderies making Venezuelan arepas and cachapas (sweet, filled corn cakes) to order. ⊕ www.arepaselcacao.com

Bubbalou's Bodacious Bar-B-Que: A quintet of local smokers serves up mounds of Southern barbecue, from baby back ribs to pulled-pork sandwiches. The restaurant on Kirkman Road and Conroy-Windermere Road is minutes from Universal Orlando. ⊕ www.bubbalous.com

Einstein Bros. Bagels: For a light breakfast or lunch, Einstein's satisfies with a menu of bagels, wraps, salads, and sandwiches. ⊕ www.einsteinbros. com

First Watch: Breakfast classics like pancakes and waffles make First Watch a popular choice for locals, who line up on weekends for Key West "crepeggs" (a crepe filled with eggs that have been scrambled with turkey, avocado, bacon, tomatoes, and Monterey Jack cheese), and Floridian French toast with bananas, kiwi, and berries. ⊕ www.firstwatch.com

Five Guys Burgers and Fries: This burger joint has a nearly cultlike following for its freshly ground beef. Fifteen toppings are available for no charge, and the fries are freshly cut. ⊕ www.fiveguys.com

Jimmy John's: Lunchtime lines are out the door at Orlando's many Jimmy John's, where the "world's greatest gourmet sandwiches" are essentially subs and clubs. ⊕ www.jimmyjohns. com

Johnny Rockets: Burgers, chili dogs, and frothy milk shakes are served in a vibrant, '50s diner–style environment here. There are three branches near the theme parks. ⊕ www. johnnyrockets.com

Panera Bread: Fresh-baked pastries and bagels are the mainstays here, although you can grab a hearty and inexpensive meal like smoked-turkey panino on three-cheese bread or a bowl of soup served in a hollowed-out sourdough loaf. ⊕ www. panerabread.com

Pei Wei Asian Diner: Bold flavors from all corners of Asia come together at these fast-casual restaurants, where a hearty noodle bowl, orange-peel beef, or sweet-and-sour tofu will come in at less than $10. ⊕ www.peiwei.com

TooJay's Gourmet Deli: A New York deli it ain't, but the TooJay's chain offers a welcome pastrami fix for those with a yen for salty meat on crusty seeded rye. ⊕ www.toojays.com

$$$$ ✕ **Le Coq au Vin.** This traditional French restaurant, owned by Sandy and
FRENCH Reimund Pitz, is a hideaway located in a small nondescript house in
South Orlando. It seats 100 people in three quaint dining rooms. Knickknacks cover the walls, creating a home-style atmosphere. The namesake dish is always available, and select entrées can be ordered in half
portions. For dessert, try the Grand Marnier, chocolate, or raspberry
soufflé. ⑤ *Average main: $32* ✉ *4800 S. Orange Ave.* ☎ *407/851–6980*
⊕ *www.lecoqauvinrestaurant.com* ⊗ *Closed Mon. No lunch* ✛ *3:D6.*

$$$$ ✕ **Norman's.** Celebrity-chef Norman Van Aken brings impressive creden-
ECLECTIC tials to the restaurant that bears his name, as you might expect from the
Fodor's Choice headline eatery in the Ritz-Carlton Orlando Grande Lakes. Van Aken's
★   culinary roots go back to the Florida Keys, where he's credited with
creating "Floribbean" cuisine, a blend that is part Key West and part
Caribbean—although he now weaves in flavors from all continents.
The Orlando operation is a formal, sleek restaurant with marble floors,
starched tablecloths, servers in ties and vests, eight certified sommeliers,
and a creative, if expensive, menu. In addition to exceptional ceviches
and a signature appetizer called Down Island French toast made with
Curacao-marinated foie gras, favorites include a Mongolian-marinated
veal chop, pan-cooked Florida snapper with citrus butter, and pork
Havana with "21st-century mole sauce." A six-course tasting menu is
$99, $49 more with beverage pairings. Covered terrace seating is also
available. ⑤ *Average main: $49* ✉ *Ritz-Carlton Orlando Grande Lakes,
4000 Central Florida Pkwy.* ☎ *407/393–4333* ⊕ *www.normans.com*
⊗ *No lunch* ✛ *2:H6.*

$$$$ ✕ **Primo.** James Beard Award winner Melissa Kelly cloned her Italian-
ITALIAN organic Maine restaurant in an upscale Orlando hotel and brought her
Fodor's Choice farm-to-table sensibilities with her. Here the daily dinner menu pays
★   tribute to Sicily's lighter foods, made with produce grown in the hotel
garden. Homemade pasta is served with spicy lamb sausage or all-nat-
ural beef-pork Bolognese; if the butternut-squash ravioli with butter-
poached Maine lobster is available, order it. Dry-aged prime New York
strip steak is enhanced with Taleggio "tater tots" and pancetta-wrapped
baby leeks. Fish plays prominently, such as a whole roasted sea bass
with black salsify, petite kalettes, and pistachio salsa. Desserts are just
as special, with the likes of warm Belgian chocolate *budino* (pudding)
cake or hot zeppole tossed in cinnamon and sugar. ⑤ *Average main: $43*
✉ *JW Marriott Orlando Grande Lakes, 4040 Central Florida Pkwy.*
☎ *407/393–4444* ⊕ *www.primorestaurant.com* ⊗ *No lunch* ✛ *2:H6.*

LAKE BUENA VISTA

Lake Buena Vista, just to the east of Downtown Disney, is essentially a
collection of mid-scale hotels, convention hotels, and chain restaurants
catering to off-site visitors to Disney World. The restaurants tend to
be well run, well kept, and affordable, with a few destination dining
rooms within convention hotels.

$$$ ✕ **American Q.** Three food themes—locally raised meats, Southern spe-
BARBECUE cialties, and Brazilian-style churrascaria service—meld at American Q,
a dimly lit, down-home hybrid housed within the sleek white B Resort.

À la carte meals blanket the southern United States, including traditional Memphis-style pork and Texas-inspired beef ribs, plus a creative hot smoked wild salmon with blackberry sauce. Most guests seem to choose the $34.95 all-you-can-eat option. Salads, soups, apple-caraway slaw, corn served with the husk on, and way more are laid out on the bed of a 1951 cherry-red Fork pickup truck. Then servers visit tables offering eight skewered meats, which might be a house-made sausage, Carolina-style flank steak, or bacon-wrapped chicken. Don't overindulge, though, because the desserts are a highlight, especially the salted caramel cheesecake and the s'mores pie topped with toasted marshmallows. ⑤ *Average main: $26* ⊠ *B Resort & Spa, 1905 Hotel Plaza Blvd., Downtown Disney Resort Area* ☎ *407/828–2828* ⊕ *www.americanq. com* ☼ *No lunch* ✣ *1:F4.*

$$$$
STEAKHOUSE
✕ **Capa.** Capa is billed as a Spanish steak house, a concept cleverly executed in a chic, modern dining area. Clean lines are the palette for ancient-looking coins creatively arranged and a decor element of red ruffles reminiscent of a matador's red flag. In a private dining room, the ceiling is covered with gold rings like those in bulls' noses, as shown in photo art on the wall. The menu spans the culinary culture gap by starting with tapas, most of them authentically Spanish, and continuing with exceptional steaks worthy of the luxury setting. The rabano is several types of radishes atop smoked crème fraîche with a hint of pomegranate; the ham croquettes with shishito pepper are especially creamy. The steak is prime, the strip and rib-eye dry-aged, and they're worth the price. End with the Valor Chocolate, an ultrarich confection with coffee ice cream, cardamom, and toffee crunch. ⑤ *Average main: $52* ⊠ *Four Seasons Resort, 10100 Dream Tree Blvd., Golden Oak* ☎ *407/313–7777* ⊕ *www.fourseasons.com/orlando/dining/* ☼ *No lunch* ✣ *1:D2.*

$$
AMERICAN
FAMILY
✕ **Covington Mill.** A polished space offering hearty buffet and à la carte breakfasts plus light lunches, Covington Mill turns into a kidfest on Sunday mornings. That's when Disney characters join the early risers, cheerfully signing autographs and posing for photographs. ⑤ *Average main: $20* ⊠ *Hilton Orlando Lake Buena Vista, 1751 Hotel Plaza Blvd., Downtown Disney Resort Area* ☎ *407/827–4000* ⊕ *ww.hiltono rlandolakebuenavistahotel.com* ☼ *No dinner* ✣ *1:F4.*

$$$$
SEAFOOD
✕ **Hemingway's.** Business travelers and vacationers put on their khakis and sundresses to dine in this quiet seafood house loosely themed around Ernest Hemingway's travels. In fact, the Papa Doble cocktail, with rum and grapefruit juice, is reputedly Papa's own creation. The woodsy dining room provides views of the Hyatt Regency's manicured grounds, a treat in summer when the sun sets late. Choose the Hemingway's "Cayo Hueso" crab cake, served with corn salsa and sweet corn coconut grits. Other options are the Duvall Street shrimp scampi, a tribute to the author's love of shrimp, here served with truffled pasta, or the paella, a nod to the time he spent in Spain. Since the Keys were another favorite spot, the baked Alaska key lime is a fitting meal ender. ⑤ *Average main: $36* ⊠ *Hyatt Regency Grand Cypress, 1 Grand Cypress Blvd.* ☎ *407/239-3854* ⊕ *www.grandcypress.hyatt.com* ☼ *No lunch* ✣ *1:F3.*

$$$
ITALIAN
✕ **La Luce by Donna Scala.** Having made a name for herself at California's Bistro Don Giovanni, Donna Scala brought the same Italian cuisine

with a Napa Valley farm-fresh flair to this upscale Hilton at the edge of Disney World. Scala has since passed, but the restaurant remains as she designed it. The walls are decorated with chalk art, which changes at least twice a year. Equal effort goes into the menu, where pastas are made fresh. Try the gnocchetti with wild porcini and sausage ragu, the grilled rib eye with gremolata butter, or a simple seared salmon fillet with a tomato-chive-butter sauce. $ *Average main: $30 ⊠ Hilton Orlando Bonnet Creek, 14100 Bonnet Creek Resort La., Bonnet Creek ☎ 407/597–3600 ⊕ www.laluceorlando.com ⊗ No lunch ⊹ 1:E5.*

$$$ ✕ **Lakeview Restaurant.** Lake views for breakfast and dinner keep this
AMERICAN hotel restaurant bustling twice a day. Yet the spot is at its peak on Tues-
FAMILY day, Thursday, and Saturday mornings when Disney characters come to visit. Two classic costumed friends visit with guests as the diners help themselves to morning specialties from the buffet, including custom omelets. The character breakfast is free for children under some lodging plans. Dinner entrées are American faves such as pan-seared salmon and New York strip steak. $ *Average main: $24 ⊠ Wyndham Lake Buena Vista Resort, 1850 Hotel Plaza Blvd., Downtown Disney Resort Area ☎ 407/828–4444 ⊕ www.wyndhamlakebuenavista.com ⊗ No lunch ⊹ 1:F4.*

$$$$ ✕ **Ravello.** Ravello is a chic modern Italian restaurant after dark. Hand-
MODERN ITALIAN tossed pizzas emerge from the oven—perhaps finished with ricotta, arugula, and truffle oil. The pastas might be familiar or ambitious, like ravioli made with veal, spinach, and wild mushrooms. And the entrées are simple yet hearty, such as pan-seared duck breast with apple-grappa mostarda, and grilled lamb chops with roasted fig–dolcetto sauce. The dining room is fresh and bright, perfect for a buffet or à la carte break-fast. On select mornings, it's also the backdrop for a Good Morning Breakfast with Goofy & Pals character meal. The $32 adult/$19 kid price tag includes a buffet with an omelet station plus a pic of each guest with Goofy. $ *Average main: $32 ⊠ Four Seasons Orlando, 10100 Dream Tree Blvd., Golden Oak ☎ 407/313–6161 ⊕ www.fourseasons. com/orlando ⊗ No lunch ⊹ 1:D2.*

$$$$ ✕ **The Venetian Room.** This fine-dining restaurant inside one of Lake Buena
EUROPEAN Vista's many convention hotels may have been designed as a place for execs on expense accounts to seal deals, but it has also become a haven for nontrendy locals seeking an old-fashioned romantic retreat. The architecture alone—it looks like Renaissance Venice—is enough to lure you. The entry door is topped by a giant copper dome, and the dining room has dark-wood furniture, crystal chandeliers, and carpets that could grace a European palace. Deep booths are surrounded on two sides by etched glass. The waiters wear tuxes. Begin with the signature lobster bisque, an ultrarich soup topped with flaky pastry. Follow that with a good filet mignon, Dover sole, or pan-roasted veal chop in porcini cream sauce. Grand Marnier soufflé is the signature dessert. $ *Average main: $40 ⊠ Caribe Royale, 8101 World Center Dr. ☎ 407/238–8060 ⊕ www. thevenetianroom.com ⊗ Closed Sun. and Mon. No lunch ⊹ 1:F5.*

$ ✕ **The Watercress Cafe.** This laid-back hotel spot is mostly a lake-view
AMERICAN place for a light breakfast or lunch. Midday meals, in fact, are mostly
FAMILY sandwiches in many forms: Vietnamese banh mi, fried chicken wraps,

Wisconsin cheddar clubs, and blackened fish inside Indian-style naan. On Sunday mornings, classic Disney characters join breakfasting guests as they eat their cinnamon-apple French toast and steak-and-egg burritos. ⑤ *Average main: $13* ⊠ *Buena Vista Palace Hotel & Spa, 1900 E. Buena Vista Dr., Downtown Disney Resort Area* ☎ *866/397–6516* ⊕ *www.buenavistapalace.com* ◌ *No dinner* ✛ *1:F4.*

SAND LAKE ROAD

This part of Orlando is an anomaly: it's a growing collection of appealing strip centers filled with restaurants—from fast-casual panini and Asian-food restaurants to fine-dining establishments—that's about equidistant from well-to-do residential neighborhoods, Walt Disney World, Universal Orlando, SeaWorld, and International Drive. The result is known as Restaurant Row, and it's the only place in town where locals dine beside convention goers and adventuresome theme-park visitors. From Interstate 4, take the Sand Lake Road exit, 74A.

$$ ✕ **Bonefish Grill.** Fish dishes served in an upscale-casual setting distinguish
SEAFOOD Bonefish Grill from other area chains. Regulars rave about the Bang Bang Shrimp, a spicy appetizer of breaded and fried shrimp tossed in a tangy, spicy, mayonnaise-based sauce. Choose one of the many wood-grilled fresh fish options with your choice of mango salsa, lime-tomato-garlic sauce, herb pesto, pan-Asian flavorings, or lemon butter. Other selections include a pecan-Parmesan-crusted rainbow trout, chicken with goat cheese and spinach, and grilled filet mignon. For the record, there's no bonefish on the menu. It's an inedible game fish, caught for sport (and usually released). The Orlando area has several additional units. ⑤ *Average main: $19* ⊠ *Plaza Venezia, 7830 Sand Lake Rd.* ☎ *407/355–7707* ⊕ *www.bonefishgrill.com* ◌ *No lunch* ✛ *2:B4.*

$$$ ✕ **Bosphorous Turkish Cuisine.** Exceptional Turkish cuisine served in a
TURKISH relaxing, indoor-outdoor setting is a welcome surprise among the big-budget chains on Sand Lake Road. Servers at this independently owned neighborhood favorite bring to the table piping-hot, oversize *lavas* (hollow bread) to dip in appetizers such as a hummus, *ezme* (a zesty, garlicky, chilled chopped salad), and baba ghanoush. Many twosomes make a meal of the bountiful mixed-appetizer platter with a lavas or two. Following are oversize platters of char-grilled whole or filleted sea bass, kebabs, and any variety of lamb dishes, each prepared expertly. Light eaters enjoy the boat-shaped spinach-and-cheese Turkish pastry. A second unit, also with alfresco tables, is in Winter Park. ⑤ *Average main: $26* ⊠ *Marketplace at Dr. Phillips, 7600 Dr. Phillips Blvd., Suite 108* ☎ *407/352–6766* ⊕ *www.bosphorousrestaurant.com* ✛ *2:B4.*

$$$ ✕ **Cedar's Restaurant.** This family-owned Lebanese eatery, set in a major
MIDDLE EASTERN upscale strip shopping center that's become part of Restaurant Row, serves Middle Eastern standards like shish kebab, baba ghanoush (an ultrasmoky variety that is the very best in town), and hummus as well as tasty daily specials. One of the most notable regular entrées is the *samak harra* (sautéed red snapper fillet topped with onions, tomatoes, and cilantro). More formal than the average Orlando-area Middle Eastern restaurant, and featuring a cocktail menu, Cedar's has tables

with white-linen tablecloths and diners who tend to sport resort-casual attire. Musicians or belly dancers perform on some Friday and Saturday nights; hookah pipes are popular on the back patio. $ *Average main: $27* ⊠ *Plaza Venezia, 7732 W. Sand Lake Rd.* ☎ *407/351–6000* ⊕ *www. orlandocedars.com* ✢ *2:C4.*

$$$$ ✕ **Christini's Ristorante Italiano.** Business travelers love to spend money at
ITALIAN Christini's, one of the city's fanciest places for northern Italian cuisine. The menu is filled with high-end versions of familiar dishes like chicken marsala and veal with lemon-wine sauce. You may be so enchanted by the rose each lady receives and the serenade by a roving accordion player that you forget to check the price of the recommended wine, which will cost you. $ *Average main: $50* ⊠ *Marketplace at Dr. Phillips, 7600 Dr. Phillips Blvd.* ☎ *407/345–8770* ⊕ *www.christinis.com* ⊗ *No lunch* ✢ *2:B4.*

$$ ✕ **Dragonfly.** Sleek and stylish, Dragonfly is a bit of everything the young
MODERN ASIAN and beautiful people want: a pretty space featuring sushi, colorful martinis, and modern, *izakaya*-style small plates, both creative and simple. Groups of dressed-up twenty- and thirtysomethings gather indoors and out to share plates of *robata*-cooked meats and vegetables, along with tempura, rolls, noodle dishes, and salads, all beautifully presented. A four-item, seasonal *omakase* menu with paired beverages debuted in 2015. The daily happy hour is hugely popular with locals. $ *Average main: $15* ⊠ *Dellagio, 7972 Via Dellagio Way* ☎ *407/370–3359* ⊕ *www.dragonflyorlando.com* ⊗ *No lunch* ✢ *2:B4.*

$$$ ✕ **Le Rouge Wine Bar and Tapas.** Determined to open a sleek tapas lounge
WINE BAR reminiscent of the ones he'd visited in Europe, owner Mounir Elidrissi decorated his with red recessed lighting and named it for the French word for the color associated with passion. With white lounge seating, it looks like a destination for a glass of wine or a first date, but foodies visiting town also find it worth seeking out. The lamb chops with currant–red wine sauce are exceptional, as is the truffle mac and cheese and the mahimahi ceviche. A three-course wine-pairing meal is $40. The wine list is comprehensive, with vintages from California to France and New Zealand. Live music plays Wednesday through Saturday. Brunch is served on Saturday and Sunday. $ *Average main: $22* ⊠ *Plaza Venezia, 7730 W. Sand Lake Rd.* ☎ *407/370–0909* ⊕ *www.lerougewinebar.com* ⊗ *No lunch* ✢ *2:C4.*

$ ✕ **Lime Fresh Mexican Grill.** What was solely a so-hot South Beach quick-
MEXICAN service joint is now a rapidly growing minichain that serves "fresh-Mex" fare. Orlando's outpost in the Restaurant Row area (there are others in Winter Park and Lake Mary) is a bright corner restaurant that serves up the signature fish tacos, steak fajita quesadillas, and tortilla soup. Six salsas, from mild (*salse verde*) to superhot (habanero), add any needed zest. $ *Average main: $9* ⊠ *Phillips Crossing, 8031 Turkey Lake Rd., Suite 100* ☎ *407/370–3810* ⊕ *www.limefreshmexicangrill. com* ✢ *2:D4.*

$ ✕ **Moe's Southwest Grill.** At this great fast-food alternative, meals cost
SOUTHWESTERN well south of $10—and come with free chips and assorted salsas. It is an immensely casual joint but by no means a dive, with a youthful vibrancy (music blares over the sound system) that makes it a great

place for a quick meal. The Moe in this equation could almost be the guy who cavorted with Larry and Curly. Dishes, such as quesadillas, fajitas, and nachos, are familiar and fresh. Burritos and burrito bowls are most popular. You get to choose what goes into each meal. The franchise has about 20 additional Central Florida restaurants. ⑤ *Average main: $6* ✉ *Dolphin Plaza, 11062 International Dr.* ☎ *407/985–5808* ⊕ *www.moes.com* ⚏ *Reservations not accepted* ⊹ *2:C4.*

$$$$ ✕ **MoonFish.** This splashy-looking restaurant caters to the convention
SEAFOOD   crowd, with private rooms, polished service, and high prices—but the food is quite good. Ten to 15 fish varieties are flown in daily and prepared with a fusion of flavors from around the world. The menu is varied, with appetizers like almond-fried lobster tail and pan-Asian steak tartare, and entrées like citrus oak-grilled, blackened, or bronzed fish; fish prepared Hong Kong–style with fresh ginger and scallions in a light sherry soy sauce; and Oscar Mignon, a steak with hollandaise and a crabmeat topping. The sushi is consistently fresh, and the wine list is extensive with about 250 labels. ⑤ *Average main: $35* ✉ *The Fountains, 7525 W. Sand Lake Rd.* ☎ *407/363–7262* ⊕ *www. talkofthetownrestaurants.com* ◷ *No lunch* ⊹ *2:C4.*

$$$$ ✕ **Morton's The Steakhouse.** This fine choice among Orlando's many steak
STEAKHOUSE houses looks like a sophisticated private club, and youngsters with mouse caps are not common at the nationwide chain's local outpost. Center stage in the kitchen is a huge broiler, kept at 900°F to sear in the flavor of the porterhouses, sirloins, rib eyes, and other cuts of aged beef. For true value, nibble on "bar bites" in the lounge area during happy hour, when they're half price, and you'll enjoy top-quality sliders and such for $6 to $7 a plate. Soufflés are a specialty here and there are four: chocolate, raspberry, lemon, and Grand Marnier (order at the beginning of your meal). The wine list has about 350 vintages from around the world. ⑤ *Average main: $46* ✉ *Marketplace at Dr. Phillips, 7600 Dr. Phillips Blvd.* ☎ *407/248–3485* ⊕ *www.mortons.com* ◷ *No lunch* ⊹ *2:B4.*

$$$$ ✕ **Ocean Prime.** From the Berries & Bubbles martinis (tart cocktails made
SEAFOOD   with citrus and berry flavors and served bubbling and smoking, thanks to dry ice) that start off the meal, to the ultrarich chocolate peanut butter dessert draped in bittersweet chocolate ganache, Ocean Prime wows at every turn. This local outpost of an upscale chain holds its own with consistently good food, if uneven service. The jumbo-lump crab cake with sweet corn cream is a good way to begin, as are the white truffle caviar deviled eggs, ahi tuna tartare, and goat cheese ravioli. Follow with a simple grilled steak, sea scallops with Parmesan risotto and citrus vinaigrette, or the teriyaki salmon. Locals find the daily happy hour to be a bargain. ⑤ *Average main: $34* ✉ *Rialto, 7339 W. Sand Lake Rd.* ☎ *407/781–4880* ⊕ *www.oceanprimeorlando.com* ◷ *No lunch* ⊹ *2:C4.*

$$$ ✕ **Peperoncino.** You'll be transported to Milan at this Dr. Phillips Italian,
ITALIAN   a slim, slightly glitzy restaurant—soon to be greatly expanded—where chef-owner Barbara Alfano puts out a fresh menu of Italian specialties every evening. The finishing kitchen is in the dining room, so diners lucky enough to snag the few indoor seats (the outside patio has extras) can see Alfano and her team composing the dishes. You might feast

on fried pecorino drizzled with honey, a lasagna worthy of a return Orlando visit, pear-and-cheese pasta pockets, wine-marinated duck breast with spicy mushroom risotto, or seared tuna with cauliflower puree. Most desserts are made in-house. $ *Average main: $25 ⊠ Dellagio, 7988 Via Dellagio Way, Suite 108 ☎407/440–2856 ⊕www. peperoncinocucina.com* ⌂ *Reservations essential* ✛ 2:B4.

$$$$ ✕**Roy's.** Chef Roy Yamaguchi has more or less perfected his own cuisine
HAWAIIAN type, using European-style cooking techniques with Asian ingredients, primarily seafood, together with lots of imagination. The menu changes seasonally, but typical dishes include Hawaiian-style butterfish (black cod) with *furikake* rice, and hibachi-style grilled Atlantic salmon with Japanese citrus ponzu sauce. If your taste buds want to stay on land, go for hearty fare like grilled filet mignon with shiso béarnaise or braised short ribs with honey-mustard. "Mixed plates" featuring two or three entrées are an option. The crunchy golden lobster pot stickers are a Roy's classic. $ *Average main: $34 ⊠ Plaza Venezia, 7760 W. Sand Lake Rd.* ☎407/352–4844 ⊕ *www.roysrestaurant.com* ☾ *No lunch* ✛ 2:C4.

$$ ✕**Seasons 52.** Parts of the menu change every week at this innovative
AMERICAN restaurant that serves different foods at different times of year, depending on what's in season. Meals here tend to be healthful yet hearty and very flavorful. The flatbreads starters are on nearly every table. For an entrée, you might have wood-roasted pork tenderloin with sweet potato mash plus French green beans tossed with a dot of bacon, or caramelized grilled sea scallops with butternut squash and leek risotto, broccolini, and lemon butter. An impressive wine list with dozens of selections by the glass complements the menu. For dessert, have miniindulgence classics like pecan pie, rocky road, carrot cake, and key lime pie served in petite portions. Although the cuisine is haute, the prices are modest—not bad for a snazzy, urbane bistro and wine bar. It has live music nightly to boot. Another Seasons is located in Altamonte Springs. $ *Average main: $21 ⊠ Plaza Venezia, 7700 Sand Lake Rd., I–4 Exit 75A* ☎407/354–5212 ⊕ *www.seasons52.com* ✛ 2:C4.

$$$$ ✕**Vines Grille & Wine Bar.** Live jazz and blues music fills the night at
STEAKHOUSE the bar section of this dramatically designed restaurant, but the food and drink in the snazzy main dining room are headliners in their own right. The kitchen bills itself as a steak house, but it really is far more than that. Entrées range from Prime steaks (alas, no longer dry-aged) to pan-seared Chilean sea bass with lobster risotto and basil *beurre blanc,* from a one-pound Wagyu burger with truffle fries to pork osso bucco. Be sure to start with the grilled octopus, which is simply prepared with red onions, capers, and roasted fennel. The wine list here is extensive, and the cocktails are serious business, too. The crowd tends to dress up, but jackets and ties are not required. $ *Average main: $62 ⊠ The Fountains, 7533 W. Sand Lake Rd.* ☎407/351–1227 ⊕ *www. vinesgrille.com* ☾ *No lunch* ✛ 2:C4.

CENTRAL ORLANDO

The center of Orlando shows what the town as a whole was like before it became a big theme park. Quiet streets are lined with huge oaks covered with Spanish moss. Museums and galleries are along main thoroughfares, as are dozens of tiny lakes, where herons, egrets, and, yes, alligators, peacefully coexist with human city dwellers. This is quintessential urban Florida. The restaurants in this area, a good half hour from the Disney tourism area via Interstate 4, tend to have more of their own sense of character and style than the eateries going full tilt for your dollars in Kissimmee and Lake Buena Vista or on International Drive.

$$
JAPANESE
✕ **Amura.** Amura, Japanese for "village of love," is a local chain of high-end Japanese restaurants; two of the three also have teppanyaki dining. The Downtown location is lively and hip, while the two suburban outposts are quieter and nearly luxurious—and priced accordingly. The sushi menu has about 40 choices, from clams to yellowtail cheek. The Mexican roll—with avocado, tempura shrimp, and jalapeño peppers—makes for an unusual appetizer. Other entrées include Tokyo orange chicken, spicy pork, and yakisoba noodles. $ *Average main: $19* ✉ *54 W. Church St., Downtown Orlando* ☎ *407/316–8500* ⊕ *www.amura. com* ⊗ *No lunch weekends* ✛ *3:D6.*

$
VIETNAMESE
✕ **Anh Hong.** Simple with dashes of glitz, this Vietnamese restaurant is among the most popular in an Orlando neighborhood filled with competitors. Asian-Americans fuel up on steaming bowls of soups, chopsticks in one hand, a spoon in the other, stopping periodically to tear fresh herbs off branches and stir them into the broth. The menu is massive and has excellent grilled meats with rice. Adventurous eaters might start with the Vietnamese carpaccio and the cabbage-and-duck salad. "Self prepare and roll your self" is essentially a make-your-own summer roll dish: you moisten a rice-paper pancake, then fill it with proteins, noodles, and herbs. The noodle soups are flavorful, and the chicken with lemongrass and hot chili and the caramel chicken with ginger are can't-miss stir-fries. $ *Average main: $11* ✉ *1124 E. Colonial Dr., Downtown Orlando* ☎ *407/999–2656* ⊕ *www.anhhongorlando. com* ✑ *Reservations not accepted* ✛ *3:E5.*

$$$$
ECLECTIC
✕ **The Boheme Restaurant.** The Grand Bohemian, a boutique, luxury hotel, is the setting for a sleek city-center restaurant. As a prelude to your main, try the calamari served with pumpkin-crab bisque or grilled Spanish octopus. For a main course, consider Florida grouper with cilantro rice, roasted pheasant with champagne cream sauce, or Alsatian choucroute garnie—a mix of meats like bacon and potatoes and sauerkraut. The Sunday brunch here is a worthwhile experience: you can get carved prime rib and snow crab as well as omelets. $ *Average main: $34* ✉ *Grand Bohemian Hotel Orlando, 325 S. Orange Ave., Downtown Orlando* ☎ *407/313–9000* ⊕ *www.grandbohemianhotel.com* ✛ *3:D6.*

$$
SEAFOOD
✕ **Cityfish.** In Downtown Orlando's trendy Thornton Park district, this casual dining spot aims to be urbane. It caters to locals, but it's loud enough and casual enough to welcome kids wearing mouse ears. With the general ambience of a city sports bar—including flat-screen TVs on all the walls—Cityfish dispenses basic, well-prepared, fresh fish, most of it simply grilled, blackened, Parmesan-crusted, or fried (your choice). Once guests select the fish and preparation, they also choose to have it served in a sandwich or plated with smoked-bacon succotash, red bliss potatoes, and jalapeño hushpuppies. The appetizers reveal creative twists. Examples are flash-fried crispy pickle slices with smoky Bloody

Mary aioli, and truffled Gouda "potato tots." The big patio filled with tables shaded by large umbrellas is a great place to spend a few unhurried hours in cool weather. Plans to add live music, games, and seafood boils are in the works. $ *Average main: $18* ⊠ *617 E. Central Blvd., Thornton Park* ☎ *407/849–9779* ⊕ *www.cityfishorlando.com* ✛ *3:E6.*

$$ ✕ **Hawkers.** Hipsters, families, and business groups dine side by side at this popular restaurant, a laid-back spot that specializes in serving Asian street food. Travel the continent with $3.50 to $8.50 appetizer-size portions of scratch-made specialties from Malaysia, Singapore, Thailand, China, Japan, Korea, and Vietnam. Musts for adventurous diners include *roti canai,* a flaky bread with a chicken-curry dip; curry *laksa,* a noodle soup with exotic flavors; and stir-fried udon noodles. More timid eaters adore the marinated beef skewers with Malaysian satay sauce, peanutty chilled sesame noodles, duck tacos, and any of the Americanized (but flavorful) lettuce wraps. $ *Average main: $16* ⊠ *1103 Mills Ave., Mills 50 District* ☎ *407/237–0606* ⊕ *www.facebook.com/ hawkersstreetfare* ✛ *3:E5.*

ASIAN
Fodor'sChoice
★

$$$$ ✕ **K Restaurant & Wine Bar.** A vibrant restaurant down the road from College Park's restaurant hub, K is a hot spot for locals, serving upscale, eclectic, American and Italian cuisine in an intimate setting. Besides lunch and dinner, K hosts flip-flop-friendly wine tastings in the garden or on the patio and popular wine dinners—generally four courses for $50. Menus change daily and feature appetizers such as fried green tomatoes with sweet corn and crab salad and grain mustard dressing, and country-fried chicken livers with caramelized onion marmalade. For entrées, check out the mushroom-dusted filet mignon with red wine sauce, the mac and cheese gussied up with lobster, or homemade sausage. $ *Average main: $34* ⊠ *1710 Edgewater Dr., College Park* ☎ *407/872–2332* ⊕ *www. kwinebar.com* ☾ *Closed Sun. No lunch Sat.* ✛ *3:C4.*

AMERICAN
Fodor'sChoice
★

$$$ ✕ **The Rusty Spoon.** Lovingly raised animals and locally grown produce are the menu foundation at this Downtown gastropub, an ideal spot for a business lunch or a pre–basketball game, -theater, or -concert dinner. The wood-and-brick dining room is a comfortable backdrop to hearty, seasonal American meals with Italian and Southern elements. Creatively stuffed eggs and buttermilk-soaked Vidalia onion rings are top starters. The salads—with ultrafresh greens—are always sensational. All pastas are made from scratch, whether a "remodeled" ravioli with roasted organic Seminole pumpkin, radicchio, and cremini mushrooms, or hand-cut wide noodles with a beef tenderloin/pork ragu with chili oil. The Dirty South seafood stew is a signature take on bouillabaisse. End with a very grown-up version of s'mores. $ *Average main: $22* ⊠ *55 W. Church St., Downtown Orlando* ☎ *407/401–8811* ⊕ *www. therustyspoon.com* ☾ *No lunch weekends* ✛ *3:D6.*

SOUTHERN
Fodor'sChoice
★

$$$ ✕ **Shari Sushi Lounge.** Resplendent with metallic leather and chic white seats, this trendy eatery has more the atmosphere of a fast-lane singles bar than of an Asian oasis, but the dishes from the kitchen—fresh sushi and cooked Asian entrées—distinguish the place as a legit dining establishment. If you're here for the sushi, the place will not disappoint. There are 25 different varieties of signature rolls alone, plus traditional sushi including sea urchin and baby octopus and a dozen interesting

JAPANESE

7

sashimi creations. The ceviche roll is especially tasty; a tribute to the Latin American fish dish, the sushi mixes the flavors of micro cilantro, a lime-chipotle sauce, plus siracha. Start with the *tako* salad, a delicious arrangement of octopus, cucumber, enoki mushrooms, mandarin oranges, and spicy kimchi sauce, or Wagyu steak that you cook yourself on a hot stone. Then move on to one of the mini-courses, like buffalo lobster tempura, or an entrée such as sake salmon: an 8-ounce fillet steamed with sake, garlic, soy sauce, lime juice, and grated ginger. Or sit at the bar and let the sushi chef pamper you with the day's multicourse omakase. ⑤ *Average main: $24* ✉ *621 E. Central Blvd., Thornton Park* ☏ *407/420–9420* ⊕ *www.sharisushilounge.com* ☺ *No lunch* ♦ *3:E6.*

$$$
AMERICAN
✕ **The Smiling Bison.** A humble hideaway located near a standard mall, the Smiling Bison is an ambitious gastropub popular with Orlando's locavores. The dining area, heavy on reclaimed woods, feels much like a living room with paintings of musicians. The owners got their start selling homemade sausages from a food cart, and you can still find smoked kielbasa, curry wurst, or other creations in sandwich form. The menu changes weekly, but poutine, a duck pizza, and a bison burger are always on offer. Dinner might be a chicken potpie, ginger-braised pork belly, or house-made papardelle with pork bison ragu. The beer menu caters to a craft-brew-centric crowd, and wines are interesting and reasonably priced. Musicians entertain several nights a week, with no cover charge, and the restaurant hosts jazz dinners every Tuesday night. ⑤ *Average main: $24* ✉ *745 Bennett Rd., Downtown Orlando* ☏ *407/898–8580* ⊕ *www.thesmilingbison.com* ☺ *Closed Mon. No lunch. No dinner Sun.* ♦ *3:G5.*

$$$
SOUTHERN
✕ **Soco.** Southern staples get mighty fancy at Soco, where both the decor and the menu mesh classic and creative in a suave way. Vegetarians get one of the best meatless entrées in town with the chicken-fried cauliflower steak, a massive dish finished with a rich tomato gravy. Meat eaters enjoy playful touches like lobster-mashed potatoes with meat loaf, Korean flavorings in fried chicken, and black-eyed peas smoked and used to fill tortellini. Be sure to end with the potato chip–crusted chocolate cake with peanut brittle and salted caramel. ⑤ *Average main: $23* ✉ *629 E. Central Blvd., Thornton Park* ☏ *407/849–1800* ⊕ *www. socothorntonpark.com* ☺ *No lunch* ♦ *3:E6.*

WINTER PARK

Winter Park is a charming suburb on the northern end of Orlando, 35 minutes from Disney. It's affluent, understated, and sophisticated—and can be pleasurable when you need a break from the theme parks. It has four restaurant hubs: Park Avenue, Orange Avenue, Hannibal Square, and Winter Park Village. To get into the area, follow Interstate 4 to Exit 87.

$
BARBECUE
Fodor's Choice
★
✕ **4 Rivers Smokehouse.** Obsessed with Texas-style barbecue brisket, John Rivers decided to turn his passion into a business upon retiring from the corporate world. The result is the über-popular 4 Rivers, which turns out barbecue standards like pulled pork and corn bread, plus more unusual items like the addicting bacon-wrapped smoked jalapeño peppers, the

Six Shooter with cheese grits, and a sausage-filled pastry called *kolache*. Old-time soft drinks such as Frostie Root Beer and Cheerwine are for sale, along with desserts like the kiddie favorite Chocolate Awesomeness, an indulgent layering of chocolate cake, chocolate pudding, Heath Bar, whipped cream, and chocolate and caramel sauces. Some units have a Sweet Shop that sells whole oversize cakes. Additional 4 Rivers are scattered throughout Central Florida. ⓢ *Average main: $13* ✉ *1600 W. Fairbanks Ave.* ☎ *855/368–7748* ⊕ *www.4rsmokehouse.com* ⌂ *Reservations not accepted* ◷ *Closed Sun.* ✣ *3:D2.*

$$
ITALIAN **✕ Brio Tuscan Grille.** Head to this trendy restaurant for wood-grilled meats and fish, Italian classics like chicken Milanese, and plenty of pasta. Try the strip steak topped with Gorgonzola, or the mushroom ravioli with champagne brown butter sauce. A good appetizer choice is the bruschetta, a wood-baked flatbread covered with toppings like sliced steak or roasted red peppers with mozzarella. The dining room's Italian archways are elegant, its frescoed walls schmaltzy in a grand trattoria sort of way, and the sidewalk tables a good option on cool days. There is another location at Orlando's Mall at Millenia and a similar, sister concept, Bravo!, on Restaurant Row. ⓢ *Average main: $21* ✉ *480 N. Orlando Ave.* ☎ *407/622–5611* ⊕ *www.brioitalian.com* ⌂ *Reservations not accepted* ✣ *3:E2.*

$$$
SOUTHERN **✕ Cask & Larder.** Firmly established as local celebs, thanks to their success at the neighboring Ravenous Pig, chef-owners Julie and James Petrakis went the Southern brewpub route for restaurant number two. It's a bustling, casual space for a wallet-friendly, home-style meal made with regional ingredients, along with several varieties of house-brewed and other craft beers plus handcrafted cocktails made with American spirits. Staples include a three-ham tasting platter with pepper jelly "ham jam," and raw oysters. After that, it's an always-changing array of small entrées, featuring familiar items like chicken and scallops and not-so-common ones like quail and lamb ribs. Plan ahead for a three-course whole-animal dinner (eight-person minimum), like a smoked suckling pig. ⓢ *Average main: $25* ✉ *565 W. Fairbanks Ave.* ☎ *321/280–4200* ⊕ *www.caskandlarder.com* ✣ *3:F2.*

$$$$
STEAKHOUSE
Fodor's Choice
★
✕ Christner's Prime Steak & Lobster. Locals like this quiet, uncomplicated, family-run steak house, which delivers carefully prepared food and attentive service in a traditional setting of red leather and dark wood. When your steak arrives—still sizzling on a hot plate—the waiter asks you to cut into it and check that it was cooked as you ordered. The menu is simple: rib eye, porterhouse, filet mignon. Seafood such as lobster, shrimp, and salmon fill out the surf side of the menu. End your meal with a big slice of mandarin orange cake. ⓢ *Average main: $45* ✉ *729 Lee Rd.* ☎ *407/645–4443* ⊕ *www.christnersprimesteakandlobster.com* ◷ *Closed Sun. No lunch* ✣ *3:C1.*

$$
ECLECTIC **✕ Dexter's.** A quartet of Central Florida restaurants, Dexter's is a low-key concept with a wildly creative menu, surprisingly low prices, a good wine list, and a faithful following among locals. Two of the best-selling entrées are the chicken tortilla pie—a stack of puffy, fried tortillas layered with chicken and cheese—and a pressed duck sandwich and a Brie sandwich. The rotating fish of the day features whatever's freshest in

season. In addition to a core menu shared by the restaurants, each has its own café menu with specialties designed by that unit's on-site chef. There's always live music on Thursday night. The other restaurants are in Windermere (just north of the Sand Lake Road area), Lake Mary, and Orlando's Thornton Park neighborhood. $ *Average main: $16* ✉ *558 W. New England Ave., Hannibal Sq.* ☎ *407/629–1150* ⊕ *www.dexwine.com* ✛ *3:E2.*

$$$ × **Luma on Park.** Indisputably one of the Orlando area's best restau-
MODERN rants, Luma on Park is a popular spot for progressive American cuisine
AMERICAN served in a fashionable setting. Every ingredient is carefully sourced
Fodor's Choice from local producers when possible, and scratch preparation—from
★ pastas to sausages to pickled rhubarb—is the mantra among its dedi-
cated clique of chefs. The menu changes daily. You might discover chestnut agnolotti with Maine lobster or a cauliflower-onion tart as starters, followed by tilefish with tangerine-fennel broth or duck breast with kale, toasted pine nuts, parsnip puree, and pickled white asparagus. The wine cellar is a high point, holding 7,000 bottles—80 varieties, all available by the half glass, glass, and bottle. The restaurant offers a three-course, prix-fixe dinner Sunday through Tuesday for $35 per person, $45 with wine pairings. $ *Average main: $30* ✉ *290 S. Park Ave., Park Ave.* ☎ *407/599–4111* ⊕ *www.lumaonpark.com* ⊗ *No lunch Mon.–Thurs.* ✛ *3:F2.*

$$$ × **Prato.** Progressive Italian cuisine in a casual, bustling wood-and-brick
ITALIAN setting immediately made Prato a local favorite. Every item from the
Fodor's Choice pancetta to the amaretti is crafted from scratch. Most are prepared in
★ one of two imported Italian wood-burning ovens, dubbed Johnny Cash
and June Cash because "they make music," the chefs say. The menu changes regularly, but standouts include the chicken-liver crostini and pastas such as shrimp ravioli and rigatoni cacciatore made with shred-ded rabbit and orange zest. The hand-tossed pizzas are also popular, as are the tiramisu and seasonal gelato. $ *Average main: $23* ✉ *124 N. Park Ave., Park Ave.* ☎ *407/262–0050* ⊕ *www.prato-wp.com* ⚱ *Reservations essential* ⊗ *No lunch Mon. and Tues.* ✛ *3:F2.*

$$$$ × **The Ravenous Pig.** A trendy, vibrant gastropub in one of Orlando's most
MODERN affluent enclaves, the Pig is arguably Orlando's most popular foodie des-
AMERICAN tination. Run by husband-and-wife chefs James and Julie Petrakis, the
Fodor's Choice restaurant dispenses delicacies such as pork porterhouse with mustard
★ glaze and pear relish, and speckle trout with romesco sauce. The menu
changes daily and always includes less expensive pub fare like rock shrimp tacos and homemade pretzels with a taleggio-porter fondue. All charcuterie is made in house, from spiced orange salami to game-bird terrine. The signature dessert is the Pig Tails, essentially a basket full of piping hot, pig tail–shaped doughnuts with a chocolate-espresso dip-ping sauce. $ *Average main: $31* ✉ *1234 N. Orange Ave., Orange Ave.* ☎ *407/628–2333* ⊕ *www.theravenouspig.com* ⚱ *Reservations essential* ⊗ *Closed Sun. and Mon.* ✛ *3:E3.*

WHERE TO STAY

Updated by Jennifer Greenhill-Taylor

With tens of thousands of lodging choices available in the Orlando area, from tents to deluxe villas, there is no lack of variety in price or amenities. In fact, narrowing down the possibilities is part of the fun.

More than 50 million visitors come to the Orlando area each year, making it the most popular tourism destination on the planet. More upscale hotels are opening as visitors demand more luxurious surroundings, such as luxe linens, tasteful and refined decor, organic toiletries, or ergonomic chairs and work desks. But no matter what your budget or desires, lodging comes in such a wide range of prices, themes, color schemes, brands, meal plans, and guest-room amenities, you will have no problem finding something that fits.

Resorts on and off Disney property combine function with fantasy, as befits visitor expectations. Characters in costume perform for the kids, pools are pirates' caves with waterfalls, and some, like the Gaylord Palms, go so far as to re-create Florida landmarks under a gargantuan glass roof, giving visitors the illusion of having visited more of the state than they expected.

International Drive's expanding attractions, including The Orlando Eye, Madame Tussauds, and a widening array of eateries, are drawing more savvy conventioneers who bring their families along for the fun.

Many hotels have joined the trend toward green lodging, bringing recycling, water conservation, and other environmentally conscious practices to the table. Best of all, the sheer number and variety of hotel rooms means you can still find relative bargains throughout the Orlando area, even on Disney property, by researching your trip well, calling the lodgings directly, negotiating packages and prices, and shopping wisely.

LODGING PLANNER

WHERE SHOULD WE STAY?

When it comes to Orlando lodging, no matter who you are and where you decide to stay, you should book months in advance (at least six months for hotels at Disney). This is particularly important for travel when rates are lowest, specifically early January to mid-February, late April to mid-June, and mid-August to early December.

Your choices include resorts on Disney property (most owned and operated by Disney), those on Universal property, and those not in or affiliated with either park. Each type of property merits consideration.

HOTELS ON DISNEY AND UNIVERSAL PROPERTY

If you're interested solely in attractions at Disney or Universal, **in-park hotels are best.** For starters, they offer such convenient transportation options that you probably won't need a rental car—a huge cost savings.

Walt Disney World's massive campus is tied together by a dizzying array of complimentary monorails, buses, and water taxis. All get you anywhere on the property you want to go. Universal provides complimentary shuttles and water taxis between its two theme parks and three on-site hotels, though the hotels and parks are also within walking distance of one another.

Universal and Disney's on-site hotels also offer many special perks—some designed to save money, some designed to save time. Note that these perks don't necessarily extend to non-Disney-owned hotels on Disney property, so ask for those specifics before booking.

HOTELS OFF THEME-PARK PROPERTY

If you plan to visit several parks or go sightseeing elsewhere in Central Florida, consider off-site hotels. Those closest to Disney are clustered in a few areas: along I-Drive; in the U.S. 192 area and Kissimmee; and in the Downtown Disney–Lake Buena Vista Area, just off Interstate 4 Exit 68. I-Drive hotels such as the DoubleTree by Hilton at the Entrance to Universal Orlando and Hyatt Place Orlando/Universal are closest to Universal.

Nearly every hotel in these areas provides frequent (sometimes free) transportation to and from Disney or even Universal. In addition, there are some noteworthy and money-saving, if far-flung, options in the greater Orlando area. One suburban caveat: traffic on Interstate 4 in Orlando experiences typical freeway gridlock during morning (7–9) and evening (4–6) rush hours.

■TIP→ Anyone can visit Disney hotels. To save money and still have on-site resort experiences, stay at a moderately priced hotel off-site and then visit the animals at the Animal Kingdom Lodge, say, or rent a boat at the Grand Floridian.

CONSIDERATIONS FOR DIFFERENT TYPES OF TRAVELERS

Whether you stay on theme-park property or off, prioritize your needs. A great spa is wonderful, but if you're running around with three young kids, will you actually use it? Do you want luxury or rustic simplicity? A splurge or a supersaver?

In addition, weigh what you get for the money. Sure, you might spend more on a room at a Disney or Universal resort than at an off-site property. But if staying at a cheaper off-site hotel means renting a car or spending a lot of money and time on cab rides, you might not ultimately be saving that much. Conversely, if you're planning to split your time between, say, Disney, Universal, and SeaWorld, you probably won't make full use of all of the Disney or Universal perks and might be better off shopping for a good-value, centrally located, off-site hotel with free theme-park shuttle service.

Finally, if you're traveling with children, be sure to mention their ages when you make reservations. Sometimes hotels have special features, such as rooms with bunk beds, just for families. Such things aren't necessarily offered up front, so be sure to ask.

■ TIP➔ **Regardless of whether you stay at hotels near the theme parks or at on-site resorts, it can take between 20 minutes and an hour to get to and from park entrances.**

FAMILIES WITH YOUNG KIDS

If this is a Disney trip, stick with Disney hotels or Hotel Plaza Boulevard properties: the transportation system makes it simple to scoot back for a nap or some downtime at the pool.

Many Disney properties are designed to appeal to kids, some with great children's facilities and programs. At the value-priced Art of Animation Resort, young kids love the familiarity of *Finding Nemo, Little Mermaid,* and *Cars* themes everywhere. The Polynesian Resort's Never Land Club has an enchanting Peter Pan–themed clubhouse and youngsters-only dinner show. Parents rave about the Sand Castle Club at the Yacht and Beach Club resorts. What's more, most of these clubs are open from late afternoon until midnight, so parents can slip out for a romantic meal while the kids play games, do art projects, and enjoy a snack or dinner.

■ TIP➔ **Surprise kids with a wake-up call from Mickey while staying at a Disney resort.**

If you do stay off-site, book a hotel geared to small children. The Nickelodeon Suites Resort, in Lake Buena Vista, offers suites whose separate kid-friendly bedrooms are decorated with images of cartoon characters. It also has live shows featuring Nick characters, a Nickelodeon-themed pool, and tons of kids' activities.

East of International Drive the connected JW Marriott and Ritz-Carlton Orlando, Grande Lakes resorts have rooms with adjoining kids' suites, complete with miniature furniture and toys. The Ritz also has a Kids Club with an engaging play area and daily scheduled activities.

WHERE SHOULD WE STAY?

	VIBE	PROS	CONS
Disney	Thousands of rooms at every price; convenient to Disney parks; free trans-.portation all over WDW complex.	Perks like early park entry, MyMagic+ and Magical Express, which lets you circumvent airport bag checks.	Without a rental car, you likely won't leave Disney. On-site buses, although free, can take a big bite of time out of your entertainment day; convenience comes at a price.
Universal	On-site hotels offer luxury, convenience, and value. There are less expensive options just outside the gates.	Central to Disney, Universal, SeaWorld, malls, and I-4; free water taxis to parks from on-site hotels.	Most on-site hotels are pricey; the Cabana Bay Beach Resort, however, is reasonable; expect heavy rush-hour traffic during drives to and from other parks.
I-Drive	A hotel, convention center, and activities bonanza. A trolley runs from one end to the other.	Outlet malls provide bargains; world-class restaurants; the Orlando Eye lifts visitors up for a bird's-eye view; many hotels offer free park shuttles.	Transportation can be pricey, in cash and in time, as traffic is often heavy. Crime is up, especially after dark, although area hotels and businesses have increased security.
Kissimmee	It offers mom-and-pop motels and upscale choices, restaurants, and places to buy saltwater taffy.	It's just outside Disney, very close to Magic Kingdom. Lots of Old Florida charm and low prices.	Some of the older motels here are a little seedy. Petty crime in which tourists are victims is rare—but not unheard of.
Lake Buena Vista	Many hotel and restaurant chains here. Adjacent to WDW, which is where almost every guest in your hotel is headed.	Really close to WDW; plenty of dining and shopping options; easy access to I-4.	Heavy peak-hour traffic. As in all neighborhoods near Disney, a gallon of gas will cost 10%–15% more than elsewhere.
Central Orlando	Parts of town have the modern high-rises you'd expect. Other areas have oak tree–lined brick streets winding among small, cypress-ringed lakes.	Locally owned restaurants, trendy hotels, vibrant nightlife, and some quaint B&Bs. City buses serve the parks. There's good access to I-4.	You'll need to rent a car. And you will be part of the traffic headed to WDW. Expect the 25-mile drive to take at least 45 minutes.
Orlando International Airport	Mostly business and flight-crew hotels and car-rental outlets.	Great if you have an early flight or just want to shop in a mall. There's even a Hyatt on-site.	Watching planes, buses, taxis, and cars arrive and depart is all the entertainment you'll get.

Wherever you stay, inquire about child equipment. Most hotels—and certainly all owned by Disney—have amenities such as cribs. (Some hotels require you to reserve cribs in advance. Ask whether there will be an additional charge, and make sure the crib meets current child-safety standards.)

8

FAMILY WITH TWEENS

With tweens you don't really need a hotel that's superclose to a theme park, so your selection is greater. Even properties that seem adult-oriented have offerings that tweens love. The "lazy-river" pools at hotels including the Omni Orlando Resort at ChampionsGate and the JW Marriott, for instance, are generally big hits.

Many hotels also have supervised camp-style programs, with trained counselors and fun, active, outdoorsy things to do. These are great for arrival and departure days, when you probably don't want to schlep to a park, but you also don't want to hear the dreaded "I'm so bored."

Standouts are at the Ritz-Carlton's Ritz Kids program, and in room camping and the Camp Hyatt program at the Hyatt Regency Grand Cypress, near Downtown Disney. The latter is a top-class resort with sprawling grounds that abut Walt Disney World property, so it's perfect for families who want to be near the Mouse but prefer to take a break from Disney each night.

FAMILY WITH TEENS

A great hotel pool is a major boon for teens, who might not want to spend all of their time in the theme parks. Stormalong Bay, the pool complex shared by the Yacht and Beach Club, has it all: a lazy river, waterslide, sandy-bottom pool, and elevated tanning deck. This location is also surrounded by the shops, restaurants, and leisure activities of Disney's BoardWalk—a great place for teens to explore on their own.

Teens are usually partial to Universal's thrills, so the *South Pacific*–themed Loews Royal Pacific Resort here is also an excellent choice. It has a lagoon-style swimming pool with a sandy beach; "dive-in" movies on select nights; a fitness center with a whirlpool, steam room, and sauna; a nightly torch-lighting ceremony; and an authentic luau. The rock-and-roll-themed Hard Rock Hotel is also a great Universal option, with underwater speakers piping rock and roll into the pool.

■ TIP→ **If at all possible, book more than one room. As they say, the family that sleeps together . . . hates each other in the morning.** Teens are used to having their own space; crabby moods stemming from cramped conditions can put a damper on the vacation. When booking, request connecting rooms—with a door linking your room to that of your teen—as opposed to adjoining rooms, which means only that your rooms are next to each other.

If booking more than one room is too pricey, look into accommodations at all-suites hotels or family suites at regular hotels. These larger quarters are often reasonably priced. Just be sure to check on the hotel's definition of "suite." Sometimes it's merely an L-shaped room with a sitting area (i.e., there's no door separating you from your teen). The key question is, "Do your suites have two separate rooms?"

SINGLES OR GROUPS OF FRIENDS

If you're traveling solo, you'll never feel lonely at a theme-park hotel. Consider one in Disney's BoardWalk area—perhaps the BoardWalk Inn and Villas, Disney's Yacht Club, or Disney's Beach Club. From here you're just steps from shopping, dining, and nightlife. Similarly,

Universal hotels like the elegant Loews Portofino Bay Hotel are just a blink away from the shopping and the hopping nightlife of CityWalk. Plus, Portofino has a spa.

If theme parks aren't your only interest, you can get your wow factor by staying at a hotel like the Gaylord Palms Resort. The interior of this place is like a Cecil B. DeMille movie—about Florida. Just walking around in the 4-acre atrium is an adventure, with indoor gardens evoking the Everglades and old St. Augustine. There's also a lot to do on-site, including dining, shopping, pampering yourself at the spa, or working out in the large fitness center.

COUPLES

Luxury properties such as the Ritz-Carlton Orlando, Grande Lakes or the Four Seasons spell romance. Ultraluxurious rooms, restaurants, and spa programs, plus championship golf courses, make these resorts among the best in the Orlando area. Another romantic option is Downtown's Grand Bohemian, with a rooftop pool, jazz in the Bösendorfer Lounge, and short-walk access to the Dr. Phillips Center for the Performing Arts and the Amway Center's NBA games and world-class concerts.

If you and your sweetie are Disneyphiles, Disney's five-star Grand Floridian absolutely drips with Victorian romance, and the Animal Kingdom Lodge offers the delights of sunsets over the savanna and giraffes and zebras munching leaves just below your balcony. The Port Orleans Resort–French Quarter, near Downtown Disney, is a great, more affordable choice for couples.

LARGE GROUPS

All-suites properties are the logical choice. If you're coming mainly for the theme parks, stay on Disney or Universal grounds, as the many perks—especially those involving transportation—definitely make life easier. Some Disney properties with suites include the cabins at Fort Wilderness Resort, the Beach Club Villas, the BoardWalk Inn and Villas, the Bay Lake Tower at the Contemporary Resort, the bungalows and studios at the Polynesian Village Resort and the villas at Animal Kingdom. At the Universal properties, Cabana Bay has 1,800 rooms, half of them suites.

If you plan to spend time away from the parks or will be shuttling between Universal and Disney, consider reserving an apartment or condo. This works best for families who thrive on the chaos of communal living. (It also works better if you assign chores. This is a vacation for everyone, and it's just not fair if one or two people consistently do all the work.)

The only potential hang-up to the apartment-condo scenario is who gets the master suite. If it's a birthday, anniversary, or retirement event, the big room naturally goes to the guest(s) of honor. Otherwise, the decision isn't so straightforward. One solution: donate it to some of the kids. The suite will be plenty big for a slumber party, and you'll love the fact that their war-torn bathroom is blissfully out of sight.

BABYSITTING IN ORLANDO

If you're staying in a room, suite, or condo and need to rent baby equipment, such as a stroller, bassinet, high chair, or even pool toys, call **Orlando Crib Rental** (☎ 407/433–7770 ⊕ www.orlandocribrental.com) for swift delivery and fair rates. You can order online. The company also provides some concierge services, such as grocery or baby-supply delivery.

If you want to plan an adults-only evening, consider the **Kid's Nite Out** (☎ 407/828–0920 or 800/696–8105 ⊕ www.kidsniteout.com) program, which works with hotels throughout Orlando. It provides in-room babysitting for children ages 6 weeks to 12 years. Fees start at $18 an hour for one child, and increase by $3 for each additional child. There's a four-hour minimum, plus a transportation fee of $10 for the sitter to travel to your hotel room. The service also rents baby equipment, such as strollers and jogging carriages, and will babysit your pet, too.

When you make a reservation, you must provide a credit-card number. There's a 24-hour cancellation policy; if you cancel with less than 24 hours' notice, your credit card is charged the four-hour minimum fee ($72 for one child, higher rates for multiple children booked). The service recommends booking from two weeks to 90 days in advance.

If your family members tend to get in each other's hair, you're better off reserving a block of hotel rooms. Add a courtesy suite, and you have all the benefits of togetherness, plus a place to retreat to when you need it. Talk to a hotel agent to figure out how many people each room can accommodate comfortably, and how many rooms you'll need.

FACILITIES AND AMENITIES

All hotels and resorts in Central Florida have air-conditioning, and most have cable or satellite TV, coffeemakers, in-room irons, and ironing boards. Those in the moderate and expensive price ranges often have bathrobes and hair dryers. High-speed wireless access (Wi-Fi) is now common even at budget properties, but some hotels still charge a daily fee for Internet service. If being connected is important, it's best to ask. Most hotels, even the budget ones, have a pool, and many have fitness facilities and business centers. Be sure to ask whether the hotel charges a resort fee. Finding a week's worth of unexpected daily fees on your final bill can be a disconcerting surprise.

If a particular amenity is important to you, ask for it; many hotels will provide extras upon request. Double-check your bill at checkout, and if a charge seems unreasonable, this is the time to have it remedied. If you're traveling with pets, note the hotel's pet policies. Some hotels require substantial cleaning fees. A big note to smokers: most of the hotels and resorts in Central Florida are entirely smoke-free, meaning even smoking outdoors on hotel property is frowned upon or prohibited.

ROOM RATES

In the Orlando area there's an inverse relationship between temperature and room rates. The hot and humid weather in late summer and fall brings lower prices and possibly hurricanes. Conversely, the balmy days of late February, March, and April attract lots of visitors; hotel owners charge accordingly. One note about hurricane season—it officially begins in June, but a hurricane in Florida before August is rare. Rates are often low from early January to mid-February, from late April to mid-June, and from mid-August to the third week in November.

Always call several places—availability and special deals can drive room rates at a $$$$ hotel down into the $$ range—and don't forget to ask whether you're eligible for a discount. You can always save by preparing a few meals in a room, suite, or villa with a kitchenette or kitchen. Websites will often offer a better room rate; so compare the prices offered on the Web and through the hotel's local or toll-free number (if one is available). Always ask about special packages or corporate rates. Don't be shy. Polite assertiveness can save you money.

The Disney Dining Plan: On-site Walt Disney World Hotels don't offer meal plans in their rates, but you can choose a Disney Dining Plan. It can be added to any on-site package, and many families swear by it. The plan saves you from having to carry around cash and—at least on the surface—masks the sting of coughing up nine bucks for a cheeseburger. To see if a Disney Dining Plan is right for your family, go to ⊕ *www. disneyworld.disney.go.com/dining* for more information.

RESERVATIONS

When booking by phone, expect a robot first, a sometimes protracted wait, then a real person who will be polite and helpful.

Walt Disney Travel Co. Packages can be arranged through the Walt Disney Travel Co. Guests can find planning tools on the website that allow them to customize vacation itineraries based on interests as well as age, height restrictions, and medical needs. ☎ *407/939–5277* ⊕ *www. disneyworld.com.*

WDW Central Reservations Office. You can book many accommodations— Disney-owned hotels and some non-Disney-owned hotels—through the WDW Central Reservations Office. The website allows you to compare prices at the various on-site resorts. ☎ *407/934–7639* ⊕ *www. disneyworld.com.*

WDW Special Request Reservations. People with disabilities can call the regular WDW reservations number, as the representatives are all knowledgeable about services available at resorts and parks for guests with disabilities. All representatives have TTY ability. The website is also a valuable source for specific needs. Go to Guest Services and search the word "Disabilities." ☎ *407/394–5277 reservations, 407/939–7838 parks* ⊕ *www.disneyworld.com.*

DISNEY AND UNIVERSAL RESORT PERKS

DISNEY PERKS

Extra Magic Hours. You get special early and late-night admission to certain Disney parks on specified days. Call ahead for details so you can plan your early- and late-visit strategies.

Free Parking. Parking is free for Disney hotel guests at Disney hotel and theme-park lots.

Magical Express. If you're staying at a select Disney hotel, this free airport service means you don't need to rent a car or think about finding a shuttle or taxi or worry about baggage handling.

At your hometown airport, you check your bags in and won't see them again till you get to your Disney hotel. At Orlando International Airport you're met by a Disney rep, who leads you to a coach that takes you to your hotel. Your luggage is delivered separately and usually arrives in your room an hour or two after you do. If your flight arrives before 5 am or after 10 pm, you will have to pick up your luggage and deliver it to the coach.

On departure, the process works in reverse (though only on some participating airlines, so check in advance). You get your boarding pass and check your bags at the hotel. At the airport you go directly to your gate, skipping check-in. You won't see your bags until you're in your hometown airport. Participating airlines include American, Delta, JetBlue, Southwest, and United.

Charging Privileges. You can charge most meals and purchases throughout Disney to your hotel room, using your MyMagic+ bands or cards.

Package Delivery. Anything you purchase at Disney—at a park, a hotel, or in Downtown Disney—can be delivered to the gift shop of your Disney hotel for free.

Priority Reservations. Disney hotel guests get priority reservations at Disney restaurants and choice tee times at Disney golf courses up to 30 days in advance, using MyMagic+.

Guaranteed Entry. Disney theme parks sometimes reach capacity, but on-site guests can enter even when others would be turned away.

UNIVERSAL PERKS

Head-of-the-Line Access. Your hotel key (except Cabana Bay) lets you go directly to the head of the line for most Universal Orlando attractions. Unlike Disney's FastPass+ program, you don't need to use this at a specific time; it's always good. Hotel guests also get early admission to the often-crowded Harry Potter attractions.

Priority Seating. Many of Universal's restaurants offer priority seating to those staying at on-site hotels.

Charging Privileges. You can charge most meals and purchases throughout Universal to your hotel room.

Delivery Services. If you buy something in the theme parks, you can have it sent directly to your room, so you don't have to carry it around.

Free Loaners. Some on-site hotels have a "Did You Forget?" closet that offers everything from kids' strollers to dog leashes to computer accessories. There's no fee for using this service.

8

WHAT IT COSTS			
$	$$	$$$	$$$$
FOR TWO PEOPLE	under $175	$175–$249	$250–$350	over $350

OUR REVIEWS

Prices: Prices in the hotel reviews are the lowest cost of a standard double room in high season, excluding taxes, service charges, resort fees, and meal plans (except at all-inclusives). Prices for rentals are the lowest per-night cost for a one-bedroom unit in high season. Note that taxes in Central Florida can be as high as 12.5%.

Maps: *Throughout the chapter, you'll see mapping symbols and coordinates (✛ 3:F2) after property names or reviews. Maps are within the chapter. The first number after the ✛ symbol indicates the map number. After that is the property's coordinate on the map grid.*

WALT DISNEY WORLD

Disney-operated hotels are fantasies unto themselves. Each is designed according to a theme (quaint New England, the relaxed culture of the Polynesian Islands, an African safari village, and so on), and each offers the same perks: free transportation from the airport and to the parks, the option to charge all of your purchases to your room, special guest-only park-visiting times, and much more. If you stay on-site, you'll have better access to the parks and be more immersed in the Disney experience.

MAGIC KINGDOM RESORT AREA

Take I–4 Exit 62, 64B, or 65.

The ritzy hotels near the Magic Kingdom all lie on the monorail route and are only minutes away from the park. Fort Wilderness Resort and Campground, with RV and tent sites, is a bit farther away from the Magic Kingdom, and access to the parks is by bus or boat.

$$$$
RESORT
The Cabins at Disney's Fort Wilderness Resort. The cabins in this 750-acre campground right across the lake from the Magic Kingdom don't exactly constitute roughing it, as they are small, air-conditioned log homes that accommodate four grown-ups and two youngsters. **Pros:** lots of traditional camping activities and a real campground community feel; you can save money by cooking, but you don't have to, as there is a three-meals-a-day restaurant and nightly barbecue; free Internet and Wi-Fi. **Cons:** shuttle to parks is free, but slow; pricey for what is really just a mobile home encased in logs; coin-op laundry is pricey, too. ⑤ *Rooms from: $413* ✉ *4510 N. Fort Wildnerness Trail* ☎ *407/824-2900* ⊕ *www.disneyworld.disney.go.com/resorts* ↩ *421 cabins* ⏪ *No meals* ✛ *1:C2.*

$
RESORT
Fodor's Choice
★

The Campsites at Disney's Fort Wilderness Resort. One of the cheapest ways to stay on WDW property is in your own tent or RV, especially considering that some of the 799 sites in this 750-acre pine and cypress forest campground can accommodate up to 10 people. **Pros:** Disney's most economical lodging; pets allowed; free Wi-Fi, free parking. **Cons:** amount of walking to reach the store, restaurants, etc. can be a bit much; shuttle rides to Disney parks take a long time; the mosquitoes can be irritating, except in winter. ⑤ *Rooms from: $99* ✉ *4510 N. Fort Wilderness Trail* ☎ *407/939–6244, 407/824–2742* ⊕ *www.disneyworld. disney.go.com/resorts* ➵ *799 campsites* ⦿ *No meals* ✛ *1:C2.*

$$$$
RESORT

Disney's Contemporary Resort. You're paying for location at this sleek, modern, luxury resort next to the Magic Kingdom, as the monorail runs right through the lobby, making park hopping a breeze, and offering quick respite for families seeking relief from the midday heat. **Pros:** monorail access; Chef Mickey's, the epicenter of character-meal world; health and wellness suites. **Cons:** a mix of conventioneers and vacationers means it can be too frenzied for the former and too staid for the latter. ⑤ *Rooms from: $571* ✉ *4600 N. World Dr.* ☎ *407/824– 1000* ⊕ *www.disneyworld.com* ➵ *1,013 rooms, 25 suites* ⦿ *No meals* ✛ *1:B1.*

$$$$
RESORT
Fodor's Choice
★

Disney's Grand Floridian Resort & Spa. On the shores of the Seven Seas Lagoon, so close to the Magic Kingdom that you can see the colors change on the Cinderella Castle, this red-roofed Victorian emulates the style of the great railroad resorts of the past with beautifully appointed rooms, rambling verandas, delicate, white-painted woodwork, and brick chimneys. **Pros:** old-Florida ambience; on the monorail route; Victoria & Albert's offers an evening-long experience in dining; if you're a couple with no kids, this is definitely the most romantic on-property hotel; right next to Disney's Wedding Pavilion. **Cons:** pricey; convention clientele and vacationing couples may be more comfortable than families with young children. ⑤ *Rooms from: $655* ✉ *4401 Floridian Way* ☎ *407/824–3000* ⊕ *www.disneyworld.com* ➵ *867 rooms, 90 suites* ⦿ *No meals* ✛ *1:A1.*

8

$$$$
RESORT

Disney's Polynesian Village Resort. This South Pacific–themed resort with its tropical backdrop of orchids, ferns, and palms, lies directly across the lagoon from the Magic Kingdom, on the monorail and water taxi routes, and has lots of kids activities, making it a good family choice. **Pros:** kids activities; on the monorail; great atmosphere; free Wi-Fi. **Cons:** pricey; lots of loud children. ⑤ *Rooms from: $493* ✉ *1600 Seven Seas Dr.* ☎ *407/824–2000* ⊕ *www.disneyworld.disney.go.com/ resorts* ➵ *844 rooms, 366 suites, 20 bungalows* ⦿ *No meals* ✛ *1:B2.*

$$$$
RESORT

Disney's Wilderness Lodge. The architects outdid themselves in designing this seven-story hotel modeled after majestic turn-of-the-20th-century lodges in the American Northwest, with a cavernous lobby, supported by towering tree trunks, an 82-foot-high fireplace made of rocks from the Grand Canyon, two 55-foot-tall hand-carved totem poles that pay homage to the region's Native American culture, all lighted by enormous tepee-shaped chandeliers. **Pros:** impressive architecture; boarding point for romantic cruises or free water taxi to Magic Kingdom; elegant dining options; children's activity center; free Wi-Fi.

BEST BETS FOR ORLANDO AND THE PARKS LODGING

Fodor's offers a selective listing of high-quality lodgings in every price range, both inside and outside the parks. Here are our top picks by price and experience. The best properties—those that provide a remarkable experience in their price range—are designated with the Fodor's Choice logo.

Fodor's Choice★

Best Western Lake Buena Vista Resort, $

The Campsites at Disney's Fort Wilderness Resort, $

Disney's All-Star Sports Resorts, $

Disney's Animal Kingdom Lodge, $$$$

Disney's Coronado Springs Resort, $$$

Disney's Grand Floridian Resort & Spa, $$$$

Drury Inn & Suites Orlando, $

Hyatt Regency Grand Cypress Resort, $$

Loews Portofino Bay Hotel at Universal Orlando, $$$$

Loews Royal Pacific Resort at Universal Orlando, $$$$

Nickelodeon Suites Resort, $$

Residence Inn by Marriott Orlando at SeaWorld, $

Ritz-Carlton Orlando, Grande Lakes, $$$$

Universal's Cabana Bay Beach Resort, $$

Waldorf Astoria Orlando, $$$$

By Price

$

Best Western Lake Buena Vista Resort

The Campsites at Disney's Fort Wilderness Resort

Disney's All-Star Resorts

Drury Inn & Suites Orlando

Residence Inn by Marriott Orlando at SeaWorld

$$

Disney's Art of Animation Resort

Hyatt Place Orlando/Universal

Hyatt Regency Grand Cypress Resort

Nickelodeon Suites Resort

Universal's Cabana Bay Beach Resort

$$$

Disney's Coronado Springs Resort

$$$$

The Cabins at Disney's Fort Wilderness Resort

Disney's Animal Kingdom Lodge

Disney's Grand Floridian Resort & Spa

Loews Portofino Bay Hotel at Universal Orlando

Loews Royal Pacific Resort at Universal Orlando

Ritz-Carlton Orlando, Grande Lakes

Waldorf Astoria Orlando

By Experience

MOST KID-FRIENDLY

Disney's All-Star Resorts, $

Disney's Art of Animation Resort, $$

Disney's Contemporary Resort, $$$$

Nickelodeon Suites Resort, $$

BEST POOLS

Hyatt Regency Grand Cypress Resort, $$

JW Marriott Orlando Grande Lakes, $$$

Loews Portofino Bay Hotel at Universal Orlando, $$$$

Ritz-Carlton Orlando, Grande Lakes, $$$$

BEST FOR BUSINESS

DoubleTree by Hilton at the Entrance to Universal Orlando, $

Hilton Orlando, $$

Hyatt Place Orlando/Universal, $$

Hyatt Regency Orlando, $$$

Westin Orlando Universal Boulevard, $$

BEST SERVICE

Four Seasons, $$$$

Hyatt Regency Orlando, $$$

Orlando World Center Marriott, $$

Ritz-Carlton Orlando, Grande Lakes, $$$$

Waldorf Astoria Orlando, $$$$

BEST NEW HOTELS

Aloft Orlando Downtown, $$

Four Seasons, $$$$

Universal's Cabana Bay Beach Resort, $$

BEST-KEPT SECRET

CoCoKey Hotel & Water Resort, $

The Florida Hotel & Conference Center, $

Floridays Resort Orlando, $$$

Staybridge Suites Lake Buena Vista, $$

BEST FOR COUPLES

The Alfond Inn, $$

Four Seasons, $$$$

Hyatt Regency Grand Cypress Resort, $$

Loews Portofino Bay Hotel, $$$$

Walt Disney World Dolphin, $$$

BEST FOR MIXED GROUPS (I.E., MULTIGENERATION)

Caribe Royale, $

Hard Rock Hotel, $$$$

Holiday Inn Lake Buena Vista, $

JW Marriott Orlando Grande Lakes, $$$

Renaissance Orlando at SeaWorld, $$

BEST FITNESS ROOM

Disney's Saratoga Springs Resort & Spa, $$$$

Hard Rock Hotel, $$$$

Hyatt Regency Orlando, $$

Orlando World Center Marriott, $$

BEST DINING OPTIONS

Disney's Animal Kingdom Lodge, $$$$

Disney's Grand Floridian, $$$$

Loews Portofino Bay Hotel, $$$$

Rosen Shingle Creek, $$

Wyndham Grand Orlando Resort, Bonnet Creek, $$

BEST VIEWS

Buena Vista Palace Hotel & Spa, $

Four Seasons, $$$$

Hyatt Regency Grand Cypress Resort, $$

Park Plaza Hotel, $

Rosen Shingle Creek, $$

BEST BUDGET

Avanti Resort, $

The Campsites at Disney's Fort Wilderness Resort, $

Disney's Art of Animation Resort, $$

Drury Inn & Suites, $

Staybridge Suites Lake Buena Vista, $$

8

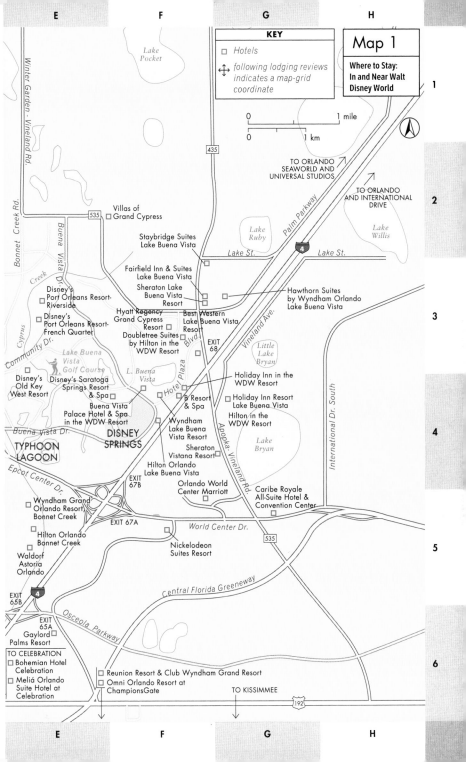

Cons: no direct bus to Magic Kingdom; no monorail. [$] *Rooms from: $431* ✉ *901 Timberline Dr.* ☎ *407/824–3200* ⊕ *www.disneyworld. disney.go.com/resorts* ↘ *727 rooms, 31 suites* ⦾ *No meals* ✛ *1:B1.*

EPCOT RESORT AREA

Take I–4 Exit 64B or 65.

From the Epcot resorts, you can walk or take a boat to the International Gateway entrance to Epcot, which deposits you right in the middle of the lands, or you can take the shuttle from your hotel or drive to the Future World (front) entrance.

$$ ⚇ **Disney's Art of Animation Resort.** This brightly colored, three-story resort
RESORT is a kid's version of paradise: each of its four wings features images from
FAMILY *Finding Nemo, Cars, The Lion King,* or *The Little Mermaid,* and in-room linens and carpeting match the wing's theme. **Pros:** direct transportation to airport; free parking; images that kids adore; free Wi-Fi. **Cons:** can be crowded; standard rooms fill up fast. [$] *Rooms from: $197* ✉ *1850 Animation Way* ☎ *407/938–7000* ⊕ *www.disneyworld.disney. go.com/resorts* ↘ *1,984 rooms, 1,120 suites* ⦾ *No meals* ✛ *1:D5.*

$$$$ ⚇ **Disney's Beach Club Villas.** Each villa in this pale-turquoise-and-white
RESORT waterfront area next to the Yacht and Beach Club Resorts has a separate living room, kitchen, and one or two bedrooms, offering families plenty of room, along with easy access to Disney's Boardwalk and boats to Epcot. **Pros:** short walk to the BoardWalk area and Epcot; regular ferries to Epcot and Hollywood Studios; in-suite kitchens let you save money on meals; free Wi-Fi. **Cons:** boat traffic can be noisy; not close to Magic or Animal Kingdoms. [$] *Rooms from: $513* ✉ *1800 Epcot Resorts Blvd.* ☎ *407/934–8000* ⊕ *www.disneyworld.disney.go.com/ resorts* ↘ *576 units* ⦾ *No meals* ✛ *1:C4.*

$$$$ ⚇ **Disney's BoardWalk Inn.** Harking back to Atlantic City in its heyday,
RESORT the striking red-and-white hotel has a wood-floored lobby filled with potted palms and looks out on a classic waterfront promenade, where ferries and water taxis tootle about the bay, the smell of pretzels and popcorn hangs in the air, and hawkers call you to arcade games. **Pros:** casual, upscale atmosphere; lots of activities just outside the door, including Epcot; free Wi-Fi. **Cons:** pricey; long bus ride to Magic Kingdom; pool can get crowded; boat whistles can intrude if you have a waterfront room. [$] *Rooms from: $553* ✉ *2101 Epcot Resorts Blvd.* ☎ *407/939–5100* ⊕ *www.disneyworld.disney.go.com/resorts* ↘ *372 rooms* ⦾ *No meals* ✛ *1:C4.*

$$$ ⚇ **Disney's Caribbean Beach Resort.** A series of palm-studded "villages,"
RESORT awash in dizzying pastels and labeled with names straight from Pirates
FAMILY of the Caribbean, makes this moderately priced Disney resort perfect for tweens smitten with Jack Sparrow. **Pros:** plenty of on-site outdoor activities give the place a lush summer-camp feel; convenient to Epcot, Disney's Hollywood Studios, and Downtown Disney. **Cons:** you don't truly feel swept away to a tropical island; the beach is for sitting on, as the only swimmable waters are in the pools, not the lake; walks from your room to the beach or a restaurant can take up to 15 minutes. [$] *Rooms*

Disney's Animal Kingdom Lodge

from: $273 ⊠ *900 Cayman Way* ☎ *407/934–3400* ⊕ *www.disneyworld. disney.go.com/resorts* ⤴ *2,112 rooms* ❍ No meals ✛ 1:D4.

$$$$
RESORT
⛼ **Disney's Yacht Club and Beach Club Resorts.** These big Crescent Lake inns next door to Epcot seem straight out of a Cape Cod summer, with their nautical decor, waterfront locale, airy, light-filled rooms, rocking-chair porches, and family-friendly water-based activities. **Pros:** location, location, location—it's easy to walk or hop a ferry to Epcot, the BoardWalk, or Hollywood Studios; free Wi-Fi. **Cons:** distances within the hotel—like from your room to the front desk—can seem vast; remote from other parks. $ *Rooms from: $560* ⊠ *1700 Epcot Resorts Blvd.* ☎ *407/934–8000 Beach Club, 407/934–7000 Yacht Club* ⊕ *www.disneyworld.disney.go.com/resorts* ⤴ *1,213 rooms, 112 suites* ❍ No meals ✛ 1:C4.

ANIMAL KINGDOM RESORT AREA

Take I–4 Exit 64B.

In the park's southwest corner, Disney's third resort area comprises a mix of high-end, moderate-range, and budget-price complexes.

$
RESORT
⛼ **Disney's All-Star Movies Resort.** Kids will delight in recognizing the scenes and characters from favorite Disney movies that dot the landscape of this large, value-priced resort: *101 Dalmatians* of all sizes scamper along railings; Mickey, in his Sorcerer's Apprentice robes, commands the waters at the *Fantasia* pool, and a larger-than-life Woody cavorts with his *Toy Story* pals. **Pros:** familiar characters and lots of activities to amuse kids; free Wi-Fi; easy access to Animal Kingdom.

Cons: at the opposite end of WDW from Magic Kingdom; food-court dining. ⑤ *Rooms from: $170* ✉ *1901 W. Buena Vista Dr.* ☎ *407/939–7000* ⊕ *www.disneyworld.disney.go.com/resorts/* ➡ *1,920 rooms* ⍥ *No meals* ✣ *1:B6.*

$ ⍨ **Disney's All-Star Music Resort.** Music rules in this colorful, value-priced resort that looks like a Florida beach hotel of the 1950s, with a

RESORT

FAMILY guitar-shaped pool and balcony railings that resemble notated musical staffs. **Pros:** good value for family holidays; free Wi-Fi. **Cons:** suites have sleeper chair and sleeper ottoman; long way to Magic Kingdom. ⑤ *Rooms from: $170* ✉ *1801 W. Buena Vista Dr.* ☎ *407/939–6000* ⊕ *www.disneyworld.disney.go.com/resorts* ➡ *1,704 rooms, 215 family suites* ⍥ *No meals* ✣ *1:B6.*

$ ⍨ **Disney's All-Star Sports Resort.** Stay here if you want the All-American,

RESORT sports-mad, quintessential Disney-with-your-kids experience, or if

FAMILY you're a couple to whom all that pitter-pattering of little feet is a rea-

Fodor's Choice sonable tradeoff for a good deal on a room. **Pros:** unbeatable price for

★ a Disney property; free Wi-Fi. **Cons:** no kids clubs or programs, because this is among the least expensive Disney resorts; distances between rooms and on-site amenities can seem vast; farthest resort from Magic Kingdom means you'll spend time on the bus. ⑤ *Rooms from: $170* ✉ *1701 W. Buena Vista Dr.* ☎ *407/939–5000* ⊕ *www.disneyworld. disney.go.com/resorts* ➡ *1,920 rooms* ⍥ *No meals* ✣ *1:B6.*

$$$$ ⍨ **Disney's Animal Kingdom Lodge.** Giraffes, zebras, and other wild-

RESORT life roam three 11-acre savannas separated by the encircling arms of

FAMILY this grand hotel, designed to resemble a *kraal*, or animal enclosure,

Fodor's Choice in Africa. **Pros:** extraordinary wildlife and cultural experiences; excel-

★ lent on-site restaurants: Jiko, Boma, and Sanaa; breakfast buffet in Boma is a bargain. **Cons:** shuttle to parks other than Animal Kingdom can take more than an hour; guided savanna tours available only to guests on the concierge level, where the least expensive room is $100 a night higher than the least expensive rooms in other parts of the hotel. ⑤ *Rooms from: $467* ✉ *2901 Osceola Pkwy.* ☎ *407/938–3000* ⊕ *www. disneyworld.disney.go.com/resorts* ➡ *972 rooms, 499 suites and villas* ⍥ *No meals* ✣ *1:A5.*

$$$ ⍨ **Disney's Coronado Springs Resort.** Popular with convention-goers who

RESORT need huge meeting spaces, and with families who appreciate its casual

Fodor's Choice Southwestern architecture; lively, Mexican-style food court; and elabo-

★ rate swimming pool, colorful Coronado Springs Resort also offers a moderate price. **Pros:** great pool with a play-area arcade for kids and a bar for adults; lots of outdoor activities, free Wi-Fi. **Cons:** some accommodations are a long trek from the restaurants; standard rooms are on the small side; as in many Disney lakefront properties, the lake is for looking at and boating on, not for swimming in. ⑤ *Rooms from: $251* ✉ *1000 W. Buena Vista Dr.* ☎ *407/939–1000* ⊕ *www.disneyworld. disney.go.com/resorts* ➡ *1,917 rooms* ⍥ *No meals* ✣ *1:B4.*

DOWNTOWN DISNEY RESORT AREA

Take I–4 Exit 64B or 68.

The Downtown Disney–Lake Buena Vista resort area, east of Epcot, has a variety of inexpensive, mid-price, and upscale hotels—some Disney owned, others not—all of which offer shuttles to the Disney parks.

$
RESORT
B Resort & Spa Lake Buena Vista. The white-and-blue tower of the B Resort on Hotel Plaza Boulevard, formerly the Royal Plaza, is the most recent addition to the cluster of hotels just outside Downtown Disney, and a stay there combines an excellent location with a reasonable price. **Pros:** walk to Downtown Disney; kids' activities; park shuttles. **Cons:** resort fee; parking fee; need a car to get to Universal or Downtown Orlando. $ *Rooms from: $152* ✉ *1905 Hotel Plaza Blvd.* ☎ *407/828–2828* ⊕ *www.bhotelsandresorts.com/b-walt-disney-world/* ⤷ *394 rooms 12 suites* ⏐◯⏐ *No meals* ✛ *1:F4.*

$$$$
RESORT
Disney's Old Key West Resort. Villas and studios resembling turn-of-the-20th-century Key West houses have full kitchens, white and pastel clapboard siding, delicate ornamental woodwork, and private balconies that overlook the waterways and golf fairways winding through the grounds. **Pros:** quiet and romantic; full kitchens in villas; accommodations with whirlpool baths; laundry facilities. **Cons:** long walks between rooms and restaurants, recreation facilities, bus stops; bus service to parks can be frustrating. $ *Rooms from: $431* ✉ *1510 N. Cove Rd.* ☎ *407/827–7700* ⊕ *www.disneyworld.disney.go.com/resorts* ⤷ *761 units* ⏐◯⏐ *No meals* ✛ *1:E3.*

$$
HOTEL
Disney's Port Orleans Resort–French Quarter. Ornate, Big Easy–style row houses with wrought-iron balconies cluster around magnolia- and oak-shaded squares in this relatively quiet resort, which appeals to couples more than families. **Pros:** authentic—or as authentic as Disney can make it—fun, New Orleans–style; moderate price; lots of water recreation options, including boat rentals; free Wi-Fi. **Cons:** even though there are fewer kids here, public areas can still be quite noisy; shuttle service is slow; food court is the only on-site dining option. $ *Rooms from: $246* ✉ *1251 Riverside Dr.* ☎ *407/934–5000* ⊕ *www.disneyworld.disney. go.com/resorts* ⤷ *1,008 rooms* ⏐◯⏐ *No meals* ✛ *1:E3.*

$$
RESORT
Disney's Port Orleans Resort–Riverside. Buildings in this family-friendly, moderately priced resort look like Southern plantation–style mansions (in the Magnolia Bend section) and rustic bayou dwellings (in the Alligator Bayou section), and you can usually pick which section you want. **Pros:** carriage rides; river cruises; lots of recreation options for kids. **Cons:** shuttle to parks can be slow; no shortage of noisy youngsters. $ *Rooms from: $246* ✉ *1251 Riverside Dr.* ☎ *407/934–6000* ⊕ *www. disneyworld.disney.go.com/resorts* ⤷ *2,048 rooms* ⏐◯⏐ *No meals* ✛ *1:E3.*

$$$$
RESORT
Disney's Saratoga Springs Resort & Spa. This sprawling Disney Vacation Club property takes its inspiration from 19th-century horse-and-spa resorts in upstate New York, where hot springs and lakes ruled the landscape, and mixes it with the more tropical feel of Florida. **Pros:** water taxis whisk you to Downtown Disney; kitchens can shave down the food bill; in-room massage available; abundance of rooms with

8

Top Spas

If you hit the ground running after arriving in Orlando, at some point you may need to shift your pace from "fast forward" to "pause." If so, head directly to one of Orlando's resort spas. The area has enough standout pampering palaces to indulge every theme park–weary parent, aching golfer, parched sunbather, and Disney princess.

Each of Orlando's resort spas is known for something special, whether it's the Balinese four-hand massage at the Mandara at Portofino Bay or customized therapies at the Waldorf. Several spas draw on Florida's citrus-producing region to offer refreshing orange, grapefruit, and lime therapies. And you can go global with massage techniques from Japan, Thailand, Polynesia, and Sweden.

Families who want to stay together can even spa together at treatment centers specializing in youth facials, massages, and manicure/pedicure (aka mani/pedi) packages. The Ritz-Carlton Orlando treats kids like royalty with manicures, pedicures, and facials. Disney's Senses Spas at Saratoga Springs and the Grand Floridian offer Magical Manicures and Princess Pedicures.

Make your spa excursion special by planning enough time to use complimentary whirlpools, saunas, and steam rooms. Most spas offer free access to impressively equipped fitness centers and relaxation rooms stocked with herbal teas, fresh fruits, and other goodies. Book treatments early, and ask about gratuities—often 18% to 20%—which may or may not be included in your treatment or package.

TOP SPAS

Blue Harmony, Downtown Disney Resort Area

Portofino Bay Mandara Spa, Portofino Bay Resort, Universal Orlando

Ritz-Carlton Orlando, Grande Lakes Spa, South Orlando

Senses Spa, Disney's Saratoga Springs Resort, Downtown Disney Resort Area

Senses Spa, Grand Floridian Resort, Magic Kingdom Resort Area

The Spa at Hilton Orlando, International Drive, Orlando The Spa at Rosen Centre, International Drive, Orlando

whirlpool baths. **Cons:** it's a fair hike from some accommodations to the restaurant and other facilities; one bar and grill restaurant. $ *Rooms from: $431* ⊠ *1960 Broadway* ☎ *407/934–7639* ⊕ *www.disneyworld. disney.go.com/resorts* ⤳ *924 units* ❍| *No meals* ✛ *1:F4.*

OTHER ON-SITE DISNEY HOTELS

Although not operated by the Disney organization, the Four Seasons, the Swan and the Dolphin, just outside Epcot; Shades of Green, near the Magic Kingdom; and the hotels along Hotel Plaza Boulevard near Downtown Disney call themselves "official" Walt Disney World hotels. Whereas the Four Seasons, Swan, Dolphin, and Shades of Green have the special privileges of on-site Disney hotels, such as free transportation to and from the parks and early park entry, the Downtown

Disney resorts may use Disney transportation, but don't have all the same perks.

MAGIC KINGDOM RESORT AREA

Take I–4 Exit 62, 64B, or 65.

$ **Shades of Green.** Operated by the U.S. Armed Forces Recreation Cen-
HOTEL   ter, this resort in the heart of Disney is open only to active-duty and retired personnel from the armed forces, reserves, and National Guard; active civilian employees of the Department of Defense; widows or widowers of service members; disabled veterans; and Medal of Honor recipients. **Pros:** large standard rooms; on Disney's shuttle bus line; Army–Air Force Exchange store discounts deeply for people with military IDs. **Cons:** prices vary based on rank. **$** *Rooms from: $125* ⊠ *1905 W. Magnolia Palm Dr.* ☎ *407/824–3600, 888/593–2242* ⊕ *www. shadesofgreen.org* ⚓ *585 rooms, 12 suites* ⦿ *No meals* ✛ *1:A2.*

EPCOT RESORT AREA

Take I–4 Exit 64B or 65.

$$$$ **Four Seasons.** The award-winning Four Seasons presides majestically
RESORT   over Disney's exclusive Golden Oak community, and its amenities and dedication to service are clear from the moment you step into the marble, flower-bedecked lobby and head for your room, which offers the option of separate quarters for nannies and/or grannies, and twice-daily housekeeping service. **Pros:** free Wi-Fi; free transportation to Disney parks; lots of on-site kids' entertainment; no resort fee. **Cons:** pricey, but then, it is the Four Seasons; long way from Universal or SeaWorld. **$** *Rooms from: $479* ⊠ *10100 Dream Tree Blvd.* ☎ *407/313–7777* ⊕ *www.fourseasons.com/orlando* ⚓ *443 rooms* ⦿ *No meals* ✛ *1:D2.*

$$$ **Walt Disney World Dolphin.** A pair of 56-foot-tall sea creatures book-
RESORT   ends this 25-story glass pyramid, a luxe resort designed, like the adjoining Swan, by world-renowned architect Michael Graves, and close enough to the parks that you can escape the midday heat for a dip in the pool. **Pros:** character meals available; access to all facilities at the Swan; free boat to BoardWalk, Epcot, and Hollywood Studios, buses to other parks; excellent on-site restaurants; MyMagic+ benefits available. **Cons:** daily self-parking fee; a daily resort fee; no charging to room key at parks. **$** *Rooms from: $335* ⊠ *1500 Epcot Resorts Blvd.* ☎ *407/934–4000, 800/227–1500* ⊕ *www.swandolphin.com* ⚓ *1,509 rooms, 114 suites* ⦿ *No meals* ✛ *1:C4.*

$$$ **Walt Disney World Swan.** With Epcot and Hollywood Studios close by,
RESORT   guests here can hit the parks in the morning, return for a swim or nap on a hot afternoon, and go back to the parks refreshed and ready to play until the fireworks. **Pros:** easy walk to BoardWalk; free boats to BoardWalk, Epcot, and Hollywood Studios; good on-site restaurants; MyMagic+ available. **Cons:** long bus ride to Magic Kingdom; daily resort and parking fee. **$** *Rooms from: $315* ⊠ *1200 Epcot Resorts Blvd.* ☎ *407/934–3000, 800/325–3535* ⊕ *www.swandolphin.com* ⚓ *758 rooms, 55 suites* ⦿ *No meals* ✛ *1:C4.*

8

DOWNTOWN DISNEY RESORT AREA

Take I–4 Exit 68.

$ 🖭 **Best Western Lake Buena Vista Resort.** Only a few minutes' walk from
RESORT Downtown Disney growing number of shops and restaurants, this tow-
FodorsChoice ering resort with its airy lobby offers luxury linens, flat-screen TVs,
★ and, in many rooms, a bird's-eye view of the fireworks, all for a bargain price. **Pros:** a quick walk to shopping and restaurants; free transportation to parks, discount shops. **Cons:** inconvenient to Universal
and Downtown Orlando; transportation to the parks can eat up time.
🕏 *Rooms from: $119* ⊠ *2000 Hotel Plaza Blvd.* ☎ *407/828–2424,
800/348–3765* ⊕ *www.lakebuenavistaresorthotel.com* ⍳ *325 rooms,
8 suites* ⎮○⎮ *No meals* ✛ *1:F3.*

$ 🖭 **Buena Vista Palace Hotel & Spa.** This towering hotel, just yards from
RESORT Downtown Disney, caters to business and leisure guests and gets kudos
as much for its on-site amenities as for its location. **Pros:** easy walk to
Downtown Disney; good restaurants and bars on-site; kids' activities;
pool is heated; spa is large and luxurious. **Cons:** inconvenient to Universal and Downtown Orlando; daily resort fee for Wi-Fi and fitness center. 🕏 *Rooms from: $164* ⊠ *1900 E. Buena Vista Dr.* ☎ *407/827–2727*
⊕ *www.buenavistapalace.com* ⍳ *1,014 rooms* ⎮○⎮ *No meals* ✛ *1:F4.*

$$ 🖭 **DoubleTree Suites by Hilton in the WDW Resort.** Price and location make
HOTEL this all-suites, Hilton-owned hotel a good choice for families and busi-
ness travelers, as there are amenities for both, and it's a quick, free bus
ride to any of the Disney parks. **Pros:** family and business traveler ame-
nities; restaurants on-site; adult pool and splash pad for kids, adults;
free shuttle to Disney attractions; quick access to Interstate 4. **Cons:**
of the properties on Hotel Plaza Blvd., this is the farthest away from
Downtown Disney; inconvenient to Universal and Downtown Orlando;
daily fee for parking, Wi-Fi. 🕏 *Rooms from: $199* ⊠ *2305 Hotel Plaza
Blvd.* ☎ *407/934–1000, 800/222–8733* ⊕ *www.doubletreeguestsuites.
com* ⍳ *229 units* ⎮○⎮ *No meals* ✛ *1:F3.*

$ 🖭 **Hilton Orlando Lake Buena Vista.** While this hotel offers full service to
HOTEL business travelers, families are not neglected, with scheduled Disney
character breakfasts every Sunday and extended theme park hours.
Pros: ergonomic work stations; 24-hour health club; character break-
fasts; free transporation to Disney parks. **Cons:** pricey resort fee, but it
includes Wi-Fi, movie rentals, coffee or water, and local and domestic
phone calls; parking fee; need a car to get to Universal and Downtown
Orlando. 🕏 *Rooms from: $169* ⊠ *1751 Hotel Plaza Blvd.* ☎ *407/827–
4000, 800/782–4414 reservations* ⊕ *www.hilton.com* ⍳ *814 rooms,
27 suites* ⎮○⎮ *No meals* ✛ *1:F4.*

$ 🖭 **Holiday Inn Lake Buena Vista.** The very modern lobby, with its glass-
HOTEL roofed, kite-filled tower atrium, muted colors, contemporary furnish-
ings, and linen sheers over floor-to-ceiling windows, is typical of the
hotel's low-key elegance; but elegance doesn't mean hidden charges, as
this hotel specializes in free stuff: free Wi-Fi, no resort fee, free break-
fast, and kids under 12 eat free breakfast, lunch, and dinner when with
parents. **Pros:** no resort fee; walking distance to Disney shopping; free
transportation to all Disney parks; free Wi-Fi. **Cons:** no free shuttle to
Universal or SeaWorld; daily parking fee; need a car to get to Orlando.

⑤ *Rooms from: $149* ✉ *1805 Hotel Plaza Blvd.* ☎ *407/828–8888, 888/465–4329* ⊕ *www.hiorlando.com* ⤵ *323 rooms* ⚟ *Breakfast* ✛ *1:G4.*

$ ⛱ **Wyndham Lake Buena Vista Resort.** Any hotel within a skip and a hop
RESORT   of Downtown Disney is a great draw, and one with a water-playground complex that can entice kids away from the Magic Kingdom during the midday heat is even better. **Pros:** good kids' programs; great views; free shuttle to all Disney parks and attractions. **Cons:** daily resort fee for parking, Wi-Fi, gym; inconvenient to Universal and Downtown Orlando. ⑤ *Rooms from: $149* ✉ *1850 Hotel Plaza Blvd.* ☎ *407/828–4444* ⊕ *www.wyndhamlakebuenavista.com* ⤵ *619 rooms, 7 suites* ⚟ *No meals* ✛ *1:F4.*

UNIVERSAL ORLANDO AREA

Take I–4 Exit 74B or 75A.

Universal Orlando's on-site hotels were built in a little luxury enclave that has everything you need, so you never have to leave Universal property. In minutes, you can walk from any hotel to CityWalk, Universal's dining and entertainment district, or take a ferry that cruises the adjacent artificial river.

The newest Universal lodging, Cabana Bay Beach Resort, with 900 family suites and 900 standard rooms, is so close to Islands of Adventure, you may see the spires of Hogwarts Castle from your room. This more affordable, motor court–style resort is designed to evoke 20th-century driving vacations with a hip, retro look.

A burgeoning hotel district across Kirkman Road and down to Sand Lake Road offers convenient accommodations and some even less expensive rates. Although these off-property hotels don't have the perks of the on-site places, you'll probably be smiling when you see your hotel bill.

$ ⛱ **Comfort Suites Universal Studios Area.** If Universal's roller coasters and
HOTEL   Diagon Alley are your destinations, these homey accommodations just outside the park should fit the bill. **Pros:** free hot breakfast; free Wi-Fi; free parking; free shuttle to Universal and SeaWorld. **Cons:** a bit of a hike to shops, restaurants; long way to Disney parks; no on-site full-service restaurant or room service. ⑤ *Rooms from: $119* ✉ *5617 Major Blvd.* ☎ *407/363–1967, 800/951–7829* ⊕ *www.comfortsuites.com* ⤵ *150 suites* ⚟ *Breakfast* ✛ *2:D1.*

$ ⛱ **DoubleTree by Hilton at the Entrance to Universal Orlando.** The name is a
HOTEL   mouthful, but it's an accurate description for this hotel, which caters to business-trippers and pleasure seekers alike, thanks to a location close to the Universal Orlando entrance and not far from the Convention Center. **Pros:** three on-site restaurants; within walking distance of Universal, shops, and restaurants; free shuttle to Universal; on I-Drive trolley route; free Wi-Fi. **Cons:** fee for parking; on a fast-lane tourist strip; need a car to reach Disney and Downtown Orlando. ⑤ *Rooms from: $149* ✉ *5780 Major Blvd.* ☎ *407/351–1000, 800/327–2110* ⊕ *www.doubltreeorlando.com* ⤵ *742 rooms, 19 suites* ⚟ *No meals* ✛ *2:D1.*

8

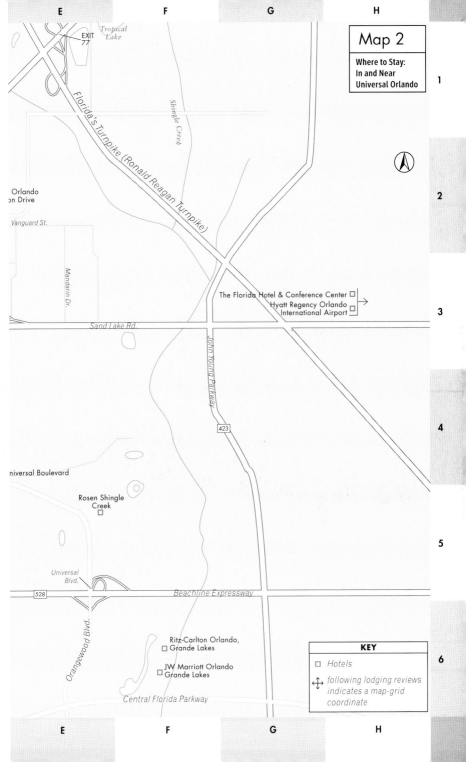

$ ☐ **Drury Inn & Suites Orlando.** This reasonably priced, centrally located
HOTEL   hotel is really shaking up the competition in Orlando with free Wi-Fi,
Fodor'sChoice   free parking, free hot breakfast, free long-distance and local phone
★   calls, and free hot food and cold beverages in the late afternoon. **Pros:**
free everything; central location; reasonable price. **Cons:** if Disney is
your destination, this might be a little far afield. $ *Rooms from: $129*
✉ *7301 W. Sand Lake Rd., at I–4* ☎ *407/354–1101* ⊕ *www.druryhotels.
com* ⤳ *238 rooms* ⫴❍⫼ *Some meals* ✛ *2:C3.*

$$$$ ☐ **Hard Rock Hotel.** Music rules in this mission-style building, from the
HOTEL   darkly amusing *Hotel California* quote above the entrance, "You can
check out any time you like. But you can never leave," to public areas
decorated with rock memorabilia, including an Elvis jump suit, Madonna's "Like a Prayer" costume, and Elton John's boots.**Pros:** shuttle,
water taxi, or short walk to Universal Parks and CityWalk; preferential
treatment at Universal rides; charge privileges extend to the other on-
property Universal hotels. **Cons:** rooms and meals are pricey; resort
fee for parking, gym, and in-room Wi-Fi; loud rock music in public areas, even the pool, but that's why you're here, right? $ *Rooms
from: $464* ✉ *5800 Universal Blvd.* ☎ *407/503–7625, 800/232–7827*
⊕ *www.hardrockhotelorlando.com* ⤳ *650 rooms, 29 suites* ⫴❍⫼ *No
meals* ✛ *2:D1.*

$$ ☐ **Hyatt Place Orlando/Universal.** Hyatt Place supports tech-savvy guests
HOTEL   in what Hyatt calls the "24/7" lifestyle, which means that essentially
any of the hotel amenities available to guests at 3 in the afternoon are
also on tap at 3 in the morning. **Pros:** walking distance to Universal
as well as a free shuttle; free breakfast, parking, and high-speed Wi-Fi
throughout. **Cons:** no kids' programs or babysitting service; no shuttles
to Disney. $ *Rooms from: $189* ✉ *5895 Caravan Ct.* ☎ *407/351–0627*
⊕ *www.orlandouniversal.place.hyatt.com* ⤳ *151 rooms* ⫴❍⫼ *Breakfast*
✛ *2:D1.*

$$$$ ☐ **Loews Portofino Bay Hotel at Universal Orlando.** The charm and romance
HOTEL   of Portofino, Italy—destination of Europe's rich and famous—are con-
Fodor'sChoice   jured up at this lovely luxury resort, where part of the fun is exploring
★   the waterfront "village" from end to end and not knowing what you'll
find around a corner or down some steps. **Pros:** Italian villa atmosphere;
large spa; restaurants on-site; short walk or ferry ride to CityWalk,
Universal; guests skip lines at Universal rides; kids' activities; shuttles
to SeaWorld. **Cons:** rooms and meals are pricey; daily fee for park-
ing. $ *Rooms from: $479* ✉ *5601 Universal Blvd.* ☎ *407/503–1000,
800/232–7827* ⊕ *www.loewshotels.com/Portofino-Bay-Hotel* ⤳ *750
rooms, 49 suites* ⫴❍⫼ *Breakfast* ✛ *2:D1.*

$$$$ ☐ **Loews Royal Pacific Resort at Universal Orlando.** The entrance—a broad,
RESORT   covered footbridge high above a tropical stream—sets the tone for the
Fodor'sChoice   Pacific Rim theme of this hotel, which lies amid 53 acres of lush shrubs,
★   soaring bamboo, orchids, and palms. **Pros:** preferential treatment and
early admission to Universal; character dining; shuttle to CityWalk
and parks; free Wi-Fi; serene, Zen-garden vibe. **Cons:** rooms can feel
smallish; fees for parking. $ *Rooms from: $404* ✉ *6300 Hollywood
Way* ☎ *407/503–3000, 800/232–7827* ⊕ *www.universalorlando.com*
⤳ *1,000 rooms, 51 suites* ⫴❍⫼ *No meals* ✛ *2:C1.*

Loews Portofino Bay Hotel at Universal Orlando

$$ · RESORT · FAMILY · Fodor's Choice ★ **Universal's Cabana Bay Beach Resort.** Universal's Cabana Bay Beach Resort takes guests back in time to a 1950s Florida beach town with a modern, ironic twist, and offers families a less expensive option to staying on-site at Universal. **Pros:** early and easy access to Universal parks; food court on property; two swimming pools. **Cons:** parking fee; access to Disney or Downtown Orlando requires a car or taxi journey via busy Interstate 4. $ *Rooms from: $199* ✉ *6550 Adventure Way* ☎ *407/503–4000* ⊕ *www.loewshotels.com/Cabana-Bay* ⤴ *900 rooms, 900 suites* ⦙⊙⦙ *No meals* ✛ *2:C2.*

ORLANDO METRO AREA

KISSIMMEE, CELEBRATION, AND POINTS SOUTH

Take I–4 Exit 64A, unless otherwise noted.

If you're looking for quaint, charming, or sophisticated, move on. Kissimmee's U.S. 192 strip—aka the Irlo Bronson Memorial Highway—has undergone a face-lift recently, but it still is primarily a neon-and-plastic swath with bargain-basement motels, fast-food spots, nickel-and-dime attractions, overpriced gas stations, and minimarts. The area nearer Disney has some upscale lodging choices, and there are several good options if LEGOLAND is also on your list.

When Disney was in its infancy, U.S. 192 was the best place to find affordable rooms. But now that budget hotels have cropped up all along I-Drive, you can often find better rooms closer to the theme parks. There are exceptions, however—some of the older hotels have maintained decent standards and kept their prices very tempting.

$$$ ⬚ **Bohemian Hotel Celebration.** Like everything in the Disney-created town
HOTEL of Celebration, this boutique hotel in the middle of the charming village borrows from the best of the 19th, 20th, and 21st centuries. **Pros:** in the heart of Celebration village; rental bikes and golf carts make touring the village a breeze; free shuttle to Celebration Golf and Fitness Center. **Cons:** steep fee for parking; need a car (or lots of cab money) to get anywhere other than Celebration. ⑤ *Rooms from: $314* ✉ *700 Bloom St., Celebration* ☎ *407/566–6000, 888/249–4007* ⊕ *www.celebrationhotel. com* ↘ *115 rooms, 9 suites* ⦿ *No meals* ✛ *1:D6.*

$$ ⬚ **Gaylord Palms Resort and Convention Center.** Built in the style of a grand
RESORT turn-of-the-20th-century Florida resort, this huge building is meant to inspire awe: inside its enormous atrium, covered by a 4-acre glass roof, are re-creations of Florida destination icons such as the Everglades, Key West, and old St. Augustine. **Pros:** you could have a great vacation without ever leaving the grounds; free shuttle to Disney. **Cons:** daily resort and parking fee; rooms can be pricey; not much within walking distance (although the hotel is so big that you can take quite a hike inside the building); shuttles to Universal and SeaWorld are available for a fee. ⑤ *Rooms from: $249* ✉ *6000 W. Osceola Pkwy., I–4 Exit 65, Kissimmee* ☎ *407/586–0000* ⊕ *www.gaylordpalms.com* ↘ *1,406 rooms, 86 suites* ⦿ *No meals* ✛ *1:E6.*

$$ ⬚ **Meliá Orlando Suite Hotel at Celebration.** Much like a European boutique
HOTEL hotel in style, the Meliá Orlando is very human in scale, minimalist in decor, and is only minutes from Disney. **Pros:** shuttle to Celebration, Disney parks, Universal, and SeaWorld; golf privileges at Celebration Golf; spa privileges at Celebration Day Spa. **Cons:** busy U.S. 192 is close by; daily resort fee; need a car to go anywhere besides Celebration and the parks. ⑤ *Rooms from: $199* ✉ *225 Celebration Pl., Celebration* ☎ *866/404–6662, 407/964–7000* ⊕ *www.solmelia.com* ↘ *240 suites* ⦿ *Breakfast* ✛ *1:D6.*

$$$ ⬚ **Omni Orlando Resort at ChampionsGate.** This huge Mediterranean-
RESORT style award-winning resort just 6 miles south of Disney, and within a 45-minute drive of LEGOLAND, includes a 1,200-acre golf club with two Greg Norman–designed courses, a David Leadbetter academy, and multi–playing field complex. **Pros:** Mokara spa; huge, water-park-style pool; five restaurants ranging from a casual café to upscale dining; golf school and two golf courses. **Cons:** remote location; daily resort fee for Internet, shuttles, gym; separate daily fee for parking. ⑤ *Rooms from: $269* ✉ *I–4 Exit 58, 1500 Masters Blvd., south of Kissimmee, ChampionsGate* ☎ *407/390–6664, 800/843–6664* ⊕ *www.omniorlandoresort. com* ↘ *720 rooms, 35 suites, 57 villas* ⦿ *Breakfast* ✛ *1:E6.*

$$$ ⬚ **Reunion Resort a Wyndham Grand Resort.** This 2,300-acre resort built
RESORT on the rolling hills of a former orange grove, 10 miles southwest of
FAMILY Disney and 45 minutes from LEGOLAND, contains three private golf courses designed by Tom Watson, Arnold Palmer, and Jack Nicklaus, along with villas and homes designed and decorated to satisfy the most discerning guest. **Pros:** secluded, upscale atmosphere; golf galore; supermarkets and drugstores within a mile; concierge grocery delivery;

excellent restaurants on-site; free Internet and parking. **Cons:** daily resort fee; remote; about a 10-mile drive to Disney parks; no theme-park shuttles, so you'll need a car. ⑤ *Rooms from: $260* ✉ *7593 Gathering Dr., I–4 Exit 58, Reunion* ☎ *407/396–3200, 866/880–8563* ⊕ *www.reunionresort.com* ⤳ *250 villas, 75 homes* |◯| *Breakfast* ✛ *1:E6.*

INTERNATIONAL DRIVE

Take I–4 Exit 72, 74A, or 75A.

The sprawl of hotels, time-shares, restaurants, malls, and dozens of small attractions known as International Drive—"I-Drive" to locals—makes a central base for visits to Walt Disney World, Universal, Sea-World, and other Orlando attractions. Parallel to Interstate 4, this four-lane boulevard stretches from Universal in the north to Kissimmee in the south.

If you're planning a day visiting I-Drive attractions, consider the I-Ride Trolley, which travels the length of I-Drive from Florida's Turnpike to the outlet center on Vineland Avenue, stopping at Universal Orlando, Wet 'n Wild, and SeaWorld. I-Ride is a more worthy transportation tool than you might think. Lots of hotels don't offer shuttle service to Disney, even for a fee, but you can take I-Ride to hotels that do offer a fee-based Disney shuttle, which, depending on the size of the family or group, can be cheaper than a cab.

$ 🏨 **Avanti Resort.** Smack-dab in the middle of all the activities on Inter-
RESORT   national Drive, this renovated resort offers families a home away from home with plenty of amenities at a reasonable price. **Pros:** scheduled shuttles to theme parks; complimentary cribs and high chairs; laundry facilities; convenient to I-Drive. **Cons:** daily resort fee, not exorbitant, covers Wi-Fi, parking, shuttles; elevators can be slow for those on top floors. ⑤ *Rooms from: $107* ✉ *8738 International Dr.* ☎ *407/313–0100* ⊕ *www.avantiresort.com* ⤳ *652 rooms* |◯| *No meals* ✛ *2:C4.*

$$ 🏨 **Castle Hotel.** In a bold move from kitsch to classy, this hotel was trans-
HOTEL   formed from a pink-and-purple cartoon castle to a sophisticated refuge of white and silver, filled with art. **Pros:** easy walk to I-Drive eateries and attractions; shuttle to Universal; free parking and Wi-Fi. **Cons:** on a congested stretch of I-Drive; not close to Disney parks. ⑤ *Rooms from: $199* ✉ *8629 International Dr.* ☎ *407/345–1511, 800/952–2785* ⊕ *www.castlehotelorlando.com* ⤳ *214 rooms* |◯| *No meals* ✛ *2:C4.*

$ 🏨 **CocoKey Hotel and Water Resort.** If swimming and sliding are among
HOTEL   your family's top vacation desires, this resort with an on-property 14-slide, three-pool water park (a heated one for adults, a separate one for teens, and a canopy-covered pool for youngsters, where families can relax without fear of sunburn or rain) could be the perfect destination. **Pros:** on-site water park; free Wi-Fi, parking, and shuttle; kids eat free. **Cons:** substantial daily resort fee; some rooms overlook noisy pools; water park closed some days in winter; on a busy stretch of I-Drive. ⑤ *Rooms from: $78* ✉ *7400 International Dr.* ☎ *407/351–2626* ⊕ *www.cocokeyorlando.com* ⤳ *391 rooms* |◯| *Some meals* ✛ *2:C3.*

$$ 🏨 **DoubleTree by Hilton Orlando at SeaWorld.** On 28 acres near the Con-
RESORT   vention Center, this hotel with Bali-inspired decor combines low

bungalow-style buildings and a 17-story tower, and offers families and conventioneers a warm welcome and a comforting escape from hectic I-Drive. **Pros:** on-site miniature golf; free theme-parks shuttles and Wi-Fi; allergy-free rooms without carpet available. **Cons:** fee for parking; few shops and restaurants within walking distance. $ *Rooms from: $189* ✉ *10100 International Dr.* ☎ *407/352–1100, 800/327–0363* ⊕ *www.doubletreeorlandoseaworld.com* ⤳ *1,094 rooms, 35 suites* ❘O❘ *Breakfast* ✢ *2:D6.*

$ 🖫 **Embassy Suites Orlando International Drive South Convention Center.** An
HOTEL   airy, eight-story atrium with palm trees and fountains lends an air of luxury to this moderately priced all-suites lodging, which offers free shuttles to all theme parks as well as free breakfast, late-afternoon drinks, and parking. **Pros:** easy walk to Convention Center, shopping, and dining; free shuttle to theme parks; free breakfast and afternoon cocktails; free parking. **Cons:** on congested stretch of I-Drive; daily Wi-Fi charge in rooms. $ *Rooms from: $169* ✉ *8978 International Dr.* ☎ *407/352–1400, 800/433–7275* ⊕ *www.embassysuitesorlando. com* ⤳ *244 suites* ❘O❘ *Breakfast* ✢ *2:C4.*

$$$ 🖫 **Floridays Resort Orlando.** This pleasant, two- and three-bedroom
RESORT   condo resort is about halfway between Universal Orlando and Disney World, with six six-story buildings, two pools, a game room, gym, business center, and café with room service. **Pros:** great, self-contained environment for a family vacation; shuttles to all theme parks; on the I-Ride trolley route. **Cons:** a car would be helpful, as it's too far to walk to almost anything meaningful; daily resort fee for Wi-Fi, parking, shuttles. $ *Rooms from: $255* ✉ *12562 International Dr.* ☎ *407/238–7700* ⊕ *www.floridaysresort.com* ⤳ *432 units* ❘O❘ *No meals* ✢ *2:C6.*

$ 🖫 **Four Points by Sheraton Orlando Studio City.** With a hard-to-miss giant
HOTEL   ball perched on top of its 20-story round tower, this hotel on the north end of International Drive is visible for blocks, and has a contemporary atmosphere, thanks to the clean, airy design of the lobby and guest rooms. **Pros:** convenient to Universal, SeaWorld, and Wet 'n Wild; shuttle to Disney, Universal; great views from upper floors. **Cons:** located on a busy stretch of I-Drive; daily resort fee for Wi-Fi, parking, park shuttles, etc. $ *Rooms from: $129* ✉ *5905 International Dr.* ☎ *407/351–2100, 800/327–1366* ⊕ *www.fourpoints.com* ⤳ *301 rooms* ❘O❘ *Breakfast* ✢ *2:D2.*

$$ 🖫 **Hilton Orlando.** Families visiting this award-winning hotel get two
HOTEL   pools, a palm-fringed lazy river to relax in, a kids' club, basketball court, tennis court, full-service spa, and a shuttle to SeaWorld; conventioneers, on the other hand, appreciate the vast meeting space, direct connection to the Convention Center, substantial restaurants and bars, work desks with Herman Miller chairs, and an on-site steak house, Spencers. **Pros:** three pools; shuttle to SeaWorld; direct walkway to Convention Center. **Cons:** about 80% of guests are conventioneers; no free shuttle to Disney World or Universal; daily resort fee; parking fee. $ *Rooms from: $189* ✉ *6001 Destination Pkwy.* ☎ *407/313–4300* ⊕ *www.thehiltonorlando.com* ⤳ *1,417 rooms, 53 suites* ❘O❘ *Breakfast* ✢ *2:D5.*

$ ⊡ **Hyatt Place Orlando/Convention Center.** Youngish, high-tech-consuming
HOTEL business travelers and vacationing families find value here because of the
location and amenities, such as 42-inch flat-panel HDTVs, work areas
with computer access panel, wet bar with minifridge, and heated pool.
Pros: free parking, Wi-Fi, and hot breakfast; convenient to Convention
Center, shopping, restaurants, and nightlife. **Cons:** no kids' program
or babysitting services; no theme-park shuttles. $ *Rooms from: $139*
✉ *8741 International Dr.* ☎ *407/370–4720, 888/492–8847* ⊕ *www.
orlandoconventioncenter.place.hyatt.com* ⤳ *149 rooms* ⦿ *Breakfast*
✛ *2:D4.*

$$$ ⊡ **Hyatt Regency Orlando.** This deluxe high-rise conference hotel, for-
RESORT merly the Peabody, offers anything a full-service resort customer could
want, with richly appointed rooms, two pools with cabanas, a full-
service spa and fitness center the size of your local Y, two large restau-
rants, and a 360-seat, glass-walled lounge overlooking the pool. **Pros:**
good spa; close to shops and more restaurants, on I-Drive Trolley route.
Cons: check-in can take a while if a convention is arriving; long walk
from end to end; daily resort and parking fees. $ *Rooms from: $299*
✉ *9801 International Dr.* ☎ *407/284–1234* ⊕ *www.orlando.regency.
hyatt.com* ⤳ *1,639 rooms, 192 suites, 5 penthouse suites* ⦿ *No meals*
✛ *2:C5.*

$ ⊡ **Parc Corniche Condominium Suite Hotel.** Set back from traffic on the
HOTEL south end of International Drive, this condo hotel offers a good deal
for a family who loves golf and theme parks, offering recently upgraded
suites with separate bedrooms, flat-screen TVs, and updated kitchens
and bathrooms. **Pros:** great for golf lovers; well-equipped kitchens;
free theme-parks shuttle; no resort fee. **Cons:** not much
within walking distance; daily $4 fee for Wi-Fi. $ *Rooms from: $119*
✉ *6300 Parc Corniche Dr.* ☎ *407/239–7100, 800/446–2721* ⊕ *www.
parccorniche.com* ⤳ *210 suites* ⦿ *Breakfast* ✛ *2:C6.*

$ ⊡ **The Point Orlando Resort.** In the center of the entertainment triangle
HOTEL bounded by Interstate 4, Florida's Turnpike, and the Beachline Express-
way, this all-suites resort is a quick walk to Wet 'n Wild and central to
Universal, outlet shopping malls, I-Drive attractions, and the Conven-
tion Center, making it a good option for family vacations, romantic
getaways, and business travel. **Pros:** central to I-Drive entertainment;
Wi-Fi throughout the resort; shuttles to theme parks; breakfast buffet
and light fare in café. **Cons:** no on-site, full-service restaurant; daily
resort fee. $ *Rooms from: $139* ✉ *7389 Universal Blvd.* ☎ *407/956–
2000* ⊕ *www.thepointorlando.com* ⤳ *244 suites* ⦿ *Breakfast* ✛ *2:D3.*

$$ ⊡ **Renaissance Orlando at SeaWorld.** With a vast and airy 10-story atrium
HOTEL full of ponds, palm trees, and, ironically, a sushi bar, this SeaWorld
neighbor offers not rubber duckies in the bath, but tiny black-and-
white Shamus. **Pros:** across from SeaWorld; free shuttles to Universal,
SeaWorld, and Aquatica; on the Lynx bus line to Disney World. **Cons:**
can be a long walk to rooms; many conventioneers; steep resort and
parking fees. $ *Rooms from: $249* ✉ *6677 Sea Harbor Dr.* ☎ *407/351–
5555, 800/468–3571* ⊕ *www.renaissanceseaworld.com* ⤳ *781 rooms,
65 suites* ⦿ *Some meals* ✛ *2:C6.*

$ 🏨 **Residence Inn by Marriott Orlando at SeaWorld.** From the bright, wel-
HOTEL   coming lobby to the well-appointed suites (including dishwasher, micro-
FAMILY   wave, pots, pans, dishes) and the parklike atmosphere around the pool,
Fodor'sChoice   this hotel is a great choice for a family if SeaWorld, Aquatica, I-Drive
★   shopping, Universal, or the Convention Center are on your to-do list.
Pros: free shuttles to all theme parks; well-equipped kitchens; free
breakfast; free Wi-Fi; no resort fee. **Cons:** not much within walking
distance; right next to busy Interstate 4. $ *Rooms from: $174* ⊠ *11000
Westwood Blvd., I–4 Exit 72* ☎ *407/313–3600, 800/889–9728* ⊕ *www.
residenceinnseaworld.com* ⤳ *350 suites* ¶○¶ *Breakfast* ✢ *2:C6.*

$ 🏨 **Rosen Centre Hotel.** Directly across from the Orange County Conven-
RESORT   tion Center, this 24-story resort pleases business customers but doesn't
ignore families: a covered sky-bridge connects the hotel to Convention
Center, and families on vacation or accompanying the conventioneer
have easy access to SeaWorld, Aquatica, and all the I-Drive entertainment complexes. **Pros:** central location; free Wi-Fi; five on-site restaurants; preferred tee times at sister resort Rosen Shingle Creek Golf Club;
free shuttles to Universal, SeaWorld, and Wet 'n Wild. **Cons:** no free
shuttle to Disney; need a car to get anywhere off I-Drive. $ *Rooms from:
$147* ⊠ *9840 International Dr.* ☎ *407/996–9840* ⊕ *www.rosencentre.
com* ⤳ *1,334 rooms, 80 suites* ¶○¶ *No meals* ✢ *2:D5.*

$$ 🏨 **Westin Orlando Universal Boulevard.** Directly across Universal Bou-
HOTEL   levard from the mammoth Orange County Convention Center, this
12-story hotel attracts scores of conventioneers, but its location near
SeaWorld and Universal and only a block from I-Drive makes it a good
choice for families, too. **Pros:** easy walk to Convention Center, Pointe
Orlando, I-Drive; kids' programs. **Cons:** 20–25 minutes from Disney
World; steep daily resort (Internet) and parking fees; conventions bring
crowds. $ *Rooms from: $219* ⊠ *9501 Universal Blvd.* ☎ *407/233–2200*
⊕ *www.westinorlandouniversal.com* ⤳ *315 rooms, 153 suites* ¶○¶ *No
meals* ✢ *2:D5.*

SOUTH ORLANDO

$$$ 🏨 **JW Marriott Orlando Grande Lakes.** This lush resort, set in 500 acres
RESORT   of natural beauty, certainly caters to a convention clientele, but leisure-
seekers and families are given equal attention: a European-style spa, a
Greg Norman–designed golf course, and a lazy river–style pool complex
offer plenty of family fun. **Pros:** pool is great for kids and adults; shares
amenities with the Ritz, including huge spa; golf course; free shuttle to
SeaWorld and Universal. **Cons:** daily resort fees for parking and in-
room Wi-Fi; the resort is huge and spread out; need a car to reach Disney or shopping. $ *Rooms from: $319* ⊠ *4040 Central Florida Pkwy.*
☎ *407/206–2300, 800/576–5750* ⊕ *www.grandelakes.com* ⤳ *1,000
rooms, 64 suites* ¶○¶ *Multiple meal plans* ✢ *2:F6.*

$$$$ 🏨 **Ritz-Carlton Orlando, Grande Lakes.** Orlando's only Ritz-Carlton is
RESORT   a particularly extravagant link in the luxury chain, which shares a
Fodor'sChoice   lush 500-acre campus with the JW Marriott, and offers exemplary ser-
★   vice that extends from the porte-cochere entrance to the 18-hole golf
course, restaurants, children's programs, and 40-room spa. **Pros:** truly
luxurious; impeccable service; great spa; golf course; award-winning

Ritz-Carlton Orlando, Grande Lakes

restaurants; transportation to theme parks. **Cons:** pricey; remote from theme parks, attractions; lots of convention and meeting traffic; resort fee. ⑤ *Rooms from: $579* ✉ *4012 Central Florida Pkwy.* ☎ 407/206–2400, 800/576–5760 ⊕ *www.ritzcarlton.com* ⟿ *582 rooms, 63 suites* ⦿⧄ *Multiple meal plans* ✛ *2:F6.*

$$
RESORT
🏨 **Rosen Shingle Creek.** Sitting amid 230 acres of subtropical landscape, including a cypress-fringed creek and a championship golf course, this award-winning luxury resort offers a golf academy, fishing, nature trails, four swimming pools, basketball and volleyball courts, and a huge spa to soothe those aching muscles. **Pros:** golf course; spa; free shuttle to Universal, SeaWorld, Aquatica; free Wi-Fi; BAGS airport check-in service; self-service coin laundry; variety of excellent restaurant options on-site. **Cons:** expansive grounds mean long walks between on-site amenities; no free shuttle to I-Drive or Disney; daily parking fee. ⑤ *Rooms from: $232* ✉ *9939 Universal Blvd.* ☎ 407/996–9939, 866/996–6338 *reservations* ⊕ *www.rosenshinglecreek.com* ⟿ *1,500 rooms, 109 suites* ⦿⧄ *No meals* ✛ *2:E5.*

LAKE BUENA VISTA

Many people stay in resorts outside the Downtown Disney area because, though equally grand, they tend to be less expensive than those right on Hotel Plaza Boulevard. If you're willing to take a 10-minute drive or shuttle ride, you might save as much as 35% off your room tab.

$
RESORT
🏨 **Caribe Royale All-Suite Hotel & Convention Center.** This big, all-suites pink palace, on 53 tropical acres just 10 minutes from Disney, melds luxurious decor, family-friendly ingredients, business-traveler amenities with

an affordable price. **Pros:** family-friendly; award-winning restaurant; scheduled shuttle to Disney and free shuttle to outlet mall; fitness center; free parking. **Cons:** a hike to other shops and restaurants; no shuttle to Universal or SeaWorld; daily fee for Wi-Fi. ⑤ *Rooms from: $152* ✉ *8101 World Center Dr.* ☎ *407/238–8000, 800/823–8300* ⊕ *www. thecaribehotelsorlando.com* ⤳ *1,218 suites, 120 villas* ⦿ *Breakfast* ✢ *1:G5.*

$ — RESORT

⊞ **Hawthorn Suites by Wyndham Lake Buena Vista Orlando.** A large, marble-columned lobby welcomes guests to this all-suites lodging less than a mile from Disney's door, and the amenities continue into the suites, most with a fully equipped kitchen, living room, and bedroom with multiple TVs. **Pros:** affordable; kitchens; walk to shops; free Disney shuttle; free Wi-Fi and parking; on public bus route. **Cons:** pool area can be noisy; no restaurant; pay shuttle to Universal or SeaWorld. ⑤ *Rooms from: $137* ✉ *8303 Palm Pkwy.* ☎ *407/597–5000, 866/756–3778* ⊕ *www. hawthornlakebuenavista.com* ⤳ *112 suites* ⦿ *Breakfast* ✢ *1:G3.*

$$ — RESORT

⊞ **Hilton Orlando Bonnet Creek.** The Hilton more than lives up to its next-door neighbor the Waldorf Astoria Orlando, with plenty of amenities, including a 3-acre lagoon pool with lazy river, rooms with deluxe bedding, flat-screen TVs, family-friendly activities, and transportation to Disney parks. **Pros:** serene setting, just moments from Disney; golf course and forest views; next door to Waldorf and its amenities; Disney shuttle. **Cons:** nothing within walking distance, so car is helpful; daily parking fee; very steep daily resort fee. ⑤ *Rooms from: $189* ✉ *14100 Bonnet Creek Resort La., Bonnet Creek* ☎ *407/597–3600* ⊕ *www.hiltonbonnetcreek.com* ⤳ *1,000 rooms, 36 suites* ⦿ *Some meals* ✢ *1:E5.*

$$ — RESORT — Fodor's Choice ★

⊞ **Hyatt Regency Grand Cypress Resort.** Sitting amid 1,500 palm-filled acres just outside Disney's back gate, this huge luxury resort hotel has a private lake with watercraft, three golf courses, and miles of trails for strolling, bicycling, jogging, and horseback riding. **Pros:** Marilyn Monroe spa; huge pool; lots of recreation options, for kids and adults, including nearby equestrian center; free Wi-Fi. **Cons:** need a car or taxi to get to Downtown Orlando or Universal; steep resort fee. ⑤ *Rooms from: $249* ✉ *1 Grand Cypress Blvd.* ☎ *407/239–1234, 800/233–1234* ⊕ *www.hyattgrandcypress.com* ⤳ *815 rooms* ⦿ *No meals* ✢ *1:F3.*

$$ — RESORT — FAMILY — Fodor's Choice ★

⊞ **Nickelodeon Suites Resort.** This 24-acre Nickelodeon-themed resort is so kid-friendly that you can barely take a step without bumping into images of SpongeBob, Dora the Explorer, Jimmy Neutron, or other Nick characters. **Pros:** extremely kid-friendly; Disney shuttles included in resort fee; mini-golf course. **Cons:** daily resort fee of $35; not within walking distance of Disney parks or Downtown Disney; way too frenetic for folks without kids. ⑤ *Rooms from: $199* ✉ *14500 Continental Gateway* ☎ *407/387–5437, 866/462–6425* ⊕ *www.nickhotel.com* ⤳ *777 suites* ⦿ *No meals* ✢ *1:F5.*

$$ — RESORT

⊞ **Orlando World Center Marriott.** With 2,009 rooms and 120 suites, this luxury resort is one of Orlando's largest, catering to conventions (nearly a half-million square feet of meeting space) and families. **Pros:** full-service spa; wide variety of on-site eateries; golf course. **Cons:** daily fee for parking, separate daily resort fee for park shuttles and Internet;

on-site restaurants have expense-account-size prices; nothing worth seeing within walking distance. ⑤ *Rooms from: $229* ✉ *8701 World Center Dr.* ☎ *407/239–4200, 800/621–0638* ⊕ *www.marriottworldcenter.com* ↝ *2,009 rooms, 120 suites* ⑩ *Breakfast* ⊹ *1:F5.*

$ 🏨 **Sheraton Lake Buena Vista Resort.** This hotel, conveniently situated near the Downtown Disney entrance to WDW, is a pool-centered oasis of cool, the perfect place to decompress after, or in the middle of, a busy day at the parks. **Pros:** short walk to shops and restaurants; Disney shuttle; small pets allowed, on-site restaurant. **Cons:** on a busy commercial strip; relatively close to Downtown Disney but a tad too far to walk in the summer heat (about 1 mile); resort fee for Wi-Fi, shuttles to parks; parking fee. ⑤ *Rooms from: $149* ✉ *12205 Apopka Vineland Rd.* ☎ *407/239–0444, 800/423–3297* ⊕ *www.starwoodhotels.com* ↝ *486 rooms, 105 suites* ⑩ *Breakfast* ⊹ *1:F3.*

HOTEL

$$ 🏨 **Staybridge Suites Lake Buena Vista.** Just minutes from a Disney entrance, this pleasant all-suites (one- and two-bedroom, two-bath) accommodation is perfect for a big family on a small budget who want a home away from home. **Pros:** free scheduled shuttle service to Disney; free hot breakfast; free Wi-Fi and parking. **Cons:** no restaurant; no shuttles to other parks. ⑤ *Rooms from: $189* ✉ *8751 Suiteside Dr.* ☎ *407/238–0777* ⊕ *www.staybridge.com* ↝ *150 suites* ⑩ *Multiple meal plans* ⊹ *1:F3.*

HOTEL

$$$$ 🏨 **Villas of Grand Cypress.** The serene views from the terraces of this 1,500-acre, award-winning golf resort's villas and suites take in the fairways of the Jack Nicklaus–designed North Course, waterways where migrating birds stop to rest, and lush tropical foliage; you'd never know you were right next door to a busy tourist area. **Pros:** upscale, golf-resort atmosphere; free transportation to all theme parks; in-room Wi-Fi; on-site golf courses; kids' activities at Hyatt. **Cons:** daily resort fee. ⑤ *Rooms from: $455* ✉ *1 N. Jacaranda St.* ☎ *407/239–4700, 800/835–7377* ⊕ *www.grandcypress.com* ↝ *191 units* ⑩ *Some meals* ⊹ *1:F2.*

RESORT

8

$$$$ 🏨 **Waldorf Astoria Orlando.** While it can't duplicate the famed Waldorf Astoria Hotel in New York, this Waldorf echoes the original with imagination and flair, from the iconic clock in the center of the circular lobby to tiny, black-and-white accent tiles on guest room floors. **Pros:** lavish and luxurious hotel with spa and golf, next to Disney; free transportation to Disney parks. **Cons:** pricey, but you knew that; if you can bear to leave your cabana, you'll need a car to see anything else in the area; steep daily resort fee. ⑤ *Rooms from: $559* ✉ *14200 Bonnet Creek Resort La., Bonnet Creek* ☎ *407/597–5500* ⊕ *www.waldorfastoriaorlando.com* ↝ *328 rooms, 169 suites* ⑩ *Breakfast* ⊹ *1:E5.*

RESORT

Fodor'sChoice
★

$$ 🏨 **Wyndham Grand Orlando Resort, Bonnet Creek.** Despite being within Mickey's gates, this family-friendly resort hotel feels serenely remote, as the entrance meanders through pristine Florida forest and bamboo-laden landscaping, creating a sense of distance. **Pros:** practically in Mickey's lap; free shuttles to Disney parks; lots of activities. **Cons:** not convenient to Universal or Downtown Orlando; daily resort fee and parking fee. ⑤ *Rooms from: $239* ✉ *14651 Chelonia Pkwy., Bonnet*

RESORT

Creek ☏ 407/390–2300 ⊕ www.wyndhamgrandorlando.com ⇲ 398 rooms, 2 suites ⦿ Breakfast ✢ 1:E5.

CENTRAL ORLANDO

Take Exit 83B off I–4 westbound, Exit 84 off I–4 eastbound.

Central Orlando, north of Walt Disney World and the I-Drive area, is a thriving business district on weekdays and attracts a club and restaurant crowd on weekend nights.

$$ **Aloft Orlando Downtown.** Just steps from the Dr. Phillips Center
HOTEL for the Performing Arts, the Amway Center, City Hall, and Church Street nightlife, this former utilities building, now an urban hotel in the middle of everything, greets guests with a sparkling lobby, floors of gleaming polished concrete, a busy bar–lounge–meeting place, and innovatively designed rooms. **Pros:** literally steps to Downtown nightlife and arts and sporting events; easy access to highways. **Cons:** if Disney is your destination, it's a 45-minute hike down Interstate 4 to get there; only parking choice is valet or street parking. $ *Rooms from: $219* ✉ *500 S. Orange Ave., Downtown Orlando* ☏ *407/380–3500* ⊕ *www.aloftorlandodowntown.com* ⇲ *118 rooms, 75 suites* ⦿ *No meals* ✢ *3:B3.*

$ ⊞ **The Courtyard at Lake Lucerne.** Four beautifully restored Victorian
B&B/INN   houses surround a palm-lined courtyard within blocks of the Amway
Center and the Dr. Phillips Center for the Performing Arts.**Pros:** great
Victorian architecture; short walk to Downtown restaurants, the
Amway Center, and performing arts center; free parking and Wi-Fi.
Cons: far from theme parks and I-Drive; walking in some parts of
Downtown at night can be a bit dicey. ⑤ *Rooms from: $130* ⊠ *211
N. Lucerne Circle E, Downtown Orlando* ☎ *407/648–5188* ⊕ *www.
orlandohistoricinn.com* ↝ *30 rooms, 10 suites* ❙◯❙ *Breakfast* ✢ *3:B3.*

$$ ⊞ **DoubleTree by Hilton Orlando Downtown.** Just north of Downtown, this
HOTEL   hotel is a gem for business guests, with easy access to the central busi-
ness district, but it doesn't neglect families, who can occupy themselves
at the nearby Orlando Science Center, Museum of Art, and Shakespeare
Theater complex. **Pros:** easy access to Downtown and Interstate 4;
close to museums and nightlife. **Cons:** no kids' program; distance and
traffic between hotel and Disney; parking fee. ⑤ *Rooms from: $209*
⊠ *60 S. Ivanhoe Blvd., Downtown Orlando* ☎ *407/425–4455* ⊕ *www.
doubletreeorlandodowntown.com* ↝ *341 rooms* ❙◯❙ *Breakfast* ✢ *3:B1.*

$$ ⊞ **Embassy Suites Orlando Downtown.** Although designed primarily for
HOTEL   business travelers, this property has nice touches for vacationers, too;
many suites have views overlooking nearby Lake Eola and its centerpiece fountain, swan boats, and jogging path, and the hotel is a short
walk from a half dozen cafés and restaurants, the Orange County History Center, the performing arts center, and the Amway Center with
its NBA basketball games and concerts. **Pros:** near Lake Eola and
Downtown; free Continental breakfast and afternoon beverages; free
Wi-Fi; on-site restaurant; nearby restaurants deliver (front desk has
menus). **Cons:** traffic can be heavy; on-street parking is hard to find, and
there's a fee for on-site parking; Disney is at least 45 minutes away (an
hour or more during rush hours). ⑤ *Rooms from: $219* ⊠ *191 E. Pine
St., Downtown Orlando* ☎ *407/841–1000, 800/609–3339* ⊕ *www.
embassysuites.com* ↝ *167 suites* ❙◯❙ *Breakfast* ✢ *3:B3.*

$$$ ⊞ **Grand Bohemian Hotel.** Decorated in a sophisticated and eclectic
HOTEL   "Bohemian" design, this European-style property is Downtown Orlan-
do's only Four Diamond luxury hotel. **Pros:** art gallery; free Wi-Fi;
quiet, adult-friendly atmosphere; great restaurant; sophisticated enter-
tainment; short walk to arts center and Amway Center, and Downtown
restaurants and clubs. **Cons:** little to attract kids; meals are pricey; fees
for parking; far from Disney and Universal. ⑤ *Rooms from: $299* ⊠ *325
S. Orange Ave., Downtown Orlando* ☎ *407/313–9000, 866/663–0024*
⊕ *www.grandbohemianhotel.com* ↝ *212 rooms, 35 suites* ❙◯❙ *No meals*
✢ *3:B3.*

ORLANDO INTERNATIONAL AIRPORT

The area around the airport, especially the neighborhood just north of
the Beachline Expressway, has a surfeit of hotels, mostly used by busi-
ness travelers and airline staff. They're worth checking out if you have
an early departure.

8

$ 🔲 **The Florida Hotel & Conference Center.** Five miles from the airport gates,
HOTEL   the hotel is midway between Orlando International and I-Drive, and if
you like to shop, you're in for a treat. **Pros:** in-room Wi-Fi and Internet access; free parking; short drive to airport. **Cons:** neighborhood
less than scenic; besides adjoining mall, little to walk to; Disney is 18
miles away; no free shuttles; pricey resort fee. $ *Rooms from: $166*
✉ *1500 Sand Lake Rd., at S. Orange Blossom Trail* ☎ *407/859–1500,
800/588–4656* ⊕ *www.thefloridahotelorlando.com* ⤴ *511 rooms, 5
suites* ❖*Breakfast* ✛ *2:H3.*

$$ 🔲 **Hyatt Regency Orlando International Airport.** If you have to catch an
HOTEL   early-morning flight or have a long layover, this hotel inside the main
terminal complex is a very convenient option; counting the time you
spend waiting for the elevator, your room is a five-minute walk from
the nearest ticket counter. **Pros:** despite being at the airport, rooms are
quiet; people-watching from terminal-side balconies can be fun; termi-
nal has 24-hour shopping and dining; shuttles to Disney and Universal
(fee); free Internet access. **Cons:** nothing around but the airport; Down-
town Orlando and theme parks at least 30 minutes away; daily fee for
parking. $ *Rooms from: $209* ✉ *9300 Jeff Fuqua Blvd.* ☎ *407/825–
1234, 800/233–1234* ⊕ *www.orlandoairport.hyatt.com* ⤴ *445 rooms,
23 suites* ❖*No meals* ✛ *2:H3.*

WINTER PARK

Take I–4 Exit 87 or 88.

Home of Rollins College, Winter Park is a charming small town just
north of Orlando. Brick streets overhung by moss-draped oaks lead
to flower-bedecked Park Avenue, the main drag. Chic shops and res-
taurants line its east side, and a beautifully landscaped park graces the
west side. It feels a million miles from the tourist trail, but it's just a
25- to 45-minute drive from the major attractions, and a great place
for people-watching from the sidewalk cafés.

$$ 🔲 **The Alfond Inn.** This serenely sophisticated building in the heart of
HOTEL   Winter Park, just steps from the shops and restaurants of Park Avenue,
combines an upscale hotel with an art gallery, and is owned by neighboring Rollins College. **Pros:** five-minute walk to Park Avenue for pleasant strolls; restaurant on property; free Wi-Fi. **Cons:** at least an hour's
drive to the theme parks; valet parking only at $18 a night. $ *Rooms
from: $229* ✉ *300 E. New England Ave.* ☎ *407/998–8090* ⊕ *www.
thealfondinn.com* ⤴ *112 rooms* ❖*No meals* ✛ *3:B1.*

$ 🔲 **Park Plaza Hotel.** Small and intimate, this beautifully updated 1922
HOTEL   establishment on Park Avenue offers the charm of fern-bedecked
wrought-iron balconies, along with free Wi-Fi and free breakfast in
bed. **Pros:** valet parking; romantic ambience; view of Park Avenue shops
and restaurants; rail station about a block away. **Cons:** railroad tracks
are close, making for train noise at night; small rooms; a long way from
theme parks. $ *Rooms from: $149* ✉ *307 Park Ave. S* ☎ *407/647–
1072, 800/228–7220* ⊕ *www.parkplazahotel.com* ⤴ *28 rooms, 12
suites* ❖*Breakfast* ✛ *3:B1.*

NIGHTLIFE

Updated by Gary McKechnie

As one of the world's leading tourist destinations, Orlando has to meet the challenge of offering entertainment to more than 50 million visitors each year—and providing memorable experiences that will bring them back again and again.

Not too long ago there was little to do after dark. Then, when Disney saw a flood of their guests heading off to a Downtown Orlando entertainment complex, they retooled their after-dark options to include Pleasure Island (now The Landing) and later West Side, now both part of the Downtown Disney (soon to be Disney Springs) entertainment complex. In response, Universal Orlando opened CityWalk. Now, with the expanded entertainment venues of the Dr. Phillips Arts Center and Amway sports arena, a good number of locals are filtering back to the city core and leaving the theme parks to tourists.

If you're here for at least two nights and don't mind losing some sleep, reserve one evening for Downtown Disney and the next for CityWalk. Disney has the advantage of being its own government entity so they can often stay open later than bars elsewhere. One difference you may detect here is that Disney's clubs are largely frequented by off-duty Disney cast members. At Universal, however, it appears to be a cross-section of young, virile club goers who work outside the theme parks. Also, to its credit, CityWalk premiered the Blue Man Group in 2007, which certainly upped the stakes. In Downtown Orlando, crowds are the usual variety pack. Club locations here are scattered, with the trendy Thornton Park district appealing to young urbanites, and serious club-goers preferring the Downtown core and the various bars and clubs along Orange Avenue and Church Street. Keep in mind that smoking is not permitted in any Florida restaurants and bars that serve food.

WALT DISNEY WORLD

When you enter the fiefdom known as Walt Disney World, you're likely to see as many watering holes as cartoon characters. After beating your feet around a theme park all day, there are lounges, bars, speakeasies, pubs, sports bars, and microbreweries where you can settle down with a soothing libation. Your choice of nightlife can be found at various Disney shopping and entertainment complexes—from the casual down-by-the-shore BoardWalk to the much larger multi-area Downtown Disney, which comprises the Marketplace, The Landing, and the West Side, with new shopping and dining options.

MAGIC KINGDOM

FIREWORKS AND NIGHTTIME SHOWS

Both in the theme parks and around the hotel-side waterways, Walt Disney World offers up a wealth of fabulous sound-and-light shows after the sun goes down. In fact WDW is one of the Earth's largest single consumers of fireworks—perhaps even rivaling mainland China. Traditionally, sensational short shows have been held at the Magic Kingdom at 10. Starting times vary throughout the year, but you can check them at Guest Relations (aka Guest Services).

Fireworks are only part of the evening entertainment. Each park hosts shows staged with varying degrees of spectacle and style. For the best of the best, head to Epcot, which hosts visiting shows that are free with admission. Regular performers include Celtic folk music at the United Kingdom, acrobats in China, exciting flag-tossing musicians in Italy, musicians in a smaller African kiosk, and a lumberjack-inspired show in Canada. Catching any of these parades and/or performances easily soothes the sting of what you may feel is an overpriced admission.

Fodor'sChoice
★

Wishes. When the lights dim on Main Street and orchestral music fills the air, you know this fireworks extravaganza is about to begin. In Wishes, Jiminy Cricket's voice comes to life and tries to convince you that your wishes really can come true. He gets plenty of support from the Disney stars of classic films such as *Pinocchio, Fantasia, Cinderella,* and *The Little Mermaid.* Portions of famous film songs play over loudspeakers, and you hear the voices of film characters like Peter Pan and Aladdin as more than 680 individual fireworks paint the night sky. Oh, and don't worry that Tinker Bell may have been sealed in her jar for the night—she comes back to fly above the crowd in grand pixie-dust style. Check the *Times Guide* for performance time, which varies seasonally. ■TIP➔ You can book a FastPass+ ahead of your visit for best viewing. The Castle forecourt and surrounding bridges offer great views; or find a place near the front of the park for a quick postshow exit. ✉ *Magic Kingdom* ☞ *Duration: 12 mins. Crowds: Heavy. Audience: All Ages.*

EPCOT

BARS

Cava del Tequila. Set inside the Mexico pavilion, this intimate bar serves tasty tapas, tequila flights, and some of the best margaritas anywhere, including the Cava Organic Skinny Lime Margarita. ✉ *World Showcase, Mexico, Epcot.*

Rose & Crown Pub. Great piano sets by the Hat Lady and, on busy nights, four-to-six-deep at the bar guarantees good times at this United Kingdom watering hole. The fish-and-chips are first rate, and the Trio of

9

United Kingdom Cheeses includes aged Irish cheddar and Stilton. (If you don't want to wait, the Yorkshire County Fish Shop next door serves the same goodies.) Grab a beer and let the fun begin! ⊠ *World Showcase, United Kingdom, Epcot.*

Tutto Gusto. This cool, cozy wine cellar adjoining Tutto Italia is a slice of Naples and the ideal place to kick back and sip a bubbly Prosecco or a glass of Italian wine while noshing on antipasto or tapas-size pastas. For quicker service, head straight for the bar. ⊠ *World Showcase Italy pavilion, Epcot.*

FIREWORKS AND NIGHTTIME SHOWS

Fodor'sChoice **IllumiNations: Reflections of Earth.** This marvelous nighttime spectacular
★ takes place over the World Showcase Lagoon every night before closing. Be sure to stick around for the lasers, lights, flames, fireworks, fountains, and music that fill the air over the water. The show's Earth Globe—a gigantic, spherical, video-display system rotating on a 350-ton floating island—is three stories tall with 180,000 light-emitting diodes. It houses six computer processors and 258 strobe lights and projects images celebrating the diversity and unified spirit of humankind. The globe opens like a lotus flower in the grand finale, revealing a huge torch that rises 40 feet into the air as additional flames spread light across the lagoon. Nearly 2,800 fireworks shells paint colorful displays across the night sky.

Although there's generally good viewing from all around the lagoon, some of the best spots are in front of the Italy pavilion, on the bridge between France and the United Kingdom, on the promenade in front of Canada, at the World Showcase Plaza, and at La Hacienda de San Angel and La Cantina de San Angel in Mexico. **For people with disabilities:** During the show, certain areas along the lagoon's edge at Showcase Plaza, Canada, and Germany are reserved for guests using wheelchairs. ■ TIP→ Limited FastPass+ reservations are offered; otherwise, for best views, find your place 45 minutes in advance and send someone in your group for ice cream or other treats. ⊠ *World Showcase, Epcot* ☞ *Duration: 12 mins. Crowds: Heavy. Audience: All Ages.*

HOLLYWOOD STUDIOS

FIREWORKS AND NIGHTTIME SHOWS

Fantasmic!. This Hollywood Studios 25-minute special-effects blockbuster is held after dark in an often-packed 6,500-seat amphitheater. Mickey Mouse in the guise of the Sorcerer's Apprentice emcees this special effect–packed revue. Performances run two or three times nightly during high season, less frequently in slow periods. ⊠ *Disney's Hollywood Studios, Lake Buena Vista.*

DISNEY'S BOARDWALK

In the good ol' days, Americans escaped their city routines for breezy seaside boardwalks. Disney's BoardWalk is within walking distance of Epcot, across Crescent Lake from Disney's Yacht and Beach Club Resorts, and fronting a hotel of the same name. You may be drawn to its good restaurants, bars, shops, surreys, and performers. After sunset, the mood is festive. ■TIP➔ If you're here when Epcot is ready to close, you can watch the park fireworks from the bridge that connects BoardWalk to the Yacht and Beach Club Resorts.

Atlantic Dance Hall. This high-energy dance club plays music from the '80s onward, with a huge screen showing videos requested by the crowd. The parquet dance floor is set off by furnishings of deep blue, maroon, and gold, and the ceiling glows with gold stars and twinkling lights. Signature cocktails are in demand, and you can sip a cognac or choose from a selection of popular beers to inspire your dance floor moves. ⊠ *BoardWalk, Epcot Resort Area* ☎ *407/939–2444* 🎫 *No cover* ☼ *Tues.–Sat. 9 pm–1:45 am.*

Big River Grille & Brewing Works. Disney World's only brewpub has intimate tables where brewmasters tend to their potions. You can order an $8 sampler with five to seven 3-ounce pours of whatever's on tap that day, usually including Red Rocket, Southern Flyer Light Lager, Gadzooks Pilsner, and Steamboat Pale Ale. Upscale pub grub and sandwiches pair well. There's also a sidewalk café. ⊠ *BoardWalk, Epcot Resort Area* ☎ *407/560–0253* 🎫 *No cover* ☼ *Daily 11–11.*

ESPN Club. The sports motif here is carried into every nook and cranny—the main dining area looks like a sports arena, with a basketball-court hardwood floor and a giant scoreboard that projects the day's big game. While you watch, you can munch on wings, nachos, and linebacker-size burgers. There are more than 100 TVs throughout (even in the restrooms). The place is packed for big games; call ahead to see if special seating rules are in effect. ⊠ *BoardWalk, Epcot Resort Area* ☎ *407/939–1177* 🎫 *No cover* ☼ *Daily 11:30 am–1 am.*

Jellyrolls. In this rockin', boisterous piano bar, comedians act as emcees and play dueling grand pianos nonstop. The steady stream of conventions at Disney makes this the place to catch CEOs doing the conga to Barry Manilow's "Copacabana"—if that's your idea of a good time. ⊠ *BoardWalk, Epcot Resort Area* ☎ *407/560–8770* 🎫 *$12 cover* ☼ *Daily 7 pm–2 am.*

TOP ATTRACTIONS

Cirque du Soleil—*La Nouba.* If you haven't yet seen one of the surreal Cirque du Soleil shows, or if you have and you were wowed, you'll love this high-energy acrobatics performance.

House of Blues. This concert hall in Downtown Disney is the best live-music venue in Orlando and always hosts major headliners.

IllumiNations. Epcot's nighttime spectacular, featuring lasers, fireworks, and floating movie screens, is a not-to-be-missed crowd-pleaser.

9

DOWNTOWN DISNEY

Walt Disney World is so much more than the Magic Kingdom and its theme-park siblings, Epcot, Disney's Hollywood Studios, and Disney's Animal Kingdom. Beyond the parks, there are enough diversions to keep you busy day and night. At Downtown Disney (soon to be Disney

Springs) alone there are dozens of stores, including the best World of Disney store on the planet, and the LEGO Imagination Center, with its life-size LEGO people and animals, retail store, and play area. Then there's the nightlife, including the Cirque du Soleil show, the sports events, the boat rides—and so much more.

WEST SIDE

West Side at Downtown Disney is a hip outdoor complex of shopping, dining, and entertainment with the main venues being the House of Blues, DisneyQuest, and Cirque du Soleil. Aside from this trio, there are no cover charges. Whether you're club hopping or not, the West Side is worth a visit for its waterside location, wide promenade, and diverse shopping and dining. Opening time is 11 am, closing time around 2 am; crowds vary with the season, but weeknights tend to be less busy. For entertainment times and more information, call ☏ 407/824–4500 or 407/824–2222.

Bongos Cuban Café. Latin rhythms provide the beat at this restaurant and bar with a pre-Castro theme owned by pop singer Gloria Estefan. Four bars are especially busy on weekends, when a Latin band kicks it up a notch with *muy caliente* music. Samba, tango, salsa, and merengue rhythms roll throughout the week. ✉ *West Side, Downtown Disney* ☏ *407/828–0999* ☉ *Sun.–Thurs. 11–10:30, Fri. and Sat. 11 am–2 am.*

DisneyQuest. In a five-story virtual-reality mini–theme park at Downtown Disney West Side, DisneyQuest lets you pay a hefty cover to participate in high-tech virtual adventures and play video games. To be fair, you can play all day, and there are cutting-edge games and interactive adventures that make the admission worthwhile. It's also a great place for teens and older tweens (children under 14 must be accompanied by a guest age 14 or older).

In **Explore Zone,** fly through the streets of Agrabah with the help of a virtual-reality helmet on Aladdin's Magic Carpet Ride. Take a Virtual Jungle Cruise down the roiling rapids of a prehistoric world, and paddle (yes, *really* paddle) to adventure amid volcanoes, dinosaurs, and other Cretaceous threats. At Pirates of the Caribbean: Battle for Buccaneer Gold, you and the gang must brave the high seas and sink pirate ships to acquire treasure.

In the **Score Zone,** battle supervillains while flying, headset firmly intact, through a 3-D comic world in Ride the Comix. Escape evil aliens and rescue colonists during Invasion! An ExtraTERRORestrial Alien Encounter. Or hip-check your friends in a life-size Mighty Ducks Pinball Slam game.

In the **Create Zone** learn the secrets of Disney animation at the Animation Academy. Create your own twisted masterpiece at Sid's Create-A-Toy, based on the popular animated film *Toy Story.* Or, at Living Easels, make a *living* painting on a giant electronic screen. Thrills await at Cyberspace Mountain, where you can design your own roller coaster on a computer screen, then climb aboard a 360-degree pitch-and-roll simulator for the ride of your dreams. At Radio Disney SongMaker, produce your own hit.

Classic free-play machines like Pac Man reside in the **Replay Zone.** You can also sit with a partner in an asteroid cannon–equipped bumper car and blast others to make their cars do a 360-degree spin in Buzz Lightyear's AstroBlaster.

All attractions are wheelchair accessible, but most require transfer from wheelchair to the attraction itself. You can, however, wheel right onto Pirates of the Caribbean: Battle for Buccaneer Gold, Aladdin's Magic Carpet Ride, and Mighty Ducks Pinball Slam. Rent wheelchairs at the DisneyQuest Emporium or at Downtown Disney Marketplace Guest Relations ($12 per day for hand operated, plus $100 refundable credit-card deposit); electric chairs are $50 plus deposit at the Marketplace location only. Guide dogs are permitted in all areas but aren't allowed to ride several attractions. Strollers are *not* permitted.

Four attractions have height requirements: Cyberspace Mountain (51 inches), Buzz Lightyear's AstroBlaster (51 inches), Mighty Ducks Pinball Slam (48 inches), and Pirates of the Caribbean (35 inches). Little ones 2–7 can enjoy a Kids' Area on the fourth floor, where they can play smaller versions of video and other games like air hockey, basketball, and bowling.

Lost and Found is at the Guest Relations window and cash is available at ATMs inside the House of Blues merchandise shop not far from the DisneyQuest entrance. ⊠ *West Side* ☎ *407/828–4600* 💲 *$45 adults, $39 children 3–9, excluding sales tax* ☉ *Sun.–Thurs. 11:30 am–10 pm, Fri. and Sat. 11:30 am–11 pm.*

La Nouba. If you've seen rave media reviews of this production, believe them. The surreal show by the world-famous Cirque du Soleil company starts at 100 mph and accelerates through 90 mesmerizing minutes of acrobatics, avant-garde costumes and staging, and captivating choreography. So much happens that even those who've seen the show once return to see what they missed last time.

The story of La Nouba—derived from the French phrase *faire la nouba* (live it up)—is alternately mysterious, dreamlike, comical, and sensual. A cast of 67 international performers—including two vocalists and six musicians who play 22 instruments from tower platforms—takes the stage in a 1,671-seat showroom of a big-top-style theater.

World-renowned jugglers manipulate balls, hoops, and clubs with breathtaking precision and speed. Another fresh act—Skipping Ropes—combines dance and acrobatics to elevate child's play to a seemingly impossible level.

The interplay is charming as the Cleaning Lady sweeps her way into a dreamworld of Technicolor characters who dance, tumble, and fly through the air on ribbons of red silk. Two silly clowns provide comic relief at intervals, and four adorable Chinese girls steal applause with their astonishing diabolo (Chinese yo-yo) performance. The jaw-dropping last act is a masterpiece of acrobatics and gymnastics synched to uplifting music.

Call ahead for good seats (there are three categories of seating), and hire a babysitter if necessary—you wouldn't want to miss one minute of this class act. ✉ *West Side, Downtown Disney* ☎ *407/939–7600 reservations* ⊕ *www.cirquedusoleil.com* 💲 *$63–$150 adults, $52–$125 children 3–9; higher holiday rates* ⊙ *Performances Tues.–Sat. 6 and 9.*

House of Blues. The restaurant serves up live blues performances and rib-sticking Mississippi Delta cooking all week long. The attached concert hall has showcased such artists as Aretha Franklin, David Byrne, Steve Miller, Willie Nelson, and Journey. Many swear by the "World Famous Gospel Brunch" each Sunday. ✉ *West Side, Downtown Disney* ☎ *407/934–2583* 💲 *Covers vary* ⊙ *Restaurant Sun.–Thurs. 11:30–11, Fri. and Sat. 11:30–1 am. Concert times vary.*

DOWNTOWN DISNEY MARKETPLACE

Although the Marketplace offers little in the line of typical nightlife, there's hardly a more enjoyable place for families to spend a quiet evening window-shopping, enjoying ice cream at a courtyard café, or strolling among eclectic Disney stores.

MAGIC KINGDOM RESORT AREA

With more than a dozen resort hotels on Walt Disney World property, the hotel-bar scene is understandably active. Depending on whether the resort is geared to business or romance, the lounges can be soothing or boisterous—or both. You do not have to be a resort guest to visit the bars and lounges, and a casual tour of them may well provide an evening's entertainment. To reach any of these hotel bars directly, you can call the Disney operator at ☎ *407/824–4500 or 407/824–2222.*

BARS

Mizner's. A stylish, refined alcove named after Florida Renaissance architect Addison Mizner is tucked away at the far end of the Grand Floridian's second-floor lobby. It's a tasteful getaway where you can unwind with a glass of champagne, a martini, or a Manhattan. The extensive drink menu includes multiple single-malt Scotch whiskies and after-dinner cognacs and ports. ✉ *Grand Floridian Resort* ⊙ *Daily 5 pm–midnight.*

Narcoossee's. Inside the restaurant is a bar that serves ordinary beer in expensive yard glasses, along with some exclusive and tasty cocktails. ■ TIP→ **The porch-side views of the Seven Seas Lagoon, the nightly Electrical Water Pageant, and the Magic Kingdom fireworks are worth the premium you pay.** ✉ *Grand Floridian Resort* ⊙ *Daily 5:30 pm–10 pm.*

Territory Lounge. The frontier theme here honors the Corps of Discovery (look overhead for a Lewis and Clark Expedition trail map). In between drinks, check out the surveying equipment, daguerreotypes, parka mittens, maps, and what the lounge claims is a pair of Teddy Roosevelt's boots. ✉ *Wilderness Lodge* ⊙ *Daily 4:30–midnight.*

DINNER SHOWS

Hoop-Dee-Doo Musical Revue. The Pioneer Hall Players perform romantic ballads, corny tunes, and slapstick—it's old-fashioned and groanworthy and kids adore it. You chow down on barbecued ribs, fried chicken, corn on the cob, strawberry shortcake, and all the fixin's. Unlimited beverages include beer, wine, and sangria for adults with I.D.

Prime-time shows sell out months in advance in busy seasons. ⊠ *Fort Wilderness Resort* 🕾 *407/939–3463 for reservations up to 180 days in advance, 407/824–2803 for dietary restrictions* 🗢 *$58.99–$67.99 adults, $32.99–$36.99 children 3–9, including tax and gratuity. Prices vary by seat selection* ⊙ *Daily 5, 7:15, and 9:30.*

Spirit of Aloha. It's an outdoor barbecue with colorful South Pacific–style entertainment. Fire jugglers and hula-drum dancers are entertaining for the whole family, and the hula dancers' navel maneuvers are something to see. ⊠ *Polynesian Resort* 🕾 *407/939–3463 for reservations up to 180 days in advance, 407/824–1593 for dietary restrictions* 🗢 *$60.99–$72.99 adults, $33.99–$39.99 children 3–9, including tax and gratuity. Prices vary by seat selection* ⊙ *Tues.–Sat. 5:15 and 8.*

FIREWORKS AND NIGHTTIME SHOWS
Electrical Water Pageant. This 10-minute floating parade of illuminated sea creatures on the Seven Seas Lagoon and Bay Lake rolls past several Magic Kingdom–area resorts. Watch it from a resort bar like Narcoossee's, the campgrounds at Fort Wilderness, or the pier at the Grand Floridian—you can hear the electronic score featuring Handel's *Water Music*.

ANIMAL KINGDOM RESORT AREA

BARS
Victoria Falls. The exotic safari theme incorporates leather directors' chairs, native masks, and the gurgling of a stream that flows from the lobby and through the lounge to cascade over rockwork into a small pool at the Boma restaurant below. This is a great spot to watch a game, sip South African wines and beers, and relax with a snack from the food menu. ■ TIP→ Arrive early and check out the zebras, giraffes, and other animals on the lodge's savanna. ⊠ *Animal Kingdom Lodge* ⊙ *Daily 4–midnight.*

9

UNIVERSAL ORLANDO

With the wide range of nightlife you'll find at Universal, you may get the feeling that you're vacationing not in Orlando but in New York City. CityWalk's stores open by mid-morning, and its restaurants come to life between lunchtime and late afternoon. Eateries that double as nightclubs (such as Pat O'Brien's, Bob Marley's, and the Red Coconut Club) start charging a cover before dusk and apply age restrictions (usually 21) around 9. For details on a particular establishment, check with Guest Services (aka Guest Relations).

UNIVERSAL ORLANDO'S CITYWALK

Blue Man Group. At their own venue, the Sharp-Aquos Theatre, the ever-innovative Blue Men continue to pound out new music, sketches, and audience interaction that is nothing like you've ever seen. Attempting to understand the apps on a GiPad (a gigantic iPad), they may appear clueless and perplexed about cutting-edge technology (which for them can be as basic as a can of paint), but they're always excited when they can drum out rhythms on lengths of PVC pipes and throw a rave party finale for all in attendance. The show is a surreal comic masterpiece, so if you have the time and a little extra in your vacation budget, this is a must. Three levels of admission (Poncho, Tier 1, and Tier 2) hint at how messy things can get when the Blue Men cut loose. ⊠ *CityWalk* ☎ *407/258–3626* ⊕ *www.universalorlando.com* ◪ *Adults start at $70 advance purchase, $85 at box office; children 9 and under from $30* ⊙ *Daily showtimes vary; call for schedule.*

Bob Marley—A Tribute to Freedom. Modeled after the King of Reggae's home in Kingston, Jamaica (even down to the air-conditioner window units), in a way this nightclub is also part museum, with more than 100 photographs and paintings showing pivotal moments in Marley's life. Though the place does serve meals, most patrons are at the cozy bar or by the patio, where they can be jammin' to a (loud) live band that plays nightly. For a nice souvenir, pose by the wonderful Marley statue outside the club. Legendary Thursdays feature drink specials for everyone, and Sunday is ladies' night from 9 pm until closing. ■TIP→ **Often on Mondays and Tuesdays, CityWalk's pace is slow enough where some clubs will offer free admission. Ask before you pay.** ⊠ *CityWalk* ☎ *407/224–2692* ⊕ *www.universalorlando.com* ◪ *$7 after 9 pm* ⊙ *Daily 4 pm–2 am.*

CityWalk's Rising Star. Here you and other hopeful (and hopeless) singers can really let loose. Instead of singing to recorded music, you're accompanied by a band complete with backup singers—in front of a live audience. Backup singers are on hand every night, while the live band plugs in Tuesday through Saturday, and a full bar is always on tap. ⊠ *6000 Universal Blvd., No. 717, CityWalk* ☎ *407/224–2961* ⊕ *www. universalorlando.com* ◪ *$7, no charge to sing* ⊙ *Nightly 8 pm–2 am.*

the groove. In this cavernous hall images flicker rapidly on several screens, and the lights, music, and mayhem appeal to a mostly under-30 crowd. Prepare for lots of fog, swirling lights, and sweaty bodies. The '70s-style Green Room is filled with beanbag chairs and everything you threw out when Duran Duran hit the charts. The Blue Room is sci-fi Jetson-y, and the Red Room is hot and romantic in a bordello sort of way. The music is equally diverse: Top 40, hip-hop, R&B, techno, and the occasional live band. ⊠ *6000 Universal Blvd., CityWalk* ☎ *407/224–2692* ⊕ *www. universalorlando.com* ◪ *$7* ⊙ *Daily 9 pm–2 am.*

Hard Rock Cafe. The Hard Rock Cafe here is the largest on Earth, which means you can see plenty of memorabilia, including such Beatles rarities as John Lennon's famous New York City T-shirt, Paul's original lyrics for "Let It Be," and the doors from London's Abbey Road, studios plus hundreds of other fascinating collectibles. And the food's great, too. For savvy locals and many surprised guests, the main attraction is found next door in the Hard Rock Live concert hall ("The Coliseum of Rock"). Frequent performances featuring comedians, solo acts, and internationally recognized bands make it a popular venue and one of the most active places at Universal. A few drawbacks: The seats are hard and two-thirds don't face the stage; if you arrive at the door carrying a large purse or bags, it won't be time to rock, it'll be time to walk—about a quarter-mile back to the parking garage to stow your stuff. For showtimes, call ☎ *407/351–5483.* ✉ *CityWalk* ⊕ *www. hardrocklive.com* 🗗 *Cover prices vary* ☉ *Daily from 11 am, with varying closing times, generally around midnight.*

Jimmy Buffett's Margaritaville. Buffett tunes fill the air at the restaurant here and at the Volcano, Land Shark, and 12 Volt bars. Inside there's a miniature Pan Am Clipper suspended from the ceiling, music videos projected onto sails, limbo and hula-hoop contests, a huge margarita blender that erupts "when the volcano blows," and live music nightly—everything that Parrotheads need to roost. Across the promenade, another full-size seaplane (emblazoned with "Jimmy Buffett, Captain") is the setting for the Lone Palm Airport, a pleasing and surprisingly popular outdoor waterfront bar. ✉ *6000 Universal Studios Plaza, No.704, CityWalk* ☎ *407/224–2692* ⊕ *www.margaritavilleorlando.com* 🗗 *$7 after 10 pm* ☉ *Daily 11:30 am–2 am.*

Pat O'Brien's. An exact reproduction of the legendary New Orleans original, this comes complete with flaming fountain and dueling pianists who are playing for highly entertained regulars and visitors—even on weekday afternoons. Outside, the cozy and welcoming Patio Bar has a wealth of tables and chairs, allowing you to do nothing but enjoy the outdoors and your potent, rum-based Hurricanes in Orlando's version of the Big Easy. ✉ *6000 Universal Blvd., CityWalk* ☎ *407/224–2692* ⊕ *www.patobriens.com* 🗗 *$7 after 9 pm* ☉ *Patio Bar daily 4 pm–2 am; piano bar daily 5 pm–2 am, 21 and up after 9 pm.*

Red Coconut Club. Paying tribute to kitsch design of the 1950s, the interior here is part Vegas lounge, part Cuban club, and part Polynesian tiki bar. It's "where tropical meets trendy." There are three full bars on two levels, signature martinis, an extensive wine list, and VIP bottle service. Hang out in the lounge, on the balcony, or at the bar. On a budget? Take advantage of the daily happy hours and gourmet appetizer menu. A DJ (Sunday–Wednesday) or live music (Thursday–Saturday) pushes the energy with tunes ranging from Sinatra to rock. Thursday is ladies' night. ✉ *6000 Universal Blvd., CityWalk* ☎ *407/224–2425* ⊕ *www.universalorlando.com* 🗗 *$7 after 9 pm* ☉ *Sun.–Wed. 8 pm–2 am, Thurs.–Sat. 6 pm–2 am.*

ORLANDO

The Downtown clubs lost their monopoly on nighttime entertainment in the area when Disney and Universal muscled their way onto the scene. As the pendulum swings, though, more locals are making their way back Downtown. Although still several years from completion, the new Dr. Phillips Performing Arts Center has changed the dynamic of Downtown. Developers are salvaging old buildings, revitalizing stalwart Church Street, and adding new nightclubs. For the time being, Downtown clubs can be quite upscale or quite the opposite. The neighborhood of Thornton Park and the community of Winter Park also have clusters of chic bars and restaurants, though no serious dance clubs.

CENTRAL ORLANDO

Outside of Downtown Disney and Universal's CityWalk, the focal point of adult Orlando nightlife is Downtown. If you stand on the corner of Orange Avenue and Church Street long enough, you can watch all types of gussied-up revelers walk by. The bars and music clubs here hop even after the 2 am last call.

AERO. You have to head up to the roof using the side staircase of The Social nightclub to reach the former Sky60 rooftop bar. Revamped and updated, it offers a hip and social view of Downtown Orlando. ⊠ *60 N. Orange Ave.* ☎ *407/246–1599* ⊕ *www.skysixty.com/* ⊗ *Thurs.–Sat. 10 pm–2 am, Sun. 5 pm–11 pm.*

Bull and Bush Pub. After more than a quarter century in the same location, this is still one of the most atmospheric places in town, where you can get a hand-drawn pint, play a game of darts, and have a (still) smoky chat. The tap lineup covers 11 imported beers and ales. Darts leagues and weekly pub quizzes make it feel like a piece of old London. ⊠ *2408 E. Robinson St.* ☎ *407/896–7546* ⊕ *www.bullandbushorlando. com* ⊗ *Closed Sun.*

Monkey Bar. You access this tiny pocket of sophistication amid the frenetic energy of the Wall Street entertainment area by walking through the WaiTiki Retro Tiki Lounge and finding the all-but-hidden elevator at the back. There's a relatively quiet room inside and an almost New Orleans–style balcony. Call ahead for happy hour times. ⊠ *19 N. Orange Ave.* ☎ *407/481–1199* ⊕ *www.wallstplaza.net/venues/monkey-bar/* ⊗ *Wed.–Fri. 5 pm–2 am, Sat. 9 pm–2 am.*

Wally's. One of Orlando's oldest bars (circa 1954), this longtime local favorite is a hangout for a cross section of cultures and ages. Some would say it's a dive, but that doesn't matter to the students, bikers, lawyers, and barflies who land here to drink surrounded by the go-go-dancer wallpaper and '60s-era interior. Just grab a stool at the bar to take in the scene and down a cold one. ⊠ *1001 N. Mills Ave.* ☎ *407/896–6975* ⊕ *www.wallysonmills.com* ⊗ *Mon.–Sat. 7:30 am–2 am.*

MUSIC CLUBS

Bösendorfer Lounge. One of only two Imperial Grand Bösendorfer pianos in the world takes center stage at this, perhaps the classiest gathering spot in Orlando. The highly civilized (but not stuffy) lounge attracts a cross section of trendy Orlandoans, especially the after-work crowd, among whom the conversation and camaraderie flow as smoothly as the champagne, beer, wine, and cocktails. Art on the walls, comfortable couches, rich fabrics, sleek black marble, and seductive lighting invite you to stay awhile. If music is what attracts you, call in advance for the schedule of jazz combos and solo pianists who perform in the lounge. Many are among the area's finest and most talented musicians. ⊠ *Grand Bohemian Hotel, 325 S. Orange Ave.* ☎ *407/313–9000* ⊕ *www.grandbohemianhotel.com* ⊗ *Fri. and Sat. 10 am–2 am, Sun.–Thurs. 10 am–1 am.*

Rollins College. The gorgeous Mediterranean-revival campus is home to cultural venues and a renowned festival. The Annie Russell Theatre produces student-acted classic and modern plays and dance programs in its beautiful (and, some say, haunted) building. The music department hosts local and international classical, jazz, and world-music artists in a multimillion-dollar performance hall. The annual Bach festival, in late February and early March, honors all things classical and is held at locations throughout Rollins College and Winter Park. ⊠ *1000 Holt Ave., Winter Park* ☎ *407/646–2000* ⊕ *www.rollins.edu.*

Fodor'sChoice
★

The Social. Beloved by locals, The Social is a great place to see touring and area musicians. Up to seven nights a week you can sip trademark martinis while listening to anything from indie rock to rockabilly to undiluted jazz. Several now-national acts got their start here, including Matchbox Twenty, Seven Mary Three, and other groups that don't have numbers in their names. Hours vary. ⊠ *54 N. Orange Ave.* ☎ *407/246– 1419* ⊕ *www.thesocial.org* 🍸 *$5–$30, depending on entertainment.*

Tanqueray's. Of all the entertainment possibilities in Downtown Orlando, the most interesting one may be the hardest to find. Housed in a former bank vault, Tanqueray's is a belowground hideaway featuring live music nightly and a full bar, including craft beers and nightly drink specials. If you don't mind the smoky atmosphere, you can enjoy a variety of entertainment from one night to the next, including reggae, funk, and high-energy blues. No food is served here. ⊠ *100 S. Orange Ave.* ☎ *407/649–8540.*

Venue 578. Originally an old automotive repair shop, this multilevel, high-energy club, the former Firestone Live, went through a very costly renovation to attract international music acts. Something's always going on to make the crowd hop: DJ mixes, big band, jazz, hip-hop, rock. Often the dance floor is more like semicontrolled chaos than a place to just listen, so be prepared. Hours and prices vary by event; check the website. ⊠ *578 N. Orange Ave.* ☎ *407/872–0066* ⊕ *www.venue578. com/.*

NIGHTCLUBS

Chillers. Known as Orlando's original party bar, Chillers features an entire wall of frozen daiquiri machines and sells craft beers and premium liquors as well. A DJ spins Top 40 dance music, and there's karaoke every Thursday. Drinks are two-for-one and three-for-one on certain nights. ⊠ *33 W. Church St.* ☎ *407/649–4270* ⊕ *www.churchstreetbars. com/chillers.*

Parliament House Resort. For those enamored of gay, lesbian, and high-camp entertainment, Parliament House is legendary and welcoming to every kind of audience. The 250-seat art deco performance space, which has been open since 1975, hosts live theater, musical acts, karaoke, cabaret, dance, and bawdy and hilarious drag shows. Le Club Disco and Dance bar, along with four other bars, draws thousands of partiers weekly. Unfortunately, Orange Blossom Trail remains a sketchy area, so wandering around the neighborhood isn't advised. ⊠ *410 N. Orange Blossom Trail* ☎ *407/425–7571* ⊕ *www.parliamenthouse.com* ⊘ *Le Club: Mon.–Sat. 9 pm–2 am, Sun. 3 pm–when they decide to close. Hrs vary at other bars.*

9

THEATER

Dr. Phillips Center for the Performing Arts. More than $500 million has gone into the new state-of-the-art Center, the Downtown home for opera, symphony, and Broadway touring spectaculars, and the addition of this artistic mecca is well on the way to changing life in Downtown Orlando completely. Already, new restaurants, galleries, and entertainment venues have sprung up around the Center, bringing crowds to Downtown who haven't ventured outside the theme parks since the heyday of Church Street decades ago. Construction of the final stages (and stage) of the Center are anticipated to be completed around 2018, but the current facilities are in full swing. ⊠ *445 S. Magnolia Avenue, Downtown Orlando* ☎ *844/513–2014* ⊕ *www.drphillipscenter.org/* ⊗ *Box office: Weekdays 10–4, Sat. noon–4.*

Mad Cow Theatre. Orlando's longest-standing professional theater company is where risks are taken. Regional premieres, new works, and thoughtful interpretations of classics such as *Death of a Salesman* make this a stage worth seeking. Local actors eager to show their talents line up to work here. ⊠ *54 W. Church St.* ☎ *407/297–8788* ⊕ *www. madcowtheatre.com.*

Orlando Shakespeare Theater. "Orlando Shakes" has four stages, where a typical season includes 11 plays covering classics (including Shakespeare, of course), contemporary, and children's productions. The theater also hosts the very popular Orlando International Fringe Festival, the oldest in America. The season runs June through April, with the Fringe Festival in May. PlayFest! The Harriett Lake Festival of New Plays offers world-premiere and staged-reading opportunities for new playwrights. The theater is in Loch Haven Cultural Park, just a few minutes north of Downtown, where the Orlando Science Center and the Museum of Art also stand. ⊠ *812 E. Rollins St., Lake Ivanhoe* ☎ *407/447–1700* ⊕ *www.orlandoshakes.org.*

INTERNATIONAL DRIVE

BARS

B.B. King's Blues Club. The blues great was doing quite well as a musician before becoming a successful entrepreneur, with blues clubs in Memphis, Nashville, Las Vegas, and West Palm Beach as well as Orlando. Like the others, this club has music at its heart. There's a dance floor and stage for live performances by the B.B. King All-Star Band or visiting musicians seven nights a week. You can't really experience Delta blues without Delta dining, so the club doubles as a restaurant with fried dill pickles, catfish bites, po' boys, ribs, and other comfort foods. Oh, yeah, and there's a full bar. ⊠ *Pointe Orlando, 9101 International Dr.* ☎ *407/370–4550* ⊕ *www.bbkingclubs.com/orlando/* ⊗ *Fri. and Sat. noon–2 am, Sun.–Thurs. noon–midnight.*

NIGHTCLUB

ICEBAR. Thanks to the miracle of refrigeration, this is Orlando's coolest bar—literally and figuratively. Fifty tons of pure ice is kept at a constant 27°F and has been cut and sculpted by world-class carvers into a cozy (or as cozy as ice can be) sanctuary of tables, sofas, chairs, and

Celebration at Night

Celebration. This community, where every blade of grass in every lawn seems perfect, is as picturesque as a movie set—although, to some critics, it would be one used in *The Stepford Wives*. But Celebration is a model of good American architecture and urban planning as well as a delightful place to spend a morning or afternoon.

Things appear nearly as faux as on Main Street, U.S.A., but as they unfold, you see signs of reality—and a pleasant one it is. Celebration is a real town, with its own hospital and school system. Houses and apartments spread out from the compact downtown area, full of restaurants, which wraps around the edge of a lake. Sidewalks are built for strolling,

restaurants have outdoor seating with lake views, and inviting shops beckon. After a walk around the lake, take youngsters over to the huge interactive fountain and have fun getting soaked.

The town has a year-round roster of special events and a noteworthy Sunday farmers' market. Starting the last Saturday in November and continuing through New Year's Eve, honest-to-goodness snow sprinkles softly down over Main Street every night on the hour from 6 to 9. ⊠ *Celebration ✛ 6 miles south of Epcot; take I–4 to Exit 64A and follow "Celebration" signs* ☎ *407/566–1200* ⊕ *www. celebrationfl.com.*

a bar. The staff loans you a thermal cape and gloves (upgrade to a fur coat for $10), and when you enter the frozen hall your drink is served in a glass made of crystal-clear ice. There's no cover charge if you just want to hang out in the Fire Lounge or outdoor Polar Patio, but you will pay $19.95 to spend as much time as you can handle in the sub-freezing ICEBAR. There's no beer or wine inside; it's simply too cold. ⊠ *Pointe Orlando, 8967 International Dr.* ☎ *407/426–7555* ⊕ *www. icebarorlando.com* ⊙ *Fri. and Sat. 7 pm–2 am, Sun.–Wed. 7–midnight, Thurs. 7–1.*

DINNER SHOWS

Dinner shows are an immensely popular form of nighttime entertainment around Orlando. For a single price, you get a theatrical production and a multicourse dinner. Performances run the gamut from jousting to jamboree tunes, and meals tend to be better than average; unlimited beer, wine, and soda are usually included, but mixed drinks (and often *any* drinks before dinner) cost extra. What the shows lack in substance and depth they make up for in grandeur and enthusiasm. The result is an evening of light entertainment, which youngsters in particular enjoy. Seatings are usually between 7 and 9:30, and there are usually one or two performances a night, with an extra show during peak periods. You might sit with strangers at tables for 10 or more, but that's part of the fun. Always reserve in advance, especially for weekend shows, and always ask about discounts although you can often find online coupons (sometimes for half off) that you can print out yourself.

9

If you're in Orlando off-season, try to take in these dinner shows on a busy night—a show playing to a small audience can be uncomfortable. Don't let the big prices fool you—there's a flood of major discount (sometimes half-off) coupons papering International Drive restaurants, hotels, and at the Orlando/Orange County Convention & Visitors Bureau. Since performance schedules can vary depending on the tourist season, it's always smart to call in advance to verify show times. When buying tickets, ask if the cost includes a gratuity—servers anxious to pocket more cash may hit you up for an extra handout.

Fodor'sChoice
★
Sleuths Mystery Dinner Show. If Sherlock Holmes has always intrigued you, head on over for a four-course meal served up with a healthy dose of conspiracy. Sleuths is a hotbed of local acting talent, with 13 rotating whodunit performances staged throughout the year in three different theaters. The comedy-mystery show begins during your appetizer, and murder is the case by the time they clear your plates. You'll get to discuss clues and question still-living characters over dinner and solve the crime during dessert. Prizes go to top sleuths. Comedy and magic shows fill up the late-night lineup on weekends. ✉ *8267 International Dr.* ☎ *407/363–1985* ⊕ *www.sleuths.com* ✉ *$59.95; 3–11 $28.95* ◷ *Performances usually daily at 7:30 but call ahead.*

KISSIMMEE

DINNER SHOWS

Capone's Dinner and Show. This musical dramedy brings you back to gangland Chicago of the 1930s, when mobsters and their molls were the height of underworld society. You'll meet Al Capone and learn that you can become a member of the "family," but you've got to help take care of a rat in the organization. Flashy costumes and musical numbers are accompanied by an all-you-can-eat American and Italian buffet that includes beer, alcoholic mixed drinks, and cocktails for kids. Check the website for a 50%-off coupon. ✉ *4740 W. Irlo Bronson Memorial Hwy.* ☎ *407/397–2378, 800/220–8428* ⊕ *www.alcapones. com* ✉ *$63.99; online discounts.*

FAMILY
Medieval Times. In a huge, ersatz-medieval manor you'll see a tournament of sword fights, jousting matches, and other exciting games. More than a dozen charging horses and a cast of 75 knights, nobles, wizards, and maidens participate. Sound silly? It is. But it's also a true extravaganza. That the show takes precedence over the meat-and-potatoes fare is obvious: everyone sits facing forward at long, narrow banquet tables stepped auditorium-style above the tournament area. Kids love eating without forks; adults are swept away by the tremendous horse-riding artistry. Check the website for discounts. ✉ *4510 W. Vine St.* ☎ *407/396–1518, 888/935–6878* ⊕ *www.medievaltimes.com* ✉ *$62.95–$82.95; 12 and under $36.95* ◷ *Castle daily 9–4, performances usually daily at 8.*

SHOPPING

Updated by
Joseph Hayes

From fairy-tale kingdoms to Old West–style trading posts to outlet malls, Walt Disney World and Orlando have a plethora of shopping opportunities that won't leave you disappointed. The colors are bright and energetic, the textures soft and cuddly, and the designs fresh and thoughtful.

Before you board any roller coaster or giggle at any show, you'll catch yourself window-shopping and delighting in the thought of making a purchase. And when it comes time to do some serious shopping, you may have a hard time deciding what to buy with all the options available. Of course, your best bet is to wait a couple of days before you buy anything; survey the scene a little before spending all the money in your budget. Better yet, save shopping for the last day of your trip.

WALT DISNEY WORLD

Even if you're not inclined to buy, the shops on Disney property are worth a look. Across the board, they're open, inviting, cleverly themed, and have beautiful displays. Of course, you could easily pick up $100 worth of goods before you've ventured even 10 feet into a store, but you're better off practicing some restraint. Enjoy the experience of just looking first. If you see something you like, think about it while you enjoy the rest of your day. You might see something even better in the next store. If you're still thinking of that beautiful stuffed Cheshire Cat or Cinderella snow globe at the end of the day, you can always go back to get it. That way you don't weigh yourself down with purchases until you're ready to leave. If you're a Disney hotel guest, you never have to carry off your purchases—Disney stores will deliver your merchandise to your room for free.

Also, don't let the price tags scare you off. Small souvenirs (key chains, pens, small toys, etc.) for less than $10 are available in almost every store. Just be careful with souvenir-hungry kids. Many attractions exit directly into gift shops. Even if you put your kid on a strict budget, he may be overwhelmed by the mind-boggling choices at hand and be completely unable to make a selection. If you return home and realize that you've forgotten a critical souvenir, call WDW's Merchandise Mail Order service at ☎ *407/363–6200.*

MAGIC KINGDOM

Everywhere you turn in the Magic Kingdom there are shops and stalls urging you to take home a little piece of the magic.

MAIN STREET, U.S.A.

Arribas Brothers. This shop dazzles with Arribas Brothers–engraved crystal pieces like a sparkling Cinderella coach or an iconic glass slipper in one of many sizes (though none will fit your foot!). ■TIP➜ **Be sure to visit the glass studio and its 2,100°F furnaces in the back, where a glassblower explains the process while creating wineglasses and bowls. Fascinating!** ✉ *Main Street, U.S.A.* ⊕ *https://disneyworld.disney.go.com/shops/downtown-disney/.*

DRUMROLL, PLEASE . . .

The number-one best store on Disney property is World of Disney in the Marketplace section of Downtown Disney. You could actually skip all of the stores in the theme parks and find everything you want here in an hour. And it may be a cliché, but there really is something for everyone, whether you're looking for something small and inexpensive, like the $3 princess pen, or a Disney collectible, like a Mickey watch or figurine.

The Emporium. At 17,000 square feet, it's one of the largest souvenir shops in any of the parks. You'll find thousands of Disney character products, from sunglasses to plush toys. Princess items rock for little girls; the costume jewelry is an inexpensive souvenir. This is the place to buy Mickey sweatshirts or T-shirts. Inquire about deals or marked-down merchandise. ✉ *Main Street, U.S.A.*

Uptown Jewelers. It's a treasure chest of jewelry, figurines, and accessories by Vera Bradley, Dooney and Bourke, and other leading designers. If dressing up is your thing, Uptown has your bling. ✉ *Main Street, U.S.A.* ⊕ *https://disneyworld.disney.go.com/shops/magic-kingdom/.*

ADVENTURELAND

Agrabah Bazaar. In addition to the expected Aladdin-wear and Jasmine costumes, you'll also find maracas and other inexpensive percussion instruments, gold- and silver-plated bangles, collectible pins, sunglasses, and snappy safari hats. ✉ *Adventureland* ⊕ *https://disneyworld.disney.go.com/shops/magic-kingdom/.*

Pirate's Bazaar. Just outside the Pirates of the Caribbean, you can stock up on pirate hats, swords, flintlocks, and hooks-for-hands. The ultimate scalawag topper is a Captain Jack Sparrow hat complete with braids. ✉ *Adventureland.*

FRONTIERLAND

Big Al's. This merchandise cart across the walkway from the Country Bear Jamboree has Davy Crockett coonskin caps, cowboy hats like Woody wears in *Toy Story*, and other gear that draws oohs and aahs from cowboy and cowgirl wannabes. ✉ *Frontierland.*

10

LIBERTY SQUARE

Ye Olde Christmas Shoppe. Christmas in July—it can happen only at Disney. Shoppers who arrive after Christmas may discover some markdowns on ornaments. Mickey, princess, and other character-themed stockings are hot items. Character ornaments, Mickey wedding top hats, and Minnie bridal veils are always in stock. ⊠ *Liberty Sq.*

FANTASYLAND

Castle Couture. Sparkly, shimmery dresses, hats, dolls, jewelry, and princess nightgowns and slippers are all the rage here. ⊠ *Fantasyland.*

TOMORROWLAND

Mickey's Star Traders. One of the largest shops in the Magic Kingdom, Star Traders trades on the purchase of all things Star Wars by Disney. Licensed merchandise with Mickey spins, and a wall-size mural with a multitude of hidden Mickeys are highlights. ⊠ *Tomorrowland.*

EPCOT

Fine goods and trinkets from all over the world, some handcrafted, are sold at the pavilions representing individual countries here. Check out the Japanese and Chinese kimonos, Moroccan fezzes, French wines, Norwegian sweaters, and Mexican wood carvings. A United Kingdom shop even helps you research your family coat of arms, which you can buy as a paper printout or dressed up with paint or embroidery.

FUTURE WORLD

Future World shopping won't tempt you to spend much money unless you're heavily into the art of Disney animation.

WORLD SHOWCASE

Fodor'sChoice ★ Each of the countries represented has at least one gift shop loaded with things reflective of the history and culture of that nation's homeland, and many of the items are authentic imported handicrafts.

If your shopping time is limited, check out the two shops at the entrance to World Showcase.

Historic Research Center. The focus at this United Kingdom outpost in the Crown & Crest is tracking down your family name and coat of arms. Take home a printout of both for $65. Drop the bigger bucks for a framed, embroidered, or hand-painted version. ⊠ *World Showcase.*

CANADA

With its recently revamped movie, Canada is worth a new look, as is its Northwest Mercantile. Along with an abundance of hockey-related merchandise and maple syrup, the shop offers a number of things not otherwise available in the United States, such as the lighthearted Hatley clothing line and the Roots fragrance and clothing line.

UNITED KINGDOM

Anglophiles will find their hearts gladdened upon entering the cobblestoned village at the United Kingdom, where an English pub sits on one side, and a collection of British, Irish, and Scottish shops beckon you on the other.

FRANCE

La Signature. In the France pavilion, follow your nose for a sniff and a spritz of high-end French perfumes. Guerlain fragrances, cosmetics, and skin-care products like the Orchidée Impériale eye cream (most recently selling for a whopping $200 apiece) draw fans from around the globe. ⊠ *World Showcase, France Pavillion* ⊕ *https://disneyworld. disney.go.com/shops/epcot/*.

Les Vins de France. Enjoy tasting some wine and shopping for a bottle or two of your favorite. A fun, practical souvenir is the sparkly Mickey wine stopper. ⊠ *World Showcase* ⊕ *https://disneyworld.disney.go.com/ shops/epcot/*.

MOROCCO

Tangier Traders. Morocco's open-air market is like something out of an Indiana Jones movie. It's a maze of shops selling straw bags and colorful carpets. It's also a great place to pick up something really different, like a Moroccan fez or belly-dancing gear, including a bright scarf, finger cymbals, and a CD with all the music you need to wow your audience. ⊠ *World Showcase* ⊕ *https://disneyworld.disney.go.com/shops/epcot/*.

JAPAN

Mitsukoshi. Hello Kitty, one of Japan's most popular toys, is on hand here. Another toy favorite is a 4-inch collectible Bebichhichi doll with pacifier. Dress up with a washable poly kimono or a more luxurious silk version ($40–$400), or check out the shimmering pearl jewelry. You'll be tempted to take home some sweets after watching a Japanese Candy Art demonstration just outside the store (see *Times Guide* for demo schedule). ⊠ *World Showcase*.

ITALY

Il Bel Cristallo. For chic Italian totes, accessories, and collectibles, stop at the Italy pavilion. You'll also find fragrances by Fendi, Prada, and Bulgari. ⊠ *World Showcase*.

Tutto Gusto Wine Cellar. This café and wine bar in the Italy pavilion is an exclusive seller of some of the country's unique wines. ⊠ *World Showcase*.

GERMANY

Weinkeller. In Germany, you can buy a wine-flight passport ($20) here for two 2-ounce samples of German wine—Rieslings and ice wines are popular—as well as two samples each of Italian and French wines at the Italy and France pavilions (or you can pick up the same passport when visiting those other two countries). ⊠ *World Showcase* ⊕ *https:// disneyworld.disney.go.com/shops/epcot/*.

CHINA

House of Good Fortune. China's sprawling bazaar has a huge selection of tea sets ranging in style from traditional to contemporary ($45 and up) and fragranced candles that are sure to align your chi. Butterfly hair combs and brocade pajamas are beautiful, but the hottest items are little Buddha statues, available for $6 and up. ⊠ *World Showcase* ⊕ *https:// disneyworld.disney.go.com/shops/epcot/*.

10

NORWAY

Puffin's Roost. In Norway, Viking wannabes go crazy for the soft toy spears and shields. The plush seals are sweet for tots, and you can find Norwegian pewter, leather goods, and colorful sweaters, along with a wide variety of character goods from the hit movie *Frozen*. ⊠ *World Showcase* ⊕ *https://disneyworld.disney.go.com/shops/epcot/*.

MEXICO

El Ranchito del Norte. Get sombreros, shirts, and multicolored maracas in this streetside bazaar just outside the Mexico pyramid. ⊠ *World Showcase* ⊕ *https://disneyworld.disney.go.com/shops/epcot/*.

Plaza de Los Amigos. As you enter the Mexico pavilion and descend the staircase, stop in the village square here to browse the hand-painted wood carvings crafted by Zapotec Indians of Oaxaca in southern Mexico. Vendors' carts offer home decor gifts, silver jewelry, sombreros, piñatas, and pottery. ⊠ *World Showcase.*

DISNEY'S HOLLYWOOD STUDIOS

HOLLYWOOD BOULEVARD

You can upgrade your look at Keystone Clothiers. Mickey's of Hollywood has something for everyone in the family.

Keystone Clothiers. This shop pops with stylish clothing and accessories for adults. Handbags and totes sport classic Mickey Mouse artwork. Colorful scarves with hidden Mickeys and other designs are popular buys. Character-theme clothing for men, including ties, hats, and even Hawaiian shirts, elicit smiles. ⊠ *Hollywood Blvd.*

Mickey's of Hollywood. The largest store in Hollywood Studios is a miniversion of the Magic Kingdom's Emporium with toys, T-shirts, and doodads. Blue velvety Sorcerer's Apprentice hats have Mouse ears, plus a moon and stars that light up. You'll also find plush Minnie Mouse and Donald Duck character key chains and lots of Disney-character-embossed tech accessories. ⊠ *Hollywood Blvd.*

Tower Hotel Gifts. After the screams and thrills of the Tower of Terror, what could be better than a mug from the Hotel bar, the actual bell from the front desk, or a key from "your" room. ⊠ *Sunset Blvd.* ⊕ *https:// disneyworld.disney.go.com/shops/hollywood-studios/*

ECHO LAKE

Almost as popular as the pirate swords and hats in the Magic Kingdom are the Indiana Jones bullwhips and fedoras sold at the **Indiana Jones Adventure Outpost,** next to the stunt amphitheater, and the Darth Vader and Wookie masks at **Tatooine Traders,** outside of Star Tours. Serious Star Wars collectors might also find the action figure that's been eluding them, as well as books and comics. It's a busy store that inspires browsing.

Indiana Jones Adventure Outpost. Almost as popular as the pirate hats in the Magic Kingdom are the Indiana Jones felt fedoras sold at this outpost near the stunt amphitheater. Small kids can get a complete Indy play set with fedora, machete, pistol, and gems for about $20. ⊠ *Echo Lake.*

Tatooine Traders. This spot outside of the Star Tours ride is jammed with kids clamoring to build their own single or double light sabers complete with crystals, hilts, and blades. Collectible pins and Vinylmation characters are popular here. ⊠ *Echo Lake.*

STREETS OF AMERICA

The Writer's Stop. A cup of coffee or a spot of tea pairs well with some browsing here, with comfy seating and fresh baked goodies. If you happen to hit it right, you might get a book signed by a celebrity author. ⊠ *Streets of America.*

ANIMATION COURTYARD

Animation Gallery. If you appreciate the art of animation, this is the place. It's loaded with interesting pieces, some valuable, some not. You can watch artists sketch characters and hand-paint animation cels; you can also buy limited-edition, hand-painted cels that include "Goofy Moments," and "Off to Neverland" ($125–$290). You'll also find statuettes, posters, and animation books. ⊠ *Animation Courtyard.*

In Character. Little girls love this open-air shop next to the Voyage of the Little Mermaid for the dolls, plush princess toys, and dress-up costumes. You can drop a small bundle on glass (plastic) slippers and a magical light-up wand or spring for the coveted Ariel mermaid costume gown. ⊠ *Animation Courtyard.*

SUNSET BOULEVARD

Sunset Club Couture. It's the one shop you don't want to miss on Sunset Boulevard. Vintage-style T-shirts of Mickey, Pluto, Donald, and Grumpy are classy alternatives to standard-issue T-shirts, and a white sequined Mickey hat adds flair to any outfit. Women's fashion tees ($30) and costume bling ($12–$30) draw lots of shoppers. Customized watches like those sold at the Magic Kingdom's Uptown Jewelers are sold here, too. ⊠ *Sunset Blvd.*

DISNEY'S ANIMAL KINGDOM

DISCOVERY ISLAND

10

Disney Outfitters. The Outfitters, near the Tip Board, features unusual keepsakes like hand-painted ostrich eggs ($85–$185). There's a broad selection of upscale men's and women's apparel as well as jewelry and pottery handcrafted by African artisans. ⊠ *Discovery Island.*

Island Mercantile. To the left as you enter Discovery Island from the Oasis, the Animal Kingdom's largest shop stocks clothing, cookware, photo frames, and logo souvenirs. Safari hats, caps, and straw hats range from $20 to $30, and you can buy a backpack or messenger bag. Load it with towels for when you emerge soaked from Kali River Rapids. ⊠ *Discovery Island ⊕ https://disneyworld.disney.go.com/shops/animal-kingdom/.*

DINOLAND U.S.A

Chester & Hester's Dinosaur Treasures. Dinophiles can't resist the finds here. It has a big display of quite large and scary-looking, yet soft and huggable, T-rex, velociraptor, and other dinosaur figures ($13–$23). Beyond the prehistoric, the shop has an attractive bin of rocks for collectors. ⊠ *DinoLand U.S.A.* ⊕ *https://disneyworld.disney.go.com/ shops/animal-kingdom/.*

ASIA

Yak & Yeti Bhaktapur Market. At this gem of a shop you'll find bejeweled sandals and thongs and gorgeous, colorful print scarves of silk, satin, or India chiffon. There's also a good chance you'll find something on the clearance shelves—anything from a calligraphy kit to a Buddha figurine. ⊠ *Asia.*

AFRICA

Mombasa Marketplace and Ziwani Traders. In Harambe Village, this is a great stop for unusual items like hand-painted dishes from Zimbabwe and South African wines such as a Chakalaka red varietal by Spice Route Winery. Young kids like to play with the small, inexpensive figurines of giraffes, elephants, rhinos, and other critters they just saw on their Kilimanjaro Safaris ride. ⊠ *Africa* ⊕ *https://disneyworld.disney. go.com/shops/animal-kingdom/.*

DOWNTOWN DISNEY

Fodor's Choice
★

Why spend valuable touring time shopping in the theme parks when you can come here (for no entry fee) on your first or last day? The perfect place for one-stop souvenir shopping, the newly revamped Downtown Disney, soon to be Disney Springs, has dozens of stores, including the vast, hard-to-top World of Disney, the super-kid-friendly LEGO Imagination Center, and the überhip Tren-D clothing and accessory shop.

MARKETPLACE

A lakefront outdoor mall with meandering sidewalks, hidden alcoves, jumping fountains that kids can splash around in, and absolutely fabulous toy stores, the Marketplace is a great place to spend a relaxing afternoon or evening, especially if you're looking for a way to give the kids a break from standing in line. There are plenty of spots to grab a bite, rest your feet, or enjoy a cup of coffee while taking in the pleasant water views and the hustle and bustle of excited tourists. The Marketplace is generally open from 9:30 am to 11 pm. If you happen to run out of cash while you're shopping, you can apply for instant Disney credit at any register. How convenient.

Chapel Hats. Disney hats and bride-and-groom ears are joined by a selection of the world's best hats at this specialty retailer new to the Disney Springs expansion of the Marketplace. Fedoras, fascinators, and floppy hats can be found, along with Mickey favorites. ⊠ *1642 E. Buena Vista Dr.*

DisneyQuest Emporium. A full day at the interactive DisneyQuest wouldn't be complete without a visit to the Emporium, with racks upon racks of collectible pins, Disney apparel, and sparkly toys. ⊠ *West Side* ⊕ *https:// disneyworld.disney.go.com/shops/downtown-disney/.*

Disney's Design-a-Tee. Tucked next to the long-standing Art of Disney gallery, this shop wows creative types with eight touch-screen computer stations where you can select your Hanes shirt (color, size, style), then choose from among hundreds of Disney images (contemporary and vintage) to complete your design ($22.95 children's size; $26.95 adult size). These are perfect for a family-reunion keepsake. ⊠ *Marketplace.*

LEGO Imagination Center. An impressive backdrop of large, elaborate LEGO sculptures and piles of colorful LEGO bricks welcomes children and their parents who want to build toy castles, cars, and pirate ships. The center, including its covered outdoor play area, has been expanded by 3,500 square feet to accommodate more brick-building stations and merchandise. ■TIP➔ **Ask a clerk to point out the discounted merchandise shelf.** ⊠ *Marketplace.*

LittleMissMatched. Girls and their moms are goofy for the candy-colored T-shirts, jammies, duffels, and miss-matched socks (a pack of three pairs of knee-high socks for $13) at this Marketplace shop. ■TIP➔ **Seasonal sales run periodically, and there's a good chance you can dress up with quirky flair for a bargain.** ⊠ *Marketplace* ⊕ *https://disneyworld.disney.go.com/shops/downtown-disney/.*

Mickey's Pantry. If you're dying to get the recipe for a Disney dish you love, explore the cookbooks at Mickey's Pantry. It's hard to resist Mickey's own brand of kitchen items, and kids clamor for a bag of Mickey-shaped pasta. Look for savory spices, gourmet teas, and seasonings from the Spice & Tea Exchange. ⊠ *Marketplace.*

Once Upon A Toy. Toy rooms are themed to boys with kinetic train displays and Star Wars sets and to girls with princess and fairy items. There are lots of classic games redesigned with Disney themes, like the Haunted Mansion Game of Life. You can test-drive many of the toys, and at the Mr. Potato Head Creation Station, you can fill a box with assorted lips, noses, and even Mickey ears ($20). ⊠ *Marketplace* ⊕ *https://disneyworld.disney.go.com/shops/downtown-disney/.*

Tren-D. This Marketplace boutique has "hip" and "eclectic" written all over it. Chic sundresses with subtle Mickey-ear designs are perfect for an evening at Cirque du Soleil or dinner at House of Blues. Designer items are from Billabong, Dooney & Bourke, Harveys (The Original Seatbeltbags), and Roxy. ⊠ *Marketplace* ⊕ *https://disneyworld.disney.go.com/shops/downtown-disney/.*

World of Disney. At *the* Disney superstore—with 50,000 square feet and nearly half a million Disney items—beware of sensory overload. Themed shopping areas like the princess room ($65 for that Cinderella dress or Ariel costume) help steer you to just the right toys, clothing, housewares, and more. The Bibbidi Bobbidi Boutique, similar to the one at the Magic Kingdom, does princess makeovers ($55–$200). Disney media, from software to CDs, is everywhere, and there's candy for every sweet tooth. ⊠ *Marketplace.*

WEST SIDE

The West Side is mainly a wide promenade bordered by an intriguing mix of shops and restaurants. There are also gift shops attached to **Cirque du Soleil, DisneyQuest,** the **House of Blues,** and **Planet Hollywood.**

Hoypoloi. It's easy to lose track of time in this little oasis of fine art, handcrafted jewelry, and Zen paraphernalia. Big sellers include solid bronze frogs by Frogman; signed, digitized paintings by Alan Foxx; Josh Simpson glass-planet art pieces; and handsome menorahs and mezuzahs. ⊠ *West Side.*

Orlando Harley-Davidson. Climb aboard an iconic hog for a photo op. Harley riders of all ages can buy biker vests, patches, and other popular gear. ⊠ *West Side* ⊕ *https://disneyworld.disney.go.com/shops/downtown-disney/.*

UNIVERSAL ORLANDO

UNIVERSAL STUDIOS FLORIDA

At Universal Studios the merchandise is geared toward the attractions themselves; nearly every themed ride channels you from the exit into a gift shop with related merchandise.

The largest collection of stores is near the park gates around **Production Central** and **Hollywood.** The Universal Studios Store offers one-stop shopping with items from different areas in the studio—and even adds some merchandise from Islands of Adventure's most popular attractions. The busiest shops can be found on Diagon Alley, in the monstrously popular Harry Potter addition to the park.

Brown Derby. Felt fedoras, bush hats that seem straight from wardrobe for *Jurassic Park,* Cat in the Hat red-and-white stovepipes, and Duff Beer mug hats are among the many novelty chapeaus for sale at this Hollywood store. ⊠ *Hollywood* ⊕ *https://www.universalorlando.com/Shopping/Universal-Studios-Florida/Hollywood-Shops.aspx.*

Kwik-E-Mart. This re-creation of the animated original from the Simpsons is one of the park's most popular shopping stops. You'll find Kwik-E-Mart (Apu Nahasapeemapetilon, proprietor) caps and smocks, Duff Beer mugs, Lard Lad donuts, Marge-style blue bouffant wigs, and Homer T-shirts packaged in Duff Beer cans. In 2013, an assortment of Springfield-inspired locales appeared, making the shop and its surroundings one of the park's best photo ops. ⊠ *World Expo Shops.*

Silver Screen Collectibles. The Queen of Comedy, Lucille Ball, still makes people smile—and makes a wonderful subject for souvenirs from cookie jars to aprons. Celebrity photos, books on TV and film, and the world's largest selection of Betty Boop souvenirs also feature prominently in this shop perfectly located near the entrance/exit. ⊠ *Hollywood* ⊕ *https://www.universalorlando.com/Shopping/Theme-Park-Shops.aspx.*

SpongeBob StorePants. There seems to be no end to the desire to own items featuring SpongeBob and friends. When you see this shop with its cartoonish nautical theme—pink jellyfish overhead, a pineapple home in the middle of the store, and SpongeBob merchandise from mugs to shorts to swimwear all around—there's scarcely a chance you can pass it by. ⊠ *Woody Woodpecker's KidZone* ⊕ *https://www.universalorlando.com/Shopping/Theme-Park-Shops.aspx.*

Super Silly Stuff. Talk about truth in advertising. This colorful gift shop tied to Despicable Me: Minion Mayhem is filled with what seems to be millions of cute minions (both one-eyed and two-eyed) on T-shirts, mugs, and stuffed dolls. Gru fans can also sport a black-and-gray scarf like the one worn by the supervillain—sold separately or silk-screened onto a T-shirt. ⊠ *Production Central* ⊕ *https://www.universalorlando. com/Shopping/Universal-Studios-Florida/Production-Central-Shops. aspx.*

Universal Studios Store. This sizable store doesn't have all the merchandise that's sold in individual park gift shops, but as the park's central shopping destination, it does have most of it—and some of the best, including T-shirts, stuffed animals, and limited-edition Universal trading pins. A big plus is that you'll also find popular merchandise sold primarily at Islands of Adventure. ⊠ *Production Central* ⊕ *www. universalorlando.com.*

Wizarding World of Harry Potter: Diagon Alley. Underneath the fire-breathing dragon atop Gringott's Bank are cobblestone streets filled with Harry Potter–themed shops. And more shops. From the stuffed pets at Magical Menagerie to the (very!) expensive clothing at Quality Quiddich supplies, everything Hogwarts can be found here, including dark arts supplies down the chilly and sinister Knockturn Alley. ⊠ *6000 Universal Blvd.* ⊕ *https://www.universalorlando.com/Theme-Parks/ Universal-Studios-Florida/Wizarding-World-of-Harry-Potter-Diagon- Alley/Shopping.aspx.*

ISLANDS OF ADVENTURE

At Islands of Adventure the merchandise varies in each section of the park. If you simply must have a Spider-Man T-shirt or Incredible Hulk coffee mug, for example, head to Marvel Super Hero Island.

The largest concentration of stores is near the gates at the **Port of Entry.** And, as at Universal Studios, a central emporium—the Trading Company—carries nearly every coveted collectible from nearly every park shop. Keep in mind that **Hogsmeade Village** in the Wizarding World of Harry Potter is the place for Potter-related memorabilia and wizard supplies, along with the train-connected Diagon Alley at Universal Studios (two-park ticket required).

TOP SOUVENIRS

Several stores carry superhero and film-themed souvenirs—from Spider-Man gear and Incredible Hulk fists at IOA to Egyptian hats and clothing from The Mummy at Universal Studios.

At Seuss Landing, Thing 1 and Thing 2 T-shirts are always a hit with couples and siblings. Or how about a couple of red-and-white-stripe *Cat in the Hat* mugs?

Visit IOA's Wizarding World of Harry Potter and you may find yourself heading home with a wand, omnioculars, a quaffle ball, Hogwarts robe, or Nimbus 2000 broomstick.

TOP SHOPS

Borgin & Burkes. Count on cracking open your wallet in the main repository of Potterabilia. There are Hogwarts school uniforms; hundreds of wands; broomsticks, including the top-of-the-line Nimbus 2000 and

10

TOP ATTRACTIONS

Downtown Disney. The perfect place for one-stop souvenir shopping, Downtown Disney now has dozens of stores, including World of Disney, easily the largest and best store on Disney property.

Epcot World Showcase. Trinkets from all over the world, some handcrafted and incredibly unique, are sold at the pavilions representing individual countries here. Check out the Japanese bonsai trees and Moroccan fez hats.

Main Street, U.S.A., Magic Kingdom. The Main Street buildings are so adorable with their forced perspective architecture, pastel colors, and elaborately decorated facades that you want to go inside

them and start examining the wares immediately. Don't waste precious touring time shopping in the morning, but definitely come back to check them out in the afternoon or evening.

Mall at Millenia. Visiting this mall is like going to New York for the afternoon. One look at the store names—Gucci, Dior, Chanel, Jimmy Choo, Cartier, Tiffany—and you'll think you've died and gone to retail heaven.

Park Avenue, Winter Park. If you have the chance to visit the upscale village of Winter Park north of Orlando, carve out an hour or two to stroll up and down this thoroughfare.

Firebolt; magical items such as sneakoscopes, spectrespecs, and omnioculars; and "all your Quidditch needs," including the elusive Golden Snitch. ⊠ *Wizarding World of Harry Potter* ⊕ *www.universalorlando.com.*

Dinostore. Above a juvenile chorus of "I want this!" are adults counseling their kids on what they actually *need*. That can be a monumental task in this large store, which is packed with dino hats, shorts, necklaces, cards, mugs, squirt guns, figurines, and the clever T-Rex T-shirt emblazoned with the helpful suggestion "Bite Me." Rest assured there are educational dino toys, too. ⊠ *Jurassic Park* ⊕ *https://www. universalorlando.com/Shopping/Islands-of-Adventure/Jurassic-Park-Shopping.aspx.*

Trading Company. The rambling emporium inside the entrance/exit of IOA is the largest store in the park; filled with a little something of everything from everywhere, even items from the attractions of Universal Studios. Here you'll find Shrek, SpongeBob, Spider-Man, the Simpsons, superheroes, and *puh-lenty* of Potter products plastered on sandals, frames, mugs, cups, caps, and clothing. ⊠ *Islands of Adventure* ⊕ *www.universalorlando.com.*

CITYWALK

This 30-acre entertainment and retail complex is at the hub of promenades that lead to Universal Studios and Islands of Adventure. Shops here sell fine jewelry, cool beachwear, fashionable clothing, and stylish accessories. The best stores are near the entrance/exit of the complex.

Fresh Produce. Featuring fashions that look right at home in sunny Florida, this boutique showcases comfortable and colorful swimwear, blouses, capri slacks, dresses, footwear, beach gear, and accessories designed for coastal comfort. ⊠ *CityWalk* ⊕ *https://www.universalorlando.com/ Shopping/shopping.aspx.*

Quiet Flight. Granted the closest beach is about 60 miles east, you can still get outfitted like a surfer at this shop, which sports an inventory featuring brand names such as Billabong, Quicksilver, Hurley, and Oakley. In addition to shorts and shirts, Quiet Flight also sells sandals, watches, sunglasses (Ray-Ban, Prada, and D&G among the featured names), and surfboards! ⊠ *CityWalk* ⊕ *https://www.universalorlando. com/Shopping/shopping.aspx.*

ORLANDO

Visitors from as far away as Britain and Brazil often arrive in Orlando with empty suitcases for their purchases. Although shopping has all but disappeared from Downtown, the metro area is filled with options. There really is something for everyone—from high-end fashion to outlet-mall chic, from the world's largest flea market to a boutique-filled town, from an antique treasure to a hand-hewn Florida find.

The College Park area, once an antiques-hunter's dream, still has some treasures to be found along North Orange Avenue and Edgewater Drive, including the largest vinyl-record shop in Florida.

The simultaneously glitzy and kitschy International Drive has almost 500 designer outlet stores and odd, off-brand electronics shops. The factory outlets on the north end of I-Drive once consisted of shops with merchandise piled on tables; today the shops here are equal to their higher-priced first-run cousins. The strip also has plenty of massive restaurants and, for those in your group who don't feel like shopping, movie theaters.

CENTRAL ORLANDO

10

SHOPPING CENTERS

Florida Mall. With 250-plus stores and 1.8 million square feet of shopping, it's big enough for you to vacation here—in fact, there's even an attached hotel. Only 7 miles from the airport, the mall attracts crowds of international visitors eager for American bargains. Anchor stores include Sears, JCPenney, Dillard's, and Macy's. An expanded food court adds a total of almost 50 casual eateries and sit-down restaurants to the shopping mix. Stroller and wheelchair rentals are available; there are even concierge services and a currency exchange. The mall is 4½ miles east of Interstate 4 and International Drive at the corner of Sand Lake Road and South Orange Blossom Trail. ⊠ *8001 S. Orange Blossom Trail, South Orlando* ☏ *407/851–7234* ⊕ *www.simon.com/mall/ the-florida-mall* ☯ *Weekdays 10–9, Sat. 10–10, Sun. noon–8.*

SPECIALTY SHOPS

Orlando Harley-Davidson. During Daytona Beach Bike Week in March and Biktober Fest in October, this is Hog Central. Anything Harley is available, from chrome pipes, leather clothing, and cycle GPS units to actual motorcycles to buy or rent—yes, rent. The staff can teach you how to ride or paint flames on the side of your bike, and the calendar includes themed events with free food and live music. There are other locations in East Orlando and Kissimmee, as well as shops selling gear on International Drive, at Downtown Disney, and at the airport. ⊠ *3770 37th St., South Orlando* ☎ *407/423–0346* ⊕ *www. orlandoharley.com* ☉ *Mon.–Sat. 9–7, Sun. 10–6.*

Rock & Roll Heaven. Vinyl records are popular again, but according to R&R Heaven, they never left. Thousands upon thousands of LPs, 45s, CDs, and cassettes, in every conceivable (and a few unbelievable) music style can be found here, starting at as little as $1. The posters rock, too. ⊠ *1814 N. Orange Ave., Lake Ivanhoe* ☎ *407/896–1952* ⊕ *www.rock-n-rollheaven.com* ☉ *Mon.–Sat. 10–7:30, Sun. 11–4.*

Washburn Imports. Here you'll find an eclectic mix of antiques, commissioned furniture, and one-of-a-kind home furnishings made in India, Indonesia, and Thailand. There's a second location in Sanford. After hours, the back room turns into the Imperial Wine Bar, a popular hipster haven of craft beers, local wine, and snacks. ⊠ *1800 N. Orange Ave., Lake Ivanhoe* ☎ *407/228–4403* ⊕ *www.washburnimports.com* ☉ *Mon.–Sat. 10–6, Sun. 11–5; Imperial Mon.–Thurs. 5 pm–midnight, Fri. and Sat. 5 pm–2 am.*

INTERNATIONAL DRIVE

FACTORY OUTLETS

The International Drive area is filled with factory outlet stores, most on the northeast end. These outlets are clumped together in expansive malls or scattered along the drive, and much of the merchandise is ostensibly discounted 20%–75%. You can find just about anything, some of it top quality, but be advised: retailers have learned that they can fool shoppers into believing they must be getting a deal because they're at a stripped-down outlet store. Actually, prices may be the same as or higher than those at other locations.

Orlando International Premium Outlets. This is a prime destination for international shoppers, who can find shoes, clothing, cosmetics, electronics, and household goods at a fraction of their home-country prices. The massive complex at the north tip of International Drive includes Saks Fifth Avenue OFF 5TH, Coach, Kate Spade New York, Victoria's Secret Outlet, and a Disney outlet. Searching for bargains works up an appetite, and there are plenty of places to eat here, either in the well-lit food court or in one of several sit-down and highly regarded restaurants. ⊠ *4951 International Dr.* ☎ *407/352–9600* ⊕ *www.premiumoutlets. com* ☉ *Mon.–Sat. 10 am–11 pm, Sun. 10–9.*

Orlando Vineland Premium Outlets. This outlet capitalizes on its proximity to Disney (it's at the confluence of Interstate 4, State Road 535, and International Drive). It's easier to see from the highway than to enter, and parking is tedious and scarce, but smart shoppers have lunch on International Drive and take the I-Ride Trolley right to the front entrance (it runs every 15 minutes). The center's design makes this almost an open-air market, so walking can be pleasant on a nice day. You'll find Prada, Gap, Nike, Adidas, Tory Burch, Polo Ralph Lauren, Giorgio Armani, Burberry, Tommy Hilfiger, Reebok, and about 100 other stores. ✉ *8200 Vineland Ave.* ☎ *407/238–7787* ⊕ *www. premiumoutlets.com* ⊗ *Mon.–Sat. 10 am–11 pm, Sun. 10–9.*

SHOPPING CENTERS

Artegon Marketplace. A new artisanal-market approach to shopping malls, Artegon replaces the old Festival Bay Mall with a shopping "village" of 250 to 300 kiosks in which artisans sell everything from leather goods to local hot sauces, and there's a weekly indoor farmers' market for local produce. Shepler's Western Wear, Bass Pro Shops Outdoor World, and Ron Jon Surf Shop continue to attract customers, as does the 20-screen Cinemark Theater and several restaurants. ✉ *5250 International Dr.* ☎ *407/351–7718* ⊕ *www.artegonmarketplace.com/* ⊗ *Mon.–Sat. 10–9, Sun. 11–7.*

Pointe Orlando. What was once an enclosed shopping center is now a dining, shopping, and entertainment hot spot—one that's within walking distance of five top hotels and the Orange County Convention Center. In addition to WonderWorks and the enormous Regal IMAX theater, the complex has specialty shops such as Armani Exchange, Tommy Bahama, Chico's, Tommy Hilfiger, Hollister, Charming Charlie, and Victoria's Secret. Restaurants have become a reason to visit, with the very high-end Capital Grille, the Oceanaire Seafood Room, Cuba Libre Restaurant and Rum Bar, The Pub, Marlow's Tavern, the popular Funky Monkey Bistro & Bar, B.B. King's Blues Club, and Taverna Opa. Blue Martini and Lafayette's provide after-hours entertainment and adult beverages. Check the website for a list of happy-hour specials. ✉ *9101 International Dr.* ☎ *407/248–2838* ⊕ *www.pointeorlando.com* ⊗ *Oct.–May, Mon.–Sat. noon–10, Sun. noon–8; June–Sept., Fri. and Sat. noon–9, Sun.–Thurs. noon–8.*

SPECIALTY STORES

Bass Pro Shops Outdoor World. Inside a 150,000-square-foot Western-style lodge—and with fishing ponds, deer tracks in the concrete, and a massive stone fireplace—the store packs in countless boats, RVs, tents, rifles, deep-sea fishing gear, freshwater fishing tackle, scuba equipment, fly-tying materials (classes are offered, too), a pro shop, outdoor clothing, and Uncle Buck's Cabin (a snack bar). If you're an outdoors enthusiast, this is a must-visit. ✉ *5156 International Dr.* ☎ *407/563–5200* ⊕ *www. basspro.com* ⊗ *Mon.–Sat. 9 am–10 pm, Sun. 10–8.*

10

KISSIMMEE

FACTORY OUTLETS

Lake Buena Vista Factory Stores. Although it has scant curb appeal, it does have a good collection of standard outlet stores for Aeropostale, Converse, Eddie Bauer, Fossil, Gap, Izod, LOFT, Nike, Old Navy, and Tommy Hilfiger. Check out the coupons on the website, too. Take Exit

68 off Interstate 4, and go 2 miles south on State Road 535. ⊠ *15657 S. Apopka Vineland Rd. (State Rd. 535), Lake Buena Vista* ☎ *407/238–9301* ⊕ *www.lbvfs.com* ⊙ *Mon.–Sat. 10–9, Sun. 10–7.*

FLEA MARKETS

192 Flea Market Outlet. With 400 booths, this market is about a fourth the size of Flea World in Sanford, but it's much more convenient if you're staying in the Disney World area, and it's open daily. The all-new merchandise includes toys, luggage, sunglasses, jewelry, clothes, beach towels, sneakers, electronics, and the obligatory T-shirts. ⊠ *4301 W. Vine St. (U.S. 192)* ☎ *407/396–4555* ⊕ *www.192fleamarketprices. com* ⊙ *Daily 9–6.*

MOUNT DORA

The Renaissance. Built in the 1920s, what was once known as the Dora Hotel is now The Renaissance, a Victorian-style shopping arcade with more than 20 shops and the Frog and the Monkey restaurant. ⊠ *411 N. Donnelly St.* ☎ *352/735–2608.*

Renninger's Twin Markets. This may be Florida's largest gathering of antiques and collectibles dealers. Atop the hill, 700 flea-market dealers sell household goods, garage-sale surplus, produce, baked goods, pets, and anything else you can think of. Below, 200 antiques booths purvey ephemera, old phonographs, art deco fixtures, antique furniture, and more. If you have the time, hit the flea market first, since that's where antiques dealers find many of their treasures. Both markets are open every weekend, but on the third weekend of the month the antiques market has a fair attracting about 300 dealers. The really big shows—drawing 800 booths—are three-day extravaganzas in November, January, and February. A Guitars, Cars, and Cycles Swap Meet is held the second Sunday of each month. You can spend a morning or all day at these events. Renninger's is busiest from October through May. From Interstate 4, take Florida's Turnpike north to Exit 267A to Route 429 east and, 8 miles later, U.S. 441 north to Mount Dora. ⊠ *20651 U.S. 441* ☎ *352/383–8393* ⊕ *www.renningers.com* ✉ *Markets and antiques fairs free; extravaganzas $10 Fri., $6 Sat., $4 Sun., $15 for 3 days* ⊙ *Antiques center: weekends 9–5; antiques fairs: Mar.–Oct., 3rd weekend of month 9–5; extravaganzas: Jan., Feb., and Nov., 3rd weekend of month 8–5.*

Uncle Al's Time Capsule. This is a great place to sift through some terrific Hollywood memorabilia and collectibles. Hottest sellers are autographed items featuring *The Wizard of Oz, Gone with the Wind,* Elvis, and Marilyn Monroe. ⊠ *140 E. 4th Ave.* ☎ *352/383–1958* ⊕ *www. awautographs.com.*

WINTER PARK

Park Avenue in downtown Winter Park is definitely a shopper's heaven. This inviting brick street has chic boutiques, sidewalk cafés, and hidden alleyways that lead to peaceful nooks and crannies with even more restaurants and shops. The last several years have seen a mass exodus of the chain stores that came to dominate shopping on Park Avenue, leaving the street open to the return of boutiques. Most of these stores are privately owned and offer merchandise that cannot be easily found elsewhere.

A stroll across the railroad tracks that run through Winter Park brings you to the gentrified Hannibal Square. Centered on the intersection of New England and Pennsylvania avenues, the upscale dining and shopping found here has revitalized the area.

Farmers' Market. Try to schedule your visit to Winter Park for a Saturday morning, so you can begin your day at the weekly farmers' market, which takes place from 7 am to 1 pm at the city's old train depot, two blocks west of Park Avenue. It's a bustling, vibrant market with vendors selling farm-fresh produce, dazzling flowers, and prepared foods. Pick up locally harvested honey, locally made cheese, and freshly baked croissants. ☒ *200 W. New England Ave.* ☎ *407/599–3397* ⊕ *www. cityofwinterpark.org.*

SPECIALTY SHOPS

Charles Hosmer Morse Museum Gift Shop. The obvious reasons to shop here are for the representations of Tiffany glass, silk scarves with stained-glass motifs, and fine-art glass that Louis Comfort himself would have treasured. There are also many objects from world museum gift collections and a wide assortment of books about the Arts and Crafts movement. ☒ *445 N. Park Ave.* ☎ *407/645–5316* ⊕ *www.morsemuseum. org/museum-shop* ☉ *Tues.–Sat. 9:30–4, Sun. 1–4.*

Kathmandu/Tribalasia. The unique items here come from exotic locales like India, Indonesia, Nepal, and Turkey. Hats, turquoise and crystal jewelry, and brass figures of Indian gods are among the merchandise. Follow your nose to the smell of patchouli and sandalwood. ☒ *352 N. Park Ave.* ☎ *407/647–7071* ☉ *Mon.–Thurs. 9:30–6, Fri. and Sat. 9:30–9, Sun. 11–6.*

FAMILY **Sassafras Sweet Shoppe.** Around a corner from Park Avenue, this quaint, old-timey sweet shop is packed with goodies from yesterday and today, from vintage candy to popcorn balls. This is a perfect pit stop for kids (and adults) after a long day of shopping or touring. ☒ *115 E. Morse Blvd.* ☎ *407/388–0101* ⊕ *www.sassafrassweetshoppe.com.*

Shoooz on Park Avenue. Mephisto, Taryn Rose, Rieker, Naot, Salpy, and BeautiFeel just begin the list of designers in this cozy, shoes-only shop. ☒ *303 N. Park Ave.* ☎ *407/647–0110* ☉ *Mon.–Sat. 10–6, Sun. noon–5.*

Ten Thousand Villages. This fascinating little store sells fair-trade, artisan-crafted home decor, jewelry, and gifts of all kinds from the smaller corners of the world. ☒ *346 N. Park Ave.* ☎ *407/644–8464* ⊕ *www. tenthousandvillages.com/winterpark* ☉ *Mon.–Sat. 10–6, Sun. 11–5.*

Timothy's Gallery. It's not a museum gallery; rather, Timothy's sells wearable, sittable, usable art. Hand-carved exotic woods crafted by local artists become jewelry; blown, fused, and shaped glass turns into showcase vases and bowls; and carved furniture can turn a room into a masterpiece. ☒ *236 N. Park Ave.* ☎ *407/629–0707* ⊕ *www.timothysgallery. com* ☉ *Mon.–Thurs. 10–5:30, Fri. and Sat. 10–9, Sun. noon–5.*

10

SPAS

MAGIC KINGDOM RESORT AREA

Senses—A Disney Spa at Disney's Grand Floridian Resort. All the senses—sound, sight, smell, touch, and taste—are engaged when you enter this new, Disney-designed and -owned, 15-room spa near the Wedding Pavilion at the Grand Floridian Resort. Soothing fruit-based elixirs start the journey toward serenity, while soft lighting, gentle music, and the aroma of lavender encourage you to shed your stress along with your clothes. Lounge chairs in separate and secluded men's and women's relaxation areas offer you a spot to further unwind as you wait. Pure silk sheets on the heated massage tables surround you in heavenly luxury. Tiny green-glass tiles form a floral mosaic on the walls and on heated lounge chairs in the restful wet room (spend some time looking for the hidden Mickey on the wall). Swimsuits are required in all wet relaxation areas. Treatments include facials, scrubs, warm-stone, Swedish, and aromatherapy massages. A whimsical Mad Hatter chair offers little princesses a special place for a pedicure. Massage from $135. Packages from $375. 20% gratuity added. ⊠ *Grand Floridian Resort, 4401 Floridian Way* ☎ *407/824–3000* ⊕ *https://disneyworld. disney.go.com/spas/grand-floridian-resort-and-spa/senses-spa/* ⏎ *Parking: complimentary self-parking.*

DOWNTOWN DISNEY RESORT AREA

Blue Harmony. Infused with the colors of ocean and sky, this spa lives up to its name from the moment you enter. Its signature treatment combines exfoliation with marine salt and oil, polishing with marine salt and lavender, and a massage based on Thai techniques. Body treatments use oil-infused seawater gels to add natural minerals to the skin, and end with a cozy wrap and massage. Two of the eight treatment rooms are outdoors near the relaxation spa garden and hot tub, taking advantage of the blue Florida sky. The serene relaxation lounge offers beverages and tea as you wait for your treatment. Bring the family, as the spa offers treatments for teens and men. Massage from $120. Packages from $140. ⊠ *14651 Chelonia Pkwy.* ☎ *407/390–2442* ⊕ *www. blueharmonyorlando.com/.*

Kay Casperson Lifestyle Spa and Boutique. At the Buena Vista Palace's 10,000-square-foot haven for the frazzled fun-seeker, you can settle back in one of 14 treatment rooms for an invigorating facial using botanicals, minerals, and ingredients from the sea, or enjoy a relaxing deep-tissue massage. The Kay Casperson philosophy balances inner health and outer beauty, so after a treatment, guests are offered a free makeup application of Casperson's hypoallergenic products. Those ages 12 and under who choose the Princess Package receive a tiara along with a mani-pedi and makeup session. The spa has a full-service salon, private steam showers, a large dry sauna, separate whirlpools, and an adults-only lap pool for serene swimming. Massage from $120. Packages from $305. There is a 20% service charge. ⊠ *Buena Vista*

Palace Hotel & Spa, 1900 E. Buena Vista Dr. ☎ *407/827–3200* ⊕ *www. buenavistapalace.com/things-to-do/spa-salon/.*

Senses Spa at Disney's Saratoga Springs Resort. The spa may share its name with the Grand Floridian's, and the senses are just as successfully nourished, but the ambience is quite different at this two-story stone-and-wood spa, inspired by the legendary lodges at the mineral springs of the Adirondacks. Fruit-infused elixirs and the scent of frankincense sooth you as you enter either the separate men's or women's waiting room. Signature treatments include the hydrotherapy package that combines water and stone to exfoliate, soak, wrap, and relax that stressed-out body, and the Bamboo Fusion massage that combines warm stones and an ancient technique using heated bamboo segments. The pure silk sheets surround you with dreamlike luxury. Don't miss the spa's two wet relaxation rooms, with steam bath, pool, and heated, glass-tile-covered lounge chairs. You can even bring the family—there's a couples' treatment room and a manicure and pedicure for kids ages 4–12. Swimsuits are required in wet rooms. Massage from $145. Spa packages from $375. ✉ *Disney's Saratoga Springs Resort, 1960 Broadway* ☎ *407/939–7727* ⊕ *https://disneyworld.disney.go.com/spas/ saratoga-springs-resort-and-spa/senses-spa-saratoga/.*

SOUTH ORLANDO

Mandara Spa at Loews Portofino Bay Hotel. Adjacent to the bustling Italian-themed square at Universal's Portofino Bay resort, the doors to this Asian-themed sanctuary waft you into a more tranquil world, with bamboo screens, exotic statuary, and silk hangings. Warm blankets comfort you while you wait in the relaxation lounge for one of the 16 treatment rooms. Try the Ceremony of the Hands and Feet, an indulgence that scrubs, exfoliates, and massages your extremities, finishing with a mani-pedi. Separate men's and women's steam rooms and saunas add to the sense of serenity, but the men needn't worry about missing a game, as their lounge sports a plasma TV. Portofino's serene sand-bottomed pool is next door, as is the fitness center. Massage therapies include four hands, deep tissue, hot stone, Balinese, or Swedish. Facials and peels are available, as are full makeup, hair, and salon services. Massages from $89. Packages from $360. ✉ *5601 Universal Blvd., Universal Orlando Area* ☎ *407/503–1244* ⊕ *www.mandaraspa.com/ spa/orlando-loews-portofino-bay-hotel-at-universal-orlando.aspx.*

Ritz-Carlton Spa Orlando, Grande Lakes. Prepare to be wowed as you enter this lavish, grand spa, Orlando's largest with 40 treatment rooms, a fitness center, salon, private pool, and café—which means it can get busy. Get here in plenty of time to take a tour and get your bearings, shed your tourist togs, don a plush robe, and prepare to unwind. Unisex and co-ed waiting areas with couches and chairs are available, each on a different floor, with tea, water, fruits, and snacks. Treatments include massage, skin therapy, and deep-cleaning HydraFacials that gently extract impurities from the skin. Massage techniques include traditional Swedish, neuromuscular, stone therapy, Ashiatsu, and even one in a hammock, under the stars. Special treatments for mothers to

10

be. Massage from $145; 20% service charge is added. ⊠ *Ritz-Carlton Orlando, 4024 Central Florida Pkwy.* ☎ *407/393–4200* ⊕ *www. ritzcarlton.com/en/Properties/Orlando/Spa/Default.htm* ☞ *Parking: valet parking discounted with spa validation.*

The Spa at Shingle Creek. The romance of Old Florida surrounds the Rosen Shingle Creek resort, and most of the spa treatments feature Florida products such as citrus and cedar oils, aloe, and an Everglades sugar scrub. The Calusa Cocoon begins with an exfoliation using grapefruit, eucalyptus, and peppermint-infused clay and ends with a moisturizing wrap rich with citrus oils that relieves stress while feeding your skin. Types of massage include Swedish, aromatherapy, warm stone, and Ashiatsu barefoot massage, in which the therapist uses gravity to reach deep into your muscle tissue. A variety of facials and salon treatments are available, and, for supreme relaxation, you can even add on a 25-minute siesta where you're wrapped in hot packs after your treatment and awakened by gentle bells. Massages begin at $110. Packages begin at $215. Gratuity is included in the cost. Parking, either self or valet, is validated for day guests. ⊠ *Rosen Shingle Creek, 9939 Universal Blvd.* ☎ *407/996–9939* ⊕ *www.spaatshinglecreek.com* ☞ *Parking: complimentary valet or self parking with spa validation.*

INTERNATIONAL DRIVE AREA

nèu lotus spa at Renaissance Orlando at SeaWorld. Let the world's cares disappear as you recline in the candlelighted relaxation area, or make use of the steam room before your treatment at this bright, modern spa. An Asian-style barefoot massage can work the knots out of the tensest muscles, while the hot-and-cold-stone massage offers a more relaxing, restorative experience. Facials and skin treatments combine skin rejuvenation with shoulder relaxation and scalp massage. The spa also has a 2,600-square-foot fitness center with the latest equipment and a full-service salon. Massages include barefoot, aromatherapy, hot and cold stone, and bamboo shoot. Massages from $75. Packages from $239. Gratuity at guest's discretion. ⊠ *6677 Sea Harbor Dr.* ☎ *407/248–7428* ⊕ *www.marriott.com/spas/mcosr-renaissance-orlando-at-seaworld/ n%25c3%25a8u-lotus-spa/5014213/home-page.mi.*

The Spa at Hilton Orlando. From the deeply cushioned chaise longues in the waiting room, where guests relax in fleecy robes and cozy blankets, to the complimentary infused water, juices, teas, and fruits, guests are made to feel cherished from the moment they enter this big (15 treatment rooms) resort spa. Orange blossom is the source of the oil for the signature Neroli massage, and essences of rosemary, pine, and lavender soothe the senses during aromatherapy treatments. Massages include Swedish, deep tissue, and heated stones, and guests are welcome to linger in the steam room, full-body showers, or full-service salon, or to have a treatment in a cabana by the pool. Special services are available for youngsters and teens. Massages from $75. Packages from $335. An 18% service charge is added. Day pass available. Self-parking is free for nonhotel guests. ⊠ *6001 Destination Pkwy.* ☎ *407/313–4300* ⊕ *www. thehiltonorlando.com/spa-recreation/spa-en.html.*

The Spa at Hyatt Regency Orlando. Getting to this 22,000-square-foot, full-service contemporary retreat, set at the heart of a huge convention resort (formerly The Peabody), can be quite a hike, so guests are happy to shed their clothes and cares, don fluffy robes and slippers, and settle in for some serious rejuvenation. The separate locker rooms offer whirlpools, steam room, and showers, and guests have access to a private serenity pool, where they can soak before and after their treatments. Massages include deep tissue, aromatherapy, and warm stone. A variety of facials and complete salon services are available. Massages from $125. Packages from $425. Gratuity added. ⊠ *9801 International Dr.* 🕾 *407/284–1234* ⊕ *orlando.regency.hyatt.com/en/hotel/activities/hotel-activities/spa.html.*

The Spa at Rosen Centre. An intimate spa in a resort right across from the convention center, the Spa at Rosen Center caters to busy, stressed-out businesspeople as well as bridal parties, girlfriends' getaways, and more. Once clothes and cares are exchanged for luxurious robes and comfy slippers in the separate locker rooms, guests move to the serene, candle-lighted, and aroma-enhanced separate relaxation rooms. The men's room has a TV for those who can't or won't miss a game or the news, but the sound is off, making sure that relaxation is the ultimate goal. If those muscles need a real workout, be sure to experience a traditional Ashiatsu massage, where the masseuse, supported by a wooden frame, uses gravity and her bare feet to reach deep into those knots. Massage techniques include Swedish, therapeutic, deep tissue, warm stone, Ashiatsu, and Asian-fusion barefoot. Massages from $125. Packages from $335. Day pass available for hotel guests and nonguests. Parking validated for nonguests. ⊠ *9840 International Dr.* 🕾 *407/996–1248* ⊕ *www.spaatrosencentre.com/.*

KISSIMMEE

Mokara Spa at Omni Orlando Resort at Championsgate. Golf courses surround the Omni Orlando Resort at Championsgate, and Mokara Spa offers special treatments to ease tension and soreness in those stressed shoulders and backs. The Sports Massage uses muscle-warming oil, massage, and stretching to make sure you're ready for another round. There are plenty of choices for the nongolfer in the group, which is good, since this resort is far, far away from anything. Separate locker rooms, steam rooms, and relaxation rooms ensure privacy and serenity while you wait for your treatment. A full-service salon offers hair and nail services, and massages include Swedish, hot stone, deep tissue, and mothers-to-be. Massages from $120. Packages from $205. A 20% gratuity is added to the bill. Parking is validated if you're a day-spa visitor. ⊠ *1500 Masters Blvd., ChampionsGate* 🕾 *407/390–6603* ⊕ *www.omnihotels.com/hotels/orlando-championsgate/spa.*

Relâche Spa & Salon at Gaylord Palms Resort. The 20,000-square-foot spa is in the Everglades Atrium of this giant, Florida-themed resort, and guests may feel like explorers in a tropical wilderness as they make the trek toward tranquility. Once inside the doors, cares and clothes shed, the soft pastels and generous chaise longues of the tearoom

10

radiate serenity. Fresh fruit and beverages keep you hydrated while you wait, then it's on to serious relaxation. Try one of the signature Florida treatments, such as Islamorada Glow using coconut milk, pure cane sugar, and tropical oils, or the Clearwater Hydrating Wrap, where warm stones are applied after exfoliation, along with a vitamin-filled moisturizing wrap. Massages include hot stone, bamboo, Thai stretching, deep tissue, aromatherapy, and more. Massages from $75. Packages from $300. A 20% gratuity is added onto bill. Day pass available for a fee. ✉ *6000 W. Osceola Pkwy.* ☎ *407/586–4772* ⊕ *www.marriott.com/hotels/hotel-information/fitness-spa-services/ mcogp-gaylord-palms-resort-and-convention-center/.*

The Spa at Orlando World Center Marriott. Finding the spa in this sprawling, multitower resort can be a challenge, but once you arrive at the lower-level entrance, tranquility rules. Robes and slippers are provided in the locker rooms, but there are no private changing rooms. If you are modest, you must retreat to the bathroom or shower. The waiting room is co-ed. Steam rooms, pool, and fitness facility are available for use before or after a treatment in one of the 14 treatment rooms. The Around the World in Eighty Minutes massage combines international massage techniques, and the World Center Aromatherapy Escape starts with tea and a deluxe cleansing of your tootsies, then proceeds to an aroma-therapy massage and wrap for total relaxation. Massage types include pressure, warm stone, and Swedish. Massages from $120. Packages from $200. Gratuity at guests' discretion. ✉ *8701 World Center Dr., Lake Buena Vista Area* ☎ *407/239–4200* ⊕ *www.marriott.com/spas/ mcowc-orlando-world-center-marriott/spa-at-world-center/5014219/ home-page.mi.*

The Waldorf Astoria Spa. Don't try to pour your own tea—your gracious valet is there to serve you and make you comfortable at this huge, 22-treatment-room spa in a very deluxe hotel. Everything is designed for the guest, from custom body treatments and facials, to plush robes and spa slippers that actually fit you. Separate waiting rooms lead to a eucalyptus steam room; experiential shower that surrounds you with water, sound, and light; and a tea lounge. Try the Diamond Body, an over-the-top decadent treatment that incorporates precious stones and gold-enriched creams. The full-service salon offers every service imaginable. Massages include warm stone, Swedish, and deep tissue. Massages from $149. Packages from $380. A 20% service charge is added, but parking is complimentary. Day pass $30 for nonguests. ✉ *Waldorf Astoria, 14200 Bonnet Creek Resort La., Bonnet Creek* ☎ *407/597–5360* ⊕ *www.waldorfastoriaorlando.com/spa* ☞ *Parking: valet only, complimentary with spa validation, but please tip.*

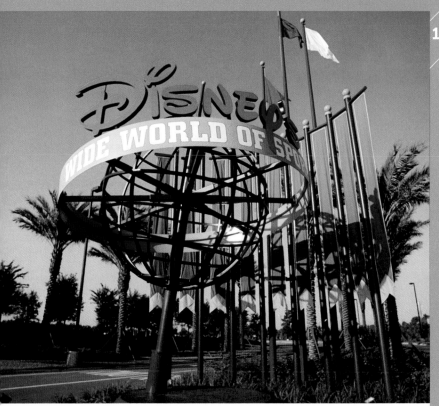

SPORTS AND
THE OUTDOORS

Updated
by Gary
McKechnie

Tennis, anyone? Or maybe you'd rather surf, parasail, or ride a horse. Should you feel the need to stretch your legs and travel outside the theme parks, you can take part in these activities and many more around Orlando.

But if your vacation is based solely at Disney, you'll have plenty of recreational opportunities to choose from. Disney is known for its championship golf courses, of course, and several lighted courts—both clay and hard—are found at five Disney resorts. Disney's Fort Wilderness is the place to saddle up for a ride through the woods, and the Contemporary Resort is number one for water sports, including parasailing.

Anglers get hooked on fishing charters; runners and bikers get their adrenaline rush on trails across the property. If you'd rather be a spectator, take yourself out to a ball game at the ESPN Wide World of Sports Complex. Popcorn? Check. Hot dogs? Check. Does it get any better than this? For Disney recreation information, call ☎ *407/939-7529.*

There are many ways to enjoy the outdoors here. You can navigate the more than 2,000 lakes and waterways, perhaps on a sportfishing excursion—something to consider in what is one of the bass-fishing capitals of the world. You can also take to the air in a glider or hot-air balloon, or stay firmly planted hiking or biking a trail.

According to the folks at the Orlando Convention and Visitors Bureau, there are more than 170 golf courses and 20 golf academies in the area. Indeed you'll probably be amazed by the country club–like golf courses (and tennis courts) run by the City of Orlando and accessible at bargain prices.

Orlando's sports arena and its three pro teams (basketball, hockey, and arena football) bring in the crowds. Throughout Central Florida, professional baseball comes down from the frozen North to warm up during spring training.

11

TOP 3 RECREATIONAL EXPERIENCES

Bob's Balloons. Think you see a lot from the top of the Tower of Terror? That ain't nothin' compared to what Bob will show you from the top of the clouds.

Sky Venture. Totally safe skydiving? That's right. In this indoor chamber, a massive turbine allows you to fly like a bird without jumping out of an airplane (or even getting that far off the ground).

Winter Summerland Miniature Golf. This is kind of what you might expect Christmas in the Bahamas to look like, minus the snowman, of course. The giant sand castle is a small replica of Cinderella's not-so-humble abode.

BALLOONING

Fodor's Choice
★

Bob's Balloons. Bob's offers one-hour rides over protected marshland and even flies over the Disney area if wind and weather conditions are right. You meet at Champions Gate, near Disney World, at dawn, where Bob and his assistant take you by van to the launch site. It takes about 15 minutes to get the balloon in the air, and then you're off on an adventure that definitely surpasses Peter Pan's Flight in the Magic Kingdom.

You'll see farm and forest land for miles, along with horses, deer, wild boar, cattle, and birds flying *below* you. Bob may take you as high as 1,000 feet, and you may be able to see such landmarks as the Animal Kingdom's Expedition Everest mountain and Epcot's Spaceship Earth sphere. Several other balloons are likely to go up near you—there's a tight-knit community of ballooners in the Orlando area—so you'll view these colorful sky ornaments from an unparalleled sightline. There are seats in the basket, but you'll probably be too thrilled to sit down. Check the website for specials and call Bob to reserve. ⊠ *Orlando* ☎ *407/466–6380, 877/824–4606* ⊕ *www.bobsballoons.com* ✆ *$175 per person.*

BASKETBALL

Orlando Magic. The most popular pro sports team in town, the Magic entertains locals and visitors in the multimillion-dollar, state-of-the art, 20,000-seat Amway Center. Many famous names have come out of this team (Shaquille O'Neal, anyone?), and although the team's fortunes have fluctuated, the Magic has consistently been one of the most successful of the NBA expansion teams. The season runs from October to June. ⊠ *400 W. Church St., Downtown Orlando* ☎ *407/896–2442* ⊕ *www.nba.com/magic* ✆ *$30–$1,400; parking $10–$20, VIP lot $50.*

BIKING

WALT DISNEY WORLD

Paved trails take you past forests, lakes, wooded campgrounds, and resort villas. If you're 18 or older, you can rent bikes at multiple locations, but you must ride them in the area where you rent them. Rental locations include Downtown Disney Marketplace (near the Rainforest Café) and nearly every moderate-to-deluxe Disney resort, including the BoardWalk Inn and other Epcot Resort Areahotels, Coronado Springs Resort near Disney's Hollywood Studios, Old Key West Resort and Saratoga Springs Resort & Spa near Downtown Disney, Animal Kingdom Lodge, Grand Floridian Resort, and the Fort Wilderness Bike Barn at Fort Wilderness Resort.

Most locations have children's bikes with training wheels and bikes with toddler seats. Surrey bikes are also an option. These look like old-fashioned carriages and are a great way to take your family on a sightseeing tour. The covered tops provide a rare commodity at Disney—shade. Rates start at $9 an hour for regular bikes ($19 for a full day) and go up to $20 to $25 per half hour for surrey bikes (depending on whether they have two, four, or six seats). Wear a helmet; it's free with each rental.

ORLANDO AREA

Thanks to the Orlando community's commitment to the nationwide Rails to Trails program, the city now has several biking, running, and in-line skating trails—converted from former railroad lines—in both rural and urban surroundings.

Orlando City Transportation Planning Division. You can get information about Orlando bike and running trails from this agency. One of the most popular trails is about 10 miles west of Downtown Orlando in the town of Winter Garden. The Orange County Parks and Recreation transformed an old railroad line into a 14-foot wide recreational trail where bicyclists, pedestrians, joggers, roller skaters, and skateboarders gather to get their share of exercise and the great outdoors. Incredibly, an estimated 150,000 people roll through town on the West Orange Trail *every month.* ✉ *Orlando City Hall, 400 S. Orange Ave.* ☎ *407/246–2821* ⊕ *www.cityoforlando.net.*

West Orange Trail. The trail runs some 22 miles from the Orange County–Lake County line, through the towns of Killarney and Oakland and the bustling center of the revived city of Winter Garden, and across U.S. 441 through downtown Apopka. Highlights are views of Lake Apopka and the butterfly garden at the Tildenville outpost. Among the trail's many access points is Chapin Station (*501 Crown Point Cross Rd., Winter Garden*). There are some great places to rest and eat in Winter Garden, which appeals greatly to the 150,000 visitors who travel the trail each month. ✉ *501 Crown Point Cross Rd., Winter Garden* ⊕ *www.ocfl.net/ CultureParks/Parks.aspx?m=dtlvw&d=44#.VMgpEFb3ry8*

West Orange Trail Bikes & Blades. Bicycles and in-line skates can be rented starting at $6 per hour and $30 per day from this full-service shop. Keep in mind several other bicycle/skate rental facilities can be

found along the trail, one of which is Winter Garden Wheel Works
(⊕ *www.wgwheelworks.com*), downtown. ✉ *17914 State Rd. 438,
Winter Garden* ☎ *407/877–0600* ⊕ *www.orlandobikerental.com.*

BOATING

Disney has one of the nation's largest fleets of rental pleasure craft.
There are marinas at the Caribbean Beach Resort, Contemporary
Resort, Downtown Disney Marketplace, Fort Wilderness Resort, Grand
Floridian, Old Key West Resort, Polynesian Resort, Port Orleans French
Quarter and Riverside resorts, and the Wilderness Lodge. You can rent
12-foot sailboats, catamarans, motor-powered pontoon boats, pedal
boats, kayaks, canoes, and tiny two-passenger Sea Racers—a hit with
children—for use on Bay Lake and the adjoining Seven Seas Lagoon,
Crescent Lake at Epcot resorts, Lake Buena Vista, or Buena Vista
Lagoon. You can also sail and water-ski on Bay Lake and the Seven
Seas Lagoon; stop at the Fort Wilderness, Contemporary, Polynesian,
or Grand Floridian marina to rent sailboats or sign up for waterskiing.
Call ☎ *407/939–7529* for more information.

FISHING

Central Florida freshwater lakes and rivers swarm with all kinds of
fish, especially largemouth black bass but also perch, catfish, sunfish,
and pike.

LICENSES

To fish in most Florida waters (but not at Walt Disney World), anglers
over 16 need a fishing license, available at bait-and-tackle shops, fishing
camps, most sporting-goods stores, and Wal-Marts and Kmarts. Some
of these locations may not sell saltwater licenses, or they may serve
non-Florida residents only; call ahead to be on the safe side. For nonresidents of Florida, freshwater or saltwater licenses cost $17 for three
consecutive days, $30 for seven consecutive days and $47 for one year.
For Florida residents under age 65, a freshwater or saltwater license is
$17 per year for each, or $32.50 for both. A five-year fishing license
costs Florida residents $79 for both. Fishing on a private lake with the
owner's permission—which is what anglers do at Disney World—does
not require a Florida fishing license.

WALT DISNEY WORLD

Disney Fishing Excursions. You can sign up for two-hour catch-and-release
excursions on regularly stocked Bay Lake and Seven Seas Lagoon. In
fact, Bay Lake is so well stocked that locals joke that you can almost
walk across the water on the backs of the bass. Departing from the Fort
Wilderness, Wilderness Lodge, Contemporary, Polynesian, Yacht &
Beach Club, Saratoga Springs, Old Key West, Port Orleans Riverside,
and Grand Floridian resort marinas, trips include boat, equipment, and
a guide for up to five anglers. Similar charters depart at the same times
from a Downtown Disney Marketplace dock by Lake Buena Vista. Your
guide is happy to bait your hook, unhook your catches, and even snap
pictures of you with your fish.

Two-hour trips for up to five people depart daily at 7, 10, and 1. The cost is $270 (per group) for morning departures and $235 at 1 pm. Live bait and fishing equipment are included; a license is not required on Disney property. ☎ *407/939–2277.*

Ol' Man Island Fishin' Hole. You can fish inexpensively from a dock at Port Orleans–Riverside. Cane poles and bait are $15 per half hour for a family of up to six. You must rent equipment here to use the dock, and you're required to release any fish that you catch. The Fishing Hole is open daily 7–2:15. ⊠ *Disney's Port Orleans, 1251 Riverside Dr.* ⊕ *www.disneyworld.com.*

ORLANDO AREA

Top Central Florida fishing waters include Lake Kissimmee, the Butler and Conway chains of lakes, and Lake Tohopekaliga—a Native American name that means "Sleeping Tiger." (Locals call it Lake Toho.) The lake got its centuries-old name because it becomes incredibly rough during thunderstorms and has sent more than a few fishermen to a watery grave. Be careful in summer when you see storm clouds. Your best chance for trophy fish is between November and April on Toho or Kissimmee. For good creels, the best bet is usually the Butler area, which has the additional advantage of its scenery—lots of live oaks and cypresses, plus the occasional osprey or bald eagle. Toho and Kissimmee are also good for largemouth bass and crappie. The Butler chain yields largemouth, some pickerel, and the occasional huge catfish. Services range from equipment and boat rental to full-day trips with guides and guarantees. Like virtually all lakes in Florida, the big Orlando-area lakes are teeming with alligators, which you'll find totally harmless unless you engage in the unwise practice of swimming at night. Small pets are more vulnerable than humans, and should never be allowed to swim in Florida lakes or rivers.

■TIP➔ Fishing on a private lake with the owner's permission—which is what anglers do at Disney—doesn't require a state fishing license.

FISHING CAMPS

A number of excellent fishing camps in the form of lakeside campgrounds draw a more outdoorsy crowd than you'll find elsewhere in the area.

Bass Challenger Guide. With Captain Eddie at the helm, BCG takes you wherever the fishing is best that day. It might be Lake Toho or the St. Johns River—Florida's longest and one of the few that runs north—which is a prime bass site. Indeed, bass is the only quarry. Half-day trips for one or two people begin at $300, six-hour trips are $350, and full-day trips begin at $400. Each additional person pays $75 more. BCG also sells bait, arranges for transportation to and from your hotel, organizes multiday trips, and books area accommodations. ⊠ *Sanford* ☎ *321/377–2013* ⊕ *www.basschallenger.com.*

11

Boggy Creek Resort & RV Park. Formerly the East Lake Fish Camp, the new name still covers the camp that includes a restaurant and country store, sells live bait and propane, and rents boats. You can also take a ride on an airboat from here. Hard to believe this much of Old Florida is just minutes from Walt Disney World. The camp has 286 RV sites ($40–$45 per night, $180 a week, or $400 per month) and simple, rustic cabins ($73 per night). Try to reserve one of their 24 cabins at least two weeks in advance in winter and spring. ⊠ *3705 Big Bass Rd., Kissimmee* ☎ *407/348–2040* ⊕ *www.boggycreekresortandrvpark.com.*

Lake Charters. This outfitter conducts trips from November to May on Lake Tohopekaliga (January through April is high season, so reserve accordingly) and has done so for more than 20 years. It's possible to catch a 14-pound bass here. Rods and reels are included in the cost, and transportation is available. Half-day freshwater trips are $275, six-hour trips are $325, and full-day trips are $375. Prices are for one to two people. A third participant costs $50 more. You can also buy your licenses here, and an informative website will fill you in on details regarding rates and what you'll catch. ⊠ *1550 Scottys Rd., Kissimmee* ☎ *407/891–2275, 877/326–3575* ⊕ *www.lakecharter.com.*

Lake Toho Resort. Although some of the full hookups at the 200 RV sites here are booked year-round, electrical and water hookups are usually available, as are live bait, food, and drinks. Sites are $30 per night or $315–$365 per month, plus electricity and an initial $100 refundable deposit. Boat slips start at $45 a month, depending on the length of your boat. ⊠ *4715 Kissimmee Park Rd., St. Cloud* ☎ *407/892–8795* ⊕ *www.laketohoresort.com.*

Richardson's Fish Camp. This camp on western Lake Toho has seven cabins with kitchenettes, 16 RV sites, and six tent sites, as well as boat slips and a bait shop. The RV sites are $30 per night; tent sites are $24.50; and cabins run $44 for one bedroom, $68 for two bedrooms, and $79 for three bedrooms. ⊠ *1550 Scottys Rd., Kissimmee* ☎ *407/846–6540.*

GUIDES

Guides fish out of the area's fishing camps, and you can usually make arrangements to hire them through the camp office. Rates vary, but for two people a good price is $250 for a half day and $350 for a full day. Many area guides are part-timers who fish on weekends or take a day off from their full-time job.

FOOTBALL

Orlando Predators. With a new home in the CFE Arena on the University of Central Florida campus, this professional arena-football team plays from March through July. The team has been in Orlando since 1991 and has reached the league playoffs for 19 consecutive seasons. ⊠ *12777 Gemini Blvd. N, UCF* ☎ *407/648–4444* ⊕ *www.orlandopredators.com* ⊠ *$12–$250; parking $10 and up.*

GOLF

With more than 170 golf courses and 20 golf academies in the area, it's no wonder the International Association of Golf Tour Operators has recognized Orlando as a top golf destination. Sunny weather almost year-round doesn't hurt, and though most of Florida is extremely flat, many of the courses feature hills that make them more challenging.

Resort hotels often let nonguests use their golf facilities. Some country clubs are affiliated with particular hotels, and their guests can play at preferred rates.

■ TIP→ Twilight discounts often apply after 2 pm in busy seasons and after 3 pm the rest of the year; the discount is usually half off the normal rate. Because golf is so incredibly popular, courses regularly raise rates.

In general, even public courses have dress codes, so call ahead for specifics and be sure to reserve tee times. Greens fees usually vary by season, and virtually all include mandatory cart rental, except for the few 9-hole walking courses.

GOLFPAC Travel. GOLFPAC Travel packages golf vacations and arranges tee times at nearly 80 Orlando courses. Rates vary based on hotel and course, and 60 to 90 days' advance notice is recommended to set up a vacation. ✉ *483 Montgomery Pl., Altamonte Springs* ☎ *407/260–2288, 888/848–8941* ⊕ *www.golfpactravel.com.*

WALT DISNEY WORLD
Disney has three championship courses, plus a 9-hole walking course. Any guest at a WDW hotel who checks in specifically to play golf gets free cab rides to the course.

Greens Fees. Rates change frequently, so confirm when booking. Disney resort guests get a price break, and you should ask about twilight discount rates. If you plan to play only once, leave the gear at home—you can rent shoes, range balls, and clubs at any location.

Tee Times and Reservations. Tee times are available daily from dawn until dusk. You can book them up to 90 days in advance if you're staying at a WDW-owned hotel, 60 days ahead if you're staying elsewhere. You must cancel at least 24 hours out. For tee times and private lessons, call Disney's central World Golf reservations line ☎ *407/939–4653.*

GREENS FEES
There are lots of variables here, with prices ranging from $20 for a youngster 17 or under to play 9 holes at Oak Trail walking course to an adult nonhotel guest paying $169 to play 18 holes at one of Disney's newer courses in peak season. Disney guests get a price break, with rates ranging from $89 for a Disney hotel guest playing Monday through Thursday at the Lake Buena Vista course to $159 for a day visitor playing the Palm, Magnolia, or Lake Buena Vista courses. All have a twilight discount rate, $30–$80 for the 18-hole courses, which goes into effect at 2 pm from October 31 to January 14 and at 3 pm from April 1 to October 26. The 9-hole, par-36 Oak Trail course is best for those on a budget, with a year-round rate of $20 for golfers 17 and under and $39 for golfers 18 and older, and can be played for

a twilight rate of $15 for adults and $10 for youngsters under 17 after 3 pm between May 14 and September 27.

Rates at all courses except Oak Trail include an electric golf cart. No electric carts are allowed at Oak Trail, and a pull cart for your bag is $6. If you've got the stamina and desire to play the same course twice in the same day, you can do so for half price the second time around, but you can't reserve that option in advance, and this Re-Play Option, as Disney calls it, is subject to availability. Golf shoes rent for $10 a pair, and range balls are available for $7 a bucket. If you'd rather not pay a baggage fee to haul your clubs onto your plane, you can rent the latest TaylorMade woods, irons, and a putter for $50. If, for some reason, you have to cancel your tee time, they'll try to fill your spot, but if not, you'll be charged. Note that golf rates change frequently, so double-check them when you reserve.

GOLF INSTRUCTION

One-on-one instruction from PGA-accredited professionals is available at any Disney course. Prices for private lessons vary: 45-minute lessons cost $75 for adults and $50 for youngsters 17 and under.

COURSES

Disney's Lake Buena Vista Golf Course. A favorite among golfers, the Lake Buena Vista course has hosted the PGA Tour, LPGA Tour, and USGA events. As you play, you'll find the course winds among Downtown Disney–area town houses and villas. Greens are narrow, and hitting straight is important because errant balls risk ending up in someone's bedroom. Be prepared for the famous island green on the 7th. This is a pleasant location surrounded by wonderful scenery. Greens fees range from $39 to $165 and includes a cart. ⊠ *Downtown Disney* 🏌 *18 holes, 6,745 yards, par 72.*

Fodor's Choice
★

Four Seasons Golf Course. Sculpted from some of the still-forested portions of the huge WDW acreage, the Tom Fazio–designed course opened in summer 2014 as part of the new Four Seasons Resort Orlando. Known to Disney golfers as the former Osprey Ridge course, the rebranded Four Seasons course has undergone contouring and bunker enhancement. Tees and greens as much as 20 feet above the fairways keep competitive players from getting too comfortable. Amenities include luxury golf carts with GPS, a Cuban-American clubhouse restaurant, driving range, and putting green. Greens fees begin at $195 in season, but drop to $125 after "twilight" play begins at 2 pm. ⊠ *Four Seasons Golf Course, 10100 Dream Tree Blvd., Golden Oak* 🏌 *18 holes, 6,968 yards, par 71.*

The Magnolia. The Magnolia has been lavished with four stars by *Golf Digest* and was certified by Audubon International as a Cooperative Wildlife Sanctuary. The long but forgiving course features extra-wide fairways, and its name stems from more than 1,500 magnolia trees that line the course. While you're working to avoid the woods, try avoiding the water hazards that are found at 11 of the 18 holes. But that's not all. There are 97 bunkers spread throughout the fairway. Greens fees range from $39 to $165. ⊠ *Shades of Green, 1950 W. Magnolia-Palm Dr.* 🏌 *18 holes, 7,516 yards, par 72.*

Oak Trail. Located across from the Grand Floridian at the Shades of Green Resort (a resort used primarily by military families), the Oak Trail was designed by Ron Garl to be fun for the entire family. It's noted for its small, undulating greens and affordable fees, from $20 to $38. ⊠ *Shades of Green, 1950 W. Magnolia-Palm Dr.* ⊕ *https://disneyworld. disney.go.com/recreation/oak-trail-golf-course/* ⚲ *9 holes, 2,913 yards, par 36.*

The Palm. Although it's not as long as the Magnolia, nor as wide, The Palm has been confounding the pros for years. The course, located across the Grand Floridian Resort, has nine water holes and 94 bunkers—including one in the iconic shape of Mickey Mouse's head. Greens fees, $39–$165, include a cart. ⊠ *Shades of Green, 1950 W. Magnolia-Palm Dr.* ⚲ *18 holes, 7,011 yards, par 72.*

ORLANDO AREA

If golf is your passion, you already know that Arnold Palmer and Gary Player—in fact, almost half of the PGA tour—make Orlando their off-road home. It's not by accident that the Golf Channel originates from here. The Bay Hill Invitational and several LPGA tourneys (the headquarters is in Daytona) come to Orlando every year. And with more than 170 public and private courses, there's ample opportunity for you to play on world-class courses such as Grand Cypress or Champions Gate.

Annika Academy. Named for world-renowned pro golfer Annika Sorenstam (its owner and chief golf guru), Annika Academy offers golf instruction, fitness training, and nutrition counseling. Some package prices are steep. Personalized instruction starts at $95 and heads north; higher-level packages allow guests to play golf with Annika herself. At the Reunion Resort, which has three championship courses, by Nicklaus, Palmer, and Watson, the academy has its own driving range and putting green. ⊠ *7450 Sparkling Ct., Reunion* ☎ *407/662–4653, 888/266–4522* ⊕ *www.theannikaacademy.com.*

Arnold Palmer's Bay Hill Club & Lodge. The course is the site of the annual Arnold Palmer Invitational, and the 18th hole is considered one of the toughest on the PGA tour. Courses are open only to those who have been invited by a member or who book lodging at the club's 70-room lodge. But with double-occupancy rates for rooms overlooking the course running as low as $130 for a double room in summer, many consider staying at the club an interesting prospect. Keep in mind this rate does not include your greens fees, which are necessary since staying here in essence buys you a day of "membership" at the club. Beyond some of the best golf in Orlando, perhaps the best perk of all is the chance that you'll meet Arnold Palmer himself. ⊠ *9000 Bay Hill Blvd.* ☎ *407/876–2429, 888/422–9445* ⊕ *www.bayhill.com* ☒ *Greens fees included in resort package* ⚲ *18 holes, 7,207 yards, par 72; 9 holes, 3,409 yards, par 36* ☞ *Restaurants, spa, salon, tennis, fitness center, heated pool, golf academy, private lessons, club rental.*

Barnett Park Golf Practice Facility. Besides having an attractive 18-hole disc (as in Frisbee) golf course, Barnett Park has a great asset: it's free. If you want to stick with traditional golf, just show up at the 159-acre

Orange County park to use the net-enclosed driving range (with 10 pads) and the two small putting greens. The drawback, though, may be its location—in a somewhat cluttered and not-so-attractive area of town. ⊠ *4801 W. Colonial Dr.* ☎ *407/836–6248* 💳 *Free.*

Celebration Golf Club. Talk about a great pedigree—the Celebration course was designed by Robert Trent Jones Jr. and Sr. Located just 10 minutes from Walt Disney World, the course is paired with the master-planned Disney community, just 1 mile off the U.S. 192 strip. Lovely, wooded, and serene, the fairways are framed by natural woods and wetlands to create what the Joneses envisioned: "Every hole a hard par and an easy bogey." ⊠ *701 Golf Park Dr., Celebration* ☎ *407/566–4653* ⊕ *www.celebrationgolf.com* 💳 *Greens fees $59–$129, depending on time of year, time of day, and whether you're a Florida or Celebration resident; daily discount rates begin at noon* ⅄ *18 holes, 6,783 yards, par 72* ⌔ *Restaurant, pro shop, private lessons, club rental.*

ChampionsGate Golf Club. The two courses at ChampionsGate were designed by Australia's Greg Norman, and there's an on-site David Leadbetter Golf Academy. The 7,363-yard International has the "down-under" style of Australia's coastal links, whereas the 7,128-yard National course is designed in the style of the better domestic courses, with a number of par-3 holes with unusual bunkers. The club is less than 10 miles from Walt Disney World at Exit 58 on Interstate 4. ⊠ *1400 Masters Blvd., ChampionsGate* ☎ *407/787–4653 Champions-Gate, 407/787–3330 Leadbetter Academy, 888/633–5323 Leadbetter Academy* ⊕ *www.championsgategolf.com* 💳 *Greens fees $45–$142, depending on time of year and time of day. Golf lessons at Leadbetter Academy are $225 per hr and $1,750 per day for private lessons; group lessons are $325 for 3 hrs; a 3-day minischool is $975; a 3-day school from 9 to 5 is $2,400, and a 3-day complete school, which includes 9 holes of golf each day, is $3,000.* ⅄ *International: 18 holes, 7,363 yards, par 72. National: 18 holes, 7,128 yards, par 72* ⌔ *Pro shop, restaurant, golf school, private lessons, club rental.*

Falcon's Fire Golf Club. Designed by Rees Jones, Falcon's Fire has strate-gically placed fairway bunkers that demand accuracy off the tee. This club is just off the Irlo Bronson Memorial Highway and is convenient to the hotels in Kissimmee's so-called Maingate area. ⊠ *3200 Seralago Blvd., Kissimmee* ☎ *407/239–5445* ⊕ *www.falconsfire.com* 💳 *Greens fees $49–$135, $39 after 3:30 pm in summer* ⅄ *18 holes, 7,015 yards, par 72* ⌔ *Tee times 1–90 days in advance. Restaurant, private and group lessons, club rental, lockers, driving range, putting green.*

Grand Cypress Golf Resort. Grand Cypress comprises three 9's: the North, South, and East courses, and the 18-hole New Course, fashioned after a Scottish glen. In addition, the Grand Cypress Academy of Golf, a 21-acre facility, has lessons and clinics. The North and South courses have fairways constructed on different levels, giving them added defi-nition. The New Course, designed by Jack Nicklaus, was inspired by the Old Course at St. Andrews, and has deep bunkers, double greens, a snaking burn, and even an old stone bridge. ⊠ *1 N. Jacaranda* ☎ *407/239–1909, 800/835–7377* ⊕ *www.grandcypress.com* 💳 *Greens* *fees $125–$175* 🏌. *North: 9 holes, 3,521 yards, par 36. South: 9 holes, 3,472 yards, par 36. East: 9 holes, 3,434 yards, par 36. New: 18 holes, 6,773 yards, par 72* ☞ *Tee times New Course 8–5; all others 7:30–5. Restaurant, club rental, shoe rental, locker room, driving range, putting green, free valet parking.*

Hawk's Landing Golf Club at the Orlando World Center Marriott. The 220-acre Hawks' Landing course includes 15 water holes, lots of sand, and exotic landscaping. Located at the monumental World Center Marriott (it's the world's largest Marriott) near the entrance to Walt Disney World. As you play you'll see they've maintained the natural surroundings and enhanced the same with vibrantly colored azaleas. A good choice if you're here on business and want to get in a round. No need to pack your clubs—Callaway rental equipment is available. Need some help? Instruction is offered at the Bill Madonna Golf Academy. ✉ *Orlando World Center Marriott, 8701 World Center Dr.* ☎ *407/238–8660, 800/567–2623* ⊕ *www.golfhawkslanding.com* ✆ *Greens fees $69– $149* 🏌. *18 holes, 6,602 yards, par 71* ☞ *Tee times 60 days in advance for public, 90 days in advance for World Center guests. Restaurants, private and group lessons at the resort's Bill Madonna Golf Academy, club and shoe rental.*

Marriott Golf Academy. The Marriott Golf Academy is an extensive-curriculum golf school and 9-hole golf course on the grounds of the corporation's biggest time-share complex, Marriott's Grande Vista. Here you can do anything from taking a one-hour, $119–$169 lesson with a certified instructor to immersing yourself in a three-day extravaganza ($999–$1,499) in which you learn more about golf technique than most nonfanatics would care to know. The Swing Studio offers high-tech teaching methods. The course, designed by Ron Garl, is geared to make you use every club in your bag—and perhaps a few you may elect to buy in the pro shop. In March 2015, they closed their 18-hole course, and students now test their newly honed skills at their 9-hole course or travel to Hawks' Landing. ✉ *Marriott Grande Vista, 12001 Avenida Verde* ☎ *407/238–7677, 855/642–2369* ⊕ *www.marriottgolfacademy. com* 🏌. *9 holes, 2,400 yards, par 32.*

Orange Lake Resort. About five minutes from Walt Disney World's main entrance, Orange Lake has two 18-hole courses (the Legends and the Reserve), two 9-hole courses (Crane's Bend, Legends Walk), and pro instruction at the McCord Golf Academy (rates start at $65). The Legends is a signature Arnold Palmer–designed championship course; the Reserve was designed by Mike Dasher and has unique land and water challenges. Crane's Bend is family-friendly. Legend's Walk is an executive walker's course open until 9 pm nightly, where children 15 and younger play free with complimentary clubs. The signature hole for the entire group of courses is the Island Oak, No. 13, a 432-yard, par-4 hole in the Pines section (the back 9) of the Legends Course. ✉ *8505 W. Irlo Bronson Memorial Hwy., Kissimmee* ☎ *407/239–1050, 888/640–6522* ⊕ *www.golforangelake.com* ✆ *Greens fees $35–$110 for resort guests; $60–$140 nonguests* 🏌. *The Legends: 18 holes, 7,072 yards, par 72. The Reserve: 18 holes, 6,670 yards, par 71. Crane's Bend: 9 holes, 1,901 yards, par 30. Legend's Walk: 9 holes, 1,581 yards, par 30* ☞ *Advance* *tee times preferred. Restaurant, private and group lessons, club rental, lighted driving range, putting green.*

Rosen's Shingle Creek Golf Club. Rosen's Shingle Creek Golf Club, designed by David Harman, lies alongside a lovely creek that is headwaters of the Everglades. The course is challenging yet playable, with dense stands of oak and pine trees and interconnected waterways. The golf carts even have GPS yardage systems. Another favorite for conventioneers, Universal Studios and the Orange County Convention Center are within a few minutes' drive. ⊠ *9939 Universal Blvd.* ☎ *407/996–9933, 866/996–9933* ⊕ *www.shinglecreekgolf.com* ✉ *Greens fees $85–$149* 🏌 *18 holes, 7,069 yards, par 72* ⌗ *Tee times 7–dusk. Restaurant, club rental, shoe rental, driving range, putting green.*

Waldorf Astoria Golf Club. Rees Jones maintained natural elements while enhancing the land's existing contours when he designed Waldorf Astoria Golf Club. Majestic stands of pine and cypress line the fairways, and it winds through a scenic wetland preserve, with bunkers reminiscent of century-old hazards. It has a five-tee system for all playing levels. ⊠ *14224 Bonnet Creek Resort La.* ☎ *407/597–5500, 888/924–6531* ⊕ *www.waldorfastoriagolfclub.com* ✉ *$65–$195 (seasonal)* 🏌 *18 holes, 7,113 yards, par 72* ⌗ *Tee times 7:30–6. Restaurant, club rental, shoe rental, locker room, driving range, putting green, free valet parking.*

Winter Park Country Club. Framing the north end of Park Avenue (picture Worth Avenue in Palm Beach or Rodeo Drive in Beverly Hills), this historic country club offers nonresidents access to its immaculate golf course. Opened in 1914, the 9-hole walking course was modeled after authentic Scottish links. Notably, within the past decade residents were given a choice to sell the golf course to developers or raise their own taxes to preserve it for the city. They chose to keep the course. With greens fees topping out at just $17, this is one of the most affordable and authentic recreational experiences in Central Florida. ⊠ *761 Old England Ave., Winter Park* ☎ *407/599–3339* ⊕ *www.winterparkcountryclub.com* ✉ *Greens fees $8 weekdays, $17 weekends.*

HORSEBACK RIDING

ORLANDO AREA

Horse World Riding Stables ⊠ *3705 Poinciana Blvd., Kissimmee* ☎ *407/ 847–4343* ⊕ *www.horseworldstables.com.*

Silver Spurs Rodeo. There's an era many natives recall as "Old Florida," and that's the time before 1971 and the arrival of the theme parks. You can still find Old Florida on Disney's doorstep, right there in neighboring Kissimmee at the Silver Spurs Rodeo. Launched here by ranching families in 1944, the largest rodeo east of the Mississippi is where you'll see bull riders and cowboys competing in a variety of high-energy, high adrenaline competitions including bull and bronc riding, steer wrestling, and barrel racing. Held at the Osceola Heritage Park each February and June, just grab a seat and watch in awe. Pure Florida goodness. From Interstate 4 Exit 77, take Florida's Turnpike south to Exit 244

(Kissimmee–St. Cloud). ⊠ *1875 Silver Spur La., Kissimmee* ☎ *321/697–3495* ⊕ *www.silverspursrodeo.com* ✉ *$15; under 15 free* ⊙ *Hrs vary.*

ICE SKATING

The Ice Factory. Ice-skating in Florida? Yup! This Olympic-class facility has two rinks. Teens are drawn to Friday's DJ Night, and there are family-night rates on Saturday. Skate rentals are included with admission, and an upgraded pair (which costs a little extra) include extra padding. Hours vary and often the rink is being used for training, so be sure to visit their website before you go for an updated schedule on public skating. ⊠ *2221 Partin Settlement Rd., Kissimmee* ☎ *407/933–4259* ⊕ *www.icefactory.com* ✉ *$5–$10; $3 skate rental* ⊙ *Daily; hrs vary by rink and day.*

MINIATURE GOLF

If mini golf is your game, Disney's Winter Summerland, next to Blizzard Beach, has 18 holes on its faux-snow "winter" course and 18 on its tropical "summer" course—sand castles and all. At the Fantasia Gardens 36-hole mini-golf course, adjacent to the Walt Disney World Swan, dancing hippos and broomsticks remind you of the classic animated film *Fantasia.* There's even a Fantasia Fairways challenge course, with sand traps, water hazards, and par-3 and par-4 holes up to 75 feet long for experienced golfers.

FAMILY **Congo River.** In this clever creation, it's mini-putt meets theme park. Multilevel courses wander amid waterfalls, rocky summits, caves, and rain forests. Popular with families and, believe it or not, couples, kids are the prime audience. They love the live alligators (not loose on the course), the arcade room, and the treasure hunt. Congo River also has locations in Kissimmee and East Orlando. ⊠ *5901 International Dr.* ☎ *407/248–9181* ⊕ *www.congoriver.com* ✉ *$12.99; 10 and under $10.99* ⊙ *Sun.–Thurs. 10 am–11 pm, Fri. and Sat. 10 am–midnight.*

FAMILY
Fodor's Choice
★
Hawaiian Rumble Adventure Golf. Who can resist miniature golfing around an erupting volcano? Hawaiian Rumble combines a tropical setting with waterfalls, tunnels, tiki gods, and flame-belching mountains. There's also a location in the Lake Buena Vista area. Enjoyed your first round? It's only a few bucks to play an additional 18 holes. ⊠ *8969 International Dr.* ☎ *407/351–7733* ⊕ *www.hawaiianrumbleorlando.com* ✉ *$9.95 (18 holes), $12.95 (36 holes)* ⊙ *Sun.–Thurs. 9 am–11:00 pm, Fri. and Sat. 9 am–11:30 pm.*

FAMILY **Pirate's Cove Adventure Golf.** Two 18-hole miniature golf courses wind around artificial mountains, through caves, beside waterfalls, and into lush foliage. The beginner's course is called Captain Kidd's Adventure; the more advanced course is Blackbeard's Challenge. There's another Pirate's Cove on International Drive. ⊠ *12545 State Rd. 535, Lake Buena Vista* ☎ *407/827–1242* ⊕ *www.piratescove.net* ✉ *$9.45 (under 10), $10.45 (18 holes), $14.95 (36 holes)* ⊙ *Daily 9 am–11 pm.*

MULTISPORT

Fort Wilderness Resort. One of the original Disney resorts (the Polynesian and Contemporary were the others), Fort Wilderness Resort offers a number of sporting and outdoors activities. For 90 minutes you can get in some target shooting with an archery guide who oversees novice and expert marksmen (ages 6 and up). Nonresort guests are welcome to join campers, and the $39 fee includes use of the compound bow and arrows, plus instruction. You can book up to 180 days in advance. But that's not all of the outdoor activities you can enjoy here.

Tame backwoods horseback trail rides from here begin at 8:30 am and continue through mid- to late afternoon. Children must be at least 9 years old and 48 inches tall to ride, and adults must weigh less than 250 pounds. Trail rides are $45 for 45 minutes; hours vary by season. You must check in 30 minutes prior to your ride, and reservations must be made at least one day ahead. Both horseback riding and the campground are open to nonresort guests.

A two-hour Wilderness Back Trail Adventure Segway tour is done on an "off-road" version of the vehicle, and begins with a training session to get you acquainted with its operation. Call ahead for reservations. The cost is $90 per person, and you must be at least 16 and carry a photo ID. If you'd prefer to rent a bicycle, stop by the Bicycle Barn where they rent for $9 an hour or, even better, $18 per day.

For fishing, rods and tackle can be found at the **Fort Wilderness Bike Barn,** open daily 9–5, for fishing in the canals around Fort Wilderness Resort. Rod and reel with tackle is about $12.50 for the day, but you must be at least 18 to rent here. If you'd like to go fishing with a guide, it costs $270 for an excursion for up to five people. ⊠ *4510 N. Fort Wilderness Trail* ☎ *407/939–7529 archery, 407/824–2742 Bicycle Barn, 407/824–2832 horseback riding.*

RUNNING

WALT DISNEY WORLD

The World has several scenic running trails from the Grand Floridian, Polynesian, and Contemporary in the Magic Kingdom area. At the Epcot resorts, you can get your heart rate up along the promenade that circles Crescent Lake past the BoardWalk and Yacht and Beach Club resorts. If you're staying at Port Orleans, you can work up a sweat on nearby trails; Coronado Springs guests run along the resort's 1-mile esplanade.

The roads that snake through Downtown Disney resorts are pleasant, and early in the morning traffic isn't too bad. At the Caribbean Beach Resort, there's a 1½-mile running promenade around Barefoot Bay. Fort Wilderness Campground has a woodsy 2-mile course with numerous exercise stations along the way.

ORLANDO AREA

Orlando has two excellent bicycling, jogging, and recreational trails, the West Orange Trail and the Cady Way Trail. Rural Orlando has some unbelievable hiking trails with long, densely wooded, nonrocky stretches that are tremendous for running, and often you can run for a half hour and not see any other living being—except wild game.

Bill Frederick Park at Turkey Lake. Named in honor of former Orlando Mayor Bill Frederick, this 178-acre park has a 3-mile biking trail that's popular with runners, a pool, disc golf course, and a lake that attracts the casual fisherman. Hard to believe this much natural goodness is just a few miles from the fast-paced world of Universal Orlando. Rental cabins and a 36-site RV campground welcome visitors. Several wooded hiking trails also make for a good run. The park closes at 5 pm November–March and 7 pm April–October. ⊠ *3401 S. Hiawassee Rd., West Orlando* ☎ *407/246–4486* ⊕ *www.cityoforlando.net/fpr/Html/Parks/BillFrederick.htm* ☞ *$4 per car.*

Cady Way Trail. Although a bit far from the attractions, this is a favorite of local bikers, joggers, and skaters since it connects eastern Orlando with the well-manicured enclave of Winter Park. The pleasant 7.2-mile trail is open sunrise to sunset, with water fountains and shaded seating along the route. The best access point is the parking lot on the east side of the Orlando Fashion Square Mall (*3201 E. Colonial Dr., about 3 miles east of I–4 Exit 83B*). The northern access is at the Orange County Recreation Center (*4863 N. Goldenrod Rd., Winter Park*). ⊠ *1360 Truman Rd.* ☎ *407/836–6160.*

SKYDIVING AND PARASAILING

Fodor'sChoice
★
iFLY Orlando. OK, so technically you aren't really skydiving, but you come pretty close in this 12-foot-high, 1,000-horsepower wind tunnel that lets you experience everything skydivers do, but closer to the ground.

The experience starts with instruction, after which you suit up and hit the wind tunnel, where you soar like a bird (or try to) under your instructor's watchful eye. It's all so realistic that skydiving clubs come to hone their skills. It's also pretty surreal as you look through the window and see people floating in mid-air. The attraction is safe for anyone under 250 pounds and older than 3. The 90-minute introductory experience includes two flights. You can purchase a video of your "jump" for $24.95. ⊠ *6805 Visitors Circle* ☎ *407/903–1150* ⊕ *www.skyventureorlando.com* ☞ *$59.95 and up, depending on package* ☉ *Daily 10–10:30.*

Sammy Duvall's Water Sports Centre. Thanks to Sammy Duvall's, you can get a bird's-eye view of Disney while parasailing on Bay Lake. Flights with 450 feet of line last 8 to 10 minutes ($95); deluxe flights with 600 feet of line last 10 to 12 minutes ($130). You must weigh at least 120 pounds, though lightweights can bulk up with the help of a lifeguard or family member and a tandem flight (without the tandem charge). But if you want to parasail with a partner from the get-go, tandem flights are $170; deluxe tandem flights are $195.

At the same location, you can try your skills at waterskiing, wakeboarding, and tubing. Up to five people can go on the ski boat, which includes equipment and an expert instructor and driver. For a group that large, instructors recommend booking two hours ($165 for the first hour and $135 for each additional hour); couples or smaller groups may want to try one hour, though half-hour rentals ($85) are available. ⊠ *Contemporary Resort* ☎ *407/939–0754* ⊕ *www.sammyduvall.com.*

SPECTATOR SPORTS

ESPN Wide World of Sports Complex. This complex is proof that Disney doesn't do anything unless it does it in a big way. The 220-acre facility (formerly known as Disney's Wide World of Sports Complex) contains a 7,500-seat baseball stadium housed in a giant stucco structure that, from the outside, looks like a Moroccan palace. There's also a 5,000-seat field house and a number of fan-oriented commercial ventures, such as the ESPN Wide World of Sports Grill, and shops that sell clothing and other items sanctioned by Major League Baseball, the NBA, and the NFL. During spring training the Atlanta Braves play here with tickets priced between $23 and $45.

The complex also hosts more than 200 amateur and professional events each year, including big-ticket tennis tournaments. In all, some 30 spectator sports are represented among the annual events, including Harlem Globetrotters basketball games, baseball fantasy camps held in conjunction with the Braves at the start of spring training, and track events ranging from the Walt Disney World Marathon to Amateur Athletic Union (AAU) championships. The complex offers bowling, softball, basketball, and other games for group events ranging from family reunions to corporate picnics. Admission is $16, sporting events cost extra. ⊠ *700 S. Victory Way, Kissimmee* ☎ *407/828–3267 events information* ⊕ *www.disneyworldsports.com.*

SURFING

Surfing? Here, in landlocked Central Florida? You bet. Early in the morning, before Typhoon Lagoon opens to water-park visitors, you can hit some man-made waves with 11 other novices and a professional instructor. Run by local surf pros, the three-hour session begins with a half-hour beachside lesson on surfing moves and basics. Before you know it, you're in the heated wave pool and headed for your first ride. You must be at least 8 years old, and lessons cost $165 per person. Soft-sided boards are provided. You must have transportation to Typhoon Lagoon; even if you're staying at Disney, buses don't run before the class begins at 6:45 am. The program is scheduled several days each week for up to 12 participants, but lesson days vary, so call ☎ *407/939–7529.*

TENNIS

WALT DISNEY WORLD

You can play tennis at several Disney hotels: Bay Lake Tower at Disney's Contemporary Resort (two hard courts), BoardWalk (two hard courts), Old Key West Resort (two hard courts), Saratoga Springs Resort & Spa (two Hydrogrid clay courts), and Yacht Club Resort (one hard court). Courts are available without charge on a first-come, first-served basis for resort and nonresort guests. All have lights, and most have lockers and racquets available to rent or borrow. At the Walt Disney World Swan and Dolphin hotels, you can get an hour-long private lesson on one of four courts for $90 from 7 am to 9 pm. Call ☎ *407/621–1991.*

ORLANDO AREA

Tennis awaits on well-tended public tennis courts and on courts in resort hotels. There are more than 50 courts run by City Parks and Recreation, some free and others reasonably priced.

Fort Gatlin Tennis Complex. Close to Downtown Orlando, Fort Gatlin has the finest city-run courts open to the public. Ten hard courts equipped for day or night play, a pro shop that's open daily, and lessons are among this beautiful facility's offerings. ⊠ *2009 Lake Margaret Dr., Downtown Orlando* ☎ *407/254–9878* ⊕ *www.mgtennis.com/ fort-gatlin-tennis-center* ✉ *$4–$6 per court per hr* ☾ *Weekdays 8 am– 10 pm, weekends 8–8.*

Orlando Tennis Center. Run by the City of Orlando and located near Downtown, this fine facility offers adult tennis clinics (18 and up), private lessons, and youth tennis programs (6 and up). ⊠ *649 W. Livingston St., Downtown Orlando* ☎ *407/246–4469* ⊕ *www.orlandotenniscenter. com* ✉ *$5 soft court per hr, $4 hard court* ☾ *Weekdays 8 am–9:30 pm, weekends 8–2:30.*

INDEX

PHOTO CREDITS

NOTES

NOTES

NOTES

NOTES

NOTES

NOTES

NOTES

NOTES

NOTES

NOTES

NOTES

NOTES

ABOUT OUR WRITERS

Rona Gindin, who worked on the Where to Eat chapter, is a freelance writer, editor, and TV personality specializing in restaurants and travel. She is the dining editor of *Orlando Life Magazine*, the author of *The Little Black Book of Walt Disney World*, and regularly talks about area restaurants on local TV shows. She also contributes to *Zagat*, *Go*, Epicurious.com, and other print and online publications.

Where to Stay writer **Jennifer Greenhill-Taylor** has been a journalist for more than two decades—working as a travel editor, theater and film critic, wire editor, and freelance writer/editor. She was born in Edinburgh, Scotland, has lived in four countries and a dozen states, and travels widely for pleasure and profit. She lives in Orlando with her partner, playwright and freelance writer Joseph Reed Hayes, and enjoys sharing her extensive research on the area's hospitality with friends and family.

Orlando and Environs writer **Joseph Hayes** has informed the world about travel, food and the arts in Central Florida for print and online publications for 20 years. He won a Florida Magazine Association Award for his work as the restaurant critic for *Orlando Magazine*. His other hat is worn in performance spaces, as an award-winning playwright produced in New York, California, Florida and the United Kingdom, a jazz event producer and advocate for new, original creative work for in-house and online audiences. Born in Manhattan, Hayes worked in publishing in New York before moving to Central Florida to take up writing and traveling as a full-time career. ⊕ *wjrhayes.net*.

Freelance writer **Jennie Hess** covered what's new at Walt Disney World and across Orlando and its environs for this edition. When she's not trekking through theme parks or exploring Orlando's many treasures, Jennie keeps us up to date on the city's growth and the evolving Disney kingdom. Born in York, Pennsylvania, she has lived in Florida since 1979 and was a newspaper journalist before enlisting as a Disney publicist during the 1990s when Walt's world experienced a decade of rapid growth. A Fodor's contributor for more than a decade, Jennie lives in Orlando with her attorney husband, Walter. Sons Nathan and Sam, now in college, are Disney water park experts and help her update all rides involving high-speed splashdowns.

Gary McKechnie, who covered all of Universal and SeaWorld, knows a lot about Florida—his native state. During his student days, he worked as a Walt Disney World ferryboat pilot, Jungle Cruise skipper, steam train conductor, double-decker bus driver, and was also an improv comedian at Epcot. He wrote the award-winning *Great American Motorcycle Tours*, the nation's best-selling motorcycle guidebook, and, following years of travel and research, National Geographic's *USA 101*, which highlights 101 iconic American places, events, and festivals. Gary also speaks on America's cultural heritage aboard the Cunard Line ships *Queen Mary 2* and *Queen Victoria* and at business and tourism meetings across America.